MW01502729

TRADE AND FREEDOM

For
Rebecca

TRADE AND FREEDOM

JAMES BACCHUS

Rob,

I look forward to working
with you for the full flourishing
of human freedom.

Jim

2022

CAMERON MAY

INTERNATIONAL LAW & POLICY

ISBN: 1 874698 59 7

Printed by Digital Books Logistics LTD

Table of Contents

Foreword and Acknowledgments 9

Preface 13

    Promenade: Morning in Geneva 13

Part One

Reflections of a Faceless Foreign Judge

Chapter One 19

    Trade Talks 19
        Proust in the Ritz 19
        Table Talk 20
        Table Manners 35

Chapter Two 51

    Trade Faces 51
        Six Wise Men 51
        The Ice Cream Man 53
        The Episcopalian 60
        The Aristotelian 66
        The European 74
        The Orchard Keeper 82
        The Silver Fox 89
        The American 98
        And Six More 106
        Crossing the Alps 113

Chapter Three 117

    Trade Secrets 117
        Trade Secrets 117
        Looking Through "WTO Glasses" 122
        The Open Society 129
        In Our Nature 138

Smith's Hand 148
Smith's Division 155
The Gains from Trade 165
Ricardo's Insight 174
Ricardo's Reach 183
The Revolt Against Freedom 190

Chapter Four **199**

Trade Fears 199
    The Fiddle and the Radio 199
    The Revolt Against Trade 203
    The Fear of Change 208
    The Fear of Technology 221
    The Fear of Growth 231
    The Fear of Capitalism 240
    The Fear of Commercialism 249
    Dostoevsky's Choice 257

Chapter Five **267**

Trade Hopes 267
    Means and Ends 267
    The Watchmakers of Ferney 275
    Voltaire's Trees 290

Conclusion **305**

The Age of Reason 305

Part Two

Further Reflections on Trade and Freedom

Chapter One 311

    The Appeals of Trade: The Making of an Old GATT Hand

Chapter Two 329

    The Bicycle Club: Affirming the American Interest in the
    Future of the WTO

Chapter Three 347

    Thoreau's Pencil: Sharpening Our Understanding of
    World Trade

Chapter Four 361

    "Woulda, Coulda, Shoulda": The Consolations of WTO
    Dispute Settlement

Chapter Five 373

    The Strange Death of Sir Francis Bacon: The Do's and
    Don'ts of Appellate Advocacy in the WTO

Chapter Six 389

    Learning and Living the Liberal Arts

Chapter Seven 403

    An Education in 404 Pages

Chapter Eight 407

    Poetry About Butter

Chapter Nine 415

    The Double Rainbow

Chapter Ten **431**

    Lone Star: The Historic Role of the WTO

Chapter Eleven **451**

    Groping Toward Grotius: The WTO and the International
    Rule of Law

Chapter Twelve **475**

    Lecky's Circle: Thoughts from the Frontier of International
    Law

About the Author **513**

Foreword

and

Acknowledgments

This book began one morning in a hotel room in the Hampton Inn at Elliston Place in Nashville, Tennessee, as a brief outline I wrote on a legal pad for a lecture I gave a few hours later at Vanderbilt University Law School. That lecture eventually evolved into "Table Talk," which is part of the first chapter of the lengthy essay that is the first part of this book.

A few months later, I mentioned to my longtime friend and fellow Vanderbilt graduate, Lauren Gilmer Rigby, that I was thinking of writing a book. Laurie, who knows me well, and who adorns her abiding friendship with candor, replied, "You have been telling me that for thirty years. When are you going to do it?"

Another few months later, I submitted an early draft of a hundred pages or so to the scrutiny of another longtime friend, my roommate from graduate school at Yale, Eric Edelman. Eric also knows me well, and his enduring friendship is likewise one that gets to the point. He asked, "So… when are you going to finish it and publish it?"

The book grew from there. On long nights in Geneva. On long rides in airplanes. On long weekends in my library at home in Florida. In the places and in the spaces between pending appeals before the Appellate Body of the World Trade Organization, the first pages of that first brief outline grew over time to become a book that expresses much of my personal philosophy of trade, and explains much about why I was willing, for eight years, to spend those long nights, take those long rides, and judge those trade appeals.

This is not a book about all of the details of all of the decision making in all of the appeals I have helped judge for the WTO. The WTO rules of conduct do not permit me to write that book.

Nor is this a book about all of the specific issues facing the WTO in ongoing dispute settlement or in continuing global trade negotiations. The future may permit me, perhaps, to write that book.

Rather, this is primarily a book about the philosophical view of the world that is the basis and the motivation for the world trading system that is served by the WTO. Further, it is a book that was written, in its entirety, during the years while I served that system as a Member and as Chairman of the Appellate Body of the WTO. The final pages were written in my final days in Geneva.

In addition to Laurie and Eric, many others have also helped make this book possible. I cannot mention all of them here, but I would be remiss if I did not say "thanks" here to some of them.

There is Lynn Watch, my "sidekick," who has, in the preparation of this book, added accomplished typing to her countless other talents that I could not do without. (She has benefited, from time to time, from the assistance of Heather Falloon-Johnson and Linda Borchardt, to whom I am also grateful.)

There is Cesar Alvarez, my friend and my law partner, who made it possible for me to finish the job I started in Geneva, and whose continuing confidence in me means more to me than I can say.

There are my other partners and colleagues at Greenberg Traurig, who have waited patiently for my return from afar.

There are, of course, the twelve wise men with whom I have served during eight eventful years at the round table of the Appellate Body of the WTO. This is their book as much as mine (although the views I express in this book are, I stress, solely my own.)

There are Debra Steger, Peter Van den Bossche, Valerie Hughes, and all of the other dedicated members of the Appellate Body Secretariat who have served with us so loyally and so well along the way.

There are the Members of the WTO, who have twice honored me by appointing me, by consensus, to a job that has been, for me, a joy.

There are former President Bill Clinton, former Vice President Al Gore, and my former Congressional colleagues —in both parties —who had the confidence in me to nominate me for appointment by the Members of the WTO as "the American" on the Appellate Body.

There are Mickey Kantor, Rufus Yerxa, Andy Stoler, and Dorothy Dwoskin, who had not a little to do with my nomination.

There are my former Congressional chief of staff, Linda Hennessee, and all of the others who served with me during my time in the Congress, shuddered whenever I uttered the word "GATT," and assumed, rightly, that I would, for better or worse, write all of my own speeches.

There was my friend, the late Professor Jon Charney, who invited me to go to Vanderbilt to give the lecture that ultimately evolved into this book, and there is Dean Kent Syverud of Vanderbilt, who fulfilled one of my lifelong dreams when he invited me later to join the Vanderbilt law faculty.

There are those other friends who have encouraged me and helped me in this effort along the way: Pat and Jim Schroeder, Rita Bornstein and Harland Bloland, Mary Tom Bass, Bruce Starling, Pete Peterson, and the man who, more than any other, made it possible for me one day to become an old GATT hand, Reubin Askew.

There is Steve Charnovitz, who first suggested to my publisher, Nick May, that he might want to approach me about publishing this book.

There is Nick May himself, who has been bold enough to publish it.

There are my brother, Tom; my sisters, Debby, Cindy, and Terri; and my mother, Christine Bacchus, who first made me believe long ago that some day I might be capable of writing a book.

There is my son, Joe, the aspiring journalist, now twenty-three, who is a much more talented writer than his father. Joe is the editor of this book. He has edited every page with his eagle eye.

There is my daughter, Jamey, now twelve. When told that I was writing a book, she asked me, "Do I have to read it?" (I assured her, "Not yet.")

And, lastly, there is Rebecca, who has made all things possible for me, and always will.

She is my double rainbow.

Geneva, Switzerland

December, 2003

Preface

Promenade:
Morning in Geneva

From my apartment in the *Paquis*, I walk up in the morning to the esplanade along the lake. The plane trees in the *Place des Alpes* trill with birdsong. The cold waters of the lake sparkle in the bright blindness of the rising sun.

On the lake's far shore, elite emporiums yield to cobblestone streets that climb up through the old town toward the solitary spire of the medieval cathedral of St. Pierre. The steep, stony slope of the Saleve shadows the old town. Mont Blanc, the highest peak in Europe, a judge robed in white, peers down from afar on the pretensions and the pursuits of those of us who live and work in Geneva.

The sun does not always shine on Geneva. But, today, the sun lifts the chill from my face as, clutching my briefcase, I cross the *Quai du Mont Blanc* and reach the esplanade that follows the shoreline of Lac Leman, the lake of Geneva. I turn and walk north, joining the busy crowd on the wide walkway for the promenade that always welcomes a sunny day in this decidedly international city near the French border of Switzerland.

Perhaps a dozen languages fill the air. As many different costumes greet my eye. Teen-age girls in hip-huggers chatter in French while they linger on the low wall that lines the lake. Jogging Africans in gym shorts share a joke. Arab mothers in veils push expensive prams. A young woman in a thong bikini chats on a cell phone as she speeds by on roller blades. Weary business travelers, in rumpled suits and jetlag, blink at the new day. Tourists in designer jeans scurry to the designer shops. Aging Swiss pensioners soak up the sun on the benches that face the lake.

And, amid the morning throng, others, like me, embark on their daily walk to work.

The world, they say, meets in Geneva. And here, in the hurried onrush on the esplanade, the world meets every morning. Together, each morning, we each go our separate ways, variations on the common theme of humanity, all part of the morning promenade.

On my right, along the lakeshore, small children feed the ducks and the swans. Crying gulls swoop and soar. Sailboats bob in the marina. Steamers sound their horns as they begin the morning's journey to Lausanne and Montreux. The famed fountain of Geneva — the *Jet d'Eau* —rockets a wind-blown stream of icy water high above the lake.

On my left, bumper-to-bumper traffic crawls impatiently along the quay. Beyond the traffic jam, a long, high row of luxury hotels and ornate apartment buildings shelters the lake. Farther on is the *Palais Wilson*, once home to the lofty dreams of the League of Nations. Newly renovated, the *Palais* shines today in the sun.

Gazing now right, now left, tracing the turn of the lake, I thread my way through the crowd and follow the esplanade for perhaps half a mile. Then the crowd thins. The traffic recedes. The human hum fades away. I reach the welcome refuge of the *Parc Mon-Repos*.

I have walked this way perhaps a thousand times. Each time, upon entering the park, I am enfolded by a leafy calm. I walk into what was once, literally, a landscape by Corot. The walkway continues to hug the meandering shore. Children laugh on a nearby playground. Church bells in the old town ring in the distance. The bright reds of the azaleas adorn well-tended flowerbeds. I walk beneath ancient oaks, towering blue cedars, and perfect parasol pines. Winding my way along the walkway, I am renewed by the soothing repose of the well-named park.

But soon this serenity ends. I turn a last corner in the glade, and, just offshore, I see a Swiss police boat, anchored in the lake, awaiting today's promised protest. Just ahead, too, a few would-be protesters are beginning to gather. They shake their fists and wave their banners at the police boat as, unnoticed, I pass by.

Beyond the protesters is the mud-gray magnificence of the vast Italianate villa that serves as the international headquarters of the World Trade Organization. This is the center of the mutual endeavor of —at last count —146 countries and other customs territories that is both hailed and assailed around the world as the "WTO."

I walk up quickly now from the lake, through the trees, and around to the heavily-guarded main entrance of the villa. High fences and high gates separate the villa from the busy *Rue du Lausanne*. Swiss policemen stand about. Barbed wire barriers abound. Black limousines from a dozen embassies line the circular driveway that curves from the gate to the villa and back. Bored drivers read and smoke while they wait. Already this morning the meetings are beginning in "the house."

I wear a plastic ID card on a chain around my neck. Seeing the ID, the police wave me through. I cross the driveway and hurry up the low steps that lead to the main entrance. Two stone statues, noble and nude — and also a bit worn by a few decades of rain —guard either side of the heavy wooden door. I open the door and go in.

A small room just past the door serves as a security safety valve for all those who seek entry. Albert, the security guard inside, does not even glance at my ID. After all these years, he knows me. He simply nods and pushes the hidden button that opens another door, of sliding glass.

Beyond this glass door is a long lobby. Gray stone walls reach to a high ceiling. At the far end of the lobby, long windows look out on a broad green lawn that leads down to the lake. This is the great common hall of the villa. This is where the world meets in the WTO.

A second security guard merely waves me through.

I pass now through a milling mix of delegates from every part of the world. They are shedding coats, shuffling papers, drinking coffee, and tugging at elbows while they wait for the first meeting of the morning to begin.

I glance to my left through the open doors of a large meeting room. Long rows of signs with the names of the Members of the WTO are arrayed in alphabetical order, up and down the long tables in the room. Some of the delegates are sitting down and settling in.

I turn to my right and make my way slowly through the crowd toward the stairway that leads to the upper floors of the villa. No one notices me. The delegates know my name. They know my work. But, because my work is done behind closed doors in what the WTO calls "confidential" proceedings, few of them know my face.

So I am stopped only by yet another security guard, who offers his daily greeting in the form of his daily weather report. "Bonjour," says Mario. "The sun is shining today." "Bonjour, Mario," I reply, and congratulate him on the sunny day.

Reaching the staircase, I walk up the carpeted steps that lead to the next floor. Murals on either side of the stairs celebrate *"La Dignite' du Travail"* —the dignity of work. A sign at the top of the stairs says "Delegates Only" in the three official languages of the WTO —English, Spanish, and French. Though not a delegate, I go on.

The hubbub of the lobby yields to a sudden silence as I reach the top of the stairs. I turn now, in the hushed upper reaches of "the house," and climb a second, winding flight of stone stairs to the next floor. Here I am greeted by a final security guard who, like the others, simply waves me along, and down a long hallway.

I arrive at last at a security door at the entrance to a quiet wing of the far corner of the villa. I press the index finger of my right hand into a security device on the wall next to the door. The device reads my fingerprint, and the door unlocks. I push it open and enter the long corridor where I spend most of my days. Tall cabinets on either side of the corridor are filled with thick gray binders containing many of the details of all that fills those days.

I walk the length of the corridor. I enter the last door on the right.

Here, my morning promenade ends.

The sun shines through the windows of a corner room that overlooks the lake, the city, and the Alps. The other six are already here, and waiting. They sit in their usual places around a large round table. They look up as I enter our chambers. The world, for me, meets around this round table.

The ID card around my neck identifies me as "James Bacchus" of the "Appellate Body."

I am one of the seven "faceless foreign judges" of the WTO.

I am also the chairman.

I pull off my coat, put down my briefcase, pull out a pile of legal briefs, sit down, and ask, "Shall we begin?"

Part One

Reflections of a Faceless Foreign Judge

Chapter One

Trade Talks

Proust in the Ritz

Where shall we begin?

Often I am asked: what is it like? What is it like to be one of the seven "faceless foreign judges" who serve on the Appellate Body of the World Trade Organization?

At such times, I am reminded of a story told by the late British diplomat and "man of letters," Sir Harold Nicolson. In 1919, the young Nicolson was posted with the British delegation to the Versailles Peace Conference following World War I. At a party at the Ritz Hotel in Paris, he was introduced to Marcel Proust. The great French writer attended the party in "elaborate evening clothes."[1] He wore "white-kid gloves" while "clasping an opera hat," and he was "universally affable."[2]

Fascinated by all the ceremony surrounding the conference, the famously reclusive Proust had left his sickbed in his cork-lined room to go to the Ritz and learn more about the work of peacemaking. Proust being Proust, he was, in all his affability, interested, above all, in the smallest details of the diplomacy. In his diary, Nicolson reported of the party:

> *A swell affair. Proust is white, unshaven, grubby, slip-faced. He asks me questions. Will I please tell him how the Committees work. I say, "Well we generally meet at 10:00, there are secretaries behind . . ."* "Mais non, mais non, vous allez trop vite. Recommencez. Vous prenez la voiture de la Délégation. Vous descendez au Quai d'Orsay.

The part of Chapter One entitled "Table Talk" appeared previously, in an earlier version, as "Table Talk: Around the Table of the Appellate Body of the World Trade Organization," in <u>Vanderbilt Journal of Transnational Law</u>, Volume 35, Number 4 (October 2002), 1021-1039.
[1] Harold Nicolson, <u>Some People</u> (Boston and New York: Houghton Mifflin Company, 1926), 101.
[2] Id.

Vous montez l'escalier. Vous entrez dans la Salle.
Et alors? Précisez, mon cher, précisez."[3]

My French lessons as an undergraduate are more than thirty years
in the past. All these years later, I claim to master only what might be
called, generously, "restaurant French." That said, my loose translation
of what Proust said to the young diplomat is this: "But no, but no, you're
going too fast. Start again. You take the car to the Delegation. You go
down to the Quai d'Orsay. You go up the staircase. You enter the room.
And then? Be specific, my dear, be specific."

Thus inspired, Nicolson continued:

> *So I tell him everything. The sham cordiality of it all:*
> *the handshakes: the maps: the rustle of papers: the tea*
> *in the next room: the macaroons. He listens*
> *enthralled, interrupting from time to time – "Mais*
> *précisez, mon cher monsieur, n'allez pas trop*
> *vite."*[4]

"But be specific, my dear sir, don't go too fast."

In trying to describe what it is like to serve on the Appellate Body
of the WTO, I will pretend that Proust is listening. To the extent that the
WTO rules of conduct permit, I will try to be specific. And I will try not to
go too fast.

Table Talk

We generally meet at ten.

We meet at ten in the morning, around a round table in a corner
room of a quiet wing of the Italianate villa that serves as the global
headquarters of the World Trade Organization in Geneva, Switzerland.
The windows of our chambers look out on the shore of Lac Leman. Across
the lake are the medieval heights of the old town. Beyond are the snowy
peaks of the Alps. We work in a picture postcard.

---

[3] Harold Nicolson, Peacemaking 1919 (New York: 1964), 175-176. *See also* Margaret
MacMillan, Peacemakers: The Paris Conference of 1919 and Its Attempt to End War (London:
John Murray, 2001), 160.
[4] Id.

We see the sun stream through the windows of our chambers in the morning. We see it make its way slowly across the southern sky throughout the day. We see it sink slowly into the darkness of the evening. Watched by the sun, we sip endless cups of a French coffee-and-milk concoction called *renversé* while we pursue the work we share.

We have met around this table, morning after morning, since 1995. We began doing so then after more than one hundred countries agreed on the treaty that transformed the General Agreement on Tariffs and Trade —the GATT —into the newly created World Trade Organization.[5] We were appointed then by the Members of the new WTO to a supposedly "part-time" job that most of us have, for several years now, done, in reality, full-time.

Since 1995, the faces around the table have changed. The table has not. The same wooden table in Geneva, with its smoothly polished surface, and with a few scratches here and there, has seen both faces and cases come and go in the first decade of the WTO.

What transpires around our table is of much interest to much of the world. In one recent month, there were thirty-five million "hits" worldwide on the official WTO website.[6] The WTO has been described as "the Supreme Court of Globalization."[7] The Appellate Body of the WTO has been described by the *New York Times* as "essentially the supreme court of international trade."[8] There is much at stake every day for all the world in the outcome of our table talk.

There is also much misunderstanding about what happens during our talk at our table. In the eyes of many around the world, the WTO is seen as "the center of a global conspiracy against all that is good and decent. According to the myth, the 'ultra-secretive' WTO has become a sort of super-governmental body that forces nations to bow to the wishes of multinational corporations. It destroys local cultures ...; it despoils the

---

[5] The Marrakesh Agreement Establishing the World Trade Organization, *done at* Marrakesh, Morocco, 15 April 1994 (the "Marrakesh Agreement" or the "WTO treaty").

[6] Information and Media Relations Division, World Trade Organization.

[7] David Ransom, The No-Nonsense Guide to Fair Trade (London: New Internationalist, 2001), 74.

[8] David E. Sanger, *New York Times*, "U.S. Defeated In Its Appeal of Trade Case," (April 30, 1996), D-1.

environment; and it rides roughshod over democracy, forcing governments to remove laws that conflict with its sinister purposes."[9]

This is the myth. This is the fear. This is the stereotype of the WTO that stirs its fearful opponents. This is the extent of the misunderstanding that somehow prevails in much of the world about the WTO. But what is the reality? What really happens around our table? How and why does it happen? And who sits at the table and makes it happen, day after day and year after year?

We are seven around the table. We are from seven different countries. We are from seven different regions of the world. We are from seven different legal traditions. We are from seven different points of view. We are representative of seven different ways of living and working and thinking. We are, in the words of the WTO treaty, "broadly representative of membership in the WTO."[10]

I am the only American among the seven. I have always been the only American. I am also the only North American. As I write, I am, moreover, the only one remaining of the original seven who were first appointed to the Appellate Body by the Members of the WTO in 1995, and who first sat together around our table in Geneva and sipped *renversé*. Then I was the youngest —by fourteen years —of the original seven. Today, eight years later, as I approach the end of my time on the Appellate Body, I remain the youngest of the current seven. (I confess that, at 54, I find it increasingly difficult to find pursuits in which I am "the youngest.") Having been asked by my six colleagues to do so, I serve now in my second term as Chairman of the Appellate Body, and, thus, I chair our meetings.

The seven original and founding Members of the Appellate Body who first worked together around our table were: Julio Lacarté-Muro, of Uruguay; Claus-Dieter Ehlermann, of Germany; Florentino Feliciano, of the Philippines; Said El-Naggar, of Egypt; Mitsuo Matsushita, of Japan; Christopher Beeby, of New Zealand; and yours truly, of the United States of America. My colleagues Lacarté-Muro, Ehlermann, and Feliciano all served six years, and retired at the end of 2001. My colleagues El-Naggar

---

[9] Paul Krugman, "Enemies of the WTO: Bogus Arguments against the World Trade Organization," online in <u>Slate</u> (November 23, 1999).
[10] Article 17.3, World Trade Organization Understanding on Rules and Procedures Governing the Settlement of Disputes (the "Dispute Settlement Understanding," or the "DSU").

and Matsushita both retired after four years, in 1999. My dear friend Chris Beeby died in Geneva in 2000 while working at the WTO.

Nearly eight years later, the seven who work together around our table today are: Georges Abi-Saab, of Egypt; A.V. Ganesan, of India; Yasuhei Taniguchi, of Japan; Luiz Olavo Baptista, of Brazil; John Lockhart, of Australia; Giorgio Sacerdoti, of Italy; and, still, yours truly. These six will remain and will continue to serve the Members of the WTO after my allotted eight years on the Appellate Body have ended.

We are aided in our work by the Appellate Body "Secretariat," which is a fancy way of describing our very fine staff. For more than five years after our initial appointment, the director of our Secretariat was a superb international lawyer and former trade negotiator from Canada, Debra Steger. She has been succeeded by another gifted Canadian lawyer, Valerie Hughes. Through the years, numerous bright young lawyers from all over the world have worked with us and joined with us from time to time in the discussions around our table.

The subject of these discussions is what we call the "covered agreements" of the World Trade Organization.[11] The "covered agreements" are the GATT and the numerous other international trade agreements that comprise the WTO treaty and that bind all WTO Members. All told, the text and the "schedules" of the "covered agreements" include about thirty thousand pages of binding international trade and other economic obligations.

These obligations are global rules on which all WTO Members have agreed, and that, by their agreement, provide the legal ground-rules for almost all of global commerce. These global rules are essentially contracts among the countries and other customs territories that are the Members of the WTO. They are the culmination of more than half a century of experience in building a "multilateral trading system" that began, first, with the GATT, in the aftermath of the Second World War, and continues, now, with the WTO.

We seven are, according to the WTO treaty, "persons of recognized authority, with demonstrated expertise in law, international trade and the subject matter of the covered agreements generally."[12] As such, our

---

[11] Article 1.1, DSU.
[12] Article 17.3, DSU.

job is to help the Members of the WTO fulfill the terms of the "covered agreements." Our job is to assist the Members of the WTO in their combined efforts "to clarify the existing provisions of those agreements in accordance with customary rules of interpretation of public international law" as a final forum of appeal in WTO dispute settlement.[13]

We do not wear robes. We do not wear wigs. We do not wear the white bibs that are often worn by jurists on other international tribunals. We do not have all of the institutional trappings that have accrued to other tribunals with the passage of time and with the accretion of tradition. We do not even have titles. The WTO treaty speaks only of a "standing Appellate Body."[14] The treaty does not say what the seven "persons" who are members of the Appellate Body should be called. So we call ourselves simply "Members of the Appellate Body."

Others seem not to know what to call us. From time to time, and from judgment to controversial judgment, we are called everything from the "seven wise men" to the "seven dwarfs." Some observers of the WTO describe us as "trade experts." Some trade experts describe us as "generalists." Journalists, in reporting our rulings, rarely mention us. To the extent that they do mention us, they usually describe us generically and anonymously as simply "the WTO."

And some, sometimes, call us *"faceless foreign judges."*

We are called *"faceless,"* perhaps, because few in the world seem to know who we are. Few in the world who write about the WTO, few who criticize the WTO, and few even who defend the WTO, know who we are. We always sign our opinions, but, for whatever reason, few ever mention our names. We may be called "faceless" as well because the WTO Members have mandated in the WTO treaty that all our proceedings must be "confidential."[15] So we meet behind closed doors. No one who has not participated in one of our appeals has ever seen us work.

We are called *"foreign,"* perhaps, because we are, by treaty, "unaffiliated with any government."[16] We were each nominated by our own countries to serve on the Appellate Body, but we do not represent our own countries in our work on the Appellate Body. Instead, each of us

---

[13] Article 3.2, DSU.
[14] Article 17.1, DSU.
[15] Article 17.10, DSU.
[16] Article 17.3, DSU.

and all of us have been appointed by *all* the Members of the WTO. We each speak for *all* the Members of the WTO by speaking *solely* for the WTO trading system *as a whole*. We are independent. We are impartial. We are required to be both "independent" and "impartial" by the WTO rules of conduct.[17]

We may be called *"judges"* because, whatever we may call ourselves, and whatever else others may call us, that word may best describe what we do. For our job is to "judge" appeals in international trade disputes affecting the lives of five billion people in the 95 percent of all world commerce conducted by the 146 countries and other customs territories that are — currently — Members of the WTO, and, thus, are bound by the WTO treaty. We may not wear robes, but we are cloaked with what amounts in most respects to a judicial responsibility.

Moreover, the scope of our jurisdiction seems to grow daily. At this point, every country in the world is either a Member of the WTO or seems to want to be. At last glance, more than two dozen additional countries had applied for admission in a process the WTO calls "accession." China and Taiwan are now Members. Russia, Saudi Arabia, Vietnam, and Ukraine are among those waiting to become Members. Among the others awaiting membership are about half of the Arab states and a handful of former Soviet republics.

Technically, the Appellate Body is rightly described as "quasi-judicial." Our rulings take the form of "recommendations" in "reports" to the Members of the WTO. To have legal effect, those reports must be adopted by the Members of the WTO sitting in their collective role as the WTO's "Dispute Settlement Body." However, a ruling by the Appellate Body in an international trade dispute will *not* be adopted only if *all* the Members of the WTO decide "by consensus" that it should *not* be — including the Member or Members in whose favor we may have ruled.[18] Thus far, this has never happened.

But whether our work is described as "judicial" or as "quasi-judicial," and whatever we may be called, we have much to do around our table in Geneva in keeping up with an ever-growing caseload of appeals in international trade disputes. We have much to do because, alone among all the international tribunals in the world, and, indeed,

---

[17] WTO Rules of Conduct, Articles II and III (2).
[18] Article 17.14, DSU.

alone among all the international tribunals in the *history* of the world, the Appellate Body of the WTO is unique in two important ways.

The *first* way in which we are unique is that we have what we lawyers call "compulsory jurisdiction." The Appellate Body has "compulsory jurisdiction" because the WTO dispute settlement system has "compulsory jurisdiction." All of the Members of the WTO have agreed in the WTO treaty to use the WTO dispute settlement system exclusively to resolve all of their treaty-related disputes with other WTO Members. A WTO Member that does not do so may be sued by another WTO Member for not doing so in WTO dispute settlement. Thus far, this, too, has never happened.

The *second* way in which the Appellate Body is unique is that the "recommendations" we make in our "reports" are upheld. Our judgments in appeals in the WTO are upheld, not by us, but by the Members of the WTO themselves. They are upheld through the power of economic suasion. Like all treaties, the WTO treaty is in the nature of a contract. Indeed, the members of the WTO's predecessor, the GATT, were often called "Contracting Parties." In every contract, there are obligations and there are benefits. And, as in every other contract, in the global contract called the WTO treaty, if a WTO member fails to fulfill all of its obligations under the contract, it risks losing some of the benefits of the contract.

The WTO does not have the power to *make* any Member of the WTO do anything. The Members of the WTO are sovereign countries and other customs territories. No Member of the WTO can ever be required to comply with any ruling in WTO dispute settlement. As the trade scholar and former American trade negotiator Judith Bello has pointed out, despite what some have suggested, "the WTO has no jailhouse, no bail bondsmen, no blue helmets, no truncheons or tear gas."[19] (Indeed, it was only recently that the Appellate Body was able to obtain an electric pencil sharpener.)

Sovereignty remains. Yet, under the WTO treaty, if a Member chooses —in an exercise of its sovereignty —not to comply with a ruling in WTO dispute settlement, it risks paying an economic price. That price is what the treaty describes as "compensation and the suspension of concessions."[20] This is a form of "damages" to the other Member injured

---

[19] Judith Hippler Bello, "The WTO Dispute Understanding: Less is More," 90 American Journal of International Law 416, 417 (1996).
[20] Article 22.1, DSU.

in that trade dispute. These "damages" consist of either additional access for the injured Member to the market of the "non-complying" Member in other sectors of trade ("compensation"), or reduced access for that "non-complying" Member to the market of the injured Member in other sectors of trade ("suspension of concessions"). As this can sometimes be a very high price to pay, WTO Members have considerable economic incentive to choose to comply with WTO judgments. They almost always do so.

These two ways in which the dispute settlement system of the WTO is unique help keep us busy around our round table in Geneva as we try to help the Members of the WTO provide what the WTO treaty calls "security and predictability to the multilateral trading system."[21] Like the WTO itself, and like the thousands of pages of WTO rules, our jurisprudential uniqueness is the culmination of more than half a century of building the multilateral trading system, first under the GATT, and now under the Dispute Settlement Understanding —the "DSU" —that is the legal linchpin among the "covered agreements" of the WTO treaty. It is the DSU that ensures our uniqueness by providing for a "dispute settlement system" with compulsory jurisdiction and with the authority to uphold WTO rules.

This "dispute settlement system" began, under the GATT, as largely a *diplomatic* system for resolving international trade disputes. It has, however, evolved in half a century into what is now largely a *legal* system, and the system's essentially *legal* nature today is reinforced by the DSU as part of the WTO treaty. We are, as a result, also kept busy around our table because WTO Members know that, when they bring a case in WTO dispute settlement that eventually reaches the Appellate Body, they will receive a *legal* judgment, and not a *political* judgment. They know that they will receive a judgment that will, in the words of the WTO treaty, "address" the "issues of law" that are "raised . . . during the appellate proceeding."[22] Nothing more. Nothing less. For, in addressing issues of law in WTO appeals, we seven have always been, and we will always be, as one observer for the *New York Times* has put it, "impartial and unflinching."[23]

For all these reasons, in the handful of years since we began working together around our table in 1995, the WTO has rapidly become

---

[21] Article 3.2, DSU.
[22] Article 17.12, DSU.
[23] Michael M. Weinstein, "Economic Scene: Should Clinton embrace the China trade deal? Some say yes," *New York Times* (September 9, 1999), at C2.

by far the busiest international dispute settlement system in all of history. Almost all of the trillions of dollars of trade that is conducted annually among the Members of the WTO is conducted *without dispute*. WTO Members have agreed on the rules for trade, and WTO Members generally abide by those rules. This is often forgotten in the many heated debates about having a rule-based world trading system. But, inevitably, there are disputes about what some of the rules for trade mean, and about how those rules apply to the ever-increasing flow of trade. And, when there are such disputes, there must be an effective way to resolve them. This is the purpose of the WTO dispute settlement system. As the WTO treaty says, "The aim of the dispute settlement system is to secure a positive solution to a dispute" involving WTO Members.[24]

With the growth of the WTO trading system, ever-increasing numbers of trade disputes have been brought to the WTO by WTO Members in search of a "positive solution." Thus far, more than three hundred formal complaints have been brought to the WTO, and more than twenty thousand pages of jurisprudence have resulted from WTO dispute settlement.[25] The number of pages that have been written in an effort to help resolve WTO disputes is increasing almost every day. Together, my colleagues on the Appellate Body and I have written many of those pages. (For several years now, I have nursed a pinched nerve in my neck from writing lengthy legal opinions in longhand.)

The parties to the proceedings in WTO dispute settlement that arise from these trade disputes are exclusively the countries and other customs territories that are Members of the WTO. No one else is entitled under the WTO treaty to participate in WTO dispute settlement. Private interests do not have "standing" to bring suits in the WTO. But, of course, the WTO Members that are the sole parties to these proceedings are always of the view that they are asserting and defending important domestic interests. Thus, for example, it is not surprising that the journalists who reported on the dispute a few years ago between Japan and the United States involving the Japanese market for photographic film routinely described that dispute as the "Kodak-Fuji case."[26] Those two competing companies each had a significant stake in the outcome of that case.

---

[24] Article 3.7, DSU.

[25] John H. Jackson, "Perceptions about the WTO trade institutions," World Trade Review, Vol. 1, No. 1, 101, 109. Professor Jackson keeps a running count of the page numbers which is, at this writing, in excess of twenty thousand,

[26] *See e.g.*, Nancy Dunne et al., "WTO's Film Ruling Angers Washington," *Financial Times* (December 8, 1997), at 3.

In these first few years of the WTO, numerous trade disputes among the Members of the WTO have been settled "out of court," so to speak, by virtue of the very existence of a compulsory dispute settlement system that can make enforceable judgments. Most disputes have been resolved before even reaching the initial formal legal stage of "consultations." And most disputes that have led to formal "consultations" have been resolved during "consultations" without the formal establishment of a "panel" to render a judgment. These are not the disputes that make the headlines. This success in resolving disputes without resort to formal litigation may well, however, be the greatest success thus far of the WTO. It is certainly persuasive evidence that the WTO dispute settlement system can do much to make a world in which countries can abide by their agreements with other countries.

Many of the other disputes that have been brought to the WTO in its brief history have led to formal international litigation, and have resulted in rulings by the *ad hoc* three-judge "panels" that are established separately for each dispute and are the WTO equivalent of trial courts. About seventy percent of these disputes have been appealed to the "standing" Appellate Body, and about sixty of these disputes have resulted in reports by the Appellate Body that have been adopted by the Members of the WTO. Moreover, almost all of the disputes that have been heard by panels and by the Appellate Body have been resolved with what the parties to the disputes have viewed as a "positive solution."

There are many who see the continued success of the WTO dispute settlement system as the key to securing the overall success of the WTO. The early successes of WTO dispute settlement inspired the former Director-General of the WTO, Mike Moore, to describe the WTO dispute settlement system as the "crown jewel" of the multilateral trading system.[27] Peter Sutherland, the former Director-General of the WTO's predecessor, the GATT, has gone so far as to say that the WTO dispute settlement system "is the greatest advance in multilateral governance since Bretton Woods."[28]

The conference at Bretton Woods in New Hampshire toward the end of the Second World War was the beginning of what has since become

---

[27] Former Director-General Moore used the phrase "crown jewel" during the "swearing-in" ceremony for new Members of the Appellate Body before the WTO Dispute Settlement Body, in Geneva, on December 19, 2001.

[28] Former Director-General Sutherland was quoted in "Rules to fight by: The US and Europe Are Looking to the World Trade Organization to Resolve Their Dispute Over Steel," *Financial Times* (March 25, 2002), at 22.

the WTO-based world trading system. It was there where the victorious Allies agreed on much of what became the architecture for the postwar economic system. Part of that architecture was supposed to be an "International Trade Organization" that would help prevent a renewal of the "beggar-thy-neighbor" trade policies that had deepened and widened the Great Depression in the 1930s and had contributed to the outbreak of the war.

The idea of an "International Trade Organization" —an "ITO" — fell victim to the isolationism that soon returned in the aftermath of the war. However, the initial international agreement that had been negotiated as a prelude to an "ITO" —the General Agreement on Tariffs and Trade —entered into force on a "provisional" basis. It turned out that, as those at Bretton Woods had anticipated, the postwar world needed some kind of an institution to establish and uphold rules to facilitate an increased flow of world trade. Thus, in time, the piece of paper called "the GATT" also became a place called "the GATT" in Geneva.

The subsequent evolution of the GATT into the WTO occurred over the course of nearly five decades. The twenty-three original "Contracting Parties" to the GATT —including the United States of America —eventually became more than one hundred. The limited coverage of the GATT eventually grew to include much of the world economy. And the "Contracting Parties" to the GATT eventually achieved much of what they originally intended when they tried to establish an "International Trade Organization" when, in 1995, they became the founding Members of the WTO.

The GATT grew into the WTO through a series of "rounds" of multilateral trade negotiations. There were eight such "rounds" during the nearly five decades between the agreement on the GATT and the establishment of the WTO. The first "rounds" were negotiations on cuts in tariffs. The later "rounds" addressed not only tariffs, but also the global proliferation of non-tariff barriers to trade. Round by round, the GATT rounds lowered many of the global barriers to trade on a multilateral basis.

The eighth such round of negotiations was the "Uruguay Round," which began in Punta del Este, Uruguay, in 1986, concluded in Marrakesh, Morocco, in 1994, and culminated in the adoption of the WTO treaty and in the creation, as one consequence of that treaty, of the WTO. The initials on the door of the world headquarters of the world trading system in

Geneva were changed from "GATT" to "WTO," and much else was changed as well by the global approval and global implementation of the WTO treaty. Among the most significant of those changes were those that established, for the first time, a binding dispute settlement system with the two unique qualities of compulsory jurisdiction and powers of enforcement.

Before the changes made in the Uruguay Round, countries were not required to submit to dispute settlement when other countries questioned their compliance with GATT rules. They could be sued only if they agreed to be sued in a particular dispute. Moreover, before the innovations of the Uruguay Round, there was no assurance that rulings in dispute settlement would be binding. A losing party in a dispute could single-handedly "block" the "consensus" needed to "adopt" a ruling. For these reasons, and for all its successes, the GATT was often derided as the "General Agreement to Talk and Talk."

The Dispute Settlement Understanding that was concluded in the Uruguay Round as part of the WTO treaty changed all this. It did so by establishing compulsory jurisdiction, and also by establishing a "reverse consensus" rule that provides that a ruling in WTO dispute settlement will be adopted automatically unless *all* of the Members of the WTO —sitting as the "Dispute Settlement Body" of the WTO —agree that it should *not* be. Because this would mean that the winning party in a dispute would have to agree to set aside its own victorious judgment in a trade dispute, this is tantamount to "automaticity," and makes the rulings of panels and of the Appellate Body in WTO dispute settlement, in practical effect, automatically binding and thereby subject to the treaty's powers of enforcement. As a result, while the WTO remains a forum where WTO Members can *talk* about trade, it is also a place where WTO Members can *take action* on trade. And much of the action at the WTO occurs in dispute settlement.

Nearly a decade after the successful conclusion of the Uruguay Round, the workload of the new WTO dispute settlement system increases while the other necessary work of strengthening the world trading system continues. In particular, a new "round" of multilateral trade negotiations is underway —the ninth since the agreement on the GATT and the first since the creation of the WTO. At their ministerial conference in Doha, Qatar, in November, 2001, the Members of the WTO "launched" the "Doha Round." The deadline for concluding this new "round" of global negotiations under the auspices of the WTO is, currently, January 1, 2005.

The negotiating agenda for this latest "round" reaches around the world and far into the future.

The "developed countries" that are Members of the WTO — including the United States —are seeking additional "market access" worldwide for their manufactured and agricultural goods beyond what they have already achieved through successive tariff cuts in previous "rounds." They are seeking market access also for the services they provide as an increasing part of their ever-evolving economies. Furthermore, they are seeking new rules in an array of other areas relating to trade such as intellectual property, investment, government purchases, and antitrust and competition policies, among others.

The "developing countries" that are a growing majority of the Members of the WTO are, in turn, seeking additional market access in the areas where they are routinely the most productive and, therefore, the most competitive in the world economy. In particular, they are desirous of lowering the barriers in developed countries —such as the United States —to additional market access for their agricultural goods and for such manufactured goods as textiles and steel. Moreover, they are intent as well on negotiating new limits on the "anti-dumping" duties, the "countervailing" duties to governmental subsidies, and the "safeguard" duties that WTO Members are permitted to impose as "trade remedies" in response to certain import surges under current WTO rules.

A "review" of the WTO dispute settlement system is also on the agenda of the "Doha Round," and some changes in the dispute settlement system may well result from the "round." But perhaps as important as the trade talks that are ongoing about dispute settlement in the new "round" are the trade talks that are occurring as a part of dispute settlement every day in Geneva. The Members of the WTO are likely to have little success in agreeing on the new rules for trade that the world needs if we are not successful in upholding the rules for trade on which the Members of the WTO have agreed previously through WTO dispute settlement. The dispute settlement system must remain the "crown jewel" of the overall WTO trading system. For what good are rules if they are not upheld?

Thus, much of the focus of the world trading system rightly remains on dispute settlement. Given the broad scope and sway of the WTO treaty, the disputes that are resolved by upholding WTO rules in WTO dispute settlement routinely involve manufacturing, agriculture, services, intellectual property, investment, taxation, and other forms and aspects of commerce of all kinds. The appeals we have judged thus far have affected literally thousands of products, and have involved as many as several dozen countries at one time. They have involved everything from apples to computers, from automobiles to airplanes, from semiconductors to supercomputers, from shrimp to satellites, and from bananas to chemicals to pharmaceuticals to oil to aerospace to lumber to textiles and to steel.

Ever more varied kinds of disputes relating to ever more complicated aspects of the complex inter-relationships between conventional trade issues and competing areas of pressing global concern are resulting in WTO dispute settlement as more agreements enter into force, more agreements are concluded, and more concessions are made. Trade and technology. Trade and the environment. Trade and labor. Trade and health. Trade and virtually anything and everything that may affect trade are, increasingly, within the growing domain of WTO dispute settlement. Beyond the border, at the border, and inside the border, the boundaries of WTO jurisdiction are ever-expanding. Thus, increasingly, the "boundaries" of WTO jurisdiction are the subject of both political and academic debate.[29] And, increasingly, too, the decisions made in WTO dispute settlement are the subject of worldwide controversy. They are controversial because, being binding, and being enforceable, they cannot be ignored.

We do not render advisory opinions on the Appellate Body. We render opinions only when there are specific trade disputes. By treaty, all WTO Members that are parties to a dispute have the automatic right to appeal "issues of law covered in the panel report and legal interpretations developed by the panel" to the Appellate Body.[30] Under the treaty, on appeal, we "shall address each of the issues raised…during the appellate proceeding."[31] In doing so, we "may uphold, modify or reverse the legal findings and conclusions of the panel."[32]

Thus, we cannot choose either the disputes that are appealed to us or the issues of law that are appealed to us in those disputes. Unlike the Supreme Court of the United States, for example, we have no

---

[29] *See* "Symposium: The Boundaries of the WTO," American Journal of International Law, Vol. 96, No. 1 (January 2002), 1 – 158.
[30] Article 17.6, DSU.
[31] Article 17.12, DSU.
[32] Article 17.13, DSU.

discretionary jurisdiction. Further, we have no power to "remand" a dispute to a panel for further consideration. In short, we have no authority whatsoever to decline to hear an appeal. Moreover, we have no authority whatsoever to refrain from "addressing" a legal issue that has been properly raised in an appeal. The WTO treaty says that we "shall address" every legal issue raised in an appeal. So we do.

And we do so within deadlines established by the treaty. Most other international tribunals have no deadlines. We not only have deadlines; we have deadlines that are strict and demanding. No matter how complicated the issues may be that are raised on appeal, generally we have no more than ninety days in which to hear and decide an appeal.[33] As our record reflects, we take seriously the need to "address" the legal issues raised in each appeal both thoroughly and appropriately within the treaty deadlines. We have met the treaty deadlines consistently, and I am persuaded that this, too, has contributed to the success thus far of the WTO dispute settlement system.

By treaty, we have been granted the authority to draw up our own "working procedures" within the deadlines "in consultation with the chairman of the DSB and the Director-General" of the WTO.[34] Eight years ago, we sat down together at our table with a blank legal pad and began writing our procedures. It took us three weeks. Since then, we have made only minor changes. Using these procedures, in each appeal, we review the panel record and the panel report, we review submissions by the WTO Members that are interested parties and third parties, we conduct an oral hearing on the legal issues that have been raised, we deliberate at length on the legal issues raised in the appeal, and we write a final report containing our judgment. And generally we do all this within no more than ninety days. (My colleagues would no doubt urge me to add that this is, actually, no more than seventy-five days, as it is our practice, when possible, to allow two weeks for mandatory translation.)

Although there are three official languages of the WTO —English, Spanish, and French[35] —as a matter of practice, the seven of us generally work in our common language —English. We conduct our oral hearings in English —unless asked by the WTO Members participating in the hearing to do otherwise. We deliberate in English —embellished by the

---

[33] Article 17.5, DSU.
[34] Article 17.9, DSU.
[35] Article 16, the Marrakesh Agreement.

occasional Latin legal phrase heard around the table. We write our reports in English. Our reports are usually translated into Spanish and French before they are released to the parties to the appeal and to the world.

We have been able to meet our deadlines in part because we have shared our growing workload among the seven. By treaty, three of us sit as a "division" to hear and decide each appeal.[36] Those three sign the report of the Appellate Body in that appeal. Before a decision is reached, however, the three on the "division" in the appeal engage in an "exchange of views" with the four others who are not on that "division." One of the three serves as "Presiding Member" of the "division" and also presides in the "exchange of views." By treaty, all seven of us "serve in rotation" in all of these roles,[37] and, by rule, we do so on an anonymous and random basis that tends to equalize our individual workloads.[38]

Whatever our individual role may be in any particular appeal, each of us strives always to reach a "consensus" in every appeal. We are not required to do so. The treaty does not prohibit dissents. The treaty provides only that "opinions expressed" by individuals serving on the Appellate Body must be "anonymous."[39] But, thus far, in all our years of working together, and in about sixty appeals, there has not been even one dissent by any Member of the Appellate Body to the conclusions or the recommendations in any Appellate Body report. Thus far, all our decisions have been by "consensus."

Table Manners

I do not believe that I betray the "confidentiality" of our table talk by saying that, in the many appeals that have been made thus far to the Appellate Body, the "consensus" we have achieved has not always been achieved easily. Nor do I think I betray any of our "confidentiality" by saying that our ability to achieve consensus around our table in our first seven years is testimony to the considerable care taken by the Members of the WTO in the elaborate, global selection process they have employed in appointing all of the Members of the Appellate Body.

Some may say that there is no accounting for my own selection. As one astute observer remarked in a letter to the editor of my hometown

---

[36] Article 17.1, DSU; Rule 6 (1), Working Procedures for Appellate Review.
[37] Article 17.1, DSU.
[38] Rule 6 (2), Working Procedures for Appellate Review.
[39] Article 17.11, DSU.

newspaper in Florida shortly after I was first appointed to the Appellate Body in 1995, "I don't understand all this fuss about Jim Bacchus. He is just another lawyer from Orlando."[40] And so I am. My colleagues who have served with me on the Appellate Body have, however, all been much more than "just lawyers." From the very beginning, I have been joined around our table in Geneva by distinguished international jurists of the very highest caliber.

My colleagues on the Appellate Body are not narrow-minded "trade bureaucrats." They are not administrative cogs in some thoughtless, heedless, global administrative machinery. On the contrary, they are decidedly determined individuals with decidedly individual ways of thinking. They are individuals who are committed to the multilateral trading system. They are also individuals with broad experience and with broad concerns that extend far beyond the commercial "widgets" of trade. They are much mindful at all times of how very much all they do in WTO dispute settlement affects billions of other individuals throughout the world.

My colleagues on the Appellate Body have, each and all, been legal thinkers and legal craftsmen of the very highest quality. They have been students of history and philosophy, as well as students of economics and jurisprudence. They have been seekers of the better world that yet can be —if we ultimately succeed in our shared efforts to sustain multilateral trade liberalization, and to secure the international rule of law. Today I remain, still, just a lawyer from Orlando. Yet, because of my colleagues, and because of all I have learned from them while working with them around our table in Geneva, I am, perhaps, more than I was when I first was appointed by the Members of the WTO to the Appellate Body.

In his later years, Sir Harold Nicolson wrote a book that he titled, quaintly, <u>Good Behaviour, being a Study of Certain Types of Civility</u>.[41] A principal theme of the book is the need for "civility" in the world, and for "the necessity of manners" as a means of achieving civility.[42] Nicolson, who survived the incivilities of two world wars (not to mention all the many incivilities of a long career in diplomacy and in politics), believed

---

[40] Wayne Lindsey, "Just Another Lawyer," *Orlando Sentinel* (December 8, 1995), at A22.
[41] Harold Nicolson, <u>Good Behaviour, being a Study of Certain Types of Civility</u> (London: Constable and Co, 1955).
[42] Id. at 1.

that the key to the manners of civility is "reasonableness."[43] The Members of the Appellate Body of the WTO share this belief. We believe in the power of human reason. We favor reasonableness as the best way of using reason, and we think that the use of reason is the best way of discovering legal truth by finding the right legal answer.

Like Nicolson, we have each read the essay <u>On Liberty</u> by perhaps the all-time champion of reasonableness, the nineteenth-century British political economist John Stuart Mill. Some of my colleagues can even recite long passages of Mill's timeless essay from memory. We all share with Mill a fervent belief in the "salutary effect" of a "collision of opinions" as the best way of finding truth.[44] Like him, we are persuaded that "truth has no chance but in proportion as every side of it, every opinion which embodies any fraction of the truth, not only finds advocates but is so advocated as to be listened to."[45] The whole of the truth we seek together is often to be found in the combination of every "fraction" or "fragment of truth" that each of us brings to our table.[46]

One of the most illustrious of the twentieth-century followers of Mill, the late American political philosopher John Rawls, echoed Mill in advancing the ideal of what he called "public reason."[47] Rawls saw "public reason" as the ongoing realization of mutual reasonableness in the making of public decisions in a pluralistic society. In particular, he said, "This ideal is realized, or satisfied, whenever judges, legislators, chief executives, and other government officials, as well as candidates for public office, act from and follow the idea of public reason and explain to other citizens their reasons for supporting fundamental political positions in terms of the political conception of justice they regard as the most reasonable."[48]

Rawls saw this ideal as applying also —and especially —to *legal* positions in judicial decisionmaking. He observed that "the idea of public reason applies more strictly to judges than to others," and that it applies to "the discourse of judges in their decisions, and especially of the judges of the supreme court."[49] Those of us who have served on the Appellate

---

[43] Id. at 9.
[44] John Stuart Mill, <u>On Liberty</u>, at 115.
[45] Id.
[46] Id. at 109.
[47] John Rawls, "The Idea of Public Reason Revisited," 64 U. Chi. L. Rev. 765 (Summer, 1997). *See also* John Rawls, <u>Political Liberalism</u> (New York: Columbia University Press, 1993), 212-254.
[48] Id. at 768-769.
[49] Id. at 768, 767.

Body do not see the Appellate Body as a "supreme court." But, in fulfilling our "quasi-judicial" responsibilities to the Members of the WTO —in our deliberations, in our decisionmaking, and in our explanations of our decisions to a waiting world —the Members of the Appellate Body have aspired to this aspect of the ideal of "public reason."

Thus, our table manners are manners of civility that rely on reasonableness. Mutual trust, mutual respect, and —above all —a relentless mutual criticism always prevail at our table. Around the table of the Appellate Body is heard a mutual criticism that flows from manners of civility that are not always heard outside our chambers. We try to reason through reasonableness. We try to think clearly. We try to think consistently. We try to think things through. And we try —always —to think *together*.

Despite what some may say, there are no representatives of the large multinational corporations at our table. There are no emissaries from countries large or small. There are no lawyers, no lobbyists, no advocates of any kind or from anywhere who join us at our table as we engage in the truth-seeking of our mutual criticism. At our table, there are only the seven of us. And there are only two things that matter to the seven of us as we seek the right answer at our table —the quality of our individual ideas, and the extent of our individual persuasiveness as advocates of our ideas.

Nothing else matters to us in the course or in the outcome of our mutual criticism. Not nationality. Not seniority. Not the length of our resumes. Not the extent of any outside controversy about the dispute before us. Not the clamor or the criticisms of the media or of others. Nothing. All that matters to us in reaching our decisions is what we say and how persuasively we say it to one another when addressing the issues that have been raised by the Members of the WTO in the process of our considerable efforts to build consensus. These are our table manners. This is the essence of our dedication to mutual criticism, and the evidence of our enduring devotion to reasonableness.

In our time together around our table, in all our efforts to achieve consensus through reasonableness, we have learned that the issues that are raised on appeal in international disputes in the WTO are rarely clear-cut. Even now, there are many important provisions of the "covered agreements," and, in fact, some entire agreements that are part of the overall WTO treaty, that have yet to be construed even once by the

Appellate Body. Moreover, legal issues are raised in almost every appeal that are, in legal parlance, issues of "first impression."

In truth, it might be said of the entirety of the ruled-based WTO multilateral trading system that, in many ways, it poses a *world* of "first impression." There are literally no precedents in the world for much that we are asked to help resolve for the world. Given this, we seven are very much of the view that we owe it to the Members of the WTO, and especially to all the people of the world that we seven serve by serving the Members of the WTO, to examine every last shade of nuance of every single legal issue that is raised in every single appeal. And we always do.

That is why our hearings sometimes last for days, our deliberations sometimes last for weeks, and our drafting sometimes lasts for draft after draft after draft. That is why we meet, day after day, around our round table. That is why we sit, hour after hour, day after day, plumbing the depths of meaning of the words of the WTO treaty, slicing the layers of logic in the interpretation of those words, and turning over and over, up and down, and inside and out, every last argument that may have been advanced about those words in an effort to reach a "consensus" on the right reasoning and the right result on every legal issue raised in every appeal. That is why we work together to forge a "consensus" up until the very limits of our ever-present and ever-pressing deadlines.

As our current chairman, I preside over our general discussions. As a practical matter, this mostly consists of keeping a list on a legal pad of the order in which we have each asked to speak about the many subtleties of the WTO treaty. Those subtleties are many, and perhaps foremost among them is the very nature of the WTO treaty.

Contrary to some popular misconceptions, the WTO treaty is *not* a free trade agreement. It does not *mandate* free trade. The WTO treaty is an international agreement for freeing trade and for preventing trade discrimination. It establishes a framework of rules that enables WTO Members to free trade by making voluntary trade concessions on a multilateral basis, and it discourages WTO Members from engaging in certain kinds of trade discrimination against trading partners that are also Members of the WTO-based multilateral trading system.

Because the WTO treaty is *not* a "free trade agreement," the job of the WTO is *not* to ensure "*free trade*." Nor is that the job of the Appellate

Body of the WTO. The job of the Appellate Body is to assist the Members of the WTO in clarifying and upholding the rules on which they themselves have agreed as an overall framework for securing *"freer trade"* within a system that also recognizes and respects other vital national and international needs and goals.

There is a very real difference. Sometimes the rules on which the Members of the WTO have agreed achieve "freer trade," and sometimes they even achieve "free trade." But sometimes they do not. Sometimes the rules uphold restrictions on trade where no trade concessions have been made, or where the Members of the WTO have agreed that such restrictions are justified to counter "unfair" trade, to provide for a period of adjustment following unforeseen import increases resulting from a trade concession, or to accomplish other legitimate objectives, such as protecting consumers, ensuring public health, and preserving the environment. At all times, our job on the Appellate Body is simply to help the Members of the WTO clarify and uphold their rules.

The more than —at last count —thirty thousand pages of WTO rules and concessions offer endless opportunities for dispute, for discussion, and for interpretation in dispute settlement. In those pages are found numerous WTO rules that are vital to the multilateral trading system. Our growing caseload is certainly evidence that the Members of the WTO do not always agree on what all of the rules mean. They would all probably agree, though, that, within the elaborate framework of WTO rules, three basic rules are perhaps the most significant and the most central to the WTO system of concessions and non-discrimination.

The first basic rule is the rule on "binding concessions." This first rule has been the key to the historic success of the WTO-based system in lowering tariff barriers to trade worldwide. This rule establishes an agreed framework for voluntary trade concessions on a multilateral basis. WTO Members are not required to make tariff concessions. But, under this vital and fundamental WTO rule, once WTO Members do make tariff concessions, and once they agree to "bind" those concessions, they are bound by them.[50] The "schedules" containing the concessions are part of the treaty. "Binding concessions" are therefore enforceable under the treaty, and cannot be changed without the agreement of other WTO Members following further negotiations.[51]

---

[50] *See* Article II, the General Agreement on Tariffs and Trade (GATT 1947) (the "GATT"), which, as the text of the GATT 1994, is part of the WTO treaty.
[51] *See* Article XXVIII of the GATT 1994.

The second basic rule is the rule requiring "most-favoured-nation," or "MFN," treatment. Despite what many in the media —and some in politics —seem to think, this is *not* a rule that requires that *more favorable* treatment be given to one trading partner than to others. Instead, this is a rule that requires that the *same* treatment be given to all trading partners that are Members of the WTO. Under this rule, WTO Members must not discriminate among different foreign producers of like imported products, but rather must give the *same* treatment to *all* foreign producers of like products from other WTO Members that is given to the producers from the "most-favoured-nation."[52]

The rule requiring "most-favoured-nation" treatment is the very heart of the multilateral trading system. When applied in concert with the rule on binding concessions, the "MFN" rule *multiplies* the potential of trade concessions for lowering barriers to trade worldwide. It does so by requiring that any concession that is made to *one* WTO Member must be made also to *all other* WTO Members on a multilateral "most-favoured-nation" basis. This is an important example of what the advocates of the WTO usually mean when we speak, as we often do, of the virtues of what is called, in WTO jargon, *multilateralism.*

As the WTO has explained with respect to "MFN" treatment, "Some exceptions are allowed. For example, countries within a region can set up a free trade agreement that does not apply to goods from outside the group. Or a country can raise barriers against products from specific countries that are considered to be traded unfairly. And in services, countries are allowed, in limited circumstances, to discriminate. But the agreements only permit these exceptions under strict conditions. In general, MFN means that every time a country lowers a trade barrier or opens up a market, it has to do so for the same goods or services from all its trading partners —whether rich or poor, weak or strong."[53] In the WTO-based trading system, this is the basic meaning of multilateralism.

The third basic rule is the rule requiring "national treatment." The "national treatment" rule prevents the favoring of domestic over foreign producers once a foreign product has crossed the border and entered the domestic market. Under this rule, WTO Members must not discriminate in favor of domestic producers, but rather must give "no

---

[52] *See* Article I, the GATT; Article 2, the General Agreement on Trade in Services (the "GATS"); Article 4, the Agreement on Trade-Related Aspects of Intellectual Property Rights (the "TRIPS Agreement").

[53] World Trade Organization, "Trading into the Future," (Geneva, Switzerland, 1998), 5.

less favourable treatment" to foreign producers than is given to domestic producers of like products.[54] This rule applies to domestic taxes and to virtually every other kind of domestic restriction or regulation. The "national treatment" rule is a good example of how WTO rules relating to international trade can also have considerable domestic implications for WTO Members in areas that do not primarily involve trade.

Those countries that are not Members of the WTO do not have the advantage of these WTO rules that share the benefit of trade concessions and that prohibit trade discrimination. They have no effective international legal remedy against trade discrimination. Even the Members of the WTO are free to discriminate against non-Members. The availability of these basic WTO rules helps explain why so many countries and other customs territories have become Members of the WTO, and also why so many more are waiting in line to become Members of the WTO. The enforceability of these and many other beneficial WTO rules in WTO dispute settlement adds all the more to the attractiveness of WTO membership. Trade benefits that can be assured through effective enforcement are benefits that are well worth having.

The disputes that are appealed to us and that are discussed around our table are about the meaning of these three basic rules, and about the meaning of the many other detailed obligations that are contained in the thousands of pages of rules in the "covered agreements." These obligations are expressed in the words of the WTO treaty, and the meaning of the words of the treaty is thus our constant focus in reaching and rendering our judgments. We are ever in search of the revealing insight and the felicitous phrase that can illuminate the meaning of the words of the treaty.

The WTO treaty instructs us to assist the Members of the WTO in their efforts to provide security and predictability to the multilateral trading system, in order "to preserve the rights and obligations of Members under the covered agreements, and to clarify the existing provisions of those agreements in accordance with customary rules of interpretation of public international law."[55] As noted in our first appeal, the customary rules are reflected in the Vienna Convention on the Law of Treaties.[56] The

---

[54] *See* Article III, the GATT; Article 17, the GATS; Article 3, the TRIPS Agreement.

[55] Art. 3.2, DSU.

[56] United States - Standards for Reformulated Gasoline, WTO Doc. WT/DS2/AB/R, at 17 (March 20, 1996) ("U. S. - Gasoline"); Vienna Convention on the Law of Treaties, *opened for signature*, May 23, 1969, 1155 UNTS 331.

interpretive approach of the customary rules that are reflected in the Vienna Convention is a *textual* approach. This approach focuses on the words in the text of the treaty. Article 31 of the Vienna Convention provides that "a treaty shall be interpreted in good faith in accordance with the ordinary meaning to be given to the terms of the treaty in their context and in light of its object and purpose."[57]

Therefore, our obsession on the Appellate Body is with the meaning of words, for our challenge in every appeal is to strive together to discern the meaning of the words of the WTO treaty. Our responsibility in every appeal is to say everything that must be said about the meaning of the words of the treaty so as to "address" the legal issues that are "raised" in that appeal, and thus assist the WTO Members in their efforts to "clarify"[58] the obligations in the treaty, and thereby resolve that dispute in a "positive solution."[59] Our aim in every appeal is to do that —only that —and no more.

"Words are tyrannical things," wrote W. Somerset Maugham, "they exist for their meanings, and if you will not pay attention to these, you cannot pay attention at all."[60] In our work on the Appellate Body, the Members of the WTO have specifically told us to submit to the tyranny of words. This is because the meaning of the obligations of WTO Members is to be found in the meaning of the words they chose to include in the WTO treaty. They agreed on those words, and, in discerning their intent in the treaty, we seven must agree on what those words mean. We must discern the meaning of the words of the treaty in order to assist the Members of the WTO in "clarifying" it.

In deciding on the words they included in the WTO treaty, the Members of the WTO drew a line. We seven must use our best efforts to see and to articulate this line for them while using the interpretive approach they said we must use in the treaty. Our shared goal in all our deliberations is to find the line they have drawn in the words of the treaty, and to reinforce that line in the words of our rulings. It is toward this end that we engage in the reasonableness of our mutual criticism.

No effort is spared in the energies we devote to reaching the conclusions that are reflected in our reports. In particular, this is true of

---

[57] Article 31, Vienna Convention on the Law of Treaties.
[58] Article 3.2, DSU.
[59] Article 3.7, DSU.
[60] W. Somerset Maugham, The Summing Up (New York: Penguin Books, 1963, 26 [1938].

our deliberations. The lively discussions around our table are the closest I am ever likely to come to the conversations that enlivened the taverns of Samuel Johnson's London and the salons of Voltaire's Paris. Intellectual sallies sail back and forth. Verbal parries go to and fro. The rhetoric around the table ascends gradually from engaging repartee to rarefied considerations worthy of the best of medieval Thomistic angel-counting on the head of a pin.[61]

Proust, the connoisseur of specifics, would not be surprised to know that the differences that must be resolved through the reasonableness of our deliberations often arise from the specifics. They arise from the ways in which specific issues in specific cases measure the depths of our individual beliefs. In Swann's Way, Proust wrote, "The facts of life do not penetrate to the sphere in which our beliefs are cherished; they did not engender those beliefs, and they are powerless to destroy them...."[62] So it is, too, with the facts and with the law in appeals in WTO dispute settlement.

In our consensus-building around our table, we must distinguish facts from law. The Appellate Body does not "find" facts in a trade dispute. The *facts* are determined by the WTO panels that precede us in dispute settlement. Only issues of *law* are "raised" in WTO appeals. Separating issues of "fact" from issues of "law" in an appeal is not always easy. Many is the legal scholar who has made an entire academic career out of analyzing the difference between issues of "fact" and issues of "law." And many has been the long afternoon in Geneva when the coffee cups and the water glasses have been emptied again and again as we seven have struggled to see the line between "fact" and "law" in a given appeal.

Once we have found that line, the question always remains: How much must we say in our report about the law in order to "address" the legal issues that have been "raised" in a given appeal? Some have suggested that sometimes we have said too much. Perhaps, at times, we have. And yet, the truth is, in any given appeal, almost all of what we agree that we could say, and almost all of what we think at first that we might say, ends up not being said at all in our report to the Members of

---

[61] According to my esteemed former colleague, Judge Florentino "Toy" Feliciano, the answer to the time-honored question, "How many angels can dance on the head of a pin?" is "None." Angels have no corporeal existence. On this, I defer to my friend Toy, who was well schooled, not only by Yale University, but also by the Jesuits in the Philippines.

[62] Marcel Proust, Swann's Way (New York: Vintage International, 1989), 162 [1913].

the WTO. We try to say only what must be said to help resolve a particular dispute.

Harold Nicolson, when a seasoned British diplomat, was sometimes asked, about the art of diplomacy, "If a foreign official asks one whether some important fact is true, what should one reply?" Nicolson answered with this advice: "If one doesn't know, one should reply, 'I have no idea at all,' but if one does know, one should say, 'You ought not to have asked me that question'."[63] We do not have those options on the Appellate Body. Our task in WTO dispute settlement is not diplomacy. It is law. In our efforts to assist the Members of the WTO in upholding the rule of law in world trade, we must find the answer to every question that is raised as a legal issue in every appeal in WTO dispute settlement.

Professor John H. Jackson of Georgetown University, who has done so much through the decades to further the development of the world trading system, and who has followed the development of the WTO dispute settlement system as closely as anyone, has speculated on what transpires around our table: "[O]ne can almost visualize the furrowed brows of the Appellate Body Members as they struggle with difficult concepts, balancing important social policies that often pose dilemmas or trade-offs, and arriving sometimes at language that is extraordinarily nuanced and delicate, sometimes discussed into late hours of the evening."[64] As my late friend and colleague Chris Beeby would undoubtedly say if he were still with us, "Indeed."

Brows furrowed, we take turns speaking in our deliberations. There are no time limits, other than those of mutual tolerance. There are no holds barred in our spirited Socratic fray. There are no occasions when we do not endeavor to take into consideration every conceivable point of view relating to every legal issue raised on appeal. There are no resources from which any one of us might not draw in our efforts to reach a "consensus" on the appropriate interpretation of the words of the "covered agreements." Through the years, I have heard everyone from Aristotle to General Ulysses S. Grant cited as authority around our table.

---

[63] Nigel Nicolson, "Foreword," to Harold Nicolson, <u>Diplomacy</u> (Washington: Institute for the Study of Diplomacy, 1988), ix [1939].
[64] John H. Jackson, "Perceptions about the WTO trade institutions," supra, at 110.

I am a reformed politician. I have not always worked in chambers of reasonableness, and I have not always had to provide reasons along with my answers. In my time in the Congress of the United States, I was rarely asked a question that I had not already been asked a hundred times before. I always had, if not a reasoned answer, then at least a ready response. In my time on the Appellate Body of the WTO, I have learned that, when I come to our table, I had better have answers, and I had better have reasons for those answers.

When I first became a candidate for the Congress, my longtime friend and mentor, former Florida Governor and former United States Trade Representative Reubin Askew, told me, "Your time for reading and reflection is over." To a certain extent, he was right about the Congress. But my experience has been entirely different on the Appellate Body. My years on the Appellate Body have been years of much reading and much reflection in search of the right reasons and the right answers.

The panel report in every appeal usually consists of hundreds of pages. The panel record in every appeal always consists of thousands of pages. The submissions by the Members of the WTO that are the parties and third parties in every appeal are lengthy. And every appeal, increasingly, involves issues that require much reading and reflection on other appeals, other rulings, and other relevant considerations. So, in every appeal, each of us brings with us to our table and to our deliberations long hours of both reading and reflection. In every appeal, each of us brings with us preparation for provisional positions in which we try to take into account all the necessary questions about all the pending issues. Then, together, through mutual thought, and through considerable mutual criticism, we try to find the right reasons and the right answers.

Our search for those right reasons and for those right answers might be compared to the fine art of fresco painting —in which water colors are applied by the artist to a surface of fresh, wet plaster, and then left to dry. Like the art of fresco, the art of reaching the right result in an appeal in WTO dispute settlement is an art that can be difficult to master. Like fresco artists, we work, so to speak, with wet plaster. Like fresco artists, we must work quickly and carefully in applying the colors of our art. Moreover, we must work with a palette comprised of the ephemeral colors of elusive legal issues that make it difficult to paint a portrait that will last long after the paint has dried. Therefore, as with fresco painting, much in decisionmaking in WTO dispute settlement depends on proper preparation and on appropriate timing. And much, as well, depends on chemistry.[65] Most of all, much depends on the chemistry of a free mutual criticism around the table.

One of the essential elements of our chemistry is listening. We try not merely to *speak* to one another in our deliberations, but to *listen* to one another. Listening is not always easy, but listening is indispensable to reaching a genuine consensus, and I would say that this is especially so for "the American" who sits at our table. After retiring from diplomacy, Nicolson devoted much of his time to writing books. In the 1930s, he went to America to research one of them. He liked Americans well enough, but one thing about Americans puzzled him. He told his wife in a letter, "Now, the oddest thing about Americans is that they never listen."[66] This remains the reputation we Americans have in the rest of the world. Today, more than ever, others in the world think we Americans do not listen. But, American though I may be, I have spent my time on the Appellate Body trying to listen, and, because I have listened, my colleagues have been much more inclined to listen to me. Because I have listened, I have been heard.

Another essential element of our chemistry is a certain measure of cultural sensitivity. We seven are far more alike than we are different. We have much in common, not only in our views on trade, but also in our views on much else. Even so, we do have distinctive cultural differences, and a constant awareness of those differences has helped me learn as I have tried to listen. One thing we seven have in common is our admiration for that advocate of reasonableness, John Stuart Mill, who once said, "It is hardly possible to overrate the value, in the present low state of human improvement, of placing human beings in contact with persons dissimilar to themselves, and with modes of thought and action unlike those with which they are familiar.... Such communication has always been, and is particularly in the present age, one of the primary sources of progress."[67] The truth of this assertion is one of many things I have learned while listening at the table of the Appellate Body.

---

[65] On fresco painting, *see* Ross King, <u>Michelangelo and the Pope's Ceiling</u> (London: Pimlico, 2003), 42-47 [2002].

[66] Nigel Nicolson, ed. <u>Harold Nicolson: Diaries and Letters, 1930-1939</u> (New York: Atheneum, 1996), 181.

[67] John Stuart Mill, <u>Principles of Political Economy</u>, Book 3, Chapter 17, Section 5, Volume 3, in J. M. Robson, ed. <u>Collected Works of John Stuart Mill</u> (London, 1981), at 594.

Ralph Waldo Emerson once said that Americans "go to Europe to be Americanized."[68] In my time on the Appellate Body, I have been "Americanized" anew in that I have been reminded, again and again, of all that we Americans have in common, and of all that, taken together, makes us distinctly American in the eyes of the rest of the world. Our sheer "can-do" confidence. Our decidedly democratic spirit. Our informality. Our practicality. Our unapologetic materialism. Our unabashed idealism. Our utter individualism. A Swiss friend told me once, in a tone of some amazement, "You Americans are willing to walk the tightrope without a net."

So we are, and, as an American, I take some considerable pride in that. Time and again in my life, I have been willing to walk the tightrope without a net. Yet, if I have been "Americanized" in my time on the Appellate Body, I have also been "internationalized." I have seen firsthand that the world needs much more of an international net. I have learned at our table in Geneva how very much the world needs an international network of ideas and institutions that can bind us, and keep us all together.

The table manners of the free mutual criticism that is the key to the success of a free and open society have also been the key to the success of our deliberations. Those who have represented WTO Members in appeals before the Appellate Body, and who have endured our interrogations in our oral hearings, can attest to the extent of our devotion on the Appellate Body to the strictures of the Socratic method. They might be pleased to know that the mutual interrogation in which we engage among ourselves in our deliberations is no less intensive. Civil as we are, we are unrelenting, and we are unsparing of one another, in our shared search for the right answers to the questions raised on appeal.

As we deliberate, the empty coffee cups accumulate. The water pitcher is filled, emptied, and filled again. The table piles high with legal briefs. The nearby blackboard fills with numbers and charts. The bright young lawyers scurry in and out of the room as we tie up loose language and loose ends. The pages of the parties' submissions on appeal are scrutinized and analyzed. The arguments made by the parties at the oral hearing in the appeal are recalled and recited. The nuances of past appeals are revisited. The implications for future appeals are considered. The debate back and forth across the table ranges from the meaning of a comma to the meaning of life. And, slowly, a "consensus" emerges.

---

[68] Ralph Waldo Emerson, "Culture," The Conduct of Life, in Essays and Lectures (New York: The Library of America, 1983), 1015, 1023 [1860].

By far the most rewarding experience for me as a Member of the Appellate Body has been the intellectual communion in which I have shared around our table. For, time after time, around our table, we have, after exhaustive mutual effort, made seven minds into one. Outside, the protesters parade with their placards. Downstairs, the negotiations continue. Here, in the quiet of our chambers, in between sips of *renversé*, we continue to shape a "consensus" that helps the Members of the WTO shape a better world.

Chapter Two

Trade Faces

Six Wise Men

Who *are* the Members of the Appellate Body of the World Trade Organization? Who are the seven jurists who gather around our round table morning after morning, day after day, season after season, year after year, to swap legal reasoning and sip endless cups of *renversé*? Who *are* the "faceless foreign judges" of the WTO?

The wider world does not seem to know who we are. This is in part because the wider world does not see us do what we do. Ours are, in the words of the treaty that binds us, "confidential" proceedings. Thus, many questions about the "faceless foreign judges" of the WTO arise that either go unanswered, or are answered in ways that often have little in common with the truth.

Are we merely the sheltered, solipsistic "trade bureaucrats" depicted by the detractors of the WTO? Are we soulless servants of a heartless trading system bent solely on a ruthless maximization of economic efficiency at any and all costs? Do we wear commercial blinders that keep us from seeing the broader concerns of the wider world? Or do we share, perhaps, a broader view? Do the "faceless foreign judges" perhaps have faces that look beyond trade and to the wider world?

The answers to these questions — the truth of who we are — may be best revealed by all we have done together in all our years together at the WTO. Yet, before we were brought together at our table in Geneva, we each led lives elsewhere that somehow brought us, in time, to the WTO. And the lives we each led before we came together in Geneva helped shape all we have done together at our table in all the years since.

For the past eight years, I have shared in the task of our table. My chair faces the corner of the room that serves as our chambers. That corner is flanked by two high windows. The two windows look out on the lawn, the lake, and the snowy peaks of the Alps beyond.

Through these windows comes much that we share around our table. The sweet smell of the grass in the summer. The stark chill of the wind in the winter. The soft drum of the rain in the spring and in the fall. The laughter of the children from the nearby *creche* as they line up, two by two, hand in hand, for their daily walk through the park along the lake.

The windows are witnesses to all we do together at our table, and all that passes through these windows becomes a part of our shared task. The rattle of the wind in the windows' wooden casements is our note of caution. The sparkle of the sun on the green leaves of the nearby trees is our illumination. The spirited song of the birds is our only applause. The darkening shadow that crawls across our table in the evenings is our recurring reminder that yet another day has passed.

As each day passes, and as each passing day diminishes the number of days that I will remain at our table, I reflect more and more on what all that has been said there and all that has been done there means, and can yet mean, for an uncertain world. And, as, once again, I pass the palm of my hand across the smoothly polished surface of our table, and as I pack up my briefcase at the end of another day, I conclude that the success thus far of the Appellate Body in serving the world by serving the Members of the WTO can be traced above all to the quality and the character of the jurists with whom I have been privileged to serve at the round table of the Appellate Body.

Our table is an American table. It is made from American wood. It is made from an American walnut tree. We Americans make tables from the wood of walnut trees in several different states. Our round table in Geneva may well have come from Oregon, or from California, or perhaps even from the forests of the northern panhandle of Florida, my home state. The smooth brown surface of our table is an ever-present reminder to me of the far horizons of my country, and of the far reach of America's international trade. The United States of America is the leading trading nation in the world.

Even so, my face is now, and my face has always been, the only American face among the jurists at our table. My voice is the only American voice at our table, and it is often the only American voice I hear all day. From the beginning, I have been the only Member of the Appellate Body from the United States. We Americans may make and export a lot of tables all over the world, but the United States is only one of 146 Members of the WTO, and there are only seven seats at our table in Geneva.

My colleagues come from every part of the world. Nowadays, when I sit down in the morning in our chambers, and when I look around our table, I see six faces smiling back at me. I see the faces of friends, the faces of admired and kindred spirits, the faces of six men who share my abiding commitment to our shared task. I see the faces of distinguished fellow Members of the Appellate Body from Egypt, from India, from Japan, from Italy, from Australia, and from Brazil.

But theirs are not the only faces I see. In the beginning, there were six others who sat with me around our table. In the beginning, there were six others who smiled back at me in the morning. I had never met any of them before we all met together for the first time in Geneva. I knew little about any of them before we began our work together for the WTO. Now, not a day passes when I do not miss their presence.

Through the years, in all our work together, they were, for me, models and mentors, as well as colleagues and friends. They were six thinkers of subtle thoughts. They were six servants of the common good. They were six seekers of a better, brighter world. They were six wise men.

Today, those six other faces are no longer to be found at our table. Yet they still smile back at me. They smile back at me today, not from across the table, but from farther across the room.

For, near the corner of the room, between the two windows, on the wall facing me, are framed photographs of the six other founding Members of the Appellate Body. From these framed photographs, those six wise men look down on all that is done in our chambers. From these framed photographs, those who once worked alongside me judge my continuing efforts to carry on without them at the table we once shared.

They each do so with a smile.

The Ice Cream Man

The biggest smile, as always, is the smile on the face of Said El-Naggar. No one smiles as much as Said. No one loves life or enjoys life any more than my dear friend from Egypt. As Said tells it, this is because life has taught him life's value. He has learned to keep smiling.

My daughter, Jamey, is now twelve. She has known my friend Said for the eight years that I have known him. She has a special place in her heart and also has a special name for her smiling "Uncle Said." She calls him "The Ice Cream Man." She does so because Said has shown a decided inclination through the years to buy her as many ice creams as she can possibly consume.

I once asked Said about this in a half-hearted effort to keep him from spoiling Jamey even more than her indulgent father has already spoiled her. He smiled, and then he explained, "I want every child in the world to be able to have an ice cream every day."[1] Knowing Said as I do, and knowing what I know of his own childhood, I believe I understand.

Said was born in another time and in another world — the Egypt of 1920. He was born in a village called Delingat in the delta of the Nile about sixty kilometers south of Alexandria. His father was a cotton merchant, and Said's family was prosperous for awhile. But his father died while Said was still small, and the family suffered from his father's debts. The depression followed, and, as Said recalls today from a distance of more than seventy years, "Times were very hard indeed."

During the depths of the depression, the impoverished family's sole source of milk was a single water buffalo. One day the water buffalo died. There would be no more milk, and there would certainly be no ice cream. Said remembers that his mother cried, and, because she cried, he cried, too.

Said's mother was his salvation. She was illiterate, as most Egyptian women were in the delta villages of the time. But she was smart, and she was shrewd. And she believed in the potential of her youngest son.

There was a primary school in Delingat, and Said completed the primary school with, as he puts it, "quite a distinction." He ranked among the top ten students in all of Egypt on his final examinations. Even so, the consensus of the elders in the village was that Said should go on to a vocational school — to become a carpenter or a mechanic — and not to the grammar school in a nearby town that could lead to a professional career.

---

[1] All of the quotations from my colleagues, both past and present, are from personal conversations, unless otherwise indicated.

Said's mother had a different idea. She was determined to see her son realize his potential. She decided to sell off what remained of the family's dwindled land holdings, piece by piece, to pay for Said's education.

Thus, at the age of twelve, Said began attending a secondary school in Damanhour, twenty kilometers from Delingat. He boarded there while attending classes during the week, and he walked the dusty roads home on the weekends to visit his mother and the rest of his family. Said strived to be first in his class at school. He believed he ought to be first. He believed he owed it to his mother. As Said remembers now, all these decades later, "Her determination to go through this hardship was matched by my determination to excel."

Excel he did. Said finished at the top of his class every year from his very first year in secondary school until he received his degree in law from the University of Cairo. He won a scholarship to study economics in London, and his mother, having silenced the village elders once and for all, saw him off at the docks of the port of Alexandria. He says now, "I could see the satisfaction in her eyes."

That was the last time Said saw his mother. He was in London for six years, and his mother died before he returned to Egypt. But he has remembered her in a way she would undoubtedly have approved. "Because of what my mother did for me," Said explains, "I became a firm believer and an activist in the promotion of the rights of women in our country."

In the first days after the Second World War, the London School of Economics was a magnet for young thinkers everywhere who hoped to prevent a third world war by making a better world. Among the brightest stars on the L. S. .E. faculty at the time was Karl Popper, the exiled Austrian philosopher. Popper had escaped the Nazi takeover of his Austrian homeland in the late 1930s. He had spent the war in exile in New Zealand, and had moved to London following the war. When Said showed up at L .S .E., Popper had just published his magnum opus, <u>The Open Society And Its Enemies</u>, a testament to freedom that excoriated the totalitarianisms of both right and left.

Popper wrote later, "The L. S. E. was in those days, just after the war, a marvelous institution. It was small enough for everybody on the staff to know everybody else. The staff, though few, were outstanding, and so were the students. There were lots of them — larger classes than I had later at L. S. E. — eager, mature, and extremely appreciative; and they presented a challenge to the teacher."[2]

One of those students was Said El-Naggar. Said, with his desire to excel, and with his insatiable desire to know all that there is to know, undoubtedly presented a challenge to all his teachers. The young scholar from Egypt worked closely with the legendary economists Lionel Robbins and James Edward Meade. He attended the lectures of the great champion of the free market, Friedrich von Hayek. However, it was Popper, the great apostle of freedom, whose lectures were etched forever into Said's thought. And it was Popper's belief in the primacy of individual human freedom that Said took back with him to postwar Egypt, along with two advanced degrees in economics.

Today, half a century later, Said still maintains that the Austrian "school" of philosophers and economists — Popper, Hayek, Joseph Schumpeter, Ludwig von Mises, and the rest — had the best understanding of economics as a human endeavor. He argues that they were distinctive among economists in that they saw human beings in their context and in all their complexity, and that they saw economics, not as mere mathematical logic, but as only one facet of the human condition, and as only one example of the human search for freedom.

Back in Egypt, in the 1950s, Said became a professor of economics at the University of Cairo. He taught economics as he knew it and as he saw it. He taught the necessity of free markets and free enterprise. He taught the indispensability of individual human freedom. He taught the need for democracy as the necessary wellspring and as the necessary safeguard of freedom. Soon this got him into trouble.

Gamal Abdel-Nasser had led a military coup in 1952 and had later become president of Egypt. In time, his authoritarian government aligned more and more with the Soviet Union. His revolutionary policy for Egypt was one he described as "Arab socialism." A government informer in one of Said's classes at the university reported that the young economics professor was not teaching "Arab socialism." Said was then told to do so. He refused.

---

[2] Karl Popper, Unended Quest: An Intellectual Biography (London and New York: Routledge Classics, 2002), 138-39 [1974].

For some time afterwards, Said was under government surveillance. He continued to teach about both free markets and freedom. Then, one day in 1965, he received a summons to the headquarters of the state security police in Cairo. Upon arriving, he was placed, alone, in a windowless room, with one chair, and with one bare light bulb. He waited — for four hours.

Then a door opened on the far side of the room. Said walked through the door and found himself facing a general — the commander of the state security police. The general sat behind an imposing desk. Said stood. "I understand that you refuse to teach Arab socialism," the general said. "The next time I hear this, no one will know where you went."

There was no next time. That day, Said decided to leave Egypt. He sought the help of an American friend, Richard Gardner, a professor of international law who has since served the United States as ambassador to several countries. With Gardner's assistance, Said secured a post in Geneva with UNCTAD — the United Nations Conference on Trade and Development.

Said did not return to Egypt at all until after Nasser died in 1970. He did not return to Egypt to live until 1993. Then, after many years of distinguished service in international organizations — first at UNCTAD and, later, notably, at the World Bank — he returned to Egypt to lead a nongovernmental organization he had founded called the "New Civic Forum." The "New Civic Forum" extolled the advantages for Egypt of free markets and freedom.

Said was busily engaged in encouraging numerous democratic reforms in Egypt when he was nominated by his country to serve on the Appellate Body of the WTO. Egypt wanted the honor of having an Egyptian named as one of the seven initial jurists on the new trade tribunal. The Egyptian government was told by other Members of the WTO that this might happen if Egypt nominated Said El-Naggar.

Said brought with him to the Appellate Body the same passion for excellence that he first learned as his mother's son in their small Egyptian village. He brought with him also his lifelong passion for freedom.

I am among the main beneficiaries of this. For Said spent no small part of his years at the WTO working with me, debating with me, sparring with me, and sharing with me his considerable understanding of the subtleties of law, economics, and freedom. Said did his very best to help "improve" me by educating me, and I have no doubt whatsoever that he did.

He did so not least by recommending that I read some of his favorite books. Some I had read before. Some I had not. Some I had read before and, at Said's urging, I now read again. The list was long. Arthur Koestler's <u>Darkness At Noon</u>. Stefan Zweig's <u>The World of Yesterday</u>. Amin Maalouf's <u>The Crusades Through Arab Eyes</u>. Hayek's <u>The Constitution of Liberty</u>. And, of course, Popper. And more Popper.

When he was not giving me reading lists, Said kept busy by reading his way through every single page of the "covered agreements." It was not long before he could recite even the footnotes to those agreements from memory. He could recite them word for word, and he could recite them also by number.

Said was seventy-five when he was appointed to the Appellate Body. Even so, he may well have worked the hardest of all of us. He rose before dawn to prepare for the day's deliberations. He was the first to arrive at our table every day. He was the most diligent — and the most ardent — in our debates.

As both a lawyer and an economist, Said aspired to a certain precision in our reasoning and in our rulings. It was almost as if he believed that there was one perfect answer to every legal puzzle, and that the right — the perfect — answer would be found if we only found the perfect combination of words. So he sought always the perfection of precision.

In an effort to inspire us to be more precise, Said would go often to the chalk board on one of the walls in our chambers. There, chalk in hand, he would explain his views at length with the aid of elaborate charts, sloping graphs, and precise mathematical formulas. In his efforts to enlighten us, Said strived for the same perfection in the work of the Appellate Body that he had achieved decades before as a schoolboy in Egypt. He wanted us always to excel.

On those few occasions when, for all his masterful efforts at the board, Said was still unable to convince us of the wisdom of his view on a particular issue, he would not fault us for our stubborn refusal to agree with him. Instead, he would blame only himself. He would conclude that somehow he had failed us. But, the fact is, he never did. Said always excelled.

Said embodies excellence. He is as durable as the Nile, as immovable as the Pyramids, as learned as the sages of antiquity who labored over the papyrus scrolls in the lost library of Alexandria. He is also a fan of small children, of Swiss ice cream, and of the mountain melodies of Dolly Parton. In his eighties, Said still savors the pleasure of every passing day, and he continues to look forward with anticipation to the future.

After four years on the Appellate Body, Said decided, in 1999, that he needed to do more for the future of Egypt. So he chose not to seek re-appointment for a second four-year term on the Appellate Body. Instead, he returned to Egypt, where he renewed his "New Civic Forum" and resumed his lectures on why Egypt continues to need free markets and freedom.

Long ago, Said developed the habit of walking alone every morning at five o'clock. He did so for years in both Washington and Geneva. He does so still, in Cairo, where his home is near the park where he walks. The park in Cairo does not open until much later in the morning. Said is held in such high regard by his countrymen that, every morning, the keeper of the park shows up at five a.m. to unlock the gate so that Said can walk.

Recently, one of his longtime friends, Saadeddin Ibrahim, a prominent human rights activist on the faculty of the American University in Cairo, was arrested and put on trial by the Egyptian government. Said volunteered to testify for him. He described on the witness stand his sorrow at "watching a scholar as honest and sincere as Ibrahim standing in a cage like a criminal." A press account of the trial reported that Said El-Naggar "broke down and wept while addressing the court."[3]

Back in Geneva for a visit, Said mentions none of this. Nor does he volunteer, without prompting, that, long years after his mother sold

---

[3] Jailan Halawi, "Who's who at Ibrahim's trial," <u>Ahram Weekly</u> (25-31 January 2001).

off the family's land, piece by piece, to pay for his education, he bought it all back — every last piece of it — and then gave it away to others in his family.

Instead, Said simply smiles. He smiles at my daughter after dinner and asks, "Jamey, would you like another ice cream?"

The Episcopalian

The smile on the face of Mitsuo Matsushita is only the mere hint of a smile. His slight smile in the framed photograph on the wall before me may best be described as one of mild amusement. This may well be because my friend Mitsuo has a special appreciation for some of the ironies of life.

He has long had need for one. For Mitsuo is a member of a small minority group. He is a Japanese Christian. And, indeed, Mitsuo is not only a Japanese Christian. He is a particular kind of Japanese Christian. He is an Episcopalian.

Mitsuo is one of a relative handful of Christians in Japan, and one of an even smaller relative handful of Episcopalians. In addition to the Anglican kneeling that this requires of him on Sunday mornings, his identity as a member of a small minority group has made Mitsuo all the more tolerant of the views of others, all the more conscious of the needs of others, and all the more mindful of all the ironies that have been evidenced in his life.

I once asked Mitsuo how it was that he became an Episcopalian. He told me that he became an Episcopalian "almost by birth." His father's father was a samurai who became a policeman and then became an Episcopalian. His mother's father was the first native Japanese bishop of the Episcopalian church. Mitsuo was baptized as a Christian by his Episcopalian family when he was three weeks old. The full import of this for Mitsuo can best be understood only in the context of the history of Japan, where Christians long have been, and still remain, very much in the minority.[4]

---

[4] On the history of Christianity in Japan, *see* Mark R. Mullins, <u>Christianity Made in Japan: A Study of Indigenous Movements</u>, (Honolulu: University of Hawaii, 1998).

For a long time, Christian missionaries and Christian converts were persecuted ruthlessly in Japan. They were tortured and executed. They were burned alive. They were even crucified.

The forward-looking modernizers of the Meiji Restoration in Japan, which began in 1868, were more tolerant of Christianity than their predecessors. But, with the rise of Japanese nationalism, and with the triumph of Japanese militarism in the 1930s, Japanese "patriotism" became identified by the Japanese government with the native rites of Shintoism, and Japanese Christians who refused to participate in Shinto rites were, once again, persecuted.

Foreign Christian missionaries were expelled from Japan on the eve of the Second World War, and arrests of Japanese Christians continued throughout the war. Then the atomic bomb that was dropped by the United States on Nagasaki in 1945 destroyed the oldest, largest, and most fervent center of Christianity in Japan. (This is one irony that Mitsuo has been kind enough never to point out to me, his American friend.)

Today, in a more tolerant time, there is much more tolerance of Christianity in Japan. Yet, less than one percent — only about one million or so — of the Japanese people are Christians. About half of these are Protestants. A fraction are Episcopalians. And one, Mitsuo Matsushita, was nominated by his country in 1995 as one of the seven founding Members of the Appellate Body of the WTO.

This could be considered comparable, perhaps, to the nomination by my country of a Hindu, a Buddhist, or a member of some obscure Muslim sect. It is testimony to how much Japan has changed in the past half century. It is testimony, too, to how highly Mitsuo is regarded not only in Japan, but throughout the world.

Mitsuo came to the Appellate Body with a broad experience of the world, and with a broad experience especially of the United States. Through the years, Mitsuo has taught for a time as a visiting professor at many American law schools in many parts of the United States. He has a particular fondness, though, for the American South. For it was to the South that he first came when he first ventured to the United States as a young man.

As a young Japanese Episcopalian, Mitsuo won a scholarship from the church to attend an Episcopalian school— the University of the South, in Sewanee, Tennessee. As a native Tennessean, I feel qualified to say: nothing is more Southern than the University of the South, an outstanding liberal arts college that is commonly call "Sewanee" and is rustically situated in the Southern piney woods atop Monteagle in rural Tennessee.

To reach Sewanee, Mitsuo took a slow cargo boat from Yokohama to California. Then he took a cross-country Greyhound bus from California to New York. Next he took another Greyhound bus, from New York down into the Deep South.

This was in 1956. The war between the United States and Japan had been over only a short time. The wounds of the war were still raw. The memories of the war were still new. In one of the saddest chapters in American history, Japanese-Americans had suffered discrimination and interdiction during the war, and there was little reason at the time to think that a young Japanese student would be welcomed with open arms anywhere in the United States.

Moreover, this was the American South of the 1950s. Having gone back and read the United States Constitution, the Supreme Court of the United States had recently decided that "separate but equal" treatment of the races in public education would no longer suffice.[5] Thus, the South was faced with a new challenge that would test the long-held views of many white Southerners on all racial issues: American Southerners, black and white alike, would, in time do much to help America begin to pass this test. But, in 1956, a young black minister named Martin Luther King, Jr., was leading the Montgomery, Alabama, bus boycott a few miles down the road from Sewanee, and much of the South, black and white alike, seemed on the verge of rebellion.

It was in the midst of all this that the young Mitsuo took his Greyhound bus ride. The trip took the better part of a week, and Mitsuo knew virtually no English at the time. Three times a day the bus stopped for meals. Three times a day Mitsuo ordered his meal using the only English words he knew: "hamburger" and "orange juice."

Eventually, after eating all the hamburgers and drinking all the orange juice he thought he could stand, he managed to learn a new English word: "soup." At the next stop, he walked up to the counter in a roadside restaurant and proudly ordered "soup." Here, however, he confronted

---

[5] *See* <u>Brown v. Board of Education</u>, 347 U.S. 483, 74 S.Ct. 686, 98 L.Ed. 873 (1954).

the unexpected. A tall woman who towered over him at the counter leaned over and asked him: "What kind of soup?"

All these many years later, Mitsuo recalls, "I was so scared that I simply said, 'Just soup.' " He adds, as a philosophical card-carrying Member of the Appellate Body might be expected to add, "This may mean 'soup' in the general and in the abstract — the Platonic concept of 'soup.' " Whether it was Platonic or not, Mitsuo does not remember today what kind of soup the woman gave him. He only remembers that he ate all of it.

At length, the Greyhound bus deposited the young Japanese scholar at a bus stop at Monteagle, just a mule's stroll from Sewanee. It was two in the morning. The bus rode away and left him alone in the dark. Mitsuo sat down on his suitcase and listened to the nightsounds until early the next morning. Then he hitched a ride on the back of a hay wagon to the nearby school, where he enrolled that day as the only Japanese Episcopalian at the University of the South.

The irony of Mitsuo's youthful presence as a student in the United States in the years just after the war becomes fully apparent when one takes into account Mitsuo's father. Like his son, Mitsuo's father was an Episcopalian. Like his son, he studied in the United States. But, unlike his son, Mitsuo's father also had another distinction: he had acted as an adviser to the Japanese Navy in the days leading up to the Japanese attack on Pearl Harbor.

During his time in the United States, Mitsuo's father had earned a doctorate in political science from Columbia University. There he had concentrated on the strategic theories of the American naval captain, Alfred Thayer Mahan, whose book The Influence of Sea Power Upon History, published in 1894, had proven influential with Theodore Roosevelt, Kaiser Wilhelm, and numerous others — including the Japanese navy.[6]

After returning to Japan, Mitsuo's father became one of the advisers to Admiral Isoroku Yamamoto, the commander-in-chief of the Japanese fleet. Admiral Yamamoto planned and carried out the attack on Pearl Harbor. But, ironically, Yamamoto opposed the attack and also opposed a war with the United States.

---

[6] Captain Alfred Thayer Mahan, The Influence of Sea Power Upon History, 1660-1783 [1894].

Having studied and lived himself in the United States, Yamamoto knew the latent strength of America. He feared that the attack on Pearl Harbor would "awaken a sleeping giant," and that an ultimate Japanese victory over the United States would be impossible. He foresaw "victory after victory" for the Japanese forces in the first year of the war. "But then," he predicted, "if the war continues after that, I have no expectation of success."[7]

Born in 1933, Mitsuo was only eight years old when the Japanese attacked Pearl Harbor. He knows that his father met with Admiral Yamamoto before the attack. He does not know what advice his father gave him. He knows only, from his childhood memories, that his father had, as Mitsuo puts it today, "a pessimistic view on the outcome of the war."

Mitsuo knows also the war's consequence for his father and his family. In the aftermath of the war, because of his role as an adviser to the Japanese navy, Mitsuo's father was purged from his post with the Japanese government. Of necessity, he embarked, in the new Japan, on a new career. He became a lawyer.

Then and now, lawyers are about as rare in Japan as Episcopalians. Unlike the United States, Japan is not a country where lawyers have, historically or traditionally, been either numerous or influential. There are nearly one million lawyers in the United States. There are only about 17,000 lawyers in all of Japan — about as many as haunt K Street in Washington on an average day of lawyer-lobbying.[8]

Some, of course, say that the United States has too many lawyers, and that there are too many lawyers in American government. (One of the charges leveled against me in the late unpleasantness of my American political campaigns was that I am — gasp — a lawyer.) With respect to Japan, though, it can be argued that there are altogether too few lawyers — in the government and in the country. In the years since the Second World War, Japan has tried to create the rule of law largely without lawyers. Many would argue today that, to ensure the rule of law in Japan, this must change.

---

[7] On Admiral Yamamoto, *see* Edwin P. Hoyt, <u>Yamamoto: The Man Who Planned the Attack on Pearl Harbor</u> (Lyons Press, 2001).

[8] *See* Carl J. Green, "Japan: 'The Rule of Law Without Lawyers' Reconsidered," remarks to the Asia Society in Washington, D.C. (March 14, 2001), online at asiasociety.org/speeches/green.html.

One who would do so is Mitsuo. After returning from his studies in the United States, Mitsuo followed in his father's footsteps by becoming a member of yet another Japanese minority group — a lawyer. In all the years since — in his university lectures, in his dozens of learned articles, in his counsel to public and private decisionmakers, and in countless other, quiet ways — he has demonstrated the many contributions that can be made to the rule of law, in Japan and elsewhere, by a Japanese lawyer.

He has demonstrated also the many contributions that can be made worldwide by someone who is devoted to the rule of a free market. Perhaps it was his own studies in economics. Perhaps it was the emphasis on individualism that is implicit in the Christian faith. Or perhaps it was his boyhood experience of a war-ravaged Japan that had tried to create economic opportunity and prosperity in other ways, and with tragic results. Whatever the reason, Mitsuo Matsushita is an apostle not only for Episcopalianism, but also for individual economic freedom within the working of a free marketplace. In particular, he is an expert on how markets are structured, how they work, and how they evolve in the face of free competition. Mitsuo is endlessly fascinated with the living, breathing, ever-changing architecture of the competitive marketplace.

Given this, not surprisingly, he has long been regarded as one of the world's leading authorities on what we Americans call "antitrust policy" and what the rest of the world calls "competition policy." It was as an expert on "competition policy" — and as one who championed the role and the rule of a freer market in Japan — that Mitsuo long advised the government of Japan. Where his father had advised the Japanese navy on the perilous pursuits of war, Mitsuo advised the Japanese trade ministry on the profitable pursuits of peace. And, laptop in hand, and economic logic at the ready, he also traveled the rest of the world as a relentless missionary for the marketplace.

Mitsuo had his own way of working toward a consensus on the Appellate Body. One Saturday morning, Mitsuo, Said, and I met in our chambers for a day of deliberations in search of a consensus in a pending appeal. To inspire us, the Secretariat placed an entire chocolate cake on the table at the beginning of our session. They thought we could all share it after lunch.

Said and I were soon diverted — as we often were — by one of our lengthy debates over some now-forgotten nuance of some knotty legal issue. While we debated, Mitsuo said not a word. An hour or so later,

Said and I finally reached an agreement. We looked across the table to discover that, while we had been debating, Mitsuo had been eating. He had eaten almost all of the cake. With a smile, he told us that he was happy that Said and I had both finally reached the right conclusion. For, while Mitsuo had been eating the cake, Said and I had talked ourselves around to agreement with Mitsuo on his position on the issue.

In the first years of the Appellate Body, Mitsuo was often our intellectual safety valve. With typical Japanese modesty and courtesy, he would, when recognized to speak at our table, always begin by saying, to whichever of his listening colleagues had just spoken, "I agree with everything you said." However, this polite disclaimer would then almost always be followed by a single pregnant word: "But...."

We would then all be reminded — ever so softly — ever so politely — of an important point we had somehow forgotten along the winding way of our deliberations. We would be recalled to renewed consideration of an obscure but critical fact, or an arcane but crucial legal argument, we had somehow overlooked. Or we would, frequently, be enlightened by a revelation from our Episcopalian friend in the form of a question that would be unexpected, a question much like: "What kind of soup?"

Sometimes Mitsuo would speak the least of us all in our deliberations, and yet, in the judgment of all the rest of us, he would contribute the most. The irony of this, when pointed out to him, would, occasionally, make Mitsuo smile.

The Aristotelian

Florentino Feliciano smiles down on me from the wall these days with the same small smile he wore when we first met at the WTO eight years ago. "Call me Toy," he said. So I did. We all did.

Everyone everywhere calls him "Toy." Everyone everywhere has always called him "Toy." Florentino Feliciano was one of the most distinguished jurists on the planet long before there was such a thing as the Appellate Body, and yet, then as now, far and wide, he is always "Toy." I am told that "Toy" is a familiar nickname in the Philippines. For my friend Florentino, it is a nickname he has had since his childhood. This is fitting. It was in his childhood in the Philippines that the beginnings were made of the great judge that Toy became.

Born in 1928, Toy was thirteen when the Japanese attacked Pearl Harbor. A few weeks later, Japanese forces overran and occupied the Filipino capital of Manila. The occupation forces closed the Catholic school where American Jesuits had been teaching the teenaged Toy. This, however, was not the end of Toy's wartime education. Toy's father, an engineer and geologist who taught at the University of the Philippines for 39 years, had studied in the United States in the 1930s at the University of Chicago. He had brought back home with him to the Philippines the five-foot shelf of classic works of science, philosophy, history, and literature that the University of Chicago called the "Great Books."

The "Great Books" program of the University of Chicago was one of the great experiments in American education of the twentieth century. In the 1930s, the university's president, Robert Hutchins, and his prolific philosopher friend, Mortimer Adler, had set out to create a new collegiate curriculum at Chicago that would focus on the "great ideas" of the "Great Books" in the Western tradition. They denounced much of what then passed for higher education. They deplored narrow specialization. They sought to impart instead the general enlightenment that they believed would surely come from an immersion in the "Great Books" of the Western liberal tradition.[9]

Hutchins advocated restructuring undergraduate education based on "a course of study consisting of the greatest books of the western world and the arts of reading, writing, thinking, and speaking, together with mathematics, the best exemplar of the processes of human reason."[10] Similarly, Adler maintained that a direct relationship with the "Great Books" would enable and empower people "to lead the distinctively human life of reason."[11]

Hutchins and Adler never fully succeeded in incorporating the "Great Books" into the curriculum at Chicago. Although the "Great Books" continue to have many enthusiasts, the ideal of a liberal arts education that would open individual minds to the vast potential of

---

[9] For a brief perspective on the "Great Books" program at the University of Chicago, *see* "The Great Ideas: The University of Chicago and the Ideal of Liberal Education," An Exhibit in the Department of Special Collections, University of Chicago Library (May 1, 2002-September 6, 2002), online at www.lib.uchicago.edu/e/spcl/excat/ideasint.html.

[10] Robert Hutchins, The Higher Learning in America (New Haven: Yale University Press, 1936).

[11] Mortimer Adler, How To Read a Book: The Art of Getting a Liberal Education (New York: Simon & Schuster, 1940).

human reason through exposure to the "great ideas" in the "Great Books" remains, in most places, only an ideal.[12]

But that was not so for Toy Feliciano in the Japanese-occupied Philippines of the Second World War. With all the schools closed, Toy continued his schooling at home by reading his way through his father's five-foot shelf of "Great Books." He participated also in "informal" study sessions on the "Great Books." These sessions employed the Socratic method of constant questioning — just as Hutchins and Adler had recommended. In this methodical approach to learning, as any lawyer who ever argued before him in later years would surely assume, Toy shined.

Through this youthful experience, through this immersion in the great thoughts in all the "Great Books," Toy chose the life of reason. He recalls now, "I did an enormous amount of reading which was ordinarily done in college." He adds, "I also learned how to think." Plato. Lucretius. Aurelius. Plotinus. Montaigne. Bacon. Hobbes. Locke. Smith. Jefferson. Mill. The reading of these, and more, were all, for Toy, part of learning how to think and to reason while he waited for the war to end.

But none of these classic authors of the "Great Books" impressed him more, or influenced him more, than the ancient Greek philosopher Aristotle. None of them, as Toy has told me many times, left more of an imprint on his own way of thinking than Aristotle. Soon after I met him, Toy told me, for the first of many times, "I am an Aristotelian."

The Aristotelian view became Toy's view. The Aristotelian way became Toy's way. Observation. Classification. Definition. Cause. Purpose. Connection. Logic. Always logic. A predisposition to proceed from particular facts to universal conclusions. A deep feeling for the natural world. And a passion, always a passion, for the natural laws that imply the existence of what Toy likes to call "natural justice." These are the constant ways of Toy, the Aristotelian.

To this, as it relates to law, and especially as it relates to how he sees law as a judge, must be added the additional ways that Toy learned following the war as a law student at Yale from his teacher and longtime mentor, the late Professor Myres McDougal. Professor "Mack" McDougal

---

[12] For an autobiographical retrospective by Adler, *see* Mortimer Adler, <u>Philosopher At Large: An Intellectual Autobiography</u> (New York: Macmillan, 1977).

was the guiding light of the "New Haven" school of jurisprudence in the 1950s. He had served as an aide to Harry Hopkins during the New Deal, had been an early advocate of the human rights efforts of the new United Nations, and, when Toy arrived in New Haven, had already begun his considerable intellectual and other efforts to re-invent legal thinking.

McDougal saw law as an open-ended process of never-ending give and take. He saw it as a process of continuous interaction in an ever-evolving world in which individual decisionmakers of all kinds weigh competing ideas of what law should be in "demand and response" to the world's constant changes.[13] McDougal saw law as consisting primarily of individual human decisions, as being "a process of decision,"[14] and thus he saw the judicial process as a process in which the judge plays, necessarily, an inevitable — and very human — part.

At Yale, Toy worked with McDougal on his classic book on the law of war (one of the "Great Books" of international law). Toy recalled later that, as a young Filipino who had lived through the Japanese occupation of his homeland, he had little faith at the outset in the existence of something that might justifiably be called a "law" of war. With McDougal's guidance, he changed his mind.

In Aristotelian fashion, Toy later helped McDougal identify and categorize the processes of decision-making and the major types of controversies that led to war. Then, with two Yale degrees in hand, he went home. Yet, even from afar, "Mack" McDougal remained his friend and his mentor for decades to come. Toy's father had died while Toy was at Yale, and McDougal became a "father figure" for the young Filipino.[15]

Back in the Philippines, Toy quickly became one of the most successful international lawyers in the Philippines and in all of Asia. He continued to write. He served as an arbitrator. He represented individuals and companies with worldwide interests. He built one of the most successful law firms in his country.

---

[13] *See*, for example, Myres S. McDougal, "The Hydrogen Bomb Tests," 49 American Journal of International Law 356, 357-358 (1955).

[14] Myres S. McDougal, *Preface* to Harold D. Lasswell and Myres S. McDougal, Jurisprudence for a Free Society: Studies in Law, Science and Policy (Student Edition, 1997), at v [1992].

[15] Florentino P. Feliciano, "In Memoriam," Tributes: Myres S. McDougal, Volume 108, Number 5 Yale Law Journal 947, 951 (March 1999).

The government of the Philippines at the time was in the hands of Ferdinand Marcos. Originally elected and re-elected as President, Marcos had abandoned democracy, declared martial law, and established a corrupt and oppressive dictatorship in 1972. Twice, the Marcos government wanted to nominate Toy for the Supreme Court of the Philippines. Twice, in his quiet way, he avoided the nomination. Years later, in typical understatement, and in his typically quiet voice, Toy said to me, "I did not support Mr. Marcos. Mr. Marcos did not support the rule of law."

The people's revolt in the Philippines in February, 1986, finally toppled Marcos after more than twenty years, and put the ousted dictator on a helicopter to a well-earned exile in Hawaii. Six months later, the new, and democratic, president of the Philippines, Carazon Aquino, named Florentino Feliciano to the country's Supreme Court. He served on the court until shortly before I first saw him smiling in Geneva in 1995.

Of us all, Toy alone had been a judge before being named to the Appellate Body, and, perhaps in part for that reason, of us all, Toy looks most like a judge. Always impeccably dressed — wearing an immaculate white shirt, a neatly knotted tie, a gray sweater vest, and a permanent pensive air — he is always supremely judicial. When he shifts back and forth between his two pairs of glasses — the one for reading and the other for judging — and when he peers over at me in utter thoughtfulness, he looks every bit a judge.

Moreover, Toy not only *looks* like a judge. He *acts* like a judge. And he has never been averse to urging his colleagues to act like judges, too. When Toy wants especially to get my attention, he calls me "James." Politely he asks, "You don't mind if I call you James, do you?" I never do. "James," he has often told me, "act like a judge. Think like a judge. Be a judge."

With Toy's help, I have tried. We all have. In his six years on the Appellate Body, Toy showed us all how to be a judge. In his time at our table, Toy tried his best to teach us all his Aristotelian ways. He brought to the round table of the Appellate Body what can only be described as an Aristotelian zeal for the task of interpreting the WTO treaty when judging appeals in WTO disputes.

Like the medieval Schoolmen who followed Aristotle, Toy schooled us all in the methodical rigors of a logical approach to legal reasoning. It was Aristotle, after all, who invented formal logic. Toy implored us to think logically. He urged us, in his frequent phrase, to "put leg over leg until the dog reaches Dover." He counseled us to have the patience to explore every conceivable angle of a legal issue until we "broke the camel's back." These quaint phrases from his genteel tradition revealed the inner workings of a rational and ordered mind.

Yet, unlike the Schoolmen, Toy beseeched us also to look beyond logic. Unlike them, he refused to divorce speculation from observation. He refused to allow us ever to descend, like the medieval Scholastics of lore, to the intellectual indulgence of Thomistic angel-counting. Remembering Aristotle's focus on the natural world, and no doubt remembering also McDougal's emphasis on the critical personal role of an individual legal decision-maker, Toy encouraged us always to focus on the observable facts, and he reminded us always to be mindful of the consequences of our decisions "in the real world where people live and work and die."[16] Toy has an empathy for others that seems — to me — to be missing in Aristotle. For my friend Toy, with his abiding passion for "natural justice," no sparrow can ever be allowed to fall in vain.

And, for Toy, justice can best be served by the best combination of words. One of those whose writings can be found among the "Great Books" is Thomas Jefferson. Like Jefferson, Toy is blessed with a felicitous pen. He would write with a quill pen if he had one. Like Jefferson, too, Toy can be inventive with words. He has even been known to *invent* a word or two for purposes of prose effect along the way. When we pointed out to him once that a "word" he had employed in one of his pleasingly elegant passages was not, in fact, a word at all, Toy was not fazed at all. He simply replied, "Well, it should be."

Peering out over his "judging" glasses, looking down from his appellate perch on some wary lawyer who has already been arguing before him for hours, seemingly futilely, in some exhausting oral hearing, Toy can appear imperious indeed. The worst for the weary appellate advocate, though, comes when Toy pauses in an interrogation and, with a disarming smile, says softly, "I'm just an old judge from a small country...." Word quickly spread beyond Geneva to all those who might one day argue before Florentino Feliciano that what this simple, unassuming sentence really means is: "Watch out!" For it is in what follows that modest phrase

---

[16] EC – Measures Concerning Meat and Meat Products (Hormones), WT/DS26/AB/R, WT/DS48/AB/R (16 January 1998), para. 187.

that Toy truly begins to teach the fine points of Aristotelian logic. It is then that he begins a merciless inquisition.

In his spare time while on the Appellate Body, Toy encouraged me to read — and re-read — the "Great Books." As Said urged me to read all that had inspired him in his youth, so Toy urged me to make my way through Hutchins' and Adler's five-foot shelf. "It is all there, James," he would say. "Read Aristotle." At his urging, I did. With his tutelage, I became a poor Alexander to his latter-day Aristotle, and I savored a special sense of accomplishment when, shortly before he retired from the Appellate Body, I was able to convince my friend Toy of the merit of my position on a legal question of causation by citing Aristotle's principle of the "final cause."[17]

Aristotle's ideal of the good life is explained in his treatise entitled The Nicomachean Ethics. His equally famous treatise, Politics, is really a sort of sequel to this treatise on ethics. (Regrettably, nowadays, many politicians, tend to forget which of the two comes first.) Aristotle saw our powers of reason as separating us from all other living things and, thus, as central to what should be our thinking on ethics. Thus, as he explains in The Nicomachean Ethics, he believed that the good life, the virtuous life, is one filled to the brim with activities which require the fullest exercise of the uniquely human powers of reason. In particular, he thought the highest good in human life could be achieved through a life of rational, philosophical contemplation. The Greeks called the highest good "eudaimonia." We call this "happiness."[18]

As an Aristotelian, Toy goes along with all of this. He seemed to see our collective struggle to find the right answer at our table as a shared experience in rational, philosophical contemplation. He seemed never to be happier than when we were laboring together to fathom the farthest reaches of the possible implications of our mutual decisionmaking. This, to Toy, is happiness.

---

[17] As Toy certainly knows, Aristotle said that each thing or event has four causes: the material cause, the efficient cause, the formal cause, and the final cause. The "final cause" is the purpose —the goal or full development of an object. For more on this, *see* Aristotle, The Ethics of Aristotle: The Nicomachean Ethics (New York: Penguin Classics, 1955), Appendix E, 355 [hereinafter The Nicomachean Ethics].
[18] Aristotle, The Nicomachean Ethics, at 328-335.

Yet Toy is mindful also that Aristotle spoke as well of the virtue of "the doctrine of the Mean."[19] According to Aristotle, a desirable "mean" for living is to be found in a path of moderation between the excesses of two extremes. This "mean," according to Aristotle, is "relative" to each of us, and is thus, presumably, "relative" to our individual circumstances and to our individual abilities.[20] It is the moderate middle way. It is the path of prudence and practical wisdom that seeks a balance between all the pushes and pulls of all the varied extremes that compete for our attention and our allegiance as we strive to live a life of reason. In following this Aristotelian path, "virtue aims to hit the mean."[21]

And so, despite his compulsion to immerse himself in the contemplation of the law, despite his determination to divine every last shade of meaning from every single legal issue we ever faced, despite his devotion to wringing every last drop of substance from every last point — however peripheral — that was ever made at our table, and despite his diehard dedication to a life lived — in every waking moment — in, and for, and ever amid, his abiding love of the law, Toy did his best, nevertheless, in his years on the Appellate Body, to aim to hit the mean.

Sometimes he even found his target. Toy loves pizza almost as much as he loves the law. And once, with typical Aristotelian precision, he and his Japanese friend Mitsuo tore themselves away from the legal mysteries of the WTO treaty long enough to conduct, evening after evening, and pizzeria after pizzeria, a mutual, methodical search for the best Italian pizza in the French-Swiss environs of Geneva. Finally, in the veranda restaurant of a small hotel near the *Cornavin* train station, they found what they were seeking.

"I've tried them all, James," Toy reported back to me, while no doubt recalling all the observations and all the classifications he had made of comparative "pizza-ness" in his gastronomic journeys throughout Geneva. With a smile of satisfaction, he explained that, at this restaurant, "The mozzarella is the best, and the crust is just right." Later, he and I shared a pizza on his newfound veranda. Toy was right — as he was so often right.

He had found the perfect Aristotelian pizza.

---

[19] Id. at 100-110.
[20] Id. at 100.
[21] Id. at 101.

The European

Looking down on me from the framed photograph on the far wall of our chambers, Claus-Dieter Ehlermann tries hard not to smile. Claus has a wonderful sense of humor, but he rarely laughs when he is reflecting on the serious work of the world. Claus knows that the world is a serious place.

Claus learned long ago just how serious the world can be. He was born in 1931, in Germany. He grew up in a small village called Scheesel, in the north of Germany, between Bremen and the great German port of Hamburg. His father was the village pharmacist. Claus was eight when the Nazis marched into Poland in 1939, ten when war was declared on the United States in 1941, and twelve when the Allies began to turn the tide of the war against the Germans in 1943.

Because there was no secondary school in the village in those days, his parents had sent Claus, at the age of ten, to a private boarding school east of Lueneberg, near the river Elbe. However, in the summer of 1943, he was out of school, back home for a visit. And one night in his little village in northern Germany, Claus saw a sight he would never forget.

Hamburg — the largest seaport in Germany, the second largest city in Germany, and a center of both submarine and aircraft production for Germany — was only fifty-five kilometers away. And, beginning one night in July, 1943, the Allied forces bombed Hamburg.

For more than a week, heavy bombing raids continued over the city. Thousands of Allied bombers dropped thousands of tons of bombs. More bombs were dropped on Hamburg during that one week than were dropped on London during the whole of the Blitz. Many of those bombs were highly explosive, highly incendiary phosphor bombs. Such bombs can sometimes create what has come to be known as a "firestorm."

Whether a "firestorm" results from phosphor bombing depends largely on weather conditions. "A firestorm is not an effect that a bombing force can achieve at will," the military historian, John Keegan, has explained, "it requires a particular combination of prevailing weather conditions and the overwhelming of civil defences."[22] The weather

---

[22] John Keegan, "Strategic Bombing," The Second World War (New York: Penguin Books, 1990) 415, 426 [1989].

conditions in July, 1943, were just right for a "firestorm" in Hamburg, and the civil defences of the city failed. The phosphor bombs from the Allied planes created an inferno. The core temperature of the "firestorm" reached fifteen hundred degrees Fahrenheit. The flames from the fires were spread, unhindered, by 150 mile-per-hour winds. Everything that could burn burst, spontaneously, into flame. The heat from the "firestorm" melted metal, glass, even the tar in the streets. There was no oxygen to breathe.

As described graphically by historian Jonathan Glover in his recent chronicle of the numerous catastrophes suffered by humanity in the twentieth century, "the firestorm sucked air out of bomb shelters, killing people inside. Some escaped through the streets, but the firestorm melted the road surface. Many found their feet were stuck in the molten asphalt. Their hands stuck too when they used them to try to escape. Trapped people were on their hands and knees screaming. Those trapped in buildings either suffocated or burned to death."[23]

And, from the sanctuary of his small village only a short distance away, twelve-year-old Claus-Dieter Ehlermann watched it all. He recalls today that "the horizon was red during the nights following the first massive attacks with phosphor bombs." Contemporary accounts say the same. Hamburg burned, and the whirling tempest of the "firestorm" stained the clouds above the city in red.[24]

Fortunately, the young Claus was not close enough to the conflagration to see everything. He did not see the sheer devastation of a great city that had been utterly consumed by flames. He did not see the wreckage and the carnage, the rats and the flies. He did not see the corpses of the forty thousand who died during the bombing — most of them women or children — or the faces of the one million who were left hungry and homeless in the aftermath of the bombing. He did not see the plowing of the dead into a mass grave in the shape of a cross.

Of such is the grim reality of war. And of such were the grim consequences of war in Hamburg in the summer of 1943. But, fortunately, Claus did not see it all in all its grimness. And, soon after the bombing, he returned to his boarding school "tucked away in the middle of

---

[23] Jonathan Glover, Humanity: A Moral History of the Twentieth Century (London: Pimlico, 2001), 78 [1999].

[24] On the fire-bombing of Hamburg, *see* "Bomber Command: Death by Moonlight," online at www.valourandhorror.com/BC/Raids/Firebomb.

nowhere." He remained there for the rest of the war, far away from all the additional destruction that followed. He remained there, too, for the first few years that followed the war, to finish his schooling.

Yet he remembered all he had seen. And he heard later the accounts of all he had not seen. He resolved to do all he could to ensure that such things would never be seen or heard again. It was thus that the young German began to become the European.

The idea of one place called "Europe" is not new. Erasmus prayed for it. Monnet dreamed of it. Churchill spoke of it — hopefully, wishfully — when he foresaw a "United States of Europe" that would save the people of Europe from the future "firestorm" of a third — and perhaps final — world war. One place called "Europe," it was hoped, would make one peaceful people who would all be called "Europeans."

Claus-Dieter Ehlermann has spent a lifetime trying to confront his memories of Hamburg by helping to make that hopeful, wishful idea a reality. In the process, he has become that new and altogether refreshing phenomenon in the long and tortured history of a continent that has seen far too many "firestorms." He has become a European. And in his lifetime of service in the making of Europe can be seen as well the motivations for his more recent service to the Members of the WTO.

Claus enlisted, early on, in the historic postwar effort to make one place called "Europe." The Treaty of Paris establishing the "European Coal and Steel Community" was signed in 1951. The Treaty of Rome establishing the "European Economic Community" was concluded in 1957. By 1961, with his law studies at Heidelberg and elsewhere behind him, Claus was in Brussels, serving in the newly created legal service of something called the "European Commission." He had volunteered as a foot soldier in the cause of a free, united, prosperous — and peaceful — Europe.

He rose rapidly in the ranks. Eventually, for ten years, he served as Director General of the legal service — the senior legal adviser to the European Commission. Then, for five years, he served as Director General of the "Directorate General for Competition" — the highest ranking civil servant of the European competition authority in Brussels. Along the way, he became, like our mutual colleague Mitsuo, one of a handful of acknowledged experts worldwide on competition policy. He became also a respected authority on the law of the European Community.

Claus became, too, the consummate European. He became one of those who made history by "making" Europe. Together with other Europeans of like inclination, he took what began as a "common market" only for coal and steel and made it — slowly, gradually, ever so incrementally — a common "single market" for a whole lot more. Product by product, year by year, the visionary idea of one European economy became the growing reality of European economic integration. Economic integration eventually led to the beginnings of political integration. And further economic and political integration led, in time, to a "European Union."

Claus was there through it all. Behind the scenes. At the side of the politicians. Whispering in their ears. Writing their lines. Writing their statements, their directives, their laws, their treaties. Nudging "Europe" along. Always nudging "Europe" along. And creating, as he did, more and more "Europeans." So that, in time, the "firestorms" of a few millennia — the religious, the ethnic, and all the many other hostilities and mutual animosities that had afflicted the continent for so long — began to yield at last — somehow, somewhat — to a half-century's labor by Claus, and by many others, in the cause of a true European union. Much more remained to be done. Much more. There were still "firestorms" in the Balkans, and in many other parts of a fearful world. But there had not yet been a third world war, and Hamburg and numerous other cities in Europe knew a security and a prosperity they had never known before.

On his retirement from the European Commission in 1995, Claus was named to the faculty of the European University Institute in Florence as Chair for European Community Law. Soon, however, he found himself in Geneva, along with the rest of us, as a founding member of the Appellate Body. He brought with him to our table in Geneva ways and wiles he had learned in thirty-five years of bureaucratic struggles in Brussels that proved equally useful in his service to the WTO.

The key to understanding Claus is to understand that Claus is a builder of institutions. He has described the ongoing development of the law of the European Union as a "physiological process."[25] In my experience with him at the WTO, this seems also to be very much his

---

[25] Claus-Dieter Ehlermann, "Differentiation, Flexibility, Closer Cooperation: The New Provisions of the Amsterdam Treaty," European University Institute (Florence, Italy) (August, 1997).

view of the continuing development of the WTO as a global institution. For Claus, the challenge confronting the WTO is a process of building an institution. It is a "physiological process." It is an organic process. It is an incremental process. It is a process that occurs over a long time. It is a process of the right nudge in the right place at the right time.

One day, a few years into our work together, Claus looked up, startled, from the sleep-inducing depths of our deliberations on some now forgotten issue, and said, as if a bright light had suddenly shone for the first time, "I see. It is 1960 again, and the WTO Treaty is the Treaty of Rome."

By this, I hasten to add, Claus did not mean to imply that the WTO treaty is in some way meant to inspire some form of global political integration. That is not his view. Rather, by this, Claus meant only to voice his realization that the task of the WTO is in some ways akin to the task of the European economic integration to which he has devoted so much of his life. He meant only to underscore that the task facing the WTO is, like the task that faced all those such as Claus who hoped to become "Europeans" all those years ago, a task primarily of institution building.

For Claus, the task of building institutions is a personal task. It is a human task. It is an individual task shared by individual people who work together toward a common goal. Like another great German — and another great European — Johann Wolfgang von Goethe, Claus believes that, "As the men, so are the institutions."[26] Of course, Claus, who is more progressive than Goethe, would surely add the women to this maxim. But, for both of them, institutions are, first and foremost, the collective creation of individual people.

So, as Claus saw it from the very beginning, our real challenge — as the founding members of a newfound institution called the Appellate Body that was part of the newborn institution called the WTO — was one of working together on an individual and personal basis. Our "quasi-judicial" institution would emerge, and would evolve into an effective international tribunal, as he saw it, from the personal workings of the "physiological process" of our unfolding mutual relationship as Members of the Appellate Body. Thus, Claus, from the outset, took it upon himself

---

[26] Goethe is quoted in Van Wyck Brooks, The Flowering of New England: 1815-1865 (New York: E.P. Dutton, 1936), 243.

to do all he could to help meld our seven into one. He did so, much to our mutual advantage, and much to the advantage also of the institution we all sought to build. He did so consistently, and he did so modestly.

Claus is modest about his considerable learning. He went off to Neuchatel one weekend, on a side trip from our ongoing deliberations, and "forgot" to mention to us that the purpose of his trip was to receive an honorary doctorate from the distinguished university there. We learned about the honor by chance from someone else several weeks later. Nor has Claus ever mentioned to me — even once — in all the years I have known him the merest possibility that he may — even once — have written something substantive on the subject of international law. On the contrary, Claus has told me more than once, "I am not a scholar." And yet the total of the articles, commentaries, and books he has written through the decades on European law, international law, and other decidedly scholarly subjects was, when last I looked, almost two hundred.

Claus is modest, too, about his considerable intellect. Perhaps inspired by a lifetime spent much in the service of mere politicians, he pretends not to be as smart or as savvy as he really is. He rarely tells you when you have told him something that he already knew. Modestly, he would rather have you think that you might have enlightened him. Moreover, he sometimes seems to strive, like Stendhal's Julian Sorel, when in the seminary in <u>Scarlet and Black</u>, *not* to look like he is thinking.[27] Claus, though, is always thinking.

His modesty as a thinker extends also to his modesty as a talker. Claus tends to listen rather than talk. He tends to say little when there is no need to say much. Yet his command of languages is as profound as his intellect. He speaks German, of course. He also speaks both French and Italian fluently. And his command of English — the language we use around our table — is at least the equal of mine.

There is a personal nuance or two to his use of English. In the first few months of our work together around our table, I noticed that, from time to time, Claus would announce that he was "shocked" or that he was "astonished" by some notion or another. In those first few months, I thought this meant that he was, indeed, "shocked" or "astonished." In time, though, I realized that, when Claus said that he was "shocked" or

---

[27] Stendhal, <u>Scarlet and Black: A Chronicle of the Nineteenth Century</u> (London: Penguin Books, 1953), 195-196 [1830].

that he was "astonished," he meant only that he was mildly surprised. I realized, too, that it would, in truth, take a lot to "shock" or to "astonish" my European friend, who had watched, in his youth, the "firestorms" of Hamburg.

With his serious view of the world, Claus may sometimes seem a bit stern to those who do not know him. He is not. In our time together around our table, Claus proved as ready to laugh at a joke as anyone — although we occasionally had to explain the punchline. And he often laughed the longest. When Claus laughs, his cheeks turn rosy, and his full head of white hair falls down toward his brow. Claus learned long ago that, the longer the laugh, the longer the respite from seriousness.

Unwittingly, too, Claus would sometimes give the rest of us reason to laugh, and thus relieve the unrelenting seriousness of our table. In the idle intellectual moments of some prolonged debate on some tedious procedural issue, I, for one, would sometimes amuse myself by simply observing the entertaining spectacle of Claus being Claus. I would watch him pour glass after glass of water from the water pitcher, while waiting for the inevitable moment — it always came — when, distracted by his own discourse, he would pour the entire contents of the pitcher across the table and into his lap. I would watch, too, for the inevitable and telltale sign, in the course of a lengthy debate, that Claus — who once brought an "egg timer" to an oral hearing to inspire the parties to stay within their time limits — had heard enough. I would wait for him to signal his impatience by beginning to drum his fingers — quietly but insistently — on the table.

Claus drums his fingers on tables in part because Claus is impatient for the future to arrive. And yet Claus knows from his own life, from his own experience, that the future is sometimes a long time in arriving. He laughs. He gesticulates. He even grins at my casual American colloquialisms. He often seems relaxed. But, somewhere deep inside, Claus is always drumming his fingers. He is always waiting for, hoping for, and working seriously for, a future without "firestorms" — a future that may be a long time in arriving.

Claus firmly believes — as I do — that the work of the Appellate Body can help hasten such a future. At one of our last dinners together, shortly before we finished our six years together around our table, and shortly before I succeeded him as Chairman, Claus, in a brief moment of uncharacteristic sentimentality, turned to my wife, Rebecca, and asked,

"Do you think that, when the Members of the WTO chose the seven of us, they chose us with the idea in mind that we seven would be able to work so well together in building a new institution?" The question was perhaps rhetorical. Claus does not know the answer. Neither do I. Yet the question itself says much about, and much for, my friend Claus-Dieter Ehlermann.

In the fall of 1944, more than a year after the bombing of Hamburg, a young first lieutenant in the United States Army Air Corps arrived at Elmswell, Great Ashfield, England. He was a member of the 549th Squadron of the 385th Bomb Group of the 8th Air Force. He was the co-pilot on a B-17 bomber called (after the popular American jazz tune of the time) the "Floogie Boo." At the tender age of twenty, he was the oldest member of his bomber crew. His name was Bacchus.

In the months that followed, First Lieutenant G.M. "Joe" Bacchus and the other, teenaged crew of the "Floogie Boo" flew from England to continental Europe on mission after mission. They bombed in the Rhineland. They bombed in the Ardennes. They bombed across Germany and across Central Europe. Along with thousands of other crews of thousands of other B-17 "Flying Fortresses," they bombed until the war's end. Then they went home to help make a new world.

My father never told me about his experiences in that war. It was not until after he died, of a heart attack, at the age of fifty, that my mother showed me all the medals he had won while a member of the crew of the "Floogie Boo." The medals were in his bedroom closet, in the back, in a shoebox, on a high shelf.

That was a long time ago. I was much younger then — not much older than my father had been when he flew all those missions over Germany. In the years since, I have often wondered what my father would say about where my life has taken me. And, in the years since I became a member of the Appellate Body, I have often wondered what he would think of my work in Geneva for the WTO — and what he would think about my working side by side with a German who, as a boy, had escaped the Allied bombing.

I mentioned this once to Claus. I told him that I thought my father would find it only fitting for Claus and me to be working, side by side, nearly sixty years later, in the cause of peace. Claus, the European, told me he agreed. Then he smiled.

The Orchard Keeper

The smile on the face of Christopher Beeby in the framed photograph before me is more like a laugh. It is as though Chris knows something that I do not know. This is not surprising. He often did.

Chris was a New Zealander, and he had a New Zealander's knack for knowing some things intuitively that many of the rest of us spend a lifetime in finding out. "Not everything is subject to debate," he once told me. "Some things are just true."

Chris also had a New Zealander's love for lamb. In all the years I knew him, and in all the many meals we shared together, he never once passed up a portion of lamb when lamb was on the menu. This, too, is not surprising. It is not surprising at all for a man from a country of perhaps four million people and perhaps forty million sheep. "The sheep," Chris said, "is a glorious animal."

But even more than he loved New Zealand sheep, Chris loved New Zealand apples. When he was not cultivating the law with us in Geneva, Chris was usually cultivating his apple orchard back home in New Zealand. He loved planting apple trees in his orchard. He loved growing New Zealand apples, he loved eating New Zealand apples, and, most of all, he loved extolling the many virtues of New Zealand apples.

Much of this extolling was done to me. In the early days of our work together on the Appellate Body, Chris and I both stayed at a small hotel across the street from the WTO. We ate breakfast there together every morning before beginning the day's work. The breakfast room at the hotel was usually blessed by an abundance of New Zealand apples, and Chris ate one every morning.

He taught me to do the same. He taught me also to appreciate some of the subtler nuances that are native to New Zealand apples and, according to Chris, enhance their virtues. "The New Zealand apple," he insisted, "has a juicy crispness, a crispy juicy-ness, if you will, that is, indeed, beyond compare." Crunching into one, I could see what he meant.

Chris instructed me, likewise, on some of the subtleties of the various varieties of the New Zealand apple. The breakfast room of the hotel usually served the luscious "Gala" apple, but Chris regaled me also with tales of the juicy crispness (or crispy juicy-ness, if you will) of the

"Braeburn," the "Fuji," the "Southern Snap," the "Southern Rose," the "Pacific Rose," and the noble "Ruby Bay Pippin."

It was with the same love, and with the same detailed precision, that Chris approached his work on the Appellate Body. Early on, over a brace of "Gala" New Zealand apples in the hotel breakfast room, I learned why. For Chris Beeby was the very first to say, at breakfast, or at any time of the day, that by far the most important thing to know about him was that he was his father's son.

Christopher Beeby was the son of Clarence E. Beeby. By his son's account, and, indeed, by most accounts, Clarence E. Beeby was one of the most important, most respected, and most beloved men in the history of New Zealand. And all that his son hoped to accomplish, all that his son hoped to be, can be seen in the life's work of his father.

Clarence Beeby was perhaps the greatest educator in the history of New Zealand, and he has been described as "an intellectual architect of modern education" by UNESCO, the education agency of the United Nations. He believed passionately in the potential of universal public education, and in the right of every person "as a citizen, to a free education of the kind for which he is best fitted and to the fullest extent of his powers." He added these and a few other famous words about the need for universal public education to the Annual Report of the New Zealand Ministry of Education as an idealistic young administrator in 1939, and, according to UNESCO, they "had a profound effect on the development of education, not only in his country but worldwide."[28]

Clarence Beeby — known to many, affectionately, as "Beeb" — served as Director of Education for New Zealand from 1940 until 1960. During that time, he led the successful effort in New Zealand to develop a broad public school curriculum, and, further, to establish the basic democratic and "human right" of all New Zealanders to the full benefit of a free public education. This is still known worldwide, in education circles, as "the Beeby principle."[29]

---

[28] "'Beeb' — an intellectual architect of modern education," UNESCO, online at www.unesco.org/iiep/news/English/1998/apre998.htm.
[29] On "the Beeby principle," *see*, for example, "Submission to the Tertiary Education Advisory Commission," The Association of Staff in Tertiary Education (ASTE) of New Zealand (June 20, 2000), online at www.aste.ac.nz/home/Offer/pdf/TEAC.pdf.

With Beeb's inspiration and leadership, New Zealand's system of public education became an example to the rest of the world. He lectured on education around the world, and his books on education were read throughout the world. Eventually, he was sent by New Zealand to serve the world. He became New Zealand's ambassador to France — and also a member of the executive board of UNESCO. There he focused his considerable energies on improving the quality of education in developing countries.[30]

Simply put, Chris Beeby idolized his father. He wanted to be just like his father. When Chris first came to Geneva to begin our work together, his father — although in his nineties — was still very much alive. And Chris spoke often to me then about his father. "Beeb is truly a great man," he said, and I did not disagree.

Before deciding to devote his life to the cause of education, Beeb had started out in life intending to become a lawyer. Chris became one. Born in 1935, he did his undergraduate studies in New Zealand, and then, following Said by a few years, he studied law at the London School of Economics. There, like Said, he fell under the spell of the economic philosophies of Popper and Hayek. There, too, he met one of Said's other heroes, the writer Arthur Koestler. Chris was fond of recalling later how Koestler told him once of the considerable pride he took in the fact that his books — which celebrated freedom and denounced totalitarianism — had been burned by the fascists and the communists alike.

Returning to New Zealand after law school, Chris joined the foreign service of New Zealand, and became a career diplomat, specializing in legal and economic affairs. Over the years, he became something of a legal and diplomatic "troubleshooter" for the New Zealand government.

Chris participated in eight sessions of the General Assembly of the United Nations. He played a principal role in the negotiation of the United Nations Convention on the Law of the Sea. He was counsel to New Zealand before the International Court of Justice at the Hague in the nuclear test case in which New Zealand and Australia challenged the legitimacy under international law of French atmospheric nuclear testing in the South Pacific. He was agent for New Zealand in the arbitration

---

[30]Clarence Beeby's most famous book is The Quality of Education in Developing Countries (1966).

between New Zealand and France arising from French destruction of the Greenpeace ship, the "Rainbow Warrior."

In addition, Chris served as New Zealand's ambassador to Iran during the Iranian hostage crisis (when he rendered, I am told, notable service to American hostages as a friend of the United States). He served also as New Zealand's ambassador to Pakistan, to Algeria, and — like his father — to France. He was ambassador as well, while in Paris, to the OECD — the Organization for Economic Cooperation and Development.

Moreover, through the years, Chris acted for New Zealand in many a twist and turn involving the GATT and GATT trade negotiations — with a special ardor, no doubt, on all matters involving either lamb or apples. He knew the GATT inside out. And he also knew the other "covered agreements" that were concluded in the Uruguay Round.

Chris retired from the diplomatic service of New Zealand upon his appointment to the Appellate Body in 1995, and we quickly became good friends as well as colleagues. Perhaps it was because of our morning apple-munching. Perhaps it was because of our many common intellectual interests. Or perhaps it was because (as Said — nearly thirty years my elder — once joked) Chris, only fourteen years older than me, was the *second* youngest Member of the Appellate Body. Whatever the reason, I soon discovered that the passion of Chris Beeby for New Zealand apples was exceeded only by his passion for the rule of law.

New Zealand is a small but supremely civilized country, and, like many of those from the small but supremely civilized countries of the world, New Zealanders have a supreme understanding of the significance to the world of the rule of law. They seem to share an almost intuitive understanding of the indispensability of the rule of law in preserving all those who are small in the world from the ravages of all those who are not. Thus, New Zealanders have contributed much to the establishment of the rule of law in the world — and Chris Beeby not least among them.

Chris was short and slight. He was freckled and often frazzled. His thinning, reddish hair framed a gaunt face. His wrinkled shirts were often untucked. His scrawny shins peeked out from below the short cuffs of his trousers. He often forgot to wear the shiny coat of what seemed to be his only suit, and I had the hardest time convincing him of the "quasi-judicial" imperative of our always wearing our coats in all our oral hearings. But Chris was never less than formal in his dedication to the law.

Chris knew the substance of the law. He knew it perhaps to an extent that none of the rest of us did. In particular, he seemed to know all there was to know about his greatest legal passion — public international law. When the rest of us were stumped for an international legal precedent, Chris would recall one at our table, from memory, and sometimes from more than a century past. When we were all held up in our deliberations by some mutual mental impasse, Chris could retrieve, from the roomy recesses of his personal legal memory banks, some half-forgotten footnote that would, as we lawyers say, be right "on point," and that, thus, would break the impasse and help move us closer to a consensus on the right answer we sought. Where a profound knowledge of the substance of the law was needed, Chris could do such things, and he often did.

However, his true strength was not the substance, but the spirit, of the law. This is what, in his spare moments, Chris tried his best to teach me. When not enlightening me on the many virtues of New Zealand apples, New Zealand lamb, New Zealand cricket, or the New Zealand "All Blacks" football team, Chris enlightened me on the virtues of the rule of law. With his luminous mind perched on his lean and angular frame, he shared with me, time and again, his impassioned belief that the rule of law is, as he put it, "the key" to securing and sustaining real human rights and, thus, real human freedom.

I do not remember ever differing with Chris on any issue that ever came before us during our time together on the Appellate Body. Maybe I did a time or two, and it is only my fond memory of him that keeps me from remembering our occasional substantive disagreements. Certainly it is accurate to say, though, that, on both the substance and the spirit of the law as it came before us on appeal, Chris and I were invariably of like mind at our table. Very often one of us would speak at length in our deliberations, and then the other would simply say, "I agree."

Where we sometimes did differ was on points of style. Chris was a connoisseur of a classic British style — a style of elegance and erudition — a style of oblique and understated indirection. I, on the other hand, am an American. I am a captive of the native American tendency to want to get to the point, and of the native American urge to be direct. Moreover, I happen also to be one American who has been much schooled in the rhetorical black art of speaking — pointedly and directly — in what the television chroniclers of American politics often call "sound bites."

So it was that my friend Chris and I were frequently at odds, not over substance, but over minor matters of style. There was, for example, one memorable occasion when we were preparing a list of questions to pose to the parties in an oral hearing. We did not differ at all on what questions to ask. We differed only on how best to ask them. Chris suggested framing the questions by asking: "Is it *not* true...?" I objected. Instead, I favored asking: "Is it true...?" I asked Chris, "Why do we need the *not*? The question means precisely the same thing without it." To the amusement of our colleagues, Chris and I debated this compelling issue for some time. He observed that my stubborn opposition to what he saw as the sheer necessity of the controversial "*not*" was "very American" of me. It was, he said, "very American, indeed." Ultimately, we compromised. Throughout the hearing the next day, we took turns asking our questions first one way, and then the other. We noticed that the answers seemed to be the same no matter how we posed the questions.

Those concerned more with the substance of the issues that come before us on the Appellate Body will no doubt be comforted to hear that Chris and I gave even more attention to the substantive issues we faced than we did to such meaningless minutiae. Yet we always had great fun when indulging ourselves in debates over such semantic whimsies. And we had great fun together in many other ways as well — until one day it all seemed to change forever for my friend Chris Beeby.

One day, in the midst of a discussion on a pending issue, Chris paused, looked over at me, and said, "You know, Jim, my father died." Beeb died on March 10, 1998. He was ninety-five years old. He was mourned by all of New Zealand. He was mourned especially, in Geneva, by his son.

Chris had talked with me about the imminence of his father's death. He had been expecting his father's death. Beeb was, after all, ninety-five. Yet somehow something went out of Chris Beeby when his father died. After that, Chris was never quite the same.

The quality of his work remained as high as ever. His work never suffered. But Chris did. He had little time now for munching apples. He had little time now for our amiable musings over eccentricities of style. He had, it seemed, little time at all, for he always seemed somehow far away.

Sometimes, on a weekend, in the midst of the day, I would see him from a passing street, sitting all alone, sipping a beer, and smoking a cigarette, in one of his favorite cafes in Geneva. He would be gazing vacantly into the distance. At such times, if he saw me, he would wave. But it was clear to me that he preferred to be alone.

Sometimes, too, he would return to Geneva to judge a new appeal, and I would ask him what he had been doing back home, "down there" in New Zealand. Always before, when I had asked that same question, he had been full to overflowing with all the latest I ought to know about his wonderful country on the other side of the world. Now, though, he always gave me exactly the same reply: "I've been in the orchard, Jim. I've been out planting trees on the hillside. I've been planting hundreds of apple trees."

I do not know the nature of all the demons that may have possessed my friend Chris Beeby. I suppose I never will. There was much of his life of which I remained — and still remain — unaware. I know only that, in the end, I lost a good friend.

One morning back home in Florida, only a few hours after I had last left Geneva, and only a few hours after I had last seen Chris, I was awakened by a phone call: Chris Beeby had died in Geneva, of a heart attack, while working there on an appeal at the WTO. The date was March 19, 2000 — two years and nine days after the death of his father. Chris was sixty-four years old. At their request, I spoke on behalf of my colleagues on the Appellate Body at the memorial service for him at the WTO.

Today, when I think of Chris, when I look at Chris in the framed photograph on the far wall of our chambers, when I study the steady way that Chris smiles down on me during our deliberations, I often ask myself: of all the many things that Chris knew, what did Chris know best? It seems to me that the answer is this: Chris knew that the world, for all its far horizons, is really a very small place. He knew that, in this small place, all we ever really have is each other. And he knew, even in his sorrow, and even in his solitude, that, in the end, this is enough.

It is enough for me to be able to remember Chris, not as a picture on the wall, but as I believe Chris wanted most to be remembered: His father's son. The good and faithful servant. Back home in his orchard. On a green hillside. In the soft southern sunshine. Planting apple trees.

Chris looked at me once with a smile on his face that seemed somehow far away. He told me that, out on the hillside, he felt closer to his Creator. He told me that, when he planted apple trees, he could hear the voice of God.

Is it not true?

The Silver Fox

And then there is Julio. The face of Julio Lacarté-Muro of Uruguay smiles broadly in the framed photograph on the wall before me. His smile seems to suggest that Julio has seen it all — because he has — and that he sees through it all — because he does. Gazing down on me, Julio smiles confidently. He smiles wryly, and oh so slyly. Like a fox.

"I hear you're going to Geneva to work with The Silver Fox," an old GATT hand in Washington remarked to me a short while before I was appointed to the Appellate Body. "The Silver Fox"? I had no idea who or what he meant at the time. Now I do. For I have become an older GATT hand myself in the years since while working with — and learning much from — Julio Lacarte, who is known in trade and other diplomatic circles throughout the world as "The Silver Fox."

I do not really know *why* Julio is known as "The Silver Fox." He was given that nickname long before he and I began to work together on the Appellate Body. Perhaps it is his silver hair. Or it may be his distinguished Latin bearing. Or it could be the long trail of all of those who have been vanquished by the rapier of his clever wit and his cunning charm in countless diplomatic duels through the long decades of his service to his country and to the world.

However, I do know why Julio *should* be called "The Silver Fox." The answer is to be found in a cryptic surviving fragment from the lost works of the ancient Greek poet Archilochus which, roughly translated, is believed to say: "The fox knows many things, but the hedgehog knows one big thing."

Some time ago, the British philosopher Isaiah Berlin drew on this poetic distinction to explain what he saw as "one of the deepest differences which divide writers and thinkers, and, it may be, human beings in general."[31] It is not, he wrote, that this distinction makes one group better

---

[31] Isaiah Berlin, The Hedgehog and the Fox: An Essay on Tolstoy's View of History (New York: Elephant, 1993) 3 [1953].

than another. It is only that it makes them different in the way they see the world. "Hedgehogs" see one big picture, while "foxes" see all the fine details. As Berlin explained it, "hedgehogs" have one big idea that explains everything and applies in all situations, while "foxes" know a lot of things that apply in particular situations. Thus, he suggested, Dante belongs to the first category, and Shakespeare to the second.[32]

As additional examples, I would suggest that Rousseau was a hedgehog, and Voltaire was a fox; Luther was a hedgehog, and Erasmus was a fox; Abraham Lincoln was a hedgehog, and Franklin Delano Roosevelt was a fox. In this sense, Julio Lacarté is also a fox. To be sure, Julio does know a "big thing" or two. He knows about the need for freedom. But so did Voltaire. He knows about the necessity for faith. But so did Erasmus. He knows, too, about the indispensability of democracy as the only means of making a world in which freedom can flourish and faith can prevail. But so did Franklin Delano Roosevelt. Foxes can also know the "big things."

What makes Julio a fox, is not that he does not know the "big things that apply to all situations," but that he — like Voltaire, like Erasmus, like Roosevelt, and like all foxes — also knows a myriad of the details of "many things" that apply in particular situations. And all the "many things" that Julio knows not only help him smile like a fox. They help him serve in a uniquely significant way.

In particular, there is nothing among all the "many things" that might be known about international trade that "The Silver Fox" does not know. No one else — no one else in all the world — knows nearly as much about the politics, the economics, the history, the diplomacy, the law, the lore, or the sheer day-to-day practical reality of the world trading system. Julio is a living library of world trade.

One reason why Julio's knowledge of trade is beyond compare is because his experience in trade is also beyond compare. As I write, Julio is eighty-five years old. Born in 1918, he will soon be eighty-six. He has been working on international trade issues for more than half a century, and he has shown no sign whatsoever of ever doing such a rash thing as "retiring." Even now, in his "retirement" from the Appellate Body, he is still taking assignments from the WTO.

---

[32] Id. at 3-4.

Julio was literally born to the trading world. He is the heir to a distinguished family name in his native Uruguay. His father was one of the great tribunes of the democratic tradition in Uruguay. His father was also a leading Uruguayan diplomat who, for many years, defended Uruguay's considerable agricultural and other trading interests in postings in many parts of the world. It was as a diplomat's son that Julio came into the world, and it was only to be expected that he, too, would become a diplomat after completing his studies in economics and law. He did so while much of the world was mired in the Second World War.

At war's end in 1945, Julio, although still in his twenties, already was a diplomat in his country's foreign service. Soon after the war, he was an active participant in the London Conference that helped solidify the new "United Nations." An old black-and-white photograph that Julio displayed in his office in Geneva all the while we worked together on the Appellate Body shows his father, in formal attire, and his mother, in a feathered hat, sitting in the front row of a conference session in London. The young Julio, eager and dapper, sits nearby.

That was only the beginning. Soon the young Julio was immersed in the international effort to create a trading system for the postwar world. He helped write the GATT at the Havana Conference in 1947 and 1948. He and others tried — and failed — at that time to establish an "International Trade Organization." Julio would try again — more successfully — nearly half a century later. Yet, despite the failure of the proposed "ITO," the world, nevertheless, needed some semblance of a trade organization, and so, at age of twenty-nine, Julio was named the first Deputy-Director General of the new quasi-organization called "the GATT" in Geneva. All this happened, I should add, before I was born.

Later, Julio served on three separate occasions as Uruguay's representative to the GATT. He served in almost every elected post of the GATT. As an official for a time with UNCTAD, and as trade minister for a term for Uruguay, he also dealt frequently with the GATT. Through many long years of work both for the GATT and with the GATT, he became, by the time I met him, the only person on the planet to have participated in all eight of the global trade negotiating rounds of the GATT.

The eighth of those rounds — the Uruguay Round — can be seen in some respects as Julio's brainchild. The formal Ministerial Declaration that "launched" that round is known as "the Punta del Este Declaration" because it was concluded at the GATT ministerial conference at the seaside beach resort of Punta del Este, in Uruguay. I have been told by a number of senior Uruguayan diplomats that it was "The Silver Fox" who convinced the elected leaders of his country to extend the invitation to host that conference, and thereby lend the name of "Uruguay" to the historic trade round that was begun there. No developing country had ever before been so bold as to do so. Thus, without Julio, the "Uruguay Round" likely would not have been known as the "Uruguay Round."

By most accounts, Julio's fingerprints are also all over the wording of the Punta del Este Declaration itself. Likewise, they can be seen throughout the pages of the "covered agreements" of the WTO treaty that was the landmark accomplishment of the Uruguay Round. It was the WTO treaty, of course, that, nearly half a century after the failure of the stillborn "ITO," memorialized the unanimous agreement of more than one hundred negotiating countries to establish, at long last, a "WTO." "The Silver Fox" is not one to give up easily.

Julio's most important contribution to the successful conclusion of the WTO treaty was his service throughout nearly a decade of negotiations as chairman of the negotiating group on dispute settlement and other "institutional" issues. These were the negotiations that led to the agreement by the negotiating countries on the Dispute Settlement Understanding — which, among many other notable innovations, established the Appellate Body.

Those negotiations were conducted by Julio at the very same round table where we sit today. So it was only fitting that "The Silver Fox" would be chosen as one of the seven founding Members of the Appellate Body. It was only fitting, too, that we would elect him as our first, and, later, our permanent "honorary" chairman.

Indeed, it seemed almost foreordained. Julio's presence on the Appellate Body ensured for us the luster of an instant credibility and the luxury of an unmatched historical and institutional memory. He was respected universally and trusted implicitly by the Members of the new WTO. Furthermore, of all of us, from all our varied backgrounds, he was certainly the one among us who knew by far the most about the world of trade.

A common charge against the WTO is that those who serve the trading system are guilty of what the philosophers call "reductionism" — that we reduce everything to trade as a single theory, a single explanation, a single operating mechanism for the world. This accusation is far from being true. And one of the many ironies of this accusation as it relates to the Appellate Body is that the most consummate trader who has served among us may also be the one among us who most clearly comprehends the multiplicity of human purposes in the world, and the manifest variety of the causes that shape human events.

Julio Lacarte is the very opposite of a "reductionist." He values the rich variety of life. He knows that one size definitely does *not* fit all. He knows that one all-purpose explanation of the world simply does not suffice. This is what makes him, not a hedgehog, but a fox.

Julio may well be the world's leading expert on the international trading system. But he is also much more than that. He is a man of very many parts who has spent a long lifetime in engagement with the world and in contemplation of the world. Julio's engagement with the world has included service in many diplomatic posts that were not solely related to trade. He has served (thus far) as Uruguay's ambassador or permanent representative to Ecuador, Bolivia, Argentina, Japan, India, Thailand, Germany (twice), the European Communities, the United States, the Organization of American States, and the European headquarters of the United Nations in Geneva, among other assignments. At one time, Julio was even the nominee of his political party in Uruguay for Vice President of his country.

Quick, decisive, endlessly shrewd from the vast experience of a lifetime of diplomatic postings, "The Silver Fox" is a dedicated lawyer and diplomat who is, to me, reminiscent of the old-fashioned school of savvy and seasoned "diplomatists" who have, of late, yielded the world stage to the political place-fillers and the mere careerists. In his wary reaction to the ever unfolding flow of events, Julio has always reminded me of a story that he once told me about the legendary French "diplomatist" Talleyrand. Told once that the Russian ambassador had just died, Talleyrand supposedly mused, "I wonder what could have been his motivation."[33] The story is perhaps apocryphal. The sentiment, as it relates to Julio, is not.

Julio is no Talleyrand (although one of his favorite books is Duff Cooper's great biography of that agile and amoral French realist). Julio is

---

[33] This particular *bon mot* of Talleyrand is perhaps apocryphal, but, for others that may not be, *see* Duff Cooper, Talleyrand (New York: Fromm, 1986) [1932].

far too modern, far too idealistic, and far too admirable in the application of his foxlike ways to be compared to the slippery Talleyrand. Yet, like Talleyrand, and like every true "diplomatist," Julio is forever pondering the motivations of men in an effort to perceive, and to understand, the manifestations of human nature that so much affect the course of world events. Julio is "worldly" in the best and the truest sense of that word. Behind the gleam in the eye of the fox is the mind of a profoundly human man. Beneath the veneer of a smooth *savoir faire* beats a rare and tender heart. His humanity and his heart alike are visible in all that Julio says and does.

When I see Julio, I picture him as my son, Joe, tells me he always pictures him, from our common memory of Julio at my surprise 50th birthday party in Geneva a few years ago. There was Julio, in his eighties, out on the lawn, sleeves rolled up, an open book in one hand, a glass of scotch in the other, kicking a soccer ball, deftly and nimbly, while playing a foxy game of "keepaway" with several laughing children. This is Julio. This is my permanent picture of "The Silver Fox."

Soccer, which he played superbly in his youth, is not Julio's only sport. Equally, he loves tennis. Even in his eighties, he plays often. He serves also on the governing board of the Latin American Lawn Tennis Association. (The Dispute Settlement Understanding notwithstanding, the Appellate Body has, I confess, been known to schedule its deliberations around Julio's annual pilgrimage to Wimbledon.)

However, Julio's real passion, among sports — his enduring passion, his consuming passion — is for baseball. As the son of the then Uruguayan consul in New York City, Julio spent much of his youth, not in Uruguay, but in the depression-era streets of New York. And much of his youthful time in New York was apparently spent in Yankee Stadium. Painful though it is for a lifelong Braves fan such as me to say, my friend Julio is that bane of all other baseball enthusiasts — a Yankees fan. Yet he comes by it honestly. As he justifies it, "Never forget. I have seen Babe Ruth play."

Like all the homeruns that Julio saw him hit all those years ago in "The House That Ruth Built," the Bambino is long gone. Yet Julio still follows the fortunes of his Yankees from afar, reading and studying the box scores of their games on line every day during the baseball season. And it was our mutual love for baseball that — despite our differing team allegiances — initially brought us together during our time together around our table in Geneva.

If Julio was much impressed by my command of the intricacies of international trade law during our first weeks together on the Appellate Body, he was somehow able to refrain from saying so. Through the years, he has seen a lot of would-be trade hotshots come and go, and doubtless more than a few of them have been Americans. He was friendly. He was gracious. He was even gregarious. He was ever the courtly and distinguished "diplomatist" in all his dealings with his new, and much younger, American colleague. However, he did not, at first, seem noticeably impressed.

Then, just when I began to think that Julio (like my wife, my children, and many of my erstwhile Congressional constituents in Florida) might be immune to the charm of my "charisma," I happened, one day, to impress him. What impressed Julio, what first seemed to spark his interest in me, and what became the real beginning of our firm and abiding friendship, was when he discovered, during the course of a casual conversation over cups of *renversé*, that I was able to name the entire starting lineup of the 1931 Philadelphia Athletics. It was Connie Mack's fabled Philadelphia A's who, in his youth, had beaten Julio's beloved Yankees in the American League pennant race three years in a row, and had thus made an indelible impression on at least one Uruguayan Yankee fan. I can still see the stunned look on Julio's face when I expounded at some length on the considerable merits of A's second baseman Max Bishop as a leadoff hitter.[34]

Fortunately, many years before I set out to memorize much of the WTO "covered agreements," I had set out, just as ardently, to memorize much of the massive "Baseball Encyclopedia." And, evidently, Julio must have decided that anyone who could rattle off, from memory, as I could, the illustrious names of Jimmy Foxx, Jimmy Dykes, Mickey Cochrane, Mule Haas, Al "Bucketfoot" Simmons, and their long-ago teammates on the old Athletics was someone who might, perhaps, be worthy of instruction. This young hotshot might, he must have concluded, have some potential. For, from then on, he took me under his wing. From then on, he endeavored to teach me the ways of "The Silver Fox."

---

[34] *See,* The Baseball Encyclopedia; The Complete and Official Record of Major League Baseball, 8th ed. (New York: Macmillan, 1990), 266. The starting lineup of the 1931 A's included Jimmie Foxx at first base, Max Bishop at second base, Jimmy Dykes at third base, Al Simmons in leftfield, Mule Haas in centerfield, Bing Miller in right field, and Mickey Cochrane at catcher. Joe Boley and Dib Williams were the shortstops. Lefty Grove and George Earnshaw were the star pitchers.

Thereafter, we were master and apprentice. We shared coffee, lunch, and sometimes dinner when we were both in Geneva. We walked together — at Julio's rapid pace — both to and from work. (Sometimes it was all I could do to keep up with his quick pace.) More often than not, we sat side by side in the deliberations at our round table. Through it all, he taught me all he could of his wisdom and his craft.

Julio tried to teach me some of the many lessons he had learned in his long engagement with the world. He told me of his meetings with Konrad Adenauer, Che Guevera, Indira Gandhi, and others who were, for me, names from the history books. He spoke to me of plump Latin dictators, lush Thai jungles, and drunken Soviet spies. He explained to me how fateful international decisions are often made, as if by afterthought, in the late afternoon hours of tedious international meetings. (For example, there was one meeting, many years ago, in which Julio, by casting a "proxy" vote for an absent Latin friend, made the one-vote difference that put the headquarters of the United Nations in New York instead of San Francisco; but I promised him I would never repeat *all* the details of that particular story.)

Julio also taught me some of the many lessons he had learned in his long contemplation of the world. He told me of his great love for my country — his boyhood home. He shared with me his love for Spain, and for the lyrical literature of the Spanish Renaissance. He introduced me to the magic of the Swedish writer Axel Munthe's memoir of the Isle of Capri, The Story of San Michele. And he spoke to me — often — of his commitment to fulfilling the promise of individual human freedom by serving the cause of democracy.

I learned that, because of his belief in democracy, Julio had contemplated the world for a number of years while in exile from Uruguay. In the late 1960s, economic conditions deteriorated in Uruguay, and the economic plight of the country led to a rising threat from the leftist Tupamaro guerrillas. The Uruguayan military intervened by overthrowing the democratically elected government. For more than a decade, from 1973 through 1984, the military ruled Uruguay. In protest, Julio went into voluntary exile. He returned to his Uruguayan home only when he knew for certain that democracy was also returning.

In all our years together in Geneva, Julio said very little to me about this. Yet it was in this act of self-exile — this act of self-sacrifice for the sake of his beliefs — that Julio may have taught me most of all.

Sometimes I reflected on this as we sat together at our table. I wondered if I would have such courage in such circumstances. And I wondered, too, if, in my eighties, I would, like Julio, still be sitting at a table somewhere in the world, striving to make a reality of democratic freedom.

At our table, Julio was a reassuring presence. He was our first recourse and our final resource. He remembered all the "many things" that others in the world of trade had long since forgotten. He knew what was written between the lines of the WTO treaty. He knew where in the thousands of pages of the treaty the most worrisome unresolved "widgets" of trade law were concealed. Arms crossed, eyelids half-shut, seemingly at ease, and yet ever alert, Julio listened intently to every single word that was said in our deliberations. He would often listen for hours while saying not a word — and then punctuate an afternoon's deliberations with a single, piercing, pungent observation.

Julio did not always take an early position on the issues we debated. But when he did take a position, he did so with determination. We would know that, definitely, he had made up his mind when he would recite one of his favorite quotes, from General Ulysses S. Grant's bloody Wilderness campaign in the American Civil War: "I will fight it out on this line if it takes all summer."[35] Sometimes it did.

Both the sheer capacity and the steely tenacity of "The Silver Fox" became evident to me once and for all one day over lunch in the WTO cafeteria. I happened to mention to Julio that I had just finished reading W. Somerset Maugham's philosophical testament, The Summing Up, which was originally published in 1938. Julio replied, "I read that book when it first came out." Then, after pausing for a moment, he proceeded to recite, from memory, the book's very last line, which is a quote from the Spanish Renaissance poet and theologian, Fray Luis de Léon: "The beauty of life is nothing but this, that each should act in conformity with his nature and his business."[36]

Julio personifies this maxim. Further, his is a perfect contemporary manifestation of the indomitable will of the man who wrote it. Fray de Léon was twice denounced before the Spanish Inquisition in the sixteenth century. The second time, he was imprisoned for "heresy."

[35] General Ulysses S. Grant, in a letter to Secretary of War Edwin Stanton, during the "Wilderness" campaign of 1864.
[36] W. Somerset Maugham, The Summing Up (London and New York: Penguin Books, 1963), 203 [1938].

He remained in prison for four years. Tradition has it that he began his lecture at the University of Salamanca on the first day after returning from his imprisonment with the words: "As we were saying yesterday...."[37] I could easily believe that my friend Julio may have said exactly the same words on the first day after he returned from his long exile from Uruguay.

Anyone who spends any time with Julio in Uruguay will soon see how highly respected he is by his countrymen. I have seen this firsthand. Everyone knows him. Everyone respects him. Even the flower vendors on the sunny streets of Montevideo greet him warmly as he passes by.

I was in Montevideo at Julio's invitation. The city leaders were hosting a hemispheric conference largely to honor him, and he had asked me to attend and speak. The conference coincided with Rebecca's birthday, and Julio hosted a lavish birthday dinner in her honor, complete with champagne toasts and plenty of *dulce de leche* cake, a traditional Latin dessert. The next morning, he introduced me at the conference. He did so by saying, "I have worked with Jim Bacchus for a number of years now. He is still a very young man, but I believe he has potential."

This may well be the highest compliment I have ever received. My immediate reaction was merely one of gratitude to my friend and mentor who was beckoning me to the podium. But, schooled as I am by "The Silver Fox," I paused long enough to ask myself, "I wonder what could have been his motivation." Then I looked at Julio. There was a gleam in his eye, and he was smiling wryly, and oh so slyly. Like a fox.

The American

The only higher compliment I have received may have been my appointment as one of the seven founding Members of the Appellate Body. The question perhaps arises: Why me? How did this lawyer from Orlando come to sit with these six wise men? How did I come to be the one who, even now, is still called "the American"?

I was raised in Florida, but I was born in Nashville, Tennessee. Nashville was built on the banks of the Cumberland River. The waters of

---

[37] Review of <u>The Unknown Light: The Poems of Fray Luis de Léon</u> (New York: State University of New York Press, 1979), online at www.barnstone.com/Books/unknownlight.htm.

the Cumberland flow through Middle Tennessee toward the mighty Mississippi, and from there out into all the far waters of the wide world. This may help explain why so many of those who have come from Nashville and from Middle Tennessee to serve our country and our world have, so often, been advocates for trade. Andrew Jackson. Cordell Hull. Albert Gore, Sr. Albert Gore, Jr. Mickey Kantor. All have stood, as I have stood, on the steep banks of the Cumberland. All have watched, as I have watched, the flow of the waters toward the distant seas.

Like my friend Mickey Kantor, I studied at Vanderbilt University in Nashville (although, as I like to remind him, I arrived there as a freshman some years after he was graduated). We both studied history there, at different times, with Professor Charles Delzell, whose father had once run — unsuccessfully — for Congress as a Democrat against Hawley of "Smoot-Hawley" fame. At Vanderbilt, I learned what had happened when the Congress of the United States enacted the "Smoot-Hawley" tariffs and the world turned away from trade during the Great Depression.

I took that lesson back home with me to Florida. Back in Florida, I soon became, at twenty-four, in 1974, the youngest aide to the reform-minded Governor of that state, Reubin Askew. In my increasingly distant youth, I had the great good fortune to serve with Governor Askew, and to help him shape the laws and the ways in which the rapidly-growing trading state of Florida began to venture out commercially for the first time into the wide world.

But it was not until 1979 that I really began to follow the path that would eventually lead me to the Appellate Body. By then, Askew had left the Governor's office in Tallahassee, and he and I had both joined the same up-and-coming Miami law firm. We had been there only a few months when the call came inviting Governor Askew to join President Jimmy Carter's Cabinet in Washington.

I was with Governor Askew at the time in his corner office overlooking the blue waters of Biscayne Bay when the call came. I was sitting directly across the desk from him, and I heard several possibilities discussed. I picked up a pen and wrote one word in big bold print on a yellow legal pad on the desk. Then I picked up the legal pad and turned it, at eye level, so that the Governor could see what I had written. The one word I wrote on the legal pad was "TRADE."

No doubt Governor Askew would have made the decision he did even if I had not been so presumptuous as to try to prompt him. His good friend Bob Strauss had just completed several years of work as chief trade negotiator for the United States in the Tokyo Round, and he had told Askew how much he had enjoyed the job. Ambassador Strauss had recommended Askew to the President as his successor, and the Governor did not really need my word of encouragement on my legal pad.

All the same, I remain glad, after all these years, that I wrote it. And I will remain forever grateful for having had the experience of working with Askew at what the trading world universally calls "USTR." The day I walked into USTR — the Office of the United States Trade Representative — was the day I was introduced to the "General Agreement on Tariffs and Trade." Someone handed me a tattered copy of the GATT and said, "Here. Read this." So I did. And I have not stopped since. I have not stopped reading about trade, studying about trade, and learning about trade in all the years since. I have never ceased since in my efforts to become an "old GATT hand."

From that first day, I rejoiced in my role as an apprentice among all the old GATT hands who worked at USTR. When they saw that I took the time to read the GATT — when they saw that I seemed to be genuinely interested in the substance of trade and trade law — those old GATT hands took the time to teach me about trade, and about what they always described passionately as "the multilateral trading system." As a *new* GATT hand, I soon shared their passion. While at USTR, I reveled in all the endless acronyms of trade. MFN. MFA. TRQ. TPM. And so many more. I relished the arcane argot of trade. "Binding." "Dumping." "Safeguards." And something mysterious called "countervail." But, most of all, I read the law and the lore of the GATT.

In his memoirs, the great historian Edward Gibbon wrote of the breadth and the depth of the youthful studies that led him later to write the many volumes of his timeless classic, The Decline and Fall of the Roman Empire. In one memorable scene, he recalled the fateful day in his boyhood when he first opened the pages of a book on the history of Rome in the library of one of his father's friends. He wrote, "I was immersed in the passage of the Goths over the Danube when the summons of the dinner-bell reluctantly dragged me from my intellectual feast."[38]

---

[38] Edward Gibbon, Memoirs of My Life (London: Penguin Books, 1990), 72 [1796].

That was precisely how I felt when I first opened the pages of the GATT. During what remained of the Carter Administration, I studied the GATT during every spare moment while I served as the "Special Assistant" to the United States Trade Representative in the Executive Office of the President. The reality was not nearly as lofty as the title, but the work seemed special to me. I had a front row seat at the unfolding drama of "globalization." I had a license to learn all I could about the "political economy" of world trade. I was immersed in the passage of the world into a new *world* economy. Then Ronald Reagan became President. And I was "reluctantly dragged" from my "intellectual feast" at USTR when the new President politely asked all of us who were Democrats to go back home.

Ten years later, my neighbors back home in Central Florida elected me to the first of my two terms in the Congress of the United States. I was the first Democrat in the history of the South elected to an open Congressional seat from a district where Republicans outnumbered Democrats. Later, I was re-elected. All the same, when I first became a member of the Democratic Caucus in the House of Representatives in 1991, I was just another freshman. So I was surprised when, soon after I arrived, I received a summons to an audience with the then Chairman of the House Ways and Means Committee, Dan Rostenkowski of Illinois.

Several decades of seniority had given Chairman Rostenkowski a private "hideaway" office on a quiet hallway in a corner of the Capitol rarely frequented by the daily throngs of tourists. The room was dark when I entered. I stood at one end of a long table. He sat at the other end. A low lamp at his shoulder cast the only light in the room. "Rosty" was reading by the lamp's light when I came in. He was bulky, burly, bespectacled — just as he looked in the newspapers. He continued to read for a minute or so, and then he removed his glasses and looked up from his reading.

He asked, "You're from Florida?" "Yes, Mr. Chairman." He continued, "I understand you've *actually read* the GATT?" "Yes, Mr. Chairman." "Well, then," he replied, "you're on the trade whip team. Thanks for stopping by." Then he put on his glasses and resumed his reading.

Evidently, having actually read the GATT, I qualified as what passed for a "trade expert" in the rowdy ranks of the House. But expertise of any kind is worthless in the Congress unless it can help attract and accumulate votes. There are 435 members of the United States House of Representatives. Some have more seniority and, thus, bigger and better offices than others. But, in the end, on the floor, all their votes count the same. A majority of the votes in the House is needed to make a law. Therefore, one of the highest accolades that one member of the House can accord to another as a lawmaker is to say, "He knows how to get 218 votes."

The sole purpose of the bipartisan trade whip team in the House was to "whip" up the needed support to get "218 votes" on the trade issues that came before the House. Emboldened by Rosty's show of confidence, I set out to employ my supposed "expertise" to help get those "218 votes" in a series of legislative struggles over trade. First came the successful vote to secure the "fast-track" negotiating authority that would enable then President George Bush to conclude international trade agreements with America's trading partners. Later came the successful vote for extending "most-favoured-nation" trading status for the People's Republic of China. Then came the endlessly controversial — but ultimately successful — vote to approve the "NAFTA" — the North American Free Trade Agreement with Canada and Mexico. In working on these and other proposals for trade legislation, I learned a lot in the following years about how to get "218 votes."

The very last vote I cast as a Member of the Congress was a vote for the implementing legislation that constituted approval by the United States of the Uruguay Round trade agreements that, among many other achievements, established the World Trade Organization as the global successor to the GATT. I was one of the six original co-sponsors of the legislation in the House. I cast that vote on November 29, 1994 — my wife Rebecca's birthday — and then walked out of the House chambers alone into the night. I have not returned to the floor of the House since.

I had decided — for family reasons —not to seek election to a third term in the House. I am one of those people who has spent a lifetime torn between two loyalties. Like Tolstoy's Anna Karenina, who was torn between her loyalty to her family and her hopes for self-fulfillment through love, I have long been torn between my loyalty to my family and my commitment to a life of public service. How much do I owe my family, and how much do I owe others? (Rebecca, loving me, has reminded me also to ask: how much do I owe myself?) In 1994, I answered this question by making a necessary choice. I chose to leave the Congress.

My decision to leave the Congress was probably made the weekend I came home from Washington and tried to sneak a quick glimpse of Jamey, who was then three years old, before leaving almost immediately to return to work. When I opened the door to her nursery, Jamey was wide awake, and standing in her crib. "Mommy, Mommy," she cried, "Jim Bacchus is here." This made everyone laugh but me. Jim Bacchus was not "Daddy" to his only daughter. I had missed five of Rebecca's birthdays in a row, not to mention my children's birthdays and many other family occasions. As I walked out of the House chambers for the last time following the vote, I hoped that this additional missed birthday would be the last.

The vote on the Uruguay Round legislation had occurred in a "lame duck" Congressional session only a few weeks before my term ended. Back in Florida a few weeks later, I wondered where life would lead me next. I knew that my decision to leave the Congress was the right one for both me and my family, and yet I still wanted very much to serve.

So, when that other watcher of the waters of the Cumberland, USTR Mickey Kantor, called me in Florida a few weeks after I had left office to ask if I would allow my name to be placed in nomination by my country for appointment by the Members of the newly established WTO to the new Appellate Body of the WTO, I did not need to be prompted by boldface print on a legal pad. I said "Yes." Soon after, I was formally nominated for the Appellate Body by the United States of America.

Mickey said some years later that I was nominated in part because of my bipartisan support, and also because of my ability to develop consensus.[39] I had worked side by side on trade issues — and on numerous other issues — with members of both parties on both ends of Capital Hill. I had contributed to quite a few bipartisan legislative victories. By saying that I knew how to develop consensus, Mickey was saying, in so many words, that he thought I knew how to get "218 votes." Knowing Mickey, my guess is that he thought this knack for "consensus" might come in handy in Geneva.

So it was that, only a few weeks after leaving the Congress, I was nominated for the Appellate Body of the World Trade Organization by

---

[39] Jeff Kunerth, "Ex-Florida politician savors role of a lifetime," *Orlando Sentinel* (February 11, 2002), A1.

the President of the United States with the bipartisan support of the leadership of both chambers and also of the committees with jurisdiction over trade issues in both the Senate and the House. The only question that remained was: having been nominated by my country, would I be appointed by the WTO?

Thirty-five people in the world had been nominated for the Appellate Body. Only two were Americans. Only seven would be appointed. Early in 1995, we all made the pilgrimage to Geneva from the far reaches of the planet to participate in the selection process that had been established by the WTO.

The selection committee consisted of the ranking ambassadors on the leading councils of the WTO. In my "interview," the committee members were considerably more probing about my knowledge of trade, and about my knowledge of trade law, than Rosty had been when I first arrived in Congress. Like Rosty, the ambassadors on the selection committee in Geneva seemed surprised — and pleased— that a former member of the United States Congress had *actually read* the GATT — not to mention GATT case law and the WTO "covered agreements."

Moreover, I was equally surprised myself when, as I started to explain some of my background in answer to one of the questions, an ambassador from an Asian country stopped me by saying, "That's all right, Mr. Bacchus. I know all about your background and your voting record. I own a time-share in a condominium in Vero Beach, and I've followed your Congressional career closely."

Vero Beach is in my former Congressional district. The last time my name appeared on a ballot, I received one of the highest percentages of the vote of any Democrat in the modern history of Indian River County — forty-two percent. The Asian ambassador knew of the unpopularity among many in Indian River County of my support for foreign aid, for the United Nations, and for many other international pursuits. He knew, too, about the time when a sweet little old lady who was a follower of Ross Perot had attacked me with her hand-held sign opposing the NAFTA. "Don't you care," she had yelled, "about the future of your children?"

Following my "interview" in Geneva, I went home to Florida, and waited. Then I waited some more. Eventually a call came from Washington. The ranking American in the WTO — Deputy Director General Warren Lavorel — had been away from Geneva when I had been there for my "interview." He was going to be in Washington and up on Capitol Hill the next day. He wanted to meet with me then. Would I fly up to meet with him?

I flew up to Washington the next day. I had known Warren years before when I had been a young "Special Assistant" at USTR. At the time, he had been a senior negotiator in the USTR mission in Geneva. But I had not seen him since. He had been in Geneva all the while I was in the Congress, and now he had gone "across the street" from USTR to work for the new WTO.

Warren and I met in an anteroom of one of the big hearing rooms on the Hill. There were just the two of us. The meeting lasted for less than five minutes. Warren told me how nice it was to see me again after fifteen years. We exchanged a few reminiscences. We swapped a few other pleasantries. Then, rising from his chair, he thanked me for coming. That was it. As I flew home to Florida later that day, I wondered why he had wanted to meet with me.

Years later, I found out. It seems that my interview in Geneva had gone well. I had become a leading candidate for appointment to the Appellate Body. The only remaining question about my candidacy was unrelated to my legal or other qualifications. The only question was my *age*. Appointments to international tribunals ordinarily are accorded to only the most senior of international jurists. The other leading candidates for appointment to this new international tribunal were literally decades older than me. Was I, at age 45, old enough?

Warren had been assured by his fellow Americans that I was old enough. However, he remembered me from my youthful days at USTR. He had not seen me in the intervening years. Thus, the sole purpose of our brief exchange of pleasantries in Washington was, I was later told, so that Warren could confirm that I had *at least some gray hair*. Fortunately, my time in the Congress — and a few close calls with sweet little old ladies waving anti-NAFTA signs — had taken care of that. Warren returned to Geneva satisfied that I had, indeed, grayed sufficiently to serve on the Appellate Body.

Evidently, the Members of the WTO also concluded that I was indeed old enough. For, a few months later, on November 29, 1995 — one year to the day after the Congressional vote for the legislation implementing the Uruguay Round trade agreements, and, once again, on Rebecca's birthday — the WTO announced my appointment as one of the seven founding members of the Appellate Body. My longtime friend Andy Stoler, then at USTR and later the Deputy Director-General of the WTO, called to tell me the news of my appointment. He said, "Tell Rebecca 'Happy Birthday.'"

A few weeks later, Rebecca and I flew to Geneva, where I was "sworn in" on a sunny December morning by the WTO's first Director General, Renato Ruggiero, from Italy. Later that same day, I sat, for the first time, with the other founding Members of the world's brand new, standing tribunal for resolving international trade disputes.

Said. Mitsuo. Toy. Claus. Chris. Julio. All were there with me. While eyeing one another warily, hopefully, we assembled then for the first time in Room F on the third floor of the WTO — the room that has since been named *"Salle Julio Lacarté."* It was then that I saw for the first time the smiling faces of the six wise men who would sit with me around our round table in the years that followed. It was then that I became "the American."

And Six More

Today, the six wise men who sat with me for so long smile down on me from their framed photographs on the wall. Today, six other faces smile back at me around our table. Today, I sit with six more wise men.[40]

Said and Mitsuo chose to retire from the Appellate Body after four years. Chris died a few months later. The three of them were succeeded in 2000 by Georges Abi-Saab, of Egypt; A.V. Ganesan, of India; and Yasuhei Taniguchi, of Japan.

Georges Abi-Saab is one of the foremost scholars of public international law in the world. After forty years of teaching at the graduate institute of international studies at the University of Geneva, he "retired" from his teaching and walked next door to sit at the round table of the Appellate Body of the WTO. Georges has served as a judge *ad hoc* on the International Court of Justice at the Hague. He has served on the Yugoslav Crimes Tribunal of the United Nations. His bookcase in the spacious

---

[40] The Members of the WTO recently appointed the first woman to serve on the Appellate Body. My successor is Professor Merit Janow of Columbia University, a former trade negotiator for the United States, a distinguished scholar of international law, and a respected expert on antitrust and competition law as well as on trade law.

study of his hillside home overlooking Lac Leman in Montreux has one shelf containing copies of the many books he has written, and another shelf — in which he takes more pride — containing copies of the many books that have been written by his students. Georges has a mind that ranges far and wide — from the intellectual intricacies of international law to what he sees as the cultural universalities in the twelve hours of "Tom and Jerry" cartoons that he has taped and preserved through the years. Most important, from my view, Georges was, in his youth in Egypt, a student of Said El-Naggar.

A.V. Ganesan is, simultaneously, one of the last products of the British Raj, and one of the first prophets of the newly emerging India of the twenty-first century. He was trained in the schools established by the British, and he spent most of his life serving in the Indian civil service that was patterned after the British system. He speaks highly of the nineteenth-century Whig historian and politician, Thomas Babington Macaulay, whose time in India led to the establishment of an Indian legal system that was modeled on that of Britain. Yet A.V. has been in the forefront of all those who have strived in recent years to break the confining bonds of the statism and the socialism that the first leaders of an independent India inherited from the last British to leave the Indian subcontinent. He brings the wisdom of that experience with him to our task on the Appellate Body. He brings also a sheer brilliance that is illumined by a photographic memory, and a sheer goodness that is evidenced by a trusting heart.

Yasuhei Taniguchi is taller, by head and shoulders, than most Japanese. He is much taller than most of the Japanese of his generation. He stands higher than six feet, which, makes him the tallest Member of the Appellate Body. Yasuhei jokes that, in Japan, he is considered a "giant." His colleagues on the Appellate Body likewise consider Yasuhei a "giant" when it comes to his particular area of expertise in international law. Where Mitsuo was an expert on competition policy, Yasuhei is an expert on procedure. And it is on questions of procedure — on difficult questions of how we make certain that the rights of the sovereign countries that are Members of the WTO are fairly exercised and fairly respected in WTO dispute settlement proceedings — that we turn most often to Yasuhei around our table. On procedure, especially, Yasuhei stands head-and-shoulders high. We turn less often to Yasuhei on questions relating to automotive mechanics. In his first week in Geneva, our new Japanese judge became the proud purchaser of a used car. In his second week in Geneva, the car died. The car bought by my Japanese friend was made in America.

After sitting with me for six years around our table, Toy, Claus, and Julio all completed their allotted terms on the Appellate Body, and retired at the end of 2001. Having drawn the longer straw in the treaty-mandated "lots" that had established the initial length of our terms, I still had two more years remaining in my term. Georges, A.V., Yasuhei, and I were now joined around our table by the Appellate Body's three newest faces: Luiz Olavo Baptista, of Brazil; John Lockhart, of Australia; and Giorgio Sacerdoti, of Italy.

Luiz Olavo Baptista is a lawyer and a law professor of considerable renown, not only in his native Brazil, but worldwide. He is self-effacing and soft-spoken. He is extraordinarily able. He speaks five modern languages and reads Lucretius in the original Latin. He is also extraordinarily committed to the work of the Appellate Body and the WTO. Luiz turned down an appointment to the Supreme Court of Brazil to be able to serve on the Appellate Body. He has "input" every single word of WTO jurisprudence into his laptop computer, which usually joins us nowadays at our table. Luiz keeps an apartment in Paris, and is an admirer of French literature. He especially admires the work of the prolific Honoré de Balzac. The great Frenchman Balzac re-created the entire world of nineteenth-century France while writing, not with a laptop, but with a quill from a raven's wing.[41] Luiz admires *"La Comedie Humaine"* of Balzac because, he says, Balzac wrote about "real people." Luiz wants to serve "real people" through the WTO.

John Lockhart is, like Toy before him, a "real judge." Blond and rangy, and descended from a long line of Scottish lawyers, he was one of the youngest judges ever appointed to the federal bench in Australia, and served for more than twenty years as a federal judge in Australia before leaving the bench to work for, first, the World Bank, and, later, the Asian Development Bank, on judicial reform and other developmental issues. Like Toy, John brings with him to the Appellate Body a wide judicial experience and a seasoned judicial temperament that serve the evolving WTO dispute settlement system well. But this is only one aspect of Judge Lockhart. Perhaps even greater than his love of the law is his lifelong love of art. John has long been one of the leading advocates of art in Australia, and his enduring appreciation for the vast cultural diversity of the world is reflected in an eclectic art collection that ranges from Australian aboriginal landscapes all the way to medieval Albanian

---

[41] W. Somerset Maugham, "Balzac and *Le Pere Goriot*," <u>Ten Novels and Their Authors</u> (London: Vintage Books, 2001) 109, 118 [1954].

sculptures. John did not seem surprised that I was impressed by his art collection. He did seem a bit surprised, though, at how impressed I was to learn that, for many years, he owned an apple orchard in the Blue Mountains just outside of Sydney.

Giorgio Sacerdoti teaches international law at the University of Milan. He has spent long years working on issues of international economic development, and especially on issues of international bribery and corruption. He has broad experience with the OECD and other international organizations. He is a legendary lecturer on the sweeping vistas of international law. Like Claus, Giorgio is very much a European. Moreover, Giorgio is every American's ideal of the elegant, articulate, and ever-gracious Italian. He is tall and distinguished, and wears a full and flowing beard. He speaks in round tones and in grandiloquent terms. He has a wry and ready sense of humor; in his office is a "hanging judge" — a puppet of a judge in a long black robe that is "hanging" by his neck on the wall. Taking us beyond the bounds of our usual *renversé*, Giorgio has installed a cappuccino machine in the corner of our chambers. He is — very patiently — teaching the rest of us how to use it.

Thus, the evolution of the Appellate Body continues. The faces have changed. The cases before us are changing, and becoming ever more controversial, and ever more complex. The many challenges confronting the WTO are changing every day. But some things about the Appellate Body have not changed, and I hope they never will.

I think it was Julio who first pointed out the similarities between our round table and the oval table that one of Julio's heroes, and one of mine, Thomas Jefferson, kept in his home at Monticello. A round table does not permit any precedence in seating.[42] Jefferson said that his table was round so that all who sat around his table would do so as equals. So it was at Jefferson's round table at Monticello, and so it is at the round table of the Appellate Body.

We seven are equals around our table. Whoever we may be, wherever we may be from, whatever may be our personal predilections and inclinations, we all sit around our table as equals. The only distinctions that matter at the table of the Appellate Body are the distinctions that flow from the quality and the persuasiveness of the thoughts that are

---

[42] Interview with Professor Merrill Peterson, Professor of History, University of Virginia, Chairman of the Federal Thomas Jefferson Commemorative Commission, online/ at/pbs.org/jefferson/archives/interviews/peterson,htm.

expressed there. In particular, we seven are equal in our commitment to carry on. The six "new members," along with "the American" who lingers on, all share equally in the desire to carry on the work that was begun by the six wise men who are no longer at our table. We all share equally in the desire to build on the firm foundation they helped establish for our still new institution.

In this, we are not only equals. We are also united. We are as one. And it is as one that we trust that the world will continue to see us when the world looks at the Appellate Body. We each have something to offer. We each have our own fund of experience. We each have our own point of view. We each have our own ways of reaching a judgment. Yet the Members of the WTO seem to have long since realized that, no matter which one of us happens to sit on an appeal, and no matter what issues may be raised in that appeal, the eventual outcome of the appeal is very likely to be the same. For, in our judgments, we strive always to be and act as one. We seek always to achieve the WTO's ideal of "consensus."

Outside the WTO, the world keeps turning in all its tumult and turmoil. Elsewhere in the WTO, the hectic hum of the continuing trade negotiations drones on, still far from consensus. Meanwhile, here in our chambers, here in our quiet room, here around our round table, the ideal of what the WTO is supposed to be emerges through the consensus that is formed case by case from the crucible of WTO dispute settlement.

As equals, and as one, those who labor at the round table of the Appellate Body seek always to serve *all* of the Members of the WTO. We are, each of us, proud citizens of our own countries. But when we walk into our chambers in the morning, when we sit down together at our table, and when we consider the issues that are raised on appeal before the Appellate Body, we leave our national citizenships behind us at the door. We are as "independent" and as "impartial" as the Members of the WTO have instructed us to be.

Like Socrates, who loved Athens too much to leave it, who preferred an unjust death in Athens to an unhappy life in exile, we each love our native lands. Julio, Said, and some of the others who have sat with me around our table have sacrificed and suffered for the hard-won freedom of their countries. I admire them for their courage. I have been required — thus far — to do much less for my own country. None of us on the Appellate Body need lessons from anyone in patriotism. It is *because* we love our countries, it is *because* we want the best for our countrymen, it is *because* we believe that each of our countries will best be served by the better world for which we are all working at the WTO, that, like Socrates, we say, in our work together, "I am not an Athenian, nor a Greek, but a citizen of the world."[43]

The Members of the WTO expect us to be "citizens of the world" in our service on the Appellate Body. This is why the WTO rules of conduct require that we be "independent and impartial."[44] We do not take "instructions" from our own countries — or from any country. We ignore political pressures of all kinds. We are sworn to uphold only the legal rules that are expressed in the "covered agreements" and the legal rulings that are made from time to time by the Members of the WTO as envisioned by the WTO Treaty.

The World Bank has said, "A judiciary independent from both government intervention and influence by the parties in a dispute provides the single greatest institutional support for the rule of law."[45] If this is so for national judges and national tribunals — and I am persuaded that it is — then this is all the more true for international judges and international tribunals entrusted with significant international responsibilities. And it is true also for a "quasi-judicial" tribunal such as the Appellate Body of the WTO. To support and strengthen the international rule of law, those who serve on the Appellate Body must remain independent and impartial in the fulfillment of our responsibilities to the Members of the WTO.

And we must also continue to pursue those responsibilities with the energy and with the enthusiasm with which, from the beginning, we have embraced them. It is remarkable to me that the wise men with whom I have served on the Appellate Body are able to work as hard as they do. If I have, indeed, proven "old enough" to serve alongside them, then it is equally true that they have all proven young enough to get the job done. In their tireless dedication to the task at hand, they have often exhausted this younger man.

That wonderful American writer from Mississippi, Eudora Welty, observed, when in her seventies, that, "Emotions do not grow old."[46] The emotions that made her writing so moving did not grow old for her. Nor

---

[43] Plutarch, "Of Banishment."
[44] WTO Rules of Conduct, Articles II and III(2).
[45] World Bank, World Development Report 2002, at 129.
[46] Eudora Welty, One Writer's Beginnings (New York: Warner Books, 1983), 57.

have the emotions that have motivated the lives of the wise men with whom I have served on the Appellate Body ever grown old for them. In their passion for trade and for freedom, they are not old, but young.

When I was young, I worked with Governor Askew and with many others in a shared effort to make a bright future for my home state of Florida. Now that I am older, I have noticed that, in the years since, many of those with whom I once worked, many of those with whom I once shared a lofty dream for our state, have abandoned the bright hopes of our youth. Pressed by circumstance, they have rationalized, temporized, and compromised. They have settled for much less than, together, we once sought. They have lowered their sights. And so has Florida. This saddens me more than I can say.

I am told that this is only to be expected in life. I am told that, though the dreams of youth may die hard, they always die. The young always set out to change circumstance and thus "change the world." Then life intervenes. Marriages, mortgages, and other such responsibilities come along to change us all. Youthful idealism gives way to a harsh realism. Middle age soon arrives. The emotions of our youth grow old.

In her classic novel Middlemarch, Mary Ann Evans — the Victorian novelist we know best as "George Eliot" — told the familiar tale of how youth tends to lower its sights with the accumulation of age. As she saw it, "[I]n the multitude of middle-aged men who go about their vocations in a daily course determined for them much in the same way as the tie of their cravats, there is always a good number who once meant to shape their own deeds and alter the world a little. The story of their coming to be shapen after the average and fit to be packed by the gross is hardly ever told even in their consciousness...."[47]

Among this multitude, I refuse to lower my sights. I still tie my cravat in my own way, and, as my colleagues will tell you, being an American, I usually loosen my tie when I sit down at our table. I still cling, too, to the bright hopes and the lofty dreams of my youth. And, if my colleagues on the Appellate Body, in all their wisdom, have taught me only one lesson in all our years together, it is the lesson they have taught me through their example. Their emotions have never grown old. Their idealism has never died. They have remained forever young. And,

---

[47] George Eliot, Middlemarch: A Study of Provincial Life (New York: Signet, 1964), 143 [1872].

thanks to their example, I know that I need not — I must not — ever lower my sights. Thanks to them, I know that I can always tie my cravat in my own way. Thanks to them, I am, at last, truly old enough to know that the hopes and the dreams of my youth need never die.

Claus-Dieter Ehlermann, my European friend, may have been right when he mused to Rebecca that the Members of the WTO may have had a certain intent when they chose those of us who first sat together at the round table of the Appellate Body. It may very well have been their intent to choose jurists of like kind and like mind. It occurs to me that, for all our varied backgrounds, for all our varied experiences, and for all our varied enthusiasms, all of those who have labored together at our table are, to borrow a familiar phrase from "the covered agreements," certainly "like products."

We are alike in our desire to serve the cause of freedom. We are alike in our shared assumption that trade serves the cause of freedom. We are alike in many of the assumptions we share about the world, alike in the future we seek for the world, and alike in the importance we see for the WTO in shaping that future. We are alike, too, in the critical role we foresee for the Appellate Body in helping the Members of the WTO shape that future.

Claus may be right. This may have been by intent. It may also have been sheer serendipity. It may have been only an act of fortuitous good fortune that brought us all together at our round table to work for trade and freedom. Whatever the reason, I am forever grateful. Whatever it was that caused life to smile at me through the smiles on their faces, I am proud to have served with all these wise men.

Crossing the Alps

Soon my allotted eight years on the Appellate Body will end. Soon I will leave our table, and someone else will sit in my chair. Soon my smiling face will join the six others on our wall. This is as it should be. "Our" table is not really ours. "My" chair is not really mine. They both belong to the world. And the world — in the guise of the WTO — will soon ask someone else to sit in "my" chair at "our" table when I, too, become a *former* member of the Appellate Body.

For now, though, I remain. Present at the creation, I am present still.

I continue to work with the six who now sit with me at our table. I continue to serve beneath the reassuring smiles of the six others who have left me here, lingering on. Yet, from time to time, in the midst of the morning, or in the length of a long afternoon, I turn away from the table, and I glance, for a moment, at the wall behind me. On this wall are three more framed photographs. They are photographs of the three different groups of seven men who have served — thus far — on the Appellate Body.

The only face in each of the three photographs is mine.

In these three photographs is the evidence, if evidence is needed, that, if my years in the Congress aged me, my years on the Appellate Body have aged me even more. These days, more and more, I look like an "old GATT hand." My hair grows ever grayer, ever whiter, with every passing day. It was still mostly dark when I first came to Geneva. It is much lighter now. The American in the most recent of the three photographs is considerably grayer than the American in the first.

In that first photograph, on the left, near the corner of the room, a younger version of me stands in the front, in the middle of the seven, smiling. Julio, Said, and Toy are to my right. Chris, Mitsuo, and Claus are to my left. Behind us in the photograph is an enormous tapestry of Hannibal crossing the Alps.

This framed tapestry hangs on the wall in the high hall upstairs on the top floor of the WTO. It was given to the GATT as a gift by Tunisia — the site of ancient Carthage — on the occasion of Tunisia's "accession" to membership in the GATT in 1990. At Julio's suggestion, the seven of us who were first chosen to serve on the Appellate Body selected that backdrop intentionally for our first photograph together on the day we were all "sworn in." At the time, Julio — our leader even then — likened our task in establishing our new international trade tribunal to Hannibal's feat long ago in crossing the Alps.

The tapestry depicts a scene somewhere south and east of Geneva, high in an Alpine pass. The time is 218 B.C., during the Second Punic War between the rival Mediterranean empires of Carthage and Rome. Hannibal, the great Carthaginian general, is crossing the Alps with his army. He hopes to launch a "surprise attack" on Rome by invading the green and fertile plains of Italy from the north.

The season is winter. Some of Hannibal's troops lie fallen and frozen in the snow. Others struggle onward. One of the war elephants with the troops trumpets a protest, his tusks raised high in the icy air. A line of shivering soldiers trails off into the distance along a precarious pass.

Hannibal made it through that pass. He crossed the Alps. He invaded Italy. He attacked the very heart of the Roman Empire. He waged war in Italy for many years. He fought battle after battle against the Romans in the Italian countryside. He never lost a one.

Yet, though Hannibal never lost a battle in Italy, in the end, Carthage lost the war against Rome. Hannibal ended his life in exile and in suicide, and the Romans eventually destroyed Carthage in the climax of yet another war. They burned the city. They slaughtered soldiers and civilians alike. They sold the survivors into slavery. As legend has it, they sowed the ground of the surrounding countryside in salt so that nothing could ever grow there again. Carthage was "wiped from the face of the earth...."[48]

I am ever mindful of the fate of Carthage when I look at the photograph of the seven of us standing and smiling in front of that tapestry. Carthage was originally a colony of the Phoenicians, the great early traders of the ancient world. Carthage, at its height, controlled much of the trade of the Mediterranean. Above all, the people of Carthage were traders. Now they are only a memory. Carthage has ceased to exist. And I wonder when I gaze at the photograph: does the same fate await the traders — and the trade judges — of today?

According to one distinguished commentator, the Appellate Body has, in our work thus far, "brought a sense of rigor and deep analysis that ... may go beyond the record of any international law tribunal known in history."[49] This is high praise indeed. Not everyone would agree, and not everyone who agrees would be so kind or go quite so far. I, for one, would readily acknowledge that the results of our work at our table have sometimes fallen somewhere short of perfection.

---

[48] John Boardman, Jasper Griffin, Oswyn Murray, eds., The Oxford History of the Classical World (New York: Oxford University Press, 1986), 418. On the Punic wars, *see generally* pages 404-419.
[49] John H. Jackson, "Perceptions about the WTO trade institutions", 1 World Trade Review 101, 110 (2002).

Imperfect though we are, we have always done our very best to find the right answers and make the right decisions. And I would maintain that all of us who have been privileged thus far to serve on the Appellate Body have every reason to smile. In our time together, we have established what promises to be an enduring institution. In our work together, we have created a foundation for the future. We have crossed the Alps. We see, in the distance, the green and fertile fields. My question now is the one that Hannibal must also have asked long ago.

What happens next?

Chapter Three

Trade Secrets

Trade Secrets

What, specifically, do we say every day around our round table in Geneva? Alas, our rules of "confidentiality" do not permit me to reveal the substance of what we say in our deliberations. But, after all my years of judging appeals in Geneva, I have concluded that what we say is often not nearly as significant as what we do *not* say.

Any historian will tell you that the most treasured beliefs of a society often are those that are *not* discussed. For such beliefs usually are not discussed because they need not be discussed; they are assumed and shared. As the British historian Norman Hampson wrote of the eighteenth century era we call the Enlightenment, "What was most significant was often what was most taken for granted .... "[1]

The British political theorist Larry Siedentop has explained further, "Few societies are good at identifying the things they take for granted. These are the things that structure their vision of the world, providing them with categories which shape their experience of fact and underpin their judgments of what is valuable. The result is that, when trying to understand ourselves, we often miss the obvious."[2]

The WTO has been indicted in spray paint on the walls of the world. The WTO has been denounced by everyone from the most deceitful of latter-day anarchists and communists to the most hopeful of well-meaning environmentalists and labor unionists. The supposed sins of the WTO —according to its critics —are legion. The absurdity of some of the many charges that have been leveled against the WTO is such that recently, while walking to work in Geneva, I saw a hand-lettered sign held by an anti-WTO protester which read, in French: *"Dieu est mort, et l'OMC l'a remplacé."*

Loosely translated, this means: "God is dead, and the WTO has replaced Him."

To this, I plead: "Not Guilty." The WTO has not replaced God.

---

[1] Norman Hampson, The Enlightenment (New York: Penguin Books, 1968), 146.
[2] Larry Siedentop, Democracy in Europe (London: Penguin Books, 2000), 81.

Nor have we killed any endangered sea turtles. As one of the most insightful observers and critics of the WTO, Professor Jagdish Bhagwati, pointed out in a recent issue of *Foreign Affairs*, "In 1999 . . . kids protesting the World Trade Organization's Seattle meeting dressed as turtles to denounce the organization – unaware that the WTO's judicial body has recently ruled in the turtles' favor."[3] He might have noted also that, since then, we have done so again.[4]

I do not contend that the judgments of the Appellate Body are free from human error. They are not. Like all human endeavors, and like all human institutions, ours is fallible. Ours is capable of error. Moreover, our judgments, whether in error or not, must, of course, be subject to criticism. Mutual criticism is not only useful in the Appellate Body; it is useful in all that all of us try to do together in the world. I contend only that those who criticize the judgments in WTO dispute settlement should be expected, first, to read them.

It is not my purpose here to parse our judgments. My purpose is not to explain how or why we ruled as we did in any particular appeals in the WTO, or to add to what we said in so ruling by explaining what we meant by saying it. Many, perhaps, may wonder: What were the mutual ruminations, and what are the enduring implications, of the "gasoline" case or the "bananas" case or the "asbestos" case or the "shrimp" case or the "steel" case, or so many other cases from the early years of WTO dispute settlement? Some of these questions I will never be free to answer because of the constraints of the WTO rules of conduct. Others I may try to answer in other ways and on other days. I will not, however, endeavor to answer them here and now.

Nor is it my purpose here to address and to assess the lengthening list of specific issues on the global trade negotiating agenda of the WTO. How should we proceed to a successful conclusion in the latest "round" of WTO trade negotiations? How should we create more market access for the goods and services of developed and developing countries alike through further trade liberalization? How should we deal with the environment, with labor, with intellectual property, with investment, with

---

[3] Jagdish Bhagwati, "Coping with Antiglobalization: A Trilogy of Discontents," Foreign Affairs (January/February, 2002), 2, 3.
[4] *See* the Article 21.5 proceeding in the so-called "shrimp-turtle" case, United States —Import Prohibition of Certain Shrimp and Shrimp Products —Recourse to Article 21.5 of the DSU by Malaysia – AB – 2001 – 4 - Report of the Appellate Body.

antitrust, and with the whole array of other trade-related issues that invite increasing multilateral attention? How should we "reform" the WTO dispute settlement system and thereby improve it? These, too, may be my topics in other, future essays. I will not, however, address them in any detail here and now.

My purpose here and now is more modest. It is more basic. It is more fundamental to an understanding of why there is WTO dispute settlement, why there are WTO trade negotiations, and, indeed, why there is such an international undertaking as the WTO. My purpose here and now is to state the obvious about the WTO — or, rather, to state what *should* be obvious about the WTO, but clearly *is not*.

For the unfortunate fact is that both the critics and the criticisms of the WTO have been aided and abetted by the undeniable fact that many of the advocates of the WTO have, in Professor Siedentop's phrase, "missed the obvious." We have not stated the beliefs we assume and share. We have not explained what we take for granted. We have not explained the view of the world that is between the lines of the WTO treaty.

Those of us who support the WTO have "missed the obvious" because, all too often, we have forgotten that what may be obvious to us about what we are doing and why we are doing it, may not be at all obvious to others. All too often, we have spoken only in the esoteric Sanskrit of "GATT-speak," and thus we have allowed others to fill in the blanks between the lines of the WTO treaty. For this reason, we have, in part, only ourselves to blame for the fact that so many in so much of the world have misunderstood and misportrayed the WTO.

That Tory exemplar of the British Enlightenment, Samuel Johnson, once took enough time away from his table talk in the London taverns to suggest the need for a philosophy of trade. "There is nothing," he said, "which requires more to be illustrated by philosophy than trade does."[5] I believe we have a philosophy of trade that fully justifies the WTO, and that fully justifies all we hope to achieve through the WTO. Unfortunately, we have neither explained nor defended this philosophy of trade. Instead, we have taken it for granted. And we can no longer afford to do so.

---

[5] Johnson is quoted in Robert L. Heilbroner, <u>The Worldly Philosophers: The Lives, Times and Ideas of the Great Economic Thinkers,</u> 4th Edition (New York: Simon and Schuster, 1972).

For this reason, my purpose, here and now, is to explain and to defend the philosophy of trade that is the intellectual foundation of the World Trade Organization.

It has been said that ours is a world in which philosophy has become "breathtakingly irrelevant."[6] This is not so. In particular, this is anything but so in the world of trade and in the work of the Appellate Body. It is impossible to understand the decisions made by the seven of us around our table in Geneva without understanding the philosophical assumptions we share. The work of the Appellate Body is mental work. An account of our work is necessarily an account of the working of the mind. Our story is a story of seven minds trying to work together as one. And crucial to this story are the mental —the philosophical —assumptions that are critical to the making of the consensus we always seek. Far more important than anything the seven of us on the Appellate Body may say to one another around our table at the WTO are the *assumptions* we bring with us to our table.

Many of the authors of the thoughts that become our assumptions in life travel through the centuries incognito. We do not always recognize them in their disguise. We do not always acknowledge them amid all that we assume in our lives. Yet they are there nonetheless. And they are always there at the table of the Appellate Body. The seven of us on the Appellate Body each proceed from assumptions that are based on the thoughts of many others who have preceded us —philosophers, economists, thinkers of all kinds. In these assumptions, these past thinkers share our table with us.

These assumptions have shaped the multilateral trading system that we serve, and they influence also the way we see the trading system as we strive to serve it. Unlike our proceedings, these assumptions are not "confidential." These assumptions are not secrets. Yet many of those who support the WTO treat them as if they were. For this reason, these assumptions might well be called our *"trade secrets."* And, in my view, it is long past time for those of us who think we understand why the world needs the WTO to be much more forthcoming in sharing these "trade secrets."

---

[6] Elizabeth Young-Bruehl, cited in Danny Postel, "The Life and Mind," Chronicle of Higher Education (June 7, 2002).

What are these "trade secrets"? They are what the logicians might call the "suppressed premises." They are what the anthropologists might call the "structures." They are what the Kantian philosophers might call the "categories." However, a better illustration of what these "trade secrets" are may be provided by describing what my daughter Jamey calls our "Christmas glasses."

Some years ago, a friend gave me, as a novelty gift for Christmas, a pair of cardboard "3-D" glasses. Jamey calls these our "Christmas glasses." When seen without the glasses, the lights of our family's Christmas tree, though beautiful, are only lights. But when seen through the "3-D" lenses of our "Christmas glasses," the lights of our Christmas tree spell out brightly, in row after lighted row, the word "NOEL." How we see our Christmas tree is changed by the lenses of our "Christmas glasses."

Through what glasses, through what philosophical lenses, do I see when viewing my work on the Appellate Body? What do I not say in any one case that applies nevertheless to my personal contribution in every case? What do I take for granted? What are my "WTO glasses?"

Before attempting to answer this question, I hasten to say that I am not so presumptuous as to presume to speak for my colleagues on the Appellate Body. On this question, I speak only for myself. Yet, perhaps I can be so presumptuous as to suggest that, although the seven of us come from seven very different places in the world, we largely share the same world view. For the most part, we see the world through lenses that are very much alike. If we did not, then the Members of the WTO would perhaps not have appointed us, and the Appellate Body would perhaps not have gone all this time without a single dissent to our consensus judgments.

Certainly, too, at the outset, I must also say that nothing I see through the lenses that I use as a Member of the Appellate Body is in any way original. Nothing at all. I think it safe to say that I have never had an original thought in my life. Like "the majority of men," I am "rich in borrowed resources."[7] (This phrase is borrowed from Montaigne.) Few of us ever have a thought that is only ours, a thought that is genuinely new. But this is precisely the point. The premises, the presuppositions —

---

[7] Michel de Montaigne, "On the Art of Conversation," Essays (London, Penguin Books, 1958), 285, 302 [1580].

the things we take for granted in life — all these are widely shared as received truths. The received truths of trade are no different.

Further, I should acknowledge as well that, as I see it, a philosophy of trade is, necessarily, a reflection of a particular philosophy of life. That relentless seeker of the truth, John Stuart Mill, told us, "If the cultivation of the understanding consists in one thing more than another, it is surely in learning the grounds of one's own opinions."[8] He once said, in his essay on his utilitarian mentor, Jeremy Bentham, that: "The first question in regard to any man of speculation is, what is his theory of human life?"[9]

I can hardly be described as a man of "speculation." Even so, I think this is also a fair first question to ask of me. For, if I presume to sit in judgment on matters affecting the lives of literally billions of people around the world, then I ought to be expected, at a minimum, to have a coherent theory of human life when viewing my responsibilities to the WTO. These reflections of a "faceless foreign judge" are "reflections" in two different senses of that word. They are reflections by me about the connection I see between trade and freedom. They are also reflections of me — of how I have tried to make that connection in fulfilling my responsibilities on the Appellate Body of the WTO.

All this said, what then are the grounds of my opinions? What is my theory and my philosophy? What do I *see* when I look through my "WTO glasses"?

Looking Through "WTO Glasses"

No one knows how many species of life there are on our planet. No one has made an exact count from the available science. As the noted entomologist and naturalist Edward O. Wilson has explained, "Somewhere between 1.5 million and 1.8 million have been discovered and given a formal scientific name .... Estimates of the true number of living species range, according to the method used, from 3.6 million to 100 million or more. The median of the estimates is a little over 10 million...."[10]

---

[8] John Stuart Mill, On Liberty (London: Penguin Books, 1985), 97 [1859].
[9] John Stuart Mill, "Bentham," in John Stuart Mill and Jeremy Bentham, Utilitarianism and Other Essays (New York: Penguin Books, 1987), 151.
[10] Edward O. Wilson, The Future of Life (New York: Alfred A. Knopf, 2002), 14.

Moreover, no one knows whether there may be other species of life elsewhere. When I served on the space committee in the Congress of the United States, I supported the ongoing work of the Hubble Space Telescope, which gazes, from an orbit high above the earth, into the depths of outer space. With the Hubble telescope, we have been able to look back in time nearly fourteen billion years to the "Big Bang" that scientists surmise was the beginning of our universe.[11] With this telescope, we have been able to confirm that there are other planets around other stars, and that ours is but a minor planet circling one of about one hundred billion stars in one among about one hundred billion galaxies that *each* consist of about one hundred billion stars.[12] Thus far, however, we have been unable to determine, by looking through the lenses of the Hubble telescope, if we are all alone in the universe.

Scientists believe the universe is expanding as the galaxies rush away from each other into the depths of a dark emptiness. They think it has been expanding for billions of years. They think they know *how* this is happening. They think they know, in a purely scientific sense, *what* caused this to happen. Yet, in a broader sense, they have no notion of *why*. They do not know what came before the birth of the universe. They do not know its fate. And, for all the new knowledge they are gleaning from the gaze of the Hubble telescope and from other scientific efforts to explore the receding reaches of beckoning space, our best scientific minds readily admit that they have no real knowledge of why there is something rather than nothing, and they have absolutely no idea why we are here, and why we alone seem to be able to wonder why.[13]

Thus, when I gaze through the lenses of my "WTO glasses," when I see myself and all the others like me in the face of the infinite, I see, first of all, the solitude of human life amid the incomprehensible vastness of the universe. And, when I gaze at our small world in our small corner of the universe, and at all that happens in our world, I see, first of all, and above all, the solitude of our species in our world. I see a singular, solitary species —the human species —that is unique in all the world, and may, for all we know, be unique in all the universe.

---

[11] Dennis Overbye, "For Astronomers, Big Bang Confirmation," *New York Times* (February 12, 2003).
[12] S. Jonathan Singer, The Splendid Feast of Reason (Berkeley: University of California Press, 2001), 33.
[13] *See* Timothy Ferris, The Whole Shebang: A State of the Universe(s) Report (New York: Simon & Schuster, 1997); for some of the most recent scientific speculations, *see* Richard Monastersky, "Recycling the Universe: New theory posits that time has no beginning or end," The Chronicle of Higher Education (June 7, 2002), A19.

We are unique because we have what John Locke described as the "power of abstracting."[14] We are not mere beasts. We know we are here. We can imagine. We can remember. We can hope. We can dream. We can create. We can think. We can conceive of transcendence. There is something special between the strands of human DNA. Whether genetically or otherwise, we have been blessed with something in our software as a species that enables us to reason. And, because we are capable of reasoning, we are also capable of choosing. As I see it, it is our capacity for choice that makes us human, and it is by making the right choices that we become most fully human.

Thus, I share the view of John Stuart Mill, as described by Isaiah Berlin. For me, like Mill, "man differs from animals primarily neither as the possessor of reason, nor as an inventor of tools and methods, but as a being capable of choice, one who is most himself in choosing and not being chosen for; the rider and not the horse; the seeker of ends, and not merely of means, ends that he pursues, each in his own fashion; with the corollary that the more various these fashions, the richer the lives of men become; the larger the field of interplay between individuals, the greater the opportunities of the new and the unexpected; the more numerous the possibilities for altering his own character in some fresh or unexplored direction, the more paths open before each individual, and the wider will be his freedom of action and thought."[15] I share with Mill —and with many others —the "passionate belief that men are made human by their capacity for choice —choice of evil and good equally."[16]

The better our telescopes become, the more stars we see. Some, when confronted with the vastness of the universe and the multitude of the stars, see our species as small and insignificant. They are ever mindful that billions of years passed before there was ever a human witness, and that billions of stars burn and die without ever lighting a human face. They see our capacity for choice leading to human progress as only an "illusion."[17] They see humans in "total solitude" and "fundamental isolation,"[18] as "only currents in the drift of genes"[19] who "can no more

---

[14] John Locke, Essay Concerning Human Understanding, Book 2, Chapter 11, paragraph 10 [1689].

[15] Isaiah Berlin, "John Stuart Mill and the Ends of Life," Four Essays on Liberty (New York: Oxford University Press, 1969), 173, 178.

[16] Id. at 192.

[17] John Gray, Straw Dogs: Thoughts on Humans and Other Animals (London: Granta, 2002), 195.

[18] Id. at 30.

[19] Id. at 6.

be masters of their destiny than any other animal."[20] They suspect that "human life has no more meaning than the life of slime mold."[21] They depict the fact of human life as the result only of a dice-roll by meaningless chance, and the fate of human existence as unworthy of wonder.

I see our species differently. I see the seeming solitude of humanity as evidence of humanity's worth. I see the uniqueness of our species on this planet as making us worthy of preservation. For, when I contemplate the universe, when I gaze at the stars, when I consider that we humans are made of the same elemental stuff as the stars, I do not see us as only more mindless matter.[22] Instead, I react in the same way as the late Cambridge philosopher, Frank Ramsey, who observed, "The stars may be large, but they cannot think and love...."[23]

We humans can think and love, in my view, because we have a spark of divinity. We have a divine element that God gave us long after He caused, in some way unknown to us, the "Big Bang" of Creation. We can think and love because we have that special spark called reason that enables us to choose. We may be, as Voltaire mused, only "insects that devour each other on a little atom of mud...."[24] Or we may be divinity's noblest creation. What makes us unique in all we know of Creation is that we are able to wonder which we are. We may live in a lesser world; yet, in all our wondering, we long for the infinite. That reasoning machine —the human brain —consists of one hundred billion neurons linked by one hundred trillion connections. And, however mundane, however mechanical all those connections may seem to be, every one of them, in some way, serves to lift us toward the infinite.

There may, perhaps, be more to what makes our species unique than merely our ability to reason. The scientists, the philosophers, the theologians, all have long debated whether there may be something else that makes us special, some spark of mutual human feeling, some instinct of mutual human sympathy, that may also be embedded in the DNA of

---

[20] Id. at 4.
[21] Id. at 33.
[22] "Virtually all of the atoms in our bodies that are heavier than hydrogen were fashioned in stars that expired before the Sun and the Earth came into being." Nigel Caldor, Einstein's Universe (London: Penguin Books, 1990), 37 [1979].
[23] F. P. Ramsey, The Foundations of Mathematics (London: Routledge and Kegan Paul, 1931), 291, quoted in Simon Blackburn, Being Good (New York: Oxford University Press, 2001), 79.
[24] Voltaire is quoted in Norman Hampson, The Enlightenment, at 76. He said this in 1738.

our human genetic code. In the very first paragraph of the very first chapter of The Theory of Moral Sentiments —the book he wrote *first* that all too many traders and others usually forget to read —Adam Smith asserted his belief in human sympathy as a part of human nature. "How selfish soever man may be supposed," said Smith, "there are evidently some principles in his nature, which interest him in the fortune of others, and render their happiness necessary to him, though he derives nothing from it, except the pleasure of seeing it."[25] Smith saw "pity or compassion" as an example of this basic human feeling of sympathy.[26] He maintained that "[t]he greatest ruffian, the most hardened violator of the laws of society, is not altogether without it."[27]

In the dark shadow of the Holocaust, in the grim aftermath of all the many inhumanities of man to man that Smith did not live to see, it is difficult for me to say with any certainty that he was right. I prefer to believe, though, that he *was* right. Certainly there is more at the wellsprings of human motivation than merely the reasoned calculations of rational self-interest. And certainly there are limits, too, to the benefits to be derived from a purely rational calculation. Recall, for example, the dilemma faced by the hypothetical "rational ass" of the fourteenth-century French philosopher Jean Buridan. The donkey in his imagined example stood equally distant from two equally appealing stacks of hay. Motivated only by rational calculation, the donkey had no reason for choosing one haystack over the other. So it starved.[28] (We Florida Democrats are, understandably, tolerant of tales about undecided donkeys.)

Man cannot live by reason alone. Reason alone cannot "bind up the brokenhearted."[29]. The head must always hear the heart. And, further, like that thoughtful French scientist, Blaise Pascal, I, too, suspect that "the heart has its reasons that reason does not know."[30] I suspect, too, that Pascal —who first conceived the notion of a computer, of a calculating machine, in the seventeenth century —may have been right in thinking that it is only through the calculations of the heart that reason can know the "first principles" of human life.[31]

---

[25] Adam Smith, The Theory of Moral Sentiments (Amherst, New York: Prometheus Books, 2000), 3 [1759].
[26] Id.
[27] Id.
[28] Alan Ryan, "The Way to Reason," The New York Review of Books (December 4, 2003), 43, 44.
[29] Isaiah 61:1.
[30] Blaise Pascal, *Pensées*, section iv, 277 [1670].
[31] Id. at 282.

Thus, to be sure, we need more than our limited capacity to reason alone can offer us if we hope to make our way forward in the world. Yet, even so, I see the reasons of the heart as best served in the day-to-day work of the world by respecting, using, and relying on our unique ability to engage in rational thought, and to act accordingly. Heartfelt passions can, undoubtedly, help give meaning and purpose to human life in ways that can transcend and transform rational calculations. Imagination, intuition, creativity, sentiment —these and other human passions have their place. But, in shaping and serving human society, I would temper human passions always with human reason. Whatever the undeniable limits of reason, I see the failures of reason as largely resulting from our failures in *using* reason. And, further, whatever its substance, and whatever its sway as a part of human nature, I see mutual human sympathy as succeeding best and succeeding most when informed and guided by reason.

Human reason is one example of how nature unfolds in a singular fashion. The American scholar Ralph Waldo Emerson once said, "Nature never rhymes her children..."[32] Every snowflake is the same, and yet every snowflake is also unique in the pattern it assumes as a passing part of Creation.[33] So it is with every aspect of Creation. And so it is with the varied verse of humankind.

Because each of us possesses the ability to reason, I see each of us as the same. Therefore, I see our species as one —one and the same — regardless of sex, race, religion, nationality, or any happenstance or other circumstance. Despite all that divides us, despite all our seeming differences, we are all, as I see it, the same, not only in the encoded strands of the double helix, but also in the watchful eyes of our Creator. We must, therefore, all be seen as the same also in the wary eyes of one another. We may live in many different places on this planet. We may live in many different ways. But what makes us human is *everywhere the same.*

We are each also the same in that we each harbor within us the entirety of the human condition. We each carry within us the culmination

---

[32] Ralph Waldo Emerson, "Character," in Emerson's Essays (New York: Harper and Row, 1926), 324, 338.
[33] The hexagonal symmetry of every snowflake is due to the shape of the water molecules of which snowflakes are made. The distinctiveness of every snowflake is due to how each snowflake is affected by temperature and pressure as it falls from the clouds. Martin Rees, "Cosmological Challenges: Are We Alone, and Where?," John Brockman, ed., The Next Fifty Years: Science in the First Half of the Twenty-First Century (New York: Vintage Books, 2002), 18, 25.

of all that humanity has ever been and the hope of all that humanity can yet be. We are each the same in our solitude. We are each the same in our isolation. We are each the same in our wonder.

And yet, because each of us possesses our own special faculty for reason, I see each of us also as unique. Nature and nurture together —in some way that is still much debated —make each of us different. We are each one of a kind. We are each an original free verse of Creation. We are, therefore, each subjects, not objects. We are each ends, not means. We are each irreplaceable, and we are each invaluable, not as means to the ends of others, but as ends in ourselves.[34] We are each invaluable because we are each uniquely human.

Because we are each the same and each also unique, because we each have that special spark that enables us to reason, and because that spark shines differently in the differing reasoning faculties of each of us, in my view, we each have certain rights. We have, to echo the far-seeing founders of the American republic, been endowed by our Creator with these rights along with our ability to reason. These rights are ours by birth. They are natural rights. They are, in the timeless phrase of Thomas Jefferson, "inalienable rights." They can never be taken away.

Because we are each unique, we naturally use our rights in unique ways of our own individual choosing. The world we make in the exercise of our own rights is, as a consequence, varied and diverse. It must be. It should be. We want it to be. Snow would not be snow if every snowflake were identical. But, because we humans are each also the same, the rights we each have —to make unique and different individual choices in life — are also the same. They are the same for all of us. They are the same everywhere. They are universal rights.

To my eyes, we have these natural and universal rights simply because we are human. These rights are human rights. And I see the best statement by far of these rights, and the best effort thus far to try to transform these natural and universal rights into positive law, in the Universal Declaration of Human Rights of the United Nations —which includes every Member of the WTO. I agree wholeheartedly with the very first article of that Declaration, which says, "All human beings are

---

[34] This is, of course, not my formulation, but rather that of the Enlightenment philosopher Immanuel Kant, as part of his famous "categorical imperative," in <u>Groundwork of the Metaphysic of Morals</u> [1785].

born free and equal in dignity and rights. They are endowed with reason and conscience and should act towards one another in a spirit of brotherhood."[35]

These are uplifting words. These are ennobling words. And the need to make these lofty words about human rights something much more than merely words is indispensable to the most basic task of being human. That task, as I see it, is for each of us to prove that we are worthy of our uniqueness by using and developing to the fullest extent what makes us unique as individuals and as a species —our capacity to choose what to think and how to live through the considered use of human reason.

As theologians and other thinkers have long observed, from the Book of Job, to the books of Kant, to the bookish musings of the latest young prodigy in yesterday's freshman philosophy class: our capacity to reason compels us to ask ultimate questions; it does not enable us to answer them.[36] We are unique because we can *know*; yet we know that we cannot know *all*. This is the unique burden of humanity. This is the unique glory —as well as the unique quandary —of our species. Yet, within these inescapable limits, we must, as I see it, apply our reason to all that can be made known and to all that can be made more reasonable in our life in this world. In how we think, in how we live, in how we wonder, through the application of reason, we must extend the reach of all we can know to the very edge of the unknowable.

Thus, in historical terms, I am a child of the Enlightenment.

I seek the "Age of Reason."

The Open Society

In seeking an "Age of Reason," I follow consciously in the footsteps of the eighteenth-century Enlightenment philosophers, and especially of the eighteenth-century Americans who followed them so consciously. Among my "trade secrets" is the fact that I share many of their assumptions.

Like them, I see reason, above all, as a capacity of the mind of an individual human being. All reason occurs initially as *individual* human

---

[35] Article 1, Universal Declaration of Human Rights.
[36] Kant, of course, made this same point in the preface to his <u>Critique of Pure Reason</u> [1781].

thought. Therefore, all reason arises necessarily *from the individual.* Consequently, it is only through the liberation of the individual human mind that we can hope to know all we are capable of knowing —to add to human knowledge, further human understanding, lift the human spirit, and reach up to the utmost boundaries of our fullest humanity.

For this reason, as I see it, human rights are individual rights, and, therefore, the common thread that interweaves all of human rights is the freedom of the individual. So I believe in "individualism." I believe, with John Stuart Mill, that "[o]ver himself, over his own body and mind, the individual is sovereign."[37] I believe in what one of the foremost contemporary advocates of human rights, Michael Ignatieff, has called the "intransigent individualism of human rights."[38]

By "individualism," though, I do not mean isolation. I do not mean a solitary and self-seeking loneliness. I do not mean a rugged individualism that ignores the needs of others and the need we all have for others. Unlike some, I do not see individualism as another name for selfishness. The individualism that I see, the individualism that I seek, is not centered on self; it is centered on others. It is accompanied by an enlightened altruism. For it emerges from a realization that our truest self cannot be achieved alone; our truest self can only be achieved through exchange with others and, most of all, through service to others. And I believe we can achieve such an individualism only when our true self-interest as individuals is rightly understood.

What I mean by "individualism" is described as "Self-Reliance" in the famous nineteenth-century essay by that eloquent child of the Enlightenment and prophet of the human spirit, Emerson.[39] My son, Joe, will attest to my admiration for what, to me, is the most memorable among Emerson's many memorable essays. In the summer before his freshman year at Vanderbilt University, I urged Joe to read only one thing before leaving home and going out into the world —Emerson's "Self-Reliance." He did —eventually. And he thanked me —eventually.

Some of the most stirring parts of Emerson's affirmation of "self-reliant" individualism will readily be recalled. "Whoso would be a man,

---

[37] John Stuart Mill, On Liberty, at 69.
[38] Michael Ignatieff, "The Rights Stuff," The New York Review of Books (June 13, 2002), 18, 20.
[39] Emerson, "Self-Reliance," in Emerson's Essays, supra, at 31.

must be a nonconformist."[40] "Nothing is at last sacred but the integrity of our own mind."[41] "To believe your own thought, to believe that what is true for you in your private heart is true for all men, - that is genius."[42] "It is easy in the world to live after the world's opinion; it is easy in solitude to live after our own; but the great man is he who in the midst of the crowd keeps with perfect sweetness the independence of solitude."[43] And, of course, and not least, "To be great is to be misunderstood."[44] Surely these are clarion calls, all, for an unrelenting and unapologetic individualism.

But what kind of individualism? As I see it, despite the ringing defiance of these timeless passages, the "individualism" of Emerson's "Self-Reliance" is not an isolated and solitary self-sufficiency. It is "not a blueprint for selfishness or withdrawal."[45] It is "not anti-community."[46] Quite the contrary. I agree with one of Emerson's most thoughtful biographers, Robert D. Richardson, Jr., that Emerson "recommends self-reliance as a starting point —indeed *the* starting point...toward self-fulfillment" on the way to a better society "through a voluntary association of fulfilled individuals."[47]

Emerson did not advocate isolation, and he did not equate individualism with isolation. No one can read the youthful Emerson's heartbroken account in his journal of standing over the grave of his beloved wife and believe that he ever wished to be alone. The sage of Concord did not seek a lonely solitude. Instead, for him, the "self-reliance" of individualism served a particular societal purpose. As Richardson explains, "Emerson was committed to the belief that unless individual reformation preceded social organization, nothing would change for the better."[48]

In "Self-Reliance," Emerson said, "We must go alone. Isolation must precede true society."[49] Yet implicit in this is the expectation that, at

---

[40] Id. at 35.
[41] Id.
[42] Id. at 31.
[43] Id. at 38.
[44] Id. at 41.
[45] Robert D. Richardson, Jr., <u>Emerson: The Mind on Fire</u> (Berkeley: University of California Press, 1995), 322.
[46] Id.
[47] Id.
[48] Id. at 345.
[49] Emerson, "Self-Reliance," supra, at 52.

some point, the isolation will end. The isolation that must precede "true society" will —and must —yield to "true society." Implicit in this also is the notion that there can be no "true society" unless there is first a true individualism. To attain a true individualism, we must be more able to meet each other as equals in a "true society." It was the "true society" to which Emerson aspired through his advocacy of individualism. Emerson's individualism is thus a "self-reliance" that leads to a personal commitment to serving others in the "true society" of a shared community based on the realization of the true individual self through mutual human fulfillment.

Another of his biographers, Van Wyck Brooks, said of Emerson that "his self-reliance was a gradual conquest."[50] This was so for Emerson as he progressed from a confining convention to a creative individuality. This may well be so for all of us in our own personal progress. To live in the "true society," we must all resolve to live truly. In "Self-Reliance," Emerson said, "If we live truly, we shall see truly."[51] As he saw it, and as I see it, in the final analysis, when the integrity of the individual in isolation finally yields to the "true society," living truly for ourselves truly means living for others. And, in my view, to find and forge such a "true society," we must, as individuals, look both "far ahead" and "far afield."[52] We must be "self-reliant" enough to see clearly what truly *is* in our self-interest as individuals. To me, this is what Emerson really meant by "self-reliance."

That great champion of democracy, in America and elsewhere, the nineteenth-century French thinker Alexis de Tocqueville, agreed with Emerson on the need for the right kind of individualism. Tocqueville understood fully "the fragility of freedom."[53] His great-grandfather, the legendary Malesherbes, had died on the guillotine after trying, unsuccessfully, to save the life of the King during the bloody excesses of the French Revolution. His father had escaped from the guillotine's blade at the last moment only because of the fortuitous fall of Robespierre. Tocqueville knew that freedom can be fleeting, and he saw a certain individual restlessness and restiveness as an inevitable consequence of

---

[50] Van Wyck Brooks, The Flowering of New England, 1815 – 1865 (New York: E.F. Hutton, 1937), 197 [1936].
[51] Emerson, "Self-Reliance," supra, at 49.
[52] These terms are borrowed from Wilson, The Future of Life, supra, at 40.
[53] This is the title of one of the most thoughtful books I have read on Tocqueville. *See* Joshua Mitchell, The Fragility of Freedom: Tocqueville on Religion, Democracy, and the American Future (Chicago: University of Chicago Press, 1995).

the footloose freedom endemic to democracy. However, he believed this could be countered by an individualism based on enlightened self-interest. He saw what he described as "the principle of interest rightly understood" as the key to the fulfillment of the promise of individual human freedom.[54]

Tocqueville saw democracy in America as a way of fulfilling the promise of human freedom. He saw what he described as "the principle of interest rightly understood" as the way Americans went about trying to fulfill that promise in the America he visited in the 1830s. What Tocqueville called "the principle of interest rightly understood" is a principle of rational, national self-interest. It is a way of seeing our self-interest that ranges both *far afield* and *far ahead*. It is a way of seeing our self-interest in our *broader* as well as our *narrower* needs, and in our needs *tomorrow* as well as our needs *today*. It is a way of *seeing* our self-interest and *seeking* our self-interest that takes the broader and the longer view.

Tocqueville saw "the principle of interest rightly understood" as finding "universal acceptance" in the America of the 1830s.[55] He saw the commitment of the American people to that principle in those early years of the youthful and idealistic American republic as "clear and sure."[56] Looking ahead, Tocqueville hoped that the self-absorbed selfishness and the self-defeating shortsightedness that can result from the wrong kind of individualism could be tempered and tamed through an enlightened education of the people and through an educated participation by the people in all the voluntary associations and in all the other institutional arrangements of democracy.

Tocqueville was hopeful that, through all the varied associations that are attendant to democracy and that lead to a shared sense of community, many more individuals in America and elsewhere would come to see that our self-interest "rightly understood" is best served by helping others as well as ourselves, and by remembering and fulfilling the needs of *all* of us tomorrow as well as the desires of *some* of us today. And, as a child himself of the Enlightenment, Tocqueville hoped that all this would be accomplished through the light of reason.

I share this hope. Thus, I also agree with my friend Said's teacher and hero, the twentieth-century Austrian philosopher and heir of the

[54] Alexis de Tocqueville, "The Americans combat individualism by the principle of interest rightly understood," Democracy in America (New York: The Colonial Press, 1899), Volume II, Second Book, Chapter VIII, 129-132 [hereinafter Democracy in America].
[55] Id. at 130.
[56] Id. at 131.

Enlightenment, Karl Popper, that the only "individualism" that will help us finally find and found our "Age of Reason" is an "emancipation of the individual" that leads to "the rise of democracy."[57] The individualism we need is one that will take us, as Popper said, "from tribalism to humanitarianism"[58] by opening all the doors that are still closed to democracy. For I believe that mutual fulfillment in a "true society" —in an enduring human community that looks both far ahead and far afield —can only be found while breathing the free air of democracy.

Popper, too, was an advocate of "reasonableness." As he saw it, human civilization is "aiming at humaneness and reasonableness, at equality and freedom ...."[59] He believed that a civilization that accomplishes such aims "sets free the critical powers of man" that are founded in human reason.[60] And, as he viewed it, "only democracy provides an institutional framework that permits reform without violence, and so the use of reason in political matters."[61] The critical powers of human reason can be set free to the fullest extent, Popper explained, only in a society in which there is "an ever-widening field" where individuals are free to make "personal decisions."[62] We will fulfill the full potential of human reason, and thus of our species —we will become fully human — only in a world where free individuals can make the most possible personal decisions in deciding for themselves how to think and how to live.

The best society —the best world —is therefore one in which individuals are free to choose, and in which individuals have the most choices. Our individual human capacity for choice does us little good in a society that limits our choices, and it does us even less good in a society that keeps us from choosing. Politically and economically, individuals must be free to choose. Individuals are free to choose —individuals have the most choices —only in a democracy. By providing an institutional framework for the fullest expression of political freedom, economic freedom, and every other manifestation of individual freedom, democracy makes "personal decisions" possible, and democracy makes the greatest possible number of personal choices available.

---

[57] Karl Popper, <u>The Open Society and Its Enemies</u>, 5th Ed. (Princeton: Princeton University Press, 1966), Volume I, 101 [1945] [hereinafter <u>The Open Society</u>].
[58] Id. at 171.
[59] Id. at 1.
[60] Id.
[61] Id. at 4.
[62] Id. at 173.

Thus, the way of democracy is the only way to human freedom. Popper described the democratic society as "the open society." Popper's "open society" is Emerson's "true society." It is the society that Tocqueville hoped democracy would make. It is the society that we are still striving to make of what the far-sighted founders of our republic hoped would become "Exhibit A" of the Enlightenment Project — the democratic republic that is known as the United States of America.

Popper's most sustained defense of "the open society" is found in the two volumes of The Open Society and Its Enemies, which was first published in 1945. He wrote the book while in exile in New Zealand during World War II. At the time, Popper wrote in support of the struggle for human freedom against the totalitarianisms of both the right and the left that then threatened to overwhelm the world. In a broader sense, he wrote also for all times. In my view, The Open Society and Its Enemies is one of the most important books not only of the twentieth century, but of any century. In those two volumes of that one book, Popper was able to distill the essence of the human struggle for freedom and the essence of the enduring Enlightenment thought that provides so many of the assumptions of the modern world.

Popper saw the human struggle not as a struggle between the right and the left, but as a struggle between closed and open societies. He saw human history as the centuries-long striving of our species for something worthy of being called "civilization" through an ongoing effort to move from closed to open societies. In Popper's view, the closed society is one in which each of us is told our place, knows our place, and stays in our place. It is a society in which our decisions are made for us by others. The "closed society" is one in which "the tribe is everything and the individual nothing."[63] The "open society," in contrast, is a society that is conducive and receptive to the use of reason through the exercise of the critical powers of humankind. It is a society in which "individuals are confronted with personal decisions."[64] It is a society in which individuals are free to make personal choices.

The "open society" is, thus, one in which the individual is liberated by the availability of personal choices. It is one in which individual freedom in all its manifestations is possible. Further, it is one in which the individual has the opportunity, as Popper put it, to prove

---

[63] Id. at 190.
[64] Id. at 173.

worthy of his freedom and "prove worthy of his liberation" by showing that "man is not merely a piece of flesh – a body," that man is not merely a beast, but that "[t]here is more in man, a divine spark, reason; and a love of truth, of kindness, humaneness, a love and beauty and goodness."[65] For, "[i]t is these that make a man's life worthwhile."[66]

Consciously or not, Popper followed Emerson in how he saw human freedom. The premise of his philosophy of freedom was profoundly Emersonian. One of Emerson's best essays is one of his last essays, "Fate." In "Fate," Emerson, like Popper, focused on the presence of choice as the essence of freedom. He maintained that "choosing or acting in the soul" is freedom.[67] He argued that the universe can be understood as "advance out of fate into freedom" through the choices we make along the way.[68]

Some say we can never escape fate. Some say we are never really free to choose. They say we are not even free to choose when we live and breathe in the free air of an open society. They say we are condemned to some predetermined destiny beyond our knowing and beyond our controlling. In their view, there is an inevitable fatalism and an inexorable futility to all of human life that makes our belief in our "free will" only an illusion. This view is typified in the thinking of Popper's lifelong intellectual adversary, the Austrian philosopher Ludwig Wittgenstein, who, when reflecting on the question of "free will," imagined a leaf falling in the autumn winds, and saying to itself, "Now I'll go this way, now I'll go that."[69]

Metaphysics is not my forte. I may be only another leaf falling in the autumn wind. I may be falling toward a fate I cannot change. But I choose to believe otherwise. And I choose to believe that this choice is made freely. I choose to believe that life is real, that I am real, and that I *can* choose. Like William James, who delved far more deeply into this issue than I can ever do, I say, "My first act of free will shall be to believe in free will."[70] Like Emerson, in "Fate," I say, "So far as a man thinks, he

---

[65] Id. at 190.
[66] Id.
[67] Emerson, "Fate," in <u>Emerson's Essays</u>, supra, 943, 953.
[68] Id.
[69] Wittgenstein is quoted in Simon Blackburn, <u>Think: A Compelling Introduction to Philosophy</u> (Oxford: Oxford University Press, 2001), 87.
[70] William James wrote this in his personal diary on April 29, 1870.

is free."[71] As I see it, freedom is found in facing our fate. It is found by looking our fate squarely in the eye.

Thus, like Popper, I choose to believe that, in an open society, we can choose to be free. And, thus, like Popper, I seek an "open society," and I oppose its enemies. As I have long since learned in a life devoted to public service, and as I am reminded every day at the WTO, the creation of an "open society" through reliance on the divine spark of reason is by no means easy. The ways of public life are not always the ways of "public reason."[72] The way forward to an "open society" is difficult. It is filled with both rational and irrational obstacles. Yet, as I see it, the difficult, democratic path to an "open society" is the *only* way forward to a life that is worthwhile. It is the only way to human rights, to human freedom, and to an Age of Reason.

Clearly, I see the potential of human reason for creating an open society as vast. I am, thus, an optimist. For me, the glass is not only always half full; it is ever on the verge of being filled to the brim. As a boy in Florida, I stood barefoot in my backyard, with the sand between my toes, and watched as the Mercury and Apollo astronauts were launched from Cape Canaveral into the beckoning reaches of outer space. So it was no accident that I was, during my years in the Congress, an ardent advocate not only of the Hubble Space Telescope, but also of the space shuttle, the International Space Station, the Superconducting Supercollider, and numerous other ambitious scientific and technological projects. I favor humanism, not tribalism. I want to live in the modern, not the medieval world. I believe in the future, and I look to the future with confident optimism.

I firmly believe that the use of reason can help us find the future we seek. I believe, as Popper did, in the tradition of Socrates, in "the tradition of criticism and discussion, and with it the art of thinking rationally"[73] that enlightened the early search for an "open society" in ancient Athens. I believe that same rational tradition can serve us still today. As I see it through my "WTO glasses," reason can help us find a bright future. Reason can help illuminate democratic self-governance, and can work wonders for humanity through science, through technology, and through enlightened political economy.

---

[71] Emerson, "Fate," supra, at 953.
[72] John Rawls, <u>Political Liberalism</u>, supra, at 212-254.
[73] Popper, <u>The Open Society</u>, Volume I, at 188.

Human progress is possible through reliance on human reason. Civilization can, after all, become civilized. Our uniquely reasoning species has only barely begun the long climb up from the primordial swamp of our past, and has only just now glimpsed that fair foreshadowing of the bright future that yet can be. The rule of reason and the rule of law can be established for an unreasonable and unruly world. Tomorrow, despite all, *can* be better than today.

All this I believe. All this I see. Yet, because I also see the potential of human reason as limited, I am also a realist. And, as a realist, I am aware —all too aware —that, as my colleague Judge Georges Abi-Saab of Egypt explained to me on September 12, 2001, "Ours is not yet an Age of Reason."

In Our Nature

As I look through my "WTO glasses," I see any serious thought about the future of the human species as resting necessarily on some basic perception of human nature. The potential of human reason is limited by human nature. As I see it, it is in our nature to do good. As I see it, too, it is in our nature also to do evil.

None of us who remember September 11, 2001, can ever doubt that there is evil in human nature. Emerson, no pessimist, nonetheless conceded, in the journal he wrote to himself, that, "Human nature is as bad as it dares to be."[74] Ninety-eight percent of the human genome is the same as that of the chimpanzee. Genetically, we are more like chimpanzees than gorillas are.[75] Our capacity for reason makes us something more than a beast. But still the beast is within us. The beast is always within us. And, as I see it through my "WTO glasses," the beast will rule us if we are ruled only by our passions. The beast will rule us unless we are ruled by the taming and restraining power of reason.

A vivid reminder to me of the capacity for both good and evil in human nature can be seen in the center of Paris. There, on the isle of the city, within just a few short feet of each other, stand two lasting monuments to the hopes and the heartbreaks of the human endeavor. One is Saint

---

[74] Emerson is quoted in Vernon L. Parrington, Main Currents in American Thought, Volume Two: The Romantic Revolution in America, 1800–1860 (New York: Harcourt, Brace and World, 1954), 383 [1927].
[75] Matt Ridley, Genome: The Autobiography of a Species in 23 Chapters (London: Fourth Estate, 1999), 28.

Chapelle, perhaps the most beautiful and glorious of all Christian chapels, a testimony in stone to the heights of human aspiration. There, I first understood fully what Henry Adams meant when he said, "The spire justifies the church."[76] The other, nearby, is the Conciergerie, the dark dungeon where the victims of the terror spent their last despairing days before their execution during the French Revolution. There, I was reminded of the depths that can be reached by human depravity. Together, these two contrasting consequences of our humanity remind us that human nature can reach both up to the sublime and down to the guillotine.

As Hannah Arendt has taught us, the revolutionaries of the eighteenth century were not "capable of dreaming of a goodness beyond virtue, just as they were unable to imagine...that there could be wickedness beyond vice."[77] We have learned that lesson since. The guillotine has given way to other devices of human degradation that were beyond their imaginings. Today, those of us who still pursue the "Enlightenment Project" do so without the *naiveté* of those who first conceived it.

The depravity in human nature —the "death and dust"[78] that is part of each and every one of us —cannot be wished away through the power of human reason. Human reason is limited because human reason cannot change what the eighteenth-century Scottish philosopher and skeptic David Hume described as "the constant and universal principles of human nature."[79] Human nature is fixed. Human behavior —which emerges from the mix of nature and nurture that we call life —is endlessly diverse and variable. But human nature is unchanging.

Some have argued otherwise. That rebel against reason, Jean-Jacques Rousseau, argued that the role of the legislator is "to change, so to speak, the nature of man."[80] That other rebel, Karl Marx, insisted similarly that there is no such thing as an enduring human nature. Marx said, "All history is nothing but a continuous transformation of human

---

[76] Henry Adams, Mont Saint Michel and Chartres (New York: Penguin Books, 1986), 355 [1904].
[77] Hannah Arendt, On Revolution (London: Penguin Books, 1990), 82 [1963].
[78] Michel de Montaigne, An Apology For Raymond Sebond (London: Penguin Books, 1993), 131 [1569].
[79] David Hume, Inquiry Concerning Human Understanding [1748], quoted in Hampson, The Enlightenment, supra, at 109.
[80] Jean-Jacques Rousseau, The Social Contract (London: Penguin Books, 1968), 84 [1762].

nature."[81]   From Condorcet to Godwin to Saint-Simon to the American flower children of the 1960s, others have likewise assumed a malleable human nature that might one day lead to the "perfectibility" of man. However, in this debate, all I know of history and all I understand of science tell me to side with Hume.

Our history as a species speaks for itself, and our science helps explain our history. Science reveals how the rational and the irrational are ever at war within us. Scientists are relentless. Even now, they are busy developing new technologies for mapping neural activity and gene-activation patterns in the brain. Perhaps one day we will know more about what makes us the way we are. But all we know now tells me that Rousseau and Marx were wrong. We are not capable of changing our nature. Nor are we capable of being educated into a selfless altruism.

I concur with that ancient realist, Thucydides, who knew nothing about human neural activity, but who knew much about human nature. Thucydides saw human nature at work in the pointless carnage of the Peloponnesian War, and he portrayed it as he saw it in the history he wrote of that war. "[H]uman nature is what it is," he wrote.[82]   Thucydides had been a general in the war before losing the political favor of the Athenian assembly. He recalled that, in the midst of the chaos of the conflict, "with the ordinary conventions of civilized life thrown into confusion, human nature, always ready to offend even where laws exist, showed itself proudly in its true colours, as something incapable of controlling passion, insubordinate to the idea of justice, the enemy to anything superior to itself...."[83]   In the ancient war between Athens and Sparta, reason succumbed to unreason. So it has been in all wars. And, alas, so it is in much of life.

My time on the science committee in the Congress suggests some caution in this conclusion. I assume, as Thucydides assumed, a fixed human nature. I am aware, though, that some suggest that, as fixed as human nature may now seem, it may be subject to change by advances in biotechnology —by genetic engineering that would make us different from what we now are —that would make us "posthuman."[84]   Perhaps. But, if

---

[81] Karl Marx, The Poverty of Philosophy (Amherst, New York: Prometheus Books, 1998) [1847].

[82] Thucydides, History of the Peloponnesian War (London: Penguin Books 1972), 242, translated by Rex Warner [1954].

[83] Id. at 245.

[84] Francis Fukuyama, Our Posthuman Future: Consequences of the Biotechnology Revolution (New York: Farrar, Straus and Giroux, 2002).

he were here now, and if he looked up from unrolling the papyrus scrolls of his history, Thucydides would no doubt remind us that no such change is likely to erase the human capacity for doing *evil* as well as for doing *good*.

My view of human nature does not keep me from seeing the possibilities for human progress. But "progress," like so much else in life, must be defined. Nearly a century ago, the British historian J. B. Bury, in his classic work, The Idea of Progress, defined "progress" as "an interpretation of history which regards men as slowly advancing... in a definite and desirable direction, and infers that this progress will continue indefinitely."[85] This notion of progress as continuing "indefinitely" seems to me to imply that we can eventually create a perfect human society —a Utopia. This is not my interpretation of history, and this is not my idea of progress. Rather, I agree with another British historian, one of Bury's critics, H. A. L. Fisher, who said, "The fact of progress is written plain and large on the page of history; but progress is not a law of nature. The ground gained by one generation may be lost by the next."[86]

Those of us who support the WTO are sometimes accused of believing in the possibility that progress through trade can create a "Utopia."[87] Although I believe in the possibility of progress through trade, I do not believe at all in the possibility of Utopia. Utopia means "nowhere," and nowhere do I perceive the possibility of the perfectibility of humankind. Human perfection is not on the horizon.

Nor do I believe in any "iron laws" of history that assure us of progress. Karl Popper characterized the belief in an inevitable historical destiny as "the poverty of historicism,"[88] I agree. There is, in my view, nothing destined, nothing foreordained, nothing absolutely certain about the future history of humanity. History, to me, is ours to make, and human "progress," to me, consists in the making of a more reasonable world of more open societies. Human "progress," to me, means more of us living in freedom. It means more of us being free.

---

[85] J. B. Bury, The Idea of Progress: An Inquiry Into Its Origin and Growth (New York: Dover Publications, 1987), 5 [1920].
[86] H. A. L. Fisher, History of Europe (1946), quoted in Sidney Pollard, The Idea of Progress: History and Society (London: Penguin Books, 1971), 205 [1968].
[87] Pierre Bourdieu, Acts of Resistance: Against the Tyranny of the Market (New York: The New Press, 1998), 94.
[88] Karl Popper, The Poverty of Historicism (London: Routledge, 2002) [1957].

However we may define it, progress is far from inevitable, far from assured. Nevertheless, I believe that, in pursuit of an overall human "progress," we must work for a material progress that makes it possible for more and more people to live in the dignity of human freedom. We must try to achieve this material progress in a way that will lead also to progress in the service of the human spirit. But we must never believe that any such progress is in any way guaranteed. If we do, we will only be disillusioned, and our disillusionment will diminish our prospects for progress.

Ours is a world of contingency. There is no guarantee of a happy ending to human history. Our powers of reason are not powerful enough to predict the future. There is no map *of* the future, and there is no map *to* the future. History is not plot. History is improvisation. History is a story that only we can tell. And the only story that can be told through history is the story we tell day by day, year by year. It is the story we write through the choices we make in exercising our free will in response to both the best and the worst in our unchanging nature.

We humans are intricate creatures. We each have about thirty thousand genes. We each have about one trillion nerve cells. We each have between one hundred trillion and one thousand trillion synaptic connections between those nerve cells. We humans are also frail creatures who have, in the timeless teaching of one human faith, fallen short.[89] We are as we were made by our Creator. Those of us who are religious may —should —must —aspire to become more. Those of us who call ourselves Christians, for example, can —and ought —to strive always and ever in imitation of Christ. Yet His kingdom, as He told us, is not of this world.[90]

In *this* world, nothing can empower human reason to change the potential for both good and evil in human nature.[91] Our capacity for reason cannot, alone, create for us the utopia of heaven; and it cannot, alone, deliver us from the dystopia of hell. "The ultimate aim of the Communist system was the transformation of human nature,"[92] and tens

---

[89] Romans 3:23.
[90] John 18:36.
[91] For a different viewpoint on this, *see* Francis Fukuyama, Our Posthuman Future: Consequences of the Biotechnology Revolution (New York: Farrar, Straus and Giroux, 2002). Fukuyama fears that biotechnology, if abused, could alter the fundamental nature of the human species.
[92] Orlando Figes, A People's Tragedy: The Russian Revolution, 1891-1924 (London: Jonathon Cape, 1996), 733.

of millions died in the past century as a result of communism's blind belief in rationalism. The ultimate aim of the fascist system was the utter submission to the irrational in human nature, and the residual power of human reason was not enough to prevent the Nazi belief in unreason from resulting in the Holocaust. The tragic consequences of both communism and fascism in the twentieth century teach us this. Expecting too much from human reason leads to the gulag. Expecting too little leads to the gas chamber. The result is the same: death, destruction, and dehumanization. The result is *not* human "progress."

Therefore, we must not rely, in seeking "progress," in shaping our institutions, or in shaping our future, on the fond but forlorn hope that our genetic instinct toward mutual human sympathy —if it exists — can somehow be made to subdue and transform the other, baser instincts that are clearly part of our nature. The institutions we create in the hope of creating an "open society" must be founded on a reasoned appreciation of the reality and the frailty of human nature. They must be founded on an understanding of our species as we are, and not as we ought to be, and on a realization of the immutable reality of both the potential and the limits of human reason. Only on such a foundation can we ever hope to base and build a real and lasting Age of Reason.

This, like all else I see, is not in the least original with me. This is a premise I share with the most renowned children of the Enlightenment, the founding fathers of that most enduring of all Enlightenment projects —the United States of America. As James Madison asked in perhaps the most famous of all the many famous passages in The Federalist Papers, in Federalist Number 51, "But what is government itself but the greatest of all reflections on human nature? If men were angels, no government would be necessary."[93] With this in mind, he and his colleagues founded a government that is framed in a Constitution that reckons with the reality of human nature by providing for a separation of powers and for a system of checks and balances such that neither too much nor too little is expected from the power of human reason as part of an unchanging human nature. Because they did so, their Enlightenment project has both succeeded and endured.

Yet, like me, the founders of my country were not only realists. They were also optimists. As Madison also observed, less famously but

---

[93] James Madison, Federalist No. 51, in James Madison, Alexander Hamilton, and John Jay, The Federalist Papers, (New York: Penguin Books, 1987), 319 [1787-1788].

no less importantly, in Federalist Number 55, "As there is a degree of depravity in mankind which requires a certain degree of circumspection and distrust, so there are other qualities in human nature which justify a certain portion of esteem and confidence. Republican government presupposes the existence of these qualities in a higher degree than any other form."[94] Madison thus reminded us that we have the potential for good as well as evil, and he argued that a recognition of the evil in our nature should not blind us to the possibility of doing good, and of doing, and being, better.

Emboldened by this balanced understanding of human nature, the American children of the Enlightenment have continued through the generations since the founding of the American republic —always imperfectly, often sporadically, yet nevertheless persistently —to seek better ways to ensure the success of the American experiment in the application of human reason to human governance. And, together with others of like mind around the world, we Americans have sought better ways, both nationally and internationally, to pursue other projects that can fulfill the hopes of the Enlightenment by appealing to what the greatest of all Americans, Abraham Lincoln, called "the better angels of our nature."[95]

I see our experiment with the making of a world trading system as akin to this American experiment. I see the World Trade Organization as yet another "Enlightenment Project," and I see the WTO treaty, like the Constitution of the United States of America, as a document born of a recognition of the unchanging reality of human nature. The WTO is an effort to appeal to "the better angels of our nature" by applying the rule of reason to world trade in ways that will further the cause of human progress through the creation of free and open societies throughout the world.

Typical of the denunciations of the WTO are the rustic, home-grown diatribes of the farmer and essayist from the American state of Kentucky, Wendell Berry. Berry's elegant essays contain much that is true about the plain virtues of the simple rural life. Unfortunately, they also contain much that is not true about the global economy, and much that is not true about the WTO. "[T]he World Trade Organization agreement," he writes, "institutionalizes the industrial ambition to use,

---

[94] James Madison, Federalist No. 55, The Federalist Papers, supra, at 339.
[95] Abraham Lincoln, First Inaugural Address (1861).

sell, or destroy every acre and every creature of the world."[96] Further, he maintains, "the World Trade Organization itself…is in effect a global government, with power to enforce the decisions of the collective against national laws that conflict with it."[97] The WTO is, he contends, "a world-government-by-economic bureaucracy…."[98]

I invite Mr. Berry to take a brief sojourn from his beloved Kentucky and join me in Geneva at the WTO. I will be happy to buy him lunch in the WTO cafeteria. He will find while there that, though picturesque, the place we call "the WTO" is hardly imperial or imposing. Several hundred people work there. Most are translators. A few might admit to being "bureaucrats." (Geneva is, after all, a French-speaking Swiss city just over the border from France, and the French, after all, did invent the word "bureaucrat.") But the vast majority of those of us who work at "the WTO" prefer to think of ourselves as international civil servants who loyally serve the Members of the WTO, and, in so doing, serve billions of people around the world.

We do so on an annual budget of, at last glance, about $100 million. This sum is less than the annual *travel* budget of the International Monetary Fund.[99] Budgetary contributions by the WTO Members are calculated annually on the basis of the previous year's share of world trade, and, accordingly, the current annual contribution of the United States of America to the operating budget of the WTO is about $20 million. This is considerably less than I used to get, on a good day, in federal appropriations for projects for my former district in Florida when I served in the Congress of the United States.

To anyone at all acquainted with the everyday reality of the WTO, the very thought of the WTO as some kind of would-be "world government" is laughable. The WTO is not a government, and no one in any way involved with the WTO has even the remotest desire to make it one. The WTO is an international organization *consisting of governments*. It is a forum where governments agree by consensus on rules to lower barriers to trade, and a way for governments to ensure compliance with those rules when disputes arise about what they mean. The WTO is also

---

[96] Wendell Berry, "The Whole Horse," <u>The Art of the Commonplace: The Agrarian Essays of Wendell Berry</u> (Washington, D.C.: Counterpoint, 2002), 236, 242 [hereinafter <u>The Art of the Commonplace</u>].
[97] Id. at 243.
[98] Id.
[99] Mike Moore, Speech Notes to Legislators Assembly, Seattle, Washington (November 2, 1999).

a *voluntary* organization. Every member of the WTO is a Member by choice. Under the WTO treaty, every Member of the WTO can withdraw from membership with six months of notice.[100] No Member has ever withdrawn from the WTO for a very simple reason —every Member desires the many economic benefits that come from being a Member.

The WTO is called, in our WTO jargon, "Member-driven." This is because it is the Members of the WTO who *are* the WTO. The relatively few of us who work at the place called "the WTO" are, only and always, the servants of the WTO Members. We do not and cannot make any decisions affecting the Members that the Members do not adopt or otherwise approve. This is as it should be, and this is the only way that every one of us, and every one of the WTO Members, ever want it to be. The WTO is, in the best tradition of Lincoln and other children of the Enlightenment, an endeavor "of, by, and for" the Members of the WTO. The WTO serves the shared interest of the Members of the WTO in their own continuing self-governance by serving the cause of the international rule of law through the establishment and enforcement of mutually agreed international rules for international trade.

The WTO is an effort by 146 countries and other customs territories to secure the rule of law for a rapidly globalizing world trading system so that we can avoid the worst excesses of human nature in what would otherwise be the rule of the jungle in world trade. As King Hassan II of Morocco, the host of the Marrakesh conference that concluded the Uruguay Round, expressed it at the signing of the WTO treaty, "By bringing into being the World Trade Organization today, we are enshrining the rule of law in international economic and trade relations, thus setting universal rules and disciplines over the temptations of unilateralism and the law of the of the jungle."[101]

Thucydides was among the first to doubt that we would ever be able to escape the law of the jungle. Realist that he was, and pessimist that he was as well because of what he saw and knew of human nature, he thought that *might* would always make *right*. In the "Melian Dialogue" that is part of his timeless history, he told of how Athens imposed its will on the tiny island of Melos. Defeated in battle, the Melians sought mercy from their Athenian conquerors. Mired in moral decline after long years

---

[100] Article XV, the Marrakesh Agreement.
[101] King Hassan II of Morocco is quoted in John H. Jackson, "Global Economics and International Economic Law," 1 Journal of International Economic Law 1, 21 at n 43 (1998).

of a ruthless war, the Athenians replied, "[T]he strong do what they can and the weak suffer what they must."[102] Showing no mercy on Melos, they "put to death all the grown men whom they took, and sold the women and children for slaves...."[103] *Might* made *right* as even the supposedly civilized citizens of classical Athens imposed the law of the jungle.

In concluding and signing the WTO treaty, in establishing and expanding the WTO, and in supporting and strengthening the WTO dispute settlement system, the Members of the WTO have rejected the law of the jungle. In all that they are doing together as the WTO, they are endeavoring to demonstrate that *might* need not make *right* in world trade, but that *right* can make *might* in the world trading system when right is enshrined in the international rule of law. The WTO is an effort to extend the reach of reason by establishing the rule of law in one of the most important arenas for the exercise of human rights —that of international trade.

I see the establishment and the enforcement by the WTO of non-discrimination and other important international rules for trade as serving the cause of human progress by serving the cause of human rights. For I see the opportunity to engage in trade as an indispensable means of making human rights a reality. The Preamble to the Universal Declaration of Human Rights of the United Nations speaks of freedom from "want" —one of Franklin Delano Roosevelt's "Four Freedoms."[104] Article 28 of the Declaration speaks of the right to a social and international order in which the rights and freedoms set out in the Declaration can be fully realized.[105] To me, this includes not only the political and civil rights listed in the Declaration, but also the social and economic rights that are also set out there. To me, the so-called "first generation" of fundamental political and civil rights and the so-called "second generation" of aspirational social and economic rights are both absolutely essential to the fulfillment of the human task of using our reasoning capacity as a species to the fullest extent. The two are, to me, interrelated, interdependent, and inseparable.[106] In my view, none of our essential

---

[102] This translation of the Melian Dialogue is from Robert B. Strassler, ed., The Landmark Thucydides: A Comprehensive Guide to the Peloponnesian War (New York: The Free Press, 1996), 352.

[103] Id. at 357.

[104] Preamble, Universal Declaration of Human Rights.

[105] Article 28, Universal Declaration of Human Rights.

[106] For a similar view, and for an enlightening and well-written history, *see* Mary Ann Glendon, A World Made New: Eleanor Roosevelt and the Universal Declaration of Human Rights (New York: Random House, 2001).

human rights can ever be fully realized if we are not free to engage, both nationally and internationally, in trade and commerce. None of our other rights can ever truly be real unless we have the right to engage in trade in free and open societies.

I was first inspired to participate in politics and in public life by the American civil rights movement. As a young white boy growing up in the changing American South of the 1950s and 1960s, I saw social and racial injustice all around me. I decided to devote my life to public service largely because I wanted to work for a just society by working for civil rights. I still do. The civil rights that were so sorely needed in the American South of my youth —and are still much needed there today —are human rights. The long struggle for civil rights for African-Americans in the South is but one example and but one episode in the continuing global struggle for civil and other vital human rights for oppressed and impoverished people everywhere in the world. In working for the WTO, I am working still for a just society, and I am working still for the cause of civil and other human rights. For it is only through the reality, and only through the exercise, of civil and other human rights that we can subdue the evil and set free the good that is in our nature.

Smith's Hand

Some critics of the WTO see those of us who support the WTO as slaves to a soulless abstraction. They portray us as heedless of the human consequences of trade and desirous only of serving the supposedly heartless logic of an esoteric trade theory. One such critic, the late French sociologist Pierre Bourdieu, saw the supporters of what he derided as "neo-liberalism" as striving to create "a utopia which, with the aid of the economic theory to which it subscribes, manages to see itself as the scientific description of reality."[107] The implication of such criticism is that our view of the world is one of cold calculation in which living people are only lifeless numbers in a ruthless economic equation.

Those who see us this way do not understand us, and they do not understand how we see economics. Economics is not a mathematical abstraction that is somehow unrelated to living, breathing, and striving people, and thus unrelated to the ongoing struggle to secure human rights and human freedom. Economics is not a matter of mere numbers —no matter how much some economists may sometimes make it seem so. Nor

---

[107] Pierre Bourdieu, Acts of Resistance: Against the Tyranny of the Market, at 94.

is the market an abstraction, a theoretical mechanism that somehow magically rules our lives without reflecting the reality of the lives we live.

Like many others who follow him consciously, and like many, many more who follow him without ever realizing it, I am a follower, in many respects, of one of the greatest tribunes of the Enlightenment, the eighteenth-century Scottish political economist Adam Smith. I see his most famous book, The Wealth of Nations, published in 1776, as largely an accurate description of how best to promote "the wealth of nations" even today. And I agree wholeheartedly with his basic insight: that "the wealth of nations" —which for him meant the wealth of the people who comprise nations —is best promoted by maximizing the mutual advantages that result from a free flow of free exchange among free individuals in a free marketplace. Like Smith, I prefer the freedom of the market to the stasis of state control. I see the pursuit of our individual interests in the marketplace as serving our common interest in securing human rights and in creating free and open societies.

For this reason, I invite the working in the marketplace of Adam Smith's "invisible hand."[108] The "invisible hand" is the hand of individual self-interest. As Smith so memorably said, "It is not from the benevolence of the butcher, the brewer, or the baker, that we expect our dinner, but from their regard to their own self interest."[109] Their intention in butchering, in brewing, and in baking is not, he noted, the fulfillment "of our own necessities but of their advantages."[110] And yet, through the working of the marketplace, each of them seems "led by an invisible hand to promote an end which was no part of his intention."[111] In this way, the pursuit of the individual interests of each of us can also serve the individual and shared interests of all of us. In this way, we cooperate without coercion.

This is no abstraction. As Smith would be the first to say, the "invisible hand" is the hand of people. Economics is people. Economics is life. The market is people in action, living their lives every day, and making their own personal choices every day about how best to live their own lives. And, to me, significant among our tasks in creating free and open societies, and in thereby fashioning and furthering an Age of Reason,

---

[108] Adam Smith, An Inquiry into the Nature and Causes of the Wealth of Nations (New York: The Modern Library, 1994), 485 [1776] [hereinafter The Wealth of Nations].
[109] Smith, The Wealth of Nations, at 15.
[110] Id.
[111] Id. at 485.

must be that of maximizing the personal choices that individuals are free to make in the marketplace. Consequently, first and foremost, I see trade as an exercise in individual human freedom. I see trade as expanding the capacity for realizing human freedom by expanding the number of individual choices that we each can make.

Smith was the proverbial absent-minded professor. He was kidnapped by gypsies as a child —and the gypsies gave him back.[112] He once wandered several miles from home in his nightshirt, in broad daylight, lost in thought. On another occasion, he was so caught up in his discourse that he fell into a tannery pit full of fat and lime; he was rescued from the pit and carried home, complaining, in a sedan chair.[113] Smith was a lifelong bachelor who lived most of his life with his mother in the small Scottish seaport of Kirkcaldy, where seagoing ships sailed to and from the harbor as Smith spent years scribbling away. He spent more than ten years writing The Wealth of Nations. Because he could wield a pen only with great difficulty, he dictated the book to an amanuensis. He walked back and forth in his study as he dictated, stopping from time to time to rub his head on the wall above the fireplace. The pomade from his hair left a dark streak on the paneling.[114]

Smith, to be sure, was an eccentric. He was, however, an eccentric who understood human nature, and who understood the unavoidable relationship between economics and human nature. Like government, economics is also a reflection on human nature. I see the propensity to trade as a part of human nature, and so did Adam Smith. In The Wealth of Nations, he wrote about people as we really are, and about commerce as it really works. He believed that trade emerges from human nature, and he did not believe that trade can be separated from the realities of human nature.

As Smith explained, we are traders by nature. We tend toward trade as "the necessary consequence of the faculties of reason and

---

[112] One of Smith's biographers, John Rae, observed, "He would have made, I fear, a poor gypsy." Rae is quoted in E. G. West, Adam Smith: The Man and His Works (Indianapolis: Liberty Press, 1976), 28.

[113] *See* Ian Simpson Ross, Life of Adam Smith (Oxford: Oxford University Press, 1995); Peter Ackroyd, "Peace and Sensibility," The New Yorker (January 15, 1996), 70; Paul Strathern, Dr. Strangelove's Game: A Brief History of Economic Genius (London: Penguin Books, 2002), 89-90 [2001].

[114] Robert L. Heilbroner, The Worldly Philosophers: The Lives, Times and Ideas of the Great Economic Thinkers, 4th Ed. (New York: Simon and Schuster, 1972), 48 [1953].

speech."[115]   The different faculties we all have for reason give rise to different talents, and these different talents make us all tend toward trade. Furthermore, the faculty we all have for speech likewise makes us tend toward trade. Smith saw the human exchange of trade as a form of communication. In fact, for Smith, "Economic life...is itself a sort of discussion."[116] For these reasons, we all have, as Smith explained, "the propensity to trade, barter, and exchange one thing for another."[117]   It is in our nature.

Smith saw our different reasoning faculties and our capacity for speech as tending us toward trade and, therefore, leading us to the specialization of a division of labor. His modern critics fault Smith for supposedly placing too much emphasis on *competition*, but, in reality, his economic thought is more accurately describing as emphasizing *cooperation*. Central to his thesis and, indeed, to all of his thought, is the inevitability of cooperation in the form of a division of labor. The very act of exchanging one thing for another is, by definition, a division of labor, and, Smith said, "[I]t is this same trucking disposition which originally gives occasion to the division of labour."[118]   We all tend toward a division of labor and, thus, toward trade. We all tend to specialize. It is in our nature.

Moreover, as Smith explained, when we all specialize, "[w]hen the division of labour has been once thoroughly established, it is but a very small part of a man's wants which the produce of his own labour can supply. He supplies the far greater part of them by exchanging that surplus part of the produce of his own labour, which is over and above his own consumption, for such parts of the produce of other men's labour as he has occasion for. Every man thus lives by exchanging, or becomes in some measure a merchant, and the society itself grows to be what is properly a commercial society."[119] The division of labor thus produces a commercial society in which we all become merchants —"in some measure" —who live "by exchanging." A commercial society necessarily emerges from the tendency toward trade that is in our nature. This commercial society is a more productive society, because "[t]he division

---

[115] Smith, The Wealth of Nations, at 14.
[116] Emma Rothschild, Economic Sentiments: Adam Smith, Condorcet, and the Enlightenment (Cambridge: Harvard University Press, 2001), 8 [hereinafter Economic Sentiments].
[117] Smith, The Wealth of Nations, at 14.
[118] Id. at 16.
[119] Id. at 24.

of labour... so far as it can be introduced, occasions, in every art, a proportionable increase of the productive powers of labour."[120]

We were all told —or we should have been told —in "Economics 101" about the pin factory that Smith used as an example of the productive powers of the division of labor in the very first chapter of The Wealth of Nations. (I can still hear Professor Rendigs Fels holding forth on Smith's pinmakers during my days as an undergraduate at Vanderbilt University.) Smith explained that there were "eighteen distinct operations" in the making of a pin.[121] He described how a division of labor among ten men performing these operations produced 48,000 pins per day —4,800 for each man.[122] Without the division of labor, Smith observed, each man could have made, on his own, "perhaps not one pin in a day."[123] Generalizing from this one example, he concluded that, "In every other art and manufacture, the effects of the division of labour are similar to what they are in this very trifling one...."[124]

Smith saw the division of labor as improving productivity by saving time, increasing dexterity, and encouraging inventiveness. He saw it as creating the potential of wealth not solely for a privileged elite, but for everyone. He saw it as creating the potential for a "universal" prosperity. "It is," he wrote, "the great multiplication of the productions of all the different arts, in consequence of the division of labour, which occasions, in a well-governed society, that universal opulence which extends itself to the lowest ranks of the people."[125] He concluded that this "universal opulence" could best be achieved by removing all artificial and arbitrary impediments to the further division of labor. Thus, he opposed those economic controls that he saw as contrary to human nature. He argued that "[a]ll systems either of preference or of restraint" should be "completely taken away."[126]

Smith maintained that, logically, this should include the elimination of all tariffs and other artificial barriers to international trade. For, logically, the greater the extent of the market, the greater the gains to be made from a further division of labor. On international trade, he

---

[120] Id. at 5.
[121] Id. at 4.
[122] Id. at 5.
[123] Id.
[124] Id.
[125] Id. at 12.
[126] Id. at 745.

reasoned, "The taylor does not attempt to make his own shoes, but buys them of the shoemaker. The shoemaker does not attempt to make his own clothes, but employs a taylor. The farmer attempts to make neither one nor the other, but employs those different artificers.... If a foreign country can supply us with a commodity cheaper than we ourselves can make it, better buy it of them with some part of the produce of our own industry, employed in a way in which we have some advantage."[127] He added, "The general industry of the country, being always in proportion to the capital which employs it, will not thereby be diminished... but only left to find out the way in which it can be employed with the greatest advantage. It is certainly not employed to the greatest advantage, when it is thus directed towards an object which it can buy cheaper than it can make."[128]

Thus, Smith was what we would call today a "free trader." In his day, he called his approach to international trade and to the rest of political economy the "simple system of natural liberty."[129] One of his most perceptive contemporary followers, the American historian of European thought Jerry Muller, has summarized this approach as follows: "Smith's basic model of the links between human propensities and the wealth of nations is... *self-interest leads to market exchange, leading to the greater division of labor, leading in turn to specialization, expertise, dexterity, and invention, and, as a result, to greater wealth.*"[130]

Like the WTO, Smith, too, is often misunderstood. And he is often misunderstood the most by some of his would-be followers. Contrary to what some in "chambers of commerce" and in "think tanks" bankrolled by the generous corporate benefactors of the Republican Party have sometimes suggested, Smith did not advocate a policy of *laissez-faire* in which government would not interfere at all in the "natural" working of the marketplace. Far from it. Smith believed that government has a vital role to play in *supporting* the "natural" working of the market. He thought the "invisible hand" of the marketplace would work best only if the "visible hand" of government was used in the right way.

---

[127] Id. at 485–486.
[128] Id.
[129] Id. at 745.
[130] Jerry Z. Muller, The Mind and the Market: Capitalism in Modern European Thought (New York: Alfred A, Knopf, 2002), 61 [hereinafter The Mind and the Market] (emphasis added).

Literally hundreds of the more than one thousand pages of The Wealth of Nations deal with the indispensability of the state to the functioning of a commercial society. Smith insisted that "liberty, reason, and the happiness of mankind... can flourish only where civil government is able to protect them."[131] In particular, Smith saw government as having "three duties" to society in his system of "natural liberty": providing for domestic security and national defense; protecting individual members of society against "injustice or oppression" by other members; and "erecting and maintaining certain public works and public institutions" that individuals need and yet cannot provide for themselves.[132]

Foremost among these necessary institutions, in his view, are those relating to education. Smith advocated the establishment of local schools to provide a universal system of public education for the "children of the common people."[133] He saw such a universal system of education as essential to the proper working of the marketplace, but he also saw it as a good in itself. He shared the Enlightenment belief in education as a means of "enlightenment." He shared the humanist belief that education can make us more fully human. He saw education as a means to a freer and more open political society.[134] Smith believed that society could be brought together through education. He did not see education as merely job training. He saw education also as a way of learning how to be free.

Moreover, because he had no illusions about human nature, Smith had no illusions about the potentially harmful effects of the working of human nature in the marketplace. He was as suspicious of the predatory tendencies of "greedy capitalists" as any contemporary populist. "People of the same trade," Smith said, "seldom meet together, even for merriment and diversion, but the conversation ends in a conspiracy against the public, or in some contrivance to raise prices."[135] It is in their nature. Thus, Smith was suspicious of what people in business would do if left entirely alone to their own devices, and, in particular, he was apprehensive of the potential predations of economic monopolies. He saw economic monopolies as resulting from artificial preferences and controls, and thus

---

[131] Smith, The Wealth of Nations, at 862. For an excellent discussion of how "the crucial significance of the state" in Smith's thinking "is often overlooked," *see* Muller, The Mind and the Market, supra, at 76-78.

[132] Id. at 745.

[133] Id. at 843.

[134] *See* Emma Rothschild, Economic Sentiments, 96-100, 112-113.

[135] Smith, The Wealth of Nations, at 148.

as contrary to nature.[136]   From this derives our contemporary notion of curbing monopolies and other combinations in restraint of trade through "antitrust" and other competition policies.

Yet, despite all of these reservations, Smith believed, generally, that "[e]very man, as long as he does not violate the laws of justice," should be "left perfectly free to pursue his own interest his own way, and to bring both his industry and capital into competition with those of any other man, or order of men."[137]   He believed in individual economic freedom as an essential part of a larger human freedom, and he was confident that the division of labor that he saw as natural for humanity would lead to a better life, not only for pinmakers, but for everyone.

Smith's Division

There have always been —and no doubt always will be —critics of Smith's "simple system of natural liberty." Many of these criticisms arise from some of the consequences of the specialization resulting from the division of labor that is central to Smith's "simple system." The fundamental question about the division of labor is this. Does the division of labor maximize human welfare by maximizing "the wealth of nations," or does it, instead, only multiply all the many manifestations of human misery in the world?

One of the most eloquent of the many critics of the division of labor was Emerson's friend and protégé, the American essayist and early environmentalist Henry David Thoreau.   Thoreau worried about the possible consequences for the human economy and for the human spirit of too much specialization.   He asked, from his refuge at Walden Pond, "Where is this division of labor to end?   And what object does it finally serve?   No doubt another may also think for me; but it is not therefore desirable that he should do so to the exclusion of my thinking for myself."[138]

This is well said, to be sure.   Thoreau, like Emerson, is one of my favorite writers.   Few can match the eloquence or the visionary insight of Thoreau.   Certainly he was right in asserting that we all must think for

---

[136] Id. at 485, 488, 501-502.
[137] Id. at 745.
[138] Henry David Thoreau, in "Economy," in Walden, in Henry David Thoreau, Walden and Civil Disobedience (New York: Penguin Books, 1983), 89 [1854].

ourselves. Yet, as I picture Thoreau writing so eloquently beneath the leafy shade of a sheltering tree in the pristine solitude beside Walden Pond, I recall a visit my wife, Rebecca, and I made some years ago to the New York Public Library. There, we saw a special exhibit about Thoreau. Among the items in the exhibit was a plain wooden pencil. It was not just a pencil that had been *owned* by Thoreau. It was also a pencil that had been *made* by Thoreau.

The exhibit explained that Thoreau's father had owned a company that made pencils in their hometown of Concord, Massachusetts. Thoreau's father had urged his son to make a career of laboring, not at writing, but at the more stable and more secure profession of making pencils in the family's pencil business. Like so many sons, Henry David Thoreau had rejected his father's advice. He preferred to play his flute, wander in the woods, gaze at the stars, and write essays at Walden Pond. He preferred writing all the timeless words that we still read today.

I wondered then, and I wonder now: what would have happened if Thoreau had taken his father's advice? What would have happened if he had ignored the call of his own uniquely individual faculties of reason and refrained from "specializing" in the labor of writing? What would have happened if Thoreau had devoted all his time and all his faculties to making *all* his pencils? Would we then have the benefit all these years later of all of Thoreau's undeniable eloquence and insight?

Adam Smith would have given Thoreau advice that differed from the advice Thoreau was given by his father. Smith knew that, "without the propensity to trade, barter, and exchange" that leads to the division of labor, "every man must have procured to himself every necessary and conveniency of life which he wanted."[139] In short, without the division of labor, we would *all* have to make *all* our own pencils. It is because of the division of labor that we need not do so.

The division of labor did not begin with Smith's pin factory. There is some evidence of a primitive division of labor in prehistoric times, and some aboriginal hunter-gatherers even today still show signs also of a division of labor.[140] Some scientists go so far as to speculate that a division of labor can result from the natural selection of evolution, for "[r]epeatedly

---

[139] Smith, The Wealth of Nations, at 17.
[140] Matt Ridley, The Origin of Virtue: Human Instincts and the Evolution of Cooperation (New York: Viking, 1997), 47 [1996].

in the history of life, replicators have teamed up, specialized to divide the labor, and coordinated their behavior."[141]

Nor was Smith the first to notice that there is an advantage to a division of labor. Perhaps the first to do so with anything approaching clarity was an eighteenth-century English gadfly of Dutch origin named Bernard Mandeville, who published a pamphlet entitled The Fable of the Bees, or Private Vices, Public Benefits in 1723 —half a century before Smith's publication of The Wealth of Nations, Mandeville surmised in his fable that "public benefits" could result from the "private vices" of self-interest.[142] He saw this as a consequence of men "learning to divide and subdivide their labor."[143] Shocked by his novel conclusion, the good people of London censured Mandeville's pamphlet as a "public nuisance."[144]

Despite this censure, Mandeville's revelation of the potential benefits of the "vice" of self-interest was not forgotten. A few years later, in 1733, in his "philosophical letters" on England, the youthful French *philosophe* Voltaire likewise defended self-interest. "It is as impossible," he wrote, "for a society to be formed and be durable without self-interest as it would be to produce children without carnal desire or to think of eating without appetite, etc. It is love of self that encourages love of others, it is through our mutual needs that we are useful to the human race. That is the foundation of all commerce, the eternal link between men. Without it not a single art would have been invented, no society of ten people formed. It is this self-love, that every animal has received from nature, which warns us to respect that of others."[145]

Smith made the pilgrimage to meet Voltaire in Geneva, and he kept a bust of his friend Voltaire in his study in Kirkaldy. Smith said of his friend Voltaire, "Reason owes him incalculable obligations."[146] In stressing the significance of the division of labor, Smith was, in a sense, merely elaborating on Voltaire. His stress on the merits of the division of labor was telling in part because of its timing. He published The Wealth

---

[141] Steven Pinker, The Blank Slate: The Modern Denial of Human Nature (New York: Viking, 2002), 167.
[142] Mandeville is discussed in Muller, The Mind and the Market, at 18.
[143] Mandeville is quoted in Smith, The Wealth of Nations, at 3, footnote 1.
[144] The censure of Mandeville by London is described in Strathern, Dr. Strangelove's Game, at 76.
[145] Voltaire, Letter 25, Letters on England (London: Penguin Books, 1980), 120, 128 [1733].
[146] Smith is quoted in Strathern, Dr. Strangelove's Game, at 98.

of Nations when the Industrial Revolution was beginning the historic transformation of Great Britain that in many ways heralded the arrival of the modern economic world. The Industrial Revolution multiplied the potential of the division of labor. It also magnified its potentially harmful consequences. The same division of labor that promised to make men far more productive also threatened to break men up into brittle parts.

Smith was not unmindful of these consequences. Few descriptions of the potentially deleterious effects of the division of labor are more compelling than the worried words of Adam Smith. He was aware of the potential human costs of an ever-increasing division of labor, and he described them "bluntly and harshly" —perhaps more so than anyone else since.[147] Smith foresaw the numbing, deadening, dehumanizing effects of the assembly line when "the progress of the division of labour" would confine the work of specialized laborers "to a few simple operations, frequently to one or two."[148] Given such rote, repetitive work, Smith said, a worker "naturally loses" the habit of inventive mental exertion "and generally becomes as stupid and ignorant as it is possible for a human creature to become."[149] Further, "the torpor of his mind renders him not only incapable of relishing or bearing a part in any rational conversation, but of conceiving any generous, noble, or tender sentiment, and consequently of forming any just judgment concerning many even of the ordinary duties of private life."[150] In such circumstances, a "drowsy stupidity...seems to benumb the understanding...."[151]

Smith saw this sad fate as one into which "the labouring poor... must necessarily fall" in every improved and civilized society" unless — unless —"*government takes some pains to prevent it.*"[152] The "pains" that Smith envisaged for government were not those that would curtail his "simple system of natural liberty." Smith saw no alternative to an ever-increasing division of labor as the best and the only way to an ever-increasing human wealth. Rather, the antidote he saw to the potentially dehumanizing effects of the division of labor was education. The "pains"

---

[147] The phrase "bluntly and harshly" is from Charles L. Griswold, Jr., <u>Adam Smith and the Virtues of Enlightenment</u> (Cambridge University Press, 1999), 17.
[148] Smith, <u>The Wealth of Nations</u>, at 839.
[149] Id. at 840.
[150] Id.
[151] Id.
[152] Id. (emphasis added).

he sought from government primarily were those that would educate the "common people" so that they might overcome those dehumanizing effects.[153] Smith saw education as the remedy that would renew the human spirit and re-forge the human bonds that were severed by the division of labor.

The line is long historically of those who have shared Smith's reservations about the division of labor without sharing his optimism that, through education —and through other "pains" by government — the harmful effects of the division of labor can be overcome. Writing some years before Smith, the romantic Rousseau trumpeted in his "discourse on inequality" the rustic self-sufficiency he saw in man's "state of nature" as the ideal —and the very opposite —of a division of labor. According to Rousseau, life was "free, healthy, good and happy" for "so long as [men] applied themselves only to work that one person could accomplish alone and to arts that did not recognize the collaboration of several hands"; however, he insisted, "equality disappeared" and "slavery and misery" flourished "from the instant one man needed the help of another."[154] For Rousseau, in contrast to Smith and Voltaire, "the bonds of servitude are formed only through the mutual dependence of men and the reciprocal needs that unite them."[155] (After reading this, Voltaire wrote in the margin of his copy of Rousseau's discourse: "What, can you not see that mutual needs have done it all?")[156]

Many others through all the years since have followed Rousseau in denouncing the division of labor. That consummate craftsman, William Blake, lamented an industrialism that threatened to "turn that which is Soul & Life into a Mill or Machine."[157] The romantic German poet Friedrich Schiller feared that the division of labor left man "a fragment... nothing more than the imprint of his occupation, of his specialized knowledge."[158] Another, later romantic, John Ruskin, argued that, with the invention of the division of labor, "It is not, truly speaking, the labour

---

[153] For a provocative discussion of Smith's concerns about the division of labor, *see* Griswold, Adam Smith and the Virtues of Enlightenment, at 17-18, 292-201; and Emma Rothschild, Economic Sentiments, at 225.

[154] Jean-Jacques Rousseau, A Discourse on Inequality (London: Penguin Books, 1984), 116 [1755].

[155] Id. at 106. For a thoughtful discussion of this issue, *see* Michael Ignatieff, The Needs of Strangers (New York: Picador, 2001), 110-120 [1984].

[156] Voltaire is quoted in Id. at 180, n. 35.

[157] Peter Ackroyd, Blake: A Biography (New York: Random House, 1995), 294.

[158] Schiller is quoted in Muller, The Mind and the Market, at 334.

that is divided; but the men: —Divided into mere segments of men — broken into small fragments and crumbs of life."[159]

Emerson, like Thoreau, voiced serious reservations about the consequences of the division of labor. In an unfinished essay, entitled "Therienism," Emerson wrote, "Society pays heavily for the economy it derives from the division of labor. Compare the Indian with his plentitude of power and his courage and cheer, and equality to all his duties, with the emaciated broken-hearted pin or stocking-maker, more helpless the further the division is carried."[160] In the sanctuary of his book-lined study in Concord, Emerson, too, seemed, in this passage, to prefer the world of the noble savage to that of the efficient worker in Smith's pin factory.

But no one has been more memorable in denouncing the division of labor than Karl Marx. Throughout his life —and especially in his youth —Marx was adamant in his denunciation of the division of labor. Marx and his lifelong collaborator, Friedrich Engels, described their views memorably in The Communist Manifesto of 1848. They explained there how, "[o]wing to the extensive use of machinery and to division of labour," the worker "becomes an appendage to the machine...."[161] The worker, they said, is "enslaved by the machine."[162] Unlike Smith, as a remedy, Marx proposed, neither education nor other "pains" of government, but, rather, "abolishing the division of labour."[163]

The division of labor must be abolished, Marx believed, because the division of labor leads to what Marx and Marxists call "alienation." It leads to an estrangement of the worker from his work and from the product of his work. With the division of labor, as Marx put it, "man's own deed becomes an alien power opposed to him, which enslaves him instead of being controlled by him."[164] With the advent of communism, he predicted, the division of labor would be abolished, and workers would no longer

---

[159] John Ruskin, from The Stones of Venice, is quoted in Wolfgang Kemp, The Desire of My Eyes: The Life and Work of John Ruskin (New York: Farrar, Straus and Giroux, 1990), 228 [1983].

[160] On "Thierenism," Emerson is quoted in Robert D. Richardson, Jr., Emerson: The Mind on Fire, at 471.

[161] Karl Marx and Friedrich Engels, The Communist Manifesto (London: Penguin Books, 1967), 87 [1848].

[162] Id. at 88.

[163] Karl Marx, The German Ideology (Amherst, New York: Prometheus Books, 1998), 86 [1845].

[164] Id. at 53.

be limited to one specialized occupation. Instead, "in communist society, where nobody has one exclusive sphere of activity but each can become accomplished in any branch he wishes, society regulates the general production and thus makes it possible for me to do one thing today and another tomorrow, to hunt in the morning, fish in the afternoon, rear cattle in the evening, criticize after dinner, as the spirit moves me, without ever becoming a hunter, fisherman, cowherd, or critic."[165]

This lyrical passage is virtually all that Marx ever said about what life would be like under communism. This vision of an end to the division of labor was central to communism and to many other utopian dreams that emerged in the nineteenth century in response to the grim growing pains of industrial capitalism in Europe. Some even seemed to exceed the extremism of Marx in the ardor of their opposition to the division of labor. The French socialist Fourier, for example, "saw human nature as based on the *papillonne* or principle of variety, and to cater for this each man should take many jobs, not merely in his life but in each day."[166] The historian of France, Alfred Cobban, observed, "Fourier, like nearly all the socialist or utopian writers of the period, was not as mad as he sounds, but he was planning for a pre-industrial world."[167]

So too are many of the most prominent exponents of "anti-globalism" today. For example, John Gray, the Professor of European Thought at the London School of Economics, maintains that "the move from hunter-gathering to farming brought no overall gain in human well-being or freedom. It enabled larger numbers to live poorer lives. Almost certainly, Paleolithic humanity was better off."[168] This, of course, is nonsense. The discovery of agriculture ten thousand years ago was the real dawn of human civilization. Does Gray wish to relinquish his academic tenure and return to hunting and gathering? I doubt it. But Rousseau would agree with Gray. And so would many others today who oppose an increasingly international division of labor by trumpeting the cause of "anti-globalism."

The differences between Smith and Marx in responding to the division of labor remain at the heart of the debate over "globalization" that is at the heart of the global economic debate in the world today. Both

---

[165] Id.
[166] Alfred Cobban, A History of Modern France: Volume 2: 1799-1871 (London: Penguin Books, 1991), 120 [1961].
[167] Id.
[168] John Gray, Straw Dogs, supra, at 156.

Smith and Marx have long since left us. All the same, their different ideas about economics remain very much with us. And it is vital to understand their ideas if we hope to understand what the division of labor means today for world trade and for the overall world economy. In particular, it is vital to understand why Smith and Marx reached such different conclusions about the division of labor.

Smith saw, in the ever-widening spread of the specialization caused by the division of labor, the prospect of deliverance from feudal dependency and the possibility of human liberation. He was mindful of the potentially negative human consequences of the narrowing of human tasks that arise inevitably from specialization. But he concluded that those negative consequences could be offset by the redeeming results of universal public education. In contrast, Marx saw, in the division of labor, only "alienation." He saw, in the division of labor, the severing of human identity from human work, and the subjection of human fate to the inhuman demands of commercial profit. He concluded that the division of labor would, therefore, lead inevitably to exploitation in the marketplace.

One reason why these two thinkers reached such different conclusions may be the different ways in which they saw the *act* of free commercial exchange. Marx saw exchange as a form of conflict; Smith saw exchange as a form of cooperation.[169] Marx thought in terms of an independence that he saw as threatened by interdependence; Smith thought in terms of an interdependence that he saw as the only way to a truly liberating independence. Marx thought the division of labor only broke men into pieces; Smith thought that the division of labor, for all its fragmentation of men, could, nevertheless, help make men whole.

Another reason why they reached different conclusions may be the different ways in which they saw the *results* of human exchange. In the contemporary idiom of game theory, Marx saw exchange —Marx saw *trade* —as a "zero-sum game." For him, in every exchange, there is a "winner," and there is a "loser." Unlike Marx, Smith saw that not all games are "zero-sum." He realized that sometimes both sides win, and that sometimes both sides lose.[170] Smith saw exchange —Smith saw *trade*

---

[169] This same point is made by Charles L. Griswold, Jr. in <u>Adam Smith and the Virtues of Enlightenment</u>, 298 at note 68, and, as Griswold notes, has also been made by others he cites there.

[170] This analogy to game theory is from Ridley, <u>The Origins of Virtue</u>, at 46.

—as a "win-win" game. He saw trade as a way to make men whole by making the whole for all men greater than the sum of their individual parts —no matter how potentially fragmented those parts might be because of the division of labor.

Still another reason why they reached different conclusions was the difference between how Smith and Marx saw the individual, and how they saw the possibilities for the liberation of the mind and the life of the individual as part of an increasingly commercial society in an increasingly modern world. Smith saw society from the point of view of the individual. Marx saw individuals from the point of view of society. Smith's "simple system" was founded and focused on the emancipation of the individual. He never lost sight of the primacy of the individual. In contrast, Marx's system ultimately subordinated individual freedom to the fashioning of what he hoped would be a perfect society.

Marx forgot what Smith always remembered. Marx was what Smith would have called a "man of system," and Marx forgot —if he ever knew —what Smith wrote about the "man of system" in one of the best passages of his *other* classic masterpiece of thought, The Theory of Moral Sentiments. Smith said, of the "man of system," that he "is apt to be wise in his own conceit, and is often so enamoured with the supposed beauty of his own ideal plan of government, that he cannot suffer the smallest deviation from any part of it," and that, as a result, "he seems to imagine that he can arrange the different members of a great society with as much ease as the hand arranges the different pieces upon a chess-board. He does not consider that... in the great chess-board of human society, every single piece has a principle of motion of its own...."[171]

For me, this evokes pleasant memories of the *Parc des Bastions* in Geneva, where giant chessboards are laid out on the ground beneath the chestnut trees and where giant, life-size chess-pieces are provided for the players. One summer evening in the park, Rebecca and I played a game of chess. Two of the life-size chess-pieces were missing. So Joe became one chess-piece, and Jamey another. Our two children were supposed to move only when Rebecca and I moved them, but we found, not surprisingly, that, as human chess-pieces, they each had a motion of their own.

---

[171] Adam Smith, The Theory of Moral Sentiments, at 342-343, *see* Rothschild, Economic Sentiments, at 49.

This is also how it is in life. In the great "chess-board of human society," what it comes down to is this. Do you believe free individuals are capable of moving on their own? Do you believe they are capable of making the right choices that will ensure their emancipation and will secure their liberation through the enjoyment of the full measure of human freedom? Do you believe they are capable of *being free*?

Smith said "Yes." Smith believed that every man must be permitted "to pursue his own interest his own way, upon the liberal plan of equality, liberty and justice."[172] Smith believed that free individuals are capable of making the right choices that will enable them to overcome the potentially harmful effects of the division of labor as well as all the other hurdles to the full enjoyment of human freedom in a free, open, commercial society.

Marx, though, said "No." Marx believed that individuals —as individuals —cannot be trusted to make the right choices. He believed that the right choices will be made only if individuals submerge their individuality and submit their individual will to the collective will of a collective society. Thus, Marx was the one who was the slave to a soulless abstraction. So, too, are all those who still follow Marx today —whether consciously or not.

All of the differences between Smith and Marx that gave rise to their different conclusions about the division of labor can perhaps be traced to the most important difference between Smith and Marx: how they viewed human nature. What was the answer of Adam Smith to the threat of human fragmentation posed by the division of labor? Education. And what was the answer of Karl Marx? Abolish the division of labor. Smith's answer is based on his acceptance of the reality of human nature —and on his hopes for appealing to the best within human nature. Marx's answer is founded on the "fantasy" of achieving an unreal —and unrealizable — utopia in which human nature will somehow be changed.[173]

---

[172] Smith, The Wealth of Nations, at 719.

[173] The word "fantasy" comes from Professor Muller in his description of Max Weber's similar view of the Marxist opposition to a division of labor. According to Weber, "Limitation to specialized work, with a renunciation of the Faustian universality of man which it involves, is a condition of any valuable work in the modern world." Weber is quoted in Muller, The Mind and the Market, at 241.

Marx labeled his answer as "scientific."[174] The truth is, it is anything but "scientific." While his children starved in a garret in London for the sake of his single-minded commitment to "scientific socialism," Marx struggled, day after long day, and year after long year, in the cavernous Reading Room of the British Museum, to prove that human nature can be changed. It cannot. The division of labor is a result of our unchanging nature. It is based on the reality of who and what we are. The conclusion of the world's leading scientific authority on societies of ants, Edward O. Wilson, on the merits of Marx's theory of communism as a way of organizing a society of people, is absolutely correct: "Wonderful theory. Wrong species."[175]

All of which brings us back to Thoreau and to his pencil. If Marx had his way, the division of labor would be abolished, and, if he wanted to write, Thoreau would have to make his own pencil. But, with Smith's way, the division of labor continues, and Thoreau is free, if he chooses, to write beside Walden Pond with a pencil made by someone else. With Marx's way, Thoreau has no choice. With Smith's way, he has a choice, and the choice is his to make. The way of Karl Marx would require us to change human nature. The way of Adam Smith takes human nature as it is, and thus enables more of us both to write *and* to have pencils.

The Gains from Trade

I prefer Smith's way.

I share Smith's confidence that individuals can make the right choices about the division of labor and about every other aspect of their economic well-being. It has been said, and, I think, said correctly, that the division of labor "is the key to human social organization."[176] Locally, nationally, internationally, the market is but the manifestation of the division of labor. And, whatever the limitations of the market may be, it is, I submit, fair to say, as the late American journalist and thinker Walter Lippmann, once said, that "[t]he first principle of liberalism... is that the

---

[174] A good summary of the supposedly "scientific" nature of Marxism is found in Peter Singer, Marx: A Very Short Introduction (Oxford: Oxford University Press, 1996) 47-58 [1980].

[175] Wilson is quoted in J. Getlin, "Natural Wonder: At heart, Edward Wilson's an ant man," Los Angeles Times (October 21, 1994), E-l; and in Pinker, The Blank Slate, at 296.

[176] This point about the division of labor is made in Richard Leakey and Roger Lewin, Origins: The Emergence and Evolution of Our Species and Its Possible Future (New York: E. P. Dutton, 1977), 222.

market must be preserved and perfected as the prime regulation of the division of labor."[177]

At the heart of Smith's insight into the need for a division of labor is an even more fundamental economic insight. The economists who have followed him in the more than two centuries since he published The Wealth of Nations refer to this insight as "opportunity cost." The basic reason why we engage in trade is explained by the concept of "opportunity cost." There are inevitable trade-offs in economic decision-making. Time spent in making a pencil is time not spent in writing an essay. Time is limited. Opportunities for employing time are, therefore, also limited. A decision to do one thing is likewise a decision not to do another. A decision to do one thing rather than another that could be done more efficiently, and thus more productively, will, therefore, have a cost —an "opportunity cost." Smith's revolutionary insight is that an opportunity cost is an opportunity lost.

The classical liberal economics of Adam Smith that is founded on this revolutionary insight sees the specialization that arises from the division and subdivision of labor as minimizing "opportunity cost" and thereby maximizing productivity in ways that enhance wealth — individually, nationally, and internationally. This helps explain why Smith entitled his classic economic treatise, in its entirety, An Inquiry into the Nature and Causes of the *Wealth* of Nations. And one very important way in which we can maximize the wealth of nations by maximizing productivity is by maximizing the gains from international trade.

Some will always prefer to "protect" local producers from the "threat" of "foreign" competition by raising tariff and non-tariff barriers to trade. They prefer the autarky of such "protectionism" to the gains from trade. And they tend always to wrap their rhetoric in the righteousness of their local flag. Monsieur Dambreuse, an aristocratic politician and financier, proclaimed to Frederic Moreau in Gustave Flaubert's A Sentimental Education, "As for me, I'm an out-and-out protectionist! Our country first and foremost!"[178] Protectionists always proclaim their protectionism in this way. But theirs is one of those business conspiracies that Smith feared. Theirs is an alliance of the privileged few

---

[177] This linkage of liberalism and the division of labor is from Walter Lippmann, Inquiry into the Principles of the Good Society (New York: Little, Brown and Company, 1937), 174.
[178] Gustave Flaubert, A Sentimental Education: The Story of a Young Man (Oxford: World's Classics, 1989), 207 [1860].

against the many at home and abroad who stand to benefit from the many gains from trade. A "creeping protectionism"[179] will only keep us from reaping the benefits of the "universal opulence" envisaged by Adam Smith.

As I see it, Smith's search for a "universal opulence" that can improve the lives of people everywhere in the world is very much the same as the shared mission of the Members of the WTO. This can be seen in the words of the WTO treaty. In the very first words of the Marrakesh Agreement of 1994 that established the World Trade Organization, the founding Members of the WTO recognized "that their relations in the field of trade and economic endeavor should be conducted with a view to raising standards of living, ensuring full employment and a large and steadily growing volume of real income and effective demand and expanding the production of trade in goods and services, while allowing for the optimal use of the world's resources in accordance with the objective of sustainable development, seeking both to protect and preserve the environment and to enhance the means for doing so in a manner consistent with their respective needs and concerns at different levels of economic development."[180]

Reading this lengthy passage aloud leaves me, for one, a bit breathless. These are ambitious words, to be sure. They are also, admittedly, words of aspiration. These words make no mention of the difficult decisions that must, inevitably, be made and the hard lines that must, inevitably, be drawn in fulfilling such lofty aspirations. Many of these difficult decisions will be made, and many of these hard lines will be drawn, by the Members of the WTO in future trade negotiations. Undoubtedly, too, the Members of the WTO will continue to make many of these decisions, and will continue to draw many of these lines, in WTO dispute settlement.

To me, clearly, "the optimal use of the world's resources in accordance with the objective of sustainable development" sought by the Members of the WTO is very much the same as the "universal opulence" for all that was envisioned by Adam Smith through reliance on his "simple system of natural liberty." Clearly, too, this "universal opulence" for all is sought by the WTO through an ever-widening and ever-deepening

---

[179] The phrase "creeping protectionism" is that of Federal Reserve Chairman Alan Greenspan in a speech to a monetary conference in Washington, D. C., on November 20, 2003.
[180] Preamble, the Marrakesh Agreement.

international division of labor. This international division of labor is emerging from what the Members of the WTO described in their Marrakesh Declaration as a "world trading system, based upon open, market oriented policies and the commitments set out in the Uruguay Round Agreements and Decisions."[181] It is emerging also from their common hope for "a new era of global cooperation, reflecting the widespread desire to operate in a fairer and more open multilateral trading system for the benefit and welfare of their peoples...."[182] The shared belief expressed by the Members of the WTO in that Declaration is "that the trade liberalization and strengthened rules achieved in the Uruguay Round will lead to a progressively more open world trading environment."[183]

Broadly speaking, the Members of the WTO seek what the economists call the "gains from trade." The "gains from trade" result from the division of labor, and the "gains from trade" internationally result from an *international* division of labor. Paul Samuelson, the Nobel Prize-winning economist whose basic treatise on economics has instructed many an undergraduate, wrote that "there is essentially only one argument for free trade or freer trade, but it is an exceedingly powerful one, namely: Free trade promotes a mutually profitable division of labor, greatly enhances the potential real national product of all nations, and makes possible higher standards of living all over the globe."[184]

Trade leads, obviously, to *direct* gains that arise from the specialization that results from the division of labor. The direct gains from trade include economies of scale, lower production costs, lower consumer prices, broader consumer choices, broader producer choices, and bigger potential markets. All this results in higher income. The many efficiencies resulting from specialization and trade result in a "higher real income" that "translates into an ability to afford more of all goods and services than would be possible without trade."[185]

These direct "gains from trade" that are sought by the Members of the WTO are not new goals for the nations of the world. They have been the goals of many in this world for even longer than there have been

---

[181] Marrakesh Declaration of 15 April 1994.
[182] Id.
[183] Id.
[184] Paul Samuelson, Economics, 11th ed. (New York: McGraw Hill, 1980), 651.
[185] Douglas A. Irwin, Free Trade Under Fire (Princeton: Princeton University Press, 2002), 30.

nations. As Thucydides tells it, these gains were among the goals of the ancient Greek city-state of Athens. He recalls Pericles as saying, of Athens, in his famous funeral oration, that "the greatness of our city brings it about that all the good things from all over the world flow into us, so that to us it seems just as natural to enjoy foreign goods as our own local products."[186] Nations today still long to be Athens.

Trade leads also to *indirect* gains. Trade serves initiative and inspires incentive. Trade leads to more, and more intensified, competition that makes domestic producers more efficient. Trade furthers the transfer of technology, and the transfer also of technical and managerial know-how. Trade inspires the research and development of new technologies. Trade stimulates a continuous flow of innovations of all kinds. Trade, in short, improves overall economic performance by promoting the growth of human productivity.[187]

One contemporary economist has summarized these direct and indirect "gains from trade" as follows: "Trade allows countries to specialize in the products they have the greatest advantage in producing. Specialization encourages learning and innovation about those products and allows nations to take advantage of economies of scale. When countries specialize and trade, the world's productive resources of labor, physical resources, and time are used more efficiently. Trade allows consumers and businesses to seek out the best deal in a global market, giving producers an incentive to compete in the market."[188]

Generally speaking, these direct and indirect "gains from trade" result in more jobs and better-paying jobs by making workers and businesses more productive and, thus, more competitive in the international division of labor. Supporters of the "protection" afforded by import restrictions often argue that trade costs jobs, and, yes, some jobs are lost because of trade. But more jobs are lost when we do not trade. Import restrictions reduce the number of jobs in the industries that produce exports —which often pay more and last longer than jobs in industries that do not export. Import restrictions also reduce the number of jobs in industries that sell imports and the number of jobs in industries that use imports as components of their own products. Most of all, import restrictions lead to lost jobs from the lost opportunities that would

---

[186] Thucydides, History of the Peloponnesian War, at 146.
[187] Irwin, Free Trade Under Fire, at 35-39.
[188] Timothy Taylor, "The Truth about Globalization," The Public Interest (Spring 2002), online at www.the publicinterest.com/current/article2,at 3.

otherwise be occasioned by the innovations inspired by competition from imports. Import restrictions and other devices of protectionism "protect" a part of the past at the expense of more and better jobs in a more productive, and thus more competitive, and thus more prosperous, future overall.[189]

There are also *other* important "gains from trade." There are "gains from trade" that are not directly economic in nature. Ever desirous of discerning *non*-economic benefits from political economy, John Stuart Mill claimed that "the economical advantages of commerce are surpassed in importance by those of its effects which are intellectual and moral."[190] He was not specific. But what he may have had in mind, in part, is that trade leads not only to the creation of prosperity. Trade leads also to the promotion of peace and to the dissemination of ideas.

The relationship between trade and peace is sometimes forgotten in the pseudo-combat of international commercial relations. As one of the most eminent of the commentators on the GATT and the WTO, John Jackson, has reminded us, "It is important to remember that the most important policy objective of the post–World War II Bretton Woods institutions and the economic structure it implied was the prevention of war and military strife (overall quite a success story for the political leaders at the end of World War II)."[191] In other words, it is far better to have what the media insist on calling "trade wars" than to have the shooting wars that have resulted from international trade disputes so often in the past.

Some have suggested that the GATT and the WTO have not been successful because international trade disputes have not been *eliminated* by the multilateral trading system. They miss the point. Given our nature, and given our freedom, human conflicts are, to some extent, inevitable. As Popper observed in his autobiography, Unended Quest, "There can be no human society without conflict: such a society would be a society not of friends but of ants."[192] Trade agreements are not intended to *eliminate* trade conflicts but, rather, to help resolve them. They are intended

---

[189] Irwin, Free Trade Under Fire, supra, 75-83.

[190] John Stuart Mill, from Principles of Political Economy, is quoted in Irwin, Free Trade Under Fire, at 29-30.

[191] John H. Jackson, "International Economic Law in Times That Are Interesting," Journal of International Economic Law, Vol. 3, No. 1 (March 2000), i, 10-11.

[192] Karl Popper, Unended Quest: An Intellectual Autobiography (London: Routledge, 1992), 133 [1974].

also to establish a means for resolving conflicts when there is a disagreement over what has previously been agreed.

Accordingly, the aim of the WTO is not to *eliminate* trade disputes. In an international economy, international disputes about trade are inevitable. The aim of the WTO is to *resolve* the inevitable international disputes about trade *peacefully*. The aim is to resolve trade disputes through the legal tedium of the courtroom instead of the lethal tragedy of combat. The aim is to make right into legal might through the international rule of law. And, as Professor Jackson has rightly noted, for more than half a century, first in the GATT and now in the WTO, this aim has been accomplished.

The relationship between trade and peace has long been recognized. Not without reason did the great British free trader Richard Cobden describe trade as "God's diplomacy."[193] Montesquieu wrote, "The natural effect of commerce is to lead to peace."[194] Tocqueville, similarly, described trade as "the natural enemy of all violent passions...."[195] Cobden's French friend and ally, Frederic Bastiat, summed up this hopeful view as follows: "When goods don't cross borders, armies will."[196]

To be sure, we have been chastened a bit by history since these men wrote in the more hopeful days of the eighteenth and the nineteenth centuries. The pointless carnage of the Crimean War diminished the pacific hopes of Cobden and other early idealists as long ago as the 1850s, and countless other conflicts have disappointed the similar hopes of those who have followed them in all the years since. It may be too much to say that trade ensures peace. However, it may be too little to say that it does not. In my view, borders that are crossed by trade are, indeed, borders that are much less likely to be crossed by troops. Trade will not end war, because trade cannot change human nature. But trade can help chain the dogs of war. A headline atop the front page of the *Financial Times* of London read recently: "Maturing Relations: Trade drives Japan and China to establish more stable relationship."[197] Precisely. And this is precisely the point that is often missed.

---

[193] Richard Cobden, in 1857, is quoted in The Economist (December 7, 1996), 21.

[194] Montesquieu, Book 20, Chapter 2, The Spirit of the of Laws [1748].

[195] Alexis de Tocqueville, Democracy in America, Volume II, at 637.

[196] Bastiat is quoted in George Roche, Free Markets, Free Men: Frederic Bastiat, 1801-1850 (Hillsdale, Michigan: Hillsdale College Press, 1993), 31 [1971].

[197] *Financial Times* (April 10, 2002), 1.

Following these earlier thinkers, the contemporary psychologist Steven Pinker makes essentially the same point, and in blunt terms. He says, "There are two ways to get something you want from other people: steal it or trade for it. The first involves the psychology of dominance; the second, the psychology of reciprocal altruism. The goal of a peaceful and prosperous society is to minimize the use of dominance, which leads to violence and waste, and to maximize the use of reciprocity, which leads to gains in trade that make everyone better off."[198]

Trade leads also to the exchange of ideas. This has always been so. In ancient times, for example, the feudalistic Persians despised the entrepreneurial Greeks for their "addiction to trade."[199] They despised them even more for "the free exchange of opinions that went with it."[200] Their failure to comprehend fully the connection between the two helped contribute to the defeat of the mighty, but arrogant, Persian Empire by the upstart Greeks. What the defeated Persians failed to comprehend was that the Greek "addiction to trade" was one and the same as the Greek addiction to freedom. The Greek word for marketplace —*agora* — originally meant "place for assembly." The Greeks made no distinction between the two.[201] Thus, the Greeks equated free markets with free ideas. And so must we.

The Enlightenment philosopher Immanuel Kant asked, "What is money? What is a book?"[202] The answer to both questions is the same. Money is a means of exchange. So is a book. Money facilitates the exchange of goods and services. A book furthers the exchange of ideas. Both money and books are "the universal instruments of exchange."[203] Both serve the universal exchange of thought, and, thus, both serve the cause of human freedom. For freedom of thought is the very essence of freedom. It is the necessary foundation for all human creativity, and, therefore, it is the first freedom. It is the freedom that makes all other freedoms possible. Freer trade leads to freer thought, and freer thought leads to more freedom.

---

[198] Steven Pinker, The Blank Slate: The Modern Denial of Human Nature (New York: Viking Press, 2002), 297.

[199] Peter Green, The Greco-Persian Wars (Berkeley and Los Angeles: University of California Press, 1996), 11.

[200] Id.

[201] Id. at 11-12.

[202] Immanuel Kant, "Illustration of relations of contract by the conceptions of money and a book," in The Philosophy of Law, quoted in Rothschild, Economic Sentiments, at 45.

[203] This insight about books and money is not mine; it is that of Emma Rothschild. *See* Rothschild, Economic Sentiments, at 45, 153.

Ancient Athens is only one of many examples of the connection between free markets and free people. In his letters from England, Voltaire departed once more from the conventional wisdom of his time and portrayed the trading floors of the new London Stock Exchange of the 1730s as "peaceful and free assemblies" where those of all factions and all faiths could meet.[204] Likewise, Hume observed, a few years later, "If we trace commerce in its progress, through Tyre, Athens, Syracuse, Carthage, Venice, Florence, Genoa, Antwerp, Holland, England, etc., we shall always find it to have fixed its seat in free governments."[205]

In all of the years since, we have seen numerous other examples of how free markets go hand in hand with free governments, and with all the other essentials of freedom: in the free market that was created by the Constitution of the United States of America; in the ever-freer "common market" that has become the European Union; and, today, not least, in the growing measure of democratic freedom that has accompanied the growing openness to trade in so many of the developing countries of the world.

In the last two decades of his long life, Voltaire made his home in the small French village of Ferney, just outside of Geneva, and on the border between Switzerland and France. From there, he could easily slip across either border, to escape the vengeance of his various accusers. While there, he continued for what remained of his life to conduct the one-man campaign for freedom that made his name synonymous with the Enlightenment. Today, the village is called, in his honor, "Ferney-Voltaire." It is a suburb of Geneva and a brief bus ride from the WTO.

A statue of Voltaire stands today in the village square. (In my first years at the WTO, when she was younger, Jamey would greet the statue when we arrived in the village by saying, "Bonjour, Monsieur Voltaire.") Every Saturday morning, bright and early, a weekly market assembles around the statue. It is in many ways a traditional French weekend market, with fresh farm vegetables, a vast variety of cheeses, and roasted chickens turning on rotating spits in a booth at Voltaire's feet.

But look around. It is also much more. There are exotic fruits from Africa, rock CD's from America, and colorful carpets from the Middle

---

[204] Voltaire, Letter 6, Letters from England, 40, 41.
[205] David Hume, "Of Civil Liberty," Selected Essays (New York: Oxford University Press, 1993), 49, 52 [1742].

East. The languages, the costumes, the wares of numerous other countries also abound. The Saturday market in Ferney-Voltaire is a global bazaar. And from the statue's pedestal in the square, Voltaire smiles down knowingly on it all. This is the exchange —this is the agora—he had in mind when he came to Ferney a few centuries ago.

Emerson, who enjoyed long walks, would have enjoyed strolling through the market in Ferney-Voltaire on a Saturday morning. Whatever his occasional reservations about the division of labor, he, too, understood the "gains from trade," economic and otherwise. In a speech he gave in Boston, in 1844, entitled "The Young American," Emerson expressed the view that eventually "the historian of the world will see that trade was the principle of liberty, that trade planted America and destroyed Feudalism, that it makes peace and keeps peace, and it will abolish slavery."[206]

In freeing trade through the work of the WTO, we are still, as Emerson predicted, abolishing slavery. We are freeing people. In opening markets to trade, we are opening minds everywhere to the boundless possibilities of living in freedom. For, in exchanging the shackles of the past for the freer choices of the open societies of the future, trade is creating a global "agora."

Ricardo's Insight

Underlying the WTO treaty is the belief that all these "gains of trade" can be maximized by relying on what the economists call "comparative advantage." Between the lines of the treaty is a tacit consensus that the world will work best if we each do what we can each do the best most efficiently, most productively, and most competitively in the world marketplace. The world will work best if we each pursue our "comparative advantage."

The notion of a "comparative advantage" was first advanced early in the nineteenth century by a follower and successor of Adam Smith named David Ricardo. Ricardo was a wealthy British financier who had been disowned in his youth by his Jewish family when he converted to Christianity in order to marry his Quaker wife. He was self-made and self-taught. Ricardo became independently wealthy while still in his

---

[206] Emerson, from "The Young American," is quoted in Richardson, Emerson: The Mind on Fire, at 394.

twenties by making a fortune on the London stock market. He decided to devote his time and his talent thereafter to the study of political economy. Then one day, during a holiday in the British resort of Bath, he happened to read The Wealth of Nations.[207]

The experience transformed his life. And Ricardo transformed forever the intellectual debate about trade with the insight that was sparked by his reading of The Wealth of Nations. Inspired by Smith's discussion of the dynamics of the division of labor, Ricardo went beyond Smith in explaining the virtues of creating an international division of labor through international trade. He proved that *all* of us can profit from international trade. He showed that removing the tariff and other artificial barriers to the free flow of international commerce can inspire an international specialization in keeping with "comparative advantage" that can profit *everyone*.

Ricardo's fundamental insight was that *all* of us can profit from international trade through an international division of labor in which *each* of us does what each of us does *relatively* the best when compared to others. This is true of all individuals. This is true also of all countries. Smith had stressed the value of trade where there is an "absolute advantage" in producing a good or a service by producing it more productively than a potential trading partner. Ricardo took one step more intellectually. He saw that it is not necessary to have an "absolute advantage" to profit from trade. Ricardo's more subtle insight was that, to profit from trade, only a "comparative advantage" is necessary, and further, and more importantly, that, for both individuals and countries, a "comparative advantage" *always exists.*

In The Principles of Political Economy and Taxation, published in 1817, Ricardo demonstrated that individuals and countries alike can profit from trade even if they have *no* absolute advantage in producing *any* good or service. He showed that, even those who are better or who are worse than everyone else at producing everything, will be better off nevertheless if they concentrate on producing what they produce *relatively* the best when compared to their trading partners —and trade for the rest. The issue is not one of *absolute* advantages. It is one of *relative* —that is, *comparative* —advantages and disadvantages in efficient production.

---

[207] On David Ricardo's life, *see* Heilbroner, The Worldly Philosophers, at 82; and Strathern, Dr. Strangelove's Game, 136-138. Surprisingly, despite his historical significance, there does not seem to be a recent full-length biography of Ricardo.

Ricardo explained that, by each specializing in producing what we each produce *relatively* — and thus *comparatively* —the best, when compared to our trading partners, we will each be our most productive, and, thus, we will each be able to afford to obtain through trade the most of all the other things that we might desire and that we might otherwise have produced less efficiently.

Ricardo's insight is almost counter–intuitive. But think about it. To borrow an example that is widely used in Economics 101 (and alter it a bit to suit my own inclinations as a devoted fan of the "Orlando Magic" basketball team): should Tracy McGrady mow his own lawn?[208] No. Of course not. Tracy McGrady should concentrate on playing basketball. He should hire someone else to mow his lawn. He may be better at mowing lawns than anyone he might hire to do the job for him, but he is also doubtless both better —and *relatively* better —than anyone he may hire at playing basketball. He should engage in a division of labor that enables him to specialize by spending his limited time doing what he does *relatively* the best. And so should we all.

At the most basic level, as individuals, we all understand this. That explains why, as individuals, we all seek a division of labor in virtually every single aspect of our daily lives. That explains why we do not all try to make all our own pencils. Or shirts. Or shoes. Or supercomputers. That explains why we pay to watch Tracy McGrady shoot basketballs rather than shooting "three-pointers" ourselves. Counter-intuitive though it may be, we all, at the most basic individual level, realize that, with a division of labor based on "comparative advantage," all of us will, in the short term, *have* more, and all of us will, in the long term, be able to *do* more, *make* more, and *be* more.

The same logic that we apply individually in our daily lives also applies internationally in the world economy. The classic example Ricardo offered of his theory of "comparative advantage" in 1817 did not involve Tracy McGrady. It did not involve shooting basketballs and mowing lawns. As most of us learned in Economics 101, Ricardo's example involved trade in wine and wool between England and Portugal. But the economics are the same even without the "three-pointers."

---

[208] For the definitive statement of this basketball analogy, *see* N. Gregory Mankiw, "Should Michael Jordan Mow His Own Lawn?," in <u>Principles of Economics</u>, 2nd Ed. (The Dryden Press, 1999).

Ricardo foresaw a world in which all would pursue their comparative advantage in an ever-widening, ever-increasing, ever-subdividing division of labor. He explained, "Under a system of perfectly free commerce, each country naturally devotes its capital and labour to such employments as are most beneficial to each. This pursuit of individual advantage is admirably connected with the universal good of the whole. By stimulating industry, by rewarding ingenuity, and by using most efficaciously the peculiar powers bestowed by nature, it distributes labour most effectively and most economically: while, by increasing the general mass of productions, it diffuses general benefit, and binds together, by one common tie of interest and intercourse, the universal society of nations throughout the civilised world."[209]

Following Ricardo, who based his initial conclusions solely on relative labor costs, other economists in the nearly two centuries since have confirmed the validity of Ricardo's theory of comparative advantage where other "factors of production" —such as land and capital —are also concerned. Today, the overwhelming consensus among economists is that, in the absence of artificial barriers to trade, a country will tend to export those goods that are produced with relatively large "inputs" of the country's relatively abundant "factor of production."[210] In other words, if he is free to do so, Tracy McGrady will tend to shoot basketballs.

In recent years, there have been attempts at additional refinements of the notion of comparative advantage. For example, Michael Porter has offered a concept of "competitive advantage" that he saw as an improvement on Ricardo's initial insight.[211] Ricardo's original focus was on those "factors of production" that are *inherited* —such as labor, land, and available capital. In contrast, Porter's focus is on how some advantages can be *created* through the productive use of "knowledge, investment, insight, and innovation."[212] Whatever the label, though, the issue is one of improving overall economic development by realizing,

---

[209] David Ricardo, The Principles of Political Economy and Taxation (New York: Everyman's Library, 1977), 81 [1817].

[210] This theory relating to "factors of production" is the Heckscher-Ohlin theory (commonly "H-O theory"), which was developed in the early twentieth century by Swedish economists Eli Heckscher and Bertil Ohlin. *See* Douglas A. Irwin, Against the Tide: An Intellectual History of Free Trade (Princeton: Princeton University Press, 1996), 177.

[211] Michael E. Porter, The Competitive Advantage of Nations (New York: The Free Press, 1990).

[212] Michael E. Porter, "Attitudes, Values, Beliefs, and the Microeconomics of Prosperity," in Lawrence E. Harrison and Samuel P. Huntington, eds., Culture Matters: How Values Shape Human Progress (New York: Basic Books, 2000), 14, 17.

recognizing, and relying on *relative* advantages in the global marketplace. The issue is one of using and making "comparative advantage."

Five American authors have written a textbook on the "economics of development" that is used in more than 400 colleges and universities worldwide. They all are, or have been, affiliated with Harvard University. They reason, from their analysis of comparative advantage, that "*any* country can engage in and benefit from international trade, including the world's highest cost and lowest producers of any good."[213] They see the "most powerful results" from comparative advantage as follows: Any country can increase its welfare by trading, because the world market provides an opportunity to buy some goods at relatively low prices. In addition, the smaller the country, the greater is this potential gain from trade. Further, a country will gain most by exporting commodities that it produces using its abundant factors of production most intensively, while importing goods whose production requires relatively more of scarcer factors of production.[214]

These economists also point out, however, that, "although every country can gain from trade in the aggregate, *not all individuals or groups within each country necessarily will gain.*"[215] They explain, "Comparative advantage theory tells us that the aggregate gains outweigh the losses for the country as a whole, but that may be cold comfort to ...[t]he losers from trade.... Therein lies the seeds of political opposition to policies that promote freer trade, even though all countries gain from it."[216] There are far more "winners" than "losers" from trade. But this is little consolation if you happen to be numbered among the "losers." Furthermore, the "winners" often "win" very *generally* by, say, benefiting from lower consumer prices, while the "losers" often "lose" very *specifically* —by losing their jobs. Thus, the "winners" do not always realize they have "won" from trade, while the "losers" are inclined to look to trade as the cause of *all* of their "losses."

One journalist for the *New York Times* has summarized the political result as follows: "[O]n the campaign trail, politicians cannot help but be swayed by the fact that people who are harmed by trade expansion have

---

[213] The five Harvard economists are Dwight H. Perkins, Steve Radelet, Donald R. Snodgrass, Malcolm Gillis, and Michael Roemer, in their Economics of Development, 5th Ed. (New York: W. W. Norton and Company, 2001), 622 [hereinafter Economics of Development].
[214] Id.
[215] Id. at 625 (emphasis is in the original).
[216] Id. at 626.

names and faces —and votes —and that the people who benefit often do not even know it."[217] This helps explain why, for example, so many Members of the Congress of the United States voice support for freer trade *in theory* but cast their votes against freer trade *in practice*. This also helps explain why the great British Whig historian of the nineteenth century, Thomas Babington Macaulay, was right —then and now —when he observed, "Free trade, one of the greatest blessings which a government can confer on a people, is in almost every country unpopular."[218]

Popular or not, Paul Samuelson may well have been right when he described Ricardo's insight into comparative advantage as the one proposition in all the social sciences that is both "true" and not "trivial."[219] Some among those who oppose the WTO —no doubt inspired in part by the apparent unpopularity of trade —question the legitimate extent of Ricardo's reach. For example, some say that the contemporary relevancy of Ricardo's theory of comparative advantage is undermined because he ignored the effects of the international ebb and flow of capital.[220] Yet, by far the prevailing view among international economists is that this is not so.[221] Economists —who agree on very little else —almost all agree on both the accuracy and the continuing relevancy of Ricardo's idea of comparative advantage, and also on the potential benefits of comparative advantage for improving the standard of living throughout the world through an international division of labor.

The difficulty in extending Ricardo's reach is largely a *political* and not an *economic* difficulty. Politics among nations is premised on a world of nations. It is premised on a world of political borders. It assumes an independence within political borders. In contrast, economics is premised on a world that takes no account of nations. It is premised on a world bordered only by the extent of the market. It assumes an

---

[217] David E. Rosenbaum, "They Support Free Trade Except in the Case of....", *New York Times* (November 16, 2003), Section 4, Page 3.

[218] Thomas Babington Macaulay, "On Mitford's History of Greece," Essays and Poems (Boston: Dana Estes and Company), Volume 1, 180.

[219] Paul Samuelson, "The Way of an Economist," International Economic Relations: Proceedings of the Third Congress of the International Economic Association (London, 1969) 1-11. Samuelson said, "That it is logically true need not be argued before a mathematician, that it is not trivial is attested by the thousands of important and intelligent men who have never been able to grasp the doctrine after it was explained to them."

[220] *See, e. g.,* John Gray, False Dawn: The Delusions of Global Capitalism (New York: The Free Press, 1998), 82.

[221] Paul Krugman, "Review of False Dawn: The Delusions of Global Capitalism by John Gray," online at www.http://web.mit.edu./krugman/www/gray.html.

interdependence that transcends political borders. The meeting place between the *political* view of the world and the *economic* view of the world is the WTO.

Ricardo's reach is extended through the WTO. The overarching goal of the WTO is to secure the "optimal" and best possible allocation and use of the world's resources, and this goal can only be achieved through the wondrous working of comparative advantage. The WTO treaty is an important step toward a world in which comparative advantage will prevail —a world in which choices will be made in the marketplace for reasons other than slavish adherence to the inefficient ways of the past or cowering obeisance to the arbitrary dictates of political power. It is toward this end that the WTO treaty seeks to establish the rule of law for world trade.

As the Chairman of the Appellate Body, it fell to me some time back to "swear in" the newest of our seven members. One of my new colleagues asked me, jokingly, just before he was sworn in, "Must we swear allegiance to the memory of Adam Smith and David Ricardo?" My answer was "No." The truth is, it was not necessary to do so. For, in many respects, in concluding the WTO treaty, the Members of the WTO have done so already. In creating first the GATT, and now the WTO, the countries and other customs territories that comprise the multilateral trading system have sought "the gains from trade" that were first described by Smith and by Ricardo. In the eight completed "rounds" of multilateral trade negotiations since the creation of the GATT by the United States and a handful of other like-minded and far-sighted countries in the years just after World War II, much has been accomplished toward eliminating needless, artificial barriers to what both Smith and Ricardo would see as the natural flow of international trade and, thus, to the creation of an international division of labor.

Since the creation of the GATT, average tariffs in industrialized countries have been cut from high double-digits to less than four percent.[222] Other tariff and non-tariff barriers to international trade in developed countries and in developing countries alike have been lowered through progressive trade "liberalization." Rules against discriminating in favor of some foreign suppliers over others, rules against discriminating in favor of domestic over foreign suppliers, and other rules against

---

[222] World Trade Organization, The Multilateral Trading System: 50 Years of Achievement (Geneva, 1998), 5 [hereinafter The Multilateral Trading System].

discrimination in international trade have been established and, increasingly, enforced. And, as time has passed, more and more countries have been brought within the framework and within the mutually agreed disciplines of the ruled-based, multilateral trading system.

The overall record of success of this system is beyond dispute. Due, in large part, to the multilateral efforts to build the trading system, global trade has increased 22-*fold* in the half century or so since the creation of the GATT.[223] During that time, this increase in world trade has supported a *six-fold* increase in global GDP.[224] On average, merchandise exports have grown by six percent annually since 1950.[225] WTO figures show that worldwide exports that accounted for only eight percent of worldwide production in 1950 account for more than twenty-six percent of worldwide production today.[226] As world trade continues to grow, this percentage continues to grow as well.

This success has contributed much to unprecedented global prosperity. Thanks in no small part to trade liberalization, millions upon millions of people in every part of the world have been lifted out of poverty. The dynamic growth of world trade has been the engine of the longest and strongest period of sustained economic growth in human history. Humanity has enjoyed unprecedented prosperity in the wake of what President John F. Kennedy, an early and ardent champion of the multilateral trading system, described rightly —and memorably —as "the rising tide of trade."[227]

One study showed that the agreements to lower trade barriers that were concluded in the most recent trade "round," the Uruguay Round, would result in an *annual* gain in GDP of $13 billion for the United States and $96 billion for the world as a whole.[228] As every year passes, those worldwide "gains from trade" are being realized increasingly through the phased implementation of the Uruguay Round trade agreements under the auspices of the WTO.

---

[223] "The WTO in Brief," World Trade Organization, online at wto.org.
[224] The Multilateral Trading System, at 21; *Financial Times* (November 29, 1999).
[225] "The WTO in Brief," supra.
[226] The Multilateral Trading System, at 21; *Financial Times* (November 29, 1999).
[227] John F. Kennedy, Presidential Address in Frankfurt, Germany (June 24, 1963).
[228] Glen W. Harrison, Thomas W. Rutherford, and David G. Tarr, "Quantifying the Uruguay Round," in Will Martin and L. Alan Winters, eds., The Uruguay Round and the Developing Countries (New York: Cambridge University Press, 1996). *See also* Irwin, Free Trade Under Fire, at 31.

The new, ninth round, the "Doha Round," is the "Development Round." The overriding aim of the "Doha Development Round" is to conclude new agreements to secure and maximize the many "gains from trade" in ways that will further "sustainable development" in both developed and developing countries alike.[229] In particular. the aim of this "Development Round" is to make certain that, in relying on comparative advantage, we secure also what the late Bela Balassa called a "ladder" of comparative advantage that all those who still live in poverty in the world will be able to climb toward prosperity.[230] For the considerable challenge confronting us everywhere in the world is that of creating capability, competency, and opportunity, so that many more of us throughout the world can climb up the liberating ladder of comparative advantage.

The WTO exists in part because even many of those who profess to oppose a world with an international division of labor based on "comparative advantage" nevertheless cannot resist its logic. For example, for all his protestations, Henry David Thoreau turned out to be someone who appreciated the compelling logic of Ricardo's insight. For all his rhetorical reservations about the division of labor, even he seemed to understand the ladder of "comparative advantage."

Thoreau preferred the quiet refuge of Walden Pond. He preferred nature to industry, and essays to enterprise. He refused his father's pleas to make a career of making pencils. But, when competition from foreign pencils threatened to drive his father's company out of business, he went back to work at "John Thoreau and Company." In the face of the foreign competition, he showed up and saved the family livelihood by creating a "comparative advantage."

Thoreau spent long hours in the Harvard Library learning the finer points of pencil technology. He developed a new grinding mill, a new pipe-forming machine, and new water wheel designs. He "bought the German clay, [and] contrived machines for cutting the hardened paste and drilling the blocks of wood."[231] He devised all sorts of "process" details. He discovered a new way of mixing graphite and clay to make a

---

[229] *See* the Doha Declaration of the WTO Ministerial Conference, Doha, Qatar (November, 2002).

[230] Bela Balassa is quoted in Jagdish Bhagwati, Free Trade Today (Princeton: Princeton University Press, 2002), 85.

[231] Thoreau's pencil-making is discussed in Van Wyck Brooks, The Flowering of New England, at 425.

superior pencil lead. But, most important of all, he discovered a way of varying the mix so that he could vary the hardness of pencil leads. This discovery saved his father's company by making it the first American company to produce pencils that varied according to their hardness. The Thoreau pencils were numbered from one, *two*, three, and four.

Thus, despite all his reservations about the division of labor, Thoreau knew what we need to do to meet the challenge of world trade. We need to create "comparative advantage." We need to make a better pencil. Make one he did. And, in making a better pencil, in making it possible to produce pencils that vary in hardness, Thoreau not only saved the family business.

He also helped give us the "Number Two" pencil.[232]

Ricardo's Reach

With the launch of the "Doha Development Round," the efforts of the WTO to extend Ricardo's reach continue. They continue in a climate in which there is an increasingly hostile reaction to the "globalization" that has been evidenced by the increasingly international division of labor. In considering, and in confronting, this backlash, it is important to understand that, although the work of the WTO supports an international division of labor, and although the success of the WTO furthers an international division of labor, the WTO *did not invent* the idea of an *international* division of labor.

The idea that specialization might be extended beyond the invisible boundaries of political borders has long been with us. An international division of labor was suggested originally by Plato and Xenophon in ancient Greece, long before Ricardo, long before Smith, and long before Mandeville's Fables of the Bees.[233] The Athenians imported much of their food, and they shipped their red and black pottery throughout the Mediterranean. The Greek vases we so much admire in

---

[232] Thoreau's prowess as an inventor and as a pencil maker is largely ignored by his literary biographers. However, *see* Henry Seidel Canby, Thoreau (Boston: Houghton Mifflin, 1939), 15-16. And, for the details from which my own summary account is drawn, *see* John H. Lienhard, "Thoreau's Pencils," online at www.uh.edu/admin/engines/epi339.htm. The latter includes a photograph of an advertisement for Thoreau's "drawing pencils" that is well worth the look.

[233] For a good summary of early thinking on the division of labor, *see* Douglas A. Irwin, Against the Tide: An Intellectual History of Free Trade, supra, at 12-14.

art museums today were commercial "containers" for a seagoing trade in olive oil and wheat.

Karl Popper maintained that "the Greeks started for us that great revolution which, it seems, is still in its beginning —the transition from the closed to the open society."[234] He saw "the trade of Athens" as the catalyst for this transition.[235] "Perhaps the most powerful cause of the breakdown of the closed society," he said, "was the development of sea-communications and commerce."[236] For Athens, trade flourished, and freedom followed, because, as Popper saw it, "trade, commercial initiative, appears to be one of the few forms in which individual initiative and independence can assert itself, even in a society in which tribalism still prevails."[237]

The trade of the Athenians. The Mediterranean trade of the Phoenicians. The Egyptian shipping along the Nile in Africa. The increasing commerce along the far-flung roads of the Romans. The caravans between Europe and Asia along the great Silk Road. The Arabian dhows. The Portuguese caravels. The Spanish galleons. The German barges on the Rhine. The British ships on so many of the world's seas. The Canadian canoes. The American transcontinental railroad. The hemispheric Pan-American highway. The trans-Atlantic cables. The Pacific clipper ships. The growing trade of India and China and Japan and Southeast Asia and all of the islands of the South Seas.

All these, and more, through the generations have been part of extending Ricardo's reach. All these, and more, through the centuries have inspired an ever-widening reach of international markets that has led as a consequence to the widening and deepening of an increasingly international division of labor. The increasingly global reach of the division of labor as a part of "globalization" today is nothing new. It is only the latest chapter in this long history of an ever-widening marketplace.

Smith saw, in the late eighteenth century, that the extent of the division of labor is limited only "by the extent of the market."[238] But,

---

[234] Popper, The Open Society, Volume I, at 175.
[235] Id. at 177.
[236] Id.
[237] Id.
[238] Smith, The Wealth of Nations, at 19.

even then, he foresaw that the extent of the market could be expanded. He noted, for example, that "by means of water-carriage a more extensive market is opened to every sort of industry," and that the advantage of water-carriage "opens the whole world for the market to the produce of every sort of labour...."[239]

The advantage of "water-carriage" is only one of the many ways in which the modern world makes possible an international division of labor. Today, there is a "global invisible hand,"[240] and, today, Ricardo's reach extends throughout the world. The whole world is opening today to every sort of industry and to every sort of labor, not only by means of water-carriage in giant standardized, containerized, sea-going vessels that are beyond anything that even such visionaries as Smith or Ricardo might have imagined, but also by means of international land transport, international air transport, and international telecommunications that can conclude an international transaction almost instantaneously.

The Internet, the computer, and countless other new technologies have changed the world profoundly. Increasingly, the potential extent of the market for all kinds of goods and services is truly worldwide. If distance has not died, it has certainly diminished. And it has done so with many and varied consequences. Only one of them is the emergence of a global economy, and, with it, the possibility for a truly international division of labor. But, of all the consequences of "globalization," this is surely among the most profound. For the global extent of Ricardo's reach can be revolutionary in helping trade serve the cause of freedom.

The emergence of a global economy is a logical consequence of our reliance on reason. The application of human reason to human life leads us, inevitably, and inexorably, to an unending endeavor to transform the world around us to serve our own ends. This has always been true of our species. Doubtless this will always be true of our species in all that we do. And because we alone of all the species on this planet have the capacity to recall and, therefore, to capitalize on, all the achievements of our predecessors, our cumulative ability to transform the world to serve our ends keeps increasing. We not only know that we are here; we also recall that we were here yesterday, and the day before. This, too, is in our nature.

---

[239] Id. at 20-21.
[240] The phrase "global invisible hand" is that of Michael Ignatieff, in <u>The Needs of Strangers</u> (New York: Picador, 1984), 129.

The source of the capacity for human reason remains a mystery. Scientists do not claim to comprehend human "consciousness." They do not know how human reason works. They do not know how or when human reason began. Anthropologists working in the bleak and forbidding desert of northern Chad recently discovered the skull of the oldest human ancestors found thus far. The skull is thought to be six or seven millions years old.[241] The discovery —a nearly complete skull, two lower jaw fragments, and three teeth —may tell us, in time, whether this ancestor of ours was capable of reason.

Yet, however and whenever it was that we acquired our unique capacity to reason, this much is clear: because we have it, we are inclined to use it. In particular, we are inclined to use it as toolmakers. The anthropologists tell us that it took five million years for our species to learn how to make tools. But since the early humans first learned how to make sharp-edged tools two and one-half million years ago, we have applied our capacity to reason constantly to create ever-newer technologies to serve humanity. This, too, is in our nature.

The earliest human tools were small, sharp, stone flakes made by striking one lava stone against another.[242] Eventually —about ten thousand years ago —we humans invented the first tools —the first technologies —that gave us agriculture, and, thus, gave us the beginnings of a settled and evolving human civilization.[243] Today, the tools of our technologies seem to know no bounds. Our tools have become all the wonders that human language, human ingenuity, and human enterprise can fashion and employ in finding ever-better ways to survive and succeed on our small planet in our little corner of the universe.

Human society has evolved, naturally, from the simple to the complex. Human technologies, likewise, have evolved, naturally, from the simple to the complex. And now our society and our technologies alike have evolved, naturally, to the point where the extent of our markets for the human exchange that is "trade" need no longer be limited by either the natural boundaries of our geography or the artificial boundaries of

[241] Guy Gugliotta, "Earliest Human Ancestors? Skull Dates to When Apes, Humans Split," *Washington Post* (July 11, 2002), A1; Clive Cookson, "Meet the parents; An ancient skull in Chad has cast fresh light on the past," *Financial Times* (July 13-14, 2002), 7; Richard Monastersky, "Fossil Discovery Taps Roots of Human Family Tree," <u>Chronicle of Higher Education</u> (July 26, 2002), A20.
[242] Richard Leakey, <u>The Origin of Humankind</u> (New York: Basic Books, 1994), 12, 36.
[243] Id. at 59.

our geopolitics. It is limited only by the boundaries of our ideas. Thus, the international division of labor that both results *from* and results *in* increased international trade is, unquestionably, in our nature.

The WTO is, therefore, not the *cause* of the ever-increasing international division of labor that is commonly called "globalization." The WTO is the *result*. The worldwide trading system called "the WTO" is the collective response of the individual countries and other customs territories that are the Members of the WTO to the many challenges posed by globalization. These challenges know no national bounds; thus, they demand *inter*national solutions. As the former WTO Director-General, Mike Moore, has said: "[G]lobalization is not a policy choice, it's a fact....The real question we should ask ourselves is whether globalization is best left unfettered – dominated by the strongest and most powerful, the rule of the jungle – or managed by an agreed system of international rules, ratified by sovereign governments."[244]

Accordingly, to those of us who support the WTO, the issue is not whether there should be globalization. To us, the issue is: what kind of globalization should there be? Through the work of the WTO, we seek a globalization that extends Ricardo's reach by embracing the international division of labor and thereby enhancing international trade in ways that will serve us all to our best mutual advantage. We believe that this goal can only be achieved through a system of international rules on which we all have agreed. And, further, and perhaps most of all, we believe also that this goal can only be achieved if we also embrace the international rule of law. For we know that the rule of law is the only way out of the jungle and the surest way to individual human freedom. We know, like that foremost Enlightenment philosopher, the Baron de Montesquieu, that, "Law in general is human reason."[245] And we know, too, like Monsieur Voltaire, that, "To be free implies being subject to law alone."[246]

In the eighteenth century, Voltaire applied this assertion to France. Now, in the twenty-first century, it applies to the entire world. The rule of law means this: the law is written to apply to all equally, and all are

---

[244] Mike Moore, Address to the Seattle Symposium on International Trade Issues in the Next Decade, Seattle, Washington (November 29, 1999).

[245] Baron de Montesquieu, quoted in Donald B. Calne, <u>Within Reason: Rationality and Human Behavior</u> (New York: Vintage Books, 1999), 119.

[246] Voltaire is quoted from his <u>Philosophical Dictionary</u> in this English translation in Harold Nicolson, <u>The Age of Reason: The Eighteenth Century</u> (New York: Doubleday, 1961), 92 [hereinafter <u>The Age of Reason</u>].

equal before the law. With the rule of law, we can have freedom. Without the rule of law, we cannot. It is as simple as that. And this simple truth is every bit as true of economic freedom as it is of any other kind of freedom we may desire. The rule of law is needed at least as much in the marketplace as anywhere else. Property rights. Contract rights. Commercial rules. International obligations. All these, and much more, must be upheld by the rule of law in order to maximize the "gains from trade" in the marketplace. As the Nobel Prize-winning economist Ronald Coase has written, "It is evident that, for their operation, markets... require the establishment of legal rules governing the rights and duties of those carrying out transactions. To realize all the gains from trade,...there has to be a legal system and political order...."[247]

Nearly one thousand years ago, in the eleventh and twelfth centuries, a rising Europe, with the makings of international commerce in an increasingly continental market economy, was in need of a legal framework for facilitating further economic growth. Scholars at the University of Bologna, while digging in the dusty stacks of their library, rediscovered am artifact of antiquity known as the Code of Justinian. This was the definitive codification of Roman law that had been commissioned centuries earlier by the Byzantine emperor Justinian. The scholars at Bologna dusted it off, and made it the basis for the civil law of Europe.[248]

Today, the world finds itself in much the same need as Europe a millennium ago. Increasingly, we have a global economy. Increasingly, therefore, we are in need of global rules to facilitate global commerce. Increasingly, we are in need of global rules that can help provide the security, the stability, and the predictability that are needed in the global marketplace to encourage the continued growth of trade. But there is no Code of Justinian to be rediscovered. Thus, of necessity, the Members of the WTO are inventing a new code for world trade to facilitate the continued growth of the world economy.

Like it or not, Popper was right in believing that "our world has become so small that everybody is now a neighbor."[249] Globalization is

---

[247] Ronald Coase, The Firm, the Market and the Law (Chicago: University of Chicago Press, 1988), chapter 5 (reprint of a 1960 article), quoted in John H. Jackson, "Global Economics and International Economic Law," Journal of International Economic Law, Volume 1, November 1 (1998), 1, 4.

[248] Norman Cantor, The Civilization of the Middle Ages: The Life and Death of a Civilization (New York: HarperCollins, 1993), 306-318 [1963].

[249] Karl Popper, The Open Society, Volume I, at 183.

taking us ever-closer to one global economy. The cause of human rights and human freedom will be served best if there are global rules for the global economy on which we all have agreed. These rules must be written to apply to all equally. They must also be applied, in actual practice, to all equally. As that other Austrian economic and political philosopher, Friedrich Hayek —another of my friend Said's teachers —would remind us if he were still with us, only with rules that are "fixed and announced beforehand," only with "rules which make it possible to foresee with fair certainty" how the rules will be enforced,[250] will we be able to achieve the "predictability" that is sought by the Members of the WTO in their efforts to make the most of international trade for all the world.

Only if we have, and if we uphold, the rule of law in the world economy will we be able to achieve all "the gains from trade" that can come from an international division of labor. Only with the rule of law will we have any real hope of creating the "universal opulence" for all that was sought first by Adam Smith through his "simple system of natural liberty," that was sought also by David Ricardo through his idea of "comparative advantage," and that is sought now by the Members of the WTO through the multilateral trading system.

Thoreau asked: What object does the division of labor "finally serve"? The answer to his question, both then and now, both in the local economy of yesterday and in the global economy of today and tomorrow, is simply this. It is the division of labor that, by spreading Smith's "universal opulence," both serves and preserves precisely what Thoreau feared would be lost by the division of labor. It is the division of labor that makes it possible for us to think for ourselves, because it is the division of labor that makes it possible for us to make more personal choices. It is the division of labor that makes it possible for the would-be Thoreaus among us to choose to write essays rather than make pencils.

Faced with the force of dire economic circumstance, confronted with the fact of sheer economic necessity, millions upon millions in the world live their lives in ways that are not of their choosing. They live in ways they did not choose deliberately. Thoreau told us that he "went to the woods" to live at Walden Pond on July 4, 1845, because he wanted "to live deliberately."[251] The division of labor makes it possible for many more of us throughout the world "to live deliberately" today.

---

[250] Friedrich Hayek, The Road to Serfdom (Chicago: University of Chicago Press, 1944), 72.
[251] Henry David Thoreau, Walden, in Walden and Civil Disobedience, at 135.

The Revolt Against Freedom

When Galileo looked through a telescope in Padua in 1610, he saw something he was not supposed to see. He saw four moons circling the planet of Jupiter. Excited by this discovery, he told his colleagues at the university in Padua what he had seen. Not surprisingly, they did not believe him. Then, when he urged them "to look through his telescope and see for themselves, they refused even to look."[252]

The refusal of the other scholars in Padua even to look through Galileo's telescope is perhaps the perfect illustration of the difference between a closed and open society. Can we conceive today of, say, a class of American schoolchildren refusing even to look through a telescope to see something new, something different, something unexpected, something exciting? They would be clamoring to see. It would be hard to stop them. They live in the freedom of an open society.

The open society is the society sought by the thinkers of the Enlightenment. It is the society that values "freedom, above all, freedom in its many forms —freedom from arbitrary power, freedom of speech, freedom of trade, freedom to realize one's talents, freedom of aesthetic response, freedom, in a word, of moral man to make his own way in the world."[253] But some men and some women, even today, are afraid to make their own way in the world. They are afraid of what they might see if they dare to look through the telescope.

I see the opposition of so many in the world to the WTO as a refusal even to look through the telescope of freedom. I see the reservations of so many about the efforts of the WTO to further an international division of labor as perhaps best understood in the light of the ambivalence toward freedom that is seen in the continuing historical tensions between closed and open societies.

As Karl Popper saw it, in the transition "from tribalism to humanitarianism,"[254] in "the breakdown of the closed society,"[255] unavoidable and inescapable tensions arise. Rigid orthodoxy yields to freedom of thought. Absolute authority yields to individual autonomy.

---

[252] Galileo's telescope is discussed in Herbert J. Muller, Freedom in the Modern World (New York: Harper and Row, 1966), 245.

[253] Peter Gay, The Enlightenment: An Interpretation: The Rise of Modern Paganism (New York: Vintage Books, 1968), 3 [1966].

[254] Popper, The Open Society, Volume I, at 171.

[255] Id. at 188.

Security becomes insecurity. Certainty becomes uncertainty. The old world in which nothing is in doubt becomes a new world in which all is in doubt. In the transitional society that is beginning to open to that new world, there is a "feeling of drift"[256] because "everything is in flux."[257] The open society is open-ended. No one knows the destination of freedom.

Popper is best known as a philosopher of science, and the empirical scientific spirit of ongoing experimentation permeates his political thought and thus his view of an open society. Unlike the "scientific socialism" of Marx, the scientific thinking of Popper can, indeed, be described as "scientific." It is "scientific" because it does not pretend to certainty. In Popper's view, by definition, an open society *must* be open-ended, because an open society is a "scientific" society, and, thus, it is, by definition, a society that depends on uncertainty. It is one that thrives on doubt.

A "scientific" society is one in which there must be both uncertainty and doubt, because there must, to be "scientific," be the possibility that the answer may turn out to be other than what we happen, right now, thus far, to think. A "scientific" society is one in which we remain free to think otherwise if what we think now is proven to be false when tested by further observation.[258] A free, open, "scientific" society is a society in which, in Lincoln's timeless phrase, we can "think and act anew."[259] It is a society in which we are not only free to make our own personal decisions by making up our own minds; it is one also in which we are free, if we wish, to change our minds.

The doubt that is essential to science leaves room for uncertainty because it leaves room for the unknown. To illustrate: scientists using more than two hundred thousand computers spent years searching for "the largest known prime number" —the largest positive number divisible only by itself and by one. Eventually, a number turned up. It is 6,320,430 digits long and would need between 1,400 and 1,500 pages to write out in full. It is more than two million digits larger than the previous largest

---

[256] Id.
[257] Id. at 198.
[258] On the nature of a "scientific" society, *see* Richard Feynman, "The Uncertainty of Science," The Meaning of It All: Thoughts of a Citizen Scientist (Reading, Massachusetts: Perseus Books, 1998), 1-28 [1963] [hereinafter The Meaning of It All].
[259] Abraham Lincoln, Annual Message to the Congress of the United States (December 1, 1862).

known prime number. The key word here is *"known."* Mathematicians and other scientists continue to allow for doubt; they continue to allow for the possibility that there may be a larger prime number that is *unknown*.[260]

The doubt of science and the certainty of faith can co-exist in an open, "scientific" society. Popper's home in Vienna stood —indeed, it stands still —just across the square from the towering St. Stephen's Cathedral. Every day, the passing crowds of shoppers and tourists pursue their freedom in the busy square between the two Viennese monuments to science and to faith. There is no reason why we cannot make up our minds to have both. To say that something is *not* "scientific" is *not* to say that it is *not* significant. It is only to say that, whatever its significance, it cannot be tested by observation, and, thus, it cannot be refuted by the "trial and error" of the scientific method. This is not the same as saying that it is not true.

The "scientific" society is not a society that values science alone. Just as there is more to human nature than reason, so too is there more to human society than science. In Turgenev's <u>Fathers and Sons</u>, the scientist —and nihilist —Bazarov rejected everything that could not "be established by the rational methods of natural science" and could not "be reduced to quantitative measurement...."[261] He believed in dissecting beetles. He did not believe in reading poetry. "A decent chemist," he explained, "is twenty times more useful than a poet."[262] The open "scientific" society is *not* the society sought by Bazarov. It is a society that values poetry —and music and art and literature and philosophy. It is a society that values faith. It is a society that values all the "reasons of the heart" —because it is a society that values science as a way of serving and furthering human freedom.

The spirit of science is the spirit of freedom. It is, as the great American jurist Learned Hand said of the spirit of liberty, "the spirit which is not too sure it is right."[263] It is not fanaticism. It is not dogmatism. It is not a cold and inflexible rationalism. It is not a means for attaining

---

[260] "Student finds largest known prime number," Associated Press, online at cnn.com (December 11, 2003).
[261] Isaiah Berlin, "Fathers and Children: Turgenev and the Liberal Predicament," Introduction to Ivan Turgenev, <u>Fathers and Sons</u> (London: Penguin Books, 1975) 7, 27 [1861].
[262] Ivan Turgenev, <u>Fathers and Sons</u>, at 97.
[263] Judge Learned Hand, <u>The Spirit of Liberty</u>, 3rd Ed. (Chicago: University of Chicago Press, 1960).

certainty or proceeding from certainty. Instead, it is a means for living in uncertainty, for living in doubt and with doubt, and for making the most of doubt through the turmoil, the torment, and the "trial and error" of life.

Like many others, I have made the pilgrimage to the Spanish steps in Rome, to number 26 in the *Piazza di Spagna*, and have made the climb up the twisting stone staircase to the third floor and to the nine-by-twelve corner room overlooking those steps where the poet John Keats died, alone and far from home, in the cold Italian winter of 1821. One warm summer day, Joe and I stood together near the poet's deathbed and waved from a window to where Rebecca and Jamey waited near the Bernini fountain in the piazza below. The trials and errors of Keats' short life ended in the sickness and solitude of one hundred days of a slow dying in that small room in Rome.[264]

Keats was only twenty-five when he died. He had been apprenticed to a surgeon in England, but had abandoned a life in surgery for a life in poetry. Even so, he understood the spirit of science. This is seen in his justly famous assertion of the need, in poetry and in life, for a "Negative Capability" that "is capable of being in uncertainties, Mysteries, doubts, without any irritable reaching after fact and reason."[265] Keats' concept of "Negative Capability" has been interpreted as "an imaginative openness of mind and heightened receptivity to reality in its full and diverse concreteness."[266] It is a willingness to acknowledge ambiguities. It is a willingness to remain in doubt. From such a "Negative Capability" flow the positive achievements of both our truest science and our truest poetry.

The spirit of science is the spirit of Keats' "Negative Capability." It is the use of reason in the form of reasonableness.[267] Such reasonableness is not an intellectual despotism but rather an intellectual modesty. It is a mild intellectual skepticism. It is an intellectual attitude that admits the inevitability of ambiguity, and that tolerates and respects the differing

---

[264] John Evangelist Walsh, <u>Darkling I Listen: The Last Days and Death of John Keats</u> (New York: St. Martin's Press, 1999).

[265] The phrase "negative capability" is from John Keats' letter to his brothers, (usually) dated December 17, 1817.

[266] Walter Jackson Bate, <u>Keats</u> (Cambridge: Harvard University Press, 1963).

[267] For a discussion of the need for "reasonableness" which makes this same point far better than I can, *see* Stephen Toulmin, <u>Cosmopolis: The Hidden Agenda for Modernity</u> (Chicago: University of Chicago Press, 1990), 80, 198-201.

opinions of other reasoning individuals. It is an attitude that is —as we seven "faceless foreign judges" always strive to be in our deliberations around our table in Geneva —open, always and especially, to the mutual criticism that is the very essence of the spirit of the open society. For the open society *always* has an open mind.

The result of having such a spirit and such a society is the possibility of human progress. The result is also a "severe strain."[268] The result is what Popper calls "the strain of civilization."[269] Invariably, in the transition from a closed to an open society, there is a tendency to hesitate at the threshold of freedom. There is an understandable and all too human tendency to want to turn back from the beckoning freedom of the "open society" of today and turn again toward the security, the certainty, and the absence of doubt that were so consoling and so reassuring in the "closed society" of yesterday. For, in the "closed society," we may not have been free, but at least we knew who we were.

The transition from a closed to an open society is another way of describing the transition from the medieval to the modern world. As Marx — who was perhaps a better poet than he was an economist —once said, in the modern world, "all that is solid melts into air."[270] Where once all was known, now all is unknown. Where once all was decided, now all is undecided. Where once the individual was nothing and no one, now the individual is someone. Now, in the modern world, in the free air of the open society, we, as individuals, can decide, for ourselves, what truly can be known. Now we are free to choose. And now we *must* choose.

This freedom of choice —this opportunity for deciding, this *necessity* for deciding, on our own, for ourselves, as individuals, what truly can be known, and what, therefore, can truly be trusted to give meaning and purpose to our individual lives — is what makes freedom so frightening. In the open society, as Popper put it so pointedly, there is, amid all the confusion of doubt and uncertainty, a "demand for personal responsibility."[271] This demand, this burden, this obligation, is the very definition of living and being free. This *is* freedom. And it is because of this newfound freedom that we suffer "the strain of civilization."

---

[268] Popper, The Open Society, Volume I, at 198.
[269] Id. at 199.
[270] Karl Marx, "Speech at the Anniversary of the People's Paper," [1856] quoted in Marshall Berman, All That Is Solid Melts Into Air: The Experience of Modernity (New York: Penguin Books, 1988), 21 [1982].
[271] Popper, The Open Society, Volume I, at 5.

Examples abound throughout history of "the strain of civilization." They are far too many and far too varied to describe in all their anguished detail. But this "strain" can be illustrated by citing a few examples from the small slice of the diverse life of the world that is reflected in the lyrical refrains of English poetry. In 1611, alarmed by the advent of science and by its potential impact on the eternal verities of the Christian faith, the Anglican priest and poet John Donne wrote a poem he entitled "An Anatomy of the World." In it, he lamented a "new Philosophy" that placed "all in doubt" and left "all in pieces. All cohaerence gone."[272] Three centuries later, in 1921, the Irish poet William Butler Yeats echoed Donne. In his poem "The Second Coming," Yeats voiced his dismay at the approaching global chaos that ultimately led to World War II. In words that are, still, often quoted today, he wrote, "Things fall apart. The centre cannot hold.... The best lack all conviction, while the worst are full of passionate intensity.... And what rough beast, its hour come round at last, slouches toward Bethlehem to be born?"[273]

In the strain of life, in the inexorable wane of life, we all want, like Keats, to cling to "the soft-dying day."[274] We all want to "think warm days will never cease."[275] We all want to keep writing the poetry of life that Keats' well-intentioned doctor would not allow him to keep writing during his dying days in Rome. We all fear that we, like Keats, will end our days in the icy loneliness of a small and solitary room. Confronting this fear, overcoming this strain day after ever-passing day, is part of the inescapable price of living, and of being human. And this ordeal is all the more difficult for all of those who live where all is "in pieces" and when "things fall apart" in the painful transition from a closed to an open society.

These poetic refrains —these poetic expressions of "the strain of civilization" —are familiar to those of us who read our poetry in English. Many other poets have expressed similar sentiments. And many have done so in many other languages, as, through the centuries, different parts of the world have been confronted with the painful human ordeal of making the transition from closed to open societies. In facing that

---

[272] John Donne, "An Anatomy of the World," The Complete English Poems (New York: Everyman's Library, 1991) 325, 335.
[273] William Butler Yeats, "The Second Coming," Immortal Poems of the English Language (New York: Washington Square Press, 1952), 489. For an interesting discussion of both Donne and Yeats in terms of the debate over "modernity," see Stephen Toulmin, Cosmopolis: The Hidden Agenda of Modernity, supra, at 62-69, 158.
[274] John Keats, "Ode to Autumn," in John Keats: Selected Poems (London: Penguin Books, 1988), 197 [1819].
[275] Id.

transition —in facing for the first time the awesome and awful burden of being free, and of somehow finding the will and the way to fulfill the responsibility of being free —different people, in part because they are different, and also in part perhaps because they face different circumstances, react in different ways.

When confronted with "the strain of civilization," some embrace freedom. Some venture on into the unknown in the determination to find and make a life of meaning and purpose. They know, like Popper, that "[t]here is no return to a harmonious state of nature."[276] For, "if we turn back, then we must go the whole way —we must return to the beasts."[277] They know that the only way forward is "into the unknown" of the open society.[278] Somehow they find the way forward to freedom.

But some falter and fall back into fear. Some succumb to the fear of freedom. They try "to close the door which had been opened."[279] They "attempt to arrest all change and to return to tribalism"[280] by creating, not the open society, but "the arrested society"[281] in which freedom is defeated and denied. This leads to what Popper calls "the perennial revolt against freedom."[282] There are many who engage in this revolt, and they revolt in many different ways. Some write poetry. Others strap on suicide bombs.

Popper opposed "the revolt against freedom."[283] He saw in that revolt the seeds of the fascism and the communism that were the totalitarianisms of his time. So do I. Moreover, I see in it, too, the seeds of the many and varied totalitarianisms that threaten our time. Like Popper, I see the strain that gives rise to the revolt against freedom as "the strain created by the effort which life in an open and partially abstract society continually demands from us - by the endeavour to be rational, to forgo at least some of our emotional social needs, to look after ourselves, and to accept responsibilities."[284] And, like him, I believe that "[w]e must...bear this strain as the price to be paid for every increase in knowledge, in

---

[276] Popper, The Open Society, Volume I, at 200-201.
[277] Id. at 201.
[278] Id.
[279] Id. at 199.
[280] Id. at 182.
[281] Id. at 194.
[282] Id. at 188.
[283] Id.
[284] Id. at 176.
[285] Id.

reasonableness, in co-operation and in mutual help, and consequently in our chances of survival.... It is the price we have to pay for being human."[285]

I am willing to pay the price for being human. So are all those who also support the WTO. But I see in those who oppose the WTO an unwillingness to pay this price. I see in the backlash against "globalization" one more example of "the revolt against freedom" that we have seen so many times, in so many places, and in so many guises, in the past.

Chapter Four

Trade Fears

The Fiddle and the Radio

The eventful past of my own native South in the United States is one example in my own experience of the perennial revolt against freedom. In the tradition of Thoreau, among the most eloquent of the twentieth-century critics of the consequences of the division of labor were the Nashville Agrarians. The Nashville Agrarians were a dozen mostly poets and professors who were mostly affiliated with Vanderbilt University. They included such literary notables as John Crowe Ransom, Allen Tate, Donald Davidson, and Robert Penn Warren. Describing themselves as "Twelve Southerners," the Nashville Agrarians issued a ringing "manifesto" against the industrialization of the American South in 1930, in the midst of the Great Depression.[1]

They called their "manifesto" I'll Take My Stand. In it, they lamented the passing of the pastoral ways of the Old South and the arrival of what they saw as the crass commercialization of the New South. They saw the New South as "groaning under industrialism."[2] They foresaw in the New South a loss of identity, a loss of personality, a loss of personal independence, and a loss of a distinctive sense of place. Looking to the future, they saw the "specialization" occasioned by the division of labor as leading, not to the progress of humanity, but, rather, to the loss of humanity on an unending assembly line. They saw in "industrialism" the makings of a dehumanizing collectivism.[3]

In the "statement of principles" that introduced their "manifesto," the Nashville Agrarians announced that "modern man has lost his sense of vocation."[4] They said, "The act of labor as one of the happy functions of human life has been in effect abandoned, and is practiced solely for its rewards."[5] Bemoaning the increasingly rapid pace of industrialization

---

[1] See Paul K. Conkin, The Southern Agrarians (Nashville: Vanderbilt University Press, 2001) [1988].
[2] Louis D. Rubin, ed., Twelve Southerners, "Introduction," I'll Take My Stand: The South and the Agrarian Tradition (New York: Harper Torchbooks, 1962), xxx [hereinafter I'll Take My Stand].
[3] Id. at xxi.
[4] Id. at xxiv.
[5] Id. at xxiii.

of the hitherto rural South, they warned, "The tempo of the industrial life is fast, but that is not the worst of it; it is accelerating."[6] Furthermore, they professed, "industrial life" is a meaningless and pointless life because "[i]t never proposes a specific goal; it initiates the infinite series."[7]

And what did these poets and professors propose instead of an industrialized and commercialized division of labor? They proposed what they called "agrarianism." "The theory of agrarianism," they explained, "is that the culture of the soil is the best and most sensitive of vocations, and that therefore it should be the economic preference and enlist the maximum number of workers."[8] In other words, back to the farm —back to the farm, supposedly, for everyone *except* the poets and the professors.

As a young Southerner studying years ago as an undergraduate at Vanderbilt, I read I'll Take My Stand more than once. I admired the Thoreau-like eloquence of the Nashville Agrarians in defending the reassuring rhythms and the soothing consolations of Southern rural life. I agreed with much of what they seemed to me at the time to be saying about the dehumanizing dangers of a society founded on mere materialism. I still do. Yet, even then, I concluded that theirs was a "lost cause" —and one that richly deserved to be lost.

My own family knew much about the rhythms and consolations of rural life. Many of my relatives were farmers who practiced "agrarianism" for generations in the rural areas just outside of Nashville. Some of them became sharecroppers when they lost their land and their homes in the rural depression of the 1920s that preceded the Great Depression. They were not in any danger of yielding to the lure of mere materialism. They were in danger of going hungry.

My grandfather left the land, abandoned the "agrarian" way of life, and, at the age of eighteen, moved to the big city of Nashville in search of opportunity. He began by pumping gas at a Packard dealership on West End Avenue just across from Vanderbilt. He told me when I was a boy about all the times when he filled the tanks of the big Packard cars of the Vanderbilt professors —including some who wrote I'll Take My Stand. They were always, he told me, very polite. They were always perfect Southern gentlemen. But they were in no danger of going hungry.

---

[6] Id. at xxvi.
[7] Id. at xxvii.
[8] Id. at xxix.

My grandfather received an eighth-grade education in a one-room schoolhouse in the rural South that was idealized by the Nashville Agrarians. He rose above those beginnings because he had the courage and the enterprise to leave the farm, go to the city, and "specialize" in the then brand-new high-tech field of automotive mechanics, which he learned while he supported his family by pumping gas. He eventually became the service manager for several states for one of the major automotive manufacturers in the world.

Tell me. Should my grandfather have remained on the farm? Should he have been denied the personal choice he made? Andrew Nelson Lytle, one of the surest stylists among the Nashville Agrarians, advised, in I'll Take My Stand, "Throw out the radio and take down the fiddle from the wall."[9] Lytle sought the authentic, the unhurried, the "unplugged" life. He was perhaps right in believing that there is more shared humanity in the mutual art of conversation than in the mutual act of listening to the radio or watching a movie. Yet any Southerner might ask today, and might have asked even then: what about the country music that has long been broadcast by radio throughout the South on the "Grand Ole Opry"? Must we give that up? Do we really need to throw out the radio? Do we really need to turn away from the modern world in order to turn toward the authenticity of the good life? Can we not find ways to use the radio and all the other machines of modern life to enhance our humanity? How many of the Nashville Agrarians left Vanderbilt and returned to the farm?

The Nashville Agrarians took their "stand" as part of the revolt against freedom. They were not all rural reactionaries. They were not all entirely of like mind. A few eventually spoke up, to some extent, for civil rights in the South. But their "manifesto" in 1930 was one that celebrated a society and an economy that lacked both justice and running water. One of the "Twelve Southerners," Frank Lawrence Owsley, lamented in his essay that "half-savage blacks were armed" during the Reconstruction of the South following the Civil War.[10] For some who contributed to the "manifesto," the lingering racism was not very far below the surface. For all their eloquence, the Nashville Agrarians were a group of "bright, white, college-educated, privileged southern young men"[11] who, comfortable with their own lives and with their own illusions, seemed all too willing

---

[9] Andrew Nelson Lytle, "The Hind Tit," I'll Take My Stand, 201, 244.
[10] Frank Lawrence Owsley, "The Irrepressible Conflict," I'll Take My Stand, 61, 62.
[11] Paul Conkin, The Southern Agrarians, supra, at x.

at the time to leave out and leave behind the Southern blacks who suffered from segregation and the poor Southern whites who struggled to survive by sharecropping —including some in my family.

In their revolt against freedom in the 1930s, the Nashville Agrarians were only echoing earlier generations of American Southerners who had also rebelled against the modern world. One such Southerner was George Fitzhugh, of Port Royal, Virginia. Fitzhugh was a planter, a philosopher, and an antebellum slaveholder whose tracts in defense of slavery included many of the same salvos against individualism, industrialism, the market, and the division of labor that were later made by the Nashville Agrarians.

Fitzhugh opposed free trade. He opposed capitalism. He feared the specializing and modernizing consequences of a division of labor that contributed to the rise of both individualism and industrialism. In words similar to those used by Karl Marx at about the same time and on another continent, Fitzhugh said of the division of labor, "By confining each workman to some simple, monotonous employment, it makes him a mere automaton, and an easy prey to the capitalist."[12]

His remedy? Slavery. Far better, in his view, to have actual slaves than to have "wage slaves." According to Fitzhugh, "To secure true progress, we must unfetter genius, and chain down mediocrity. Liberty for the few —Slavery, in every form, for the mass."[13] Some few, in other words, would drive Packards. The vast majority would pick cotton. Or pump gas. Shorn of its poetry, the message of the Nashville Agrarians nearly a century later was essentially the same.

Among the "anti-globalists," Wendell Berry, for one, fancies himself nowadays as a latter-day follower of the Nashville Agrarians. He favors a fuzzy "agrarianism" over what he sees as a deracinating and dehumanizing "industrialism." And he sees in the long-ago "manifesto" of the Nashville Agrarians a prophetic warning to an unwitting world of the ominous approach of the WTO (slouching, apparently, toward Geneva).[14] For evidence of such a foretelling, he points to the "Introduction" to I'll Take My Stand, where the "Twelve Southerners"

---

[12] Fitzhugh is quoted in Eugene D. Genovese, The World the Slaveholders Made: Two Essays in Interpretation (New York: Vintage Books, 1971) 159-160 [1969].
[13] Id. at 160.
[14] Berry, The Art of the Commonplace, at 243.

foresee that "the true Sovietists —if the term may be used in the European sense —are the Industrialists themselves. They would have the government set up an economic super-organization, which in turn would become the government."[15]

What Berry sees as prophecy, I see only as hyperbole. The Nashville Agrarians were no more right in their supposed prophecies of an approaching world government than they were about many other things. The Nashville Agrarians were good poets. They were probably good professors. But they were bad prophets, and they were definitely bad economists. I am confident that, if he were here today, my grandfather would agree.

Like my grandfather, I prefer freedom. And I prefer freedom for everyone. I prefer the opportunity to engage in the exchange of trade that gives rise to "specialization," and thus to the opportunities that are offered by a modern economy in a modern world. I prefer the "infinite series" of an open and open-ended society because it is an infinite series made by individual personal choices to further individual personal goals. I prefer running water. And so, too, I suspect, would all of the many millions around the world who have never had it.

The Revolt Against Trade

In their revolt against freedom, the Nashville Agrarians were not the last to celebrate a society without justice and an economy without running water. Their intellectual successors are among those who protest today in the streets of Seattle and Genoa against the WTO as "the Supreme Court of Globalization."[16] In the protests of those who revolt against trade are echoes of the lament of the Nashville Agrarians at the arrival of the new division of labor that made the New South. The revolt against trade is one of the many guises of the revolt against freedom. For it is inspired by fear of the freedom that is created through the application of human reason in the making of the open societies of the new world.

Some of the anti-WTO protesters are violent and hardened revolutionaries. They are latter-day anarchists in revolt against the values and the institutions of the modern world, or they are unrepentant Marxists

---

[15] Id., quoting Twelve Southerners, I'll Take My Stand, at xxiii.
[16] David Ransom, The No-Nonsense Guide to Fair Trade (London: New Internationalist, 2001), 74. Regrettably, this "no-nonsense" guide is filled with nonsense.

offering only a rehash of Marxism in the guise of a vague "anti-globalism." Marx and Engels, in The Communist Manifesto, announced their undying opposition to "that single, unconscionable freedom —Free Trade."[17] Among the most agitated of the "anti-global" agitators are successors to Marx and Engels who carry on the Marxist struggle against free trade today through their opposition to the WTO. In truth, there is very little that has been said by anyone in the "anti-global" movement, Marxist or otherwise, that was not said better in 1848 in the twelve thousand words of The Communist Manifesto.

But most of those in the varied array of "anti-globalizers" who resist the rational logic of the international division of labor, and who thus oppose the work of the WTO, are not revolutionaries. Instead, like the Nashville Agrarians, they are reactionaries, for what they really want is to deny people their freedom by denying them the opportunity to make more personal choices in their own lives by embracing the mutually beneficial specialization of an international division of labor. As Virginia Postrel has observed in The Future and Its Enemies, "The alternative to specialization is the great reactionary dream: a return to peasant life."[18] This dream can be appealing —unless you happen to be a peasant.

The Nashville Agrarians drove their big Packards. Many of the anti-WTO protesters wear their expensive Nikes. In their opposition to "globalization," they are trying "to protect the poor against the process that delivered their own remarkable prosperity."[19] Whatever we call them, whatever they call themselves, and whatever their intentions, their message is nevertheless much the same: they have theirs, and, intentionally or not, they are willing, through the advancement of the policies they advocate, to deny to others the additional choices that they can only have in open societies in a modern world. Thus, they condemn millions upon millions, in whose names they profess to protest, to continue to live, barefoot and hungry, as peasants.

The reactionary dream appeals to all those who think the world was better when more of us were peasants. It appeals to all those who sing, in many different languages and in many different tunes, the timeless lament for a simpler life. It entices all those everywhere who listen to the lure of "once upon a time" and who long for the lost certitudes of a simpler,

---

[17] Marx and Engels, The Communist Manifesto, at 82.
[18] Virginia Postrel, The Future and Its Enemies (New York: Touchstone, 1999), 91.
[19] Martin Wolf of the *Financial Times* quoted in Rosemary Righter, "Free For All," Times Literary Supplement (September 26, 2003), 6.

Golden Age. Call it the Old South of the Nashville Agrarians. Call it the Walden Pond of Thoreau. Call it Eden or Camelot or Arcadia. Call it "The Deserted Village" of the British poet Oliver Goldsmith, "Sweet Auburn," the "loveliest village of the plain," where we once knew what we know no longer, that "trade's proud empire hastes to swift decay."[20] Call it, as Marx did, "communism" —a world of self-sufficient and totally self-sustaining human communion in which we can do as we like and somehow have all we need and want without having a division of labor.

Call it whatever you like. But, whatever it may be called, wherever it may have been, and whenever it may have been, it is always and everywhere the same. It is "the world we have lost."[21] It is the idyllic dream of the world we hope one day to find yet again. It is the lost and lamented Golden Age. The trouble is, the Golden Age that the poets describe is an age that never was. And the men and women who lived and worked in that dim and distant time that the poets idealize with such wistful lyricism were far from free.

A statue of Jean-Jacques Rousseau adorns a small island amid the River Rhone where it flows from Lac Leman and divides the modern urban center of Geneva. Sometimes, on a weekend, I sit on the terrace of a café nearby, sip *renversé*, and watch the birds he loved pay their homage to the original romantic. Jean-Jacques fled the forbidding Calvinism of his native Geneva in his youth, and embraced for many years thereafter the wandering life of a vagabond. But he is honored in concrete by the *Genevois* today.

Just a few kilometers away, on a hillside outside the city, is the suburb of Bossey. It is noteworthy now for its sloping green golf course, which offers a sweeping vista of the broad valley between the Jura and the Saleve. It was on the site of this golf course that Rousseau became a romantic. As he recounts in his Confessions, when a small boy, Rousseau was sent away from the old city of Geneva, after his mother died, to stay with relatives for a '[t]wo years' sojourn in the village...."[22] There he first learned about the "simplicity of... rural existence...."[23] In Bossey today, golfers endeavor daily to plant a hole in one. In Bossey then, according to

---

[20] Oliver Goldsmith, "The Deserted Village," Immortal Poems of the English Language, supra, 211, 222.
[21] Peter Laslett, The World We Have Lost: England Before the Industrial Age, 3rd Ed. (New York: Scribner, 1984).
[22] Jean-Jacques Rousseau, The Confessions (London: Penguin Books, 1953), 23 [1781].
[23] Id. at 24.

Rousseau, "our natural belief" was "that it was a finer thing to plant a tree on a terrace than a flag in the breech."[24]

In time, Rousseau became the defender of all things pristine and pastoral, and the champion of the noble savage. Years later, not long before the French Revolution, he wrote his stirring statement that men had been "born free" but were "everywhere in chains."[25] He idealized an idyllic "state of nature" in which men were everywhere free, happy, and content during a blissful Golden Age that blessed humankind before the sad advent of the iniquities and the inequities of a civilized society. Then man lived, he wrote, in "the simple, unchanging and solitary way of life that nature ordained for us."[26] Then man spent his time "casting his gaze over the whole of nature and measuring with his eyes the vast expanse of the heavens."[27] Man's "first language," rhapsodized Rousseau, was "the cry of nature."[28]

But there is little evidence that such a "state of nature" ever existed. Anthropologists continue to debate the details of the dawn of humanity, but the seventeenth-century English philosopher Thomas Hobbes probably came much closer than Rousseau to the truth of our history as a species when he wrote that the "state of nature" was one in which human life was "solitary, poore, nasty, brutish, and short."[29] The Arcadian antiquity of "peaceable, egalitarian, and ecology-loving natives"[30] that was portrayed by Rousseau and that is posited still by all those in the atavistic "anti-global" movement who echo Rousseau today was probably not the "state of nature." What Rousseau saw as the pleasant pastoral dream world of a supposedly Golden Age of early humanity was much more likely, in reality, a world in which human life was brief and cheap. It was a world in which human life was, for most, simply and solely a grim struggle to survive.

And, alas, for all too many desperate millions in the world today, that is, still, all they know of life —a struggle for survival. Only a fortunate few in the world can afford the big, gas-guzzling cars that have long since

---

[24] Id. at 32.
[25] Jean-Jacques Rousseau, "The Social Contract," The Essential Rousseau (New York: Meridian Books, 1983), 8 [1762].
[26] Jean-Jacques Rousseau, A Discourse on Inequality, at 85.
[27] Id. at 81.
[28] Id. at 93.
[29] Thomas Hobbes, Leviathan (London: Penguin Books, 1968), 186 [1660].
[30] Steven Pinker, The Blank Slate, supra, at 56.

replaced my grandfather's Packards. Only a fortunate few in the world can afford Nikes. The World Bank reports that there are 1.2 billion people in the world who live on less than $1 per day, and that there are 2.8 billion people in the world who live on less than $2 per day.[31] About half of all our species who live today —about three billion living, breathing, thinking, reasoning human beings —live with the hunger, the disease, the ignorance, and all the other lethal consequences of the despair and the deprivation that are part of a grinding and unrelenting poverty. They do not live in freedom.

I once heard the former United States Trade Representative, my friend Charlene Barshefsky, give a speech to an American audience in which she pointed out what should be the obvious: because only four percent of the people in the world are Americans, it necessarily follows that 96 percent of the people in the world *are not.* We Americans are not all fortunate. (To the shame of my beloved State of Florida, for example, there are three million Floridians without basic health insurance.) But, all in all, we Americans are far more fortunate than the vast majority of others in the world. We are among the fortunate few. And, as well-intentioned as we usually are, and as generous as we often are when we are at our best, far too often we Americans tend to forget how truly fortunate we are, and we tend to forget also how many, many millions there are elsewhere in the world who do not live in the freedom that far too many Americans tend to take for granted.

The vast majority of those of our species who have ever lived have not lived in freedom. They have been slaves or serfs or lackeys or peasants of some kind who have been denied the right to choose freely how to live. And far too many of the people in the world remain peasants today. Far too many are not yet free to choose. We were not, as a species, "born free." We were born in the chains of countless closed societies — each of our own ignorant and superstitious and fearful making. But, over time —over a long time —some of us have gradually *become free.*

We have become free by applying our unique capacity to reason to the task of making *tools* that can help shape the world to human ends. We have become free by applying our reason to the task of making *rules* for living together that we call "the rule of law." We have become free also by employing our faculties of reason to engage in trade and all the many other pursuits of freedom that can open the closed doors of closed

---

[31] World Bank, Human Development Report 2001 (Washington D.C.), 9.

societies. We will remain free, and more of us will become free, only if we have the courage to continue to make tools, to make rules, and to engage in trade and in all the many other productive pursuits of freedom.

Those who dream the reactionary dream are those who yearn for the return of a lost Golden Age in which there was no freedom. They long for the return of the closed society in which men and women were dutiful and docile, and were easily led, like sheep. Rousseau's rival, Voltaire, once said, "Sheep live very quietly in society."[32] They do not live freely. Like Rousseau, Voltaire spent many years of his life in and around Geneva. His statue in Ferney-Voltaire is not far away. But, unlike Rousseau, Voltaire did not idealize the "state of nature." He was an optimist, but he was also a realist. And, as he reminded us, however much we may be inclined to idealize the past, "[t]he republic of sheep is the faithful image of the golden age."[33]

I see all of human history as a struggle to overcome the meek quietude of closed societies and overthrow "the republic of sheep." I see history as a struggle to reach the point where we can, as individuals and as a species, choose to be free. We must reach the point where we *all* will be able to *choose* who we are, and not be *told* who we are. We must *all* be able, as Thoreau said, to choose for ourselves what we think, and not be told what we think. We must *all* be able to choose *for ourselves* how we wish to live, and not be *told* how to live by some mullah, some commissar, some "Sun King," some sanctimonious "televangelist" or "talk show host," or some other self-important potentate who has somehow persuaded himself that he alone knows the one and only way in which we *all* should live. When we reach that point, when we are *all* able to make that choice for ourselves, then perhaps —just perhaps —we will be at the threshold of a real Golden Age in a true Age of Reason.

The Fear of Change

Many of those who dream the reactionary dream have enlisted in the revolt against trade. They have done so for many different reasons: a distaste for the urban and the cosmopolitan; a distrust of the large and the complex; a disgust with the license and the licentiousness that sometimes pose as freedom; a disapproval of the many ways in which freedom can undermine the verities of traditional societies; a

---

[32] Voltaire, Philosophical Dictionary, at 287.
[33] Id.

disappointment at the many ways in which the uniformities that arise from a commercial society seem to dissolve the distinctiveness of both culture and place; a dislike for the mundane and the practical that are the commonplaces of a commercial society; and a dismay at the shades of gray that shadow everything and everywhere in the free and open society of the modern world. All these are among the many motivations for the revolt against freedom that is the revolt against trade.

But, among the many reasons inspiring this revolt, I see some as most significant. One is the natural human apprehension about change. We humans want change. But we also want things to stay just the way they are. We don't want to grow old. We don't want our children to grow up. We don't want the last lingering days of summer to end. We don't want the life we know and love to slip away forever. Mark Twain, the American pessimist who posed as a humorist, may have summed up this all too understandable human trait, as only he could do, when he supposedly suggested that we are all for *progress*, and that it's *change* we don't like.[34]

Like many of us, Twain manifested a lifelong ambivalence toward change. He favored the advance to the future, and yet he lamented the loss of the past. He welcomed the world of the railroad, and yet when, in his later years, he revisited the scenes of his youthful steamboat days on the Mississippi River, he "was oppressed by a sense of change and loss. The levee at St. Louis, once packed solid with steamboats, was empty now except for half a dozen, their fires banked or dead."[35] Twain, like many of us, feared change in part because he was apprehensive of an encroaching sameness in the surrounding world. He regretted what he perceived as a loss of the sheer diversity of the world that resulted from the loss of his boyhood "culture" along the river-banks.

"[T]he change of changes was on the 'levee,'" said Twain when he returned to St. Louis after twenty-one years away from the river. "Half a dozen sound-asleep steamboats where I used to see a solid mile of wide-awake ones! This was melancholy, this was woeful."[36] Once the familiar shout all along the Mississippi had been, "Steamboat's coming!" Steamboats were coming; now they were gone. In considering their

---

[34] Although this remark is widely attributed to Mark Twain, I have been unable to find a precise source for it in his voluminous writings.
[35] Justin Kaplan, Mr. Clemens and Mark Twain (London: Penguin Books, 1967), 374 [1966].
[36] Mark Twain, Life on the Mississippi (New York: Penguin Classics, 1986), 172 [1883].

absence, Twain observed, philosophically, that, first, steamboats had replaced keelboats, and, now, railroads had replaced steamboats.[37] Today, of course, the railroads have, in many instances, been replaced as well, by cars and by trucks on highways that Twain did not live to see. This is what he meant when he wrote in his day of the inexorable progress of "infinite change."[38]

Similarly, in one of the musings of his later years, Sir Harold Nicolson expressed a fear that "the whole earth is menaced by uniformity...."[39] Those who fear change fear uniformity. They fear homogenization. They fear a "loss of culture." They see Golden Arches on every horizon —and they do not see them as harbingers of a Golden Age. Like Twain, I am not altogether unsympathetic to such sentiments. Nicolson was right, I think, in saying that "mankind has progressed owing to difference rather than sameness, owing, not to similitude, but to variation."[40] We need diversity. We need variety in the world around us. And there is, undeniably, some "loss of culture" along the way as the world embraces trade and "globalization." The distinctive regional ways of the American South of my youth —to cite just one example —have been blurred by the years through the homogenization of modern American life.

As they say, "culture matters."[41] But, in my experience, culture also persists. In my experience, while there is some "loss of culture" from trade and from globalization —while nowadays, unlike in the days of my lost youth, fewer Southern children sip Nehi "Big Oranges" and eat "Moon Pies" on lazy summer afternoons —nevertheless, the distinctiveness of cultural differences somehow persists. Indeed, as I see it, the richness of culture is often enhanced by a plenitude and a pluralism of cultural choices resulting from trade and from globalization. The "Moon Pies" that were once sold only in the American South are now, I have noticed, sold worldwide. And beneath the Golden Arches in Geneva is a menu that offers hamburgers and other sandwiches with a choice of several different kinds of Swiss cheese.

It is not, however, the fear of a monotonous uniformity in the world that is the most powerful fuel for the fear of change. Whatever the

---

[37] Id. at 173.
[38] Id. at 204.
[39] Harold Nicolson, <u>Good Behaviour</u>, supra, at 1.
[40] Id. at 1-2.
[41] This is the title of a recent collection of provocative essays. *See* Larry E. Harrison and Samuel P. Huntington, eds., <u>Culture Matters</u>, supra.

depth of such cultural concerns, the fear of change probably penetrates most deeply in the fear of the impact of change on the work that we do, and that is so much a part of who we are. Many fear "the ringing grooves of change" most of all because they fear that change will cost them their jobs.[42] This is partly because so many of us in this world see our personal identity and our personal worth as depending so much —I would say far too much —on the kind of work we do and on the amount of money we are paid to do it. Doubtless this is mostly because almost all of us depend on our work for the means of making a living, and thus for the means of making some of the choices we want to make about how we will live.

This makes it harder for us to do something different —something that may change our status, something that may affect our income, something that may alter our way of life. This makes it harder for us to do something new. The late longshoreman and philosopher Eric Hoffer described, from his personal experience, how "the ordeal of change" grips the worker who must do something new. He recalled a year he spent picking vegetables as a migrant worker in the Imperial Valley of California during the Great Depression. "I started out," he said, "picking peas as they ripened, until I picked the last peas of the season.... Then... for the first time I was going to pick string beans. And I still remember how hesitant I was that first morning as I was about to address myself to the string bean vines. Would I be able to pick string beans? Even the change from peas to string beans had in it elements of fear."[43]

No doubt the same elements of fear gripped my grandfather when he decided to stop being a farmer and start being a mechanic. No doubt they also grip all those Americans today who make shoes or steel or textiles whenever they think about doing something new. Many have done the same job all their lives. Many have never done anything else. Many have never known anything else. Many are growing older, and are watching all they have done and known and loved slip, perhaps forever, away. Surely they must ask: can I survive the ordeal of change? Can I pick string beans? Can I really do something new?

These questions are asked, not only in America, but throughout the world. One of the Austrian economists much admired by my friend Said —Ludwig von Mises —taught that "in economic life nothing is

---

[42] Alfred, Lord Tennyson, "Locksley Hall," in <u>Alfred, Lord Tennyson: Selected Poems</u> (London: Penguin Classics, 1991), 96, 103.
[43] Eric Hoffer, <u>The Ordeal of Change</u> (New York: Harper and Row, 1967), 3 [1963].

permanent except change."[44]   In an even shrewder insight, he observed also that "the great mass of people are incapable of realizing this."[45]   On the surface, the revolt against trade reflects a fear of the economic consequences of an international division of labor and increased international trade for local workers, local producers, and local economies throughout the world. And, thus, on the surface, the revolt against trade in our new age of "globalization" is only the contemporary telling of the familiar historical tale of the confrontation between the relentless advance guard of endless economic innovation and the recalcitrant rear guard against economic change. Much that I see in the revolt against trade can thus be seen as a manifestation of the fear of doing something new that is part of the natural and human apprehension of change. And thus, as I see it, in response to this revolt, we must, above all, address and overcome this fear.

The notion of, in some way, easing "the ordeal of change" by easing the impact of change on workers who are displaced by trade is not new. Adam Smith favored easing the impact of change by phasing out protectionism through the *gradual* lowering of tariffs. In one of *his* shrewder insights, Smith said, "Humanity may... require that the freedom of trade should be restored only by slow gradations, and with a good deal of reserve and circumspection."[46]   Here, too, he revealed his profound understanding of human nature. His recommended approach of gradual tariff reductions was generally followed under the GATT and is still generally followed under the WTO. The tariff cuts of the Uruguay Round have been made *gradually* over the course of a decade.

For the same reason, in the debate over the repeal in 1846 of the protectionist Corn Laws in Great Britain, John Stuart Mill went so far as to advocate compensation for those who would be adversely affected by lower tariffs. Following Mill, the United States has, for the past several decades, had laws and governmental programs relating to "trade adjustment assistance."[47]   For the most part, these laws and programs have been neglected, and thus they have worked poorly, if at all, for workers who have been displaced by trade in the United States. Recently, however, attention has focused anew on providing "trade adjustment

---

[44] Ludwig von Mises, in <u>Socialism: An Economic and Sociological Analysis</u> (1922), quoted in Muller, <u>The Mind and the Market</u>, at 358.

[45] Id.

[46] Smith, <u>The Wealth of Nations</u>, at 499.

[47] Irwin, <u>Against the Tide</u>, at 92-93.

assistance," and on making it work. The Congress has authorized spending $12 billion over ten years for new programs of "trade adjustment assistance" for workers displaced by trade in the United States.

This is encouraging. It is not enough to lecture to those who are displaced by trade about the undeniable virtues of comparative advantage. It is not enough to explain to them about the undeniable necessity of what yet another of the Austrian economists, Joseph Schumpeter, memorably described as the "creative destruction" of capitalism in a churning, ever-evolving, and ever-changing free marketplace.[48] Through education, through training, and through transitional assistance, we must do much more to help those who suffer everywhere in the world from the economic consequences of change find the ways and the means to do something new.

And, further, in response to the revolt against trade, we must explain more clearly what the considerable "opportunity cost" is for all of us of *not* doing something new. We must understand the true costs of the tariffs, the quotas, the tariff-rate quotas, the domestic content requirements, and all the other assorted dodges and devices that are used to restrict trade and, thus, limit competition in the marketplace by limiting imports of goods and services. Locally, nationally, and internationally, in making decisions about trade, we must know what the true trade-offs are between meeting and not meeting the challenge of change. In developed and developing countries alike, we must know the answer to the question: what is the cost of *not* changing?

Above all, those who would presume to lead us must understand that cost. In one of his essays, the nineteenth-century British writer William Hazlitt observed in passing that "a few of the principles of Adam Smith, which every one else had been acquainted with long since, are just now beginning to dawn on the collective understanding of the two Houses of Parliament."[49] That was in 1826. Today, we can only hope to see the same dawning in, for example, the acts of the two chambers of the Congress of the United States. Perhaps a closer reading of Adam Smith would give more of our elected representatives a better understanding of "opportunity cost" and, thus, of the cost to the American people of *not* reducing the trade barriers we have raised against the rest of the world.

---

[48] Joseph A. Schumpeter, Capitalism, Socialism, and Democracy (New York: Harper, 1975), 82-85 [1942].
[49] William Hazlitt, "On the Difference between Writing and Speaking," The Fight and Other Writings (London: Penguin Books, 2000), 459, 469 [1826].

Tariffs are only one of the many kinds of trade barriers, and tariff costs are only one of the many kinds of costs associated with trade barriers. Even so, tariffs offer a telling example of how those costs can be hidden from public view and thus from a public understanding of the "opportunity costs" that are wrought by barriers to trade. Tariffs are simply *taxes* that are charged at the border as the price of importing a foreign good. These taxes are simply added to the overall price of that good after it is imported and when it is sold in the domestic market. The purchaser of the good usually pays this price without being told of this "hidden" tax. Thus, the purchaser usually has little or no understanding that the price of the good would be lowered by further trade liberalization.

This regressive "hidden" tax falls heavily on the poor. Further, overall, the consequences of tariff and other trade barriers are considerable, to say the very least. Economically, "the deadweight losses associated with trade barriers" that have been imposed by the United States alone are high.[50] In 1996, the U. S. International Trade Commission calculated that the net cost —"the deadweight loss" — of existing U.S. trade barriers at that time was about $12.4 billion.[51] And these are *annual* costs.[52] These are costs that, in the absence of the removal of these trade barriers, will recur every year from now on —*in perpetuity*.[53] And, as Irwin has pointed out, "such estimates understate the true costs of trade barriers, in part, because they fail to consider the productivity and variety benefits of trade."[54]

Economically, for the United States and for other developed countries, the cost of *not* seizing the opportunities that are offered by continued trade liberalization would be even higher. For example, one recent study, at the University of Michigan, concluded that, if the new trade round reduced global tariffs on agricultural and industrial goods and barriers on services trade *by one third*, the gain for the United States alone would be $177 billion —almost two percent of US GDP.[55] The same study concluded that, if *all* the global barriers to trade in goods and services

---

[50] Irwin, Free Trade Under Fire, at 55.

[51] Id. at 55-56.

[52] Id. at 60.

[53] Id.

[54] Id.

[55] Brown, Drusilla K., Alan V. Deardorff, and Robert M. Stern, "Impact on NAFTA Members of Multilateral and Regional Trade Arrangements and Initiatives and Harmonization of NAFTA's External Tariffs," Research Seminar in International Economics Discussion Paper No. 471, University of Michigan (June 2001). *See also* the excellent discussion relating to this study and to the gains from trade in Irwin, Free Trade Under Fire, at 29-35.

were eliminated, the gain for the United States alone would be $537 billion —almost six percent of US GDP.[56] Clearly, the potential gains from further trade liberalization for the United States, as well as for other developed countries, are enormous.

Yet, economically, for the many *developing* countries that are Members of the WTO, the cost of *not* seizing the opportunities from further trade liberalization would be even higher than it would be for the United States and other *developed* countries. Some say that an international division of labor helps the rich and hurts the poor. In the first lines of his book Open Veins in Latin America, the Uruguayan journalist and "anti-globalist" Eduardo Galeano wrote, "The division of labor among nations is that some specialize in winning and others in losing."[57] But this is not so. The clear and compelling evidence is that an international division of labor helps both rich and poor alike, and perhaps helps the poor even more than the rich. Indeed, the Organization for Economic Cooperation and Development has concluded that developing countries would benefit the most from a new round of trade liberalization. According to the OECD, the GDP of India would grow by 9.6 percent, the GDP of China would grow by 5.5 percent, and the GDP of Sub-Sahara Africa would grow by 3.7 percent.[58]

In 2001, at a summit meeting of the United Nations, the world established some ambitious global goals for the year 2015. Among the world's goals for "Millennium Development" are: cutting by half the proportion of people living on less than $1 per day; cutting by half the proportion of people without access to safe water; rolling back HIV/AIDS, malaria, and other diseases; reducing maternal mortality by three-fourths; reducing child mortality by two-thirds; eliminating gender disparity at all levels of education; and ensuring that boys and girls alike complete primary schooling.[59] The World Bank and the International Monetary Fund estimate that reaching all seven of these ambitious Millennium Development goals will require an additional $54 billion annually worldwide.[60] By any reckoning, $54 billion is a lot of money. Yet, by one

---

[56] Id.

[57] Eduardo Galeano, Open Veins in Latin America: Five Centuries of the Pillage of a Continent (Monthly Review Press, 1998), 1 [1973].

[58] Mike Moore, Opening Address, WTO Ministerial Conference, Seattle, Washington (November 30, 1999).

[59] James Wolfensohn, Address at the Woodrow Wilson International Center for Scholars, Washington, D.C. (March 6, 2002).

[60] Mike Moore, Address to the United Nations Financing for Development Conference, Monterrey, Mexico (March 21, 2002).

estimate, it is just *one-third* of the gains that could be made by developing countries through further trade liberalization in the Doha Development Round.[61]

The truth is, no poor country has ever become rich by resisting trade liberalization and isolating itself from the rest of the world economically. In fact, the evidence indicates that developing countries have suffered from too little "globalization" through international economic integration, and not from too much. Those developing countries that do not have access to world markets are far worse off than those that do. Contrary to the claims of the cheerleaders for the "anti-globalization" movement, the best evidence from the World Bank is that those developing countries that have been open to trade "have grown faster," and, moreover, that "greater openness to international trade and investment has in fact helped narrow the gap between rich and poor countries rather than widen it."[62]

World Bank economists David Dollar and Aart Kraay have concluded from their research that "openness to foreign trade and investment, coupled with complementary reforms, typically leads to faster growth."[63] They have concluded also that, although the growth in global wealth "was distributed very unequally up to about 1975… since then growing equality has taken hold." Moreover, they maintain, "So far, the current wave of globalization, which started around 1980, has actually promoted economic equality and reduced poverty."[64]

As the WTO has noted, "Since 1960, child mortality rates have been almost halved. Malnutrition rates have declined by almost one third."[65] Between 1960 and the end of the twentieth century, adult literacy was reduced by nearly three fifths, and "about 4 to 5 billion people" gained access to basic education and health care.[66] World Bank data show that, during the past decade of accelerated "globalization," about *800 million people* have escaped from poverty worldwide. And much of this success can be traced to the success of first the GATT and now the WTO in lowering barriers to trade. I see much truth in the assertion by *The Economist* of

---

[61] Id.
[62] David Dollar and Aart Kraay, "Spreading the Wealth," Foreign Affairs (January/February 2002), 120, at 126, 127.
[63] Id. at 126.
[64] Id. at 120.
[65] WTO, The Multilateral Trading System, supra, at 23.
[66] Id.

London that the GATT and the WTO have "in all likelihood, done more to attack global poverty and advance living standards right across the planet than has any other man-made device."[67]

Yet I see all we have done thus far as only a bare beginning in attacking the persistence of global poverty. The President of the World Bank has called on developed countries to double their current aid to the developing world.[68] I agree. Indeed, if left to decide alone, I would more than double current aid, although I would deliver and monitor aid very differently. Yet, all that might be done through additional aid is little compared to all that clearly can be done through increased trade. And this is especially true if both developed and developing countries alike agree to mutual and increased market access in more of the most politically sensitive sectors of international trade.

The scheduled implementation of the remaining trade concessions made in the Uruguay Round is expected to facilitate continued economic growth that will lift an additional *600 million people* worldwide out of poverty. In addition, in economic terms, cutting barriers to trade in agriculture, manufacturing, and services by only *one third* in the new trade round would boost the world economy by *$613 billion dollars.*[69] As Mike Moore has said, "That's like adding an economy the size of Canada to the world economy."[70] Moreover, the World Bank has estimated that, if *all* trade barriers were abolished, the new trade round that is just now getting underway, coupled with related market reforms, could add *$2.8 trillion dollars* to global income by 2015.

Annual global income is approximately $30 trillion dollars. So this would be an increase in overall global income of *nearly 10 percent*. Of this additional global income, most, *$1.5 trillion dollars,* would be in developing countries, lifting an additional *320 million people* in developing countries out of poverty. The elimination of *all* tariff and non-tariff trade barriers could result in gains for developing countries of $182 billion in services, $162 billion in manufactures, and $32 billion in agriculture.[71]

---

[67] "Who Needs the WTO?", The Economist (December 4, 1999), 74.
[68] James Wolfensohn, Address at the Woodrow Wilson International Center for Scholars, Washington, D.C. (March 6, 2002).
[69] Mike Moore, "To Doha and Beyond: A Roadmap for successfully concluding the Doha Development Round," Address to the Evian VII Plenary Meeting, Montreux, Switzerland (April 12, 2002).
[70] Id.
[71] Id.

Thus, unquestionably, the cost to developing countries of *not* continuing with trade liberalization would, in very human terms, be high. It would be appallingly high.

The World Bank has also reported some more modest numbers for a more modest conclusion to the "Doha Development Round" that, as some see it, may be more politically achievable. Assume that the developed countries cut tariffs by only five percent in manufacturing and by only ten percent in agriculture. Assume also that developing countries reciprocate with tariff cuts of only ten percent in manufacturing and only fifteen percent in agriculture. Assume further that developed and developing countries alike eliminate agricultural export subsidies, "decouple" domestic agricultural subsidies to minimize trade distortions, and eliminate the use of certain specific tariffs, quotas, and anti-dumping duties.

Under such a scenario, *developed* countries would gain *$170 billion* in additional income by 2015. Furthermore, *developing* countries would gain *$350 billion* in additional income by 2015. According to the World Bank, "At the world level, the number of persons living on $1/day or less would decline by 61 million, or 8 percent of the current forecast for 2015 of 734 million.... The number living on $2/day or less would decline by 144 million. The greatest reduction in absolute terms would come in Sub-Saharan Africa.... The largest percentage fall would occur in the Middle East."[72]

Numbers such as these reveal the arguments of the "anti-globalists" for what they are: cruel betrayals of those who are mired in poverty throughout the world. Additional trade liberalization will not hurt the poor. Continued trade liberalization will help the poor —because there will be fewer of them. Likewise, more trade liberalization will also help the rest of us, because it will raise our overall incomes as well. Additional trade liberalization will add worldwide to the overall "wealth of nations." And it is the overall "wealth of nations" that must be our overriding concern. The *prosperity* of other nations is not a threat to us; the *poverty* of other nations is a threat to us.

As I see it, the question is not whether the world will benefit from further trade liberalization. The question, rather, is one of political

---

[72] World Bank, Global Economic Prospects 2004: Realizing the Development Practice of the Doha Agenda (Washington, D.C. 2003), 52.

will. I see much of our failure thus far to achieve more for the world through still more trade liberalization as a mutual failure of political will. In developed and developing countries alike, but especially in the larger trading countries such as my own that must continue to help lead the world toward freer trade, this is primarily a failure of political leadership. All too often, we seem to me to be apologizing for policies favoring trade liberalization when we should be advocating them. I am not surprised when protectionists advocate protectionism; I am surprised —and dismayed —that so few in the world who know better are willing to stand up and speak up for trade.

Politicians in every country that is a Member of the WTO routinely pretend that "the WTO" is an alien venture that someone somewhere else has somehow compelled them to support. American politicians, for instance, act as if American membership in the WTO is something that was in some way imposed on Americans by the rest of the world. This puzzles the rest of the world. For they, in turn, like to pretend that their membership in the WTO was in someway imposed on them by "the Americans." The truth is, the WTO is a shared effort in pursuit of the shared international interest of all of the Members of the WTO in lowering the remaining barriers to world trade. And it would be refreshing, to say the least, if more political leaders in more WTO Members were willing to stand up and say so.

But I see our failure also as a failure of political persuasion. Even when we have been willing to defend trade politically, we have sometimes failed to state both the gains from trade and the considerable costs of turning away from trade clearly. In addition, we have often failed politically to state the compelling case for freer trade candidly. Economist Paul Krugman, with his customary candor, has usefully explained, "[I]nternational trade is not about competition, it is about mutually beneficial exchange."[73] Furthermore, "[I]nternational trade is an economic activity like any other and can indeed usefully be thought of as a kind of production process that transforms exports into imports."[74] Thus, "imports, not exports, are the purpose of trade. That is, what a country gains from trade is the ability to import things it wants. Exports are not an objective in and of themselves: the need to export is a burden that a

---

[73] Paul Krugman, "What Do Undergrads Need to Know About Trade?", Pop Internationalism (Cambridge, Massachusetts: MIT Press, 1996), 117, 120.
[74] Id.

country must bear because its import suppliers are crass enough to demand payment."[75]

Krugman makes these basic points in an article in which he attempts to explain what "undergrads need to know about trade." He would no doubt agree with me that those of us who advocate trade, those of us who negotiate and legislate and adjudicate on trade, must also know these basics. Further, we must both remember and explain these basics of trade in all we do relating to trade. Yet, all too often, we have stated the case for freer trade as if it were a case only for exports, when in fact the overriding purpose of trade is to be able to maximize real national wealth through the international exchange of goods and services that leads to imports as well as to exports. We have argued the case for trade as if it were only about "more jobs," when, in fact, the result of trade, inevitably, is also "different jobs." We have spoken only of the "winners" from trade while omitting any mention of the "losers." And this has caused some to suggest, not altogether unfairly, that we have sometimes implied that there are none.

More candor is needed to quell the revolt against trade. In both developed and developing countries alike, more candor is needed to create the credibility and the negotiating leverage to make the difficult changes that can maximize the gains from trade. To conclude the Doha Development Round successfully, to continue multilateral support for all the other ongoing efforts of the WTO, and especially to sustain support among WTO Members for upholding the international rule of law through the WTO dispute settlement system, we must summon the political will to engage in the political persuasion that can only succeed if we are committed to a much greater measure of political candor.

As a consequence of the international division of labor, there will always be both "winners" and "losers" from increased trade. There will be uncertainty. There will be disruption. There will be the cultural and economic uprooting that the Nashville Agrarians denounced as "deracination."[76] All this must be acknowledged by the advocates of trade if we hope to make the case for further trade liberalization successfully. All this must be addressed as well through effective transitional and trade policies, both domestically and internationally, if we hope to still the fear of change.

---

[75] Id. at 120-121.
[76] Twelve Southerners, I'll Take My Stand, at 6.

Moreover, we must also address the deeper concerns that give rise to the revolt against trade. Superficially, the revolt against trade is about the fear of the economic consequences of trade. Deeper down, as I see it, it is about much more.

The Fear of Technology

Deeper down, the revolt against trade reflects not only a fear of the economic consequences of trade, but also a fear of the consequences of the continued development of technology. It results from a fear that we will be unable to control, for human purposes, the changes that will be wrought by technology in human life. Perhaps the most extreme expression of this fear has been voiced by one of the most prolific of the many fearmongers in the revolt against both trade and technology, Jeremy Rifkin. In one of his numerous jeremiads against the modern, scientific world, Rifkin has gone so far as to predict, "A technological revolution is fast replacing human beings with machines in virtually every sector and industry in the global economy."[77]

Rifkin and others who fear technology have written admiringly of the revolt of the Luddites —the displaced workers who smashed the looms that heralded the arrival of the industrial revolution in Great Britain in the early nineteenth century.[78] He would doubtless be the first to proclaim this statement as a proud echo of the Luddite spirit. Like the Luddites, Rifkin and others of like mind today fear a future in which we humans will become the hapless and hopeless tools of all the tools we have made. Indeed, some of them seem to think we already are.

Rifkin is not the first to sympathize with the Luddites. He is the heir to a long intellectual tradition. Through the windows of our chambers at the WTO, we look out across the lake to the green slope of Cologny on the far shore. There the romantic poet George Gordon, Lord Byron, spent a memorable holiday with his friend and fellow poet, Percy Shelley, in the summer of 1816. Sometimes, as I gaze through those windows, I can

---

[77] Jeremy Rifkin, "New Technology and the End of Jobs," in Jerry Mander and Edward Goldsmith, ed., The Case Against the Global Economy: And for a Turn Toward the Local (San Francisco: Sierra Club Books, 1996), 108.

[78] *See*, for example, Jeremy Rifkin, The End of Work: The Decline of the Global Labor Force and the Dawn of the Post-Market Era (Putnam, 1996); and Kirkpatrick Sale, Rebels Against the Future: The Luddites and Their War on Industrial Revolution (Addison Wesley Longman, Inc., 1995).

almost see the two of them out there sailing in their small boat on the smooth waters of the lake.

Lord Byron, too, was a defender of the Luddites. In 1812, a few years before his summer idyll with Shelley in Geneva, he delivered a speech in the House of Lords in opposition to a proposed law that would have applied the death penalty to anyone who deliberately broke a machine. He summarized the reasons for his opposition in a letter that same year to his fellow aristocrat, Lord Holland. "Surely, my Lord," Byron wrote, "however we may rejoice in any improvement in the arts which may be beneficial to mankind, we must not allow mankind to be sacrificed to improvements in machinery."[79]

And yet, although he defended them, Byron was not a Luddite. As his letter made clear, the poet "understood the advantages of mechanized progress."[80] He was motivated, not by a fear of technology, but rather by his concern for "the plight of these miserable men,"[81] and no doubt also by the severity of the proposed penalty for their actions. The law was passed —with only three votes against it.[82] To the best of my knowledge, my forebears fled England for America a century or so before that vote, perhaps one step ahead of the Lords' noose. Scion of poor Southern sharecroppers that I am, I am no supporter of anything remotely resembling aristocratic entitlement. However, had I been there, and voting alongside Lord Byron, in the House of Lords, mine would have been a fourth vote against that draconian measure.

Today, all these many years later, what most remains of interest is the broader issue that Byron raised then about the need to make certain that machines serve people —so that people will not be sacrificed to machines. Machines are tools. Technology *is* a tool. The digital communications, the advanced pharmaceuticals, the genetic engineering, the information technology, and all the assorted space shuttles, space satellites, and space stations of today are the sharpened stone tools of humanity's yesterday.

---

[79] George Gordon, Lord Byron, <u>Selected Poems and Letters</u> (New York University Press 1977), 448-449; reprinted as "Appendix I" in Neil Postman, <u>Building a Bridge to the Eighteenth Century: How the Past Can Improve Our Future</u> (New York: Vintage Books, 1999), 175-176.
[80] Postman, <u>Building a Bridge to the Eighteenth Century</u>, at 37.
[81] Id. at 175.
[82] Id. at 37.

They are tools we have created in our continuing efforts to shape our world to our own purposes through the methodical application of reason that we call "science." Science, as Adam Smith told us, "is the great antidote to the poison of enthusiasm and superstition...."[83] Science is simply a way of thinking that substitutes human reason for enthusiasm and superstition, and applies human reason to the way we live. And technology is simply the result in our daily lives of the applied reason of science.

Moreover, the technological tools that result from our science not only add to the way we live; they also add to the domain of human knowledge. Technology is a tool for obtaining knowledge. We humans are a curious species. We are inquisitive. We want to *know*. We can never be satisfied if we do not know. Although we can never know *all*, we want always to know *more*. This is the inescapable fate of our species. The desire to know is also in our nature.

We children of the Enlightenment accept this fate. And we see our desire to know as the source for what can yet become the ultimate civilizing of our species. The Enlightenment philosopher from the trading town of Konigsberg, Immanuel Kant, was asked once, "What is Enlightenment?" He replied, quoting Horace, "Dare to know."[84] Prometheus dared to steal the fire. Daedalus dared to make wings and fly. Ulysses dared to set sail "to seek a newer world."[85] Lord Byron's "Childe Harold" sought "pleasure in the pathless woods" and "rapture on the lonely shore."[86] In fact and in fable, in history and in myth, in poetry and in prose, we have honored always those who have dared to know. We have honored them even when they have dared and failed. By daring to know, by applying human reason in the pursuit of more knowledge, we have created all the new tools that today are called new technologies.

In seeking new knowledge, and in making new technologies, we have relied, since the earliest days of what became the Enlightenment, on

---

[83] Smith, The Wealth of Nations, at 855.

[84] Immanuel Kant, "An Answer to the Question: What is Enlightenment?", in Perpetual Peace and Other Essays on Politics, History, and Morals (Indianapolis: Hackett Publishing Company, 1983), 41. The Latin phrase he used, from the Epodes of Horace, was "*Sapere Aude!*".

[85] Alfred, Lord Tennyson, "Ulysses," Immortal Poems of the English Language (New York: Washington Square Press, 1952), 375, 377.

[86] George Gordon, Lord Byron, "Childe Harold's Pilgrimage," The Viking Book of Poetry of the English-Speaking World (New York: The Viking Press, 1958), Volume Two, 723,728.

the applied reasoning that we call "the scientific method." The scientific method is the concrete expression of the scientific spirit that is essential to a free and open society. In the open society, "We have lost the need to go to an authority to find out whether an idea is true or not."[87] Instead, we test the truth of an idea by observation. If the idea passes the test, then we take it as true, tentatively, provisionally, and subject always to additional testing. If the idea fails the test, then we think of a new idea, a new "hypothesis," that can, in turn, be tested by observation.

As a history major serving on the science and technology committee in the Congress, I learned to be very cautious when using the word "scientific." The late American physicist and Nobel laureate Richard Feynman explained that an idea cannot be called "scientific" if it cannot be subjected to the test of observation.[88] A method that does not subject an idea to observation through the crucible of experiment and through the ongoing criticism of experimental "trial and error" is *not* a scientific method. Science is "a method of finding things out" in which "observation is the judge of whether something is or is not."[89] In science, "observation is the ultimate and final judge of the truth of an idea."[90]

Some ideas that may be important to us cannot be tested by observation. This does not mean that these ideas are not important. This does not mean that concepts that are not "scientific" are not valuable. This does not mean that they are not, ultimately, metaphysically, "true." This only means that they are not "scientific." Of such are the ideas of faith. We, as individuals, may make the "leap to faith."[91] We may summon the "will to believe" that faith inspires.[92] But, as the scripture of one faith says, "faith is the substance of things hoped for, the evidence of things *not seen.*"[93] Faith cannot be tested by observation. The kingdom of faith lies somewhere beyond the realm of reason.

Faith is a way to understand ourselves by trying to understand what lies *beyond us.* Science is a way to use human reason in the ongoing

---

[87] Richard Feynman, The Meaning of it All, at 21.
[88] Id. at 16.
[89] Id. at 15.
[90] Id.
[91] This is the famous phrase of the great Danish theologian Soren Kierkegaard, from Fear and Trembling [1846].
[92] This is the equally famous phrase of the American philosopher William James, from the title of his essay, "The Will to Believe," in William James, Pragmatism and Other Essays (New York: Washington Square Press, 1968), 193 [1876].
[93] Hebrews 11:1 (emphasis added).

observation of the world *around us*. There is room for both faith and science in an open society. Indeed, Karl Popper's home in Vienna still stands just a few steps across the square from the towering glories of St. Stephen's cathedral. In his thinking, Popper saw the beginnings of the open, "scientific" society in the classical Athens of the fifth century before Christ," and especially in the philosophizing of the Athenian gadfly, Socrates. It was Socrates, according to Popper, who "taught the lesson" that, in seeing and shaping the world around us, "we must have faith in human reason, but at the same time beware of dogmatism."[94] It was also Socrates who, Popper thought, first taught that "the spirit of science is criticism."[95]

Since the life and the tragic death of Socrates, we have climbed up slowly from our savage past through the mutual criticism that is central and essential to the scientific method. We have hypothesized. We have experimented. We have gathered facts. We have built on our successes. We have tried, and we have erred. We have learned from our mistakes. By relying on the scientific method, we have added to the realm of human knowledge. And, by applying science to daily human life, we have made ever-newer tools in the form of ever-better technologies. These tools have served as our "lever of riches"[96] as we have lifted ourselves up from the swamp of our savagery to some semblance of what ought to be humanity.

While I served in the Congress, I was better known (to the extent that I was known at all) as an advocate for space and technology than as an advocate for trade. I still remember with pride our success in the last important pivotal vote on the floor of the House of Representatives in 1993 to authorize building an international space station. We won —by one vote. Today, I sometimes take Jamey outside at night to see the stars. On a clear night, I am able to show her the "star" called the International Space Station. Perhaps it will be said, in the fine print of some future footnote to some future history of the ongoing human exploration of space, that I was among those who helped put it there. If so, I hope it will also be said that, as I see it, we humans have the capability of employing our reason to create still more new technologies that can, in the generations to come, continue to lift us up from savagery all the way to the stars.

---

[94] Popper, The Open Society, Volume I, at 185.
[95] Id.
[96] This is the title of a fascinating book that I highly recommend by Joel Mokyr, The Lever of Riches: Technological Creativity and Economic Progress (New York: Oxford University Press, 1990).

In my view, technology is inseparable from trade. It is technology, most of all, that is driving trade in our new era of "globalization." Much of what is attributed to trade can actually be traced to advances in technology. Technological transformation and economic globalization are mutually reinforcing. Technological progress propels "globalization" by shrinking the world. It makes possible the international division of labor that gives rise to increased international trade. At the same time, as the World Bank has explained, "Globalization propels technological progress with the competition and incentives of the global marketplace and the world's financial and scientific resources. And the global marketplace is technology based, with technology a major factor in market competition."[97]

This interrelationship between trade and technology is rarely acknowledged by those who oppose trade. It is much easier to oppose "unfair trade" by "foreigners" than it is to oppose a better mousetrap. A few in the revolt against trade are candid enough to acknowledge that they are also in revolt against technology. A few, such as Rifkin, proudly and candidly claim the label of "Neo-Luddites."[98] But most do not. Most of those in the revolt against trade say little about the consequences of technology while saying much about the supposed consequences of trade.

This is inconsistent. Given the mutually reinforcing relationship between trade and technology, logically, those who oppose "globalization" through trade should either oppose *both* trade *and* technology, or *neither* trade *nor* technology. Logically, they should not oppose one but not the other. Those who *oppose* trade cannot, logically or consistently, claim also to *support* technology. The fact that so many do is evidence either that they do not fully comprehend the implications of their own contentions, or that they realize that people everywhere in the world want the many blessings that technology can provide.

People want a better mousetrap. They want to live longer. They want to work smarter. They want to be more prosperous. They want the new opportunities that new technologies can provide. They want to be able to make a better life for their children. As my fellow traveler in the world trading system Mike Moore has put it, in the most human of terms,

---

[97] World Bank, Human Development Report 2001 (Washington, D.C.), 31.
[98] *See*, for example, Lionel Basney, "Questioning 'Progress': The Resurrection of Ned Ludd," Christianity Today (September/October 1998), at www.christianitytoday.com; and Ronald Bailey, "Rage Against the Machines: Witnessing the Birth of the Neo-Luddite Movement," Reason (July 2001), at www.reason.com.

"Everyone is a globalist when their child is sick. They want the best medicine the world can offer."[99]

The Victorian poet Alfred, Lord Tennyson was as puzzled as I am about why some people are persuaded that the embrace of technology must necessarily lead to a loss of faith, a loss of roots, and a loss of all of the moorings in their lives. Looking through a microscope, he once remarked, "Strange that these wonders should draw some men to God and repel others."[100] In his biography of Tennyson, Sir Harold Nicolson wrote of the poet's delight at the novelty in his new house in Sussex of a high-tech "hot-water bath." After moving into the house, Tennyson "would at first indulge four or five times a day" in a hot bath while reading and, no doubt, contemplating the mysteries of the Almighty.[101]

We all want hot baths. People everywhere in the world know that technology can be a positive force in their personal lives. They know that the creation of new knowledge through science, and the practical application of new knowledge through new technologies, can help provide them with the additional choices they want to have in making their own decisions about how best to live. They know that technology can help liberate them by giving them the freedom to choose. Those who revolt against trade because they fear technology would deny people everywhere their freedom to choose.

The ways in which we choose to use new technologies are up to us. Those ways are bounded only by our imagination. Harold Nicolson, as a boy, was much impressed to discover that his uncle, Lord Dufferin, when the British ambassador to France in the 1890s, had, in his personal carriage, an electric light. He was told that "when driving from the Quai d'Orsay or to the Spanish Embassy my uncle would beguile his traverse by reading Greek and Persian poets under the dim and ineffective bulb. It seemed to me the acme of modernity."[102] We, too, can choose to pursue modernity in our own ways in the brighter lights of the new technology of today.

Like Lord Byron, I am not unmindful that new technologies can lead to job losses for the unlucky successors to the Luddites. These job

---

[99] Mike Moore, Address to the Australia-Israel Chamber of Commerce (February 2, 2001).
[100] Tennyson is quoted in Gertrude Himmelfarb, <u>Darwin and the Darwinian Revolution</u> (Chicago: Elephant Books, 1996), 390 [1959].
[101] Harold Nicolson, <u>Tennyson</u> (Arrow Books, 1960), 184 [1923].
[102] Harold Nicolson, <u>Helen's Tower</u> (New York: Harcourt, Brace and Company, 1938), 15.

losses from embracing new technologies are, clearly, human costs. But this is no reason not to embrace those new technologies. In many instances, the human costs, the "opportunity costs," of not doing so would be far greater. Nobel economics laureate Robert Solow, along with others who have followed him since, demonstrated definitively that, while new labor-saving technologies do throw some workers out of work, workers *as a whole* are better off with newer labor-saving technologies.[103]

In the nineteenth century, in reply to the Luddites and to others who would cling to the old technologies rather than embrace the new, the French advocate of free trade Frederic Bastiat penned a fictional and satirical petition to the rulers of France that was ostensibly on behalf of the Parisian candlemakers. He proposed that the light of the sun be banned —because it posed unfair competition for the candlemakers.[104] Similarly, the "candlemakers" of today, who depend for their livelihoods on old and antiquated technologies, would, in all of their fearfulness, deny us the innovating, the labor-saving, the product-creating —and, yes —the job-creating light from the "sun" of new technologies. If we did as they wish, we would dim the brightness of all our futures.

I am not unmindful that we sometimes underestimate the impact of new technologies. This has always been so. In the 1830s, as Americans began to build railroads to replace Mark Twain's steamboats, the New Englander Nathan Hale was considered wildly fanciful in his forecasts for railroad travel. He suggested, in a speech in Faneuil Hall in Boston, that, "if people could come from Springfield to Boston in five hours, an average of nine people would come every day", and this was regarded at the time as a "preposterous statement."[105] Similar "preposterous" statements have been made many times since then about the automobile, the airplane, the computer, and the Internet. Even so, is the fact that we cannot ever accurately predict the extent of the impact of technological change a sufficient reason to oppose it? If so, we would all still be riding from Springfield to Boston in a "horse and buggy."

Likewise, I am not unmindful that there may be great risks as well as great rewards in the continued development of new technologies. As the scientist (and humanist) Freeman Dyson has said, "The ways in

---

[103] William Easterly, The Elusive Quest for Growth: Economists' Adventures and Misadventures in the Tropics (Cambridge, Massachusetts: MIT Press, 2002), 51-54.
[104] George Roche, Free Markets, Free Men: Frederic Bastiat, 1801–1850 (Hillsdale, Michigan: Hillsdale College Press, 1977), 33-34 [1971].
[105] Hale's speech is discussed in Van Wyck Brooks, The Flowering of New England, at 173n.

which science may work for good and evil in human society are many and various."[106] There is Dr. Jekyll, but there is also Mr. Hyde.[107] What human reason creates can be used by the human beast to destroy. The beast that ever lurks within us can spill more blood with a machine than with a sharpened stone. And the machines that we create can be used by the human beast not only to destroy others of our own species. They can be used as well to destroy other species, and to destroy other essential parts of the irreplaceable natural environment of our planet on which the continued survival of our species depends.

Yet, as Feynman reminded us, "this power to do things" that we call science, this seemingly fathomless power that gives us technology, "carries with it no instructions on how to use it, whether to use it for good or evil. The product of this power is either good or evil, depending on how it is used."[108] Science gives us technology. Science does not give us our values. Unquestionably, the beast within us must not be unleashed. Technology must be taught by reason. Where I differ with those who fear technology is that I believe that technology *can* be taught by reason. I believe that, through the mutual criticism of a free, open, and democratic society, we can make the right choices about how we wish to employ the technological products that result from the mutual criticism of science. Moreover, I fear for the fate of humanity if we turn away from science and from technology. For then we will no longer dare to know. And then, surely, we will be but beasts.

We will use our machines, our tools, our technologies —and not be used by them —only if we remember our human limitations. Science and technology will serve humanity well, and best, if we always remember that science and technology are, indeed, capable of serving either good or evil, depending on how they are put to use by human minds and by human hands. And we will be far more likely to use both science and technology for good than for evil if we are always humble in the recognition of human limits, and if we are always careful to remember that science cannot give us the absolute authority of total, absolute knowledge.

Science cannot give us certainty. Science can only help us live with uncertainty and with doubt. Science can only take us to the limited boundaries that we can reach through the use of human reason in the

---

[106] Freeman Dyson, Imagined Worlds (Cambridge: Harvard University Press, 1997), 197.
[107] Robert Louis Stevenson, The Strange Case of Dr. Jekyll and Mr. Hyde [1886].
[108] Feynman, The Meaning of It All, at 5-6.

pursuit of our uniquely human curiosity. But we must try to reach those limits. In my view, we were given our curiosity as a species in the hope that we would use it. It was the English lawyer and philosopher, Sir Francis Bacon, in the seventeenth century, who first saw clearly that science could be applied for human purposes, and who thus prepared the way for the rise of modern science and modern technology. He said that human history "must be made to the measure of the universe. For the world is not to be narrowed till it will go into the understanding... but the understanding is to expand until it can take in the image of the world."[109]

I once stood high up on the gantry of the launching pad at the Kennedy Space Center where the space shuttle is sent into orbit around the earth as part of our ongoing human effort to explore the full measure of the universe. I looked down through the openings in the metal grates of the gantry beneath my feet and into the pit where the flames flare during a launch. I looked out on the sands of the nearby beach and on the waves of the ocean as they beat their relentless tattoo on the sands. The breeze from the ocean seemed to make the gantry sway.

I can only imagine the courage it must take for the astronauts I so much admire to step from that gantry into the shuttle and to strap themselves into the shuttle for a launch. When I first ran for the Congress, I was asked whether, like my predecessor, I would become an astronaut by going into space on a shuttle mission. As Rebecca had instructed, I replied, "My wife says that I can go to Washington, but I cannot go into orbit."

No doubt I would not make much of an astronaut. I am no more skilled in astrophysics than I am in metaphysics. And yet there remains in me all these years later much of what made me the vice president of the "space club" of South Seminole Junior High School when I was an eighth-grader more than forty years ago. The truth is, I would go if I could.

For I do not fear science. I do not fear technology. I do not fear the measure of the universe. I do not fear venturing "into the unknown."

I want to know.

---

[109] Bacon is quoted in Freeman Dyson, "Science and Religion: No Ends in Sight," The New York Review of Books (March 28, 2002) 4, 6.

The Fear of Growth

Deeper still, the revolt against trade represents a fear, not only of the economic change that may result from trade, and of the other changes that may result from technology, but also of the changes that continued economic growth may cause in our natural environment. Human beings are unique and irreplaceable. But so too is our natural environment. The fate of both is fragile. The fate of both is intertwined.

My son, Joe, learned this by walking on a glacier. Early in my tenure at the WTO, we took a side trip from Geneva to Interlachen, where we took a rickety railroad ride up from the lakes, past the rocky face of the *Eiger*, and through a range of icy gorges to the top of the *Jungfrau*. There, Joe walked out from the observatory at the "top of Europe" on to the frozen slope of an ancient glacier. It was, for my son, the thrill of a young lifetime. The glassy ice of the glacier soaked through the soles of the sneakers he had brought with him all the way to Switzerland from Florida. From the face of the glacier, he gazed out on the face of the world.

Recently, as I neared the end of my time at the WTO, we made a second journey up the same Alpine peak. Joe walked once more on the same glacier. But this time he could not go out nearly as far on the slope. This time the way was barred. It is no longer safe to walk out as far on the glacier as he could before. Even at that height, the ever-increasing human toll on our planet can be seen. Global warming is shrinking and melting the glaciers even at the very summit of the Swiss Alps.

Emerson, for one, fully understood the unbreakable bonds between humanity and nature, not to mention the frailty of both. Unlike Joe, he may never have walked on a glacier, but he knew that our human nature is inseparable from the rest of nature that surrounds and envelops us. "To go into solitude," he said, "a man needs to retire as much from his chamber as from society.... [I]f a man would be alone, let him look at the stars."[110] Each of us, as an individual, is a part of the whole of nature, and, to create the true society of individuals that is the result of true "self-reliance," we must each be as one with nature. As Emerson told us, like previous generations, we must behold "nature face to face," and we must each "enjoy an original relation to the universe."[111]

---

[110] Emerson, "Nature," in Essays and Lectures (New York: The Library of America, 1983), 9 [1836].
[111] Id. at 7.

Some of those today who, like Emerson, understand the fundamental connection between humanity and nature, fear that those of us who seek continued growth through trade and technology may not. In particular, they fear that the WTO is an effort to achieve economic growth at any and all costs to the natural environment. For example, The Friends of the Earth (whose friendship for the earth I have always valued) have listed "10 reasons why the world trade system is bad for people and the planet."[112]   The first of the ten reasons is this: "The trade system pursues growth at all costs, through trade and investment liberalization, and sees economic growth and increasing consumption as ends in themselves."[113]   Yet, this is not what I see as the purpose of the WTO-based trading system. Nor is this, based on my experience, at all an accurate description of what others see who, like me, are working for growth through trade under the auspices of the WTO.

As a former Congressman who represented the "Space Coast" of Florida, I have always tried to see the relationship between trade and the environment as I would if I were orbiting the earth as a passenger in the space shuttle. The astronauts I have been privileged to know have told me how small the earth seems from space, and how thin and how fragile the shell of the earth's biosphere appears from space. Without the special mix of chemical and biological ingredients in that biosphere, there would be no human life. An end to the biosphere would bring an end to human life.

Unquestionably, the human species is a part of nature. Our man-made world tends to make us think that we are somehow separate from the world God made. But this is an illusion. We have a kinship with the earth. We are but a part of a larger Creation. Should we, in all our pride, in all our ambition, and in all our avarice, ever forget this, it surely would bring an end to human life. The degradation of nature reveals some of the worst in our species. A respect, a reverence, a realization of our oneness with the rest of nature can reveal some of the best. Our fidelity to ourselves demands that we sustain also our fidelity to nature.

There are two hundred different species of trees in the *Parc Mon Repos* in Geneva next to the WTO. They must all survive. Like Emerson, like Thoreau, like Rousseau, like John Muir, like Aldo Leopold —like all

---

[112] The Friends of the Earth, "The World Trade System: How It Works and What's Wrong With It," at http://foci.org/campaigns/TES/ideas/WTO_1.htm, 1.
[113] Id.

those who have treasured our natural environment and who have trumpeted our relationship with our natural environment —I believe that a communion with nature can help bring out the best in *our* nature. As I see it, if we are as one with nature, then we will be better able to be as one with ourselves, and better able also to be as one with all the many others who share our nature and our world. And we will perhaps also have a better understanding of *who* we are, of *why* we are, and, maybe, of *what* we are supposed to do with the marvelous, and yet mysterious, gift of life.

It is understanding —it is knowledge —that we need if we hope to live in harmony with the rest of nature. Indeed, it will be recalled that the original motivating force for the reliance on reason by the Enlightenment thinkers was their belief that reason could lead to an understanding of nature that would help us build a better society. They were devoted to science, in part, because they saw the applied reason of science as the key to understanding nature. They believed that, by understanding nature, we could learn to shape our conduct and our law in accordance with nature and, thus, be true to the true nature of humankind.

Yet, as Sir Francis Bacon wrote at the dawn of our modern, "scientific" age, "[t]he subtlety of nature," for all our inquiries and investigations, "is far beyond that of sense or of the understanding."[114] A challenge that has long faced our species, and now faces us as never before, is how best to make use of our understanding of nature without destroying the delicate balance of nature that makes human life possible. As I see it, genuinely enlightened thinking today must proceed from an understanding that nature has its limits, and that the global biosphere on which we all depend is endangered as never before, in large part because of the short-term thinking of our species. The thinkers of the eighteenth century largely did not foresee this. Those of us who presume to think about the fate of our species and the fate of our planet in the twenty-first century cannot afford to ignore it.

But in remembering the limits of our natural environment, we must remember also how often we have underestimated our potential for economic growth. As Schumpeter first reminded us, the entrepreneurialism that thrives in a free marketplace inspires not only

---

[114] Francis Bacon, Novum Organum, First Book, 10.

the "creative destruction" of capitalism, but also what might be called the *creative construction* of capitalism by transforming into useful "resources" what were previously useless things.[115] The simple grains of sand that make the silicon chips that drive our computers are the foundation of the new information age. Time and again, we have reached "the limits of growth" —only to find that we have not. The limits of our resources are less because there are no limits to our ideas.

Economist Paul Romer has pointed out that ideas are "nonrival goods." They consist of information. They are not limited by the process of exchange. As Romer has explained, "Every generation has perceived the limits to growth that finite resources and undesirable side effects would pose if no new recipes or ideas were discovered. And every generation has underestimated the potential for finding new recipes and ideas. We consistently fail to grasp how many ideas remain to be discovered. The difficulty is the same one we have with compounding. Possibilities do not add up. They multiply."[116] We must never forget the multiplier effect of the human mind.

Those who fear economic growth because they cherish our natural environment need not be concerned that I will ignore nature. I am ever mindful that our efforts to understand nature must not lead to the sabotage of nature, and that our efforts to achieve growth must not diminish our ability to sustain growth. Moreover, I am ever mindful that the limits of our natural resources must be taken into account in considering both the nature and the extent of all we hope to accomplish through trade. Yet I am aware, as well, of the unforeseeable possibilities of continued technological innovation as a lever for continued —and environmentally sound —economic growth.

Adam Smith was among the Enlightenment thinkers who *did* seem to understand that there must be a balance between economy and environment. He did not articulate his understanding in the contemporary terminology of "ecology." Even so, his philosophy of trade was based in part on the assumption that there will always be a scarcity of resources.

---

[115] Joseph Schumpeter, Captialism, Socialism, and Democracy (New York, 1942), at 117; Schumpeter is quoted in Muller, The Mind and the Market, at 309; *see also* the same book at 391.
[116] Paul Romer and R.R. Nelson, "Science, Economic Growth, and Public Policy," in B.L.R. Smith and Claude Barfield, eds., Technology, R&D, and the Economy (Washington: Brookings Institute, 1996); and *see also* the discussion on this point in Steven Pinker, The Blank Slate, supra, at 236-239.

And, as I read Smith, this assumption of scarcity applies to natural as well as human resources. In my view, his "simple system of natural liberty" is a system that should be seen as including an appreciation of nature.

The Members of the WTO understand this as well. The economic growth foreseen by WTO Members is *sustainable* growth. That is why the WTO treaty speaks of *sustainable* development. As they explained in the very first paragraph of the Preamble to the Marrakesh Agreement establishing the World Trade Organization, the Members of the WTO seek "sustainable development... both to protect and preserve the environment and to enhance the means for doing so in a manner consistent with their respective needs and concerns at different levels of economic development."[117]

I do not see any inherent conflict between freer trade and a better, cleaner, safer, sustainable natural environment. And neither do the Members of the WTO. As the trade ministers decided at Marrakesh when establishing a permanent Committee on Trade and Environment in the WTO, "[T]here should not be, nor need be, any policy contradiction between upholding and safeguarding an open, non-discriminating and equitable multilateral trading system on the one hand, and acting for the protection of the environment, and the promotion of sustainable development on the other...."[118] I am confident that every Member of the WTO would readily agree with the World Bank that "a development policy that puts a priority on growth at the expense of the environment may be short-sighted, incurring avoidably high future costs."[119]

These official pronouncements are reflections of the understanding of WTO Members of what historians know —that environment is often a decisive factor in determining the pace and the extent of economic growth. In Guns, Germs, and Steel, for example, the historian Jared Diamond concludes that "the striking differences between the long-term histories of peoples of the different continents have been due not to innate differences in the peoples themselves but to differences in their environments."[120] History reminds us to remember that —as I

---

[117] Preamble, the Marrakesh Agreement.

[118] The trade ministers are quoted in United States —Import Prohibition of Certain Shrimp and Shrimp Products, WTO Doc. WT/ DS58/AB/R, 12 October 1998, para. 154.

[119] World Bank, Globalization, Growth, and Poverty: Building An Inclusive World Economy (Washington, D.C., 2002), 131-132.

[120] Jared Diamond, Guns, Germs, and Steel (New York: Norton, 1997), 405.

wrote so many times in speeches I crafted for Governor Askew so long ago, and as I have said so many times in so many of my own speeches since —our future economically cannot be separated from our future environmentally.

These treaty testaments are tangible evidence of a common awareness among WTO Members that considerations of environment cannot be separated from considerations of growth. The Indian economist and Nobel laureate Amartya Sen echoes many other economists in asserting that "environment and development are inextricably linked."[121] Further, he asserts, "After acknowledging the role of trade and exchange in human living, we still have to examine what the other consequences of market transactions actually are."[122]

Clearly, among the other consequences we must examine are those for the environment. Where the environment is concerned, the "invisible hand" of the market must often be restrained by the visible hand of government. Markets will not always, or automatically, consider environmental costs. As Professor Bhagwati has noted, markets will lead to an efficient allocation of resources only if markets produce prices reflecting true social costs, including environmental costs. Thus, he has said, "If there are market failures, as when a producer pollutes the air but does not have to pay for this pollution, then the Invisible Hand can lead you in the wrong direction."[123]

In his classic economic treatise, The Theory of Economic Growth, published nearly half a century ago, in 1955, W. Arthur Lewis quite rightly identified the objective of economic development as increasing "the range of human choice."[124] It is by increasing the range of human choice that we increase the range of human freedom. Lewis went on to say that "the growth of output per head... gives man greater control over his environment and thereby increases his freedom."[125] But we know more about the environment today than we did half a century ago. We should all know by now that, to be desirable, economic growth must be environmentally sustainable.

---

[121] Amartya Sen, "Freedom Makes All the Difference," *International Herald Tribune* (August 15, 2002), 4.

[122] Amartya Sen, Development as Freedom (New York: Anchor Books, 2000), 126 [1997].

[123] Jagdish Bhagwati, "Free Trade: What Now?", Address at the University of St. Gallen, Switzerland (May 25, 1998).

[124] W. Arthur Lewis, The Theory of Economic Growth (London: Allen and Unwin, 1953), 9-10.

[125] Id. at 420-421.

We should all know this in the WTO. But do we? It has been noted before in the trade debate that "the devil is in the details."[126] Surely this is so. However, I would suggest to all those who fear the environmental consequences of the growth that results from trade that they should spend more time reading the details of what we have actually ruled thus far about the relationship between trade and the environment in WTO dispute settlement, and less time reading the press releases of some supposed defenders of the environment who have distorted those details for their own self-serving purposes. Some who have actually taken the time to *read* the rulings of the Appellate Body have seen them as examples of "the greening of the WTO."[127]

More significantly, I would suggest also, and especially, that those who fear growth should work more closely together with those who favor growth to make certain that we get all the details right in the WTO. I am pleased, for instance, to see that the Friends of the Earth have been among those participating in recent WTO-sponsored discussions on the relationship between trade and the environment. Other such efforts are needed. The "green room" of the WTO where important negotiations are held must be a place where the "green issues" of the environment are taken into account.

Topics worthy of discussion are many. Air and water pollution. Ocean pollution. The loss of forests. The loss of wilderness. The loss of wetlands. The loss of endangered species. Climate change. Exploding population growth. Declining fisheries. Declining supplies of fresh water. The degradation of land through erosion and other kinds of abuse. Bio-safety in all its many manifestations. These are among the many serious international environmental concerns that demand the attention of the world. The details of all these environmental concerns —and many more —are not unrelated to international trade.

Should there be specific legal "linkages" between trade and the environment? Should some among the two hundred or so existing multilateral environmental agreements be accorded specific legal status by the WTO? Should some of those agreements be given recognition through legal interpretation in WTO dispute settlement? Should

---

[126] This is, of course, the favorite phrase of that outspoken American skeptic of trade, Ross Perot.

[127] Michael M. Weinstein and Steve Charnovitz, "The Greening of the WTO," Foreign Affairs (November/December, 2001).

"environmental impact" studies be conducted when considering new trade concessions? How can we make what some environmentalists fear will be a "race to the bottom" instead a "race to the top" that will continue to free trade while also assuring needed national and international environmental protections? These are among the important questions that must be asked, and that can only be answered, by engaging with all the seemingly intractable "devils" of the details in an ongoing effort to make the right choices in the relationship between trade and the environment.

In my view, we should approach environmental issues in the WTO in much the same way as we approached environmental issues in Florida while I worked for Governor Askew in the 1970s. We should seek the right balance between economy and environment that will sustain and strengthen both. In Florida, under Askew, this led to the Land and Water Management Act of 1972, the Water Resources Act of 1973, the Local Comprehensive Planning Act of 1976, the adoption of a "State Comprehensive Plan," the purchase of environmentally endangered lands, the purchase of long miles of endangered coastline, the establishment of coastal construction "setback lines," the protection of endangered species, and many more environmental initiatives that furthered and facilitated both environmental protection and economic growth. Regrettably, Florida has turned away from protecting the state's precious environment in recent years, but, as I see it, it is not too late for Florida to turn back toward "sustainable development" —and it is not too late for the world to turn toward it as well.

Economists often describe environmental considerations as "externalities," because such considerations are external to the basic process of buying and selling that is the essence of economic exchange. Some, in so describing them, seem sometimes to dismiss them. I agree with former United States Vice President Al Gore, an ardent advocate of both trade and the environment, that there is a "blindness" in our economic calculations and computations that can sometimes prevent decisionmakers from taking fully into account the environmental consequences of economic actions.[128] But I believe also that this can change.

---

[128] Al Gore, Earth in the Balance: Ecology and the Human Spirit (New York: Houghton Mifflin,, 1992), 185.

As I see it, many trade decisions cannot be made without taking into account their possible environmental consequences. The calculations of our decisionmaking must take into account more than merely GNP. Those calculations must include concerns for "sustainable development." Over time, the sum total of the "gross national product" of every Member of the WTO will be much less if GNP is produced in ways that diminish nature or in ways that cannot be sustained compatibly with nature. But growth we must have in GNP. Unquestionably, it is true what some environmentalists say: "You can't eat GNP."[129] Yet it is also true that you cannot eat very much without it. Moreover, it is also true —though many environmentalists tend to forget it —that growth in GNP and growth in environmental consciousness usually go hand in hand.

Impoverished people living in impoverished countries are often so preoccupied with the sheer necessity of somehow surviving from day to day that they can afford to give little thought or consideration to the broader and longer-term considerations of environmental consciousness. As Professor Bhagwati has put it, "Growth enables governments to tax and to raise resources for a variety of objectives, including the abatement of pollution and the general protection of the environment. Without such revenues, little can be achieved, no matter how pure one's motives may be."[130] No doubt many of the protesters in the turtle costumes in the streets of Seattle had the purist of motives. No doubt, too, they were almost all loyal citizens of the United States and other developed countries with a high GNP. And no doubt the environmental consciousness that inspired their protests was perhaps, in part, a consequence of economic growth.

Inevitably, there will be tradeoffs in the details of the many difficult decisions that must be made on matters that affect both trade and the environment. This is true of any economic or environmental decision. But these decisions need not be "either/or." Nor is there any reason for environmentalists or anyone else to assume, based on the limited experience thus far, that legitimate environmental concerns will necessarily be sacrificed to trade concerns in WTO dispute settlement. In dispute settlement, and in all the other work of the WTO, we can maximize

---

[129] Eric A. Davidson, You Can't Eat GNP: Economics As If Ecology Mattered (Cambridge, Massachusetts: Perseus, 2000).
[130] Jagdish Bhagwati, "The Case for Free Trade," in Bhagwati, A Stream of Windows: Unsettling Reflections on Trade, Immigration, and Democracy (Cambridge, Massachusetts: MIT Press 1998), 231, 233.

the gains from trade without having to minimize the future of the environment. The last time I looked, for example, the American ban on imports of shrimp caught in ways that endanger sea turtles remained very much in force —with the full legal approval of the WTO.

If anything, the need for global environmental rules is even greater than the need for global economic rules. Many environmental concerns are intrinsically international, and increasingly so. They require international solutions, and imminently so. Through cooperative and multilateral efforts, we can find such solutions, in the WTO and elsewhere. The question is one of striking the right global balance between economic growth and environmental protection and preservation. The question is one of making the right choices. We can strike the right balance if we make the right choices. I am persuaded that we will make the right choices if we remember what that early advocate of using science and technology to create economic growth, Sir Francis Bacon, told us about our efforts to command nature: "Nature, to be commanded, must be obeyed."[131]

The Fear of Capitalism

Deeper still, the revolt against trade reflects a fear of capitalism. It reveals a fear of the sheer productive power of the market forces of a "globalized" capitalism. And it reveals also a fear that those powers will be unleashed in a reckless and rapacious way.

The fear of capitalism is not new. There were apprehensions about capitalism even long before Karl Marx, while scribbling in the sanctuary of the Reading Room of the British Museum, coined the word "capitalism" during the height of the Industrial Revolution in nineteenth-century Europe.[132] Both capitalism and the supposed consequences of capitalism have long been suspect in the eyes of those who wish that human nature were other than it is, and who therefore exhort us to change our nature.

The revolt against trade offers little that is new in the traditional critique of capitalism. Little, that is, except the scale provided by the worldwide distribution of propaganda via the Internet. And little, that is, except an ersatz economics adorned by a trendy "post-modern" rhetorical flourish that echoes Marx without embracing Marxism, and

---

[131] Francis Bacon, Novum Organum, First Book, 129.
[132] This point about Marx is made in Robert Gilpin, Global Political Economy: Understanding the International Economic Order (Princeton: Princeton University Press, 2001), 14.

that denounces capitalism without endorsing communism. Like Marx, the "anti-globalists" critique capitalism. Unlike Marx, for the most part, they do not even attempt to offer a coherent alternative.

Those who fear capitalism denounce what they dismiss as a "neoliberalism" that would give free markets an absolutely free rein to do whatever might seem to be in the short-term self-interest of the mercenary capitalists who manipulate those markets —and who, by the way, allegedly also control the WTO. They see the global governmental momentum toward freer trade as merely a consequence of widespread governmental capitulation to mindless market forces and to the manipulations of greedy capitalists.

The self-styled "agrarian" Wendell Berry is typical of those who fear capitalism in fearing also that the World Trade Organization is merely a bureaucratic creature of such a "neoliberalism." Berry sees the WTO as wholly controlled by the capitalists who control the large multinational corporations. He asserts that the global economy "is the property of a few supranational corporations."[133] He refers to these corporations as "the corporate sponsors" of the WTO.[134] He maintains, "The World Trade Organization enlarges the old idea of the corporation-as-person by giving the global corporate economy the status of a super government with the power to overrule nations."[135]

Yet this would only be so if the nations —the national governments —that are the Members of the WTO identified their individual national interests solely and entirely with the corporations that claim their nationality. There is no evidence that this is so — either in WTO dispute settlement or in any other activity of the WTO. To be sure, the Members of the WTO often see their national interests as *coinciding* with certain domestic corporate interests. However, almost always, there are *competing* domestic corporate interests within the national territories of individual WTO Members whose interests differ and conflict in the assertion of particular national interests by those WTO Members in the WTO. Indeed, this is true, to cite only one example among many I might cite, of every single "anti-dumping" claim that has ever been brought in WTO dispute settlement.

---

[133] Berry, "The Idea of a Local Economy," The Art of the Commonplace, 249, 254.
[134] Id. at 243.
[135] Id. at 255-256.

The fact is, I have yet to see any representatives of any corporation anywhere in the world appear before us in any appeal before the Appellate Body. Those who appear before us are all duly designated members of the delegations of the countries and other customs territories that are the only Members of the WTO. To the extent that corporate interests are asserted in WTO dispute settlement, the Members of the WTO alone assert them. And, to the extent that any Member of the WTO may fall short in representing the national interests of their citizens by representing the corporate interests of certain corporations, that is the fault and the failure of the national government of that Member, and *not* of the WTO. It is entirely up to the WTO Members to determine what their national interests are.

I might add that I have yet to hear Berry or any other critic of the supposed influence of the multinational corporations on the WTO explain how it transpired that, in what has been widely described as the most significant case thus far in WTO dispute settlement, the Members of the WTO adopted successive rulings by panels and by the Appellate Body holding that by far the biggest international tax benefit that is given to many U.S.-based multinational corporations by the United States of America has not been in compliance with WTO rules.[136] To the best of my knowledge, those who accuse the WTO of being a creature of the multinational corporations have simply ignored these rulings. Doubtless this is because the results in these rulings refute their view of the WTO as merely a bureaucratic mechanism for a knee-jerk "neoliberalism" that exists solely to serve the interests of such corporations.

Leaving aside for the moment the question of whether there *is* such a *laissez-faire* straw man as "neoliberalism," it is worth asking first: what do those who fear the free markets and the free trade of capitalism propose in their stead? The answer —to the extent that there is an answer —seems to be the contemporary equivalent of the Nashville Agrarians' bucolic agenda of "back to the farm." Some favor the familiar protectionism of high tariffs and other non-tariff trade barriers. Others suggest a return to the top-down state control of what Lenin —no fan of capitalism — once called the "commanding heights"[137] of the economy.

---

[136] *See* United States —Tax Treatment for "Foreign Sales Corporations," AB–1999–9, WTO Doc. WT/DS108/AB/R (February 24, 2000); United States —Tax Treatment for "Foreign Sales Corporations" – Recourse to Article 21.5 of the DSU by the European Communities, AB–2001–8, WTO Doc. WT/DS108/AB/RW (January 4, 2002).

[137] Daniel Yergin and Joseph Stanislaw, The Commanding Heights: The Battle Between Government and the Marketplace That Is Remaking the Modern World (New York: Simon and Schuster, 1998), 12.

Still others advance an avant-garde version of local, "small is beautiful"[138] self-sufficiency that is sometimes called "eco-regionalism."

All offer various ways to protect the various and vested public and private interests in the way things were. None offer anything new. And none offer anything that will work. Traditional, tariff-based protectionism was rejected after the Smoot-Hawley tariffs of the United States prolonged and deepened the Great Depression, and worsened the global economic conditions that contributed to the outbreak of World War II. State controls were rejected after state control of the "commanding heights" led numerous national economies to collapsing depths in the post-World War II decades. And the siren call of local self-sufficiency, while appealing to poets, is much less appealing to other people, who must somehow afford to feed and clothe their children. The call for "localism" has been heard many times and in many places through the centuries; but it has largely gone unheeded since ancient men first discovered the advantages of a division of labor for improving their standard of living.

What does work? Capitalism works. Capitalism does not work perfectly. Capitalism does not work automatically. Capitalism does not always work quickly, evenly, consistently, or, in the eyes of history and equity, "fairly." Capitalism, as Alan Greenspan has reminded us, can lead both to "irrational exuberance" and to "infectious greed."[139] But capitalism works. Capitalism *alone* works. Capitalism *alone* works because, to turn a phrase borrowed from Winston Churchill, capitalism is the worst form of economics —except for all the rest. Capitalism works, and capitalism *alone* works, as a system of economics, because capitalism is the only form of economics that is consistent with, and compatible with, the unchanging reality of human nature.

Like many who revolt against trade because of their fear of capitalism, I, too, wish that human nature were other than it is. But it is not. I, too, would exhort a suffering, striving, struggling humanity to change our wicked ways by changing our nature. But we cannot. Human

---

[138] E. F. Schumacher, Small is Beautiful: Economics As If People Mattered (New York: HarperCollins, 1989) [1974].
[139] Alan Greenspan used the phrase "irrational exuberance" in a speech at the annual dinner of the American Enterprise Institute in Washington D.C. on December 5, 1996; he used the phrase "infectious greed" in testimony to the House and Senate committees on banking on July 17, 2002.

nature will not change. And, because capitalism is founded on a practical and realistic understanding of an unchanging human nature, capitalism *alone*, among all the many nostrums and panaceas of political economy that have ever been advanced, has been able to create something more than merely an economic fantasy. Capitalism *alone* has been able to create something more than the distant hope of a cornucopia for humankind.

Those who fear capitalism fail to appreciate this connection between capitalism and human nature, and they fail to appreciate also what a liberating force capitalism can be for human freedom and for social justice. Far too many of the critics of capitalism, for some reason, do not see all the many ways that the political favoritism and the privileged protectionism of inward-looking autarchic and mercantile societies stand in the way of both freedom and justice. And, as Professor Bhagwati has reminded us, far too many of those critics "do not see that capitalism can destroy privilege and open up economic opportunity to the many."[140] Capitalism can and does serve the cause of social justice in an unjust world. It does so every day.

Those who fear capitalism also fail to appreciate the virtues of competition. They regret the rough and tumble of dog-eat-dog. They lament "what makes Sammy run."[141] They denounce what they see as, in the words of one of them, "the falseness and the silliness of the economic ideal of competition, which is destructive both of nature and of human nature because it is untrue to both."[142] Those who fear capitalism prefer the soothing salve of cooperation to the painful, relentless spur of competition. They forget that what they see solely as competition is also a form of cooperation that arises from the necessary crucible of human exchange. And they forget, too, that we humans need the spur that is competition. For, despite what they may want to think, this, too, is in our nature.

As a society, we need the spur of competition because we need all of the benefits that can be derived from the initiative, the incentive, and the endless stream of new innovations that are inspired by competition. We need all of the gains from trade and all of the many other bounties of the marketplace that only a division of labor in the

---

[140] Bhagwati, <u>Free Trade Today</u> (Princeton: Princeton University Press, 2002), 6.
[141] This, of course, was the title of the book by Budd Schulberg about Sammy Glick, the quintessential American "go-getter" with a passion for getting ahead, published in 1941.
[142] Berry, "Economy and Pleasure," <u>The Art of the Commonplace</u>, supra, 207, 208.

competition of capitalism can make possible. And we need also the full extent of human creativity that can only come from the spur of competition. Competition is indispensable to scientific and other efforts to create new knowledge and new know-how because, as Friedrich Hayek explained, "The mind can never foresee its own advance."[143] Far better, then, to have many minds working and competing on different plans than to have every mind following just one plan. For that one plan may very well be wrong.

These are among the virtues of competition, and, thus, of capitalism. Yet it is not correct to say that, because we defend competition, and because we defend capitalism, those of us who work for trade and for the WTO are working also for "neoliberalism" —or for some other form of market fundamentalism —that would leave the world a helpless prey to the predations of an utterly free market left untouched by the restraining hand of government. The Members of the WTO are trying to establish and uphold rules for trade. The Members of the WTO are *not* trying to abolish government. (Indeed, it seems, to me, a bit incongruous to accuse the WTO of trying both to *abolish* all government *and* to *become* one.)

The opponents of the WTO accuse the supporters of the WTO of allegiance only to the market —only to an absolutely *laissez-faire* economics. But this is not so. There is absolutely nothing in the WTO treaty that in any way requires any Member of the WTO to pledge allegiance to *laissez-faire*. Furthermore, I have never known anyone in any way associated with the WTO who would. The WTO does not dictate domestic policy choices to the sovereign countries that are Members of the WTO on such topics as the extent of a social safety net or the allocation of income distribution. These choices are left solely to domestic governments. The WTO treaty fully allows for an active, purposeful, and ongoing role for government in the domestic economies of WTO Members.

The straw man of "neoliberalism" is, indeed, made of straw. Market forces are liberating. Reliance on market forces is essential. The competition created by market forces is endlessly useful. But, as we have seen, Adam Smith was among the first to point to the harm done by monopolies and other combinations in restraint of trade. Likewise, today he would doubtless be among the first to say that reasonable restrictions

---

[143] Friedrich Hayek, The Constitution of Liberty (Chicago: University of Chicago Press, 1960), 24.

are needed to curb the harmful excesses of global market forces, and thereby serve the other human values that we seek to further by freeing the global marketplace. And there is absolutely nothing in the WTO treaty that prevents such reasonable restrictions.

I have no doubt whatsoever that everyone involved in the work of the WTO would agree that the "invisible hand" of Adam Smith should, as he suggested, be stayed —from time to time —by the visible hand of government. Certainly I would. I, for one, would never raise my hand in a salute to *laissez-faire*. I am that stubborn variety of American known as a Florida Democrat. I have voted —when they have let me vote —for the market. I have also voted for public education, public investment, reasonable regulation, and a strong social safety net. I support both markets and reasonable restraints on markets. I favor both the New Deal and the new, global economy. As a former Member of Congress, I have the voting record and the political scars to prove it. If you doubt it, please go and read the Congressional Record.

As I see it, the problem is not too much capitalism; it is too little effective democratic governance. We need appropriate and effective countervailing efforts to smooth the roughest edges of capitalism —both nationally and internationally. We need a "ladder" up for those who are climbing toward more comparative advantage. We need a "safety net" for those who fall off the ladder. We need fully funded and fully effective transitions to ease the impact of changing patterns of trade on human lives, and also to maximize the gains of trade by maximizing the vast potential of comparative advantage. We need numerous health, environment, labor, consumer, investor, and other regulatory protections of all kinds. And I believe we can apply all the reasonable regulations we reasonably need without undermining the liberating forces of the free market that are furthered by freer trade.

The Enron and other Wall Street scandals in the United States are only the latest reminder that there must be a balance between free markets and governmental regulation, and that we must, as Joseph Stiglitz has put it, "get the balance right."[144] There must be the right balance between market freedom and market controls, between private enterprise and public concerns, between unchained initiative and careful and reasoned regulation, and between the need for risk and risk-taking and the understandable human desire for some modicum of personal security.

---

[144] *See* Joseph Stiglitz, "Crony capitalism American-style," online at project-syndicate.org.

This is true both nationally and internationally. The difficulty is in finding and striking the right balance.

Personally, I do not subscribe to the philosophical tenets of either socialism or "Social Darwinism."[145] My doubts about human perfectibility keep me from believing in the "heaven on earth"[146] promised by the prophets of socialism. Tens of millions of people worldwide died in the twentieth century at the hand of governments that called themselves "socialist." Likewise, my devotion to individual human dignity keeps me from accepting the harsh notion of "the survival of the fittest" that is advanced by the contemporary advocates of "Social Darwinism." Millions of people worldwide are suffering today because they have been left out, left over, and left behind in the advance thus far of capitalism. Like Darwin himself, I am not a "Social Darwinist." My reading of the painful history of the past few centuries tells me that the right balance is somewhere in between the excesses of these two extremes.

Lionel Trilling, the American literary critic, was accused once of avoiding the extremes of ideology, and of always being "in between." He replied, "Between is the only place to be."[147] Like Trilling, I, too, usually find myself somewhere "in between" the ideological extremes. The extremes are heard most often these days in the corridors of power, and, especially, in the media. And sometimes it may be necessary to take stands that may seem to some to be extreme —such as stands in defense of the freedom of speech or the freedom of the press or other basic human rights. But, to me, the middle ground is more often the solid ground; moreover, it is often the only ground for those of us who value reasonableness.

In the Congress, I usually stood in the middle. I was someone who actually had to *decide*. I was someone who actually had to stop and think before I voted. I have tried to do the same all the while I have been at the WTO. In both places, this has led to attacks against me by extremists. While in the Congress, I was often denounced by extremists on the right

---

[145] *See*, for example, the classic work by Richard Hofstadter, <u>Social Darwinism in American Thought</u> (Boston: Beacon Press, 1955) [1944].

[146] Joshua Muravchik, <u>Heaven on Earth: The Rise and Fall of Socialism</u> (San Francisco: Encounter Books, 2002). Muravchik credits the phrase "heaven on earth" to the early communist, Moses Hess, in <u>A Communist Confession of Faith</u>, in 1846. Hess wrote, "The Christian...imagines the better future of the human species...in the image of heavenly joy.... We, on the other hand, will have this heaven on earth."

[147] Trilling is quoted in Kamalakshi Mehta, "Middle Ground," <u>World Link</u> (World Economic Forum), online at worldlink.co.uk.

as a man of the left. While at the WTO, I have often been denounced by extremists on the left as a man of the right. Neither accusation is correct.

The most populous part of my former Congressional district was Brevard County on the "Space Coast" of Florida. Brevard County is a marvelous county. Brevard County is also a conservative county. I carried the county in each of my election campaigns, but, as a Democrat, I paid a price in doing so. One of my Brevard constituents once told me, for example, that although he knew that I had saved his job, he could not vote for me because I was a "leftist." Another, fortunately, reached a different conclusion based on similar thinking. "Jim," he told me, "I know you're a socialist, but you're *my* socialist."

In contrast, a few years later, in Geneva, I stood with my friend Said at a window in the WTO, and watched a rowdy "May Day" protest against the WTO by the assembled communist parties of Europe. These were the true "leftists." Red flags flew everywhere, their hammers and sickles slicing the air. Poster portraits of Karl Marx sneered from over the shoulders of the protesters below. The bearded Marxists raised their clenched fists and shouted up at us in anger. I turned to Said and asked, "Where were these people when I needed them to protest against me in Brevard County?"

The truth is, I am very much a man of the middle ground. I am a man "in between."

Thus, to me, the question about capitalism, always and everywhere, is: Where "in between" should we strike the balance? And, moreover, are we capable of doing so? Can we make all the right choices that will draw all the right lines and, thus, strike the right balance that we need? Where I differ with all those who fear capitalism and, thus, participate in the revolt against trade, is that my answer to each of these questions is "Yes."

I do not profess, in all cases, to know where the lines should be drawn. It may be that, as we often say in Geneva, many of the lines must, of necessity, be drawn on a "case-by-case" basis. But I believe we *can* draw the right lines. I believe we *can* make the right choices. I believe we *are* capable of striking the right balance. Because I do, I do not fear capitalism.

I support it.

The Fear of Commercialism

Deeper still, the revolt against trade reflects what Popper described as "the fear of commercialism."[148] It reflects a fear of the human consequences of the increasingly commercial society that results from increased trade and other aspects of "globalization." It is revealing of a deep-seated fear that an ever-increasing commercialism will make it ever more difficult to resist an overpowering materialism that already threatens to overwhelm human life.

In some respects, I see the fear of commercialism as a familiar reaction to what Emerson described in "Self-Reliance" as "the smooth mediocrity and squalid contentment of the times."[149] It is a form of restlessness on the part of some of an intellectual bent who believe that there should be more to life than the mundane satisfactions and the bourgeois complacencies of the commercial society. In our material world, they long for the life of the spirit.

Some of this is pose. There lingers in certain intellectuals an anachronistic whiff of the disdain typical of the landed aristocrats in Jane Austen's novels for those who engaged "in trade." They cling to the illusion that they are not. Thus, they look down on those who work with "widgets." They will line up to order their *lattes* every day at Starbuck's, but they would never stoop to anything so crass as selling coffee.

But some of this is principle. Some seek more from life than seems to be offered by "trade." Some believe that life should be devoted to loftier, nobler pursuits than those that seem to consume the average consumer in the commercial society. They yearn for the heroism not seen in the day-to-day humdrum of modern life. They despair of a society that seems satisfied with only an ever-increasing number of channels on cable TV. They long to hear the trumpet's sound.[150] And, in the Babbittry[151] of the "booboisie,"[152] they see only the tranquillizing tameness and the shallow sameness of mediocrity.

---

[148] Popper, The Open Society, supra, Volume 1, at 184.
[149] Emerson, "Self-Reliance," in Emerson's Essays, supra, at 43.
[150] For a thorough and thoughtful exploration of certain aspects of this phenomenon, *see* Mark Lilla, The Reckless Mind: Intellectuals in Politics (New York: New York Review of Books, 2001).
[151] The allusion here, of course, is to George F. Babbitt, the archetypal American business "booster" who is the eponymous protagonist in Sinclair Lewis, Babbitt (New York: Bantam Books, 1998) [1922].
[152] H. L. Mencken, American Language, 4th Edition (1946), volume xi, 560 [1922].

Notable among the many intellectuals who have despaired of the mediocrity of a commercial society was Gustave Flaubert. The passion of the great French writer for the perfect sentence may have been exceeded only by his perfect contempt for the commercial society. He asked, "When everything is reduced to the mere counter-balancing of economic interests, what room will there be for virtue?"[153] For Flaubert, virtue was to be found, and heroism to be shown, in a single-minded and lifelong devotion to his art. In his home near Rouen, on the banks of the River Seine, he would labor, night after night, late into the night, in search of the perfect sentence. "The bargemen floating down the Seine would take the light shining in his window as a landmark on the black shore."[154] A large paper mill now stands where his home once stood in symbol of the continued ascendancy of the commercial society.[155] But Flaubert heard the trumpet's sound.

I confess that, from time to time, I, too, long to hear the trumpet's sound. I, too, believe that, ideally, life should be devoted to higher, nobler pursuits. Where Flaubert was devoted to his art, I have been devoted to public service. I have searched all my life for the genuine community that I believe can only be created through common human purpose. Like William James a century ago, and no doubt like many who fear commercialism today, I seek a "moral equivalent of war" that can unite humanity in peaceful rather than martial pursuits.[156] That is one reason why, Saturday after Saturday, I organized and participated in 150 community service projects that I called "Citizen Saturdays" while I served in the Congress. That is why I spend my time now at the WTO instead of on a golf course. To me, lifelong service is an essential ingredient of the good life.

Yet, unlike some who are devoted to other pursuits, I do not fear the supposed mediocrity that results from a commercial society. For, to me, lifelong study through reading and reflection is also an essential ingredient of the good life. Consequently, I have read, and I have reflected on, the reason why a German political thinker of some time back named Arthur Moeller von den Bruck opposed what he described as "liberalism." By this, he meant both the political "liberalism" of democracy and the classical economic "liberalism" of the commercial society. Liberalism, he

---

[153] Flaubert is quoted in Julian Barnes, Flaubert's Parrot (London: Picador, 1985), 214 [1984].
[154] Henri Troyat, Flaubert (New York: Viking, 1992) (translated by Joan Pinkham), 114 [1988].
[155] Barnes, Flaubert's Parrot, supra, at 12.
[156] William James, "The Moral Equivalent of War," Pragmatism and Other Essays, supra, 289.

wrote, with undisguised distaste, is the "liberty for everybody to be a mediocre man."[157]

Indeed it is. And indeed it should be. Bruck was the man who coined the phrase "Third Reich." He was the patron saint of "national socialism." Neither he nor the Nazis who admired him could abide such a philosophy of "liberalism." But I can. The Nazis sought a world without mediocrities, a world made only for Nietzschean heroes, a world made only for Nazi "supermen." I seek a world in which men are free to be mediocre —if they choose.

For, after all, one man's mediocrity is another man's happiness. In a free and open society, in a world in which we are free to choose, it is not for me to say how another man or a woman should choose to pursue the good life. I might wish, for example, that my neighbor would spend more of his time reading and reflecting, and less of his time playing golf. But he, in turn, may think that I spend too much of my time with the likes of Popper and Emerson and Thoreau and Smith. He may think that I am a bit of a nag and a bit of a bore. And he may, just possibly, be right. The point is, we should each be free to choose.

In other respects, though, I see the fear of commercialism as more deserving of consideration. "Things are in the saddle," wrote Emerson, "and ride mankind."[158] Some who fear commercialism and therefore revolt against trade echo Emerson in their antipathy to what they see as the saddle-riding rule of *things*. They see us as becoming nothing but traders and merchants. They see ours as becoming *nothing but* a commercial society in which "the cash nexus" is the only connection among us. They see us as succumbing to the lure of a mere materialism that makes us *value* only things and, worse, makes us *into* only things by making our economic value in the marketplace the only measure of our value as individual human beings.

The fear of commercialism is not new. In his sad histories of the Roman Empire, Tacitus despaired that, in Rome, "Everything was for sale."[159] Throughout all the many centuries since, the scholars, the sages,

---

[157] Bruck is quoted in Ian Buruma and Avishai Margalit, "Occidentalism," The New York Review of Books (January 17, 2002) 4, 6.

[158] Emerson, "Ode: Inscribed to W. H. Channing," in Carl Bode, ed., The Portable Emerson (New York: Penguin Books, 1981) 646, 648.

[159] Tacitus, The Histories, quoted in Rothschild, Economic Sentiments, at 243.

the priests, and the pensive "men of letters" have all warned us time and again of the perils that a rampant commercialism poses for virtue. But those perils are greater in our modern world. They are greater in part due to the pace of our world, and due also to the omnipresence of commerce within our world.

"Men think that it is essential that the Nation have commerce, and export ice, and talk through a telegraph, and ride thirty miles an hour," grumbled Thoreau.[160] So they do. "Life goes headlong," warned Emerson.[161] So it does. And, in the hurried, harried, headlong rush of humanity today, the most worthy critics of commercialism would have us pause and ponder how best to live. They would have us ask ourselves whether we can find the meaning of life in things. As one such critic has asked, must we forever be "looking for fulfillment by acquiring more stuff?"[162]

I say "No." As I see it, a life spent only in acquiring things is a life misspent. In my view, we often pursue material wealth because we do not realize that there is other, better, enduring wealth to be found. To me, wealth consists in finding contentment in what one has, and not in having a great deal of material wealth, or, much less, in always wanting more. Most certainly, in my view, the individual self-fulfillment that Emerson had in mind when he wrote of the need for "self-reliance" cannot be found by getting "more stuff." It cannot be found in things. My daughter, Jamey, will confirm that I am so paternally imperious on this point that often, before I break down and buy her a new thing of some kind, I beseech her to recite a familiar family maxim: "Things are not the most important things in the world."[163]

Given this, how, then, do I reply to the critics generally on the issue of commercialism, and how do I reply to them especially on the abiding passion that materialism fuels within us for more and more things? I reply first by saying that I see a certain measure of materialism as an intrinsic part of human nature. We are possessive. We are acquisitive as well as inquisitive. We tend to want things. We tend to want *more* things.

---

[160] Thoreau, in <u>Walden</u>, in <u>Walden and Civil Disobedience</u>, supra, at 136.

[161] Emerson, "Character," in <u>Emerson's Essays</u>, supra, 324, 342.

[162] On "stuff," *see* Brent Tantillo, "Postrel's <u>The Future and Its Enemies</u> Worships at the Empty Altar of Materialism," <u>Houston Review</u> (July/August 2000), online at www.houstonreview.com/articles, at 3.

[163] To the best of my knowledge, this thought in this form should be attributed to the American humorist Art Buchwald.

This, too, in my view, is in our nature. And, like the rest of human nature, the part of our nature that desires things is not likely to change.

Despite the pleas of generations of prophets and theologians of virtually every global religious faith, we still want things. And we always will. St. Francis of Assisi may, for example, have been able to resist this natural human temptation. He may have been emulated by a few other sages and saints along the way. But few of us are sages. And even fewer of us are saints. Deep down, those who believe that we can abandon altogether our desire for things still dream the illusory dream of human perfectibility. They would try to change our nature.

"You must change your life," insists the archaic torso of Apollo in the poem by Rainier Maria Rilke.[164] It speaks to us about the eternal things that are not "things." It speaks to us across the ages. It speaks to us in the voices of all of those who have exhorted us to change our lives through the ages. And we can try our best to change our lives. But not even by changing our lives can we ever hope to change our nature.

On this, we would all do well to remember the wisdom of George Orwell. Orwell was no capitalist. He was no particular friend of commercialism. He was no particular believer in either economic or technological progress. He worried about the prospects of a world in which "the logical end of mechanical progress is to reduce the human being to something resembling a brain in a bottle."[165] But he worried even more about a world in which human beings tried to become saints by attempting to change their nature and achieve perfection.

In an essay he entitled "Reflections on Gandhi," Orwell wrote, "The essence of being human is that one does not seek perfection, that one *is* sometimes willing to commit sins for the sake of loyalty, that one does not push asceticism to the point where it makes friendly discourse impossible, and that one is prepared in the end to be defeated and broken up by life, which is the inevitable price of fastening one's love upon other human individuals....[S]ainthood is...a thing that human beings must avoid."[166]

---

[164] Stephen Mitchell, editor and translator, Rainier Maria Rilke, "Archaic Torso of Apollo," The Selected Poetry of Rainier Maria Rilke (New York: Vintage International, 1989), 61 [1907, 1908].

[165] Orwell is quoted in Bernard Crick, George Orwell: A Life (London: Penguin Books, 1992), 309 [1980].

[166] George Orwell, "Reflections on Gandhi," The George Orwell Reader: Fiction, Essays, Reportage (New York: Harcourt, Brace and Company, 1984), 328, 332.

The truth is the timeless truth: We cannot all become saints. We all want things. We all want the earth and the fullness thereof.[167]

The good life can assume many guises, and it can consist of many parts. Must our brief time in this world be an ordeal to be endured, and not a life to be lived to the fullest of its many parts? Must we choose between an extreme asceticism and an extreme materialism? Must we, in rejecting an all-consuming and an all-embracing materialism, become so ethereal that we cannot be free to choose to find at least some part of the good life in the material world we have made? Must we become so sour, so dour, so joyless that we cannot be free to choose to find some measure of joy in our individual lives in the mere things of that material world?

On a sunny morning back home in Orlando, Rebecca and I stand side by side on the sidewalk of "Main Street, U.S.A." in the "Magic Kingdom" of Walt Disney World. In the street before us is a long parade of parents pushing strollers filled with excited children looking forward to spending a long and long-awaited day with their good friend Mickey Mouse. In the emporiums all around us, seemingly everything is for sale.

The bright eyes of the children in the parade in the street are all fixed on the soaring spectacle of Cinderella's Castle straight ahead. But Rebecca's eyes, and mine, are focused in the other direction. Our eyes are on the children. Perhaps we might be able to suggest something else, something perhaps more edifying, something perhaps more socially redeeming, that the parents of those children could have done with the money they used to pay for their tickets to the "Magic Kingdom." And perhaps we could suggest something more rewarding that those parents could have done with the time they spent making the money they used to pay for those tickets. But no such suggestions come to mind as we watch the parade in the street. Is there no part of the good life to be found in the material making of the joy reflected in the sweet smiles and the shining eyes that we see? Here, too, I submit, the answer is somewhere "in between" the extremes.

Further, to the critics of commercialism, I reply as well that there remain many throughout the world —far too many —who do not share in the bounty of the earth or in its fullness. There remain many who are much in need of *more things*. Despite the relative prosperity of the countries of the developed world, many millions in the United States and other

---

[167] Psalm 24:1.

developed countries still live in poverty. And, from the depths of their utter destitution, billions more in the poorer developing countries of the world can only envy from afar the poverty of Americans and others in the developed world. As the WTO has reported, "Despite the remarkable technological achievements of the last two hundred years, we still live in a world of pervasive human poverty and underdevelopment."[168]

According to the World Bank, of the 4.6 billion human beings who live in developing countries, more than 850 million are illiterate, nearly one billion lack access to running water, and 2.4 billion lack access to basic sanitation. Nearly 325 million children in developing countries do not attend school. Every year, eleven million children under the age of five die from preventable causes in developing countries —an average of more than thirty thousand deaths every day.[169] The trumpet's sound cannot be heard above the din of such deprivation. No doubt even those who fear commercialism would agree with me that all of these people need more things.

I am a fortunate man. I can afford to buy my daughter more things. I can afford to buy her an ice cream any time I like along the busy esplanade of the lake of Geneva. I want a world in which every other father will be as fortunate as I am, a world in which every other father will be able to buy his child an ice cream. To be sure, an ice cream will not ensure individual self-fulfillment. An ice cream will not ensure happiness. But it will bring a smile to a child. And, certainly for me, and surely for many others, bringing a smile to a child is one sure way of finding both fulfillment and happiness.

The more telling critique of commercialism is one that speaks primarily, not to the impoverished of the planet, but to the affluent among us who live mostly in the developed world. It speaks to those of us who can already afford all the ice cream we want. The more thoughtful critics of commercialism focus on the ability of commercialism to fashion a fancied need from a fabricated desire. Like Dorian Gray in Oscar Wilde's novel, The Picture of Dorian Gray, they despair of "an age when unnecessary things" sometimes seem to be "our only necessities."[170] They wonder at our ability to discern need from desire. And they wonder

---

[168] World Trade Organization, World Trade Report 2003, at 78.
[169] World Bank, Human Development Report 2001 (Washington, D. C.), 9.
[170] The quoted words are the thoughts of Dorian Gray in Oscar Wilde, The Picture of Dorian Gray (New York: Penguin Books, 1985), 104 [1891].

especially at our ability to do so in an increasingly media-drenched society in which a "torrent of images and sounds overwhelms our lives."[171]

The nineteenth-century New England of Ralph Waldo Emerson was not by any means as media-drenched as our modern commercial society. All the same, and not surprisingly, Emerson may have given the most eloquent expression to this aspect of the fear of commercialism. He said, "A question which deserves examination now is the Dangers of Commerce. This Invasion of Nature by Trade with its Money, its Credit, its Railroad, threatens to upset the balance of man, and establish a new, universal Monarchy more tyrannical than Babylon or Rome."[172] This question of "the Dangers of Commerce" gives voice, of course, to Emerson's deeply felt environmental concerns. However, it also gives voice to his lifelong concern that an ever more intrusive commercialism that offered an ever greater variety of things could eventually topple "the balance of man."

Perhaps I can illustrate this concern as follows. My daughter's favorite flavor of ice cream is French vanilla, or, as she puts it, *vanille*. One of her favorite purveyors of ice cream has a new television commercial. First, a voice asks: "Do you want some ice cream?" Then, a bowl of French vanilla ice cream appears on the screen. It is everything a bowl of ice cream should be. The voice says: "Now you do."

This is usually enough to entice Jamey into eating a bowl of ice cream. Or two. But what about the rest of us? Are we capable of resisting the temptation of a bowl of ice cream that we do not really need? Are we capable of resisting the manufactured desires of a relentless commercial society? Are we capable of resisting what Bacon called "the Idols of the Market"?[173]

Those who fear commercialism say "No." They would "protect" us from ourselves by removing the temptation. They would, thus, deny us the increased choices that increased trade can help provide. Despite

---

[171] *See* Todd Gitlin, Media Unlimited: How the Torrent of Images and Sounds Overwhelms Our Lives (New York: Metropolitan Press, 2002).
[172] Emerson, from his journals, is quoted in Vernon L. Parrington, Main Currents in American Thought, Volume II: The Romantic Revolution in America, 1800-1860 (New York: Harcourt, Brace and World, 1927), 378.
[173] Francis Bacon, Novum Organum, First Book, 43, 59; *see also* Crane Brinton, The Shaping of Modern Thought (Englewood Cliffs, New Jersey: Prentice-Hall, 1963), 103 [1950].

the evidence to the contrary of my own waistline, I say "Yes." I prefer a world in which we all have the right to choose. So I would not "protect" us from the lure of temptation. I would leave the temptation, and, thus, I would leave us all also with the right to choose.

In reply to the critics of commercialism, I say that we can maintain "the balance of man" by making the right choices. Commercialism tempts us into the marketplace. Modern commercialism, in all its ever-present ubiquity, tempts us all the more. The endless application of human creativity and human ingenuity in the market is marvelous at making more things, and is marvelous at giving us the choice of more things. The freer market that results from freer trade gives us even more choices. But we are the ones who choose. To be sure, the market tries its very best to seduce us into desiring more things. But it remains true nevertheless that the market merely makes things available. The market, despite its best efforts, does not make us slaves to things. We make that choice ourselves.

Those who fear freedom do not believe we are capable of making the right choices. They see us as too weak to resist the enslavement to materialism that they see as among the worst of "the temptations of the trading world."[174] So they fear commercialism, and they revolt against trade. Those who embrace freedom believe, like me, that we are capable of making the right choices. We believe that, if we have the wisdom to take Emerson's sound advice about individual "self-reliance," we will be capable of resisting the enticing lure of all the things we do not need. We will remember, like Jamey, that "things are not the most important things in the world."

Dostoevsky's Choice

Ultimately, at every level, and in every respect, the revolt against trade is part of the revolt against freedom. We would be less fearful of change, technology, growth, capitalism, commercialism, and all else that inspires the revolt against trade, if we were less fearful of freedom. We will embrace trade only if we first embrace freedom. And we will embrace freedom only if we believe that we are capable of making the choices that come with being free. At the very deepest level, the revolt against trade reveals a fear that we, as individual human beings, are not capable of making the right choices, and that, thus, we are not capable of being free.

---

[174] Joseph Conrad, Nostromo (Oxford: Oxford University Press, 1984), 3 [1904].

In every respect, in every form of their fear, those who revolt against trade fear that we are not all capable of making the right choices. And they fear that we can never all become capable of making the right choices. Moreover, many of them firmly believe that they, and they alone, are among the privileged and anointed few among us who know the right choices that must be made. Therefore, they believe also that freedom consists in living, acting, thinking, and choosing only as they do.

The threat to freedom that is posed by the revolt against trade is real. Granted, many among those who revolt against trade are *not* in revolt against democracy. Yes, they would have us surrender our freedom to choose, and, yes, they would have us accept their distorted version of freedom. But they would have us do so by legitimate democratic means of persuasion. They are misguided. They are misinformed. They are misled. They are perhaps naive. But, no, they are *not* dangerous.

There are, however, others in the revolt against trade who most definitely *are* dangerous. Others would, like Rousseau, in his chilling phrase, have us be "forced to be free."[175] They would compel us, by force, to accept their ersatz economics and their artificial freedom. Therein lies the source of the black hoods that hide the faces of some of those who protest around the world against the WTO. Therein lie the seeds of the sporadic violence that has shamed the protests of those who revolt against trade. And therein lie the seeds, not of freedom, but of totalitarianism. Totalitarianism is the ultimate outcome of fanaticism, and fanaticism is the eternal enemy of freedom of thought. Fanaticism forbids thought. Fanaticism dictates thought.

These words say it all: "Fanaticism, the bastard begotten out of brain and power, fancies itself dictator in the realm of thought, so that only what it thinks is acceptable and must be forced upon the whole universe; it thus splits the human community into friends or foes, adherents or opponents, heroes or criminals, believers or heretics; since it recognizes no other system than its own and no other truth than its own, it needs must resort to violence in order to curb and bridle the divine multiplicity of phenomena and to bring everything under one yoke. The forcible curtailment of mental latitude, of freedom of opinions, every kind of inquisition and censorship, of scaffold and stake —these evils were not brought into the world by blind violence, but by rigidly staring fanaticism,

---

[175] Rousseau, The Essential Rousseau, supra, at 20.

that genius of one-sidedness, that hereditary enemy of universality, that captive of a single idea which would shut the whole world up in a cage."[176]

I quote these words at length because they deserve to be quoted at length. These are not my words. These are the words of yet another of Said El-Naggar's favorite writers, Stefan Zweig. They can be found in the faded pages of Zweig's long-forgotten biography of Erasmus of Rotterdam, published in 1934, which I found on the bottom shelf in the back of a used bookstore on a rainy Sunday in Geneva, and bought for five francs. This book is hard to find, but these words are hard to forget. They deserve not only to be quoted; they deserve also to be remembered.

Zweig wrote in German. He was an Austrian. He lived and wrote on a bluff overlooking the Salz River and the winding medieval streets of the Austrian city of Salzburg. He wrote these words while he was on the run from the Nazis, who had invaded and poisoned his country with their special brand of fanaticism. They had banned his books. They had searched his home and seized his manuscripts. They had destroyed his world.[177] At one level, the book Zweig wrote in exile the following year was about his "revered master of an earlier century,"[178] Erasmus, the tolerant humanist, the mild advocate of the middle ground, who had opposed the fanaticisms of the extremes of his own time. At another level, though, his book was about the madness of the fanaticism that had sent Zweig into flight in his time. More, it was about the choice we all face at all times between fanaticism and freedom.

In the end, a despairing Zweig committed suicide. He left his last book, a biography of another man of the middle ground, Montaigne, unfinished. In the darkest days of 1942, in mid-passage on an ocean voyage from Europe to Brazil, he plunged over the side of a ship. He chose to end his own life because he could not bear to live in exile when all of Europe had been imprisoned in the cage of fanaticism. We know, with hindsight, that he might have been less despairing if he had waited a little longer. Despair is never the answer. Whatever the seeming strength of fanaticism, hope always remains for freedom.

Zweig was in many ways an intellectual heir of yet another writer who feared fanaticism, Fyodor Dostoevsky. Like the German Zweig, the

---

[176] Stefan Zweig, Erasmus of Rotterdam (New York: Viking Press, 1934), 115.
[177] Stefan Zweig, The World of Yesterday (Lincoln and London: University of Nebraska Press, 1964), 387-389 [1943].
[178] Id. at 229.

Russian Dostoevsky knew that, as his literary creation, Ivan Karamazov, said, upon learning of the latest atrocities committed by man against man, "A wild animal can never be as cruel as man, as artistic, as refined in his cruelty."[179] Dostoevsky also lived in a time when freedom was threatened by fanaticism. He understood from his own experience the choice we face between fanaticism and freedom. And, in writing of that choice for the Russians of his time, he, too, wrote of the choice we all face at all times.

The choice we face is the choice offered by the Grand Inquisitor in the story told by Ivan Karamazov to his brother Alyosha in Dostoevsky's The Brothers Karamazov. The tale will be recalled. It is the sixteenth century in Seville during the worst days of the Spanish Inquisition. The funeral pyres crackle with the corpses of the heretics. Suddenly, unexpectedly, Christ returns. He walks, silently, among the people of Seville. He says not a word. Even so, everyone recognizes Him for who He is and for what He is. The Grand Inquisitor, aged and weary, now appears. He has the silent stranger arrested and thrown into prison. Then he visits Him in the prison to explain why.

The Grand Inquisitor denounces Christ for allowing humanity the freedom to choose. He offers Him his own view of "human nature."[180] Humanity, he maintains, is not capable of choosing and, thus, is not capable of living in freedom. "[P]eace and even death," he explains, "are dearer to man than freedom of choice in the knowledge of good and evil.... Indeed, nothing is more beguiling to man than freedom of conscience, but nothing is more tormenting either."[181] We are, he says, by nature, "slaves"[182] who can overcome this torment and find happiness only by surrendering our freedom and submitting to others who will lead us "like sheep,"[183] and who will make all our choices for us.

The choice we face in the world today is Dostoevsky's choice. The issue is human freedom. The struggle is the timeless struggle between those who embrace freedom and those who fear freedom's torment. The question is the question asked by Dostoevsky's Grand Inquisitor: is it truly in our nature as a species to be capable of living in a free world of

---

[179] Fyodor Dostoevsky, The Karamazov Brothers (Oxford: Oxford University Press, 1994), 299 [1880].

[180] Id. at 316.

[181] Id. at 319.

[182] Id. at 321.

[183] Id. at 322.

open societies in which we must bear "the great burden and terrible torment of personal and free choice...."?[184]

My answer is "Yes." I believe the Grand Inquisitor was wrong. Unlike the Grand Inquisitor, and unlike those who revolt against trade, I believe we are capable of bearing the burden of freedom. I believe we are capable of choosing, and capable of making the right choices, for our species, for our planet, and for our future. I believe, above all, that we are capable, as individual human beings, of choosing between good and evil by making what Dostoevsky described as "a free decision of the heart."[185]

Emerson called it "self-reliance." Smith called it "self-command."[186] The ancient Stoics called it "self-rule."[187] Others might call it self-awareness, self-knowledge, self-confidence, self-discipline, self-control, or self-respect. Whatever it may be called, the individual self of the individual human being is, I believe, capable of discerning the true self-interest "rightly understood," and thus of making the individual personal decisions that are, as I see it, the very definition of freedom.

If an individual is not free to choose, then that individual is not free. To be free, we must be able to act on our own, and of our own free will. We must be able to make a free commitment to rationally chosen ends. I agree with Isaiah Berlin that freedom is "a state of affairs in which men freely choose,"[188] and in which "every human being is assumed to possess the capacity to choose what to do, and what to be...."[189] I agree with him also that a state of freedom is when "we think of human beings as capable of pursuing ends for their own sakes by deliberate acts of choice...."[190] I agree further, and again, with Adam Smith that "[e]very individual... can in his local situation judge much better than any statesman or lawgiver can do for him."[191] To be worthy of being called freedom, there must be the uncertainty, the unpredictability, and the sheer serendipity of free individual choice. That is the burden and the torment, but also the enduring and the potential glory, of human freedom.

---

[184] Id. at 325.

[185] Id. at 320.

[186] On "self-command," *see* Adam Smith, <u>The Theory of Moral Sentiments</u>, at 349.

[187] On "self-rule," *see*, for example, Marcus Aurelius, Book Four, <u>Meditations</u> (London: Penguin Books, 1964), 63-76.

[188] Isaiah Berlin, "On Human Dignity: A Letter to George Kennan," <u>The New Republic</u> (January 28, 2002), 23, 24 [hereinafter "On Human Dignity"].

[189] Id. at 23.

[190] Id.

[191] Smith, <u>The Wealth of Nations</u>, at 485.

There is much we can do to become more capable of making the right choices in the exercise of individual freedom. Ignorance is the great enemy of freedom, because ignorance feeds the fear of freedom. An ignorant mind is a frightened mind, inclined to superstition, closed to reason, and thus open to hate. Thus, like Smith, and like every child of the Enlightenment, I see universal public education as a necessary and universal means of helping humanity become more capable of living in freedom. I see education as the best way to the right choices.

We live in disguise, and education is a way of helping us discover and reveal what we really are. Education is a way of helping us overcome the ways in which the division of labor, whatever its undeniable benefits, can nevertheless diminish us by reducing us to the rote of reduced and repetitive tasks. Education is a way of helping us take Tocqueville's timeless advice and see our self-interest as individuals "rightly understood." Education is, as Smith thought, a way of helping us learn how to be free, and a way of helping us decide, as individuals, what our freedom is *for*.

Another way is trade. There is a crucial connection between trade and freedom. Like education, trade, too, can help us become more capable of being free. Trade can give us more choices that will help us make more of the right choices while living free. Moreover, trade can, by giving us more choices, help us create more capability for becoming and remaining free. Trade helps create freedom, and trade helps sustain freedom. The equation between trade and freedom is this. More trade equals more choices equals more freedom.

As Eric Hoffer said, "[T]rading is… a sort of subversive activity; undoctrinaire, unheroic and uncoordinated, yet ceaselessly undermining and frustrating totalitarian domination. The trader… has been a chief agent in the emergence of individual freedom…."[192] Similarly, Tocqueville saw "a hidden relation between these two words: liberty and commerce." Writing in 1835, in the journal of his voyage to England from Ireland, he perceived this "hidden relation" in the fact that, to be free, we must become accustomed to "an existence full of agitation, of movement, of danger; to be always watchful, and at every moment to look around one uneasily; this is the price of liberty. All these things are equally necessary to success in commerce."[193] Popper, likewise, saw trade and commerce as "the worst

---

[192] Hoffer, "The Practical Sense," The Ordeal of Change, supra, 48, 58.
[193] Tocqueville is quoted in Rothschild, Economic Sentiments, at 249-250.

danger to the closed society."[194]   And rightly so. For, throughout the centuries, where trade has gone, freedom has followed. And so it can be in this century, through the work of the WTO.

Amartya Sen rightly sees "development as freedom."[195] Like me, he sees a world of "unprecedented opulence" but also of unspeakable deprivation.[196]   He sees a world much in need of the right kind of "development." Sen defines "development" as "a process of expanding the real freedoms that people enjoy."[197]   He contends that development will be freedom only if it enhances human capabilities. And he sees both economic freedom and political freedom as linked to such development. In particular, Sen sees "individual agency" as "ultimately, central" to overcoming all the obstacles that deprive so many in the world of both freedom and development.[198]   I believe that this is the only right way to see global economic development, and, further, that this is the only right way to see trade, which is only one form of development. I believe, too, that the global impoverishment that Sen so appropriately labels as "unfreedom"[199] will become real freedom only if we quell the revolt against trade.

The economic growth that results from trade cannot tell us what our freedom is for. Yet, without that growth, far fewer among us will even have the opportunity to wonder. For that opportunity can only come with the emancipation of the individual from the perennial, bestial struggle to survive. If you are a child with no real chance of growing up, then you have no freedom. If you are a woman with no real say in your own life or in your own livelihood, then you have no freedom. If you are someone who has no job, no food, and no personal economic choices, then you have no freedom. If you are someone who has no means to create the opportunity for a good education, a clean environment, decent working conditions, quality health care, and the other basic ingredients of a life lived in dignity, then you have no freedom. And, if you have no freedom, then you need not wonder what freedom is for.

Go to one of the many blighted, benighted places in the world. Ask one of the poor children —sold in slavery to repay a parent's debt.

---

[194] Popper, The Open Society, Volume I, at 176.
[195] Amartya Sen, Development As Freedom (New York: Anchor Books, 1999).
[196] Id. at xi.
[197] Id. at 3.
[198] Id. at xi.
[199] Id. at 15.

Ask one of the poor women —sold into the dehumanization of prostitution. They will tell you. Like the "Old South" of the Nashville Agrarians, the revolt against trade is a cause that richly deserves to be lost. The reactionary dream can seem a beautiful dream. It can seem an idyllic dream. But it is, in reality, a dangerous dream. For it offers nothing to the billions in the world who prefer freedom to "unfreedom." The dream of a world without an international division of labor is a dream of a world without running water. Those who dream this dream truly are the enemies of the future.

Those of us who support the WTO are sometimes described, by our adversaries, as reactionaries or, at best, as defenders of the status quo. But, in fact, we are the real reformers. In truth, we are the real liberators. We are the real revolutionaries. For we seek a world in which the "specialization" arising from an international division of labor will create many more personal choices for many more millions of people everywhere about how best to live their lives. We labor in the continuing human struggle to create freedom by creating open societies in which individual human beings can choose —freely —whether to play the fiddle *or* play the radio. We serve loyally in the long struggle for freedom that was begun long ago. We are the heirs to those in Athens, in Jerusalem, and in many other places perhaps untold throughout the world, who first made the revolutionary discovery of the worth, the dignity, and the unique, irreplaceable, divine promise of *every* individual human being.

The struggle has never been easy. The struggle will never be easy. There has always been a price for human progress. The examples are many. The land enclosure movement in late medieval England. The creation of the French state under Cardinal Richelieu. The reforms introduced by Peter the Great in Russia. The Meiji Restoration in Japan. The industrialization of Europe. The industrialization of the United States following the Civil War —a lengthy process that eventually reached the New South and inspired the elegant reaction of the Nashville Agrarians. All caused cultural and economic uprooting. All had a human cost that came from change. All were part of the long, hard struggle to transform the medieval into the modern world.

From the window on the world that I am privileged to have today in Geneva, I see similar struggles occurring today in China, in Vietnam, in sub-Sahara Africa, in eastern Europe, in post-Soviet Russia, in the Middle East, and in many other places where closed societies still stand in the way of human freedom. I see the approach at last of the modern world to the most distant corners of the earth. As I watch, I recall my undergraduate course more than thirty years ago at Vanderbilt in "The Politics of Modernization." It was then and there that Professor James Bell first taught me about "the revolution of rising expectations" in the developing world. Today, I see the continuing turmoil of "the revolution of rising expectations" in the determined struggle of so many people in so many developing countries to succeed somehow in making the transition from closed to open societies in the modern world.

No, the struggle will never be easy. But, from the struggle for freer trade that is part of the continuing struggle for freedom, we can make a freer and better world. Trade can help us rise above the brute struggle to survive. Trade can help us make the most of human reason. Trade can help give us the capability —and the courage —to resist the surrender of our freedom that is sought by all the many modern forms of the Inquisition. And, lastly, by freeing us from the constant contemplation of mere survival, trade can help free us as well to fulfill the ultimate goal and the ultimate responsibility of human freedom. Trade can help free us to rise up from our fallibility, and rise up from our finitude, to confront the unknowable, and contemplate the ultimate.

We may begin with only an ice cream in exchange for a child's smile. But that is only the beginning. We can choose, through trade, to help create the human capability of doing much, much more. The choice is ours to make.

Chapter Five

Trade Hopes

Means and Ends

By the 1930s, Harold Nicolson was long since disillusioned by the Proustian details of the outcome at Versailles. During the doldrums of a diplomatic exile to a far-flung outpost of the British Empire, he passed the time by writing a fond memoir of his famous uncle, Lord Dufferin, who had served Queen Victoria loyally as a globetrotting diplomat in earlier, happier days.

He wrote of a sightseeing trip that the young Lord Dufferin took in Ireland in 1846, during the darkest days of the Irish potato famine. The road to Cork was lined with coffins, and his stagecoach "was surrounded by crowds of wretched creatures begging for something to eat. Wan little faces thrust themselves in the window."[1] Later, Lord Dufferin "stood at the window of his Inn and threw loaves of bread to the rabble that fought and screamed below him."[2] In Ireland, he saw "unfreedom" firsthand.

During the famine, the British government did little to help. At one point, the British tried to assist the starving Irish peasants by sending them pamphlets containing excerpts from Adam Smith's The Wealth of Nations. Many of the hungry peasants were illiterate, so, as much as they might have profited from an understanding of Smith's "simple system of natural liberty," they could not read the pamphlets that explained Smith's revealing philosophy of trade. They certainly could not eat them.[3]

More than one million died of starvation during the Irish potato famine, but those who starved in Ireland then were few in number when compared to the starving millions in the world today. Hunger, today, still gnaws at the empty bellies of the world. Clearly, having a philosophy of trade is not enough. The words of our trade philosophy must be made to nourish the world, and this cannot be done merely through pamphlets.

---

[1] Harold Nicolson, Helen's Tower (New York: Harcourt, Brace and Company, 1938), at 71.
[2] Id.
[3] Cecil-Woodham Smith, The Reason Why: The Incredible Story of the Light Brigade (New York: Barnes and Noble, 1998), 126. Ms. Smith's fascinating book, originally published in 1953, was, like many others I have read in recent years, recommended to me by my late friend and colleague on the Appellate Body, Chris Beeby.

Transforming the words of our trade philosophy into the reality of global prosperity is the work of the WTO, but it is also work that extends far beyond the limits of what can be directly accomplished through the WTO.

Typical of the thinking of many WTO opponents is that of British polemicist Noreena Hartz. In her widely-read book, The Silent Takeover, she portrays the WTO as the unthinking minion of a global corporate combine that seeks to maximize trade in order only to maximize corporate profits and corporate power.[4] She sees the WTO as utterly indifferent to broader human values, and as mindful only of the exclusively economic values of the corporate bottom line. She sees those who serve the WTO as the trade equivalent of what Reubin Askew describes as "mules with blinders on." She thinks that when we see the world, we see nothing but trade, and we plow straight ahead, with no thought whatsoever to those broader values.

No doubt even Hartz and many of the others who oppose the WTO would agree that it is too much to expect a trader *not* to seek profits from trade. It is too much to expect that commerce *not* be commercial, and that economic transactions *not* be concerned with economic values. Emerson put it pointedly in one of his more commercial moments, observing that, "The trade in our streets believes in no metaphysical causes, thinks nothing of the force which necessitated traders and a trading planet to exist: no, but sticks to cotton, sugar, wool, and salt."[5] Whatever else it may accomplish, trade is supposed to result in profits; without profits, there would be no trade.

As someone who has sat in judgment in trade disputes involving cotton, sugar, wool, and numerous other products that are part of world trade, I can attest that "metaphysical causes" are rarely discussed in appeals in WTO dispute settlement. Appeals in the WTO address the legal issues that are raised in economic disputes about trade. But does this mean that we are "mules with blinders on" at the WTO? Does this confirm the view of the "anti-globalists" that the "faceless foreign judges" of the WTO are concerned only with the economic means of life, and not at all with the human ends of life? Are we concerned only with "the calm moral arithmetic of cost effectiveness" and not at all with "actual human

---

[4] Noreena Hartz, The Silent Takeover: Global Capitalism and the Death of Democracy (London: Arrow Books, 2001), 103-113.
[5] Emerson, "Montaigne; or, the Skeptic," Representative Men, in Essays and Lectures, supra, 690, 691.

beings who live the lives and suffer the deaths of concrete individuals"?[6] Or do we acknowledge that there are limits to trade?

In my view, there *are* limits to trade. Obviously, I see the claims of trade as considerable — as *very* considerable. But I also see the claims of trade as limited. My philosophy of trade is one that acknowledges trade's limits. As I see it, there is a world beyond trade. There is a wider world beyond the "widgets" with which we deal daily at the WTO, and to achieve the true ends of trade — to fulfill all of our many hopes for trade — we must have more than merely a philosophy of trade. We must reap more from trade than mere economic profits.

Like all of my thinking, this is not in any way a thought that is new with me. Trade has long been seen to have limits as a part of human life. Aristotle, in his Nicomachean Ethics, described "[t]he life of money-making" as "one undertaken under compulsion."[7] Certainly, many in today's world would echo him by saying, in contemporary terms, that we engage in money-making and widget-making in order "to make a living." But, be it individual wealth, or, if you will, "the wealth of nations," the material wealth itself is not the goal. As Aristotle said, "[W]ealth is evidently not the good we are seeking; for it is merely useful and for the sake of something else."[8]

More recently, in the century just past, Hayek, the great proselytizer for free markets and for free trade, readily conceded, "Economic considerations are merely those by which we reconcile and adjust our different purposes, none of which, in the last resort, are economic...."[9] Similarly, the Edwardian English journalist and author, G. K. Chesterton — who was no economist, but who was something of a philosopher — explained that "economic systems are not things like the stars, but things like the lamp-posts, manifestations of the human mind and things to be judged by the human heart."[10] However bright it may be, the light that illumines the lamp-posts does have its limits.

---

[6] Isaiah Berlin, "Fathers and Sons: Turgenev and the Liberal Predicament," the Romanes Lecture (1970), reprinted in Ivan Turgenev, Fathers and Sons (London: Penguin Books, 1975), 7, 54.

[7] Richard McKeon, Introduction to Aristotle (New York: The Modern Library, 1947), "Nicomachean Ethics," Book I, Chapter 5, 313.

[8] Id.

[9] Hayek, The Constitution of Liberty, supra, at 35.

[10] G. K. Chesterton, Dickens (New York: Schocken Books, 1965), 229 [1906].

We humans shine from the light within us. We are not merely money-makers and widget-makers. We are not commodities, and we are not concerned only with commodities. The economics of a free market is an essential part of our freedom, but it is only one form of our freedom. The exchange of goods and services that we call "economics" is only one form of the human endeavor. There are others, and those other redeeming human endeavors must also be served by the "economics" that we call "trade" if we are to have the full measure of our freedom.

This notion, too, is not new with me. Here is Thoreau again, pencil in hand, from his essay on "Life Without Principle": "[W]e are warped and narrowed by an exclusive devotion to trade and commerce and manufactures and agriculture and the like, which are but means, and not the end."[11] Here, Thoreau is absolutely right. The economic means of trade must be made to serve human ends. Trade is not an end in itself, but a means to an end. That end is all of the human enjoyment, the human achievement, and the human happiness that will come from attaining the full measure of human freedom.

Thoreau and I are not alone in this view of trade. My six colleagues who work with me around our round table in Geneva also see trade as a means for this hoped-for end. They are not "mules with blinders on." They are not narrow advocates only of trade, or only of the growth of trade. They, like me, have devoted their lives to much else in addition to trade. They, like me, seek the end of an expanding, sustaining, fulfilling, and lasting human freedom. It is not entirely without justification that the most esteemed of the true trade gurus sometimes describe the Members of the Appellate Body as "generalists." In upholding the rules of world trade, we are upholding the specific efforts of the Members of the WTO to create more trade by establishing and upholding rules for trade. But, in serving the world trading system, we see ourselves as also serving the general cause of creating more freedom.

I am confident, as well, that every Geneva delegate of every Member of the WTO shares this view of trade. Many of them serve not only as delegates to the WTO, but also as delegates to the European headquarters of the United Nations, and to the entire alphabetic array of other agencies and assemblies that seek a vast assortment of vital human ends every day in Geneva. One of the many ironies of a familiar accusation

---

[11] Thoreau, "Life Without Principle," in Wendell Glick, ed., <u>Great Short Works of Henry David Thoreau</u> (New York: Harper Perennial, 1993), 404, 423 [1863].

of the "anti-globalists" —that the advocates of the WTO think and care only about trade —is seen in the simple daily fact that the delegates to the WTO do not, by any means, spend all of their time in a given day working only on trade. Most of the very same people in Geneva who represent their countries at the WTO also work tirelessly every day on human rights, women's rights, children's rights, arms control, land mines, global warming, AIDS, illiteracy, and much more.

Those of us who serve the cause of trade by serving the WTO do not wear blinders that keep us from seeing all of the many other needs of the world. We do not simply plow straight ahead for trade, heedless of other compelling human concerns. Do we seek economic growth through increased trade? Yes. Is that all we seek? No. In the words of the WTO's "World Trade Report" for 2003, "Growth in real income is an important means of expanding freedom but it is not the ultimate objective. The means and ends of the development process should not be confused.... Ultimately the development process is about expanding the opportunities of people to choose a life they have reason to value."[12]

I am not alone among the advocates of the WTO in seeing trade as a means to an end. At the WTO, we *all* see trade as a means to an end, and the end we all see is more individual human freedom. The end we all seek is a world in which millions more individual human beings are both seen and treated, not as means, but as ends in and of themselves. And we all firmly believe that this end cannot be achieved in a world in which individuals, wherever they may be in the world, are not free to trade, and thus are not free to make all the individual personal choices that the freedom to trade can help create.

Ultimately, the hopes we have for trade are hopes for a true community. Those of us who serve the world by serving the WTO all know that trade alone will not suffice to summon a true community in an Age of Reason. To fulfill all of our ambitious hopes for trade, we will need more than just trade. We will need more than merely an increase in the exchange of goods and services across international borders. Our real need as a unique and endangered species on this shrinking planet is for the broader and deeper human exchange that goes far beyond the simple exchange of goods and services. That alone will lead to the creation of an enduring bond among all of humanity. That alone will give us the

---

[12] World Trade Organization, <u>World Trade Report 2003</u>, at 79.

open society that is also Emerson's "true society," and that alone will give us a true community.

We do not need the false community of the closed society, a community in which we seek a trembling and temporary refuge in inwardness and isolation because of our common inability to overcome our fear of freedom. We need the true community that is only provided by an open society, a community in which we find liberation *because* of our embrace of freedom. This true, free, and open community cannot be created through freer trade alone. It can only be created when freer trade is accompanied by the exercise of human reason in a true individual, Emersonian "self-reliance" that transforms *all* of the global tragedies of "unfreedom" into the full measure of a real and lasting freedom for *all* of humanity.

Rhetoric can often be telling. Those who revolt against freedom and against trade see trade as a "threat" rather than as the chance that it is for more freedom for all of us. They see trade as a "threat" to the local, and they see only the local as true, as authentic, and as having a legitimate claim to our concern. In particular, they are inclined to rhapsodize on the supposed virtues of local "self-sufficiency." They favor local "self-sufficiency" in every part of the world. They favor local products and local producers over those from elsewhere. They ask: Should we not grow all our own food? Should we not make all our own tools? Should we not rely only on ourselves for all we need?

They forget to ask: Who are "we"? Are "we" only you and me? Are "we" only those in our own family, our own neighborhood, our own city, our own state, our own country, or our own hemisphere? Where, in our supposed local "self-sufficiency," do "we" draw the dividing line of "we" between ourselves and the foreign, alien, excluded "other"? And what price are "we" willing to pay for drawing that line as an "opportunity cost" of an artificial allocation of our limited economic resources? Will "we," in the end, be better off because "we" draw that line? Will "we" be better off if, for the sake of a supposed "self-sufficiency," we favor a privileged local few at the expense of the local many, not to mention the many who are beyond the line that we draw of "we"?

We erect a mirror at the border of where we draw the line of "we." When considering that border, "we" see only our own reflection. The protectionism that persists in trade is only one example of how we distort our view of the world by seeing only that mirror's image. The supporters of the protectionism that parades as "self-sufficiency" assume that "we" will profit from protectionism. They assume that "we" will gain by relying primarily on local producers in local economies, and by giving precedence to local producers through protectionist public policies. They assume that this will lead to a greater prosperity and to a better life. It will not. It may profit some of us, at the expense of others of us, in the short run, but it will lead to a lesser prosperity and to a lesser life for all of us in the long run. Whoever "we" may be, we cannot profit for long by clinging to yesterday at the expense of tomorrow.

Local producers, local economies, and local communities cannot remain strong for long by turning away from trade and by otherwise trying to hide from the rest of the world. Likewise, national producers, national economies, and national communities cannot remain strong if they do not participate fully in the world economy. The "strength" of an insular and isolated community is not really strength. It is weakness. It is failure waiting to happen. The supposed "self-sufficiency" of such an inward-looking community is insufficient to the outward-looking and forward-looking true community that we need in every part of the world.

Emerson, the self-reliant individualist, warned us to "beware of the man" who indulges in an "egotism" that tends to "shut him up in a narrower selfism, and exclude him from the great world of God's cheerful fallible men and women."[13] Such "egotism" is not individualism. It is not "self-reliance." It is not "self-sufficiency." It is, instead, a self-defeating isolationism that turns inward by turning away from all that is offered by the wider world. The inwardness of a "self-sufficient" protectionism in trade is but one manifestation of such a self-defeating "egotism" that turns away from the true community.

The true community *will* be local. It will respect individual differences. It will respect individual distinctiveness. It will be capable of preserving, at the local level, the rich diversity of ways in which individuals give expression to freedom in different local communities throughout the world. And it will be capable of doing so even in the face of the seemingly irresistible impulse toward global homogenization and standardization that is inspired by "globalization." We may decide that we want to have only one Internet. We may decide that we want to have only one standard width for an industrial bolt or screw. However, this

---

[13] Emerson, "Culture," The Conduct of Life, in Essays and Lectures, supra, 1015, 1016.

does not mean that we must all look alike, act alike, think alike, and live alike everywhere in the world. This does not mean that we must have only one kind of human being. This does not mean that we must have only one way to live.

The true community will also be national. The demise of the "nation-state" has been much exaggerated.[14] The Treaties of Westphalia of 1648, which first gave precedence to the "nation-state," still have meaning for the modern world. The WTO is not alone among international institutions in being "Member-driven" by "nation-states." But, in the true community we seek, "nation-states" will exercise their strength in ways —such as the WTO —that will serve the cause of international community. Through international cooperation, in trade and in numerous other areas of global concern, the governments of "nation-states" can find better ways of preserving their national identities and prerogatives, while also sharing in strengthening the sense of community both locally and internationally. Thus, the true community will be a community of nations.

The true community will also be international. Unquestionably, most of the economic, environmental, health, labor, population, and other challenges we face in the world transcend national borders. Consequently, our efforts to meet those challenges must also transcend national borders. In the free and open society that more freedom can help create, we must work together locally, nationally, and internationally to find more and better ways to serve freedom. The round table of the Appellate Body in Geneva is just one of many tables where citizens of different countries must sit and reason together in search of a consensus. The story of the WTO is just one chapter in the much longer story that must be written in the creation of a true international community.

In my view, there are other important chapters to this story. If all of our hopes for trade are to be realized, more open markets must be part of more open societies. Trade must be accompanied by the democratic and other domestic institutional reforms that trade can help inspire. Market forces will only work over an extended period of time if they are embedded in a framework of freedom in which free people can choose to make the most of those forces in their own lives. So we must do more than merely lower the barriers to trade. We must also lower the many other barriers to freedom.

---

[14] *See* Robert Gilpin, Global Political Economy: Understanding the International Economic Order (Princeton: Princeton University Press, 2001), 362-363.

We can try, each of us, to retreat toward our purely private concerns. We can seek refuge in the bosom of our families, in the haven of our book-lined studies, or in the contemplation of our annual personal bottom line. But how will we hide? How will we convince ourselves that there can be such a thing as an inward and isolated "self-sufficiency" in a world in which there can be no secure and lasting refuge? Beyond the window of our retreat is a world in which reason is slain by passion, a world in which the extremes overwhelm the "golden mean" of the "in between," a world in which the right balance and the tempered tolerance and the measured moderation of a mutual human respect are daily defeated by the forces of unreason and "unfreedom," by a world in which, alas, there is all too little reasonableness.

We sit, each of us, in silent communion with all of the hopeful voices of ages past. They speak to us across the centuries. They whisper to us in our quiet moments. They urge us onward. Will we listen, or will we turn away? Will we simply accept and endure the disappointing and increasingly dangerous world in which we find ourselves? Will we try only to save what we each can salvage personally from such a world in the embrace of the false security of a fake "self-sufficiency"? Or will we hear and heed the voices from the past that urge us to venture beyond the window in search and in service of a free and open and more reasonable world? Will we turn at last toward a world where our hopes for trade will be fulfilled by a true community?

The Watchmakers of Ferney

In flight from the fearful adversaries of freedom, in search of a place where he could continue to work for the hopeful cause of freedom, Voltaire settled in 1759 in the French village of Ferney. He spent the last twenty years of his life there. When he arrived in Ferney, there were only about forty or fifty villagers. When he died in 1778, there were more than one thousand. In the interim, largely at his instance, Ferney became a thriving center of commerce that prepared the way for today's prosperous "Ferney-Voltaire."

Voltaire was "the great Doer in the midst of the Dreamers."[15] "True philosophy," he wrote, "makes the earth fertile and the people happier. The true philosopher cultivates the land, increases the number

---

[15] Quoted in S. G. Tallentyre, The Life of Voltaire (New York: Loring and Mussey, 1903), 489 [hereinafter The Life of Voltaire].

of the ploughs, and so of the inhabitants; occupies the poor man, and thus enriches him; encourages marriages, cares for the orphan; does not grumble at necessary taxes, and puts the laborer in a condition to pay them promptly."[16] In brief, the true philosopher is the builder of the true community. And that is precisely what Voltaire became with his sustained stewardship of Ferney.

In doing rather than merely dreaming during his two decades in Ferney, Voltaire built his local community, first of all, by engaging in trade. Voltaire the writer had long also been Voltaire the businessman and Voltaire the capitalist. His investment in the emerging modern world of trade and commerce in the eighteenth century was not only philosophical but was also financial. As early as 1730, long before he settled in Ferney, "he became part of a company that imported grain from North Africa to the French port of Marseilles, and then re-exported it to Italy and Spain. The company also imported cocoa, sugar, tobacco, and indigo from America to France."[17]

Voltaire continued to engage in trade after he moved to Ferney. There were hurdles, though. The France of the time was anything but a center of free trade. Throughout the country, there were "toll-gates, so numerous that fish brought from Harfleur to Paris paid eleven times its value *en route*."[18] Moreover, when he arrived, Ferney was "a mean hamlet … devoured by poverty, scurvy, and tax-gatherers!"[19] But, because of his initiative, by the time he died, Ferney was a crossroads for trade and commerce.

First he cultivated silkworms. The silk they produced was one of the coveted luxury goods of his time. Dramatist though he was, Voltaire turned the theatre in Ferney into a thriving silkworm nursery. To make use of the silk, he brought in weavers from Geneva, built homes for them in Ferney, and put them to work making silk stockings. He created a market for the stockings by sending free samples and flattery to the duchesses among his aristocratic friends in Paris.[20] Soon the silk stockings from Ferney became all the Parisian rage.

---

[16] Id.
[17] This summary of Voltaire's trading ventures is from Muller, The Mind and the Market, supra, at 39.
[18] Tallentyre, The Life of Voltaire, at 489.
[19] Id. at 356.
[20] Id. at 491.

Then he brought in the watchmakers. Voltaire's world was a world that had only recently discovered "time," and discovered as well the advantages of precision in time. The specialized skill of watchmaking was the newest "high-technology" of the day, and nearby Geneva was the "global" center of the watchmaking industry. But Geneva then was also what Karl Popper would have called a "closed society," and many of the skilled watchmakers of Geneva had to flee from the political and other consequences of the severe stringencies of Genevan Calvinism.

With an eye to the future, Voltaire invited them to flee only a few miles and to live with him in Ferney. He built homes for them in the village, and sheltered some of them in the safety of his own chateau. He bought them the gold, the silver, and the jewels they needed for their work. He loaned them what today we would call "start-up capital," and "[i]n six weeks he had watches ready for sale —of exquisite workmanship, artistic design, and to be sold at least one third cheaper than they could be in Geneva."[21]

The great self-promoter that he was, Voltaire realized that the watchmakers of Ferney needed aggressive promotion for their wares, so he conducted something resembling a modern advertising campaign. He sent to all of the ambassadors in Europe a circular from "THE ROYAL MANUFACTORY OF FERNEY" (in just such capital letters) in praise of Ferney's watches. He sold one to Catherine the Great, the Empress of Russia. He asked her to help him promote a watch trade between Ferney and China —and she did. "Ferney was soon sending watches not only to China, but to Spain, Italy, Russia, Holland, America, Turkey, Portugal, and North Africa, besides carrying on an enormous trade with Paris."[22]

We can learn much today from recollecting the efforts of Voltaire on behalf of the watchmakers of Ferney, and from contrasting his attitude toward watches with that of his contemporary and rival, Rousseau. The elusive Rousseau was ecstatic when he sold his watch; he felt free of the clockwork demands of an open-ended society.[23] In contrast, the enterprising Voltaire was elated at the prospect of being able to sell watches to others; he felt free in being able to meet the demands of such a society. Rousseau felt free when he lost his watch; Voltaire felt free when he found

---

[21] Id. at 492.
[22] Id. at 493.
[23] On the sale of Rousseau's watch, *see* Muller, <u>Freedom in the Western World</u>, supra, at 332-333.

a way to help others make and sell their watches. Therein, perhaps, lies the essence of the fundamental difference between those two rival eighteenth-century paragons, respectively, of the closed and the open society. Therein also may be found part of the difference as well between their two contrasting approaches to the making of human society.

Where Rousseau thought people should be "forced to be free"[24] in a world without watches, Voltaire thought people should have the chance to keep their own time and to choose their own way to freedom. Moreover, he was willing to help give them that chance. Voltaire once told Cardinal Richelieu, "Give me a chance and I am a man to build a city."[25] So he was. And so he did —with the help of the watchmakers of Ferney. But Voltaire knew that building a city —building a true community —requires more than just trade. Fulfilling our hopes for trade requires a broader commitment, a broader investment, a broader framework for a solid foundation for a true community. It requires, in echo of our required approach to treaty interpretation on the Appellate Body, what might be called "context."

Voltaire understood the need for "context" as a necessary condition to the fulfillment of his hopes for trade. While peasants starved throughout France in the lean years leading up to the French Revolution, he created an unprecedented prosperity in Ferney. In his two decades in the village, he built houses and roads for his workers, and he built "manufactories" for the flourishing of his workers' watchmaking skills. He freed them from oppressive tolls and other onerous taxes. He rid them of needless regulations. He provided a doctor to tend to their health. He even provided them with entertainment. "Every Sunday the young people of the colony used to come up to the chateau to dance. Their host provided them with refreshments, and was the happiest spectator of their happiness."[26]

Voltaire also built a school for the children of his workers, and he paid for the schoolmaster. Reproved by one of his numerous correspondents, who argued that all would be lost if the children of common working people were taught to think that they, too, could reason, Voltaire replied in words that are well worth recalling today. "No, Sir, all is not lost when the people are put into a condition to see that they too

---

[24] Rousseau "The Social Contract," <u>The Essential Rousseau</u>, supra, at 20.
[25] Tallentyre, <u>The Life of Voltaire</u>, at 493.
[26] Id. at 490.

have a mind. On the contrary, all is lost when they are treated like a herd of bulls, for sooner or later they will gore you with their horns."[27]

Adam Smith, who visited Voltaire several times at Ferney, would have agreed. He was among the few of that time who did. But flash forward a few centuries to our time, and, in the face of the rage of a world in which far too many are far too often treated as if they were less than human, the prophetic nature of Voltaire's reply should be apparent to everyone. Because they failed to heed his words, those who followed Voltaire reaped a whirlwind in the reign of terror that was the climax of the French Revolution. If we, too, fail to heed them today, we, too, will reap only terror as a result.

Today, too, it is all about "context." As he often does, the globetrotting American journalist Thomas Friedman gets it right. He contends that "[t]he dirty little secret about globalization —and it takes a lot of countries a long time to figure it out —is that the way to succeed in globalization is to focus on the fundamentals. It's not about the wires or about bandwidth or about modems. It's about reading, writing, and arithmetic. It's about churches, synagogues, temples, and mosques. It's about rule of law, good governance, institution building, free press, and a process of democratization. If you get these fundamentals right, then the wires will find you and the wires will basically work. But if you get them wrong, nothing will save you."[28]

In this, as he would doubtless acknowledge, Friedman echoes much of the thinking of one of the most thoughtful of the contemporary followers of Adam Smith and David Ricardo, the retired Harvard economist and historian David Landes. In <u>The Wealth and Poverty of Nations: Why Some Are So Rich and Some So Poor</u>, written after long decades of study and observation, Landes, in echo of both Smith and Ricardo, attempts to list for contemporary policymakers the qualities of a successful modern, open society.[29] In attempting to explain why some societies prosper and others do not, he observes that, like our "trade secrets" in Geneva, the "values and institutions" that go into the making

---

[27] Id. at 490-491.
[28] Thomas Friedman, quoted in "States of Discord: A Debate Between Thomas Friedman and Robert Kaplan," <u>Foreign Policy</u> (March/April 2002).
[29] David Landes, <u>The Wealth and Poverty of Nations: Why Some Are So Rich and Some So Poor</u> (New York: W.W. Norton and Company, 1998), 215-219 [hereinafter <u>The Wealth and Poverty of Nations</u>].

of a successful modern society "are so familiar to us ... that we take them for granted."[30] What he has concluded about the necessary ingredients of an "ideal" society for creating the kind of economic growth and development that will foster a true community, is well worth quoting at length.

"Let us begin," writes Landes, "by delineating the ideal case, the society theoretically best suited to pursue material progress and general enrichment.... This ideal growth-and-development society would be one that.... Knew how to operate, manage, and build the instruments of production and to create, adapt, and master new techniques on the technological frontier." It would also be one that "[w]as able to impart this knowledge and know-how to the young, whether by formal education or apprenticement training," and that "[c]hose people for jobs by competence and relative merit; promoted and demoted on the basis of performance." It would be one as well that "[a]fforded opportunity to individual or collective enterprise; encouraged initiative, competition, and emulation," and also that "[a]llowed people to enjoy and employ the fruits of their labor and enterprise."[31] Landes sees these standards as implying what he calls "corollaries: gender equality (thereby doubling the pool of talent); no discrimination on the basis of irrelevant criteria (race, sex, religion, etc.); also a preference for scientific (means-end) rationality over magic and superstition (irrationality)."[32]

He maintains that, therefore, "[s]uch a society would also possess the kind of political and social institutions that favor the achievement of these larger goals...." Such a society would, for example, "[s]ecure rights of private property, the better to encourage saving and investment," and "[s]ecure rights of personal liberty —secure them against both the abuses of tyranny and private disorder (crime and corruption)." It would "[e]nforce rights of contract, explicit and implicit." Such a society would also, as he sees it, "[p]rovide stable government, not necessarily democratic, but itself governed by publicly known rules (a government of laws rather than men)." And, "[i]f democratic, that is, based on periodic elections, the majority wins but does not violate the rights of the losers; while the losers accept their loss and look forward to another turn at the polls."

---

[30] Id. at 215, 217.
[31] Id. at 217.
[32] Id.

Further, such an ideal society would "[p]rovide responsive government, one that will hear complaint and make redress," and "[p]rovide honest government, such that economic actors are not moved to seek advantage and privilege inside or outside the marketplace." He adds that, "[i]n economic jargon, there should be no rents to favor and position." In addition, such a society would "[p]rovide moderate, efficient, ungreedy government. The effect should be to hold taxes down, reduce the government's claim on the social surplus, and avoid privilege."[33]

Landes adds, "This ideal society would also be honest. Such honesty would be enforced by law, but ideally, the law would not be needed. People would believe that honesty is right (also that it pays) and would live and act accordingly."[34] Further, he sees "[m]ore corollaries: this society would be marked by geographical and social mobility. People would move about as they sought opportunity, and would rise and fall as they made something or nothing of themselves. This society would value new as against old, youth as against experience, change and risk against safety. It would not be a society of equal shares, because talents are not equal; but it would tend to a more even distribution of income than is found with privilege and favor. It would have a relatively large middle class. This greater equality would show in more homogeneous dress and easier manners across class lines."[35]

Thus, Landes argues that "culture makes almost all the difference."[36] He suggests that, far from fearing the loss of the static culture of a closed society, we should be doing all we can to encourage the creation of the fluid culture of an open society. We should be striving to establish a context in which the full flourishing of freedom can succeed. We should not be simply seeking excuses for why freedom has failed in failed societies in which "[i]t is always easy to blame the Other."[37]

With *almost all* of what Landes says, I agree. In his listing of the prerequisites of an open society, he sets forth the needed context that can help fulfill our hopes for trade. He identifies the necessary ingredients. Basically, these are the basics of an open society. Essentially, these are the essentials for continued human progress toward a free, open, modern

---

[33] Id. at 217-218.
[34] Id. at 218.
[35] Id.
[36] David Landes, "Culture Makes Almost All the Difference," Culture Matters, supra, at 2.
[37] Id. at 4.

world, and toward an Age of Reason for the world. Fundamentally, these are the ways to secure the fundamentals for attaining the full measure of human freedom. I would, however, take exception in two important respects.

First, I do not agree that "the ideal society" is one that necessarily "would value new as against old, youth as against experience...." Perhaps it is only the onset of my middle age. Perhaps it is one of my mentors from Florida, the late Congressman Claude Pepper, the great champion of the "senior citizen," speaking to me in his rich and rolling tones from beyond the grave. Perhaps it is my fond recollection of working with Pepper and with numerous other very able senior colleagues in the Congress. Or perhaps it is my more recent experience of eight years in working so closely with my considerably older colleagues around our table in Geneva —colleagues who still have much to offer, and who still have much of significance to say. Whatever the reason, my "ideal society" —unlike that of Landes —would be one that values both new *and* old, both youth *and* experience. I would not value age and experience simply because they *are* age and experience, but I feel that, in many societies, and especially in my own, the wisdom of both age and experience are, to our detriment, often needlessly discarded.

Second, I would also, and especially, take exception to the notion that democracy is not indispensable to "the ideal society." Landes says that "the ideal society" is "not necessarily democratic." But I believe that it is necessarily so. I believe that democracy *is* indispensable. I believe that no society can truly call itself "free" if it is *not* a democracy.

Watches are much more precise in keeping time today than they were when Voltaire was busy peddling the wares of the watchmakers of Ferney. Today's atomic clocks are accurate to a millionth of a second a day.[38] The world's time is kept by such a clock in Greenwich in Great Britain. After making the steep climb on a windy day up the winding path of the hill leading up from the Thames to the observatory in Greenwich, Joe, Jamey, Rebecca, and I have, like so many other tourists, stood astride the Prime Meridian of our clockwork society and watched firsthand the relentless passing of today's "Greenwich time" in all its persistent precision.

---

[38] Nigel Calder, Einstein's Universe: The Layperson's Guide (London: Penguin Books, 1990), 60 [1979].

Emerson, Thoreau, and even Voltaire would remind us that we do not need *too much* precision in the workings of a free society. We are men and women; we are not machines. We are ends; we are not means. Freedom always needs a little elbow room. Yet freedom also needs sufficient precision to hold society together by keeping our elbows from becoming too sharp, and by keeping us from elbowing each other out of the way. And the only form of governance that can hold a free society together —the only way of living together that can keep a free society ticking with sufficient precision —is democracy.

To maximize the potential "gains from trade" in the "ideal society," we must, as both Friedman and Landes suggest, focus on all of the fundamentals *besides trade.* To maximize the gains from trade, in addition to freeing trade, we must also find and free the way to social and political modernization, as well as to other economic reforms. We must create stable, responsive, honest governments. We must create honest and independent judiciaries that respect and enforce individual rights. We must establish public support for the obligation of contract and for other private property rights. We must create a public climate that is conducive to free enterprise, free inquiry, and, above all, free thought. We must create both attitudes and institutions that are part of mutually reinforcing cultures that can provide the societal context to support and to sustain freedom.

But, in my view, we can do none of this successfully if we do not also create democracy. We are not free if we do not govern ourselves. We are not free if we are not free to choose. Whatever else we may choose to be, we must be democrats, and we must have democracy. If it is true, as Professor Sen suggests, that we must see "development as freedom," then it is also true, as he asserts, that "[d]eveloping and strengthening a democratic system is an essential component of the process of development."[39]

Harold Nicolson was perhaps more of an aristocrat than a democrat. He believed in popular elections, to be sure, but he seemed to believe even more in the need for *noblesse oblige* by the educated classes of Britain who were, as he saw it, those who were best fit to rule. His support for democracy was perhaps more intellectual than emotional. From my reading of his published diaries and his letters of several decades, I have concluded that Sir Harold *tolerated* democracy as a second-best alternative

---

[39] Sen, <u>Development As Freedom</u>, at 157.

to the rule by the enlightened few that he preferred, but could not create, in twentieth-century Britain.

Like me, Nicolson sought elected office. He stood for the House of Commons on the eve of World War II, was elected, and served — admirably —on the back bench as a strong supporter of Winston Churchill's war policies for a number of years. He could never, however, reconcile himself to all of the ham-handed pleasantries and all of the glad-handing redundancies that pass for graciousness in the day-to-day pursuits of elective politics. Nicolson won his first election by only 87 votes. In his diary at the time, he described his first campaign for election to Parliament as an immersion in "the mud-baths of ignorance and meanness."[40] So it was for him. So it was for me. So it is for anyone who presumes to seek elected office. But what is the alternative if we hope to live in a free and open society?

"Never let anyone vote on you," my mother advised me when I first contemplated a campaign for election to the Congress. Hers was sound advice, perhaps, for someone as stubborn and as strong-willed as I am. My mother knows me well. And yet hers was advice I chose not to take, for I wanted to serve as a representative of the people of my community. And how could I serve them as their representative if I was not accountable to them through the periodic exercise of their votes? Like a watch, democracy is not an absolutely precise instrument, but it is one that we have made more precise over time. It is one that must have all the right pieces in order to work, and one, further, that we must somehow keep ticking if we hope to make ours a society that will truly serve the cause of freedom.

In considering the prospects for democracy in some of the closed societies of the world, there are those who fear the creation and the consequences of "illiberal democracy."[41] They foresee a "world on fire"[42] with a "coming anarchy"[43] occasioned by too much democracy too soon in too many parts of the world. They do not perceive the people in those

---

[40] Nigel Nicolson, ed., Harold Nicolson, <u>Diaries and Letters, 1930-1939</u> (New York: Atheneum, 1966), 223.

[41] Fareed Zakaria, <u>The Future of Freedom: Illiberal Democracy At Home and Abroad</u> (New York: Norton, 2003).

[42] Amy Chua, <u>World on Fire: How Exporting Free Market Democracy Breeds Ethnic Hatred and Global Instability</u> (New York: Doubleday, 2003) [hereinafter <u>World on Fire</u>].

[43] Robert D. Kaplan, <u>The Coming Anarchy</u> (New York: Random House, 2000) [hereinafter <u>The Coming Anarchy</u>].

parts of the world as being prepared for the use of reason in the self-rule of democracy. They urge, in part, that our hopes for the establishment of democracy in those places be postponed until, for example, "free markets produce enough economic and social development" in those places "to make democracy sustainable."[44]

These fears for the fate of democracy are not altogether unjustified. Real democracy is not simply a plebiscite. Representative democracy will not work if it is only an opinion poll. Elections are essential to democracy, but democracy depends on more than merely having elections. Elections can be rigged, and the electorate can be rigged as well through a combination of ignorance, demagoguery, and misinformation that can make of the electorate only a mob. As James Madison, ever skeptical of too much "pure democracy," put it in Number 55 of The Federalist Papers, "Had every Athenian citizen been a Socrates, every Athenian assembly would still have been a mob."[45]

Likewise, democracy depends on more than free markets. For all our fond hopes for trade, it cannot be said that free markets alone can create a free people who will be capable of making a democracy work. Nor have those of us who favor freer trade ever said that. As long ago as 1845, Lord Macaulay rightly remarked, "No friend of free trade is such an idiot as to say that free trade is the only valuable thing in the world; that religion, government, police, education, the administration of justice, public expenditure, foreign relations, have nothing to do with the well-being of nations."[46] More recently, Amartya Sen has, similarly and rightly, said, "[T]he market mechanism has to work in a world of many institutions, provided by democratic practice, civil and human rights, a free and open media, facilities for basic education and healthcare, economic safety nets, and of course, provisions for women's freedom and rights...."[47]

Some of those who fear democracy say, too, that democracy is a Western invention, and that democratic freedoms are only possible in a Western context. They maintain that democratic values have no universal origins and, thus, have no universal significance. Here, too, Professor

---

[44] Chua, World on Fire, at 261, citing Kaplan, The Coming Anarchy, at 63-78.
[45] James Madison, Number 55, The Federalist Papers, supra, at 335, 336.
[46] Macaulay is quoted in Irwin, Free Trade Under Fire, supra, at 68.
[47] Amartya Sen, "The Affront of Relegation," Harvard Magazine, Vol. 103, No. 1 (2000), 66 (published excerpts from his commencement address at Harvard University in 2000).

Sen tries to set us straight. He argues, with some persuasiveness, that if we look beyond the act of voting, if we take a "broader view" of democracy, if we see it in the broader scope of Rawls' concept of "public reason," then there is reason to conclude that the intellectual heritage of democracy extends beyond the West to include much of the rest of the world.[48]

As a Florida Democrat, I am, perhaps not surprisingly, much attached to the notion of voting as an indispensable aspect of democracy. I want every vote to count. Also, I give Western civilization its historical due. I am mindful, for example, of all that the Greeks did for us. Nevertheless, I am aware that there is much more to history and much more to the world than the West. And I share Sen's view that there are historical antecedents to certain aspects of democratic thought and practice to be found in parts of the world other than those that share the benefit of a lineal heritage from Periclean Athens.

Again, the question is one of context. Democracy depends on context. Democracy depends on having the right kind of supportive institutions and practices. Democracy depends on having the right kind of leaders. Democracy depends, too, on having the right kind of followers. Democracy depends, above all, on having the right kind of citizens. Democracy depends on having active, engaged, and informed citizens who are willing to choose and to follow leaders who strive to serve all citizens through an allegiance to the broad view and the long view of Tocqueville's "principle of interest rightly understood."

Thus, democracy depends on having the right kind of education that will produce such citizens. By this, I do not mean merely technical training in how to make the watches and the other "widgets" of trade. By this, I mean education in critical thinking. I mean education that enables emerging citizens to develop fully their individual powers for using human reason. Such education alone can keep democratic elections from becoming merely money-driven and media-driven plebiscites, and such education alone can keep democratic citizenries from becoming merely mobs.

For such education to succeed, it must be readily and equally available *to all*. No one has ever expressed this better than Clarence Beeby,

---

[48] Amartya Sen, "Democracy and Its Global Roots: Why democratization is not the same as Westernization," The New Republic (October 6, 2003) 28, 29.

the father of my late friend and colleague Chris Beeby. What he wrote in the Annual Report for the Ministry of Education of New Zealand in 1939 revolutionized education in New Zealand, and won for "Beeb" his lasting worldwide fame as an educator. In that report, he said, "The Government's objective, broadly expressed, is that every person, whatever his level of academic ability, whether he be rich or poor, whether he live in town or country, has a right, as a citizen, to a free education of the kind for which he is best fitted and to the fullest extent of his powers. Formal education beyond primary level is no longer a special privilege... but a right to be claimed by all who want it to the fullest extent that the State can provide. It is not enough to provide more places in schools of the older academic type that were devised originally for the education of the gifted few. Schools that are to cater for the whole population must offer courses that are as rich and varied as are the needs and abilities of the children who enter them."[49]

What we want is *not* an elite. What we want is *not* Nicolson's intellectual aristocracy of the few. What we want —intellectually, educationally, and, above all, democratically —is, in the phrase of the American thinker on "globalization," Benjamin Barber, "an aristocracy of everyone."[50] We can hope to achieve this only through universal education. Barber has said, "Public education is democracy's answer to Plato,"[51] who thought of democracy only as mindless mob rule. Only through mass public education —more specifically, only through the right kind of mass public education that inspires the crucial critical thinking of responsible citizenship —can we keep democracy from degenerating into mob rule, in America and elsewhere.

The first question to be asked is always the first and age-old question of all political philosophy: who should rule? Should it be Plato's "philosopher kings"? Should it be those who, in echo of the Melian Dialogue of Thucydides, have the might to make their own form of "right"? Or should it —somehow —be all of us? My answer is: the people should rule. I would have the people rule, locally and nationally, through popularly elected and representative democracies in every single Member of the WTO. I would have the work of the WTO benefit

---

[49] Clarence Beeby is quoted in "'Beeb —an intellectual architect of modern education," online at unesco.org/iiep/news/english/1998/apre998.htm.
[50] Benjamin R. Barber, <u>An Aristocracy of Everyone: The Politics of Education and the Future of America</u> (New York: Oxford University Press, 1992), 265.
[51] Id. at 266.

internationally from the full and effective participation of such democracies as WTO Members. And I would have the WTO continue to be responsive, and endeavor to be even *more* responsive, to the will of WTO Members in their mutual efforts to reflect the principles of democracy and to serve the cause of democracy in and through the work of the WTO.

Those who dwell on the shortcomings of democracy seem to suggest that we all might be better served by some kind of plutocratic, aristocratic, or autocratic rule. In so doing, they forget the far greater shortcomings of every form of governance other than democracy. The absence of democracy, ultimately, leaves us at the mercy of those who happen to have might, and who are therefore able to exercise at whim some form of arbitrary power. At the height of the Habsburg Empire, in the midst of the nineteenth century, the imbecilic Habsburg Emperor, Ferdinand, exclaimed one day, "I'm the emperor and I want dumplings!"[52] Sometimes those who hold an arbitrary power over us only want dumplings. But sometimes they want weapons of mass destruction. All in all, I prefer to take my chances with a democracy of educated, informed, and active citizens.

Thus, as I see it, our hopes for trade will be realized, and the human story will have a happy ending, only if we realize that the true community is a democratic community. Moreover, our gains from trade will be maximized only if the choices created by trade are maximized for all of us in a democratic community blessed by democratic self-governance. Economic freedom and the political freedom of a democratic community go hand in hand. Trade does not guarantee political freedom. Trade alone is not enough to establish and maintain political freedom. All the same, freer trade, over time, requires —and often demands —a context of other important freedoms. Freer trade feeds the human desire for other freedoms. This is one of the most important reasons why I have chosen to spend nearly a decade of my life in Geneva in building the WTO.

Still another important reason why I have chosen to devote so much time to building the WTO is my abiding belief in another indispensable part of the context of democracy, and of the context of fulfilling all of our hopes for trade. I see the cause of democracy —locally,

---

[52] A. J. P. Taylor, The Habsburg Monarchy, 1809 – 1918: A History of the Austrian Empire and Austria-Hungary (London: Penguin Books, 1990), 53 [1948].

nationally, and internationally —as being served, not only through education, but also through the rule of law. And, thus, I see a true, free, and open community as being created only through the rule of law. The people can rule *only* if there is the rule of law. The rule of law is needed everywhere and at every level of governance. Yet, as I see it, with the arrival, and with the ever-accelerating pace, of "globalization," the rule of law is needed especially, and increasingly, *internationally*.

In his *chateau* in Ferney, Voltaire's bedroom was also his study. The appointments of his study revealed the multiplicity of the passions of his life. "The room contained five desks. On each were notes for the various subjects on which the author was working; this desk had notes for a play; this, for a treatise on philosophy; a third for a *brochure* on science; and so on. All were exquisitely neat and orderly; every paper in its place."[53] (I think of Voltaire's study sometimes when I consider the spectacle of my own, cluttered with separate piles for each separate pending WTO dispute, and littered with the remains of accumulating memories of previous panel reports and appellate submissions.)

Voltaire's study was not a place of retreat. Voltaire, as we have seen, was not one to seek a cloistered refuge from the world in the snug sanctity of his study in Ferney. His study was not a refuge from the cares of the world; it was a staging ground for changing the world. And, in his mind, by far the best way of changing the world was by eliminating the exercise in the world of the capricious sway of arbitrary power. Even the margins of the books in his personal library were filled with his protests against arbitrary power.

Voltaire knew that the true community is one in which decisions about the future of the community are made in the right way and for the right reasons, and he knew that no such rightness would rule so long as there remained the rule of arbitrary power. What is needed, he knew, is the rule of law. And thus it may have been that, one day when he was not engaged in his worldwide watch trade, and one day when he was not engaged in one of the myriad of other pursuits that combined to make him all that was the embodiment of "Voltaire," he sat down at one of those desks and wrote, in a single sentence in his <u>Philosophical Dictionary</u>, the classic definition of the rule of law and the classic expression of the lasting connection between freedom and the rule of law.

---

[53] Tallentyre, <u>The Life of Voltaire</u>, at 360.

Wrote Voltaire, in the usual English translation: "To be free implies being subject to law alone."[54] This one sentence sums up why I chose to serve the Members of the WTO as a Member of the WTO Appellate Body.

Voltaire's Trees

One day, toward the end of his life, a friend said to Voltaire, "You have done a great work for posterity." Voltaire replied, "Yes Madame. I have planted four thousand feet of trees in my park."[55]

When he was not writing or otherwise agitating, and when he was not conducting his worldwide trade in watches and other wares, Monsieur Voltaire spent much of his spare time at Ferney planting trees. One of his many biographers recalled, "As if he had not hobbies enough, he soon became an enthusiastic tree-planter —begging all his friends to follow his example —and sending wagons all the way to Lyons for loads of young trees for his park. After a while that park stretched in three miles of circuit round the house, and included a splendid avenue of oaks, lindens, and poplars. In the garden were sunny walls for peaches; vines, lawns, and flowers."[56]

"The best thing we have to do on earth," Voltaire wrote, "is to cultivate it."[57] He added, "I have done only one sensible thing in my life —to cultivate the ground. He who clears a field renders a better service to humankind than all the scribblers in Europe."[58] And cultivate his ground he did, even as he continued to scribble in the service of freedom to all of Europe. Although he was in his seventies, Voltaire worked in his park with his hands, planting his avenues of trees. There were occasional setbacks. "Four times over he lined his drive with chestnut and walnut trees, and four times they nearly all died...."[59] He was, however, undaunted. He said, "To have cultivated a field and made twenty trees grow is a good which will never be lost."[60] And, in time, he made, not twenty, but four thousand trees grow in his park in Ferney.

---

[54] Voltaire is quoted from his <u>Philosophical Dictionary</u> in Nicolson, <u>The Age of Reason</u>, supra, at 92.

[55] Tallentyre, <u>The Life of Voltaire</u>, at 363.

[56] Id at 362.

[57] Id. at 487.

[58] Id. at 363.

[59] Id. at 488.

[60] Id.

I can understand, in some small part, the satisfaction that Voltaire derived from planting trees in his park. From time to time, on the "Citizen Saturdays" that I organized in Central Florida while I served in the Congress, we planted trees. On one memorable Saturday, we planted long rows of trees along the road that led to the entrance to the Orlando Naval Training Center. I remember the detailed instructions we were given by the tree-planting experts of the City of Orlando about how best to plant trees that would take root and grow. We needed the right mulch. We needed the right depth. We needed to keep "air pockets" out of the mulch that nourished the young trees. ("Air pockets are the enemy," observed my close friend and chief-of-staff, Linda Hennessee, as she hoisted her shovel.) Today, more than a decade later, the naval base is no longer there —but the trees are. I drive by them from time to time with Jamey on the way to the movies or to the bookstore, and, whenever I do, I remember anew the lessons that Voltaire and many others have taught me about cultivation. In planting trees, we are planting the future. And we can never know precisely how the future will take root and grow.

In the work of the Appellate Body of the World Trade Organization, we are engaging in the human cultivation of a human institution. We are planting trees. We are planting the seeds of the international rule of law, and we are hoping that those seeds will take root and grow into trees that will, in the future, offer shade and shelter and sustenance to all the world. We cannot know if we will succeed. Whether we seem to be succeeding, in our eyes, and in the eyes of a watching world, changes from day to day, and from dispute to dispute.

But things, they say, are not always as they seem. From a distance, the architectural lines of the Parthenon on the Acropolis in Athens seem to be all in symmetry. The truth is, the ancient Athenian architect, Phidias, only made it *seem* that way; the Parthenon contains scarcely a single straight line. Furthermore, what may seem to some to be insignificant at the time may later seem to others to be of profound significance. For example, in all that remains of what was written in antiquity there is not one single reference to the frieze of the Parthenon —the stately sculptured procession that is thought now to be one of the artistic marvels of all time. Would the sculptors of classical Athens have guessed that, millennia later, I would stand, as I have, for hours in the British Museum and gaze at the broken remnants of their handiwork?

In our efforts to help the international rule of law take root in the world by helping it grow and flourish in the world trading system, all that the Members of the Appellate Body can do is to keep planting trees. We can measure our progress case by case. We can consider the facts we are given in any given case. We can contemplate the issues of law that relate to those facts. We can do our best to discern the meanings of the words that comprise the law. We can do our best —as we always do —to find just the right words for just the right ruling. But we cannot know at the end of the allotted ninety days around our table in any given appeal if our ruling in that appeal will take root to grow and bear the fruit of the international rule of law.

Emerson visited Ferney during his first trip to Europe, in 1833, when he was only thirty. That was about half a century after Voltaire's death. Emerson professed at the time to his traveling companions his "unworthiness" to make the pilgrimage to Voltaire's home.[61] While there, he must have seen Voltaire's trees. Later, back home in Concord, he had trees of his own. Emerson, like Voltaire, had an orchard. In his orchard, Emerson had more than one hundred fruit trees. Chris Beeby smiled when I told him that more than thirty of Emerson's fruit trees were apple trees, and he laughed when I told him that Emerson named one of the varieties of apples on his trees "Thoreau."[62]

The fruit of the trees we have planted already on the Appellate Body is likewise varied. It ranges across the whole cornucopia of trade concerns. It is the fruit of a principled independence and a sustained consensus among all of those who have sat together around our table in Geneva, studied the "covered agreements," sliced logic, and sipped *renversé*. In between planting, tending, and growing the fruit trees in his orchard, Emerson told us, in "Self-Reliance," that "[a]n institution is the lengthened shadow of one man."[63] This may be so of some other institutions, but this is not so of the Appellate Body of the WTO. The Appellate Body is the lengthened shadow of all of those who have established it, supported it, and served it. It is the lengthened shadow of all of the Members of the WTO. It is the lengthened shadow of all of the hard-working members of the Appellate Body Secretariat. And it is the lengthened shadow especially of all of the Members of the Appellate Body who have sat together and served together around our table in Geneva.

From the beginning, the Members of the Appellate Body have kept separate and apart from the day-to-day give and take and ebb and

---

[61] Richardson, Emerson: The Mind on Fire, supra, at 138.
[62] Id. at 433-435.
[63] Emerson, "Self-Reliance," in Essays and Lectures, supra, 257, 267.

flow of the overall WTO. We may not be called "judges," but we have, from the beginning, tried to act as if we were judges in the exercise of our discretion and in the practice of our decorum. Part of that shared effort has consisted of maintaining our independence from the rest of the ongoing process of the trading system. Indeed, for the first few years, so as to maintain our independence, the Members of the Appellate Body did not even eat lunch in the WTO cafeteria. Further, for the first few years, so as to maintain our solidarity, we refrained from any and all public speaking. (This is not easy, I must admit, for an American politician, however reformed.) We spoke only as the Appellate Body and only in the pages of our reports to the Members of the WTO.

From the beginning, too, we have strived to *stay* together in part by *being* together. Not only have we spent long hours of many days sitting together, and slicing logic together, around our table in our shared effort to discern and "clarify" the meaning of the "covered agreements." In addition, in our "off hours," we have socialized in Geneva, to the extent that we have socialized at all, largely with one another. It was not at our round table in the WTO, but at his dining room table in his apartment in Ferney, where my friend Said first explained to me some of the subtler nuances of international economics. Our only rule in the discussions of our "off hours" has been that those discussions can include everything *except* the legal issues that have been raised in our appeals. This self-imposed rule has helped us to understand one another all the more, and, thus, has been the source, I am persuaded, of much of our enduring consensus.

When I visited the law school of the University of Virginia a few years ago, I met one of the professors there who is an expert on the early history of the Supreme Court of the United States. He compared the early years of the Appellate Body to the early years of the Marshall Court that established the principle of judicial review as well as so many other basic principles of constitutional interpretation that have now long been accepted in American law and life. It seems that, when he became Chief Justice, John Marshall deliberately set out to strengthen the struggling new Court and make it the vital and indispensable institution it has long since become for the United States.

Marshall insisted that he and his colleagues on the previously badly-divided Supreme Court reside "together under one roof" in the same rooming house in Washington. They lived together. They took all their meals together. They spent all their spare time together. The result?

The same Court which, in the first decade of the new republic, had been known for diminishing its effectiveness by issuing separate opinions by every single justice in every single case, proceeded, in the first few years after Marshall was appointed, to issue forty-six consecutive unanimous "opinions of the court" —without a single dissent.[64] Marbury v. Madison and many other landmark decisions were issued without dissent, and most American legal scholars are of the view that this did much to establish the foundation of the Court's subsequent stature and effectiveness during the decades that followed.

The professor from Virginia asked me if we had consciously emulated the early Marshall Court in the early years of the Appellate Body of the WTO. In answer, I could only say then, and I can only say now, that the Appellate Body has made every conceivable effort to create a cohesion among the Members of the Appellate Body that facilitates the making of a consensus. As a result, where the Marshall Court issued forty-six consecutive opinions without a dissent, the Appellate Body of the WTO, in its first eight years, has now issued sixty.

The time will come, no doubt, when there will be a dissent to an Appellate Body report. The time will come, no doubt, when the Appellate Body will fall short, on some issue, of a consensus. But perhaps, by that time, it will be, as it was with the Marshall Court, at a time when the basic legitimacy of the Appellate Body as a global tribunal for resolving trade disputes has been firmly established. That time is not quite yet, if I can judge from what I still sometimes hear from those who are affected by our judgments. This does not surprise me. Nor would it surprise Marshall.

Today, John Marshall is immortalized in marble at the end of a long white corridor on the basement floor of the Supreme Court of the United States. Symbolically, the edifice of the entire Court rests on his shoulders. In marble, as in life, he remains unmoving, unwavering in support of the judicial branch of the United States Constitution. The tourists who file by his statue simply assume the legitimacy of the Supreme Court as the final and ultimate arbiter of the meaning of our Constitution.

It has not always been so. When Marshall was appointed Chief Justice in 1801, "[t]he Court had no library, no office space, no clerks or secretaries."[65] Additionally, "[i]nitially there was no bench for the justices,

---

[64] Jean Edward Smith, John Marshall: Definer of a Nation (New York: Henry Holt, 1996), 284-293.
[65] Id. at 285.

and they sat at individual desks placed on a raised platform."[66] The official reporter for the Court resigned rather than make the trip to the muddy backwater of Washington, and cases sometimes had to be cancelled for lack of a quorum.[67] In 1801, there was no marble.

Marshall spent the next thirty-five years of his life planting the trees of the rule of law for what has become an enduring and an essential institution. But it was not easy. He earned his immortality in marble. In recalling the emergence of the Marshall Court, Henry Adams, the eloquent American historian of the era, described unavoidable conflict between order and chaos, and between unity and multiplicity, resulting in "the perpetual effort of society to establish law and the perpetual revolt of society against the law it had established."[68] All of this sounds only too familiar to those of us who hear the seeming ambivalence to the international rule of law that is sometimes voiced in response to the rulings of the WTO.

Yet, however loud they may sometimes seem, these voices of ambivalence must not obscure for us the day-to-day reality of what is happening in WTO dispute settlement. The rule of law prevails in WTO dispute settlement. Compliance with WTO rulings is not yet happening routinely, but it is happening consistently. Even in the most seemingly intractable of the international trade disputes that lead to dispute settlement, the result, after all of the loud voices are heard, seems almost always to be a resolution of the dispute through compliance with a "positive situation" reached in dispute settlement and adopted by the Members of the WTO.

I recalled the question I was asked by the scholar of the Supreme Court from Virginia, and I remembered the solid feel of the smooth surface of the white marble of John Marshall's statue in the Supreme Court, when I read an article that appeared in the *New York Times* a few days before the end of my eighth and last year as a Member of the Appellate Body. I had just completed my work in my final division in my final appeal in WTO dispute settlement. I had served as the Presiding Member of the division in the appeal relating to a safeguard measure applied by the United States of America on imports of steel from a number of other WTO Members.[69]

---

[66] Id.

[67] Id. at 283.

[68] Henry Adams, The Education of Henry Adams: An Autobiography (New York: Houghton Mifflin, 2000), 458 [1907].

[69] United States – Definitive Safeguard Measures on Imports of Certain Steel Products, AB – 2003 – 3 (November 10, 2003).

The day before the article appeared, the President of the United States had announced his decision to comply with our recommendation that the United States bring its steel safeguard measure into compliance with its obligations under the WTO treaty.

As I packed my books, perused my papers, and prepared to leave the WTO after my eight eventful years on the Appellate Body, I read this "news analysis" of the outcome of my last appeal by the *New York Times*: "While the White House was loath to say so, Mr. Bush's decision to comply fully with the ruling helped establish the trade organization's authority, showing that even the world's largest economic power, and the nation that spurred its creation, had to bend to its rulings. For the organization that conservatives, and some liberals, once denounced as an 'unelected bureaucracy' that should never be given power over American jobs, this case was the rough equivalent of Marbury v. Madison, the 1803 decision that established the Supreme Court as the final arbiter of the Constitution, able to force Congress and the executive branch to comply with its rulings."[70]

We shall see. In the meantime, whatever the dispute, and whatever the occasional ambivalence that is aroused in others as a consequence of our rulings, there is no ambivalence whatsoever in the continuing commitment of the Appellate Body to fulfilling the responsibilities of the Appellate Body to the Members of the WTO under the WTO treaty. The Members of the Appellate Body share with Voltaire a belief in the necessity of constant cultivation, and, especially, a belief in the necessity of the constant cultivation of the international rule of law.

In perhaps his most famous words, the very last words on the very last page of his tale of the travails of Candide, Voltaire has Candide say, "[W]e must cultivate our own garden."[71] Through the centuries, there have been many who have suggested that these words are an admission by Voltaire of the foreordained failure of all human efforts at reform, and an admonition to retreat into the "garden" of purely private concerns. But when we realize that Voltaire was busy writing Candide when he moved to Ferney, and when we remember all of the thousands of trees that Voltaire planted in his park there, then we understand that Voltaire

---

[70] David E. Sanger, "Backing Down on Steel Tariffs, U.S. Strengthens Trade Group," New York Times (December 5, 2003), 25.

[71] Voltaire, Candide, Zadig, and Selected Stories (New York: Signet, 1981), translated by Donald Frame, 101 [1759].

was simply advising us at the conclusion of <u>Candide</u> to keep cultivating a garden for all of us. The "we" he had in mind was all of us, and "our own garden" is all the wide world.

The Appellate Body continues to cultivate this garden by planting the trees of the international rule of law. We do not do so without criticism. Indeed, we cannot do so without criticism. Because we are required to rule on every appeal, and because we are required to rule on every legal issue raised in every appeal, we cannot possibly avoid criticism. If no one else, the party that does not happen to prevail in any particular dispute surely can always be expected to criticize us. So, too, of course, can others. On the Appellate Body, we have only a choice of critics. And, given that we are fallible —given that we are, like all of our fallible species, less than perfect —I would be the first to acknowledge that such criticisms may, from time to time, be justified. No one has offered thus far to immortalize us in marble.

And yet, I learned long ago in the Congress, and I have been reminded anew on the Appellate Body, the truth of something I was told many times by my role model and wry mentor, Reubin Askew, when I was too young to comprehend such truth fully. Governor Askew told me more often than I can remember, "Jimmy, there is a difference between an opinion and a decision." And so, I now know, there is. In the Congress, we usually had only fifteen minutes in which to make a decision and to cast a vote. On the Appellate Body, we usually have only ninety days. With both, the hardest part of the job is not always finding the right answer. With both, the hardest part of the job is often translating the right answer from an "opinion" into a "decision."

Foreshadowing Askew, Dr. Benjamin Rush of Pennsylvania, one of the founding fathers of the American republic, wrote, in 1776, a few weeks after becoming a Member of Congress, "I find there is a great deal of difference between sporting a sentiment in a letter, or over a glass of wine upon politics, and discharging properly the duties of a senator."[72] As it was then for Rush with politics and with the Congress, so it is now for me and my colleagues on the Appellate Body with trying to make the right "decision" in a WTO appeal. Translating an "opinion" into the right "decision" takes not only the patience to *see* what's right, but also the resolve to *do* what's right.

---

[72] Rush is quoted in David McCullough, <u>John Adams</u> (New York: Simon and Schuster, 2001), 146.

Public decisionmaking is not armchair philosophy. As Askew knows, as Rush discovered, and as I have learned along the way, it is one thing to have an "opinion" about what is "right" when there is no necessity of making a "decision." It is quite another to be able to reach a reasoned "decision" about what is "right" when confronted with the responsibility of making that "decision" for others in particular factual and legal circumstances. Such a responsibility is shared in every appeal in WTO dispute settlement by the Members of the Appellate Body.

Public decisionmaking, furthermore, requires something more than academic courage. It is one thing to be able to *discern* what is "right" in particular factual and legal circumstances, and it is quite another to have what it takes to *do* what is "right" by actually making that "decision." Both "independence" and "impartiality" are required of each of the seven Members of the Appellate Body, but the real test of whether those words have any real meaning is whether every Member of the Appellate Body has the personal resolve not only to reach, but also to support the shared consensus that will, in every appeal, result in the "right" answer in the "right" decision.

Providing the Members of the WTO with the "right" answer in the "right" decision requires a continuing commitment to *objectivity*. Adam Smith compared his "impartial spectator" to a judge. He described "the impartial spectator" as the quiet voice of conscience in each and every one of us.[73] To be "independent," to be "impartial," the Members of the Appellate Body must be, each and every one, an "impartial spectator" for the whole of the global trading system. Whatever the issue, whatever the criticism, and whatever its source, the seven Members of the Appellate Body must, at all times, each transcend their own nations, their own regions, and their own personal backgrounds in their mutual service to the Members of the WTO. They must each serve all of the Members of the WTO equally by serving the entire trading system exclusively. They must each fulfill faithfully their sworn responsibility to an "independent" and an "impartial" objectivity. Where the "right" answer in the "right" decision is concerned, to be true to the oath they have each given to the Members of the WTO, each Member of the Appellate Body must always be as unmoving as marble.

As we have learned in the first years of the Appellate Body, being unmoving in the resolve to reach the "right" answer by making the "right"

---

[73] Adam Smith, The Theory of Moral Sentiments, at 27.

decision can be habit-forming. One "right" answer can lead to another. One "right" decision can lead to another. Emerson said, "A great part of courage is the courage of having done the thing before."[74] Having done the thing before, having evidenced the resolve to find the "right" answer and to make the "right" decision before, the Members of the Appellate Body are inclined to do so again. It becomes a habit.

This habit serves the cause of freedom by serving the cause of trade. Like Tennyson, when he was not dipping in his "hot-water bath" in Sussex, we can dip "into the future, far as human eye [can] see," and see "the Vision of the world, and all the wonder that would be...."[75] Like him, all of us on the Appellate Body, and all of us who serve the WTO, can see "the heavens fill with commerce, argosies of magic sails, pilots of the purple twilight, dropping down with costly bales...."[76] Knowing, as we do, the crucial connection between trade and freedom, we can, in this bright vision of the future of the world, see that more trade will lead to more freedom. We can see, as Tennyson saw, a world "where Freedom slowly broadens down from precedent to precedent."[77] We can see freedom taking root, we can see freedom growing, we can see freedom rising, precedent by precedent, case by case, and tree by tree. In this way, the trees that are planted by the Appellate Body will take root and grow into the international rule of law.

Many in the world —including some even in my own country, which was founded on a belief in the rule of law —still doubt that there can, or should, be such a thing as the international rule of law. They subscribe only to the *realpolitik* of power. For example, the current Under Secretary of State for Arms Control and International Security for the United States, John R. Bolton, has, in opposing the new International Criminal Court, asked, "Why should anyone imagine that bewigged judges in The Hague will succeed where cold steel has failed?"[78] He misses the point. There must be international judges such as those in The Hague —whether "bewigged" or not —to help enforce the rule of law in the world. Otherwise, *all we will have will be cold steel. And that cold steel may not always be our own.*

---

[74] Emerson, "Culture," The Conduct of Life, in Essays and Lectures, supra, 1015, 1019.
[75] Tennyson, "Locksley Hall," Alfred, Lord Tennyson: Selected Poems (London: Penguin Books, 1991), 96, 101.
[76] Id.
[77] Tennyson, "On a Mourner," Alfred Tennyson: Poetical Works (London: Oxford University Press, 1959), 60.
[78] John R. Bolton, "The United States and the International Criminal Court," remarks at the Aspen Institute, Berlin, Germany (September 16, 2002).

We are a long way from Tennyson's Victorian vision of a world where the war drums throb no longer and the battle flags are furled.[79] We are a long way as well from his lofty vision of "the Parliament of man, the Federation of the world."[80] We may never get there. We may never want to get there. I know of no one in any way involved with the WTO who sees the WTO as a way to get there. But, even if we do not seek a federation of the world, we certainly do seek the preservation of the world. To ensure global preservation in this new and newly "globalized" world in which we find ourselves, we must have the rule of law. And, in this world that remains very much a world of *nations*, we must therefore have the *international* rule of law.

We must also have an Appellate Body that continues to serve the Members of the WTO by helping them to uphold the international rule of law. The continued development of the international rule of law through the work of the WTO is essential to meeting the many challenges of a "globalized" economy in ways that can help serve democracy, and that can help make possible a true international community that will truly serve the cause of human freedom. Furthermore, the success thus far of our efforts to serve the international rule of law through the WTO is important also because it demonstrates, perhaps for the first time in all of history, that there really can be such a thing as "international law."

Through the years, some have seen the law of the GATT, and now the law of the WTO, as somehow self-contained in the world of "widgets" that was for so long the seemingly separate province of those who dealt with GATT law and with GATT lore. Yet our brief experience with the WTO has clearly shown that the work of the WTO cannot be seen as separate and distinct from all that is not directly related to trade in "widgets." And it follows, logically and necessarily, that WTO law likewise cannot be considered as separate and apart from other international law. WTO law is a part of international law. As we said in the very first ruling of the Appellate Body, and as we have reiterated often in the years since, WTO rules cannot be viewed or interpreted in "clinical isolation" from the broader corpus and the broader concerns of the rest of international law.[81]

Nor are WTO rules the only rules the world needs. There are many other international agreements, in addition to the WTO treaty, that

---

[79] Tennyson, "Locksley Hall," supra, at 101.
[80] Id.
[81] U.S. —Gasoline, supra, at 17.

have legitimacy, and that are also deserving of enforcement. There are hundreds upon hundreds of multilateral international agreements dealing with human rights, women's rights, children's rights, workers' rights, the environment, health, intellectual property, investment, crime, corruption, genocide, and numerous other areas of compelling and continuing international concern that deserve due credence and due consideration by both national and international tribunals. And there is need for more.

The world needs more international law, not less. The world must find more and better ways both to make and enforce international law in order to meet the historic challenge of "globalization." The continued success and strengthening of the WTO dispute settlement system must be seen, not as a substitute for other efforts by the world to establish and enhance the rule of law internationally, but rather as an example to the world that, at long last, after long centuries of wishful thinking and seemingly futile hoping, such efforts really can succeed. The WTO dispute settlement system must be seen by the world for what it is: real evidence that something worthy of being called "international law" finally exists.

In 1651, in the midst of the bloody fratricide of the English Civil War, Thomas Hobbes observed in his Leviathan that, in thinking of how we can make the world work for humanity, we must take into account that there is no "common power" in the world.[82] For, he said, "Where there is no common Power, there is no Law...."[83] Today, nearly four centuries later, there is still "no common power" in the world. It therefore falls on the nations of the world both to shape and to share a "common power" that not only will be sufficient to address the needs of global trade in a global economy, but also will be sufficient to address the other common needs of global humanity. Although still new, the WTO is proof that such a "common power" can serve the common cause of human freedom.

As explained by a leading theorist on international security, Professor Michael Mandelbaum of The Johns Hopkins University, "The world that we want to see evolve today is not a world of one, two or three contending powers, but rather a world governed by rules. That is already increasingly true in economics, and... security affairs will eventually

---

[82] Hobbes, Leviathan, supra, at 188.
[83] Id. at 188.

mirror that. The idea is not to end competition, which is enduring, but to regulate it. We want a world where countries apologize when they are wrong, but we don't want a world where countries are coerced to apologize when they are not wrong."[84] As with the WTO, the aim in other areas of common human concern must be to resolve international disputes by relying on international rules on which all have agreed. The aim must be to beat our "swords into ploughshares"[85] —and into all the other "widgets" of the world economy and of all our other world concerns —through the international rule of law.

International law. The rule of law. Democracy. True community. The many ends of human freedom that are served by the means of trade. No, trade alone is not enough. Trade alone is not nearly enough. Much more is needed. I am confident that Thoreau would be eager and willing to put down his pencil long enough to join me in saying emphatically: we can claim much for trade, but trade has its limits. Trade cannot teach us how to live. Trade cannot give meaning and purpose to our lives. Trade cannot fill the emptiness in our hearts.

Even so, trade can help fill the emptiness in our stomachs. Trade can help keep us from being hungry. And this, perhaps, is enough to begin. For only when we are no longer hungry can we begin to overcome the fear of freedom. Only then can we begin to seize freedom, embrace freedom, and use freedom in finding the mutual human fulfillment that can only be achieved through the full measure of freedom. Only then can we begin to become capable of rising up from the brute struggle for survival to become truly human by asking: what is our freedom for?

Not all those who fear freedom are hungry. Osama bin Laden is not hungry. Saddam Hussein is not hungry. Slobodan Milosevic is not hungry. Hitler and Stalin may never have missed a meal. Yet it remains true, nevertheless, that hungry people have no time for freedom. Hungry people have time only for fear. And hungry people become fodder for all those who fear freedom, and who would turn fear into prejudice, prejudice into intolerance, intolerance into hate, and hate into terror.

The "war against terror" we are waging worldwide is a war *for* freedom, and it is a war *about* freedom. It is *not* a war *between* civilizations.

---

[84] Michael Mandelbaum, interview with Thomas Friedman, *International Herald Tribune* (April 11, 2001).
[85] Isaiah 2:4.

It is a war *within* civilizations between the partisans of open and closed societies. It is a war *within* civilizations between the future and the past. It is a war *within* civilizations between those who embrace freedom and those who fear it. It is a war *within* civilizations between those who would create freedom in an effort to liberate humanity and those who would deny freedom in order to keep humanity chained in all the prisons of the past. The "war against terror" is a war *within* all the many civilizations of the world between those who believe we are capable of living in freedom and those who believe we are not.

In this war, the World Trade Organization is on the side of the future, and on the side of freedom.

So am I.

Sometimes, on Saturdays, when I am on my own in Geneva, I walk up to the Cornavin and take the "F" bus across town and across the border to Ferney. The fare each way is four francs. Sometimes then I stroll from the bus stop at the *mairie* in Ferney through the cobblestone streets of the village to the weekly agora of the Ferney market, soaking up along the way the scents and the sounds that have traveled there from all the far places of the world. When I see a stall where Swiss watches are for sale, I stop, and I smile.

Sometimes, I walk on beyond the market, and, when he is not in Egypt working for democracy, I go over to see my friend Said at his Ferney apartment. His Norwegian wife, Gerd, prepares a feast. We eat roasted lamb and Egyptian beans to our fill. Then Said and I sit together on his balcony, enveloped by the embrace of the Jura and the Alps, musing on Popper and Schumpeter, on Mill and Smith, and pondering the ways of making freedom from "unfreedom" in all the closed societies of the world. I still have much to learn from Said.

And, sometimes, I climb up, step by step on the long stone staircase, from the streets of the village, past the playground where Jamey likes to swing (an ice cream in hand), past the cemetery where Joe likes to read the faded tombstones, past the garden where Rebecca likes to see the multi-colored flowers, up to the vestige of what remains of the once vast estate of the sage of Ferney, up to the ancient *chateau* of Monsieur Voltaire. The French government has recently purchased the *chateau* and what remains of the surrounding park. The residents of Ferney and other nearby villages helped raise the money to purchase and to preserve it.

There, in my own pilgrimage, I join the usual jumble of tourists waiting for the *chateau* to open at noon. In due course, the door opens. I buy a ticket, go inside, and follow the tour guide for an hour or so through those rooms of the *chateau* that are open, at appointed times, to the public. The tour is conducted, not surprisingly, in French. I strain to hear and to discern the meaning of every second or third word. The tour guide, though, speaks French much more rapidly than the waiters in the restaurants I frequent across the border in Geneva. So, mostly, I look around me at what is left in the *chateau* of Voltaire. His portrait. His dressing gown. His pens. His desks.

Then, the formal tour over, I go outside into the garden. I gaze, as he once did, at the imposing snow-capped prospect, in the distance, of Mont Blanc. The park that adjoins the *chateau* just beyond the garden is much smaller now than it was in his time. Of the hundreds of acres of the park of his time, today little more than a dozen are left. And yet the park enfolds me, it is sufficient even now to console me, as I walk out past the low walls of the garden.

For, as I walk out into the park in the lengthening shadows of the afternoon, I walk in the shade of Voltaire's trees.

Conclusion

The Age of Reason

All this I see through my WTO glasses. All this I recalled as I stood with my colleagues at the WTO, one sunny September day, watching, in shock and in silence, as CNN repeated, again and again, the hellish horror of two airplanes flying —from the fear of freedom, from the fathomless pits of despair, from the darkest depths of human nature —into the twin towers of the World Trade Center. And all this I recalled soon after as I sat with my colleagues around our table in Geneva through three minutes of silence in honor of all those who were killed by the attacks of September 11, 2001. All this I still remember as I sit with them today, slicing logic and sipping *renversé*.

Recently, the Swiss government replaced all the casements in the windows of our chambers. The view through the windows is still the same, but the new casements are better than the old at keeping the winds from the lake from scattering the papers that pile ever higher on our table. Sometimes the wind that rises from the lake is the *"bise,"* the sharp glacial wind that cuts like a knife. At other times, it is the *"foehn,"* the warm, dry, unexpected, ill wind that gusts down from the mountain slopes and into the valley below even in the midst of winter. What wind, I wonder, will be blowing next on the work of the WTO?

The winds of the world seem to threaten the future of the "multilateral trading system" that is served by the WTO. The pages of the world press are nothing if not ominous. Trade talks are "stalled." Trade disputes "fester." Trade "wars" are said to "loom." Trade advocates are few, and trading nations seem only to make apologies for trying to trade. As the days grow shorter, as another winter arrives, and as I prepare to turn and go from the WTO, the chill winds of the world seep through the cracks in the new casements of our windows.

In a history he wrote of the Congress of Vienna of 1815 that followed the end of the Napoleonic Wars, Sir Harold Nicolson spoke of how the leading European powers of the time, after long years of continental conflict, were in common search of "repose."[1] They wanted

---

[1] Harold Nicolson, The Congress of Vienna: A Study in Allied Unity: 1812-1822 (New York: Grove Press, 2000), 225, 227 [1946].

to make time stand still. They sought to assert "static principles" that would hold off the onset of the modern world.[2] From our point of view, nearly two centuries later, theirs was an old-fashioned world, and their desire for "repose" can only be seen as an old-fashioned notion. There is no "repose" in our world. There can be no "repose" in our world —and certainly there cannot be after the events of "9-11."

There are now more than six billion of our unique species in the world. We are adding another two hundred thousand to our numbers every day. At the current rate of population growth, the total number of the human species will peak at between nine billion and ten billion unique, irreplaceable, individual, reasoning souls sometime late in the twenty-first century.[3] More than 99.99 percent of all the species that ever existed on our planet are now extinct.[4] Our species —our daring, dreaming, striving, questing, reasoning species —somehow still survives. For now. But for how much longer? As both an optimist and a realist, I find myself wondering: what is our fate? Will we, in the face of the fear of freedom, and in the face of the terror that results from the fear of freedom, somehow find that our capacity to reason is enough to help ensure our continued survival and our continued success as a species? Or will we, too, tumble into the abyss of extinction?

Harold Nicolson wondered as well. Toward the end of his life, more than forty years after his encounter with Proust in the Ritz Hotel in Paris in 1919, after eating many more macaroons at many more diplomatic conferences, and after writing dozens of thoughtful books about diplomacy and history, Nicolson wrote, in his retirement, one of his last books. It was a study of Voltaire and a number of the other Enlightenment luminaries of the eighteenth century. It was called The Age of Reason.

And what was his conclusion? What was his bottom line after a lifetime spent in both action and reflection in pursuit of a world that would be ruled by reason? Nicolson said this: "The more one studies The Age of Reason, the more one realizes that the majority were utterly unreasonable: that it was but a small elite that possessed any good sense at all."[5] Nicolson said this about the eighteenth century. It might be said as well about the nineteenth century. At least one hundred million dead

---

[2] Id. at 258.
[3] Wilson, The Future of Life, supra, at 28-31.
[4] Richard Leakey, The Origin of Humankind, supra, at 58; Bill Bryson, A Short History of Nearly Everything (New York: Broadway Books, 2003), 3.
[5] Harold Nicolson, The Age of Reason, supra, at 187.

from the excesses of various extremisms of both right and left should be enough to persuade us that it can also be said about the twentieth century. For all our hopes, for all our efforts, for all our progress, ours is not yet an Age of Reason.

But what of this new century, the twenty-first century? Will this also be said about our brand new century another hundred years from now? Will the same sad verdict apply? Or will we, in this new century, at last be able to keep the divine promise of our humanity? Will we, in this new century, in a new Enlightenment, prove ourselves worthy of our special spark of divinity and somehow summon, at last, the better angels of our nature to greet the dawn of an Age of Reason?

In the long history of our planet, and in the much longer history of our universe, the short life of our unique human species is only a moment. The human species is still in its infancy. Human civilization is still in its infancy. The new institution we have created in the work of human civilization —the new institution that we call the WTO —is also still very much in its infancy. Who can say —who can know —what winds will blow next in the life of the WTO?

In 1995, shortly after my appointment to the Appellate Body, and shortly before my first official trip to Geneva and to the new WTO, my friend Mickey Kantor, who was then the United States Trade Representative, told me, "I envy you in your task. You will be present at the creation." He was right. I have been "present at the creation" of the WTO. And much has been created by the WTO for the world, and for the future of the world, since I first traveled to Geneva to sit at the round table of the Appellate Body and serve the Members of the WTO. Yet we must remain mindful that, where the historic task of the WTO is concerned, we are all still very much "present at the creation." There is much more that must be done. There is much more that must be created.

The poet W. H. Auden wrote of the aged Voltaire in his last days at Ferney: "Perfectly happy now, he looked at his estate. An exile making watches glanced up as he passed and went on working; where a hospital was rising fast, a joiner touched his cap; an agent came to tell some of the trees he'd planted were progressing well. The white alps glittered."[6] Was Voltaire, in the end, content with the number of trees he had planted? Was he satisfied with the extent of his contribution to the creation of an Age of Reason? If anyone could be, then surely he should have been. But

---

[6] W. H. Auden, "Voltaire at Ferney."

what about me? As I stroll in the shade of Voltaire's trees, am I content with the extent of my own contribution?

Like so many of the answers I have found to all of the many questions I have asked during my time in Geneva, the answer to this question has been suggested to me by one of the wise men who have sat with me for so long around our table. When he left our table, and when he left the WTO, Julio Lacarté did not even consider the possibility of "retirement." Even in his eighties, he had more, much more, that he hoped to do. Today he is busy doing it. Julio explained to me sometime afterwards, "I can't seem to do nothing." Nor can I. Not if, as part of my own trade hopes, I hope to live up to Julio's example, and to the enduring example of all of the other wise men with whom I have sat and served at the round table of the Appellate Body of the WTO.

When he left Walden Pond after two years, and moved in with his friend Emerson, Thoreau explained that he did so because he "had several more lives to live."[7] In leaving the Appellate Body, in turning to go from the WTO, I, too, do so in the belief that I, too, have "several more lives to live." There are other trees that need planting. But, in leaving, I leave content with the extent of my own contribution to the work of the WTO, and I leave confident about the future of the WTO, even as I am confident about the future of all our hopes for trade and for freedom.

The promenade continues. The WTO is a work *in* progress of the work *of* progress. The work of the WTO will not, alone, enable us to greet the dawn of an Age of Reason. Yet the success of the WTO is one indispensable means for helping all who pass by in the promenade to see, some day, such a dawn. The white Alps can glitter for all of us. A bright morning in Geneva can become a bright morning for all the world.

This, as I see it, is the most important of all our "trade secrets."

It is certainly the most hopeful of all of the reflections of this "faceless foreign judge."

Geneva, Switzerland

December, 2003

---

[7] Henry David Thoreau, Walden, in Walden and Civil Disobedience, supra, at 371.

Part Two

Further Reflections on Trade and Freedom

Chapter One

The Appeals of Trade:
The Making of an Old GATT Hand

"Why are they doing it?"

"Why are they doing it?"

This question has been asked by one of the many critics of the World Trade Organization, a Canadian writer named Naomi Klein. Her question deserves an answer. So I will try my best to answer it.

Writing a few weeks after the tragedy of September 11, 2001, and a few days before the WTO ministerial conference in Doha that "launched" a new "round" of global trade negotiations, Ms. Klein wondered in print what it was that made so many American and other international trade negotiators willing to fly to the very middle of the Middle East at that dangerous time.[1] Watching from afar, she tried to comprehend this. In the reputable pages of the Toronto Globe and Mail, she asked the question: *"Why are they doing it?"*

She was puzzled. There was absolutely nothing in any of her assumptions about the WTO to help her understand this show of courage. There was nothing in anything she thought she knew about the WTO to help explain why the supporters of the WTO would be willing to risk personal sacrifice for what must have seemed to her to be merely the widgets that are the usual subjects of global trade negotiations.

Why were so many people from so many countries willing to risk their very lives for the mere chance of concluding something so seemingly mundane as an international trade agreement?

Why are so many talented people in USTR and in the trade ministries and the trade missions of so many other Members of the WTO willing to endure, year after year, "round" after "round," and decade

---

This chapter is adapted from an address to a conference of the American Bar Association at Georgetown University Law School on January 21, 2003.
[1] Naomi Klein, "Kamikaze Capitalists," Toronto Globe and Mail (November 7, 2001), reprinted in Naomi Klein, Fences and Windows: Dispatches from the Front Lines of the Globalization Debate (New York: Picador, 2002), 176. The quotes from Klein are all from this article.

after decade, all the sleepless nights, all the endless commercial fights, and all the increasingly dangerous flights that are the common and inevitable plight of every international trade negotiator?

And why, after all these years, am I still willing to brave all those imposing piles of trade agreements and legal briefs and panel reports in my office at the WTO —while, outside my window, Swiss police boats bob up and down in the blue waters of the Lake of Geneva?

What *are* the appeals of trade? Why *are* we doing it?

Despite her puzzlement, Ms. Klein suggested a possible answer. Indeed, she suggested an interesting and provocative answer: "Probably for the same reason people have always put their lives on the line for a cause: they believe in a set of rules that promises transcendence."

As she sees it, the "rigid rules" that inspire the supporters of the WTO are rules that promise "salvation" through trade. In her eyes, the "only god" of the "true believers" in trade "is economic growth," and the "transcendence" that is promised by trade is the "transcendence" of a "Kamikaze Capitalism."

Clearly, many of those who oppose the WTO do not see us for who we truly are. So they cannot see why so many of us would be willing to sacrifice for the sake of trade.

We certainly are *not* doing it because we hope to find transcendence through trade. Trade is not transcendence. Trade is only an exchange of goods and services. All the many "things" that are traded in the world every day are, for all their seeming significance, only "things." Widgets are only widgets.

We do not seek transcendence through trade. We seek something else. We seek something more. We seek what has always been sought by all those who understand the appeals of trade. We seek what has always been sought by every old GATT hand.

The answer to why we are "doing it" is found in what we *are* seeking through trade. And perhaps the best way I can begin to explain what it is that we *are* seeking through trade is by explaining, first, how it was that I first heard and first heeded the appeals of trade long ago, and why it is that I have long wanted nothing more than to be known one day as an old GATT hand.

I was raised in Florida, but I was born in Nashville, Tennessee. Nashville was built on the banks of the Cumberland River. The waters of the Cumberland flow through Middle Tennessee toward the mighty Mississippi, and from there out into all the far waters of the wide world. This may help explain why so many of those who have come from Nashville and from Middle Tennessee to serve our country and our world have, so often, been advocates for trade. Andrew Jackson. Cordell Hull. Albert Gore, Sr. Albert Gore, Jr. Mickey Kantor. All have stood, as I have stood, on the steep banks of the Cumberland. All have watched, as I have watched, the flow of the waters toward the distant seas.

Like my friend Mickey Kantor, I studied at Vanderbilt University in Nashville (although, as I like to remind him, I arrived there as a freshman some years after he was graduated). We both studied history there, at different times, with Professor Charles Delzell, whose father had once run —unsuccessfully —for Congress as a Democrat against Hawley of "Smoot-Hawley" fame. At Vanderbilt, I learned what had happened when the Congress of the United States enacted the "Smoot-Hawley" tariffs and the world turned away from trade during the Great Depression.

I took that lesson back home with me to Florida. Back in Florida, I soon became, at twenty-four, in 1974, the youngest aide to the reform-minded Governor of that state, Reubin Askew. In my increasingly distant youth, I had the great good fortune to serve with Governor Askew, and to help him shape the laws and the ways in which the rapidly-growing trading state of Florida began to venture out commercially for the first time into the wide world.

But it was not until 1979 that I really began to follow the path that would eventually lead me to the Appellate Body of the WTO. By then, Askew had left the Governor's office in Tallahassee, and he and I had both joined the same up-and-coming Miami law firm. We had been there only a few months when the call came inviting Governor Askew to join President Jimmy Carter's Cabinet in Washington. I was with Askew at the time in his corner office overlooking Biscayne Bay. I was sitting directly across the desk from him, and I heard several possibilities discussed. I immediately picked up a pen and wrote one word in big bold print on a yellow legal pad on the desk. Then I picked up the legal pad and turned it, at eye level, so that he could see what I had written. The one word on the legal pad was "TRADE."

No doubt Governor Askew would have made the decision he did even if I had not been so presumptuous as to try to prompt him to do so. His good friend Bob Strauss had just completed several years of work as the chief trade negotiator for the United States in the Tokyo Round, and he had told Askew how much he had enjoyed the job. Ambassador Strauss had recommended Askew to the President as his successor, and the Governor did not really need my bold word of encouragement on my legal pad.

All the same, I remain, after all these years, glad that I wrote that one word. And I will remain forever grateful for having had the experience of working with Askew at what the trading world today universally calls "USTR." The day I walked into USTR —the Office of the United States Trade Representative —was the day I was introduced to the "General Agreement on Tariffs and Trade." Someone handed me a tattered copy of the GATT, and said, "Here. Read this." So I did. And I have not stopped since. I have not stopped reading about trade, studying about trade, and learning about trade in all the years since. I have never ceased since in my efforts to become an old GATT hand.

From that first day, I rejoiced in my role as an apprentice among all the old GATT hands who worked at USTR. And when they saw that I took the time to read the GATT —when they saw that I seemed to be genuinely interested in the substance of trade and trade law —those old GATT hands took the time to teach me about trade, and about what they always described passionately as "the multilateral trading system." As a *new* GATT hand, I soon shared their passion. While at USTR, I reveled in all the endless acronyms of trade. MFN. MFA. TRQ. TPM. And so many more. I relished the arcane argot of trade. "Binding." "Dumping." "Safeguards." And something mysterious called "countervail." But, most of all, I read the law and the lore of the GATT.

In his memoirs, the great historian Edward Gibbon wrote of the breadth and the depth of the youthful studies that led him later to write the many volumes of his timeless classic, The Decline and Fall of the Roman Empire. In one memorable scene, he recalled the fateful day in his boyhood when he first opened the pages of a book on the history of Rome in the library of one of his father's friends. He wrote, "I was immersed in the passage of the Goths over the Danube when the summons of the dinner-bell reluctantly dragged me from my intellectual feast."[2]

---

[2] Edward Gibbon, Memoirs of My Life (London: Penguin Books, 1990), 72 [1796].

That was precisely how I felt when I first opened the pages of the GATT. And, during what remained of the Carter Administration, I studied the GATT during every spare moment while I served as the "Special Assistant" to the United States Trade Representative in the Executive Office of the President. The reality was not nearly as lofty as the title, but the work seemed special to me. I had a front row seat at the unfolding drama of "globalization." I had a license to learn all I could about the complex and ever-changing "political economy" of world trade. I was immersed in the passage of the world into a new *world* economy. Then Ronald Reagan became President. And I was dragged reluctantly from my "intellectual feast" at USTR when the new President politely asked all of us who were Democrats to go back home.

Ten years later, my neighbors back home in Central Florida elected me to the first of my two terms in the Congress of the United States. I was the first Democrat in the history of the South elected to an open Congressional seat from a district where Republicans outnumbered Democrats. Later, I was re-elected. All the same, when I first became a member of the Democratic Caucus in the House of Representatives in 1991, I was merely another freshman. So I was surprised when, soon after I arrived, I received a summons to an audience with the then Chairman of the House Ways and Means Committee, Dan Rostenkowski of Illinois.

Several decades of seniority had given Chairman Rostenkowski a private "hideaway" office on a quiet hallway in a corner of the Capitol rarely frequented by the daily throngs of tourists. The room was dark when I entered. I stood at one end of a long table. He sat at the other end. A low lamp at his shoulder cast the only light in the room. "Rosty" was reading by the lamp's light when I came in. He was bulky, burly, bespectacled. He was just as he looked in the newspapers. He continued to read for a minute or so, and then he removed his glasses and looked up from his reading.

He asked, "You're from Florida?" "Yes, Mr. Chairman." He continued, "I understand you've *actually read* the GATT?" "Yes, Mr. Chairman." "Well, then," he replied, "you're on the trade whip team. Thanks for stopping by." Then he put on his glasses, and returned to his reading.

Evidently, having *actually read* the GATT, I qualified as what passed for a "trade expert" in the rowdy ranks of the House. However, expertise of any kind is worthless in the Congress unless it can help attract and accumulate votes. There are 435 members of the United States House of Representatives. Some have more seniority and, thus, bigger and better offices, than others. But, in the end, on the floor, all their votes count the same. A majority of the votes in the House is needed to pass a bill and, thus, help make a law. Therefore, one of the highest accolades that one member of the House can accord to another as a lawmaker is to say, "He knows how to get 218 votes."

The sole purpose of the bipartisan trade whip team in the House was to "whip" up the needed support to get "218 votes" on the trade issues that came before the House. Emboldened by Rosty's show of confidence, I set out to employ my supposed "expertise" to help get those "218 votes" in a series of legislative struggles over trade. First came the successful vote to secure the "fast-track" negotiating authority that would enable then President George Bush to conclude international trade agreements with America's trading partners. Later came the successful vote for extending "most-favoured-nation" trading status for the People's Republic of China. Then came the endlessly controversial —but ultimately successful —vote to approve the "NAFTA" —the North American Free Trade Agreement with Canada and Mexico. In working on these and other proposals for trade legislation, I learned a lot in the years that followed about how to get "218 votes."

The very last vote I cast as a Member of the Congress was a vote for the implementing legislation that constituted approval by the United States of the Uruguay Round trade agreements that, among many other achievements, established the World Trade Organization as the global successor to the GATT. I was one of the original co-sponsors of the legislation in the House. I cast that vote on November 29, 1994 —my wife Rebecca's birthday —and then walked out of the House chambers alone into the night. I have not returned to the floor of the House since.

I had decided —for family reasons —not to seek election to a third term in the House. My decision to leave the Congress was probably made the weekend I came home from Washington and tried to sneak a quick glimpse of my daughter, Jamey, who was then three years old, before leaving almost immediately to return to work. When I opened the door to her nursery, Jamey was wide awake, and standing in her crib. "Mommy, Mommy," she cried, "Jim Bacchus is here." This made everyone laugh but me. Jim Bacchus was not "Daddy" to his only daughter. I had missed five of Rebecca's birthdays in a row, not to mention my children's birthdays and many other important family occasions. As I walked out of the House chambers for the last time following my vote for the WTO, I hoped that this additional missed birthday would be the last.

The vote on the Uruguay Round legislation had occurred in a "lame duck" Congressional session only a few weeks before my term ended. Back in Florida a few weeks later, I wondered where life would lead me next. I knew that my decision to leave the Congress was the right one for both me and my family, and yet I still wanted very much to serve. So, when that other watcher of the waters of the Cumberland, USTR Mickey Kantor, called me in Florida to ask if I would allow my name to be placed in nomination by my country for appointment by the Members of the WTO to the new Appellate Body of the WTO, I did not need to be prompted by boldface print on a legal pad. I said "Yes."

So it was that, only a few weeks after leaving the Congress, I was nominated for the Appellate Body of the World Trade Organization by the President of the United States with the bipartisan support of the leadership of both chambers and also of the committees with jurisdiction over trade issues in both the Senate and the House. The only question that remained was: having been nominated by the United States of America, would I be appointed by the Members of the WTO?

Thirty-five people in the world had been nominated for the Appellate Body. Only two were Americans. Only seven would be appointed. Early in 1995, all thirty-five of us made the pilgrimage to Geneva from the far reaches of the planet to participate in the selection process that had been established by the WTO.

The selection committee consisted of the ranking ambassadors on the leading councils of the WTO. In my "interview," the committee members were considerably more probing about my knowledge of trade, and about my knowledge of trade law, than Rosty had been when I had first arrived in the Congress. But, like Rosty, the GATT hands on the selection committee in Geneva seemed surprised —and pleased —that a former Member of the Congress of the United States had *actually read* the GATT —not to mention GATT case law and the numerous other WTO "covered agreements."

Moreover, I was equally surprised myself when, as I started to discuss some of my background, an ambassador from an Asian country stopped me by saying, "That's all right, Mr. Bacchus. I know all about your background and your voting record. I own a time-share in a condominium in Vero Beach, and I've followed your Congressional career closely."

Vero Beach is in Indian River County in my former Congressional district. The last time my name appeared on a ballot, I received one of the highest percentages of the vote of any Democrat in the modern history of Indian River County —forty-two percent. The Asian ambassador knew of the unpopularity among many in Indian River County of my support for foreign aid, for the United Nations, and for many other international pursuits. He knew, too, about the time when a sweet little old lady who was a follower of Ross Perot had attacked me with her hand-held sign opposing the NAFTA. "Don't you care," she had yelled, "about the future of your children?"

Following my "interview" in Geneva, I went home to Florida, and waited. Then I waited some more. Eventually a call came from Washington. The ranking American at the WTO —Deputy Director General Warren Lavorel —had been away from Geneva when I had been there for my "interview." He was going to be in Washington and up on Capitol Hill the next day. He wanted to meet with me then. Would I fly up to meet with him?

I flew up to Washington the next day. Warren was one of the old GATT hands I had known years before as a young "Special Assistant" at USTR. At the time, he had been a senior negotiator in the USTR mission in Geneva. But I had not seen him since. He had been in Geneva all the while I was in the Congress, and now he had gone "across the street" from USTR to work for the new WTO.

Warren and I met in an anteroom of one of the big hearing rooms on the Hill. There were just the two of us. The meeting lasted for less than five minutes. He told me how nice it was to see me again after fifteen years. We exchanged a few reminiscences. We swapped a few other pleasantries. Then, rising from his chair, he thanked me for coming. That was it. As I flew home to Florida later that day, I wondered why he had wanted to meet with me.

Years later, I found out. It seems that my "interview" in Geneva had gone well. I had become a leading candidate for appointment to the Appellate Body. The only remaining question about my candidacy was unrelated to my legal or other qualifications. The only remaining question was my *age*. Appointments to international tribunals ordinarily are accorded only to the most senior of international jurists. The other leading candidates for appointment to the new international tribunal for trade were literally decades older than the American from Florida. Was I, at age 45, old enough? Was I enough of an *old* GATT hand?

Warren had been assured by his fellow Americans that I was old enough. But he remembered me from my youthful days at USTR. He had not seen me in all the intervening years. Thus, the sole purpose of our brief exchange of pleasantries in Washington was, I was later told, so that Warren could confirm that the years had aged me enough that I had *at least some gray hair*. Fortunately, my time in the Congress —and a few close calls with sweet little old ladies waving anti-NAFTA signs —had taken care of that. Warren returned to Geneva satisfied that I had, indeed, grayed sufficiently to serve on the Appellate Body.

Evidently, the Members of the WTO also concluded that I was old enough. For, a few months later, on November 29, 1995 —one year to the day after the Congressional vote for the legislation implementing the Uruguay Round trade agreements —and, once again, on Rebecca's birthday —the WTO announced my appointment as one of the seven founding members of the Appellate Body. My longtime friend Andy Stoler, then at USTR and later the Deputy Director-General of the WTO, called to tell me the news of my appointment. He said, "Tell Rebecca 'Happy Birthday.' "

A few weeks later, Rebecca and I flew to Geneva, where I was "sworn in" on a sunny December morning by the WTO's first Director General, Renato Ruggiero, from Italy. Later that same day, I sat, for the first time, with the six wise men who had been selected to serve with me as founding Members of the world's brand new, standing tribunal for resolving international trade disputes. The seven of us assembled, for the first time, in "Room F" on the third floor of the WTO. Room F has since been named *"Salle Julio Lacarte"* in honor of one of those six wise men, the legendary Uruguayan jurist and diplomat who is the oldest — and the wisest —of all the old GATT hands. At the time, I was —by sixteen years —the youngest Member of the new Appellate Body.

Eight years later, I am the only remaining original Member of the Appellate Body. The six wise men who first served alongside me in Geneva are no longer there. Today, I serve with six more. Present at the creation, I am present still. There is no other Member of the Appellate

Body, nor even any member of our hard-working Appellate Body Secretariat, who has been there nearly as long as I have. Today, I remain the youngest Member of the Appellate Body, but my hair grows ever grayer, and ever whiter, with every passing day.

When I first left for Geneva, Amy Porges, a GATT hand and a good friend from my days at USTR, gave me, as a thoughtful "going-away" gift, a little light reading: a copy of the "Analytical Index" of GATT law that she had helped prepare during her time in Geneva. Eight years on, that "Analytical Index" still sits nearby on my desk. But now there is much more to all I need to know about the WTO. Now there is much more to the law of the WTO trading system than the GATT *acquis* that is summarized in that Index.

Eight years after the creation of the WTO, there are, altogether, about 30,000 pages of rules and concessions in the GATT 1994 and in all the other "covered agreements" of the WTO. There are also —at last count —more than 20,000 pages of reports from WTO dispute settlement. Many of those pages contain the rulings and the recommendations made by the Appellate Body in nearly sixty reports resulting from a vast range of complex appeals that have consumed nearly a decade of my life. As some here today may have noticed, we added another hundred or so pages to this ever-increasing tally just the other day.

One of the most eminent of all the old GATT hands, Professor John Jackson, of Georgetown University, has described the opinions of the Appellate Body as "an amazing group of reports."[3] Some seem to find them more "amazing" than others. But there can be no denying the growing significance of WTO reports to an ever-growing multilateral trading system that —at last count —affects the lives and the livelihoods of five billion people in 146 countries and other customs territories that account for ninety-five percent of the world economy.

Today, all the world seems to have an opinion on the opinions of the Appellate Body. This is as it should be. Even as politics is too important to be left to the politicians, so too is trade too important to be left entirely to the trade diplomats, the trade lawyers, and all the other old GATT hands. The WTO must work for *all* the world. The WTO trading system must truly serve *all* of those five billion people.

---

[3] John Jackson, "Perceptions about the WTO Trade Institutions," World Trade Review, Volume 1, Number 1, 101, 110.

But to serve them all well, to serve them all best, all of us who serve the WTO and support the WTO must do a much better job of explaining exactly how our world of widgets serves the wider world of all our many other urgent global concerns. We must do a much better job today, and in the days to come, of answering the question: *"Why are they doing it?"*

The answer to this question —the reason why I first responded years ago to the appeals of trade —the reason why I have strived for so long to become an old GATT hand —is not found in the text of the GATT itself. The answer to why we are "doing it" is not found in the pristine prose of "Article XIII," in the subtle syntax of "Ad Article III," or in the long rows of numbers in the long lists of schedules of tariff and other trade concessions that can glaze the gaze of even the oldest GATT hand.

As much as I am committed to every single page of the GATT, it must be admitted: there is very little poetry in the pages of the GATT. The thirty-eight articles of the GATT, the handful of annexes to the GATT, and even the other, newer "covered agreements" that, along with the GATT, are part of the overall WTO treaty, contain few ringing phrases for the ages. This may be one reason why so few have actually read it.

No, the answer is not in the text of the GATT itself. The answer, instead, is in what the GATT stands for. The answer is in what we "quasi-judges" of the WTO might call the "object and purpose" of the rule-based multilateral trading system that is served by the WTO. It is in the way that all old GATT hands see the relationship that *does exist* between trade and transcendence.

As a Christmas gift, Rebecca gave me, for my very own, the two thick, shiny new volumes of the long-awaited Fifth Edition of the Shorter Oxford English Dictionary. It has been suggested by some that those of us on the Appellate Body think of the Shorter OED as tantamount to one of the "covered agreements." This is not so. Yet we *do* work with words on the Appellate Body. We *do* try always to discern the meaning of words. The meaning of words is discerned in how they are defined. And the words of the English language are nowhere better defined, in my view, than in the OED. (The new edition of the Shorter OED even includes the word "Klingon" —in reference to the bellicose alien species of the "Star Trek" television series. At last glance, the Klingon Empire was not yet a Member of the WTO. But who knows what the future holds?)

My shiny new copy of the Shorter OED defines "transcendence" as "the action or fact of transcending; the condition or quality of being transcendent." It defines "transcendent" as something "that transcends, surpassing or excelling others of its kind, supreme; beyond the range or grasp of human experience, reason, belief, etc."[4] One example given for "transcendent" is: "In Kantian philosophy, something *not realizable in experience.*"[5]

To me, this dictionary definition of "transcendence" evokes images of Plato holding forth on the "forms" beneath the ancient porticos in Athens, of Augustine bending in an ascending prayer in the early churches in Hippo, of Emerson musing on the immanence of nature beneath his beloved apple trees in Concord, or of Kant himself contemplating the "oughts" of the "categorical imperative" during his daily afternoon stroll through the streets of Konigsberg.

When viewed from the everyday, workaday world of the WTO, these images of "transcendence" may seem a bit much to many old GATT hands —not to mention this former Member of Congress. Kant does not stroll through the pages of the GATT. The word "transcendence" does not appear in the "covered agreements." Our world of widgets in the WTO is *not* a world of human "transcendence." It is a world of human experience. It is a world that most definitely *is* "realizable in experience."

The world that concerns all of us who are privileged to serve the Members of the WTO is, as my distinguished former colleague on the Appellate Body, Florentino Feliciano, of the Philippines, has been known to express it, "a real world in which people live and work and die." It is a real world of hard facts. It is a real world in which real people try to put bread on the table, put their kids through school, and put —and keep — hope for the future in their hearts. It is a real world in which the many gains that are made from trade make a real difference in improving real lives.

The gains from trade can be seen throughout the history of the human experience with trade. The evidence is in every economics textbook. The division of labor that is derived from the human exchange of trade is a division that multiplies human productivity and, thus, human

---

[4] Shorter Oxford English Dictionary, 5th Edition (Oxford: Oxford University Press, 2002) ("Shorter OED").
[5] Emphasis added.

prosperity, and, thus, human opportunity. The *international* division of labor that results from *international* trade is only the natural extension of the ever-extending arm of human opportunity in hope for the future.

The *"invisible hand"* of Adam Smith is served by the outstretched hand of the GATT. So is the economic logic of "comparative advantage" advanced by Smith's handy follower, David Ricardo. Between the lines of the GATT is the belief that by lowering the barriers to worldwide trade we are lifting Smith's "invisible hand" to help make more worldwide prosperity. Between the lines, too, is the belief that we will all be more prosperous —that the world will work best —if we all do what we all *do best* when compared with others, consistent with our relative, "comparative advantage."

Yet, the *"visible hand"* of government can likewise work together with the hand of the GATT. Effective and responsive democratic governance is not only *compatible* with the GATT; it is *indispensable* to the ultimate success of the GATT, and of the WTO. Opponents of the WTO frequently accuse supporters of the WTO of "market fundamentalism."[6] They accuse us of allegiance only to the market —only to an absolutely *laissez-faire* economics. Yet there is absolutely nothing in the WTO Treaty that in any way requires any Member of the WTO to pledge allegiance to *laissez-faire*. And I have never known anyone in any way associated with the WTO who would.

I, for one, would never raise my GATT hand in such a salute. I am neither a socialist nor a Social Darwinist. I am that stubborn variety of American known as a "Florida Democrat." I have voted —when they have let me vote —for the market. I have also voted for public education, public investment, reasonable regulation, and a strong social safety net. If you doubt me, go read the Congressional Record. Or, better yet, go ask any Republican in Indian River County.

I have also voted for trade. I have voted for trade, I have heeded the appeals of trade, I have followed in the footsteps of the old GATT hands of trade, for the one compelling reason that explains the one all-embracing "object and purpose" of trade: *because trade makes more choices possible.* Trade makes more choices possible for a lot more people in a world in which far too many people have far too few real choices. And,

---

[6] Naomi Klein is one who used this phrase, for example. *See* Klein, <u>Fences and Windows</u>, at 243.

by making more choices possible for more people in our all too real world, trade also makes possible *more real freedom.*

GATT hands tend to the real world. GATT hands are practical. GATT hands are as mundane as the mundane prose of the GATT itself. We are realists. But, the real truth of who we truly are is this. We realists of trade are also idealists. The real world of trade is a world that serves an ideal. This ideal is trade's real appeal. This ideal is *freedom.*

The ideal of freedom is the ideal of every GATT hand. Trade is not the end we seek. Trade is not an end at all. Trade is a *means* to an end. Trade is a means to all the many ends of human freedom. In lowering the barriers to trade, we are serving the ends of freedom. In lowering the barriers to trade, we are raising the hopes of all humanity for having and living in freedom.

The struggle in the world today is a struggle *for* freedom. It is *not* a struggle *between* civilizations. It is a struggle *within* civilizations *between* those who believe in freedom and those who do not. It is a struggle *within* every country, *within* every culture, and *within* every civilization *between* those who believe in *closed* societies in which people are *told* how to live, and those who believe in *free and open* societies in which people are free to *choose* how to live.[7]

The struggle for freedom is a struggle of *ideas.* It is a struggle that can only be won by the power of an idea. As another of the six wise men who first served with me on the Appellate Body, Said El-Naggar, of Egypt, has said, "History tells us you cannot kill an idea by repression. Ideas have to be killed by ideas."[8] All the ideas that imprison the minds of so many in all the closed societies of the world can only be defeated by the idea of freedom that is the *very essence* of a free and open society.

My dear friend Said, now in his eighties, has devoted his entire life to the struggle to create free and open societies in the world. In his retirement from the Appellate Body, he is back in Egypt, and still engaged in the struggle for freedom. In his youth, he learned about freedom as a student of that great philosopher of freedom, Karl Popper. Popper taught Said —he taught us all —that a free and open society is one in which

---

[7] In this paragraph and in those that follow, I am, of course, using the familiar terms that Karl Popper first used in his classic work, The Open Society and Its Enemies (1945).

[8] Said is quoted in Caryle Murphy, Passion for Islam: Shaping the Modern Middle East: The Egyptian Experience (New York: Scribner's, 2003), 146.

individuals are free to make their own choices. Freedom is about choosing. Freedom is about making personal decisions about how best to live. The more personal decisions we make, the freer we are. And the more choices we have, the more personal decisions we can make.

What we seek *through trade* is the opportunity for more people to have more choices so they will be free to make more personal decisions in free and open societies. What we seek through the *rules of trade* is the assurance that the five billion people who are served by the WTO will have the full benefit of all the choices of trade that the Members of the WTO have chosen to include in the WTO Treaty.

It is true that those of us who support the WTO believe in a "set of rules." We believe in a "set of rules" because we believe in the rule of law. The rules we follow in establishing the rule of law in trade are rules on which all the Members of the WTO have *voluntarily* agreed. They are rules for trade that are —by their own *voluntary* agreement —binding on all WTO Members. They are rules for making binding trade concessions, rules for preventing trade discrimination, rules for countering unfair trade practices, rules for permitting certain environmental and other measures that affect trade, and rules for resolving disputes when there are the inevitable international disagreements about the meanings of the rules of trade. The "set of rules" in which we believe establishes an agreed international framework for securing the many benefits of all our existing agreements on trade, and for concluding new agreements that will reduce the remaining barriers to trade.

We are "true believers" in these rules of trade, because we believe these rules of trade are essential to the ends of freedom. We are "true believers" in upholding these rules of trade by upholding the rule of law, because we believe the rule of law is essential to the ends of freedom.

Our long historical experience with trade, our half-century of experience with the GATT, and our experience thus far with the WTO, all tell us that we have more choices when we have more trade, and that we have more assurance of having the benefit of those choices when we have more adherence to agreed trade rules in a multilateral trading system. By creating more choices, trade creates more freedom. And, by assuring the availability of the benefit of the additional choices that trade creates, the multilateral trading system that is served by the WTO fulfills an essential role in the struggle for freedom within all the civilizations of the world.

No, trade is *not* transcendence. But, because trade provides more choices, because trade permits more personal decisions, because trade creates more freedom, each of us, in every part of the world, can have, *through more trade*, more of all the freedom we each need as individuals to find our own way to transcendence. This is the ultimate end of trade, because this is the ultimate end —this is the ultimate purpose —of human freedom. This is the real relationship between trade and transcendence.

The struggle for freedom is unending. In this struggle, there are always those who fear freedom. And, thus, there are always those who fear the additional choices that are made possible by trade. In one of the early chapters of his epic history of Rome, Gibbon described the annual voyage of a huge Roman fleet to bring back to the Romans the silks, perfumes, and precious stones of India. In a foreshadowing of many such debates to come, some of the Romans feared the loss of the silver they exported to India in exchange for these imports. Gibbon —who served for a time on the British board of trade —concluded that, despite these fears, the supply of silver in Rome actually increased during the course of this trade. It was not trade that caused the decline and fall of the Roman Empire.[9]

In all the centuries since, variations of this ancient story have been repeated many times and in many places. But, in every time, and in every place, the ends of human freedom have always been served best by creating more choices by creating more trade. In creating more trade, we create more freedom to choose from all the many ways of life in all its many marvelous manifestations. In furthering trade, we further the flow of freedom into all the waters of the wide world. And further freedom we must. For, as Gibbon said in the memoirs he wrote while gazing out on the snow-covered peaks of the Alps from his hillside villa overlooking the Lake of Geneva, "Freedom is the first wish of our hearts; freedom is the first blessing of our nature..."[10]

Those who would have us turn away from trade would have us turn away from freedom. They would have us turn away from the wide world. They fear to go where the waters flow. But those of us who understand the appeals of trade have no such fears. We do not *fear* freedom. We *choose* freedom. We *choose* freedom because we believe we

---

[9] Edward Gibbon, The Decline and Fall of the Roman Empire, abridged version (London: Penguin Classics, 1988), Chapter 2, 79-80 [1776].
[10] Gibbon, Memoirs of My Life, at 74.

are each capable as individuals of making the *right* choices among all the many choices that freedom makes possible. We believe we are each capable of *being free*.

Not too long ago, I returned to Nashville to speak at Vanderbilt University Law School. Afterwards, I was approached by a bright young law student from China. He told me about the choice he had made. He told me he was studying trade law because he wanted to return to China to work for freedom and democracy. He told me he believed he could best work for freedom and democracy in China by working for freer trade between China and the rest of the world. As he turned to go, he told me, too, "I enjoyed listening to you. I learn by listening to an old GATT hand."

As I prepare to turn to go from the WTO, as I approach the end of my allotted eight years on the Appellate Body, I think more and more about all I have learned about all it means to be an old GATT hand. And, as I begin to consider the personal choices I will soon have to make about how best to use my own newfound freedom in my own future, I consider also the future of the still new institution I will leave behind me when I leave the Appellate Body.

Like all human institutions, the WTO has human imperfections. Like all efforts to serve human freedom, the WTO is much in need of more and better efforts by all of us who try our very best to serve freedom by serving the cause of trade. On some other day, I will have more to say about what I believe some of those efforts should be. On some other day, I will have a lot more to say.

Today, I will leave you with just this from an old GATT hand who looks forward to getting a lot older, and who looks forward also to finding new ways in the future to continue to serve the cause of trade: *"Why are they doing it?"* We are doing it to free all of humanity. The appeals of trade are the appeals of humanity. The hand of the GATT is the hand of freedom.

Chapter Two

The Bicycle Club:
Affirming the American
Interest in the Future of the WTO

I am the only American member of the Appellate Body of the World Trade Organization —the WTO. I am the only American who has had the privilege thus far of serving on the Appellate Body of the WTO. Thus, I am uniquely placed to affirm the *American* interest in the future of the WTO.

This interest can be illustrated by a bicycle. We all know about this bicycle. We all talk about it every time we talk about the future of the WTO. We all ride it every time we try to make the case *for* the future of the WTO.

I seem to remember hearing about the bicycle for the first time when I first went to work at USTR with Reubin Askew in 1979. To the best of my knowledge, it was Fred Bergsten who first referred to the bicycle, earlier in the Seventies.[1] By the late Eighties, the bicycle was so well known that Jagdish Bhagwati was writing about what he described as the "bicycle theory."[2] Today, all of us who support the WTO ride the bicycle, and all of us who work for the future of the WTO subscribe to the "bicycle theory."

The bicycle, of course, is simply a way of describing the trading system that is served by the WTO. It is simply a way of referring to the WTO-based, treaty-based, multilateral world trading system. And the "bicycle theory," of course, is simply this: Like a bicycle, the world trading system must always go forward. For, if it ever stops going forward, it will surely fall and fail.[3]

This chapter is adapted from a speech to the Washington International Trade Association on November 12, 2002, and appears under the same title and in slightly different form in the Journal of World Trade, Volume 37, Number 3, 429-441 (2003).

[1] *See* Fred Bergsten, Toward a New International Economic Order (Lexington, Mass.: Lexington Books, 1975).

[2] Jagdish Bhagwati, Protectionism (Cambridge, Mass.: The MIT Press, 1988), 41.

[3] *See* Ben Zissimos, "Gradualism, the Bicycle Theory, and Perpetual Trade Liberalization." This paper was first presented at the "Asian Crisis II" conference in Seattle, Washington, on January 4-5, 2000.

According to the "bicycle theory," the history of trade, and of trade policymaking, teaches us that a failure to move steadily forward toward freer trade condemns the world trading system to topple over and fall due to the accumulating pressures of protectionism. According to the theory, we must move steadily, gradually, incrementally forward on the bicycle, because, if we do not, the world will be overwhelmed by all the many reactionary forces that would have the nations of the world retreat from trade. If we do not, the world will *turn away* from growing economic integration, *turn away* from the mutual prosperity of growing economic interdependence, and *turn inward* toward all the self-deceiving illusions and all the self-defeating delusions of an isolating and enervating economic autarchy. According to the theory, we must keep *lowering* the *barriers* to trade or we will risk *losing* all the many *gains* from trade.

Thus, whatever the pressures, whatever the economic happenstances, and whatever the political circumstances, we must always keep the bicycle we call the "world trading system" going forward by making ever more progress toward ever freer trade. We must keep pedaling. We must pedal neither too fast nor too slow. We must steer carefully. We must go straight ahead. We must avoid all the wrong turns. And, above all, we must never, *never* stop.

It has never been easy riding the bicycle. It took many centuries to get to the point where the world even had a bicycle. It took half a century of riding and eight long rounds of pedaling through all the many complications of seemingly endless multilateral trade negotiations to create the mutual international endeavor called the WTO. No doubt it will take many more years of hard pedaling to make the WTO all that so many nations of the world and so many billions of people in the world so much need it to be.

There have been more than a few bumps in the road we have followed along the way. Many of you can recall more than a few of them. The difficulties in concluding the Tokyo Round in the Seventies. The long struggle to conclude the Uruguay Round —and create the WTO — in the Eighties and Nineties. The disruptions and the disappointments at Seattle in 1999. The road ahead will be no easier. We can all look forward to a very bumpy ride. Just how bumpy the road ahead will be will depend on how well we steer the bicycle.

The bicycle today is even harder to steer than in the past because our bicycle today is not what it used to be. Because of all our past successes, our bicycle today has bells and whistles, gears and speeds it did not have in the past. The world trading system that originally included only a few countries and only a small fraction of world trade today serves five billion people and includes about ninety-five percent of the world economy.

Our bicycle today is not a bicycle built for one, or for two, or for only a few. Nowadays, it is a bicycle built for one hundred and forty-six. There are —at last count —146 Members of the WTO. There will soon be more. Almost every country in the world is either a Member of the WTO or wants to be. And, together, *all* the Members of the WTO must continue to steer the bicycle toward freer trade through the process we call "consensus."

But a corollary, if you will, to the "bicycle theory" is this. As the largest trading nation in the world, the United States of America must help the other Members of the WTO in a shared effort to steer the bicycle in the right direction. However many countries may be sharing in the steering, *our* country must always be *one* country with a firm grip on the handlebars of the bicycle. And we Americans must always be willing to do our fair share of the pedaling.

Worldwide, there are many adherents to the "bicycle theory" and to this corollary. Worldwide, there are many who agree that the bicycle must keep going forward, and that the United States must help with the steering and with the pedaling. Worldwide, there are many members and many chapters of what might be called "The Bicycle Club."

In Washington especially, there are many charter members of "The Bicycle Club." Lawyers. Economists. Scholars. Former trade negotiators. Those who have worked hard through the years in the House, in the Senate, in USTR, and in other executive agencies to try always to move the bicycle forward. Those who are still pedaling the bicycle as hard and as well as they can.

And no other chapter of "The Bicycle Club" is the focus of more of the world's attention today than the chapter in Washington. The chapter of the club in the capital of the United States is a focus of the world's attention today because there is increasing concern throughout the world that the United States may be on the verge of loosening its grip on the handlebars, lifting its feet from the pedals, and letting the bicycle tip and fall.

All those who are members in good standing of the Washington chapter of "The Bicycle Club" fully understand that keeping the bicycle moving steadily forward is not only in the common *international* interest of all the Members of the WTO. It is also very much in the *national* interest of the United States of America.

But not everyone in Washington understands this. Not everyone in Washington — nor in America — comprehends the compelling American interest in the future of the WTO. Not everyone in our country knows why we Americans must keep riding the bicycle.

And it is time they were told.

Some in the Congress of the United States are trying to tell them. And they are having some success. The recent approval by the Congress of trade promotion authority for the President of the United States should not be overlooked by those either in the United States or elsewhere in the world who are looking for evidence of a continuing American commitment to world trade and to the future of the WTO.

I am not some metaphysical theorist. I am not unmindful of the practical realities of pressing political concerns. In the parlance of the Hill, I have "run for sheriff." I am a former Member of Congress. I was a Democrat from a heavily Republican Congressional district. I know what it is like to cast a tough vote.

Thus, I wish to commend Senator Tom Daschle, Senator Max Baucus, my own Senators Bob Graham and Bill Nelson, and those among my many other friends and former colleagues in both parties in the House and in the Senate who cast a very tough vote for trade promotion authority in the midst of an economic slowdown and on the eve of an election season. The vote for trade promotion authority is, indeed, evidence of the continuing American commitment to moving the bicycle forward.

Some in the executive branch in the United States are also trying to tell America why we Americans must keep riding the bicycle. And they, too, are having some success. Like the recent Congressional approval of trade promotion authority, the American contribution to the decision at the WTO Ministerial Conference in Doha to launch a new round of multilateral trade negotiations must not be overlooked by those in search of evidence of the continuing American commitment to trade.

As an alumnus of USTR, I was proud of the considerable courage shown by the dedicated trade negotiators from USTR in even going to Doha in the face of the dire difficulties for all Americans at that time. And I believe every other Member of the WTO would agree with me that the United States Trade Representative, Ambassador Robert Zoellick, and all those who work with him at USTR, did much in Doha to help secure the successful launch of the new round, and have done much more since Doha to try to keep the bicycle going forward.

New negotiating authority has been secured. A new round of global trade negotiations has been launched. The new negotiations have already begun, and are continuing, in Geneva. The bicycle *is* still moving forward. The United States *does* still seem to be holding on to the handlebars and pushing down on the pedals. Why, then, all the concern, both here in the United States and in the rest of the world? Why, then, the worry that "the Americans" —as we are called in Geneva —will let the bicycle fall?

Fundamentally, the worry is that, despite these recent accomplishments, there will, in the end, simply not be the *political will* in the United States to conclude the mutually beneficial trade agreements that will enable the United States and all the other Members of the WTO to maximize the many gains they all can make from increased world trade. This fear is fueled especially by an accumulating frustration at the seeming reluctance of some who should be among the foremost American advocates of trade to support and defend the trading system as faithfully and forcefully as they should.

On the merits, this reluctance is difficult to understand. The American interest in the future of the WTO, and in the future of the world trading system served by the WTO, can hardly be overstated. Economically, the case for freer trade is irrefutable. Statistically, the potential gains from freer trade are overwhelming. Politically, the alternative to a worldwide rule-based system for serving the American interest in freer trade is simply non-existent. In very many ways, the future of America *is* the future of the WTO.

At the most basic level, trade is a manifestation of human nature through what Adam Smith famously described in 1776 in <u>The Wealth of Nations</u> as the human "propensity to trade, barter, and exchange one thing for another."[4] Trade results from a *division of labor* that arises from human nature. As the psychologist Steven Pinker says in his thoughtful new book, The Blank Slate, "There are two ways to get something from other people: steal it or trade for it. The first involves the psychology of dominance; the second, the psychology of reciprocal altruism. The goal of a peaceful and prosperous society is to minimize the use of dominance, which leads to violence and waste, and to maximize the use of reciprocity, which leads to gains in trade that make everyone better off."[5] Thus, the mutual reciprocity of trade —the mutual exchange that *is* trade —is an act of mutual and enlightened self-interest in pursuit of the *"gains from trade."*

There are many "gains from trade." Smith first taught us that trade leads to *direct* gains that arise from the specialization that results from an *international* division of labor. David Ricardo later instructed us, through his enduring explanation of "comparative advantage," that we can maximize these direct gains by specializing in those economic pursuits in which we are relatively the most productive when compared to others. We always *do* best by doing *what* we do best when compared to others.

The direct gains from trade include economies of scale, lower production costs, lower consumer prices, broader consumer choices, broader producer choices, and bigger potential markets. All this results in higher income. As one contemporary follower of Smith and Ricardo, the Dartmouth economist Douglas Irwin, has reminded us, the many efficiencies resulting from specialization and trade result in a "higher real income" that "translates into an ability to afford more of all goods and services than would be possible without trade."[6]

Trade leads also to *indirect* gains. Trade serves initiative and inspires incentive. Trade leads to more, and more intensified, competition that makes domestic producers more efficient. Trade furthers the transfer of technology, and of technical and managerial know-how. Trade inspires the research and development of new technologies. Trade stimulates a continuous flow of innovations of all kinds. Trade, in short, improves overall economic performance by promoting the growth of human productivity.[7]

---

[4] Adam Smith, The Wealth of Nations (New York: The Modern Library, 1994), 14 [1776].
[5] Steven Pinker, The Blank Slate: The Modern Denial of Human Nature (New York: Viking, 2002), 297.
[6] Douglas A. Irwin, Free Trade Under Fire (Princeton: Princeton University Press, 2002), 30.
[7] Id. at 36-39.

Another contemporary economist, Timothy Taylor, has summarized these direct and indirect "gains from trade" as follows: "Trade allows countries to specialize in the products they have the greatest advantage in producing. Specialization encourages learning and innovation about those products and allows nations to take advantage of economies of scale. When countries specialize and trade, the world's productive resources of labor, physical resources, and time are used more efficiently. Trade allows consumers and businesses to seek out the best deal in a global market, giving producers an incentive to compete in the market."[8]

There are also other important "gains from trade." John Stuart Mill claimed that "the economical advantages of commerce are surpassed in importance by those of its effects which are intellectual and moral."[9] Trade leads not only to the creation of prosperity. Trade leads also to the spread of ideas and to the spread of peace. That old GATT hand, the Enlightenment philosopher Immanuel Kant, put it this way: "The spirit of trade cannot co-exist with war, and sooner or later this spirit dominates every people."[10]

An enlightened and visionary view of the mutual self-interest of all nations in securing the "gains from trade" motivates the United States and every other Member of the WTO. The WTO is not something that has somehow been *imposed* on the United States or on other Members of the WTO. The WTO is something that the United States and the other Members of the WTO have *voluntarily created*. It is a common assertion of their shared self-interest in working together to maximize the gains from trade. And it is a common acknowledgment that the gains from trade will be maximized *only if* they work together.

The United States and the other Members of the WTO have created the WTO because the United States and the rest of the world very much need a global trading institution such as the WTO. The German statesman, Otto von Bismarck, once said of the Kingdom of Italy in the nineteenth century, "If the Kingdom of Italy did not exist, we should have to invent it."[11] Likewise, today, if the WTO did not exist, we would have to invent

---

[8] Timothy Taylor, "The Truth about Globalization," The Public Interest (Spring, 2002).
[9] Quoted in Irwin, Free Trade Under Fire, at 45.
[10] Immanuel Kant, "To Perpetual Peace: A Philosophical Sketch," Perpetual Peace and Other Essays (Indianapolis; Hackett, 1983), 107, 125 [1795].
[11] A. J. P. Taylor, Bismarck: The Man and the Statesman (New York: Vintage, 1967), 49 [1955].

it. We would *need* to invent it in order to have any hope of attaining all the many potential "gains from trade."

The overarching goal of the WTO is to serve the mutual self-interest *of* all WTO Members by maximizing the "gains from trade" *for* all WTO Members through the best possible allocation and the best possible use of the world's limited resources. In the very first paragraph of the preface to the Marrakesh Agreement that established the WTO, the United States and the other Members of the WTO identified as their common goal "the optimal use of the world's resources in accordance with the objective of sustainable development."[12]   The goal of the WTO is "sustainable development" for the benefit of everyone on our shrinking planet. It is toward this goal that the WTO treaty seeks to lower the barriers to world trade and to establish the rule of law in the world trading system.

In creating, first, the GATT, and, now, the WTO, the countries and other customs territories that comprise the world trading system have sought and secured the "gains from trade" that result from an international division of labor. Since the creation of the GATT-based trading system, average tariffs in industrialized countries have been cut from high double-digits to *less than four percent*.[13]   In the half century or so since the creation of the GATT, global trade has increased *14-fold*, and this historic increase in world trade has supported a *six-fold* increase in global GDP.[14]   WTO figures show that worldwide exports that accounted for only eight percent of worldwide production in 1950 account for more than 26 percent of worldwide production today.[15]   As world trade continues to grow, as the wheels of the bicycle keep turning, this percentage continues to grow as well.

Through the lowering of tariffs and other trade barriers, millions upon millions of people in America and in every other part of the world have been lifted out of poverty since the establishment of the multilateral trading system in the aftermath of World War II. The dynamic growth of world trade in the past five decades has contributed significantly to the longest and the strongest period of sustained economic growth in human history. Much of humanity has enjoyed unprecedented prosperity in the

---

[12] The Marrakesh Agreement establishing the World Trade Organization, done at Marrakesh, Morocco (15 April 1994).

[13] World Trade Organization, The Multilateral Trading System: 50 Years of Achievement (Geneva: WTO, 1998),5.

[14] Id. at 21.

[15] Id.

wake of what President John F. Kennedy, an early champion of the multilateral trading system, described rightly —and memorably —as "the rising tide of trade."[16]

The eighth, and most recent, of the "rounds" of global trade negotiations was the Uruguay Round, which was concluded in 1994, and which led to the transformation of the GATT into the WTO in 1995. I am proud that I was one of the original co-sponsors in the United States House of Representatives of the American implementing legislation for the Uruguay Round trade agreements. One study at the time showed that the agreements to lower trade barriers that were concluded in the Uruguay Round would result in an *annual* gain in GDP of $13 billion dollars for the United States and $96 billion dollars for the world as a whole.[17] Those "gains from trade" for the United States and for other Members of the WTO are being realized now through the phased implementation of the Uruguay Round trade agreements. For example, according to USTR, since the conclusion of the Uruguay Round and the creation of the WTO, American exports of goods and services have risen by more than *$300 billion dollars*.[18]

Many more gains can be made by lowering the many barriers that remain to trade worldwide. Here in the United States, what Professor Irwin calls "the deadweight losses associated with trade barriers" of all kinds that have been imposed *by the United States alone* are high.[19] In 1996, the United States International Trade Commission calculated that the net cost —"the deadweight loss" —to the American people of existing U.S. trade barriers at that time was about $12.4 billion dollars.[20] As Irwin stresses, these are *annual* costs. These are costs that, in the absence of the removal of these trade barriers, will recur every year from now on —in *perpetuity*.[21] Moreover, as he has pointed out, "such estimates understate the true costs of trade barriers, in part, because they fail to consider the productivity and variety benefits of trade."[22]

---

[16] John F. Kennedy, Presidential Address in Frankfurt, Germany (June 24, 1963.).
[17] Glen W. Harrison, Thomas W. Rutherford, and David G. Tarr, "Quantifying the Uruguay Round," in Will Martin and L. Alan Winters, eds., The Uruguay Round and the Developing Countries (New York: Cambridge University Press, 1996). *See also* Irwin, Free Trade Under Fire, at 31.
[18] Office of the United States Trade Representative, "America and the World Trade Organization," 2, online at ustr.gov.
[19] Irwin, Free Trade Under Fire, at 55.
[20] Irwin, Free Trade Under Fire, at 55-66.
[21] Irwin, Freer Trade Under Fire, at 60.
[22] Id.

One recent study, at the University of Michigan, concluded that, if the new trade round reduced global tariffs on agricultural and industrial goods and barriers on services trade *by one third*, the gain *for the United States alone* would be $177 billion dollars *annually* —almost two percent of US GDP.[23] According to the President's Council of Economic Advisers, that is about $2500 dollars *annually* for the average American family of four.[24] The same Michigan study concluded that, if *all* the global barriers to trade in goods and services were eliminated, the gain *for the United States alone* would be $537 billion dollars *annually* —almost *six percent* of US GDP.[25]

Cutting barriers to trade in agriculture, manufacturing, and services by *one third* in the new trade round would boost the *world* economy by *$613 billion dollars annually*.[26] As former WTO Director-General Mike Moore has said, "That's like adding an economy the size of Canada to the world economy."[27] Moreover, the World Bank has estimated that, if *all* trade barriers were abolished, the new trade round that is just now getting underway, coupled with related market reforms, could add *$2.8 trillion dollars* to annual global income by 2015.[28] As annual global income in 2000 was approximately $30 trillion dollars, this would be an increase in overall annual global income of *nearly 10 percent*.[29]

All this helps explain why the United States has always been in the forefront in world efforts to lower the barriers to world trade. The potential gains to the United States alone from continuing to lower the barriers to freer trade are enormous. Furthermore, and although my focus today is on the benefits of trade to the United States, I would be remiss if I did not mention also that, while a successful conclusion of the new WTO round would benefit the United States and other *developed* countries substantially, lowering the remaining barriers to trade would undoubtedly benefit the people of the world's many *developing* countries *even more*.

---

[23] Drusilla K. Brown, Alan Deardorff, and Robert M. Stern, "Impact on NAFTA Members of Multilateral and Regional Trade Arrangements and Initiatives and Harmonization of NAFTA's External Tariffs," Research Seminar in International Economics Discussion Paper No. 471, University of Michigan (June 2001). *See also* Irwin, Free Trade Under Fire, at 29-35.
[24] Council of Economic Advisers, "Trade and the American Economy: The Case for Trade Promotion Authority" (February 12, 2002), 14, online at whitehouse.gov/cea/pubs.html.
[25] Brown et al, University of Michigan study, supra.
[26] Mike Moore, "To Doha and Beyond: A Roadmap for Successfully Concluding the Doha Development Round," Address to the Evian VII Plenary Meeting, Montreux, Switzerland (April 12, 2002).
[27] Id.
[28] Id.
[29] Id.

Trade is a means to an end. The end is human freedom. The cause of trade is the cause of freedom. The "gains from trade" can give us the means to give more real meaning to freedom in America and in all the world. The "rising tide" of trade can also be the rising tide of humanity.

Given all this, why would there be any reluctance at all within the United States to move the bicycle forward?

Every member of "The Bicycle Club" knows the answer. The "gains from trade" are *general.* The dislocations that result from the changing patterns of trade and the changing terms of trade are *specific.* And this has political consequences. Moreover, in trade, as in so much else, the way we *are* is often far more vocal and far more influential than the way we *should be.* In trade, as in so much else, the implacable weight of inertia can be a very powerful force in opposition to needed change. And this, too, has political consequences.

The challenge facing the Washington chapter of "The Bicycle Club" and all the other American members of "The Bicycle Club" is the challenge of confronting and overcoming these consequences. The "bicycle theory" is not an *economic* theory. The "bicycle theory" is a *political* theory. "The Bicycle Club" is, therefore, a *political* club. And the challenge facing every card-carrying, dues-paying, hard-pedaling American member of "The Bicycle Club" is the challenge of summoning and sustaining the *political will* to move the bicycle forward in the face of all the powerful political opposition to freer trade.

This challenge is greater during hard economic times, because the weight of the political opposition to trade is greater during hard economic times. And these are hard times. These times are harder than some would have us think. In hard times, we need freer trade the most. But, in hard times, it is harder politically to find the political will to be for freer trade. In hard times, it is harder politically to acknowledge and articulate the verities of trade and the virtues of the trading system.

An example is WTO dispute settlement. The United States of America has long maintained in international trade negotiations —and continues to maintain consistently within the councils of the WTO —that the key to securing all the many "gains from trade" for all WTO Members is having a multilateral trading system based on agreed rules that are fairly and effectively enforced. The key is having a *system* in which we have the *rule of law.* And that is precisely what the United States and the other Members of the WTO *now have* as a result of their establishment and their support of the WTO dispute settlement system.

WTO dispute settlement serves the shared interest of *all* WTO Members in establishing and enforcing the rule of law in world trade. And yet no other Member of the WTO has a greater interest in ensuring the rule of law in world trade than the largest trading nation in the world —the United States of America. For, without the rule of law, there will be neither security nor stability nor predictability in the trading system. And, without security, without stability, without predictability, the ability of the millions of people of the United States to continue to make the gains they can and should make from trade through continued trade expansion and through continued development of an international division of labor will be greatly at risk.

A world without the rule of law is *not* a world in which we Americans can maximize the many gains we can make from trade. Trade makes the economic pie larger. The freer trade is, the larger the pie. But only if there are agreed rules for trade will the economic pie be as large for everyone as it can be. And only if those rules are fairly and effectively enforced through the rule of law will our share of the pie be as large as it ought to be.

All this has long been a premise of American trade policy. It has been an assumption of Democratic and Republican administrations alike. It has been a bipartisan assumption of the leadership of the Congress. And we Americans must remember this basic premise of our longstanding national trade policy. We must keep it ever in mind if we hope to have the political will to keep moving the bicycle forward.

The political philosopher Hannah Arendt, who fled Nazi Germany and became an American citizen, once lamented what she saw as a tendency of her adopted country toward forgetfulness. She described this tendency as "the American failure to remember."[30] She was not referring to trade. But what she saw and said about America can be seen in the attitude of some Americans toward trade and —especially —in the attitude of some Americans toward the rule of law in trade through WTO dispute settlement. Some Americans *do* seem to fail to remember —some Americans *do* seem to evidence an American tendency toward

[30] Hannah Arendt, On Revolution (New York: Penguin Books, 1990) 220, 319 [1963].

forgetfulness —when they express what they see as the American interest in WTO dispute settlement.

In affirming the American interest in the future of the WTO, I am not free today to say all that I might wish to say. Yet I am free today to say *this much* about what we Americans must all realize —and what we Americans must all *remember* —about WTO dispute settlement.

Seven members of "The Bicycle Club" serve the 146 Members of the WTO as Members of the Appellate Body of the WTO. Six are among the most dedicated and most distinguished international jurists in the world. One is a hard-pedaling American. We seven are servants of the world.

In our work together in WTO dispute settlement, we seven are ever mindful of *all* our responsibilities to *all* the Members of the WTO. We do our very best to assist the WTO Members in their mutual efforts — in the words of the WTO treaty —"to preserve the rights and obligations of Members under the covered agreements, and to clarify the existing provisions of those agreements in accordance with customary rules of interpretation of public international law."[31] We do no more. We do no less.

We seven are each bound by the WTO Rules of Conduct. The "Governing Principle" of those rules is that we must each *always* be "independent and impartial."[32] We always are. One reporter from the *New York Times* has gone so far as to say that we are both "impartial and unflinching."[33] We always will be. We seven serve the world, the world trading system, and every Member of the WTO best by being always independent, impartial, and unflinching.

We do not choose the cases that are resolved in WTO dispute settlement. The Members of the WTO that are the parties to a particular trade dispute decide for themselves whether to engage in dispute settlement. We do not choose which cases in dispute settlement are appealed to the Appellate Body. The parties to a dispute have an absolute right to appeal, and they decide whether to appeal. Moreover, we do not

---

[31] Art 3.2, WTO Dispute Settlement Understanding.
[32] *See* Article II and Article III, Rules of Conduct for the Understanding on Rules and Procedures Governing the Settlement of Disputes, World Trade Organization.
[33] Michael M. Weinstein, "Economic Scene: Should Clinton Embrace the China Trade Deal? "Some Say Yes," *New York Times* (September 9, 1999). at C2.

decide which legal issues are appealed to us. The parties to a dispute have the exclusive right to decide which legal issues, if any, are appealed.

And, once the parties to a dispute decide to appeal a legal issue to the Appellate Body for a final ruling, we seven have absolutely no authority *not* to rule on that issue. Under the WTO treaty, we "shall address each of the issues raised" on appeal.[34] In accordance with this treaty obligation, we address *every* issue that is raised on appeal. We address *only* those issues that are raised on appeal. We rule *only* on what is *necessary* to resolve the dispute on appeal. We always exercise a considerable measure of what I would describe —and what I believe almost any objective observer would also describe —as "quasi-judicial" restraint. And we always explain our reasoning.

Thus far, there have been thousands of pages of reasoning and rulings in WTO dispute settlement. Thus far, on the Appellate Body, we have reasoned and ruled in about sixty appeals. Some may disagree with some of our reasoning. Some may disagree with some of our rulings. However, this is in the very nature of an appellate legal process. This is unavoidable under the rule of law. There have been, for example, some rulings of the Supreme Court of the United States with which some Americans might not agree. We Americans must always remember: The *real* test of our commitment to the rule of law is *not* whether we comply with the rulings with which we *agree*. The *real* test is whether we comply with the rulings with which we *may not agree*.

We seven on the Appellate Body of the WTO serve *all* the Members of the WTO. We serve all the Members of the WTO *equally*. We serve them all equally by treating them all equally and by assisting them all equally in their mutual efforts to establish and uphold the international rule of law through WTO dispute settlement. And, in serving the rule of law, we serve the *real national interest* of the United States of America.

Those Americans who wish to serve the *real national interest* of America in world trade would do well to read again the masterpiece of the great French thinker Alexis de Tocqueville, <u>Democracy in America</u>. Alexis de Tocqueville never rode a bicycle. He died a few years before the bicycle was invented. However, he believed that we Americans have a special way of seeing our self-interest. And I believe that, if we Americans

---

[34] Article 17.12, WTO Dispute Settlement Understanding.

see our self-interest in that way, if we define our self-interest as he believed we define it, we will remember to keep riding the bicycle.

Tocqueville saw democracy in America as a way of fulfilling the promise of individual human freedom. He saw what he described as "the principle of interest rightly understood" as the way Americans went about trying to fulfill that promise in the America he visited in the 1830s.[35] What Tocqueville called "the principle of interest rightly understood" is a principle of rational, national self-interest. It is a way of seeing our self-interest that ranges both *far afield* and *far ahead*. It is a way of seeing our self-interest in our *broader* as well as our *narrower* needs. It is a way of seeing our self-interest in our needs *tomorrow* as well as our needs *today*. It is a way of *seeing* our self-interest and *seeking* our self-interest that takes the broader and longer view.

Tocqueville saw "the principle of interest rightly understood" as finding "universal acceptance" in the America of the 1830s.[36] He saw the commitment of the American people to that principle in those early years of our youthful and idealistic republic as "clear and sure."[37] To be able to ride the bicycle, we must be able to say the same of America today. In all that we do in world trade, we must, as Americans, remember to be true to "the principle of interest rightly understood." In all that we do relating to the WTO, we must never forget our *real national interest*. And, in all that we do relating to WTO dispute settlement, we must take the broader and longer view.

Listen to this. On dispute settlement, *here* is the broader and longer view:

"To ensure that the United States secures the full benefits of the WTO Agreements, the United States sought and obtained a strong, binding and expeditious dispute settlement process for the WTO. The dispute settlement process provides certainty for American businesses and workers that their disputes will be heard by a panel of impartial experts, and that the defending foreign government will not be able unilaterally to derail the process.

---

[35] Alexis de Tocqueville, <u>Democracy in America</u> (New York: The Colonial Press, 1899), Volume II, 129 [1840].
[36] Id. at 130.
[37] Id. at 131.

"As a result, under the WTO we have better enforcement of U.S. rights and more certainty that our trading partners will abide by the rules and open their markets to American exports. The WTO dispute settlement process has proven valuable in achieving tangible gains for American companies and workers, across a broad range of sectors, including agriculture, manufacturing, services and intellectual property protection.

"It has also served as a deterrent —our trading partners know it is ready and available to us if they do not fulfill their obligations. We have been successful in reaching rapid resolution of our complaints through early settlement, and have also achieved substantial benefits from litigation and resulting panel decisions which enforce our rights."[38]

These are not *my* words. These are the official words of the Office of the United States Trade Representative in the Executive Office of the President of the United States of America. You can read them —just as I did —on the official USTR website. These words are a worthy summary and an accurate expression of the broader and longer view of the *real national interest* of the United States in WTO dispute settlement. They are a statement of our real interest "rightly understood."

Many able attorneys from many countries appear before us in Geneva. Every other Member of the WTO would agree that the appellate advocates for the United States are among the very best in WTO dispute settlement. The attorneys from USTR and other American agencies who argue before us in appellate proceedings always do so ably and aggressively. In every case that comes before us, they make the very best case they can for the legal position of the United States.

But, as any attorney will tell you, some cases are better than others. And we Americans must always remember that our *real national interest* as Americans is *not* in the outcome of any *one* case in WTO dispute settlement. Our real interest is in having a dispute settlement system in which *every* case can be resolved, and can be resolved fairly, through the rule of law. Our real interest is in *the system.* Our real interest is in the system, because the system *establishes and upholds* the international rule of law.

In dispute settlement, and in all else relating to trade, our *real national interest* is in taking the broader and longer view by working for

---

[38] USTR, "America and the World Trade Organization," supra, at 5-6.

the future of the WTO. And this interest will best be served by keeping our hands firmly on the handlebars, keeping our feet securely on the pedals, and always moving the bicycle forward. Of all times, now is not the time, and, of all countries, ours must not be the country, to let the bicycle fall.

But we will be able to move the bicycle forward only if we continue to benefit from the very best efforts of every member of "The Bicycle Club." All of us who are loyal members of "The Bicycle Club" must keep riding. We must keep steering. We must be out in the forefront, pedaling as hard as we can. "The Bicycle Club" must meet more frequently. We must enlist more members. We must add more chapters. We must continue to pay our dues.

Some may fear that America will fail to remember. Some may worry that America will not be able to summon the political will to keep the bicycle going. Some may be concerned that we Americans will forget America's real national interest, and that we will forget to take the broader and longer view.

Those of us who are members of "The Bicycle Club" know better. We know that Americans will remember the real American interest in the future of trade and in the future of the WTO. Because we know, as everyone ought to know, that no one ever forgets how to ride a bicycle.

Chapter Three

Thoreau's Pencil:
Sharpening Our Understanding of World Trade

I brought my "power point" with me today.

I even sharpened it.

This is a "Number Two" pencil.

This "Number Two" pencil makes the point I wish to make today about the power of trade.

This pencil belongs to me.

But in another, broader, truer sense, this pencil belongs to Henry David Thoreau.

In truth, we might rightly describe this "Number Two" pencil as "Thoreau's pencil."

Why? Why is this "Thoreau's pencil"? And why does an understanding of why this *is* "Thoreau's pencil" help sharpen our understanding of the significance of world trade?

Like the answers to so many other questions, the answers to these questions about Thoreau's pencil are found where they keep the books. They are found in the New York Public Library.

A few years ago, on a visit to New York, my wife, Rebecca, and I went to the New York Public Library. There we saw a special exhibit about the best American books by the best American writers. One of the writers featured in the exhibit was Henry David Thoreau.

Among the items in the exhibit were the handwritten pages from Thoreau's journals, the earliest drafts of Thoreau's essays, and an early edition of Thoreau's timeless classic, <u>Walden</u> —his lyrical account of the

---

This chapter is adapted from an address to the Association of American Publishers in Washington, D.C. on February 27, 2003, and appears under the same title and in slightly different form in the <u>*Florida State University Law Review,*</u> *Volume 30, November 4 (Summer, 2003), 911.*

months he spent in self-imposed solitude in the 1840's in a homemade hut in the woods beside Walden Pond.

Also among the items in the exhibit was a plain wooden pencil.

It was Thoreau's pencil.

However, the pencil in the exhibit was not just a pencil that had been *owned* by Thoreau. It was also a pencil that had been *made* by Thoreau.

The exhibit explained that Thoreau's father had owned a company that made pencils in their hometown of Concord, Massachusetts. The exhibit explained also that Thoreau had worked for a time in the family business of making pencils, and that his father had urged his son to make a career of laboring — not at writing essays — but at the more stable and more secure profession of making pencils.

Of course, like so many sons, Henry chose not to take his father's advice. He chose to make his living as a writer. He chose to write the essays we still read today. He chose to go to Walden Pond.

This choice made long ago by the youthful Thoreau helps sharpen our understanding of the significance of world trade today. It does so in a way that helps clarify what is really at stake for all of us in world trade.

Here is why.

Some time after my visit to the New York Public Library, I was re-reading Thoreau's Walden for the "umpteenth" time when I was struck by this question Thoreau posed in the provocative first essay in Walden, on "Economy":

"Where is this *division of labor* to end? And what object does it finally serve? No doubt another may also think for me; but it is not therefore desirable that he should do so to the exclusion of my thinking for myself."[1]

I wondered then, and I wonder now: What would have happened if Thoreau had acted in his own life on the basis of his own obvious reservations about a division of labor? What would have happened if he

---

[1] Henry David Thoreau, Walden and Civil Disobedience (New York: Penguin Books, 1986), 89 [1854].

had taken his father's advice, ignored the call of his own unique talents as a writer of essays, and chosen to minimize the division of labor in his own life by spending *all* his time making *all* his pencils? Would <u>Walden</u> and all of Thoreau's other enduring essays even have been written if Thoreau had not been able to benefit in his own life from the very division of labor that he denounced?

Whether consciously or not, many of those who oppose world trade today are only echoing Thoreau's reservations about a division of labor. They need to know more about Thoreau's pencil.

For the choice Thoreau faced in his life is the same choice we all face in our lives every day with every kind of trade. Will we do it ourselves? Or will we pay someone else to do it — whatever "it" is — so that we can have more time and more freedom to do something else? Will we choose to pay the "opportunity cost" of doing it ourselves, or will we choose a division of labor?

Trade is nothing more than the consequence of this choice. Trade is nothing more than a division of labor.

Trade is about pencils. Trade is about making pencils. Trade is about buying and selling pencils. Trade is about the *division of labor* that is evidenced in every pencil that is made and bought and sold in every part of the world.

In all our debates about "globalization" —in all our discussions about the "pros" and "cons" of the World Trade Organization —in all our understandable attention to all the "ins" and "outs" of international trade negotiations, international trade agreements, and international trade disputes —in all our day-to-day attention to all the many arcane details of world trade —we have a tendency at times to forget what trade really *is*.

Trade is simply the exchange that results from a division of labor. Trade is simply the exchange of pencils. Some of our pencils are called "goods." Some are called "services." Some are the ideas that we call "intellectual property." Yet, whatever we may call what we trade, everything we trade is some kind of a pencil.

Sometimes it is only a simple matter of the teenager next door mowing your lawn. Sometimes it is the clerk at the corner grocery selling you a carton of milk. Sometimes it is the bookseller at the local bookstore selling you a book.

Sometimes the trade resulting from the division of labor is only a simple local exchange. But, many times, it only seems that way. Oftentimes, it is really much more. Often, the division of labor is a complex matter of buying a complicated "high-tech" instrument such as this "Number Two" pencil.

This pencil is the end result of the application of centuries of increasingly sophisticated technology. This pencil is a combination of highly-crafted parts from all the far corners of the world. This pencil has been assembled and finished and brought into the marketplace through the unique talents of many different individuals who all came together and worked together to make it.

Often, our pencils do come from just next door. But, more often, our pencils come from somewhere else. Frequently, and increasingly, trade is "world trade." "World trade" is called "world trade" only because some part of the pencil that is traded happens to cross some arbitrary and artificial political border. Apart from that, "world trade" is no different, economically, from hiring the kid next door to mow your lawn, or maybe make your pencil.

I am not the first to use a pencil to illustrate this point.

In an essay written in the 1950s entitled "I, Pencil," Leonard Read assumed the persona of a pencil. His pencil tells the tale of all its many parts and many makers, and declares proudly that "not a single person on the face of this earth knows how to make me."[2]

Here is the point. Even the simple pencil is the complex product of the individual talents of many different people in many different places working together in many different ways. *All* of them know *something* about making a pencil. But *not one* of them knows everything that needs to be known to make *even one* pencil. And the same is true for virtually *every other* good and service that is exchanged in world trade.

Milton Friedman praised Read's essay for illustrating, with the simple pencil, the possibilities of cooperation without coercion through the workings of the "invisible hand" of the market economy, and the impossibilities of an insular self-sufficiency that depends for success on

---

[2] Leonard Read, "I Pencil: My Family Tree," online at ww.econlib.org/library/Essays/rdPncl1.html.

having a breadth of knowledge that often is so dispersed among so many people in so many places that it is only available to everyone *through cooperation.*[3]

I agree. As I see it, this is the key to understanding the significance of world trade. And, as I see it, this key can be turned only when we understand the indispensability of an international division of labor to all that we hope to achieve in the individual lives of all humanity.

Thoreau told us, in Walden, that he "went to the woods" because he "wished to live deliberately."[4] That is the common aim of all humanity. That is what we all wish for. Whoever we may be, wherever we may be, however we may define the good life, we all wish "to live deliberately."

We all want to make life happen for us, and not just let life happen to us. We all want to use the unique talents that God gave each of us in ways that will help each of us give our lives more real and lasting meaning. And we all ask ourselves: how best can we do this?

In search of meaning in his life, Thoreau sought solitude. He sought the simplicity of self-sufficiency in the woods beside Walden Pond. His sojourn in the woods seems to suggest that the best way "to live deliberately" is to live alone, to work alone, to be alone. The message of Walden seems to be that we are most likely to find meaning in human isolation.

I keep reading and re-reading the writings of Henry David Thoreau because I believe that Thoreau understood human freedom. He understood that human freedom is, ultimately, about the autonomy, the integrity, and the dignity of the free individual. He understood that human freedom is *individual* freedom.

Thoreau understood also the real purpose of individual freedom. Human life *is* about living "deliberately." It *is*, as he wrote, about confronting "the essential facts of life," about learning what life has "to teach," so that we will not, in the end, discover that we have not lived.[5]

But Thoreau did *not* understand how we can *each best secure* the meaningful individual freedom that will enable each of us "to live

---

[3] Id.
[4] Thoreau, Walden and Civil Disobedience, supra, at 135.
[5] Id.

deliberately." We cannot "live deliberately" if we choose to live in isolation. We can "live deliberately" only if we choose to live in ways that *further cooperation*.

If we take Thoreau's advice and think for ourselves, if we think clearly, and if we think things through, then surely we will realize that we need the human cooperation of a division of labor.

Thoreau urged each of us to find meaning in life by trying to do it all ourselves. He thought it best "to oversee all the details yourself in person; to be at once pilot and captain, and owner and underwriter; to buy and sell and keep the accounts; to read every letter received, and write or read every letter sent; to superintend the discharge of imports night and day...."[6]

Thoreau would have us all seek self-sufficiency — down, as in Walden, to the last half-cent. He would not have us depend on other people. He would have us depend only on ourselves. He would have us *all* make *all* our own pencils.

But, the truth is, we can never be entirely self-sufficient, either economically or otherwise. The truth is, we must depend on other people. We need other people. We each need other people if we hope to be able to fulfill the divine promise that is embedded deep within each and every one of us.

This was true of Thoreau — who needed someone else to make at least some of his pencils, so that he would have more time and more freedom to make all his magical essays. This is true of all of us — in as many individual ways as we have individual talents and individual dreams of using them.

Thoreau was inclined —as he once put it —to "measure distance inward and not outward."[7] He was right in thinking that it is essential for each of us to look inward to learn who we are —and who we hope to become —as individuals. Yet, as I measure it, we must then look outward, and use what we have learned about ourselves in cooperative ways that diminish our distance from others.

---

[6] Id. at 62.

[7] Thoreau's journal, quoted in Robert D. Richardson, Jr., Henry Thoreau: A Life of the Mind (Berkeley: University of California Press, 1986), 84.

Thoreau was fond of paradox. He was intrigued by all the apparent contradictions in life. But one paradox he failed to see is this. Very often in life, simplicity needs complexity. The simplicity we seek as a way of inspiring self-discovery and self-fulfillment can only be found through the complexity of mutual cooperation.

For none of us can ever become all we might become unless all of us are able to develop fully all the "special" individual ways in which we all are unique. And none of us can ever develop fully as unique individuals without economic and other associations with other people.

This means we need the "specialization" of a division of labor. This means we need trade. The division of labor that is trade is a liberating force that is essential to unleashing the unique power of human thought through human initiative, incentive, invention, innovation, inspiration, imagination, ingenuity, and enterprise. It is a force for freeing the vast untapped potential for the singular creativity of humankind.

In one of his later essays, "Life Without Principle," Thoreau lamented that — as he expressed it — "we are warped and narrowed by an exclusive devotion to trade and commerce and manufactures and agriculture and the like, which are but means, and not the end."[8]

Thoreau was right in concluding that the chief ends of life are not producing and consuming. He was right to urge us to look beyond mere materialism to see everything that truly can give life real meaning. But he was wrong to think that the true ends of life are not served by the means of trade.

Trade is a means to all the many ends of human freedom. Trade is a means of making more choices available to more people so they can make more personal choices about how they wish to live. Freedom is about choices. Freedom is choosing. The equation between trade and freedom is this. More trade equals more choices equals more freedom.

The *division* of labor *multiplies* human *productivity*, and, thus, human *prosperity*, and, thus, human *opportunity*. It multiplies human choices, and, thus, multiplies *human freedom*. It empowers more of us "to live deliberately." This is equally so whether we hire the teenager next

---

[8] Henry David Thoreau, "Life Without Principle," in Wendell Glick, ed. , Great Short Works of Henry David Thoreau (New York: Harper Perennial, 1993) 404, 423 [1863].

door to mow our lawn, or the worker on the other side of the planet to make our pencil.

By dividing our labor, by creating an ever-widening and ever-deepening *international* division of labor through world trade, we are establishing an economic foundation for uniting all the world in the deliberate life of freedom.

We are limited only by the reach of the market. And, more and more, the reach of the market is limited by less and less. More and more, we have more *world* trade in what is more truly a *world* economy characterized by the ever-dividing subdivisions of a more truly *international* division of labor.

In the midst of all the many controversies about world trade, we tend to forget *why* we trade. We tend to forget all the positive effects of an increasingly international division of labor in furthering and facilitating human freedom. We tend to forget what the world would be like if we *all* had to make *all* our own pencils.

In his definitive study of the history of the humble pencil — entitled <u>The Pencil: A History of Design and Circumstance</u> — Henry Petroski had much to say about Thoreau's pencil and all it illustrates. He pointed out that, before Thoreau left to go to the woods, he made an exhaustive list of everything he needed to take with him — but he forgot to mention his pencil. And, yet, Thoreau kept his pencil with him, in his pocket, all the time.[9]

Trade, too, is with us all the time, and we tend to take the positive effects of trade for granted. We take the positive effects of trade for granted when trade is the kid next door who wants to mow our lawn. And yet we fret about trade when trade is someone in some other country who wants to help make our pencil. We fret endlessly about the competition that is an inevitable part of world trade.

I have this "Number Two" pencil only because my twelve-year-old daughter, Jamey, has not yet "borrowed" it. Pencils often disappear mysteriously from the pencil box on my desk at home. Jamey likes to sharpen the pencils she "borrows" in the pencil sharpener on the corner

---

[9] Henry Petroski, <u>The Pencil: A History of Design and Circumstance</u> (New York: Alfred Knopf, 1992), 4.

of my desk. She sometimes sharpens a whole handful of pencils at once. I have read that the average pencil can be sharpened seventeen times, but I'm not sure this is so with the pencils that Jamey grinds so eagerly in my pencil sharpener.[10]

The competition in world trade is like the grinding of a pencil sharpener. It makes a lot of noise. It uses up a lot of pencils. Yet it is absolutely necessary in order to make proper use of a pencil. Only with the relentless spur of free and fair competition can trade succeed. Only with the sharpened pencils of trade can we write all the words of human freedom.

But there must be rules to ensure free and fair competition in world trade. There must be rules to help free us to make more trade so that we can make more freedom. And that is why we have created the World Trade Organization. That is why we have created the much-needed but much-debated, much-maligned, and much-misunderstood "WTO."

One common misunderstanding about the WTO is much like one common understanding about the pencil. We commonly speak about a pencil "lead." Yet the "lead" of a pencil is not really made of lead. It is made of a mixture of graphite and clay. Likewise, we commonly speak of the "WTO" as if it were some all-powerful, supra-national organization that is somehow able to impose its arbitrary will on us by telling the sovereign countries of the world what to do. Yet the WTO is really nothing more than those very sovereign countries working together as the "WTO" to provide the right mix of rules the world needs to make more trade and, thus, more freedom.

The WTO is a cooperative effort by 146 countries and other customs territories to ensure the best mix of all the graphite and all the clay that will be needed to make all the many pencils that are needed by the world. This mix is made in a world trading system that serves five billion people in ninety-five percent of the world economy.

This is where I come in. I help the Members of the WTO clarify the rules of world trade, and I help them uphold the rules of world trade, so that the grinding competition of world trade will be freer, will be fairer, and will continue to make more trade and, thus, more freedom.

---

[10] "Interesting Pencil Facts," online at www.pencils.net/facts.cfm.

There are seven of us who have been appointed by the Members of the WTO to serve on the Appellate Body of the WTO. We seven work for all the Members of the WTO. We seven are independent and impartial.

When there are disputes about what the rules mean, the countries that make the rules, and that are bound by the rules, have the right to resolve those disputes in what we call the WTO dispute settlement system. The seven of us on the Appellate Body help the Members of the WTO uphold the rules by assisting them in their efforts to decide what the rules mean by drawing all the right lines in WTO dispute settlement.

Pencils are made for drawing lines, and the world needs rules for trade that draw all the right lines. The average pencil can write 45,000 words.[11] The average pencil can draw a line thirty-five miles long.[12] We need rules for trade that will have all the right words to draw all the right lines to take us all the long miles to freedom.

We need rules for trade on which the countries of the world have agreed. We need rules for trade that can help lower the barriers to trade, and help resolve trade disputes. We need rules for trade that can help provide the stability, the security, and the predictability that are needed for trade to be as successful as it can be in creating more freedom.

We already have many of the rules the world needs for trade. There are 30,000 pages of trade rules in the WTO Treaty. There are 20,000 pages of reports on these trade rules that have resulted thus far from WTO dispute settlement. Along with my six colleagues on the Appellate Body, I have helped the Members of the WTO draw many of the lines we need by writing many of those pages.

The many countries in the world are busy now trying to agree on the additional lines that need to be drawn in world trade. In the new worldwide trade negotiations under the auspices of the WTO, many countries are working together to make new rules for trade in the same way that many people work together to make a pencil.

But having all the rules we need for trade will not be enough.

---

[11] Steve Ritter, "Pencils & Pencil Lead," <u>Science and Technology, Volume 79, Number 42</u> (October 15, 2001), at 3, online at wwwpubs.acs.org/cen/whatstuff/7942sci4,html.
[12] Id.

The rules must be fair. The rules must be the same for everyone, and they must be applied to everyone in the same way. This is what is called the "rule of law."

And the rules must be upheld. Rules are not really rules unless they are upheld. In upholding the rules for trade, we are upholding the "rule of law." Freedom is only possible within the "rule of law." We cannot write without some kind of pencil, and we cannot be free without the lines that form the freeing framework of the law.

Only if we draw all the right lines, only if we have all the right rules, only if those rules are fairly written and fairly applied, and only if those rules are upheld, will we be able to *maximize* all the many gains that can be made for freedom through the many gains from trade. Only then will we be able to make it possible for millions more people in every part of the world "to live deliberately."

The more trade we have, the more gains from trade we will have to maximize, and the more "deliberately" we will all be able to live. And we will have the most trade —we will have the most personal choices — we will have the most freedom — if we trade in ways that enable — that empower — each of us to do what we each do the best when compared to others. The world will work best if we each do what we each do the best, when compared to others.

This is what the economists call our relative, "comparative advantage." This is also the way for each of us to have the best chance to choose "to live deliberately." Because a world in which we are each free to do what we each do the best when compared to others, is the world in which we will each be the freest to make a *deliberate* choice about how best to live.

At some basic level, Thoreau understood this. At some fundamental level, he understood the need for a division of labor that enables each of us to meet and beat competition by using and making "comparative advantage." The evidence is not in what he *said*. It is in what he *did*. It is in what Thoreau did about Thoreau's pencil.

Thoreau rejected his father's advice to make a career of making pencils. He preferred to wander in the woods and write essays at Walden Pond.

But Thoreau was an American writer of American books. He was very much an American. And, when the going gets tough, we Americans don't go live alone in the woods. We don't flee the world. And we don't fear the world. We face the world, and we face all the tough challenges the world presents.

Sometimes those challenges are in trade. Sometimes those challenges are in space. Sometimes those challenges are in some far dark corner of the world. Wherever and whatever those challenges are, we Americans always — always — meet them.

Thus, when competition from foreign pencils threatened to drive his father out of business, Thoreau went back to work at his father's pencil company. In the face of the foreign competition, he showed up to save the family livelihood.[13]

Thoreau spent long hours in the Harvard library studying the finer points of pencil technology. He developed a new grinding mill, a new pipe-forming machine, new water wheel designs, and all sorts of new processes for making pencils. He discovered a new way of mixing clay with graphite to make a superior pencil lead. But, most important of all, he discovered a way of varying the mix so that he could vary the hardness of the pencil lead.

This discovery saved his father's company by making it the first American company to produce pencils with grades that varied according to their hardness. The Thoreau pencils were numbered one, *two*, three, and four.[14]

Thoreau knew what we need to do to meet the challenge of world trade.

We need to make a better pencil.

Make one he did. And, in making a better pencil, Thoreau showed why this pencil I hold today truly is "Thoreau's pencil."

---

[13] *See* John H. Lienhard, "Thoreau's Pencils," online at www.uh.edu/engines/epi 339.html; and Van Wyck Brooks, <u>The Flowering of New England: 1815 – 1865</u> (New York: E .F. Dutton, 1937), 425.

[14] Henry Petroski, <u>The Pencil</u>, supra, at 119.

By making it possible to produce pencils that vary in hardness, Henry David Thoreau helped give us this —and every other —"Number Two" pencil.

Chapter Four

"Woulda, Coulda, Shoulda":
The Consolations of WTO Dispute Settlement

Many talented lawyers have appeared before me during my time on the Appellate Body. One of the most talented is Scott Andersen.

Mr. Andersen was formerly an advocate for one of the Members of the WTO, the United States of America. Today, he employs his considerable legal talents in private practice with a large law firm in Geneva.

Yet, as talented as he is as a lawyer, Mr. Andersen is perhaps even more talented as a musician. Indeed, he is perhaps best known in and around Geneva as a member of a popular band of musicians called "The Swing Solicitors."

"The Swing Solicitors" is an international band of mainly international trade lawyers who devote their days to the considerable depths of the WTO "covered agreements" and their nights to the consoling rhythms of swing music.

From time to time, I have been known to emerge from the depths of my own explorations of the "covered agreements" to go and hear them swing.

As one of "The Swing Solicitors," Mr. Andersen plays what *he* calls an "acoustic bass," and what those of us who happen to have been born in Nashville, Tennessee, call a "bass fiddle."

Sometimes Mr. Andersen sings while he strums his bass fiddle. My favorite among the songs he sings is his unique rendition of the old swing tune, "Do I love you? 'Deed I do."[1]

No doubt the lyrics of this old tune appear somewhere in the thousands of pages of the "covered agreements." Everything else does. You will all, of course, recall the words.

This chapter is based on an address to the International Bar Association at the Richemond Hotel in Geneva, Switzerland, on March 20, 2003.

[1] " 'Deed I Do," words and music by Fred Rose and Walter Hirsch (1926).

"Do I love you? Oh my. Do I. Honey, 'deed I do."

Surely these words are worthy of inclusion in the musical pages of the GATT.

In his own riff to these words from this old swing standard, the bass fiddle player of "The Swing Solicitors" sings a recurring refrain of regret about all that *"woulda," "coulda,"* and *"shoulda"* happened if only he had been able to show his true feelings to the true love of his song.

This refrain made such an impression on me when I first heard it that, some time later, when Mr. Andersen, shorn of his bass fiddle, was so bold as to advance, on behalf of his country, an equally lyrical, but somewhat less impressive, riff to an argument in an oral hearing before the Appellate Body, I could not resist saying to him in reply, "Woulda, coulda, shoulda, Mr. Andersen. Woulda, coulda, shoulda."

In recounting this exchange, I trust that I neither embarrass Mr. Andersen nor betray the sanctity of the "confidentiality" of dispute settlement proceedings in the World Trade Organization. The particular argument he made and the particular appeal in which he made it, will forever remain safely "confidential" —if for no other reason than that I have forgotten what they were.

But I have not forgotten the riff. I still remember the recurring refrain of "woulda, coulda, shoulda," and I am reminded of that refrain again today as I reflect on the future of WTO dispute settlement. For, it seems to me that "woulda, coulda, shoulda" may well be an appropriate refrain for all those who strum the chords today for the future of WTO dispute settlement.

I play "bass fiddle" in another swing band in Geneva. Our band is called "The Appellate Body." Our band is not nearly as popular as "The Swing Solicitors." For some reason, everyone always seems to want to re-write our lyrics.

The members of our band are not allowed to say a lot about our lyrics or about our performances. We do not sing solos on the Appellate Body. Moreover, there is nothing in our repertoire under the WTO Dispute Settlement Understanding to suggest that Members of the Appellate Body should be singing at all about what "woulda," "coulda," or "shoulda" be done to improve WTO dispute settlement.

The Members of the WTO have their own band that sings those songs. They call their band "The Dispute Settlement Body." Their band is busy now, rehearsing. The Dispute Settlement Body is in the midst of a jam session in which the Members of the WTO are trying their best to sing in harmony on a discordant song called "DSU Review."

Clearly, all of us who support the WTO and the WTO trading system need to sing in harmony on WTO dispute settlement, and, clearly, there is much that "woulda, coulda, shoulda" be done in DSU review to improve the WTO dispute settlement system.

There is much we *would* do if we had the will to do it. There is much we *could* do if we had the will —and the resources —to do it. There is much we *should* do to strengthen and sustain the dispute settlement system so that the multilateral trading system will be able to meet all the many challenges the Members of the WTO will face going forward.

Clearly, too, after eight years of strumming my bass fiddle on the Appellate Body, I have my own views about what "woulda, coulda, shoulda" be done to improve WTO dispute settlement.

But that is *not* the song I will sing today.

I will be leaving our band for a new "gig" at the end of this year. Next year, as a *former* Member of the Appellate Body, I will be free to play my own improvisations and sing my own tunes about how we might find the harmony we seek in dispute settlement.

Today, I will sing a different tune.

My tune today is not a foot-tapping tune that is intended to drum a downbeat for the current review of the WTO dispute settlement system. Rather, my tune today is a consoling tune that is meant to mark a back beat of reassurance about the many successes, thus far, of the WTO dispute settlement system. My tune today is meant to offer some much-needed perspective in the hope that it will inspire some much-needed confidence in the midst of DSU review.

It goes like this.

Nearly a decade after the creation of the WTO dispute settlement system, there is a growing chorus of criticism of the system. Lawyers, scholars, journalists, politicians, and trade diplomats —not to mention a global choir of activists of all kinds and all persuasions —have all joined in a rising crescendo of competing and cacophonous voices and views about what *would* and *could* and *should* be done to improve WTO dispute settlement. This crescendo has risen to still higher octaves in recent months as the members of that other Geneva band —the Dispute Settlement Body —have "tabled" literally dozens of proposals for changing the arrangements of the dispute settlement system as part of their DSU review.

But, for all the talk all over the world about all that "woulda, coulda, shoulda" be done to improve WTO dispute settlement, there is considerably less talk about all that the Members of the WTO have already done for the world in the first decade of WTO dispute settlement. There is considerably less talk about all the many successes that are our *consolations* for all our many efforts in WTO dispute settlement.

The riff in my tune today —the refrain that I hope will be remembered —is this. The steady back beat of reassurance that reminds us of all our recent successes in WTO dispute settlement is needed to set the tempo for more successes in the future. But the back beat is hard to hear in the current debate about DSU review. And, my worry is that, without the back beat, the WTO will play out of tune.

As Mr. Andersen surely knows, every time he hums when he strums his bass fiddle, he is harmonizing with an ancient Roman philosopher named Boethius.

In the sixth century of our era, Boethius wrote a treatise on musical theory that became a basic textbook for musicians for a thousand years. His account of sound, pitch, scale, and syncopation informs the strumming of every bass fiddle player, even today.[2]

More famously, Boethius was also a politician who was wrongly imprisoned and brutally executed after a fatal fallout with his Gothic king. While in prison, bravely awaiting his fate, he wrote another influential book that is still widely read today, The Consolation of Philosophy.[3]

---

[2] "Boethius," online at www.stfrancis.edu/ph/hauser/boethius/boeinfo2.htm; *see generally* Averil Cameron, The Mediterranean World in Late Antiquity, 395-600 (London and New York: Routledge, 1993), 42; and Bertrand Russell, A History of Western Philosophy (New York: Touchstone, 1972), 370 [1945].

[3] Boethius, The Consolation of Philosophy, Loeb Classical Library (Cambridge, Mass: Harvard University Press, 1973).

As we strum away today on the subject of WTO dispute settlement, we, too, should be mindful of our *consolations.* We should remember the example of that ancient musician, Boethius, and we should pause to ask ourselves: In addition to those that may be offered by philosophy, what *other consolations* do we have as we await the fate of DSU review?

Our greatest consolation is one that is very much on my mind because of world events on this very day. In my view, as someone who has spent nearly eight years strumming the bass fiddle for the Appellate Body of the WTO, the most consoling of all the many consolations of WTO dispute settlement is the success of the dispute settlement system in serving its original and most fundamental purpose. That purpose is to resolve international trade disputes *peacefully.*

More than half a century on, we tend to forget sometimes why we created our rule-based multilateral trading system, and why we invented a mechanism for dispute settlement within that trading system. We did so to keep "trade wars" from becoming real wars.

The aim of the WTO is not to *eliminate* trade disputes. In an international economy, international disputes about trade are inevitable. The aim of the WTO is to *resolve* the inevitable disputes about trade through the hums and strums of WTO dispute settlement so that we will be less likely to hear the drums of war.

It may be too much to say that trade ensures peace. It may be too little to say that it does not. Trade cannot end war, because trade cannot change our unchanging human nature. But trade can help silence the drums of war. Trade can help chain the dogs of war.[4]

Even as we meet today, the dogs of war strain at their chains. For all our hopes for harmony in the world, the cry of havoc is still heard in the world. But where are these cries heard? The world is threatened by war, but the world is *not* threatened by war *between Members of the WTO.*

Despite all that is happening to the world as we meet today, we can be consoled by this particular refrain of reassurance. We must be

---

[4] "Cry 'Havoc,' and let slip the dogs of war." William Shakespeare, <u>Julius Caesar</u> (Act III, Scene 1).

ever aware that, in settling trade disputes, we are serving the cause of peace.

Yet another consolation of WTO dispute settlement is how *relatively little* there really is in the world trading system that is in dispute. If we only read the headlines, we might conclude that there is no harmony at all in the trading system. And yet the humming, strumming, day-to-day reality of the trading system reveals the reassuring back beat.

Almost all of the trillions of dollars of international trade that is conducted annually in the 95 percent of the world economy that is generated by the 146 countries and other customs territories that are Members of the WTO is conducted *without dispute*.

The Members of the WTO have agreed —at last count —on *thirty thousand* pages of rules and concessions that comprise the "covered agreements" of the WTO. The Members of the WTO have adopted —at last count —about *twenty thousand* pages of rulings in reports that have resulted from WTO dispute settlement.

Often overlooked in all the discord about the WTO —and especially in all the debate about WTO dispute settlement —is the fact that, on a daily basis, as a matter of mundane commercial routine, every single Member of the WTO tries to abide by *virtually every single one* of the rules *and* the rulings that have been agreed and adopted by the Members of the WTO. Furthermore, every other Member acknowledges that this is so —*without dispute*.

Our consolation from this refrain of my tune today is the knowledge that the growing global volume of all of this *undisputed* trade creates a growing volume of unprecedented overall wealth for the five billion people who are served every day by the WTO trading system.

There is consolation, too, in the knowledge that the *very existence* of the WTO dispute settlement system helps *prevent* trade disputes. The *very existence* of the dispute settlement system encourages WTO Members to sing from the same page, and sing in the same key.

WTO Members generally trade in unison in accordance with WTO rules and rulings, because they know there will be consequences from dispute settlement if they sing off key. In this way, WTO dispute settlement helps provide the "security and predictability to the multilateral trading system" that WTO Members sought in writing the arrangements of the Dispute Settlement Understanding.[5]

Still another consolation of WTO dispute settlement is the *consistency* with which WTO Members take their disputes with other WTO Members to the WTO dispute settlement system in an effort to resolve them. Where there *are* trade disputes, those disputes are largely resolved through WTO dispute settlement.

To be sure, all of the Members of the WTO are supposed to play in the band. They have all *agreed* in the WTO treaty to use the WTO dispute settlement system to resolve all their treaty-related disputes with other WTO Members. But all of us who sing so ardently for international law know only too well that it is one thing to *agree* to a treaty, and quite another to *abide* by it.

Our consolation from WTO dispute settlement is that, for the most part, after only a few years on stage with the new WTO system, everyone *is* playing in the band. For the most part, it is now *simply assumed* that trade disputes between and among the Members of the WTO will be resolved through the arrangements of WTO dispute settlement.

Further, an additional grace note of consolation is afforded by the fact that this is especially so for the developing countries that comprise the majority of the membership of the WTO. Developing countries are increasingly featured in the performances of the Dispute Settlement Body.

We can be consoled as well by the *frequency* with which WTO Members have used the WTO dispute settlement system. Professor Andreas Lowenfeld has said that the WTO dispute settlement system is "the most complete system of international dispute settlement in history."[6] It can also safely be said that the WTO dispute settlement system is by far the *busiest* system of international dispute settlement in history.

Here, too, though, it is important to listen for the back beat. Here, too, if we only read the headlines, we might conclude from the *sheer busyness* of the system that WTO dispute settlement reverberates with an

---

[5] Article 3.2, Understanding on Rules and Procedures Governing the Settlement of Disputes (the "Dispute Settlement Understanding").

[6] Andreas F. Lowenfeld, International Economic Law (Oxford: Oxford University Press, 2002), 150.

unrelenting drumbeat of unresolved and unresolvable disputes. And, yet, here, too, the reality of what happens daily in dispute settlement reveals the consoling and reassuring rhythm of the back beat.

According to the DSU, "The aim of the dispute settlement mechanism is to secure a positive solution to a dispute."[7] The WTO dispute settlement system achieves this aim *in almost every dispute.*

Many —perhaps even most —of the international trade disputes that are brought to the attention of the WTO are resolved in a "positive solution" *without* formal consultations. Most of the disputes that result in formal consultations are resolved *without* the formal establishment of a panel. (To be more precise, the Legal Affairs Division of the WTO Secretariat reports that, thus far, a panel has been established in only about *40 percent* of the disputes in which there has been a request for consultations.[8])

Furthermore, *almost all* of the trade disputes that are addressed by a panel and, if appealed, by the Appellate Body, result in what all the WTO Members that are parties to those disputes agree is a "positive solution" within a reasonable period of time after the adoption of the dispute settlement reports by the Dispute Settlement Body.

Not surprisingly, many of those throughout the world who follow the performances of the WTO from afar tend to focus on the *mere handful* of disputes in which it has been most difficult to achieve a "positive solution." Those of us who play in the band have a better perspective, because we can hear the reassuring back beat of the dispute settlement system. So we know that the difficulties, thus far, have been, in fact, in only a mere handful of disputes. We could count them on the fingers of the hand we might use to strum a bass fiddle.

The *efficiency* and the *sufficiency* of WTO dispute settlement as sources of consolation can be seen in how *very few* disputes there have been, thus far, that have truly tested the limits of the dispute settlement system in achieving the aim of a "positive solution." No doubt there will

---

[7] Article 3.7, Dispute Settlement Understanding.
[8] According to the records of the Legal Affairs Division of the WTO Secretariat, as of February 10, 2003, there had been 281 requests for consultations in WTO dispute settlement, and there had been 105 panels established in WTO dispute settlement covering 129 disputes.

be more in the future. Even so, there is reassurance for the future in the steady back beat of all that occurs in the daily rhythm of dispute settlement.

I would hope, too, that the Members of the WTO would find some consolation as well in the services that those of us who have been privileged to serve them as Members of the Appellate Body have rendered through the years as performers in the WTO dispute settlement system.

Like any band, from time to time, we may have missed a beat or two. But we have always heard the back beat on the Appellate Body. We have been consistent in our interpretations of the complicated arrangements of the "covered agreements" of the WTO, and we have been consistent, too, in our common commitment to serving all the Members of the WTO.

Our band sings on cue. We meet the deadlines the Members of the WTO have given us for addressing the legal issues that are raised on appeal.

Our band sings in harmony. In nearly sixty appeals, there has *never once* been a dissent by any Member of the Appellate Body to the conclusions and recommendations in any Appellate Body report.

And our band sings our own songs. In nearly eight years, there has *never once* been a suggestion by any Member of the WTO that the Appellate Body is anything but independent and impartial in reaching and rendering our judgments in dispute settlement.

The WTO rules of conduct require the Members of the Appellate Body to be both "independent" and "impartial." The Members of the WTO have put this important requirement in the rules of conduct in two separate places —perhaps as an accent for emphasis.[9]

True to their trust in us, and true to our obligations to them, we have stressed what they have stressed in the rules of conduct. We perform for *all* the Members of the WTO. We play for *all* the trading system. We are always independent. We are always impartial. We will always be. We will always sing our own songs.

---

[9] WTO Rules of Conduct, Articles II and III (2).

There is consolation also in knowing that our efforts to assist the Members of the WTO in clarifying the obligations of WTO Members under the "covered agreements" have helped clarify also the commitment of the Members of the WTO to *the international rule of law.*

To my musical ear, this soothing note of consolation sounds sure and true in the tones of every performance in WTO dispute settlement. Admittedly, some shrill solos are sometimes heard in the performances of the Dispute Settlement Body. But, despite the occasional solos, the reports from dispute settlement have always been adopted, and the Members of the WTO have shown an admirable and remarkable consistency in following the score of the DSU by complying with the rulings and recommendations of the Dispute Settlement Body. In upholding the rule of law in international trade, the Members of the WTO have, consistently, played the right notes in the right pitch to the right beat.

This is an historic achievement. This is an unprecedented achievement. Moreover, this is an achievement that must become a cadence for all the world. The "automatic" beat of the "automatic" adoption of WTO dispute settlement reports is a beat that must be heard and heeded throughout the world.

We are proving that the rule of law can prevail in international trade. We must prove also that the rule of law can prevail as well in many other arenas of compelling international concern.

In their clear regard and in their consistent respect for the international rule of law, the Members of the WTO have set an example for all time and for all the world. All of us who continue to have high hopes for the WTO must hope that this example will endure, and that WTO dispute settlement will, like the musical treatise of Boethius, become a textbook that will be read for a thousand years.

Even Boethius might be consoled by the extent of all of these many consolations of WTO dispute settlement. These many successes so far in WTO dispute settlement give the Members of the WTO every reason for confidence that there can be many more. These refrains of my tune today offer ample reassurance to the Members of the WTO that, if they keep rehearsing, if they keep trying to play together, and if they play in tune, they will find the harmony they seek.

For all their difficulties thus far in harmonizing on the melody of DSU review, the Members of the WTO seem to me to know this. They seem to me to be aware of the rhythm of the back beat. They may not be singing about it. But they do seem to hear it.

Dozens of changes to the DSU have been proposed as part of DSU review. Changes have been suggested in almost every single article of the DSU. Changes are being debated in almost every single provision of the DSU.

But listen closely to the subtle back beat of DSU review. Listen to the revealing and reassuring back beat.

No one has proposed dismantling the Dispute Settlement Understanding. No one has proposed reversing the "reverse consensus" rule that has been the source of so much of the success of the Understanding. No one has proposed abolishing the Appellate Body. No one has proposed a single change with the professed intent of altering the *basic architecture* of WTO dispute settlement.

Because no one wants to break up the band.

An accomplished amateur musician —and philosophical successor to Boethius —named Johann Wolfgang von Goethe once described architecture as "frozen music."[10] I do not know if Goethe ever played the bass fiddle. I do know that his well-known description of architecture does *not* apply to the architecture of WTO dispute settlement.

The music of WTO dispute settlement is not frozen. It is alive. It is alive with the life that flows from trade. It is alive with the life of the world. It swings.

"Woulda, coulda, shoulda, Mr. Bacchus?" Of course. But the din of the downbeat of all that *"woulda," "coulda,"* and *"shoulda"* be done to improve WTO dispute settlement must not keep us from hearing the reassuring rhythm of the back beat of all we have already done for the world through WTO dispute settlement. If we hear the back beat, if we seek consolation in all we have already done, we will, indeed, find the harmony we need to do much more.

---

[10] Johann Wolfgang von Goethe, Letter to J. P. Eckermann (March 23, 1829).

What consolation do I have as I prepare to set my bass fiddle aside, and as I turn to leave the bandstand after eight years on the Appellate Body? As I prepare to leave, do I believe the WTO dispute settlement system has been a success, and do I believe that it can be an even greater success in the years to come?

"Oh my. Do I. Honey, 'deed I do."

Chapter Five

The Strange Death of Sir Francis Bacon: The Do's and Don'ts of Appellate Advocacy in the WTO

The case was styled in the customarily cryptic way of the World Trade Organization: "EC —Measures Affecting the Importation of Certain Poultry Products, WT/DS69/9."[1]

In other words, it was a chicken case.

It was a case arising from an international trade dispute between the European Communities and Brazil about restrictions the Europeans had imposed on imports of chicken from Brazil. The appeal in the case occurred early in my tenure on the Appellate Body of the WTO, and, through the workings of our system of anonymous and random rotation, I was anointed to sit as one of the division of three Members of the Appellate Body that would hear the appeal.[2]

On the morning of the oral hearing in the appeal, the delegations from the European Communities and from Brazil filed into the hearing room in Geneva. They had long been preparing for this last legal showdown over their chicken trade. And yet they obviously were not looking forward to the lengthy legal interrogation they rightly anticipated from our division of the Appellate Body.

Faces were grim. Jaws were set. Lips were pursed. Brows were furrowed. Nervous hands shuffled sheafs of paper as all in attendance awaited the onset of the long ordeal. This air of tension was sustained throughout the parties' opening statements and throughout the initial questions that were posed to the parties by my two colleagues on the division. The ordeal of the oral hearing promised to be long indeed.

This chapter is adapted from remarks at a conference on international trade law at the Barber-Surgeons Hall in London, United Kingdom, on June 20, 2003, and appears under the same title and in slightly different form in Legal Issues of Economic Integration, *Volume 31, Number 1 (2004).*

[1] The text of the Appellate Body Report in this appeal is online at wto.org.
[2] Article 17.2, Understanding on Rules and Procedures Governing the Settlement of Disputes (the "Dispute Settlement Understanding" or "DSU").

Then it was my turn to pose a question. I removed my glasses. I turned to gaze at one of the delegates. I wore my gravest face. I summoned my most serious voice. And I asked:

"Did you know that Sir Francis Bacon was killed by a frozen chicken?"

From the frozen response on his face, one might have thought that *he* had been slain by a frozen chicken. He said not a word. He simply sputtered. Elsewhere in the room, others muttered. But no one anywhere in the room answered my question. And no one laughed.

It was then and there that I learned the extent to which the Europeans and the Brazilians take their chicken *seriously*.

It is not surprising that they would. Annual exports of broiler meat by the European Communities are 720,000 tons; annual exports by Brazil are 2.3 million tons.[3] This is definitely *not* chicken feed.

My question, though, was a joke. It was an attempt to introduce a little levity into the proceeding that might lighten the occasion, and might thereby make it possible for the participants in the hearing to relieve some of their tension, lighten up a little, and perhaps be able, in response to our questions, to enlighten us a little more about some of the subtler nuances of the legal issues they had raised on appeal in their chicken case.

I was not joking, however, about the strange death of Sir Francis Bacon. Those who know me best know that I take the philosophy of Sir Francis Bacon *seriously*.[4]

Certainly we are all familiar with the seriousness of quite a few longstanding and ongoing disputes in the WTO —about chicken and about much else. Like trade lawyers and trade diplomats, historians also have

---

[3] "Livestock and Poultry: World Markets and Trade," Foreign Agriculture Service, United States Department of Agriculture (March, 2003).

[4] There are numerous biographies of Sir Francis Bacon. The best of the most recent are, on Bacon's personal life, Lisa Jardine and Alan Stewart, Hostage to Fortune: The Troubled Life of Francis Bacon (New York: Hill and Wang, 1998); and, on Bacon's philosophy, Peter Zagorin, Francis Bacon (Princeton: Princeton University Press, 1999). A less probing but well-written biography of some time back is Catherine Drinker Bowen, Francis Bacon: The Temper of the Man (Boston: Little, Brown and Company, 1963).

their longstanding and ongoing disputes. One such dispute is over Bacon's strange death, and whether Bacon was, in fact, slain by a frozen chicken.

For those who know more about chicken than about Bacon, it may be worth recalling that Sir Francis Bacon was one of the makers of our modern world. In early 17th century England, his ardent advocacy of the rigorous methods of science and the practical applications of science helped lay the philosophical foundation for the modern world.[5] Bacon was an early champion of the Scientific Revolution in the Age of Reason. He saw the "trial and error" of the scientific method as the surest way to secure human progress. He believed in inductive reasoning through experiment. He believed in observing facts through experience. He believed in the open minds of the open societies that are sought by the modern world. Bacon was a philosopher of science. He was an eloquent essayist. He was also a gifted jurist who, after many years of striving, rose, at last, to become, first, the Attorney General, next, the Lord Keeper, and, eventually, the Lord Chancellor of England under King James I.

"All rising to great place is by a winding stair," Bacon warned us,[6] and, after his long climb, he soon fell from his great place. It was revealed that Bacon had accepted bribes while on the judicial bench. He was dismissed in disgrace. He was imprisoned briefly in the Tower of London, banned from public office, and banished from the court. (Undoubtedly, Sir Francis Bacon would have had difficulties with the WTO Rules of Conduct.)

Bacon's loss of high office was, however, a gain for higher learning. His disgrace freed him for his philosophy. He decided to devote the remainder of his life to his long-postponed literary and scientific pursuits. It may have been his passion for these pursuits that cost him his life in a fatal confrontation with a frozen chicken.

As the story goes, during the spring snow of 1626, the aging, ailing Bacon was returning by coach one night from London to his country estate when he suddenly decided to conduct a scientific experiment. He stopped the coach, bought a gutted chicken from a local villager, and stuffed the chicken with snow with his bare hands. His aim was to show with this

---

[5] For an informative and provocative discussion of Bacon's thoughts on the scientific method, *see* Herbert Butterfield, The Origins of Modern Science, 1300-1800, revised edition (New York: The Free Press, 1965), 113-122 [1957].
[6] Francis Bacon, The Essays (London: Penguin Books, 1985), "Of Great Place," 91, 92-93.

experiment that food could be preserved when frozen. This experiment proved fatal for Sir Francis Bacon. From the damp of the snow, he caught a chill from which he never recovered. A week later, he died. In recounting the sad ending to this story, the historian Thomas Macaulay later declared, "The great apostle of experimental philosophy was destined to be its martyr."[7]

Perhaps. And perhaps Bacon was *not* killed by a frozen chicken. The dispute about the accuracy of this story continues to this day among historians. Some historians doubt that there ever was a frozen chicken.[8] Fortunately, the settlement of this particular longstanding and ongoing dispute is clearly beyond the jurisdiction of the Appellate Body of the WTO.

However he may have died, my intent in telling this story of the strange death of Sir Francis Bacon then was merely to move all those involved then toward the achievement of a "positive solution" in that particular dispute about the chicken trade between the European Communities and Brazil. Further, my intent in recalling this story of Bacon's strange death now is to move others now to a positive awareness of all the many strange legal deaths of so many ardent advocates who have engaged in appellate advocacy in the WTO during my time on the WTO Appellate Body.

I was one of the seven founding Members of the Appellate Body in 1995. I am the last of the founding Members remaining on the Appellate Body. I am the only Member of the Appellate Body who has served since the very beginning of WTO dispute settlement. In the past eight years, I have participated in varying roles in nearly sixty appeals in the WTO. I have served on more divisions in WTO appeals than anyone else. I have seen many, many legal advocates suffer all kinds of strange legal deaths in oral hearings before the Appellate Body.

An oral hearing before the Appellate Body of the WTO is an inquiry by the Appellate Body in search of legal meaning and, thus, legal truth. It is an extended exercise in the classic Socratic method for finding truth. It is a rigorous exercise in relentless questioning in pursuit of truth

---

[7] Thomas Babington Macaulay, Essays and Poems: Critical, Historical and Miscellaneous, in Three Volumes (Boston: Dana Estes and Company, ___), Volume II, "Lord Bacon," 336, 434.

[8] *See especially* Jardine and Stewart, Hostage to Fortune, at 502-511.

in the form of the right legal answers that will enable the Appellate Body to help the Members of the WTO "clarify" the legal obligations in the "covered agreements" of the WTO treaty.[9]

The questioning of advocates in hearings before the Supreme Court of the United States usually lasts for only a few minutes. The questioning of advocates in hearings before the Appellate Body of the WTO always lasts for hours, and sometimes lasts for days. I have heard renowned, experienced advocates who have also appeared before many of the other notable international and other tribunals of the world say that no other tribunal in the world is as demanding, as exhausting, as inquisitive, or as downright persistent as the Appellate Body of the WTO in the pursuit of legal truth.

I take this as a compliment. I, for one, would not be eager at all to try to answer my own persistent questions, much less those of my distinguished colleagues on the Appellate Body, in the "quasi-judicial" quest for legal truth in our oral hearings. In my checkered past, I was at different times both a journalist and a politician. I have long since repented and reformed. But I learned long ago that it is much easier to ask the questions than to answer them. No doubt Socrates would agree.

And yet, for all the strange hearsay about the Appellate Body, and for all the strange legal deaths before it, very little is really known in the world about what really happens in appellate advocacy in the WTO. Even now, after eight years, only a handful of lawyers in the world have appeared before the Appellate Body. Indeed, even now, after eight years, *the majority of the Members of the WTO* have never even seen a proceeding of the Appellate Body.

The chicken case was resolved in a "positive solution" some time ago.[10] In the years since, the word has no doubt spread to many of those who appear for the first time before the Appellate Body to beware the occasional odd question from the occasionally odd American who serves on the Appellate Body. Nowadays, some of the participants in our oral hearings sometimes laugh at my jokes —or at least pretend to laugh.

Still, all too little seems to be known in the world about the supposed mysteries of the Appellate Body's "confidential" proceedings.[11]

---

[9] Article 3.2, Dispute Settlement Understanding.
[10] Article 3.7, Dispute Settlement Understanding.
[11] Article 17.10, Dispute Settlement Understanding.

Very little seems to be known about the purely practical approaches that advocates would be advised to pursue in appeals in the WTO so as to avoid being numbered along with Sir Francis Bacon among those who have suffered strange deaths. Very little seems to be known about the *dos* and *don'ts* of appellate advocacy in the WTO.

What are those *do's* and *don'ts*? What *are* some of the *do's* and *don'ts* of appellate advocacy in the WTO?[12]

First of all, *do* remember to file your notice of appeal on time. Bacon said, "There is surely no greater wisdom than well to time the beginnings and onsets of things."[13] There are deadlines in the WTO Dispute Settlement Understanding. Know them. Meet them. The Appellate Body does. Moreover ...

Don't forget that, in accordance with the DSU, the Appellate Body has promulgated its own Working Procedures for Appellate Review. Every successful advocate knows that the small matter of procedure is often the largest matter of all. As Bacon said, "[S]mall matters win great commendation."[14] Read those Working Procedures. Follow them. The Appellate Body does.

Do state your claims clearly in the notice of appeal. Both the other participants and the Appellate Body need to know what your appeal is about. They should not be left to wonder. But ...

Don't feel that you need to set out your whole case in the notice of appeal. It is, after all, only a *notice* of appeal.

Do, by all means, file all necessary preliminary motions. Some concerns simply cannot wait until the oral hearing. But ...

Don't file needless or frivolous preliminary motions. The Appellate Body has only ninety days to produce a report in an appeal. In

---

[12] Accustomed as I am to *asking* questions, before trying to *answer* this question, I took the time to pose it to my six colleagues on the Appellate Body, and also to the loyal and long-suffering lawyers who serve on our Appellate Body Secretariat. Their answers were all very much the same. Thus, in answering this question, I offer a view that, to a certain extent, can be considered as a "consensus" view that is shared by all the Appellate Body. I stress, however, that my attempted expression of this view is mine alone. I confess, moreover, that all my references to frozen chicken are, most definitely, mine alone.

[13] Sir Francis Bacon, The Essays (London: Penguin Books, 1985), "Of Delays," 125.

[14] Bacon, The Essays, "Of Ceremonies and Respects," 213.

practice, this includes two weeks for translation. As Bacon said, "[A]n unseasonable motion is but beating the air."[15]

Do use big print to make your points in your written submissions. I am the youngest Member of the Appellate Body, and even I can barely read the smallest print. Even with my bifocals, it looks like so much "chicken scratch."

Don't fail to respond to the points that are made by the other party in its written submissions. Failure to acknowledge these points will not keep the Appellate Body from addressing them. Silence is not golden in WTO dispute settlement. Bacon said, "Silence is the virtue of fools."[16]

Do be on time for the oral hearing. I may be best known within the WTO, not for my jokes, but for my insistence on starting our hearings on time. A clock on the title page of the first edition of Bacon's book, New Atlantis, showed truth being brought forth by time.[17] Best then, in search of truth, to get started on time.

Don't take too much time in your opening statement. The Appellate Body reads every word of the written submissions. There is no need to repeat them word for word. Bacon observed of opening remarks, "To use too many ... ere one come to the matter is wearisome ...."[18] Perhaps with this in mind, my former colleague on the Appellate Body, Claus-Dieter Ehlermann, once brought an egg timer with him when he presided in an oral hearing. In that particular case, the egg came before the chicken.

Do assume that the Appellate Body is prepared to hear the appeal. Usually, by the time of the oral hearing, the members of the division in an appeal have each spent many hours, on their own and together, preparing for the oral hearing. They are always prepared. And...

Don't assume that the members of the division have already made up their minds by the time of the oral hearing. They have not. They are always mindful of Bacon's admonition that, "Surely there is in some sort a right in every suit...."[19] They always have open minds. And...

---

[15] Bacon, The Essays, "Of Dispatch," 134, 135.
[16] Sir Francis Bacon, De Dignitate et Augmentis Scientarum, I, vi, 31.
[17] *See* the Francis Bacon Research Trust online at fbrt.org.uk/pages/truth-time.
[18] Bacon, The Essays, "Of Discourse," 160, 161.
[19] Bacon, The Essays, "Of Suitors," 207.

Do know that the Members of the Appellate Body are independent and impartial. As the DSU requires, Members of the Appellate Body are "unaffiliated with any government" and "broadly representative of membership in the WTO."[20] They are each there to represent *all* the Members of the WTO by representing *all* the world trading system. So ...

Don't assume from the nature or the slant of the questions asked by the members of a division of the Appellate Body in an oral hearing that they do *not* have open minds or that they are *not* independent and impartial. Their questions are not intended to reveal *their* thinking; they are intended to provoke *yours*.

Do answer the questions. If they are not answered, the members of the division will keep asking them until they are answered. As I have said many times to many advocates in our oral hearings, "Humor me."

Don't tell the members that their questions are irrelevant. They choose the questions, and they have their reasons for asking them. Trust me.

Do answer the questions even if the answers seem obvious to you. The answers may not seem as obvious to the members of the division. Thus, be prepared to tell them, if they ask, why the chicken crossed the road.

Don't keep talking when you have finished answering a question. Stop. If you don't stop, you may say something you will later regret. "For he that talketh what he knoweth," said Bacon, "will also talk what he knoweth not."[21]

Do expect to be interrupted when you are answering a question. Bacon, the seasoned jurist, explained, "A sudden, bold, and unexpected question doth many times surprise a man, and lay him open."[22] The Appellate Body's aim in interrupting by asking such a question is to lay the way open to legal truth.

Don't ask questions of the other parties. Only the Appellate Body asks questions of the parties in an oral hearing. Bacon's first act as Attorney

---

[20] Article 17.3, Dispute Settlement Understanding.
[21] Bacon, The Essays, "Of Simulation and Dissimulation," 76, 77.
[22] Bacon, The Essays, "Of Cunning," 126, 128.

General was to outlaw the practice of dueling in England.[23] An oral hearing of the Appellate Body is *not* a duel between the parties.

Do argue the law. An oral hearing before the Appellate Body of the WTO is a *legal* proceeding. The job of the Appellate body is to address each of the *legal* issues raised in the appeal.[24] That is their job, and that is their only job.

Don't argue politics or policy. The Members of the Appellate Body leave the politics and the policy entirely to the Members of the WTO. That is *not* their job.

Do argue WTO law. The law that interests the Appellate Body by far the most is the law that is found in the WTO "covered agreements." WTO law is where WTO obligations are found.

Don't simply assume that a provision in WTO law will be interpreted in precisely the same way as a similar provision in your own municipal law. It may be. It may not be. What matters most in interpretation is whether the "covered agreements" say that it *must* be.

Do argue other international law —when it is relevant. As the Appellate Body has said from the very beginning, WTO law is a part of international law and cannot be viewed in "clinical isolation" separate and apart from other international law.[25] But ...

Don't assume the *relevance* of other international law. Whether other international law *is* relevant may be subject to debate in the WTO. To the extent that this debate will be resolved in WTO dispute settlement, it will be resolved, like so much else, on a case-by-case basis.

Do know the "covered agreements." The "covered agreements" contain WTO law. Bacon advised, "[S]ome books are to be read, but not curiously; and some few to be read wholly and with diligence and attention."[26] Read the whole of the "covered agreements" with diligence and attention.

---

[23] Jardine and Stewart, Hostage to Fortune, at 341-342.
[24] Articles 17.6, 17.12, and 17.13, Dispute Settlement Understanding.
[25] United States – Standards for Reformulated and Conventional Gasoline, WT/DSU/AB/R, at 16 (May 20, 1996), 35 I.L.M. 603.
[26] Bacon, The Essays, "Of Studies," 209.

Don't assume that it will be easy to discern the legal truth of the legal obligations of WTO Members from the "covered agreements." If the right answer were obvious, the issue would never have reached the Appellate Body. As Bacon recalled, *"What is truth?* said jesting Pilate, and would not stay for an answer."[27] Stay awhile, and help the Appellate Body find the answer.

Do come prepared to stay a *long* while. The hearings *do* go on for hours and, frequently, for days. The Appellate Body asks *many* questions in search of the *right* answer. "Stay a little," urged Bacon, "that we may make an end the sooner."[28]

Don't be impatient if, in the methodical asking of their many questions, the members of the division do not seem to be proceeding with haste to the issue you see as most important. Be patient. They will get there. Bacon cautioned, "[M]easure not dispatch by the times of sitting, but by the advancement of the business."[29]

Do argue the case law when it supports your claim. Yes, yes, it is true that there is no *stare decisis* —no rule of precedent —in public international law. However, in my experience, when the case law supports a party's claim, that party argues the case law; and when the case law does not support a party's claim, that party reminds the division hearing the appeal that there is no *stare decisis* in public international law. Moreover...

Don't merely ignore the case law when it does *not* support your claim. You are free, of course, to argue that the Appellate Body erred egregiously in its ruling in a previous case. You can argue that. Or, instead, you may wish to argue that your case can be distinguished from the previous case —if it can be.

Do know your brief. Know every single detail there is to know about the dispute. This will not be easy. Panel reports include hundreds of pages. Panel records include thousands of pages. But the lawyer who does the best is usually the lawyer who knows the brief the best. Bacon said, "Knowledge itself is power."[30]

---

[27] Bacon, The Essays, "Of Truth," 61.
[28] Bacon, The Essays, "Of Dispatch," 134.
[29] Id.
[30] Sir Francis Bacon, Religious Meditations, "Of Heresies."

Don't contest the facts as found by the panel. The members of the division can discuss with you the endless nuances of what is "law" and what is "fact". They can discuss with you how the law should be applied to the facts. But they are bound on appeal by the facts as found by the panel. Thus, like Bacon, they prefer, on appeal, "that reason which is elicited from facts ...."[31]

Do rely on the customary rules of interpretation of public international law. The Members of the WTO have instructed the Members of the Appellate Body to do so when assisting them in their efforts to "clarify" the provisions of the "covered agreements."[32] They do. So should you.

Don't bother arguing that the Appellate Body should embrace some "teleological" approach to interpretation that would enable the members to impose their purely personal views on the meaning of the "covered agreements." They don't. They won't.

Do know the measure. A dispute in every case involving a claim of a violation of the "covered agreements" is always about the application of some kind of a statute, regulation, administrative practice, or other governmental "measure." The very first question in an oral hearing is almost always, "What is the measure?" Know the answer. But ...

Don't look at the measure without seeing it in relation to the claims. My former colleague on the Appellate Body, Florentino "Toy" Feliciano, is fond of saying that a measure is a prism that can be viewed from the perspective of many possible claims. As usual, I agree with Toy. Whether a measure, when viewed, is a violation, often depends on the nature of the claim.

Do know the difference between the *claims* that have been made, and the *arguments* that have been made about the claims. The Appellate Body will address all your claims. It will not necessarily give equal attention to all the arguments you make in support of your claims. Some arguments are better than others.

Don't confuse eloquence with persuasiveness in making your arguments. Bacon said, "Discretion of speech is more than eloquence."[33]

---

[31] Sir Francis Bacon, <u>Novum Organum</u>, Book I, Aphorism 26, Section 5.
[32] Article 3.2, Dispute Settlement Understanding.
[33] Bacon, <u>The Essays</u>, "Of Discourse," 160, 161.

One precise sentence that makes a legal point effectively will be far more persuasive than a glittering effusion of eloquent sentences that are beside the point.

Do pursue your best arguments —even if the panel seemed to give them short shrift. You will never know which, of all your arguments, may, in the end, prevail. "For if there be fuel prepared," Bacon said, "it is hard to tell whence the spark shall come that shall set it on fire."[34] But...

Don't cling to the weakness of your weakest arguments. Bacon said, "For what a man would like to be true, that he more readily believes."[35] This does not mean, though, that the Appellate Body will believe it.

Do be flexible. Be ready to improvise in your oral argument at the drop of a question. It is not enough to know the law and to be able to argue the law. To be truly effective, an advocate must be able to seize the opportunity to improvise while arguing the law. Bacon said, "A wise man will make more opportunities than he finds."[36]

Don't overlook the small but telling detail —the question not asked by the division, the question not answered by the other party, or perhaps the grudging concession by the other party in a buried footnote. Bacon reminded us, "The way of fortune is like the milken way in the sky, which is a meeting or knot of a number of small stars, not seen asunder but giving light together."[37] So too with the small but telling details that shed a revealing light in an appeal in the WTO.

Do be willing to admit the obvious. Concede what cannot credibly *not* be conceded. You may not wish to make any concession at all, but, as Bacon told us, even "princes many times make themselves desires, and set their hearts upon toys...."[38] If you deny that the sky is blue, then the Appellate Body may be less likely to believe you when you say later that the rain is wet.

Do be aggressive in your advocacy. The Appellate Body will not make your case for you. You must make it yourself. One advocate in a

---

[34] Bacon, The Essays, "Of Seditions and Troubles," 101, 103.
[35] Sir Francis Bacon, Novum Organum, Book I, Aphorism 49, Section 59-9.
[36] Bacon, The Essays, "Of Ceremonies and Respects," 213, 214.
[37] Bacon, The Essays, "Of Fortune," 181.
[38] Bacon, The Essays, "Of Empire," 115.

recent appeal made a point of reminding me that he expected to win or lose solely on the strength of his own arguments. He did. All do. But ...

Don't be so aggressive as to be arrogant in your advocacy. Perhaps the worst show of arrogance in my experience was when one young lawyer from one large country told one of my learned colleagues in a patronizing tone, "I know this is difficult for you to understand, but ...." My colleague —forty years his senior and the author of numerous legal treatises —was too polite to reply. Bacon, the *former* Lord Chancellor, might have told that young lawyer that pride sometimes goes before a fall.

Don't get your hopes up if you ask the Appellate Body to recommend a means of compliance with its ruling. Under the Dispute Settlement Understanding, the Appellate Body "may suggest ways" to implement its recommendations.[39] To date, the Appellate Body has never done so. As Bacon noted, "[t]he predominancy of custom is everywhere visible...."[40]

Do know specifically what you are asking the Appellate Body to go and do at the conclusion of the oral hearing. Do you want a ruling that a statute is in violation of WTO obligations, or only that the statute *as applied* is in violation of those obligations? Do you want a ruling on *all* your claims, or only on *some* of them if the Appellate Body otherwise rules in a certain way? The members of the division may very well ask you in the oral hearing precisely what you want them to do. Know your answer. And, lastly...

Don't take too long with your concluding statement. Bacon took *thirty years* to complete his famous essays from which I have been reciting so freely. You should take considerably less time to complete your concluding remarks in an oral hearing in the WTO. As I have reminded advocates more than once toward the end of a long and arduous hearing, parties have prevailed more than once on appeal in the WTO *without making* a concluding statement. You may be the next.

These are only a few of the *do's* and *don'ts* of appellate advocacy in the WTO. I will save the others for another day. Notably, there are also *do's* and *don'ts* for those who happen to sit in judgment in appeals in the WTO. Bacon, for example, was of the view that, "Judges ought to be

---

[39] Article 19.1, Dispute Settlement Understanding.
[40] Bacon, The Essays, "Of Custom and Education," 179.

more learned than witty."[41] He would probably *not* have laughed at my joke about his strange death. No doubt he would have advised me to tell fewer jokes and show more learning in our oral hearings. But what should we expect from a man who was so learned as to allow his learning to expose him to death by frozen chicken?

I had hoped, before leaving the Appellate Body, to have one more chance to tell my "frozen chicken" joke in an oral hearing. I watched and waited with anticipation as another dispute about the chicken trade — this time between Brazil and Argentina —made its way all the way through the WTO dispute settlement system. But, alas, that one last chance was plucked away. The Panel Report was adopted without an appeal. The dispute was settled.[42]

I am consoled by the knowledge that the purpose of the WTO dispute settlement system *is*, after all, the settlement of disputes. I am consoled also by some of the last words of Sir Francis Bacon. In his last letter, written after his fatal confrontation in the snow, and written on the eve of his strange death, Bacon reported that, for all its unexpected consequences, his experiment with the frozen chicken had "succeeded excellently well."[43] I think, too, that, for all the unexpected consequences that sometimes result from appeals in the WTO, and for all the strange legal deaths that sometimes occur in our oral hearing in those appeals, the experiment with WTO dispute settlement has also, thus far, "succeeded excellently well."

Yes, there are some who do take their chicken too seriously. There are some who seem always to be saying that "the sky is falling" on the WTO. But this is not so. The world needs the WTO. The world will continue to need the WTO, and, in the truly Baconian spirit of "trial and error," the world will continue to make the WTO work for the world as a crucial part of the work of human progress. Moreover, the Appellate Body will continue to do its part to make the WTO dispute settlement system work for the world as a crucial part of the WTO.

---

[41] Bacon, The Essays, "Of Judicature," 222.

[42] Argentina —Definitive Anti-Dumping Duties on Poultry from Brazil, WT/DS241/R.

[43] In a letter to the Earl of Arundel, Bacon wrote, "As for the experiment itself, it succeeded excellently well." The letter is quoted in Jardine and Stewart, Hostage to Fortune, at 504, and also in Macaulay, "Lord Bacon," at 434.

Macaulay said that Bacon aimed, above all, at "the multiplying of human enjoyments and the mitigating of human suffering."[44] In a world where 1.2 billion people live on less than $1 per day, in a world where 2.8 billion people live on less than $2 per day, that, of course, is likewise our aim today in the WTO.[45] That is why we have the WTO. That is why we have appellate advocacy in the WTO. And that is why it is imperative that the historic international experiment that we call the WTO continue to succeed "excellently well."

Do remember that.

And —oh, yes —do remember also one last suggestion I have for achieving success in appellate advocacy in the WTO.

Don't forget to laugh at the jokes. Or, at least, pretend to laugh — even when the joke is about a frozen chicken.

---

[44] Macaulay, "Lord Bacon," at 436.
[45] World Bank, Human Development Report 2001 (Washington, D.C.), 9.

Chapter Six

Learning and Living the Liberal Arts

I first learned of Vanderbilt University from the stories my grandfather told me when I was a boy.

Grandaddy was not much more than a boy himself when he married my grandmother and left the impoverished tobacco country of southern Kentucky for the lights of Nashville in 1925. Nanny and Grandaddy had shared the same bareback mule to and from the same one-room schoolhouse, where they completed the eighth grade. In time, they would share nearly sixty years of marriage.

They were both just twenty, just beginning, when they arrived in Nashville. A daughter, my mother, had just been born. With a family to feed, Grandaddy found a job pumping gas at a Packard dealership on West End, across the street from Vanderbilt.

Decades later, Grandaddy would often puff on his pipe and recall to my youthful wonderment how Robert Penn Warren, John Crowe Ransom, Allen Tate, Donald Davidson, and other famous Vanderbilt professors wheeled in their big black Packards for fill-ups every Saturday.

"They were always real gentlemen," he would say. "They treated me just like I was somebody."

Nearby, Nanny would smile and continue to rock in her quiet way as Grandaddy told me about Vanderbilt one more time.

With only eight years of formal schooling, Grandaddy eventually rose through hard years and hard work to become a regional service manager for Ford Motor Company in charge of several states. In his later years, he taught aspiring mechanics at the automotive-diesel college in Nashville. I always thought Grandaddy was the best mechanic in the world. He always felt he could have been something else, something more.

This chapter appears under this title and in slightly different form in Vanderbilt Magazine (Fall 1994).

Denied a chance for even a high school diploma, my grandfather believed emphatically in the worth of a college education. He believed especially that an education at Vanderbilt could transform a nobody into a "somebody" who could be and do something more in the world.

So it was that Vanderbilt University became for me a symbol of the something more I sought, the something more that no one in my family had ever had, the something more that I feared was beyond my reach, even as it had been beyond the reach of my Grandaddy.

And so it was that when Vanderbilt reached out to me during my senior year in high school and offered me the chance to become the first person in my family to earn a college degree, I did not hesitate. Grandaddy told me that the day I accepted a full academic scholarship from Vanderbilt was just about the happiest day of his life.

I had been born just two blocks from Vanderbilt in the old Saint Thomas Hospital, where my mother had studied nursing. I had gazed at the clock atop Kirkland Hall and at the other red brick spires of the university from time to time from passing car windows. Yet I never actually set foot on the Vanderbilt campus until I became what Vanderbilt grandly called a "Founder's Scholar."

Raised hundreds of miles away in Central Florida, I was by all accounts the first person from what was then still a small semirural high school ever to attend any college remotely resembling Vanderbilt. Yellowed clippings from the local newspapers in celebration of this fact can still be found in the family scrapbook.

A snapshot a few pages later in the scrapbook shows me standing that first fall with two newfound friends on the steps of Mims Hall, books in hand. What that photo does not show is how confused, how lonely, how frightened, how excited, how determined I was as a newly arrived undergraduate, away from home for the first time.

Nanny and Grandaddy lived nearby, in East Nashville. But I felt all alone at the university on West End, and I was all alone every night in Room 238 of Mims Hall. I tried to subdue my home sickness by studying while, across the hall, my neighbor in the dormitory played his favorite Jackie Wilson record, "Higher and Higher," over and over, late into the night.

I was not alone in my confusion.

My first fall at Vanderbilt was one of those confused "between" times in American college life. We freshmen were suppose to wear "beanies" during the first week of the fall semester, though few of us did. At the same time, we were also invited to attend a "teach-in" about a widening war in a faraway place many of us had never heard of, Vietnam.

Buttoned-down conservatives mingled with bearded, would-be radicals in the shade of the magnolias on the winding walks of the campus. Fraternity and sorority rows were joined by Landon House, the University's first coed facility. On the weekends, most students cheered, as always, for the slowest halfbacks and the smartest point guards in the Southeastern Conference; yet some took time out weekly to offer polite protest against the martial drills of the Vanderbilt ROTC. The plaintive pleas of Jackie Wilson had to compete more and more with the defiant guitar chords of Jimi Hendrix.

This casual mix of the old with the new, of tradition with rebellion, of quiet conformity with ever probing, ever increasing, and ever more unsettling questioning, was evident as well in the classrooms of Vanderbilt.

For the most part, the professors who taught us dressed and looked like the souls of consoling conservatism. Yet they were the spiritual heirs of the Fugitive poets and the Agrarian philosophers my grandfather had so much admired. They were unwilling to embrace the world's ways and the world's wishes solely because it was expected of them. They were much inclined to question just about everything.

These teachers, writers, and iconoclastic intellectuals called the consequences of the Vanderbilt curriculum a "liberal arts education." And soon it became clear that I was to get one.

I first became aware of this while taking notes feverishly in a crowded pew in drafty, church-like Neely Auditorium. Up front, in well-worn sneakers and an open sportshirt, Professor Alexander Marchant endeavored to introduce me and a few hundred other novices to the muses and the mysteries of Western civilization. He asked question after question that few of us had ever before thought or dared to ask ourselves. He told us again and again that asking questions, asking hard questions, asking uncomfortable questions, asking unthinkable questions, was the only way to discover the truth about life and how to live it.

In the ancient agora of Athens, Socrates sat on one end of a bench and his student on the other. At Vanderbilt in 1967, Marchant held forth from a lectern at the front of Neely Auditorium. As if from a pulpit, he professed the gospel of the never-ending search for the truth that is the source and soul of all philosophy. Like Socrates, he argued eloquently that the "examined" life, the life engaged in the passionate and purposeful pursuit of understanding, is the only life worth living.

From my dutiful place in the pew, it seemed to me that in all his talk about Socrates, Plato, Aristotle, and all the rest whose dusty thoughts we deciphered and dissected, this man with the booming baritone voice was challenging directly, and even gleefully, every single conviction I had brought with me from my small-town Southern upbringing.

And so, of course, he was. For, as the eminent Yale historian and classicist Donald Kagan has put it, "[A] liberal education needs to create a challenge to the ideas, habits, and attitudes that students bring with them, so that their vision may be broadened, their knowledge expanded, their understanding deepened. That challenge must come from studies that are unfamiliar, sometimes uncomfortably so, and from a wide variety of fellow students from many different backgrounds, holding different opinions, expressing them freely to one another, and exploring them together."[1]

Like others in my class, I soon accepted Marchant's challenge and began what would become a lifelong search for understanding through the study and the practice of the liberal arts. I read the required readings. I read the recommended readings. I read the footnotes. With other confused denizens of the dormitories, I debated endlessly the enduring undergraduate questions of philosophy, history, religion, and life.

Perhaps most important, I discovered that timeless temple of the liberal arts, the library. I went there to try to find the answers to my questions.

Thomas Carlyle said that "[t]he true university... is a collection of books."[2] Enter a library, and all time and all humanity are arrayed in front of you. Voices from all ages, all faiths, all races, and all places cry

---

[1] Donald Kagan, "An Address to the Class of 1994," Commentary (January, 1994), 48.
[2] Thomas Carlyle, "The Hero as a Man of Letters," in Heroes and Hero-Worship [1841].

out from the seemingly endless stacks. The pain, the fear, the hope, the ecstasy, the divine spark of being a passing part of a confused species in search of elusive answers is there in the wondrous words of countless beckoning books.

Like John Keats on first reading George Chapman's *Homer*, I felt, when I first entered the Joint Universities Library at Vanderbilt, as though I had seen a new planet swim into the sky. I disappeared into the sacred stacks. For six days of every week, when not eating or sleeping or listening to a lecture in a classroom, I virtually lived in the "JUL". I lived among the musty books —reading, writing, exploring, thinking, searching for the answers that would lead to understanding.

On Sunday, I attended church across town with my grandparents. I went home with them afterwards to eat Nanny's country ham and homemade biscuits while I listened to Grandaddy rail against the frailties of all the lazy politicians in Washington.

There appeared to me to be few frailties among the professors at Vanderbilt who guided me along the path toward understanding. It has been said that "[o]nly the great universities can take students to the brink of uncertainty."[3] Marchant's lectures on the unfolding logic of Western life and thought had made me a history major and a political science minor, and now he, Harold Bradley, Charles Delzell, Howard Boorman, Jacque Voegeli, Riordan Roett, and others helped take me to the brink of uncertainty where certainty is sometimes found.

Typical of the Vanderbilt approach to teaching the techniques of the liberal arts was one memorable independent study course taught by snowy-haired Henry Lee Swint. He entitled it simply "Readings in American Social and Intellectual History."

After enrolling in the course in the fall of my junior year, I went to Professor Swint's office in Calhoun Hall at the appointed time during the first week of the semester. He looked me over, gave me a syllabus several pages long, and said, "Go and read these books. Come back when you're done." A few weeks later, I returned. Like a surgeon with a scalpel, he sliced up my brain for several hours with his questions. Then he handed

---

[3] Charles W. Anderson, <u>Prescribing the Life of the Mind: An Essay on the Purpose of the University, the Aims of Liberal Education, the Competence of Citizens, and the Cultivation of Practical Reason</u> (Madison, Wisconsin, 1993), 67.

me another syllabus, smiled, and said, "Go and read these books. Come back when you're done."

Years later, some of those who knew me only casually when I was reading my way through Swint's syllabus are astonished at what they see as my decidedly unlikely pursuit of a decidedly public life. In their eyes, I seemed far more likely at the time to spend my life delivering scholarly lectures in the cloister of the academy than giving stump speeches in the pit of the political arena. To some extent, I share their astonishment.

They knew me when I was first engaged in the often private pursuit of asking the most fundamental questions. I was trying to discover the truth about myself at least as much as I was trying to discover the truth about the rest of the world. I was proving the validity of Ralph Waldo Emerson's admonition that, in the pursuit of understanding, a scholar must sometimes "embrace solitude" before he can face the world.[4]

Inspired by Swint, I devoured dozens of books I might otherwise never have known. I pursued self-reliance with Emerson, pondered nature with Thoreau, praised democracy with Whitman, and preached the social gospel with Rauschenbusch. I shared the education of Henry Adams, and many more, in the logic of their philosophy, the lyrics of their poetry, and the power of their prose.

Professor Swint understood that the point of teaching is to teach students those ways of thinking that will help them escape from the chains of ignorance and the shackles of sophistic relativism and climb up with Socrates and others from Plato's classic cave toward the light of understanding. In the books he gave me, and in the way and the ways he taught me, I glimpsed for the first time the distant light.

This approach was mirrored in many other courses I took as well. On European history. On Chinese history. On English literature. On political theory. On philosophy, art, and humanities. In Swint's course and in others like it throughout the university, and in the far reaches of the "JUL", I read the "great books" of civilization. And I received in four short years that most treasured of assets, that most valued of personal possessions —a liberal arts education.

---

[4] Ralph Waldo Emerson, "Friendship," in Emerson's Essays (New York: Harper and Row, 1951), 137, 139 [1841].

At Vanderbilt, I learned how to discipline my mind. I learned how to find patterns, see connections, make deductions, and reach reasoned judgments. I learned how to order my thinking. I learned some of the ways of thinking that have worked best in understanding the erring heart of humanity and the eternal meaning of the world.

At Vanderbilt, I learned the wisdom of William James' warning that unless they are understood in the connected context of humanity's unending search for understanding, "literature remains grammar, art a catalogue, history a list of dates, and natural science a sheet of formulas and weights and measures."[5] I learned as he did that "[a]ll our arts and sciences and institutions are but so many quests for perfection on the part of men...."[6]

I learned too the absolute necessity of constant questioning in the pursuit of understanding. I learned that prejudices, perceptions, predilections, and presuppositions of all kinds must be subjected to relentless questioning if we are to have any real hope of advancing from the dark confusion of the cave toward the light we seek.

Many of the convictions I brought with me to Vanderbilt as a freshman were still with me when I left. Yet, by the time I left, those adolescent beliefs were much closer to becoming real convictions. And, when I left, I took with me as well some new convictions, convictions that have sustained me and served me in all the years since.

Among them is the belief that the effort to attain an education is only barely begun in four fleeting years at even the best university. The pursuit of understanding is a lifelong journey. And, for me, that journey, of necessity, has been one of service.

For, most of all, at Vanderbilt I learned that a life truly devoted to the liberal arts is a life devoted to service. Those who embrace solitude must in time emerge from isolation to confront the world. The pursuit of understanding leads ultimately to the conclusion that the best way by far to discover the truth about ourselves is by devoting our lives to serving others. The best way to find individual understanding is by seeking the common understanding that can enable us *all* to climb up and out of the cave.

---

[5] William James, "The Social Value of the College Bred," in Bruce Kuklick, ed., William James Writings, 1902 – 1910 (New York: Library of America, 1987).
[6] Id.

Knowledge is indeed "its own end," as John Henry Newman expressed it so succinctly in the title to his fifth discourse in *The Idea of the University*.[7] But Newman also said "that training of the intellect, which is best for the individual himself, best enables him to discharge his duties to society."[8] The "practical end" to a university education in the liberal arts "is that of training good members of society. Its art is the art of the social life, and its end is fitness for the world."[9]

The academy and the arena are forever linked. When Plato founded the first Academy, the world's first university, the ancient model for all the rest, he did so not to retreat into reclusion and solitary contemplation, not to embrace solitude, but rather to establish a training ground and a staging ground for citizenship. Appalled by the judicial murder of Socrates and by the other mindless excesses of mob rule, he established the Academy to teach citizens how to go forth and restore the rule of reason in Athens.

Fearful of the ignorance of the masses, Plato opposed the Athenian form of democracy. Yet his invention of the university and of the concept of universal education helped make the eventual success of democracy possible. All these centuries later, ignorance remains the enemy, and education remains the answer.

The liberal arts truly are the arts of liberty. If we remember the vital connection between education and democracy, if we remember to make education serve democracy, then we can still create the common understanding that will permit each of us to pursue our own individual understanding in what Benjamin Barber has called "an aristocracy of everyone."[10] We can still escape together from the cave.

My four years at Vanderbilt culminated in a lengthy inquisition for which my tutorials with Swint had helped prepare me. To earn distinction in the independent honors program, I was required to submit a thesis, and to submit as well to the prolonged questioning of a panel of professors that, alas, included the formidable Marchant himself. All these many years later, I still recall with satisfaction his words at the end of the panel's scrutiny: "Anyone who knows so much about the Clark

---

[7] John Henry Newman, "Fifth Discourse," The Idea of a University [1854].
[8] Id.
[9] Id.
[10] Benjamin Barber, An Aristocracy of Everyone: The Politics of Education and the Future of America (Oxford: Oxford University Press, 1992).

Memorandum deserves not merely 'honors' but 'high honors' in history." And so it appears on my diploma.

Honorable or not, I appear just once in the 1971 edition of the *Commodore* yearbook, in the mugshots of the senior class. Page 317. Row 4. Last photo. I'm the serious one with the horn-rimmed glasses, the curly black hair, the stylishly long sideburns, and the moustache. In part to please Grandaddy, I shaved the moustache the day before the commencement exercises in June of that year.

Leaving Vanderbilt, I may have left my moustache behind. Yet, like many of my classmates, I took with me an education that had supposedly made me fit for the world. And, in a life that has called me to confront many parts of the world, in a life that has found me practicing the liberal arts successively, and sometimes successfully, as among other pursuits, a journalist, a history teacher, a governor's aide, an international trade negotiator, an attorney, a community activist, a Member of Congress from Florida, and more, I have been reminded again and again through the years of the value of my Vanderbilt education.

I was reminded of it once again as I sat at my desk in Washington while in the Congress and read the report of the Wingspread Group on Higher Education.[11] I noticed at the time that one of the members of the group and an author of the report was the then Chancellor of Vanderbilt University, Joe B. Wyatt.

Much has changed in the years that have passed since I stalked the stacks of the "JUL", and the report of the Wingspread Group reflects those changes. In a compelling call to action, the report declares, "The American imperative for the 21st century is that society must hold higher education to much higher expectations or risk national decline.... Education is in trouble, and with it our nation's hopes for the future. America's ability to compete in a global community is threatened. The American people's hopes for a civil, humane society ride on the outcome."[12]

Chancellor Wyatt and his colleagues in the Wingspread Group depict an atmosphere of crisis: Declining standards. Creeping credentialism. Trivialized curricula. Worthless degrees. Spreading

---

[11] "An American Imperative," Report of the Wingspread Group on Higher Education (1993).
[12] Id.

psuedo-scholarship. Needlessly narrow specialization. A preoccupation with the parochial, the peripheral, and the ephemeral. An increasing intolerance for unpopular and unorthodox views on campus. A growing lack of engagement with the principal ideas and events that have been the sources and the sustenance of civilization.

As evidence of this crisis, the Wingspread Group cites an analysis of college transcripts by the U.S. Department of Education: More than 26 percent of recent recipients of bachelor's degrees did not earn a single undergraduate credit in history, nearly 31 percent did not study mathematics of any kind, nearly 40 percent earned no credits in either English or American literature, and more than 58 percent were graduated without any exposure to a foreign language.[13]

They conclude, "The simple fact is that some faculties and institutions certify for graduation too many students who cannot read and write very well, too many whose intellectual depth and breadth are unimpressive, and too many whose skills are inadequate in the face of the demands of contemporary life.... The harsh truth is that a significant minority of these graduates enter or reenter the world with little more than the knowledge, competence, and skill we would have expected in a high school graduate scarcely a generation ago."[14]

In my efforts to serve, I have seen firsthand how the challenges we face as a nation in the world economy have changed in the past generation. As the Wingspread Group emphasizes, we live in "a knowledge-based economy with a shortage of highly skilled workers at all levels and a surplus of unskilled applicants scrambling to earn a precarious living. Many of those unskilled applicants are college graduates, not high school dropouts."[15]

Whatever else my classmates and I may have questioned in 1971, we simply assumed that a college diploma was a one-way ticket to a good job with a bright future. We assumed that an expanding economy would keep expanding. We assumed that the wars, the weapons, and the other woeful injustices of the day would yield to the inexorable march of progress toward the inevitable realization of the American Dream. We assumed that tomorrow would be better than today.

---

[13] Id.
[14] Id.
[15] Id.

Now that tomorrow is here, today's graduates make no such assumptions. In the new world in which we find ourselves, we need urgently to be smarter, and to work smarter, than ever before if we hope to win our fair share of the world marketplace. Yet far too many of the young men and young women leaving our colleges today are, as the Wingspread Report so aptly puts it, "uneducated graduates."[16]

Uneducated, uninvolved, unaware, and all too often unemployed, many of today's graduates face the future with little more than the mere rudiments of the broad general knowledge and the critical thinking skills that it will take to succeed in the new century. Worse, they lack a common understanding. They lack the shared educational cement that has held America together in the past, and that is desperately needed now to bring this country together and hold it together as we confront the future.

In short, they lack a good liberal arts education.

As the Wingspread Group summarizes, "[E]very student needs the knowledge and understanding that can come only from the rigors of a liberal education. Such an education lies at the heart of developing both social and personal values. If the center of American society is to hold, a liberal education must be central to the undergraduate experience of all students. The essentials of a liberal education should be contained in a rigorous, required curriculum defined on each campus."[17]

For "[d]emocratic societies need a common ground, a shared frame of reference within which to encourage both diversity and constructive debate about the common good. A free people cannot enjoy the fruits of its liberty without collaborative efforts in behalf of community. Higher education has a central obligation to develop these abilities."[18]

In many ways, the report of the Wingspread Group is a restatement and a reaffirmation of much that my professors tried to teach me at Vanderbilt years ago. No doubt this can be attributed in no small measure to the participation of Chancellor Wyatt in the group's deliberations. Doubtless he had some significant say also in the soundness of the group's broad recommendations —to take the values of liberal learning seriously again in higher education, to put student learning first once more in the nation's colleges and universities, and to reach beyond

---

[16] Id.
[17] Id.
[18] Id.

the confines of educational tradition to find more collaborative and cost-effective ways of creating a nation of lifelong learners. Both implicit and explicit in these recommendations is the belief that heeding them will help solidify the common ground in America that seems to be fast slipping away.

During my time in the Congress, I worked with many others in trying our best to hold and harden our common ground. Numerous economic and educational initiatives of recent years have in common the goal of strengthening our democracy by investing in our people and by enhancing the sense of community we share as a people: Added investments in Head Start, child nutrition, and other children's programs. Fiscal overhaul of the Pell Grant program. Reform of the overall student loan program. New emphasis on school-to-work programs and on training and retraining programs of all kinds. Creation of the America Corps as the vanguard of a new national service program. The enactment of the Goals 2000 legislation that established lofty national educational standards to take us into the new century.

All these programs, all these advances, and many more, have been aimed at achieving common understanding by adding to our common ground. Many of them remain at risk. But there are many who still serve in Washington who realize that only common understanding and common ground can yield the common purpose we need to survive and succeed as a democracy.

The Wingspread Report remains a needed reminder of the urgency of focusing much more of our governmental attention on improving higher education. Yet what is most striking about the report, and perhaps what is most enduring about the report, is its realization that, however helpful and however desirable they may be, programmatic advances by the federal government are not in any way an anodyne for what ails higher education in America. The recommendations of the Wingspread Group are not aimed primarily at the President and the Congress. They are aimed primarily at the prevailing powers within higher education itself.

In fact, the group's most important contribution is its challenge to each and every one of America's several thousand colleges and universities to conduct a "self-assessment" of its success in responding to the American imperative for higher expectations and higher standards in higher education. The report even includes a detailed checklist of questions for those institutions that may not know what questions to ask. Somewhere, Marchant and Swint are smiling.

My guess is that Vanderbilt conducts such "self-assessments" every day. I'd be surprised if it did not. After all these years, I'm still asking questions and still trying to find the answers, and I'm confident that Vanderbilt is as well. For both of us, the search for understanding continues.

As we summon our energy and our creativity as a nation to meet the challenge issued by the Wingspread Group, I don't know what questions are on Vanderbilt's checklist. Yet I do know this: I for one would be content if every young man and every young woman in America could have the same opportunity I had to receive a liberal arts education at a university such as Vanderbilt.

I was able to seize that opportunity only because Vanderbilt reached out to me and gave me a chance. And the best way I know to thank my alma mater is by working to give others the same chance I had for a quality liberal arts education.

Like my grandfather, and like the Wingspread Group, I believe emphatically in the transforming potential of a college education. I know the difference a college education made in my life. I can only imagine the difference such an education might have made in the life of my grandfather.

At the top of our national checklist must be this: We must remember the vital connection between education and democracy. We must give every American the chance to become something more as an individual so that, together, we can become something more as a nation. We must "teach liberty" by teaching the liberal arts, and by teaching how, in their highest form, the liberal arts lead most truly to a life of democratic service. And, above all, we must learn how to serve others best, and thus serve democracy best, not only by *learning,* but by *living* the liberal arts.

Teaching is one way to serve. Serving in the Congress is another. There are many other ways to serve as well. Everyone can serve in some way. Everyone can practice the highest form of the liberal arts. Everyone can join in the search for common understanding and common ground.

There is often a tendency in higher education to believe that to escape mediocrity, we must embrace elitism. There is often an inclination to believe that the privilege of an education should be limited to the privileged. There is often a temptation to believe that we must choose somehow between "equality" and excellence.

In America, we must choose both. Vanderbilt has chosen both. I know. I'm proof of it. And I'm just one of many. I'm just one of many who have been challenged and changed by Vanderbilt's commitment to both equality and excellence in education.

In my own ongoing "self-assessment," I find that I miss Vandy more and more as time passes by. I miss the magnolia blossoms, the musty books, and the night music in Mims Hall. I miss the electric excitement of a classroom afire with thought. I miss the scholar's life.

The education ideal is still Socrates at one end of the bench and the student at the other. It will remain so. But I might be persuaded that the philosopher's bench can be found beneath a magnolia tree not far from Kirkland Hall at Vanderbilt University. And if he were still here, I know my Grandaddy could be.

Chapter Seven

An Education in 404 Pages

If asked what America needs most today, I would reply: America needs a good liberal arts education.

But a good education is getting ever harder to find and afford, and not everyone can find the time to get a good education by reading all the "Great Books."

With this in mind, I suggest the following list for the consideration of all who feel in need of a good liberal arts education. This list can provide an education, not by reading a few hundred books, but by reading only a few hundred pages.

My recommended reading list for all Americans is:

Ralph Waldo Emerson, "Self-Reliance." ... We must be true to ourselves. Only by being true to ourselves as individuals will we be able to build a true society of individuals that will be worth sharing. We must never be afraid to stand alone in the crowd. (26 pages)

Alexis de Tocqueville, "The Principle of Interest Rightly Understood," from Democracy in America. ... Our real self-interest, as individuals and as a society of individuals, is in our broader as well as our narrower needs, and in our needs tomorrow as well as our needs today. We need others, and we have obligations to others. (4 pages)

Thucydides, "The Melian Dialogue," from History of the Peloponnesian War. ... "The strong do what they can and the weak suffer what they must." We may be stronger than others, but that does not make us right. All of history is an effort to prove that might does not make right. (6 pages)

James Madison, Number 10 and Number 51, The Federalist Papers. ... For government to help make right into might for all of us,

---

This chapter appears under this title and in slightly different form in Vanderbilt Magazine (Spring 2003).

government must be founded on an understanding of the reality of human nature. "If men were angels, no government would be necessary." We are capable of both good and evil. We can always make progress. We can never achieve perfection. (11 pages)

Adam Smith, "Of the Division of Labour," from The Wealth of Nations. ... Like government, all economics must begin with an awareness of our unchanging human nature. We tend toward exchange, trade, and an ever-expanding and ever-deepening division of labor. It is in our nature. (21 pages)

Voltaire, Letter 15, "On the System of Gravitation," from Letters on England. ... Unique to human nature is human reason. Reason made science. Science made the modern world. Science can help us make an even better world. (9 pages)

Richard Feynman, "The Uncertainty of Science," from The Meaning of It All. ... Science gives us our technology. Science does not give us our values. And science does not give us certainty. Science is a way of living with uncertainty and also with doubt. (26 pages)

Plato, "The Cave," from The Republic. ... We must doubt. The world may not be as it seems. We live in shadows, and we must search for the light of the truth. (9 pages)

Michel de Montaigne, "Of Cannibals," from The Essays. ... Local custom is not necessarily eternal truth. There are other ways to live and think. There are other ways to search. We Americans do not have a monopoly on wisdom, virtue, or truth. (15 pages)

John Stuart Mill, "Of the Liberty of Thought and Discussion," from On Liberty. ... Truth emerges from free and open discussion among free individuals in a society that cherishes the freedom of thought. Truth welcomes debate. Truth welcomes criticism. (44 pages)

Karl Popper, Chapter 10, The Open Society and Its Enemies. ... In the "closed society," there is no freedom of thought. In the "open society," the individual is free to think and to choose. The freest society is the "open society" where the individual is free to make the most possible personal decisions about how to live. (32 pages)

Fyodor Dostoevsky, "The Grand Inquisitor," from <u>The Brothers Karamazov.</u> ... In deciding how to live, we have a choice as individuals. We can choose to let others think for us, and be slaves. Or we can choose to think for ourselves, and be free. Choose. (24 pages)

Martin Luther King, Jr., "Letter from the Birmingham Jail." ... We *all* must be free to choose. Freedom belongs to everyone. Lest we forget. (6 pages)

Virginia Woolf, Chapter 6, <u>A Room of One's Own</u>. ... And "everyone" includes women. Again, lest we forget. (20 pages)

Abraham Lincoln, "The Gettysburg Address." ... A lot of good people have died so that we can be free to choose. A lot. Never forget. (1 page)

Suetonius, "Augustus, Afterward Deified," Sections 61-96, from <u>The Twelve Caesars.</u> ... Be skeptical of those you choose to entrust with your freedom. They, too, are human. Even Caesar Augustus, to seem taller, wore lifts in his sandals. (20 pages)

George Orwell, "Politics and the English Language." ... Some of our leaders will lie to us. They will use words without meanings. They will hide behind empty phrases. Make them accountable. (12 pages)

Edmund Burke, "Letter to the Sheriffs of Bristol." ... The best leaders will help keep us free by telling us what we truly need to hear — and not just what we want to hear. We need their judgment, and not just their echo. (35 pages)

Samuel Johnson, Number 21, <u>The Rambler.</u> ... We are none of us immune to the frailties of human nature. We each imagine that we are superior in some way to others. We are not. Be humble. (5 pages)

Immanuel Kant, "On Perpetual Peace." ... Despite our nature, despite our frailties, we can be better than we are. Thus, the world can be better than it is. Keep trying. (33 pages)

Henry David Thoreau, "On Seeing," from his <u>Journal.</u> ... Try to see. Seeing is understanding. "We cannot see anything until we are possessed with the idea of it, and then we can hardly see anything else." Keep looking. (3 pages)

Plutarch, "On Contentment." ... Look not for fame or fortune. Fame is hollow. Fortune is fickle. We must find contentment in life no matter what blows life deals us. Keep living. (28 pages)

Soren Kierkegaard, "The Story of Abraham," from <u>Fear and Trembling</u>. ... Reason alone does not suffice for living. Reason can only take us just so far toward understanding. Beyond that, we must make the "leap to faith." Keep believing. (8 pages)

William Hazlitt, "On the Feeling of Immortality in Youth." ... But believe in this world as well as the next. When we are young, we all think we will never die. We will. Life is short. Life is meant to be lived. So seize the day. (6 pages)

This is my list.

Total: 404 pages.

Of course, much is missing here. Poetry. Fiction. Song. Scripture. Shakespeare. The Bill of Rights. The Sermon on the Mount. And a whole library filled with a whole lot more.

My list could go on. Your list would surely be different. But try starting here. Starting with this list will give you —and will give every American —an education in 404 pages.

Chapter Eight

Poetry About Butter

In the darkest days of the Second World War, the French philosopher Simone Weil was in exile in England. She went to work there for General Charles De Gaulle's Free French in London. Although Hitler and the Nazis occupied France, Weil was given the task of thinking and writing about what a free France should be following the war. The result was one of her finest works, The Need for Roots.[1]

In the report that became that book, Weil focused her decidedly original mind on numerous timeless political, social, and economic issues. One of those issues was the choice that nations always face between martial and peaceful pursuits —the choice between "guns and butter." She wrote, "When men are offered the choice between guns and butter, although they prefer butter so very much more than guns, a mysterious fatality compels them, in spite of themselves, to choose guns. There isn't enough *poetry about butter...*"[2]

Poetry about butter? Who would bother to write poetry about butter?

The sheer unlikelihood of the question suggests the answer. Just how much poetry is there about the "guns" of war? Just how much is there about the "butter" of trade? And what are the consequences?

Writing was invented by scribes in ancient Mesopotamia to record the results of commercial transactions. It was the accounting of the traders of antiquity that made it possible for the first time for us to express the poetry within us in cuneiform with a stylus on tablets of clay. Almost all of the ancient Sumerian texts we have discovered are contracts, bills of sale, and the like.[3] Back then, we might have expected our poetry to be about butter. Since then, far more often, our poetry has been about guns. From the ancient siege of Troy to the recent siege of Baghdad, from the

---

[1] Simone Weil, The Need for Roots: Prelude to a Declaration of Duties Towards Mankind (London and New York: Routledge, 2002) [1949].
[2] Id. at 96.
[3] By one reckoning, ninety-five percent. *See* Chester G. Starr, A History of the Ancient World, 3rd Ed. (Oxford: Oxford University Press, 1983), 49 [1965].

epic songs of Homer to the epic "shock and awe" on CNN, we have, far more often than not, glorified, not butter and trade, but guns and war.

The six hundred of the Light Brigade charge valiantly into the valley of death.[4] The stained stones are kissed by the English dead.[5] Some corner of a foreign field is forever England.[6] In Flanders fields, the poppies grow.[7] In English poetry, in all our poetry, war is glorified and trade is trivialized. Even the poetry that denounces war is nevertheless always *about* war.

"Do not weep, maiden, for war is kind."[8] But is it? Is it really? We all march to the metered memory of "John Brown's Body,"[9] but how many of us might profit from having other poems to march by? Where is the measured meter about the marketplace?

We have poetry aplenty about battles and barricades, about blood and bones, and about "the stench of corpses rotting in front of the front-line trench."[10] At battle's end, the tattered flag still waves in glory over "the land of the free and the home of the brave."[11] But, amid "the rockets' red glare,"[12] amid all the stars that spangle, where are the poetic bars about the glories of trade that help keep the flag flying?

Where is the poetry about cross-country freight trains, about seagoing cargo-container ships, and about long-haul semi-tractor trailers? Where is the poetry about letters of credit, about bills of lading, and about customs declarations? Where is the poetry about, yes, the ching-ching of the ring of the cash register? Where is the poetry about butter?

Poetry about butter —poetry about trade —is essential to us if we hope to make the right choices between guns and butter. For trade is not only about butter. Trade is about life. Trade is about freedom. Trade helps make us free. Trade helps keep us free. The ways of trade are ways and means to the full flourishing of life that can be facilitated by the wise exercise of freedom.

---

[4] Alfred, Lord Tennyson, "The Charge of the Light Brigade."
[5] Wilfrid Owen, "Greater Love."
[6] Rupert Brooke, "The Soldier."
[7] John McCrae, "In Flanders Fields."
[8] Stephen Crane, "War is Kind."
[9] Stephen Vincent Benet, "John Brown's Body."
[10] Siegfried Sassoon, "The Aftermath."
[11] Francis Scott Key, "The Star-Spangled Banner."
[12] Id.

In my youth, in my time in law school, I read the American court cases from the 1930s about butter and oleomargarine in which federal judges in the United States first came to terms with the broad regulatory reach of the interstate commerce clause in the United States Constitution. I learned much from those cases about the many nuances of "butter-fat content." There is much at stake, I learned, in simply defining "butter."

Years later, in my time as a Member of the Congress of the United States, I dealt with the esoteric statutes that provide for federal price supports for butter and other dairy products. The eloquence of the debates over butter in the Congress can occasionally evoke echoes of the likes of Webster and Clay. At one time, I knew precisely how many creameries there were in the 15th Congressional District of Florida.

In the past eight years, in my time as a Member of the Appellate Body of the World Trade Organization, I have considered contentious cases involving international trade in butter and other dairy products involving all the far corners of the world. I have been immersed in recent years in the many mysteries of the global butter trade. Not least, I have learned in my time at the WTO that the trading nations of the world take their trade in butter *seriously*.

Thus, I have had occasion in my life to ponder much that there is to ponder on butter. However, I have yet to see even one single line of poetry that has been written *about* butter. I have seen much poetry about the supposed glories of war. I have yet to see any poetry about the glories of trade.

One of Weil's French forebears, Gustave Flaubert, once said that "every lawyer carries within him the broken remnants of a poet."[13] If so, this can scarcely be seen in what I have seen of what lawyers have written about butter. Much of it does not rise to the level of prose, much less poetry.

Why does this matter? This matters because poetry itself matters. Poetry is the outer manifestation of our inner life. Poetry reveals a world far more real to us than the semblance of any outer seeming. Poetry is our wishful expression as a striving, struggling species of the world that ought to be. Nothing reveals more about who we are and who we hope to be than what inspires our poetry.

---

[13] Gustave Flaubert, Madame Bovary, translated by Gerard Hopkins (London: Oxford World's Classics, 1998), 267 [1856].

For this reason, poetry has consequences. The abundance of poetry about war has consequences. Equally, the absence of poetry about trade has consequences. The glorification of war helps lead to an habituation to war. The trivialization of trade helps lead to a denigration of trade. Our children learn to prefer conflict over commerce, guns over butter.

This is nothing new with humanity. Recall some among the Greek inheritors of Homer. In classical Greece, trade was encouraged by Solon in Athens, but forbidden by Lycurgus in Sparta. The Athenian port of Piraeus welcomed the world. Landlocked Sparta shunned the world. The Athenian pottery "globalized" the Mediterranean. The Spartan army militarized the Peloponnese. The Athenians invented the idea of a free and open society. The Spartans invented nothing.

Athens was an open society where art, architecture, music, drama, science, mathematics, philosophy, and poetry all flowed from free and open minds, and flourished amid a prosperity that was created in no small part by trade. Sparta was a closed society where trade was forbidden largely because trade would have led to the spread of all the creative ideas of freedom. The citizens of Athens included traders whose ships sailed all the surrounding seas. The obedient and disciplined citizens of Sparta were not traders; they were soldiers. To be sure, both Athens and Sparta engaged in war. The nearly thirty years of war between them did much to destroy them both. But the Athenians tolerated war as a necessity; the Spartans glorified it as a way of life.[14]

The Athenians and the Spartans manifested two endlessly competing tendencies in our unchanging human nature. Given what we know of our nature, the power of war as an inspiration for poetry is understandable. War is a fundamental, elemental struggle among men. War has stakes that are ultimate. The risks of war are risks of life and limb. The risks of trade usually are risks only of livelihood. Since the time of the Greeks, since the epic time of The Iliad, there has been poetry about war. There always will be.

The unavoidability of war as an inspiration for poetry is likewise understood. Simone Weil was a bit of a pacifist and perhaps also a bit of a saint. Even so, she did not insist that we should not have fought Hitler. Indeed, she died while serving in her own way in the struggle against

---

[14] *See* H.D.F. Kitto, The Greeks (London: Penguin Books, 1951), 90-91, 100-101.

Hitler. She died in England in 1943, at the age of just thirty-four, soon after writing her call for "poetry about butter." As T.S. Eliot put it, she died "partly, it would seem, as the result of self-mortification, in refusing to take more food than the official rations of ordinary people in France...."[15] Quite literally, she starved herself to death. She died in service to a principle.

I would not have us starve ourselves to death. Rather, I would have us all have plenty of butter. Still, some principles are worth dying for. Some wars are worth fighting. Some wars serve the cause of freedom and, thus, the cause of life. Our ability to engage in trade and in the many other enriching and ennobling pursuits of peace sometimes depends on our willingness to engage in war. Hitlers will always be among us, and the Hitlers among us must always be stopped.

The unhappy fact that war is sometimes necessary does not, however, make war glorious. War is sometimes necessary. War is never glorious. War may *seem* glorious. But there is no glory in war. There is glory only in what enriches and ennobles life. War does not enrich or ennoble life. War only destroys life. "The paths of glory lead but to the grave."[16] Trade may *seem* tedious, not glorious. But trade is filled with life. Trade creates life by creating freedom. Trade enriches and ennobles life by making it possible for us to be more fully and more freely human. The Athenians lived; the Spartans merely survived. Athens still lives; Sparta has long since turned to dust.

Some say that trade turns the individual human being into a commodity —into a thing. This is not so. Trade helps give each of us, as individuals, the chance to choose, and, thus, trade helps make it possible for each of us, as individuals, to choose *not* to be a thing. It is war that transforms the individual human being into a thing. As Weil wrote in one of her memorable essays, on The Iliad, the force of war turns everybody who is subject to war into a thing. "Those who use it and those who endure it are turned to stone."[17] War is not glorious, because war robs us of all that makes us human.

Consider the lament in The Iliad of Andromache, the noble wife of Hector, the heroic prince of Troy, when she learns that her husband has

---

[15] T.S. Eliot, "Preface," Weil, The Need for Roots, supra, at X.
[16] Thomas Gray, "Elegy Written in a Country Churchyard."
[17] Simone Weil, "*The Iliad* or the Poem of Force," Sian Miles, ed., Simone Weil: An Anthology (New York: Grove Press, 1986), 162, 184.

been slain by Achilles of Greece. Summoned from her loom by the sounds of the Trojan women weeping for their slain hero on the ramparts of the besieged city, she watches as the vengeful and victorious Achilles drags the body of her beloved husband behind his chariot and before the horrified eyes of the grieving Trojans.

Andromache vows to burn all of Hector's fine clothing in a last tribute. In Robert Fagles' splendid translation of Homer, she promises her slain husband, "Now, by god, I'll burn them all, blazing to the skies! No use to you now, they'll never shroud your body —but they will be your glory burned by the Trojan men and women in your honor!"[18]

Yet where is the glory in this? For all of her promises to him, her husband was dead. He was gone forever. "And a thick cloud of dust rose up from the man they dragged, his dark hair swirling round that head so handsome once, all tumbled low in the dust...."[19] In Weil's words, even "the hero becomes a *thing* dragged behind a chariot in the dust...."[20] The "glory" of war turns all that is human into dust.

If we took Weil's advice, if we wrote more "poetry about butter," we would be more human, because we would have less need for fighting wars. If we wrote more poetry about how trade leads to life, we would need to write less poetry about how war leads to death and dust.

Poets make many choices in writing poetry. Weil explained that, in arranging words, and in choosing words, poets "must simultaneously bear in mind matters on at least five or six different planes of composition."[21] The number of syllables in the verses. The grammatical sequence of words. The logical sequence of words. The purely musical sequence of the sounds of the words. The rhymes and the rhythms of the words. These, she explained, are among the many choices a poet must make.

Like poets, we, too, have many choices to make in choosing between guns and butter. What will we choose? Will it be guns? Or will

---

[18] Homer, The Iliad, translated by Robert Fagles (New York: Penguin Books, 1990), 558.
[19] Id. at 554.
[20] Weil, *The Iliad* or the Poem of Force," supra, at 164.
[21] Weil, The Need for Roots, supra, at 214.

it be butter? Will it be war? Or will it be trade? Do we have a "rendezvous with death,"[22] or do we have a rendezvous with life?

The choice is ours to make.

What rhymes with "butter"?

---

[22] Alan Seeger, "I Have a Rendezvous with Death."

Chapter Nine

The Double Rainbow

I was roused from my reading on a lazy Sunday afternoon in Geneva by my wife's voice at the window.

"Look," she said. "A double rainbow."

I put aside my book, rose from my chair, and rushed over to join her. She pointed outside our sixth floor window, past the plane trees in the *Place Des Alpes* below, and over to the blue sky above the nearby lake of Geneva. There, in the aftermath of the afternoon's rain, was the dual arc of a double rainbow.

I had never seen a double rainbow before. Neither had Rebecca. Our eyes on the sky, our faces pressed to the pane of the window, we gazed, transfixed, at this sudden burst of color and light into the familiar routine of our lives. Together, we called to our daughter in the next room. "Jamey. Quick. Look. There's a double rainbow."

In what passes for haste in a twelve-year old, Jamey strolled into the room and up to the window. Her head phones in place, her music in her ears, she peered out the window, and pronounced a considered judgment.

"Cool," she said, and then she turned and strolled away.

Rebecca and I remained, rapt, at the window, watching this strange new sight in the Swiss sky. As the sun began to sink toward the west, we continued to look toward the east, through the mist of what remained of the rain. We marveled at the bright colors, the striking shape, and the sheer surprise of what we saw so unexpectedly, and so extraordinarily, on what we had expected would be an ordinary Sunday afternoon.

The sky was filled to overflowing with the curve of two translucent arcs. One embraced the other in a cradle of color. The long curve of the cradle ascended from the smooth surface of the lake to the rocky heights of the hill called the Saleve that looms beyond the lake and beyond the slope of the old city of Geneva.

The colors of the inner arc were bold and vivid. They emblazoned the sky. The colors of the outer arc were less striking, but were no less stirring. The fainter colors of the outer arc seemed to our watching eyes more furtive, more fleeting, more suggestive of the passing fancy that a rainbow often seems to be to human eyes.

Rebecca was the first of us to notice that the colors in the two arcs were reversed. On the inner, brighter bow, the colors ranged from violet on the inside to red on the outside. On the outer, dimmer bow, the colors ranged, instead, from red on the inside to violet on the outside. The second of the two bows seemed to us to be somehow a mirrored reflection of the first. Together, the two arcs adorned a deep blue sky that still shimmered with a scattered memory of the recent rain.

"My heart leaps up when I behold a rainbow in the sky."[1] So said the romantic poet, William Wordsworth, in one of his most famous poems, "The Rainbow." Having beheld the double rainbow, I know now what Wordsworth must have been trying to say some two hundred years ago with those well-known words.

I know, too, that Wordsworth cannot have beheld too many rainbows from the windows of Dove Cottage, his rustic home in the "Lake District" of northwest England where he lived when he wrote so many of his "lyrical ballads" about nature. Even today, very little light passes through the small windows of Dove Cottage. What is more, according to the matronly Wordsworthean who spends her days trying to enlighten American tourists on the special sensibilities of the Lake Poets, the windows of Dove Cottage are considerably larger today than they were in Wordsworth's time.

Thus, Wordsworth must have seen the rainbow that inspired the single stanza of his poem while walking outside, in the garden behind his cottage at "town's end" in Grasmere, or in the hills overlooking the meres where he hiked long hours of every day in search of poetic inspiration. Perhaps it was in those hills where the sight of a rainbow inspired the realization he expressed in his poem that "the child is father of the man."[2]

Perhaps, after seeing that rainbow, he hurried back from the hills, as he so often did, to immortalize his realization on paper before the

---

[1] William Wordsworth, "My Heart Leaps Up," or "The Rainbow."
[2] Id.

inspiration passed. Perhaps he returned quickly through the private door that had been carved in the back of the cottage so that the day-to-day domestic interruptions of his household would not cause him to lose his inspirations before he could put them to paper in the favorite writing chair upstairs where he kept a faithful record of all his heart's leapings.[3] Perhaps this was how we came to have the timeless truth of this timeless verse.

But, I wonder: did Wordsworth ever see a *double* rainbow? And what was the height of his heart's leaping if he did? Two centuries later, sitting here in my own favorite writing chair, I wonder, too: can *our* hearts leap in quite the same way as his did at the sight of a rainbow today?

Back then, another poet, Wordsworth's younger contemporary, John Keats, also wrote a rhyme about rainbows. Keats worried that the continued march of science would, in the future, prevent our hearts from leaping at the sight of a rainbow. In his poem, he warned:

> Do not all charms fly
> At the mere touch of cold philosophy?
> There was an awful rainbow once in heaven:
> We know her woof, her texture; she is given
> In the dull catalogue of common things.
> Philosophy will clip an angel's wings.
> Conquer all mysteries by rule and line,
> Empty the haunted air, and gnomed mine
> Unweave a rainbow.[4]

Keats feared that science would diminish beauty and defeat wonder. He was concerned that the ever-unfolding scientific insistence on finding an explanation for the natural world would deprive us of our heart-leaping delight in all that God gave us in His gift of nature. Keats worried that, in weaving an answer to *how* the natural world works, the "cold philosophy" of science would "unweave a rainbow" and leave the colorful spectacle of a rainbow as only one more colorless listing in "the dull catalogue of common things." Although, to my knowledge, Keats never said so, presumably these worries would apply equally to the unweaving of a *double* rainbow.

---

[3] Wordsworth lived in Dove Cottage from 1799 to 1808. His poem "The Rainbow" was written in 1802 and published in 1807. *See* Hunter Davies, <u>William Wordsworth</u> (Thrupp, Gloucestershire: Sutton Publishing, 2003) [1980].
[4] John Keats, "Lamia."

As Keats foresaw, scientists have done much since his day to clip the angel's wings. In their precise and prosaic way, in the mundane matter-of-factness of their experimentalism, in the cumulative process of their relentless empiricism, scientists have proceeded, since his day, to unmask, one by one, the mysterious marvels of the natural world. As a result, marvels have ceased, for many of us, to be marvels. Scientists have unwoven many of the previous mysteries of the universe. The unweaving of the rainbow is but one example of the ongoing unraveling of the scientific *how* of the world around us.

But, even in Keats' day, scientists had already learned a lot about the *how* of rainbows. They had learned much about the science of rainbows in the many centuries since one of the first of the poets was inspired to tell us, in the Book of Genesis, of Noah's ark, and of the reassuring rainbow's arc that followed the flood from a great rain.[5] They had learned much over a long time about *how* it is that rainbows sometimes follow a rainfall.[6] It was an awareness of this knowledge, an apprehension of this knowledge, and an anticipation of the eventual impact of this knowledge, that caused Keats to worry.

As Keats knew, this knowledge about the *how* of rainbows had been acquired gradually. In ancient times, Aristotle, in classifying the natural world, classified rainbows with echoes and with reflections in mirrors. He concluded that the rainbow, whatever its cause, was a reflection of colors from sunlight in the clouds. He noticed also that a rainbow always has seven distinct colors —ranging outward across a spectrum of colors from red to orange to yellow to green to blue to indigo and to violet.[7]

In the Middle Ages, in the thirteenth century, that curious Englishman, the Franciscan scholar Roger Bacon, realized that rainbows only occur when the sun is low in the sky. As part of his innovative experiments applying geometry to the study of optics, he measured the

---

[5] *See* Genesis 8:13 – 9:12.

[6] The standard scientific textbook on rainbows and other atmospheric optical effects is Robert Greenler, Rainbows, Halos, and Glories (Cambridge: Cambridge University Press, 1990). For more on this distinguished scholar of rainbows, *see* Professor Greenler's eloquent memoir, Chasing the Rainbow: Recurrences in the Life of a Scientist (Elton Wolf, 2000). And *see also* Carl Boyer, The Rainbow: From Myth to Mathematics (Princeton: Princeton University Press, 1957).

[7] Aristotle, *Meteorologico* III, and *De sensu et sensibili*, IV, 442.

maximum elevation of a rainbow at 42 degrees above the horizon. He observed that, if the sun is any higher, there is no rainbow.[8]

Later, in the fourteenth century, Theodoric of Freiberg, a Dominican monk who was equally curious about rainbows, conducted experiments that showed that light bounces off drops of water, and also that light bends when it bounces off drops of water. From these experiments, he concluded that rainbows result from the convergence of the light of the sun with the water of a rain.[9]

Like so much else of that medieval time, Theodoric's work was, unfortunately, lost. It remained lost for half a millennium. However, his experiments and his conclusions were largely duplicated, unknowingly, in the seventeenth century by the French philosopher and polymath Rene Descartes. In his Discourse on Method, in 1637, Descartes explained how he peered at the passage of sunlight through a large sphere he had made to test his own theories of optics. Like Theodoric, he concluded that a rainbow results from sunlight passing through a spherical drop of rainwater.[10]

Then, in 1704, in his famous experiments with optics, Isaac Newton showed how light streaming through a prism is broken into a whole spectrum of colors ranging from red to violet. Moreover, he showed how light, when it passes through raindrops, is dispersed into an array of different colors that are all at different angles and that, therefore, are all on slightly different paths. Hence, he said, we see a rainbow in stripes of different colors.[11]

Thus, by Keats' time, scientists had reached some tentative conclusions about the scientific secrets of the rainbow. By his time, scientists had learned much about just *how* it is that a rainbow happens to appear sometimes in the sky after a rain. And those of that time who knew something of science —such as Keats, a former medical student — were well aware that scientists had largely unwoven the scientific *how* of the rainbow.

---

[8] For details on the fascinating life of Roger Bacon, a man far ahead of his time, *see* Brian Clegg, The First Scientist: The Visionary Genius of Roger Bacon (London: Carroll & Graf, 2003).

[9] *See* Stephen Kramer and Daniel Mark Duffy, Theodoric's Rainbow (W.H. Freeman, 1995).

[10] Rene Descartes, Discourse on Method (1637).

[11] Isaac Newton, Optics (1704).

Since Keats' time, those tentative scientific conclusions have largely been confirmed. Today, two centuries later, the secrets of the rainbow are revealed for all of us to read in the pages of virtually every basic science textbook. Moreover, today, those of us who are in too much of a hurry to take the trouble of finding and reading a textbook, can simply consult the rainbow of information that is readily available about rainbows on the Internet.[12] Any one of us, if we wish, can read the scientific explanation of *how* rainbows happen. Today, we *all* can know the secrets of the rainbow.

It turns out that the scientific surmises of Keats' time were largely right. Scientists continue to tell us today that rainbows are caused by the bouncing back (reflection) and the bending (refraction) of sunlight within raindrops. This process of reflection and refraction in a raindrop is, as Newton concluded, similar to what happens when light passes through a prism. When sunlight passes through a raindrop, as when any light passes through a prism, its different wavelengths are bounced and bent by slightly different amounts so that the light separates into all the colors of the light spectrum. These separate colors are sent by this process on slightly different paths, thus spreading into the bright array of all the different colors of a rainbow.

Theodoric and Descartes were right, then, in concluding that rainbows require both water and light. This explains why rainbows only occur in the sky after a rain, and why they only occur there when the sun is shining. Moreover, the physics of optics are such that a rainbow can only be seen in the sky when the sun is at your back, as it was when Rebecca and I gazed out our apartment window in Geneva at the double rainbow. Further, and, again, because of the peculiar physics of optics, rainbows only occur when the angle between the incoming sunlight and the raindrop is within a very narrow range. Roger Bacon was right about that angle of 42 degrees.

More, a rainbow is not really a bow. A rainbow is a circle. The bouncing and bending of sunlight within a raindrop actually creates a whole circle of colors. A rainbow looks like a bow instead of a circle only because the surface of the earth gets in the way when we see it. The higher we are when we see a rainbow, the more we see of the circle. If we were high enough —if we were much higher than Rebecca and I were in

---

[12] *See* online, for example, skyscapes.com/Sky or wonderquest.com/rainbow.circle.

our apartment building in Geneva —we might be able to see the whole circle of the rainbow.

What then, causes a *double* rainbow?

Scientists inform us today that a double rainbow is caused by *two* reflections and, thus, *two* resulting refractions of a ray of sunlight within a raindrop. Sometimes, not all of the incoming light is reflected out of a raindrop after only one bounce. Sometimes, some of the light remains in a raindrop after the first bounce, and so is bounced and bent inside that raindrop a second time. When this happens, there is a double rainbow.

The particular characteristics that we see in a double rainbow are likewise explained by scientists. The colors of the second, outer bow in a double rainbow can be reversed because the second reflection can cause a reversal of the image of the colors of the light —much like a mirror inverts an image. Further, the second, outer bow is dimmer than the brighter inner bow because some of the light is lost in the first of the two reflections.

Scientists insist that double rainbows are *not* unusual. Supposedly, they are commonplace. Supposedly, they are as routine as my reading on a Sunday afternoon. Supposedly, double rainbows are *not* rare. Double rainbows have, however, been rare for me. In my more than half a century of watching the skies after rainstorms, I have seen only the one that I happened to see on that Sunday afternoon when I was roused for once from my routine in Geneva. I may see another one tomorrow. I will certainly be watching. But, for me, for now, seeing a double rainbow remains a rare moment.

What have I concluded from this rare moment in my life? Does science really "unweave a rainbow"? Did my knowledge of some of the scientific secrets that explain the *how* of the double rainbow diminish for me its beauty, or dispel for me its wonder, when I saw *my* double rainbow? When I saw my double rainbow, did I really see *less* than others saw in the days before we knew all about all the reflections and all the refractions that contrive to make a double rainbow?

Was Keats right?

Philip Fisher, a distinguished professor of English literature at Harvard University, says "No." Professor Fisher has written an entire book in an effort to confront Keats' concern. He concludes that this concern is unfounded, and that science is not incompatible with an ongoing aesthetic appreciation of beauty, or with a continuing human expression of wonder, when confronted with the heart-leaping splendour of the natural world.[13]

Likewise, Richard Dawkins, the noted British science writer, says "No." He, too, has written an entire book on Keats' worries about the unweaving of the rainbow, and, he, too, concludes that these worries are unfounded. He claims that science helps us see more beauty. He claims, too, that the pursuits of science are inspired by wonder, and can lead us to still more wonder, as we continue to explore the natural world.[14]

For my part, I also say "No." For the most part, I believe that both of them are right. Keats was, I think, certainly right to worry that science might "unweave a rainbow." But, as I see the rainbow, it need not be that way. There is much that nature's weaving of a rainbow in the sky can yet mean to those who see it —whether they happen to know the scientific explanation of *how* a rainbow happens or not. I believe, too, that this is all the more so for a double rainbow.

I value the scientific method. Science is the foundation for the modern world. Science is indispensable to all we seek for humanity in the modern world. I did not serve for as long as I did on the science committee in the Congress of the United States without subscribing to a strong belief in the significance of the methods of science to the modern world. But there is, I am persuaded, more to us, there is more to all we seek, there is more to all we strive for, there is more to all we hope for from being human in our "modern" world, than can ever be revealed by the scientific method.

Soren Kierkegaard, the Danish theologian, shared this view. Kierkegaard was no scientist, but he gave much thought to what it means to be human in the modern, scientific world. Somewhere he said, "The whole of science is a parenthesis."[15] By this, he meant that science does not address —much less answer —the ultimate questions of human life.

---

[13] Philip Fisher, <u>Wonder, the Rainbow, and the Aesthetics of Rare Experiences</u> (Cambridge: Harvard University Press, 1999).

[14] Richard Dawkins, <u>Unweaving the Rainbow: Science, Delusion and the Appetite for Wonder</u> (New York: Houghton Mifflin, 1998).

[15] Quoted in T. M. Kirkwood, <u>What Is Human?</u> (London: Inter-Varsity Press, 1970), 58.

Our reliance on the ever-unfolding results of the scientific method has revolutionized how we live. Our application of science to how we live has made the modern world. Because of science, because of our adherence and our allegiance to the scientific method of trial and error, of testing by observation, we know more now than we have ever known before. And yet we know nothing at all about what we most want to know.

For not all things can be tested by the trial and error of observation. Knowing *how* does not help us to know *why*. We may know *how* a rainbow happens, but we do not know *why* it happens. The truth is, we do not know *why* anything happens. The methods of science, though powerful, though necessary, are, nevertheless, necessarily limited. Science may help improve *how* we live, but science cannot explain *why* we live. Science can show us the reflections and the refractions of the light of the natural world, but science cannot illuminate for us what we truly see when we study our own image in the mirror. What is more, science cannot tell us *why* we are here to see it. Science does not minister to that part of our heart that leaps at the sight of a rainbow.

Thus, we live within the parenthesis. We live in the confines of the world of science. The modern, scientific world is a world of our own making. It is a world we think we can know. It is a world we believe we can understand. And yet, still, at moments, at rare and unexpected moments, we see beyond the world of our own making. We see the sheer beauty of the natural world around us. We see the sheer miracle of the very existence of the world. And, in these rare and unexpected moments, we are reminded that there is far more to the world than we will ever begin to know or understand.

Living within the parenthesis, most of us tend not to think too often or too much about ultimate questions of knowledge or understanding. Living within the hurried humdrum of the modern, scientific world, we tend, as Robert Louis Stevenson once put it, to miss "that rainbow work of fancy that clothes what is naked and seems to ennoble what is base."[16] But, in rare moments, in all too rare moments, we are surprised by the sight of a rainbow. And, in the very rarest of moments, we are, some of us, so fortunate as to be surprised on a Sunday afternoon by the sudden sight of a double rainbow. And then our heart leaps.

---

[16] Robert Louis Stevenson, "The Lantern-Bearers," Across the Plains (London: Chatto and Windus, 1916), 138, 151.

William Hazlitt, the eloquent English essayist, was a friend of Keats and a critic of Wordsworth. Like them, and like me, he, too, shared the view that there is more to life, and more to being human, than science can teach us. Hazlitt was no theologian. Indeed, he was, despite his devout religious upbringing, undoubtedly a bit of a skeptic. But he, too, gave much thought to the ultimate question about what it means to be human in our modern, scientific world. And he, too, was a man who valued the rare moments of sudden insight in his own life.

Hazlitt was also a bit of a painter, and, for him, such moments often involved the beauties and wonders of paintings. He wrote rhapsodically "On the Pleasure of Painting." He valued the very act of painting as a way of seeing and, thus, as a way of knowing. In the act of painting, he wrote, "the dream and glory of the universe is made 'palpable to feeling as to sight.' —And see! A rainbow starts from the canvas with all its humid train of glory, as if it were drawn from its cloudy arch in heaven."[17]

Loving painting as he did, in his youth, Hazlitt roamed the English countryside, going from manor house to manor house, knocking on doors, and asking to be allowed to see the private art collections of the landed aristocrats. Once inside, he studied the pictures on their walls, and then kept the moments that became his memories of those pictures alive ever afterwards. One of his biographers relates that, "On each occasion he came away 'richer than the possessor' because the treasures he had come to see were 'stamped on his brain,' and lived there thenceforward, a clue to nature, and a test of art."[18]

Keats was much influenced by Hazlitt, and Keats might have been reassured by this thought. If Hazlitt was right, if we can keep such moments alive, if we can stamp them indelibly, and forever, in our memories, then Keats, perhaps, need not have worried. And, if this can be true of those rare moments when we see the beauty and wonder in the art of a painting, then surely this can also be true of those moments when we see the beauty and wonder in the arc of a rainbow. Surely this can be true of those moments when we see nature's art in painting a palette of

---

[17] William Hazlitt, "On the Pleasure of Painting," The Fight and Other Writings (London: Penguin Classics, 2000) 15, 18 [1821].

[18] A. C. Grayling, The Quarrel of the Age: The Life and Times of William Hazlitt (London: Phoenix Press, 2001), 64 – 65 [200], quoting P. D. Howe, ed. The Complete Works of William Hazlitt (in 21 volumes), Volume 8, page 14.

colors in the rainbow. And surely, too, this can be doubly true of the rare moment when we see a double rainbow. The beauty and wonder of a double rainbow can likewise be a clue to nature and a test of art. But more. The very *moment* when we chance to see a double rainbow can be a clue to, and a test of, what it means to be human.

The poets may be better than the rest of us at discerning this clue and passing this test. They, oftentimes, have a larger vision than the rest of us. They may come closer than the rest of us to making the most of such moments for themselves, and, through their poems, for all of us. Hazlitt, a writer, for the most part, of prose, not poetry, said that the poet "steals colours from the rainbow."[19] Wordsworth, the poet, was not by any means the only one of us whose heart has leaped up at the sight of a rainbow, but, in the stolen colors of his poem, he was able to tell the stirring story of such a sight, of such a rare moment, in a way that speaks to, and for, all of us. Had he seen a double rainbow, he might very well have written a second stanza to his poem that would have spoken to, and for, all of us all the more.

As "the child is the father of the man," so is the unexpected sight of a rainbow a creative spur to a poetic expression that speaks and soars in the most basic, the most fundamental language of what it means to be human. The sudden surprise, the sudden presence, the sudden arrival, of a rare moment of awareness of the surpassing beauty and the surpassing wonder of the world around us, the sudden occurrence of a rare moment of insight into the surpassing miracle of life itself, is a recurring source of human inspiration and human affirmation.

The poets can speak to this in their poetry. Hazlitt said, "The finest poetry…is…a bold and happy enunciation of truths and feelings deeply implanted in the mind…."[20] The finest poetry is an enunciation of truths that, in some measure, in some way, in some deep well of knowing, are known to all of us. Those truths are gleams in our eye; they are glimpses of the *why*. They are double rainbows that suddenly appear in the sky. The poets simply help us to see them.

The poets have been blessed and burdened by what it takes to take from our rare moments of insight —however rare and however

---

[19] William Hazlitt, "On the Prose-Style of Poets," The Fight and Other Writings, supra, 393, 398 [1826].
[20] William Hazlitt, "Poetry," The Fight and Other Writings, supra, 208, 210 [1829].

fleeting they may be —a truly human inspiration. The very best of them can take from such moments an inspiration that lasts, an inspiration that endures in undying words of truth that continue to speak to, and for, us all long after they themselves are gone. Wordsworth did so. So did Keats. So have many others in stanzas that continue to speak and soar through the ages. Such is the gift of the poets. Such is the gift that makes the finest poetry an abiding affirmation of the human spirit.

And yet, there is, I am persuaded, some poetry in each of us. Each of us, whether we happen to be a poet or not, harbors some measure of the human spirit. Each of us has some share of something that can be summoned from deep within us to express the human spirit. Each of us is numbered among those rare creatures that we call "human." Each of us experiences those rare moments of insight in our lives when we are reminded of what it means to be human. And each of us is capable of making such moments last.

I am neither a scientist nor a theologian. I am certainly no poet. Even so, I am human. I am only one among the billions who harbor, and who can express, the human spirit. But I am decidedly, determinedly human. I play my small part as a living part of a suffering, struggling, striving humanity. And I, too, have been blessed. For I have seen a double rainbow. I have seen it in a rare moment, and I intend to make that moment last. I intend to use whatever portion of poetry I can find within me to make of that moment a lasting memory of what it means to be human, and, thus, of what it means truly to be alive.

"The rainbow comes and goes," wrote Wordsworth.[21] And so it does. But, amid all the comings and goings of rainbows in billions of human lives, the memory of the moment in our own life when we saw a double rainbow can be made to last. And, thus, so, too, can our memory of the beauty we saw, the wonder we felt, and the sudden leap of our heart at the sheer surprise, the sheer delight, the sheer beholding of such a revealing and beckoning sight.

In the afternoons of our lives, we become accustomed to routine. The glory of the world around us is such that only rarely do we stop to

---

[21] William Wordsworth, "Ode on Intimations of Immortality." Wordsworth apparently began writing this famous poem on the day after he wrote "The Rainbow" in 1802. *See* Lionel Trilling, "The Immortality Ode," in Leon Wieseltier, ed. , The Moral Obligation to Be Intelligent: Selected Essays, Lionel Trilling (New York: Farrar Straus, Giroux, 2000) 33, 41 [1941].

notice it. The very miracle of life is such that only rarely do we pause to ponder it. We live on the surface; we surrender to routine. Then suddenly, unexpectedly, a voice calls from the window, a loving voice summons us from the somnolence of the routine of our lives, a reassuring voice wakens us from the dream of our drowsy superficiality, and the glory of the world and the miracle of life are revealed to us, and beckon to us, all at once in the radiant vision of a double rainbow.

Then we see the hitherto unimagined possibilities that await us in the firmament. Then we recollect what was, what is, and what may yet be. Then we remember what it really means to be alive. For, behold. Here, before us, is all we would ever have and hold. Here is joy. Here is life. Here is the moment that makes life worth living. Here is the world in which we ought to be living. Here is the very essence of being human. Here is the very height, the very hope of all our humanity. Here, before us, is the double rainbow.

The significance of the double rainbow is not the scientific *how*. The significance of the double rainbow is the glimpse it gives us of the everlasting *why*. In the bright colors of the double rainbow is the brief glimpse we are given on only a few occasions in life to see with our very own eyes the *why* of our lives. In the colors of the double rainbow, the invisible becomes visible, the unseen becomes the seen. Like Wordsworth, "We see into the life of things."[22] We see into the hidden heart of things. The *why* shines suddenly, briefly, before us. And here is our chance to see it, to seize it, and to make it last.

Because we *are* human, we *can* make it last. This brief glimpse of true knowledge, this brief glimpse of true understanding, can abide with us ever after. It is our humanity that makes this possible. The sky above us may be graced by a rainbow. The lake before us may mirror the image of a rainbow. The birds around us may adorn a rainbow with their flight. But only those of us who are human can really *see* a rainbow, because only we really *know* that it is there. And because we alone know that it is there, we alone can make it last.

This is the uniqueness of being human. For, like the rainbow, we humans are a rare painting of nature. We are a rare and special work from the palette of the natural Creation. We are nature's most various artifice; we are nature's most mysterious secret. In our solitary human

---

[22] Id.

consciousness, in our unique awareness that we are "here" and that the rainbow is "there," in our ability truly to *see* a rainbow, we may very well be nature's masterpiece.

And, just as humanity is unique in all of Creation, so is every single one of us who is human unique as an individual part of Creation. In this, we also resemble the rainbow. Every rainbow, the scientists tell us, is unique. It is a rainbow that is seen from our own unique angle of vision; it is seen from our own unique point of view. Thus, the rainbow that each of us sees is a rainbow that is all our very own. It is one of a kind. And, when each of us sees a rainbow, we are reminded that we, too, are each one of a kind.

In the colors of the rainbow, we see, for a moment, a numinous vision of the true colors of our unique, our very own selves. We see, for a moment, the enduring truth that is there deep within ourselves. We see, for a moment, who and what we truly are. We are snatched, for a moment, from the mud and the motion of our mundane lives, to catch a glimpse, a glimmer, a shimmer, a rainbow's ray, of the way we are supposed to be. When we see a rainbow, we see, for just a moment, the *why*.

Further, in being human, we not only resemble the rainbow. We also resemble the raindrops. For, like the raindrops, we shine for a moment in the sun, and then we fade away. But also, like the raindrops, throughout that moment, throughout that all too brief moment, the light of life is reflected and refracted within each and every one of us. And, when we see a double rainbow, when we see those two bright bows in the sky, we are reminded that, like the raindrops, we, too, each have it within us to make of our life a rainbow, and that somehow we must each strive to make such a rainbow of our life that it will never fade away.

Life seems to fade away. As it fades, we ask, like Wordsworth, "What then remains?"[23] What moments remained with Keats as, just twenty-six, he lay dying, his finest melodies perhaps still unheard, in a rented room overlooking the Spanish Steps in Rome in 1821? What moments remained with Hazlitt as, only fifty-two, he lay dying, his noblest essays perhaps still unwritten, in the back room of a boarding house in Soho in London in 1830? And what moments remained with Wordsworth as, at eighty, he lay dying, his mind and his memory ebbed away, his

---

[23] William Wordsworth, "The Excursion."

happy years of roaming the hills behind him, his brightest rainbows perhaps still unseen, in an honored bed not far away from his beloved Dove Cottage?

What rare moments remained for them as their lives faded away? What redeeming light remained for them? What rainbows did they still see? And, when life fades for us, when the last light lingers in the fading, what rainbows will we still see that have inspired our own hearts' leaping?

Most moments are soon forgotten. One moment is always slipping away into the past to make way for another. Our memory paves the way for the passage of the moments by clearing away the accumulating clutter in the memory banks of our brains to make way for yet another "here" and for yet another "now." Scientists assure us that all our memories are still there, locked away, stored away, somewhere deep inside us. No memory, they say, is ever erased. Our memory does not fail us, they say. It only seems so.

Still, we do seem to forget. Life, though short, is long enough to allow us to forget. The moments, the minutes, the hours, the days, the years of our lives all slip surely away into the silent safekeeping of a vast forgetting. So much seems lost. So much seems to fade. So very much seems forgotten forever along the way.

Most moments go. But some moments stay. Some moments last. Some few moments we never forget. Some few moments we remember ever afterwards. Some rare moments remain in the fading. Some of these moments are the signal moments in our lives. His last words. Her first smile. Some, though, are those moments when we think we might just have seen a fleeting, fugitive glimpse of another "here" and another "now" than the one we think we know. Some are those rare moments of intuition, of insight, when, for a brief moment, we think we catch a glimpse of the *why* in the sky. Some are moments when we see a double rainbow.

Like a rainbow, life is real. Like a rainbow, life may also, perhaps, be a reflection. Perhaps, in the double rainbow, we are permitted to see, for only a moment, our true and best selves in our true and best lives. Perhaps, in the double rainbow, we can, for a moment, see past the vast forgetting to catch a glimpse of eternity. It may be a reminiscence. It may be a foreshadowing. It may be only a pleasing arrangement of light and water in the sky. It may be only a moment. But, if we are fortunate, we can make that moment last. We can keep it from fading away.

"I must have a picture of this," said Rebecca, half to me and half to herself, as we continued to gaze, together, at our double rainbow.

She turned from the window, grabbed her camera, left our apartment, and went down to the street below. I followed her. Together, we stood outside on the sidewalk, and looked up at the luminous sky.

"It is fading," she said, and she put her camera away. The voice I heard was the voice I first heard on that day when she first smiled at me and first spoke to me all those years ago.

Fading, yes. Fading it was, fading fast away from the bright colors of its former radiance. In the fading of the light, in the fullness of the afternoon, the double rainbow vanished from our view. Yet somehow we both still knew that it was there. We both still saw the double rainbow, there in the sky, and there always in our minds' eye, forever painted there in all its brightness. The moment has passed. The double rainbow has faded. And yet still, for the two of us, it remains.

Yes, some moments do stay. Some moments do last. Some moments do remain, as life fades away, and as time, uncaring, unheeding, unfeeling, fades away, like the fading of a double rainbow. These moments are irretrievable. But they are also imperishable. These moments live on, ever after, within us. For these are the moments when we come as close as any of us can ever come in this world to knowing why we live.

We must cling to these moments. We must somehow make them last. We must still see the double rainbow long after it has faded from the afternoon sky. For the double rainbow is the enduring evidence that, after all, and despite all, we have lived.

Chapter Ten

Lone Star:
The Historic Role of the WTO

The last time I was in Austin, Texas, *I was carried off on a stretcher.*

I was not in Austin then to speak to a symposium on international law. I was in Austin then to march in a parade.

It was the spring of 1961. I was eleven years old. And I was a Cub Scout.

I was a Cub Scout in Pack 510 in Irving, Texas, near Dallas, and I traveled by train from Dallas to Austin one Saturday to march with thousands of other Texas scouts in a statewide parade.

I had not been feeling well on the day before the trip, and my mother had suggested that I might want to stay at home. But I did not seem to be all that sick, I was excited at the prospect of my first train ride, and I was determined to go to Austin and march proudly with my "pack" in the parade.

The bluebonnets were in bloom that spring, and the train ride through the Texas countryside was everything I had hoped it would be. So was the parade in Austin. Flags were flying. Bands were playing. Scouts were marching. The parade route was lined by cheering crowds. To my eleven-year-old eyes, the path of that statewide parade seemed long, and it seemed glorious.

All in all, it was a memorable day. And the day became all the more memorable for me when, midway through the parade, I suddenly felt a sharp pain, like a knife, in my right side. I tried to keep marching. I was determined to keep marching. I managed to keep marching for a few more steps. Then I collapsed in a heap in the street.

The next thing I knew, I was being carried off on a stretcher, and driven back, by ambulance, to the train. I stayed on that stretcher, and I

This chapter is based on a keynote address to a symposium on "Globalization and the Judiciary" at the University of Texas School of Law in Austin, Texas, on September 5, 2003. It will appear in a forthcoming symposium issue of the <u>Texas International Law Journal</u>.

struggled with the pain in my side, all the while the train traveled all the way back to Dallas. Despite all my boyish determination, *I did not finish the parade.*

Back home, I soon learned that the knife in my side was an attack of what a doctor in a Dallas hospital called "appendicitis." The doctor removed my appendix. I remained in the hospital —with my mother constantly at my bedside —for nearly two weeks. And I missed hearing how the parade turned out at the next "den meeting" of Cub Scout Pack 510.

I was devastated at the time by the fact that I had not finished the parade. I vowed to return to Austin the next year to march again. But, that summer, soon after my twelfth birthday, my father was transferred from Dallas to a small but fast-growing city in Florida called Orlando. So I grew up to become, not a Texan, but a Floridian. I never returned to Austin to finish that parade.

Thus it was that I was later sent from the State of *Florida*, and *not* from the State of *Texas*, to serve in the Congress of the United States of America. Even so, when I arrived for my first congressional term in Washington, and when some of my new Congressional colleagues from Texas discovered that I had spent part of my boyhood in their beloved state, they declared me, unofficially, an "honorary" member of the Texas delegation. I worked closely with many members of the Texas delegation of both parties on trade, space, defense, and other issues all the while I remained in the Congress.

So, perhaps it is proper, even now, for me still to see myself as an "honorary" Texan. And perhaps it is especially appropriate for me to recall and to reassert my boyhood affiliation with Texas and my abiding affection for Texas today in returning, at long last, to the city in Texas where I was, all those many years ago, unable to finish that statewide parade.

For, in recent years, in the eight eventful years in my life since I chose to leave the Congress, I have been busy marching in another parade. This parade is, for me, a parade that has passed, most often, not through Austin, Texas, but through Geneva, Switzerland. This parade is not statewide; it is worldwide. It is a parade that is watched by almost all of the world. Yet, this parade reminds me, all the same, of that statewide parade on that springtime Saturday long ago in Austin. For this parade is also long. This parade seems also —to my now middle-aged eyes —to be glorious. And this parade remains also unfinished.

Marching in this parade are the United States of America and the 145 other countries and other customs territories that are the Members of the World Trade Organization. The Members of the WTO are trying to lower barriers to world trade by negotiating and establishing rules to help facilitate and help increase world trade.

Marching alongside the Members of the WTO are those of us who have been chosen by them to serve them in WTO dispute settlement. The seven of us who serve on the standing Appellate Body of the WTO are trying to assist the Members of the WTO in their global and ongoing efforts to resolve international trade disputes by upholding the rules they have established for world trade. Marching with us are all those many others throughout the world who seek a world in which all kinds of international disputes can be resolved by establishing and upholding all kinds of international rules through the international rule of law.

All of us in this long and glorious worldwide parade are marching in different ways. We are marching in many different roles and in many different places. We are each marching to our own tune. We are each marching to our own cadence. *But we are all marching in the same parade.*

We are all marching in the same parade, because we are all marching toward the same finish line. The finish line for all of us is freedom. The parade's end for all of us is the fullest measure of the fullest extent of the fullest enjoyment of human freedom. In marching in this worldwide parade, we are all seeking a world in which all of humanity can be free to benefit from such a flourishing of freedom. And, whatever our tune, or whatever our cadence may be as we march, we are all the same in knowing that such a world will be possible only if we fill the world with free and open societies that uphold fundamental human rights; and we are all the same in knowing also that such a world will be achievable, and will be sustainable, only if we establish and uphold the international rule of law.

Some say the WTO is not marching in this parade. Some critics of "globalization" question whether the WTO is truly doing the work of freedom. Some of these critics even suggest that the WTO is an adversary of freedom. These critics do not understand the WTO. They do not understand "globalization." And, clearly, they do not understand what really connects the WTO, "globalization," and freedom.

By lowering barriers to worldwide trade, the WTO is raising opportunities for worldwide freedom. True freedom is founded on individual freedom. More trade makes more individual choices possible. More choices make more individual freedom possible. The very essence, the very definition, of freedom for an individual human being in a free and open society is having the most possible choices in making the most possible *personal decisions* about how best to live.[1]

The work of the WTO increases global trade. Increased global trade contributes to increased global economic growth. Increased growth is vital to the process of overall global development. And freedom is "both...the primary end and...the principal means of development."[2] The Nobel Prize-winning economist Amartya Sen underscored this important fact about development in the very title of his book entitled Development as Freedom. Sen's book should be required reading for everyone marching in our parade, and for anyone presuming to explain how the WTO, "globalization," and freedom are connected.

To be sure, development requires much more in addition to economic growth. Start with the ambitious "Millennium Development" goals of the United Nations: An end to extreme poverty and hunger. Universal primary education. Gender equity and the empowerment of women. Reduced child mortality. Improved maternal health. Success in the struggle against HIV/AIDS, malaria, tuberculosis, and other major diseases. Environmental sustainability. A true global partnership for development.[3] Real progress toward all these goals, as well as many others, must be made to achieve real development that will result in real freedom.

Moreover, and not least, I, for one, would add to this imposing list the indispensability of an independent judiciary that respects the rule of law as an essential element of both development and freedom. A respect for property rights, a respect for the obligation of contract, a respect for the rule of law in all its manifestations by an impartial and independent judiciary is a prerequisite everywhere to the right kind of "globalization."

But economic growth is, unquestionably, a key to development, because economic growth can help unlock for individuals a life in which there are *more* possible choices and, thus, *more* possible personal decisions. As Sen has explained, "Development consists of the removal of various

---

[1] This, of course, is precisely the view that was voiced by Sir Karl Popper in his classic work, The Open Society and Its Enemies, in 1945. *See* Karl Popper, The Open Society and Its Enemies, two volumes, (Princeton University Press, 1966) [1945].

[2] Amartya Sen, Development as Freedom (New York: Random House, 1999), xii.

[3] World Trade Organization, World Trade Report (2003), 80, online at wto.org.

types of unfreedoms that leave people with little choice and little opportunity of exercising their reasoned agency. The removal of substantial unfreedoms...is *constitutive* of development."[4] The economic growth that results from increased trade can help remove all those "unfreedoms."

Those without a copy of Sen's thoughtful book can find his words about the link between development and freedom on page 79 of the WTO's "World Trade Report 2003," which is online at wto.org.[5] Anyone who takes the time to read, with an open mind, this 270-page report on how the WTO, "globalization," and freedom are connected, will begin to understand that the work of the WTO is critical to the creation of more freedom in more free and open societies in a world that is becoming increasingly "globalized." The work of the WTO is an important part of the work of freedom, and the WTO, therefore, has an important role to fulfill in our worldwide parade.

Some others say the WTO is a latecomer in this parade. They point out that the worldwide parade toward worldwide freedom under the international rule of law has been progressing for centuries. And they see the WTO as arriving late, at the tail end of the parade, to tag along as an intrusive international afterthought in the continuing progress toward the parade's end.

But the WTO is not an afterthought. The WTO is the culmination of considerable international forethought and considerable international experience in trying to make international rules that can be upheld through the international rule of law. It is true that the WTO itself is less than a decade old. The WTO, however, is the inheritor of an *acquis* of half a century's experience under its predecessor, the General Agreement on Tariffs and Trade. Likewise, the GATT was the beneficiary of literally centuries of experience in making and upholding the international rule of law through a long evolution of international commercial agreements.

From the barter of the ancient Greeks, to the transit of luxury goods along the Great Silk Road, to the early reliance on the notion of "most-favored-nation" status by the Hanseatic League, to the negotiation of countless "friendship, commerce, and navigation" treaties by numerous trading nations, to the visionary negotiation of bilateral trade agreements

---

[4] Sen, <u>Development as Freedom,</u> supra.
[5] World Trade Organization, <u>World Trade Report</u> (2003), supra, at 79.

by Cordell Hull, and, finally, to the historic conference at Bretton Woods, the international legal ground was prepared over a long time for what became, initially, the GATT, and, ultimately, the WTO.

Trade has long been a part of the parade. Reinforcing this judgment, Abram Chayes and Antonia Handler Chayes, two of the most respected marchers in the parade toward freedom under the international rule of law, wrote, "Of all the international regimes, the GATT has the most developed and most active system of formal dispute settlement."[6] They wrote this *in 1995* —before the first appeal was ever filed before the new Appellate Body of the new WTO.

Still others insist that the WTO really belongs in some other parade. They acknowledge the connection between trade and freedom. They see the need for trade rules and trade rulings arising from trade agreements. But they do not really see international trade law as an appropriate part of a parade toward international law, and, thus, they do not see the WTO as appropriately belonging to the worldwide parade toward freedom under the international rule of law.

On this, one of many possible examples may suffice. I cite the first volume of the eighth edition of a deservedly classic international legal treatise, Oppenheim's International Law, published in 1967, when the GATT as a treaty among "Contracting Parties" was very much in force, and when the GATT as a growing institution was already established as an increasingly effective forum for international dispute settlement. According to that treatise at that time, "The details of commercial treaties are, for the most part, purely technical, and are, therefore, outside the scope of a general treatise on International Law."[7]

This attitude is changing. But only slowly. Some of the newer editions of the standard textbooks and treatises on public international law include some treatment of international trade law. But only briefly.

---

[6] Abram Chayes and Antonia Handler Chayes, The New Sovereignty: Compliance with International Regulatory Agreements (Cambridge, Massachusetts: Harvard, 1995), 218.

[7] H. Lauterpacht, ed., Oppenheim's International Law, 8th edition (London: Longmans, Green and Co., 1967), Vol. I, Peace, 971; this same point, using this same quote, was made by one of the ablest of the scholars on international trade law, Professor Donald M. McRae, in his excellent Hague course in 1996. *See* Donald M. McRae, "The Contribution of International Trade Law to the Development of International Law," *Recueil des cours*, Volume 260, Hague Academy of International Law (The Hague: Martinius Nijhoff Publishers, 1996), at 112.

Many of those who are marching in the worldwide parade toward international law are not yet persuaded that the WTO truly belongs.

For our part, in the WTO, we are of the view that, as it is expressed in the WTO's <u>World Trade Report</u> for 2003, the WTO-based world trading system is "a set of principles and rules, underpinned by binding arrangements for settling trade disputes."[8] And, on the Appellate Body of the WTO, we are of the view as well that, as it was expressed in our very first Appellate Body Report, when settling trade disputes, this set of principles and rules is "not to be read in clinical isolation from public international law."[9] As we see it, the WTO definitely belongs in the parade.

And still others worry that the WTO will cause the parade to take a wrong turn. They fear that a proliferation of various specialized international tribunals such as those of the WTO dispute settlement system will cause a proliferation in competing interpretations of fundamental principles of international law. It has even been suggested that WTO and other international tribunals may wish to refer points of general international law for interpretation to the International Court of Justice in the Hague.[10]

I see no basis for such referrals in the WTO treaty,[11] which is the sole source of all authority in WTO dispute settlement. Furthermore, I agree with Judge Rosalyn Higgins of the International Court of Justice that such proposals are not only "cumbersome and unrealistic," but also are unnecessary.[12] I agree with her that there will be not be any threat to the basic identity or the basic integrity of international law so long as those of us who are entrusted with making judgments in the various specialized international tribunals show "friendly mutual respect" and

---

[8] WTO, <u>World Trade Report</u> (2003), at 78.

[9] Report of the Appellate Body, United States – Standards for Reformulated and Conventional Gasoline, WT/DS2/AB/R, adopted May 20, 1996, at page 17.

[10] *See* Address to the Plenary Session of the General Assembly of the United Nations by Judge Stephen M. Schwebel, President of the International Court of Justice, 26 October 1999, A/54/PV 39; and "The Proliferation of International Judicial Bodies: The Outlook for the International Legal Order," Speech by Judge Gilbert Guillaume, President of the International Court of Justice, to the Sixth Committee of the General Assembly of the United Nations, 27 October 2000, available online at icj-cij.org. *See also* David J. Bederman, <u>The Spirit of International Law</u> (Athens and London: University of Georgia Press, 2002), 196-198.

[11] The "WTO treaty" is the Final Act Embodying the Results of the Uruguay Round of the Multilateral Trade Negotiations, done at Marrakesh, Morocco, on April 15, 1994.

[12] Judge Rosalyn Higgins, "The ICJ, the ECJ, and the Integrity of International Law," International and Comparative Law Quarterly 1, 20 (2002).

"keep ourselves well informed," and so long as we try to march together with some consistency —to the extent that doing so is consistent with our various specialized obligations.[13]

Thus far, this seems to be precisely what those of us who are marching in the parade are doing. Before he was taken from us, my late friend, the very distinguished professor of international law at Vanderbilt University, Jonathan Charney, gave a series of lectures at The Hague addressing the question: "Is International Law Threatened by Multiple International Tribunals?"[14] His answer was "No." Like Judge Higgins, Professor Charney acknowledged the potential harm of such proliferation. So do I. But, after a thorough review of the reasoning and the results in the decisions of a whole array of varied international tribunals, he concluded that "the variety of international tribunals functioning today do not appear to pose a threat to the coherence of an international legal system."[15] That was in 1999. I know of nothing that has happened since that justifies questioning this conclusion. There may be some crossroads ahead, but, thus far, in the worldwide parade, we have not taken a wrong turn.

In sum, I say this to all those who would question the role of the WTO in the worldwide parade toward freedom under the international rule of law: The WTO is in the parade, and the WTO has been in the parade for a long time. The WTO belongs in the parade, and the WTO will not make the parade take a wrong turn. Far from it. For the truth seems to be: *The historic role of the WTO is to help lead the parade.*

In my memories of the unfinished parade of my boyhood in Texas, leading the parade —alongside the "Stars and Stripes" of the American flag —was the famed "Lone Star" flag of the State of Texas. The "Lone Star" flag of Texas has long been a symbol of freedom. Those who have followed that flag have long marched in freedom's parade.

As we all march together for freedom today, there are many stars that shine in our parade. Among the numerous international tribunals that are doing the work of freedom are the International Court of Justice,

---

[13] Id. at 19, 20.
[14] Jonathan I. Charney, "Is International Law Threatened by Multiple International Tribunals?," in 271 *Recueil des Cours* 101 (Hague Academy of International Law) [1998].
[15] Jonathan I. Charney, "The Impact on the International Legal System of the Growth of International Courts and Tribunals," Vol. 31, No. 4, <u>New York University Journal of International Law and Politics</u> 697, 700 (Summer 1999).

the European Court of Justice, the European Court of Human Rights, the court of the European Free Trade Association, the International Tribunal for the Law of the Sea, the new International Criminal Court, and more. A number of these tribunals are represented at this symposium.

The parade toward freedom under the international rule of law has been progressing for centuries. The evidence of the recent progress of the parade is to be found, in part, in the proliferation of international tribunals to fulfill many international needs. More than ever before, the world knows that the world needs both international law and the international rule of law.

Even so, as Professor David Bederman has recently written, "International law remains a primitive legal system."[16] And no doubt this is how the current status of international law is best described in terms that are familiar to theorists of jurisprudence. But, in terms that are perhaps more familiar in Austin, international law might best be described as having "gone to Texas." International law might best be described as being, so to speak, out on the legal frontier.

And, out on the legal frontier, out where the bluebonnets grow, out where the lonesome prairie stretches as far as the eye can see, *out there* is international law. Out there are the wide open spaces of jurisprudence. Out there are the open ranges of lawlessness that are still awaiting the fences of law that, alone, can secure true freedom. And, out there, above the far horizon, shining brightly in the big sky, is *the "lone star" of the WTO.*

No, the WTO is not by any means the *only* star that shines in the firmament of international law. And the WTO is not by any means the only star that *must* shine if we hope to shed light on the darkness of all the wide open spaces that face all those who would free humanity by building the fences of law. But the WTO is, for now, the brightest star. It is, for now, a "lone star" helping to lead our parade.

Ours is a time of "aggressive unilateralism." Ours is a time of retreat from "multilateralism." Ours is a time when the hopes of all those who march for freedom depend on a renewed internationalism that relies on international law. And, at this time when we are so much in need of increased support for international law, the WTO is a "lone star." Because

---

[16] David J. Bederman, The Spirit of International Law, supra, at 26.

the WTO is, often alone among global tribunals, proving that international law can work, that international law can be real, and that international law can be upheld. The WTO is offering new and needed proof to the world *every day* that multilateral approaches to multilateral challenges can result in multilateral successes.

The "lone star" of the WTO shines so brightly in the sky of international law largely because of the success, thus far, of WTO dispute settlement. The extent of this initial success is such that, in less than a decade, the WTO dispute settlement system has become, in the words of one of the foremost scholars of international law, Professor Andreas Lowenfeld, "the most complete system of international dispute resolution in history."[17]

Certainly the WTO dispute settlement system is the most *prolific* system of international dispute settlement in history. There are about *thirty thousand pages* of rules in the "covered agreements" of the WTO treaty. And, thus far, in less than a decade, the WTO dispute settlement system has produced more than *twenty thousand pages* of rulings on the obligations in those rules in those "covered agreements." During that time, hundreds upon hundreds of international trade disputes of all kinds have been brought to the WTO by WTO Members for dispute settlement. And, during that time, hundreds upon hundreds of those disputes have been resolved.

Professor Louis Henkin famously observed that "almost all nations observe almost all principles of international law and almost all of their obligations almost all of the time."[18] This is certainly true of international law and international obligations as they relate to the rules of the WTO. Almost all WTO Members endeavor to comply with almost all WTO rules almost all of the time. Their compliance with the rules furthers the flow of world commerce and, thus, increases the level of world prosperity. Inevitably, though, disputes arise among WTO Members about the precise nature of their obligations under the rules. The Members of the WTO have established the WTO dispute settlement system so that they can resolve those inevitable disputes.

Understandably, the focus of public attention at any given time is usually largely on the most significant and the most seemingly

---

[17] Andreas Lowenfeld, International Economic Law (Oxford: Oxford University Press, 2002), 150.
[18] Louis Henkin, How Nations Behave (New York: Columbia University Press, 1979), 47.

intractable disputes that have not yet been resolved. But, undeniably, the WTO dispute settlement system has proven, thus far, to be both highly effective and highly efficient in achieving the overriding aim of the Members of the WTO in establishing the system. That aim "is to secure a positive solution to a dispute."[19]

The WTO dispute settlement system achieves this aim *in almost every dispute*. Many —perhaps even most —of the international trade disputes that are brought to the attention of the WTO are resolved in a "positive solution" *without* formal consultations. Most of the disputes that result in formal consultations are resolved *without* the formal establishment of a dispute settlement panel.[20] Furthermore, *almost all* of the trade disputes that are addressed by a panel, and, if appealed, by the Appellate Body, result in what all of the WTO Members that are parties to those disputes agree is a "positive solution" within a reasonable period of time after the adoption of the dispute settlement reports by the WTO Dispute Settlement Body.

There are many reasons for the shining success of the WTO dispute settlement system in its first few years. The WTO has built on the cumulative success of the GATT. The WTO has also benefited from the continued commitment of the Members of the WTO to the continued success of WTO dispute settlement. Moreover, by achieving a "positive solution" in so many difficult disputes, the WTO has laid the foundation for continued success by reinforcing the belief among WTO Members that more such difficult disputes can be resolved through the WTO in a "globalizing" world economy where effective and efficient international dispute settlement is sorely needed.

But the most important reason for the success of the WTO, the most important reason why the WTO is a "lone star" in the forefront of the worldwide parade toward freedom under law, is the *uniqueness* of the WTO dispute settlement system as a global tribunal. Alone among all the global tribunals in the world, and, indeed, alone among all the global tribunals in the *history* of the world, the WTO dispute settlement system is unique in two significant ways.

---

[19] Article 3.7, WTO Understanding on Rules and Procedures Governing the Settlement of Disputes (the "Dispute Settlement Understanding"), which is one of the "covered agreements" of the WTO treaty.

[20] To be more precise, the Legal Affairs Division of the WTO Secretariat reports that, thus far, a panel has been established in only about 40 percent of the disputes in which there has been a request for consultations.

First, the WTO has compulsory jurisdiction. All WTO Members have agreed in the WTO treaty to use the WTO dispute settlement system *exclusively* to resolve all their treaty-related disputes with other WTO Members. They are subject to WTO dispute settlement if they do not. And, *second*, the WTO makes rulings that are upheld. The Members of the WTO comply with rulings in WTO dispute settlement because there can be consequences for them if they do not. Under the WTO treaty, a WTO Member that chooses *not* to comply with a WTO ruling can face significant economic consequences through the loss of the benefits of previous trade concessions by other WTO Members. The potentially high price of these possible consequences encourages compliance with WTO rulings.

The Members of the WTO have enhanced the historic force of this uniqueness by the strength of their common commitment to the international rule of law. So too, through the strength of the same commitment, has the Appellate Body of the WTO. The Appellate Body is not, strictly speaking, part of the global "judiciary" that is confronting "globalization." We are not "judges" on the Appellate Body. We are not part of a "judicial" system. WTO dispute settlement is, technically, a "quasi-judicial" system. Rulings and recommendations in dispute settlement are subject to adoption by the Members of the WTO by means of the WTO's unique rule of "reverse consensus."[21] Even so, we bow to no one in our shared commitment on the Appellate Body to upholding the international rule of law while serving the Members of the WTO in fulfillment of the terms of the WTO treaty.

In 1995, when the WTO was created, and when the Appellate Body of the WTO was first appointed, Judge Gilbert Guillaume predicted otherwise. He suggested that, although the new Appellate Body resembled a judicial institution, when faced with a decision on trade law,

---

[21] More specifically, the reports containing the rulings and recommendations of WTO panels and the WTO Appellate Body in WTO dispute settlement are subject to adoption by the Members of the WTO when sitting in their capacity as the WTO Dispute Settlement Body. Such reports are adopted and thereby made binding by a so-called "reverse consensus" in which a report will *not* be adopted only if *all* the Members of the Dispute Settlement Body agree by consensus that it should not be. Thus far, this has never happened. Therefore, in effect, dispute settlement reports have, thus far, always proven to be final. This is perhaps the most significant innovation of WTO dispute settlement. Under the WTO's predecessor, the GATT, a panel report was adopted only if all the "Contracting Parties" of the GATT agreed by consensus that it should be; not surprisingly, under the GATT, parties that lost in dispute settlement often "blocked" a consensus. See Article 17.14, Dispute Settlement Understanding.

"considerations of law will perhaps not be the only factor it will have to take into account when taking such a decision."[22] Respectfully, I would submit that the record of the Appellate Body thus far simply does not support this prediction.

Nor is there any basis for such an assertion in the instructions that have been given to the Appellate Body by the Members of the WTO in the WTO treaty. The WTO treaty clearly provides that appeals to the Appellate Body "shall be limited to *issues of law* covered in the panel report and legal interpretations developed by the panel."[23] Under the treaty, "The Appellate Body shall address each of the issues raised,"[24] and "may uphold, modify or reverse the *legal findings and conclusions* of the panel."[25]

The Members of the WTO have not instructed the Members of the Appellate Body to "take into account" any considerations other than those of law. So we do not. Further, the Members of the WTO have specifically instructed us —not once, but twice —in the WTO Rules of Conduct to be both "independent" and "impartial" in WTO dispute settlement.[26] So we are. Eight years on, I believe that even Judge Guillaume would say that the Appellate Body has made the WTO's star shine all the more brightly because of our continuing commitment on the Appellate Body to the international rule of law.

In particular, the Members of the Appellate Body try to demonstrate our commitment to the rule of law through our commitment to a reliance of reason. We rely on reason as we strive to assist the Members of the WTO in their efforts —as the WTO treaty expresses it —"to preserve the rights and obligations of Members under the covered agreements, and to clarify the existing provisions of those agreements in accordance with customary rules of interpretation of public international law."[27]

Some may question a reliance on reason. Some may doubt that reason can help ensure the rule of law. We do not. By relying on the mutual exercise of reason, we have reached a consensus on our legal conclusions in every single one of our —to date —about sixty appeals.

---

[22] Judge Gilbert Guillaume, "The Future of International Judicial Institutions," 44 International and Comparative Law Quarterly (1995), 848, 960.

[23] Article 17.6, Dispute Settlement Understanding (emphasis added).

[24] Article 17.12, Dispute Settlement Understanding.

[25] Article 17.13, Dispute Settlement Understanding (emphasis added).

[26] WTO Rules of Conduct, Articles II and III (2).

[27] Article 3.2, Dispute Settlement Understanding (emphasis added).

Largely because of our mutual efforts to reason together, no Member of the Appellate Body has —to date —ever dissented to even one of our ultimate rulings and recommendations. This has added to the credibility of our judgments, and this has also, I believe, added to the historic force of the uniqueness of WTO dispute settlement.

As my friend and colleague Georges Abi-Saab once said to me as we sat together at our round table in Geneva, "If we refute reason, what remains? Only power." Our worldwide parade is about many things. One of the things it is about is replacing the rule of *power* in the world with the rule of *law*. There can be no lasting freedom while freedom remains at the mercy of the whims of arbitrary power. There is lasting freedom only where reason prevails over power, and where reason is enshrined in the rule of law.

But if, in our worldwide parade, we hope to make law prevail over power, if we hope to make freedom triumph over "unfreedom," if we hope to continue to move the parade forward, if we hope finally to finish the parade, then *the WTO must not remain a "lone star."*

One morning recently, I opened the pages of my hometown newspaper, the *Orlando Sentinel*, and read that the lights are going out in the universe. The number of stars in the sky is diminishing. As the universe is aging, old stars are burning out faster than new stars are being born. This, according to the *Sentinel*, is the conclusion from the latest studies of starlight by the Royal Astronomical Society of Great Britain.[28]

There is more. While I was in the Congress, some of my friends in the Texas delegation and I worked together in support of the ongoing joint American and European mission of space exploration called Ulysses, which was launched in 1990. Now, according to that same newspaper story, the Ulysses spacecraft is sending scientific data back to earth indicating that a huge cosmic storm of stardust from the remains of dying stars is heading straight for our solar system.[29]

Back here on earth, in our worldwide parade, the lights are likewise going out, the stars are diminishing, and a storm is approaching. The "lone star" of the WTO still shines. But it will not shine much longer

---

[28] *Orlando Sentinel* (August 23, 2003), reporting on the published results of an astronomical study in the monthly notice of the Royal Astronomical Society of Great Britain, dated August 21, 2003, entitled "Dim Future for the Universe as Stellar Lights Go Out."
[29] *Orlando Sentinel*, supra.

if other stars do not also shine in our parade. Other stars must also shine, and they must shine ever more brightly if we hope to ward off the storm out on the horizon.

Despite the successes, thus far, of WTO dispute settlement, the front of the storm that is approaching the WTO alone fills the horizon. As the Members of the WTO readily acknowledge in their World Trade Report for 2003, "Despite the remarkable technological achievements of the last two hundred years, we still live in a world of pervasive human poverty and underdevelopment."[30] The landmark agreement by the Members of the WTO that will give developing countries more access to inexpensive life-saving medicines to fight AIDS and other epidemic diseases, will help calm the storm threatening the WTO.[31] But there are many other ominous clouds on the horizon of the multilateral trading system.

A successful conclusion of the Doha Development Round is essential to clearing some of those clouds away. Equally essential, not only to the WTO, but to all those in the parade, is a continuing commitment to ensuring that WTO dispute settlement remains continuing proof to a doubting world that multilateral approaches to resolving global disputes can be successful. But continued progress in the trading system will not alone suffice. Our continued progress will depend as well on the progress we also make in clearing away many of the other dark clouds on the other global fronts that threaten to rain on our parade.

To scatter the clouds, to weather the storm, to finish the parade, the nations of the world must do much more, together, on trade, but they must also do much more, together, to establish and uphold the international rule of law in numerous other areas of shared global concern. In particular, they must do much more, together, in those other areas of concern, to strengthen the ability and the authority of the "global judiciary" to meet the many and increasingly complex challenges of "globalization."

The WTO must not remain a novelty among global tribunals in having an assured jurisdiction. The WTO must not remain a rarity among global tribunals in rendering rulings that are followed routinely with the full force of law. The WTO must not remain the lonely example that it often seems to be of a global tribunal where international law can work,

---

[30] WTO, World Trade Report (2003), at 78.
[31] Elizabeth Becker, "Poor Nations Can Purchase Cheap Drugs Under Accord," *New York Times* (August 31, 2003), A-6.

can be real, and can be upheld. The "lone star" of the WTO must not shine alone. It must be merely one star in a constellation of stars that all shine brightly in our parade.

My boyhood memories of Texas include a memory of a postcard picturing a map of the United States —*from the point of view of Texas*. On this map, Texas is larger than all the other states combined. Florida, for example, is only a small speck with a palm tree in a far corner of the map on the postcard of Texas and its "adjacent provinces." Representing the state capital of Austin, the "lone star" of Texas is in the very center of the postcard.[32]

Every "lone star" tends toward such a myopic view. This is true of states such as Texas. This is true of international institutions and, moreover, of international tribunals. This is even sometimes true of the very greatest of countries. The tendency of all of us —even some of us who serve the Members of the WTO —is to think that our own role in the parade is larger than it really is. And down this route truly is the wrong turn for the parade. For down this route is the dangerous temptation to *go it alone.*

In his memoir of his boyhood in Texas, that great poet laureate of the frontier, Larry McMurtry, recalls that, out alone on the frontier, out in the wide open spaces, the early settlers of Texas had "the freedom of the skies."[33] But, in telling the story of his own family's early experiences in Texas, he goes on to explain how those who settled the state ultimately realized that, to make their freedom have any lasting meaning, they needed to build fences in embrace of a long, hard "effort to rear something...that wouldn't blow away...."[34]

So too with those of us in the parade for freedom under the international rule of law. In a world of solitary nations, international law has long been at "the vanishing point of jurisprudence."[35] In a world of wide open spaces, international law has often seemed to be on the verge of vanishing and blowing away. Today, it still seems that way. But, today,

---

[32] This postcard, circa 1959, can be seen online at: www.txgenes.com/TxPostcards/Texas/TexasMap_Replace1959.jpg.

[33] Larry McMurtry, Walter Benjamin at the Dairy Queen: Reflections at Sixty and Beyond (New York: Simon & Schuster, 1999), 53.

[34] Id. at 65.

[35] Sir Thomas E. Holland, The Elements of Jurisprudence, 13th edition (Oxford: Clarendon Press, 1924), quoted in W. Michael Reisman, Law in Brief Encounters (New Haven and London: Yale University Press, 1999), 15.

ours is much less a world of solitary nations, and much more a world of "globalization." Thus, today, we are much more in need of international law and the international rule of law than ever before. And, to keep international law from vanishing and blowing away, we must, like the early settlers of Texas, build the fences among us that will help make it last. To do so, *all* of us must understand that *none* of us can go it alone.

Even the proud "lone star" State of Texas decided ultimately that it could not go it alone. The sheer singularity of Texas remains, but the "lone star" of Texas has long been one among fifty stars. Like Texas, we must all come to see, as countries, as international institutions comprised of countries, and as international tribunals serving those countries by serving those institutions, that none of us can go it alone. In pursuit of freedom, we must all stand together and march together in the worldwide parade.

All of us in the parade who happen to be Americans should, especially, try to remember this. Sometimes I think that some Americans carry around in their heads a mental postcard of America's supposed place on the map of the world that resembles that old postcard of Texas from my boyhood. On their mental map, America is *most* of the world, and perhaps even *almost all* of the world But their map is *not* a map of the world as it really is. In reality, four percent of the people in the world are Americans; this means that ninety-six percent are not. We Americans should keep this in mind whenever we are tempted to go it alone.

As we Americans keep marching in the parade, with our proud flag, with its fifty stars, we must come to see that there is really only one way the parade can ever hope to make it to the finish line. And that one way is for Americans to see the world as it really is, and to act together in the world in concert and in cooperation with others of like mind. America cannot be a "lone star" in the world. Our continued freedom as Americans depends, in part, on our success in sharing freedom with others in the world. Our continued independence as Americans depends, in part, on our success in coming to terms with our interdependence with others in the world. Our star, too, must shine with other stars.

I believe that the greatest of all Americans, Abraham Lincoln, was right. At its best, America *is* "the last, best hope of earth.[36] But our *confidence* as Americans must not become *arrogance*. We Americans do

---

[36] Abraham Lincoln, Annual Message to the Congress of the United States (December, 1862).

not have a monopoly on either wisdom or virtue in the world. And we Americans certainly do *not* have a monopoly on the love of freedom. If America stands for *anything*, it stands for the abiding belief that *the love of freedom is universal.*

America has a sovereign right to stand alone. America remains a sovereign nation. America must always remain a sovereign nation. America is in no danger of *not* remaining a sovereign nation. But, beyond all the demagoguery, the issue with our sovereignty as a nation is not whether we will *lose* it. The issue with our sovereignty is how we will choose to *use* it. Will we choose to use it in shared efforts with others who seek the same ends of freedom for the world? Or will we choose, myopically, needlessly, recklessly, to go it alone, and to try to stand alone in the world, at great risk and at great sacrifice, when there are still billions of others in the world who are willing to stand with us?

One of the reasons why my Congressional colleagues from Texas made me an "honorary" member of the Texas delegation was because they knew that, like all grade school students in the public schools of Texas of my youth, I had taken two years of Texas history. So they knew that I had been taught what Texans mean when they say, as they sometimes do, that there are *"thirteen days to glory."* The phrase "thirteen days to glory" refers to the thirteen days of the siege of the Alamo in the fight for freedom in Texas in 1836. But, for every true Texan, the phrase refers also to what it truly means to be willing to make a lone, last stand for freedom.

Thirteen Days to Glory is the title of a book about the fall of the Alamo that my mother gave me to read while I recovered from my stay in the hospital after my unfinished parade long ago.[37] I read the book cover to cover. Then I read it again. It was, at the time, the longest book I had ever read. I still have a copy of Thirteen Days to Glory. I marveled then, and I marvel now, that there are those in the world who are willing to risk and to sacrifice their very lives by standing alone for freedom.

On the faded cover of my copy of Thirteen Days to Glory is a dramatic picture of the last moments of the last, thirteenth day of the fateful siege, when the outnumbered defenders of the Alamo fell, one by one. One lone man, obviously meant to be the legendary Davy Crockett, is at the center of the picture, surrounded by assailants, wielding his

---

[37] Lon Tinkle, Thirteen Days to Glory (New York: McGraw-Hill, 1958).

flintlock rifle, "Old Betsy," like a club, fighting, to the very last, amid the hail of bullets and bayonets that will make his a lone, last stand.[38]

No doubt I was not the only boy in the Texas of my boyhood to imagine myself as Davy Crockett, the "King of the Wild Frontier," fighting on, to the end, in a lone, last stand for freedom beneath the "lone star" flag that flew over the Alamo. When I was not wearing my Cub Scout uniform, I was often wearing a Davy Crockett tee shirt and a "coonskin" cap. I suppose there is something in all of us that makes us long for the chance to prove that we would be willing, in the end, to stand alone, to the last, for freedom.

Sometimes we must stand alone. But, at other times, we must be willing to march much harder so that we can stand, and then march, together. And, at all times, we must be willing to stand and march together with others in the world who share our love for freedom if we hope to serve the cause of freedom as we should. For those of us who are marching in the parade for freedom, now is one of those times.

We can weather the approaching storm only if we stand together. We can move the parade forward only if we march together. We must make our stand, not by going it alone, but by going together, by marching side by side to ensure the forward progress of our worldwide parade. For, if we do not, *this* stand will be a *last* stand for freedom, and it will be a last stand *without glory*.

Glory is a word much misused. Glory is not only to be found in a brave stand on a battlefield. Glory is also to be found in having the courage and the wisdom and the vision to take other brave stands. Glory is also to be found, for example, in the stand we must make together to further the progress of freedom by establishing and upholding the international rule of law.

---

[38] Precisely how and where Davy Crockett fell in the final defense of the Alamo is, of course, much debated. The cover of <u>Thirteen Days to Glory</u> depicts the traditional version that was etched in the memories of my time by the Walt Disney television series. In contrast, the recently published diary of a Mexican army officer who fought at the Alamo suggests that Crockett survived the "last stand," surrendered along with several others, and was executed. Numerous other conflicting stories abound. *See*, among many other accounts, Tinkle, <u>Thirteen Days to Glory</u>, supra, at 224-225; Michael Lind, "The Death of David Crockett," <u>The Wilson Quarterly</u> (Winter, 1998); and William C. Davis, <u>Three Roads to the Alamo: The Lives and Fortunes of David Crockett, James Bowie, and William Barret Travis</u> (New York: HarperCollins, 1998), 563, 568, 589n, 737-738n.

In such work, in such quiet but essential work, we can also find glory. For glory is making what matters. Glory is creating what lasts. Glory is building what will not blow away. Glory is doing whatever must be done to grace the gift of life with the blessings of freedom throughout the world. To find such glory, to make freedom that will matter, to make freedom that will last, to make freedom that will not blow away, we need a six-gun at our side, but we also need a law book in our hand.

It will take many more than "thirteen days to glory" for our unfinished parade. The finish line where we will find the glory of lasting human freedom is still far away. We have a long march ahead of us. The parade will be long. The crowds lining the parade route will not always be cheering. The clouds are threatening. The storm is upon us. But our parade can yet be glorious.

On this one day on the way to glory, I can promise only this: Soon I will be leaving the WTO. I will be resuming the practice of law. I will also be assuming a new role in teaching law. Come the new year, I will be looking for new ways to keep marching in the parade. And, come what may, I will keep trying to finish the parade —*until I am carried off on a stretcher.*

Chapter Eleven

Groping Toward Grotius:
The WTO and the International Rule of Law

The tale is familiar to all those who seek a world that truly values international law.

The time is the early seventeenth century, at the dawn of what historians — despite considerable evidence to the contrary — often call "The Age of Reason." The place is the Netherlands, in revolt against Spain, on the verge of a civil war, and in the grip of a divisive religious discord.

The hero is Huig de Groot — better known to us by his Latin name, Hugo Grotius. The heroine is Maria — his loyal and long-suffering wife, and the mother of his five children.

The tale is a tale of escape. It is a tale of an escape *to freedom.*[1]

In 1619, at the beginning of our tale, our hero, Grotius, was imprisoned in a gloomy and forbidding fortress in the Netherlands. Grotius was no ordinary prisoner. In his youth, he had been described by no less than the King of France as "the miracle of Holland."[2] He was a poet, a playwright, a theologian, a diplomat, and, not least, a renowned lawyer and jurist. He was, all in all, one of the most learned men in all of Europe.

Grotius was also a Christian humanist. He not only believed in Christianity. He believed also in what he saw as a necessary corollary to Christianity. He believed in human freedom. In this, Grotius was at least

---

This chapter appears under the same title and in slightly different form in Harvard International Law Journal, Volume 44, Number 2 (Summer, 2003).
[1] Much of this account of the escape of Grotius — including the quotations — is taken from the lively telling in chapters 21 and 22 of The Life of John of Barneveld by John Lothrop Motley, published in 1874. Now largely forgotten, Motley was — along with Parkman, Prescott, and Bancroft — one of the great American narrative historians of the nineteenth century. He was a novelist, a diplomat, an historian, and a quintessential "man of letters" whose most famous work was his multi-volume history of the rise of the Dutch Republic. Motley was also a Harvard graduate. He entered Harvard College at the age of thirteen, and studied law, but never practiced. On Motley, *see* Van Wyck Brooks, The Flowering of New England, 1815 – 1865 (New York: E.P. Dutton, 1936), 334 –342.
[2] These quotations are from Motley.

a few centuries ahead of his time. Thus, in the fallout from a Dutch political power struggle, he was condemned as a religious heretic and sentenced to life imprisonment. As one historian put it, Grotius was now "cut off in the flower of his age and doomed to a living grave."

Enter our heroine, Maria, a resourceful woman devoted to her husband. She proved it when she agreed to be locked up with him every night in the fortress. She proved it all the more when she engineered his escape.

For two years, Grotius continued his scholarly studies while in prison. To further his studies, his friends outside the prison sent him stacks of heavy books. The books were taken to and from the fortress in a large, locked chest. After awhile, the prison guards grew accustomed to the steady flow of books to and from their studious prisoner and "gradually ceased to inspect the chest."

The sharp-eyed Maria noticed this, and told her husband. Together, they developed a plan for his escape. Grotius would take the place of the books inside the chest. The chest was just large enough to hold the imprisoned scholar. A single keyhole allowed just enough air for breathing. In preparation, Grotius lay "in the chest with the lid fastened, and with his wife sitting upon the top of it, two hours at a time by the hour-glass."

Finally, on a rainy and windy morning in March, 1621, when the gale "beat with unabated violence in the turrets," and when the prison commandant was conveniently away, Grotius fell on his knees and prayed for an hour, and then had his wife lock him in the chest. Curled up inside, he used a copy of the New Testament as a pillow.

Maria kissed the lock, gave the key to the chest to their maidservant, and then summoned the guards. The guards joked about the weight of the heavy chest, but they carried it away. They carried it through thirteen "barred and locked doors," until, finally, they were outside the fortress. Then they placed it on a boat that waited on the bank of a nearby river.

The maidservant sat on the chest while the boat crossed the river. Then she had the chest taken to the home of one of the scholar's supporters. There she unlocked the chest, and Grotius emerged, gasping for air. Later, disguised as a journeyman bricklayer, he made his escape from the country. Soon his wife and children joined him, in freedom.

As dramatic as this tale of the daring escape of Grotius may be, even more dramatic is the sequel. For the sequel to the escape of Grotius is a tale, too, of an escape to freedom. It is the unfinished tale of our own escape to freedom — through the embrace and the establishment of the international rule of law.

It was *after* his dramatic escape from his imprisonment in the Netherlands that Grotius wrote the masterpiece for which he is most remembered by students and scholars of international law. It was *after* his escape, while living in exile in Paris, and while surviving on a small pension from the French king, that he wrote his classic treatise On the Law of War and Peace.[3]

It was in this treatise — written after his escape — that Grotius made his claim to be remembered today. For it was in this work that he had the most to say about freedom, about how freedom depends on the rule of law, and about how the hopes we have for the rule of law in an unruly world depend on having something that can truly be called "international law."

There are others, besides Grotius, who helped lay the intellectual foundation for international law. Vitoria. Gentili. Suarez. And more. Yet it is Grotius who is generally proclaimed as "the father of international law." In part, this is because of his insight and his foresight relating to the need for the international rule of law in On the Law of War and Peace.[4]

In his treatise, Grotius set forth the first modern formulation of international law. His treatise, as its subtitle indicates, is not only about the law of war and peace. More broadly, it is about "the law of nature and of nations." More precisely, it is about how what Grotius saw as the law of nature should affect what he foresaw as the law of nations. It is about how international law must serve as the foundation for universal human freedom.

As a Christian and as a humanist, Grotius taught that human law, like God's law, must be just. He believed that we humans are God's creatures, endowed with the capacity of reason and blessed with the

---

[3] Or, in the Latin, De Jure Belli ac Pacis (1625).
[4] For a more detailed discussion of this treatise, *see* "Hugo Grotius," in Leo Strauss and Joseph Cropsey, ed., History of Political Philosophy, 3rd Ed. (Chicago and London: University of Chicago Press, 1987), 386 –395 [1963].

opportunity of sharing the gift of life. Therefore, he believed that we humans are — in our nature — both rational and social. From this, he concluded that what is *just* for humanity must be what is *natural* to our society of rational creatures trying our best to live together in the world God gave us.

Thus, Grotius stressed the significance of "natural law." In his view, natural law is "the dictate of right reason." It is what is necessary to our rational and social nature. It is that system of rights and duties that flows necessarily from our essential nature as rational creatures living together in society. It is *natural* law that is *just* law.

The implications of this insight are considerable and far-reaching. For it follows that whatever is necessary for our rational existence — whatever is necessary for our productive participation in society — is necessarily *ours* under natural law. It is ours by natural *right*. And, thus, a just society is a society that both respects and realizes our natural rights.

More, it follows as well that those who would govern our rational efforts to make a just human society — those we call today "nation-states" — must both respect and realize our natural rights. Further — and crucially — it follows likewise that our natural rights — call them our "human rights" — must be both respected and realized in spite of, and irrespective of, the individual inclinations of individual "nation-states."

For Grotius, "the dictate of right reason" is a demanding dictate that applies at all times to everyone everywhere. For him, we each have — by our very nature — as individual humans — an equal claim to individual human rights. And, for him, these equal human rights are exactly the same for each and every one of us.

This is an idea that assumes a *shared* humanity. This is a notion that assumes a *single* humanity, a *common* humanity that transcends the artificial and ever-changing limits of national borders, and that binds us together above and beyond all the boundaries of nationality, race, religion, or any other superficial distinction that might somehow obscure our basic oneness. This, to say the least, is a potentially revolutionary thought.

From Grotius, this was a Christian thought, founded on the universal teachings of his own faith. Yet even Grotius argued that what he characterized as the universal law of nature would be valid even if there were no God. *Then* — as Grotius himself acknowledged at the time

— such a suggestion was blasphemous in the context of a Christian Europe.[5] *Now* — as we all might acknowledge today — the revolutionary thought that universal laws should apply to a humanity that is universally one and the same is by far the most compelling argument in favor of universal human rights in the context of our much more diverse modern world.

Reasoning from this decidedly revolutionary proposition, Grotius saw the substance of natural law — in part — in the operation of human reason in human experience. He saw it in custom. He saw it in what we would describe today as "rule-making." He saw customs and rules as transcending national borders, and as constituting some of the most significant elements of "international law." He implied that sovereign states can be fully and truly legitimate only if they acknowledge the duties they owe to each other — and to a common humanity — by acting in accordance with the customary rules of "international law."[6]

Reasoning further, Grotius argued that sovereign states must not only act in accordance with "international law." They must also act together to make "international law." Grotius wrote of what he described as "the law of nations."[7] He saw "the law of nations" as law that is developed by the collective will of all or many nations, and that draws its obligatory force from the combined will of all or many nations. Thus, he emphasized the potential of cooperative *international* efforts as a means of making *international* law.

Grotius saw sovereign states as sharing a common interest in making international law, and also in enforcing international law through strict adherence to the international rule of law. Implicit in his revolutionary thought that there are universal human rights is the equally revolutionary thought that human rights can prevail universally only if the rule of law prevails universally.

It is this implicit corollary to his thinking on international law that is perhaps most telling for us today. Not only nationally, but internationally, freedom only exists under the law. Not only nationally, but internationally, it is the certainty of the rule of law that, alone, can

---

[5] Id. at 388.

[6] For a thoughtful and thorough discussion of this point, and of several others relating to this treatise by Grotius, *see* Philip Bobbitt, The Shield of Achilles: War, Peace, and the Course of History (New York: Alfred A. Knopf, 2002), 513 – 518.

[7] Or, in the Latin, *jus gentium*.

enable us to escape from all the confining fortresses that imprison us. Not only nationally, but internationally, it is the certainty of the rule of law that, alone, can set us free.

Following his daring escape, Grotius never returned to the Netherlands. In France, in Sweden, and elsewhere he continued his humanistic scholarship. He continued to work for peace, and he continued to work for freedom. Yet, despite all his work, despite all his treatises, and despite all his scholarly and other accomplishments, at his death he thought his life a failure.

Grotius died in exile. He died of exhaustion and exposure following a shipwreck a few years before the conclusion of the Peace of Westphalia that ended the senseless religious fratricide of the Thirty Years' War in Europe in 1648. Thus, he did not live to see the first faint glimpse of the future he foresaw through international cooperation and through the international rule of law. He did not live to see the ascendance of "nation-states" in the advent of what the theorists of international affairs commonly call the "Westphalia System."

The "Westphalia System" is a system in which the principal actors in the world are all "nation-states." It is a system that depends for its success on the constructive cooperation of "nation-states." The "Westphalia System" has lasted now for the better part of four centuries. It has provided the fundamental framework for the conduct of world affairs ever since 1648. The "Westphalia System" has created the possibility for cooperative action through international law. Yet the "nation-states" of the "Westphalia System" are only now starting to see some of the most profound of the implications of what Grotius really meant by "international law," only now starting to realize some of the vast potential of international law, and only now starting to make some of the connections that Grotius made between the need for the international rule of law and the hope for human freedom.

In all the years since the creation of the "Westphalia System," we have been trying to make these connections. In all the years since he wrote his famous treatise on international law, we have been groping toward Grotius. In all the centuries since he made his escape, we have been trying to make our own escape to the full measure of human freedom that he believed could be found through the international rule of law. But we have yet to escape. We have yet to find that freedom. We have yet to free ourselves from the confines of our own imprisonment. And, thus, ours remains a world locked in a confining fortress of our own fierce making. Ours remains a world gasping for air.

For all our concerted efforts, for all our centuries of allegiance to the lofty ideal of international cooperation, the hard reality is that we have yet to find the full flourishing of human freedom that can only be found through the international rule of law. Indeed, in reality, we have yet even to agree that there can, in reality, truly be such a thing as "international law."

From the very beginning, there have been skeptics. In his Leviathan, published in 1651, just a few years after the death of Grotius, and just a few years after the birth of the "Westphalia System," the English political theorist Thomas Hobbes stated what many have long thought to be obvious about the fond hopes of internationalists and other idealists for the international rule of law. "Where there is no common power," Hobbes said, "there is no law."[8] In the minds of such skeptics, because there is "no common power" in the world — because there is no single global sovereign power — there can be no international custom, or rule, or standard of any kind, worthy of being called a "law."

Typical of the Hobbesian line of thinking on this issue was the nineteenth century English thinker on jurisprudence, John Austin. Austin defined a "law" as a rule laid down by a sovereign power for which obedience can be enforced — because there is some penalty for failing to obey it. Thus, as he saw it, for a "law" to be regarded as a "law," there must be some legal sanction for *not* obeying it.[9]

By this reasoning, much that is often described as "international law" is not really law at all. Although it is nominally binding, although it has been agreed and signed and ratified, although the "nation-states" may have convened a colorful ceremony to celebrate it, there is, in reality, no penalty for *not* obeying it, and thus there is no assurance that it will be enforced. It is, in the familiar jargon of today's successors to Grotius, not "hard law," but "soft law." Consequently, what we call "international law" is, as Austin put it, actually "a law in name only."[10] It is a form only of what he called "positive morality," because whether it is enforced or not depends entirely on whether "nation-states" are willing to obey it.[11]

---

[8] Thomas Hobbes, Leviathan (New York: Penguin Books, 1985), 188 [1651].
[9] Dennis Lloyd, The Idea of Law (London: Penguin Books, 1991), 183 [1964].
[10] Quoted in Bobbitt, The Shield of Achilles, at 565.
[11] Lloyd, The Idea of Law, at 179, 187.

Thus, in this view, it is not law, but power, that really matters in the world. And a world in which it is power that really matters is the very opposite of the world that Grotius sought through the international rule of law. It is the cold world of the ancient Greek sophist, Thrasymachus, who told Socrates, in the first book of Plato's <u>Republic</u>, that " 'right' is always the same, the interest of the stronger party."[12] It is the harsh world of the Melian Dialogue of Thucydides, where "the strong do what they can and the weak suffer what they must."[13] It is the sorrowful world of an endless series of endless variations on the Thirty Years' War that Grotius tried so hard to end — a world in which *might* always and ever makes *right*.

Because of the decisive role of power in the world, Raymond Aron, the French political thinker, concluded that international society is "an anarchical order of power in which might makes right."[14] In the absence of real international law, and in the absence of the real international rule of law, international society is destined always to remain "anarchical."[15] We have been reminded all too vividly of this lately. We have been reminded by recent events how very far we have still to go to escape from the international anarchy that characterizes our continuing imprisonment, and to secure the international rule of law through "the dictate of right reason." As my friend and colleague on the Appellate Body, that great and eloquent champion of international law, Judge Georges Abi-Saab of Egypt, reminded me on September 12, 2001, "Ours is not yet an Age of Reason."

Our only escape from anarchy into freedom is through "the dictate of right reason." Our only chance to achieve all that might be achieved through our common humanity is through the enduring vision of Grotius. And yet, in far too may ways, in far too many places, and in far too many instances, the international rule of law is only a fiction and a fantasy. Seemingly at every turn — on pressing international issues ranging from crimes against humanity to crimes against the environment, and on urgent global security issues ranging from defense against the continuing threat of nuclear missiles to defense against the new, nightmarish threat of

---

[12] Plato, <u>The Republic</u> (New York: Penguin Books, 1987), 77 – 78.
[13] Robert B. Strassler, ed., <u>The Landmark Thucydides</u> (New York: The Free Press, 1996), 352.
[14] Raymond Aron, "The Anarchical Order of Power," in Stanley Hoffmann, ed., <u>Conditions of World Order</u> (1968), 25, 47.
[15] *See* Hedley Bull, <u>The Anarchical Society: A Study of Order in World Politics</u> (New York: Columbia University Press, 1977).

unprecedented acts of terror — the desire for the international rule of law is subordinated to the demands of the international rule of power. Seemingly at every turn, *might* still seems to make *right*.

The centrality — the sheer indispensability — of the international rule of law to all our brightest hopes for the future can hardly be exaggerated. On this, the civilized nations of the world seem to agree. To cite only one example: the third clause in the Preamble to the Universal Declaration on Human Rights states emphatically that "it is essential, if man is not to be compelled to have recourse, as a last resort, to rebellion against tyranny and oppression, that human rights be protected by the rule of law."[16] In her wonderful book on the drafting of this Universal Declaration, A World Made New, Harvard Law Professor Mary Ann Glendon highlights the way in which this clause "gives prominence to a key concept: the importance and the fragility of the rule of law."[17]

And yet, all too often, in our "anarchical" world, the international rule of law for the sake of a common humanity seems only to be an afterthought to the exercise of power. It seems only to be a soothing, reassuring, rhetorical footnote to the continued rule of *realpolitik*. International law still leads what the American jurist, Justice Benjamin Cardozo, once described as a "twilight existence."[18]

But, much like Grotius, Justice Cardozo also held out the hope that international law might emerge from the twilight. It can do so, he said, when "at length the *imprimatur* of a court attests to its jural quality."[19] Something akin to this is happening now. At long last, there is evidence for the hope that international law can, indeed, emerge from its "twilight existence." At long last, there is evidence that Grotius, and all those who have followed Grotius in all the long years since his escape to freedom, have been right: there can be the international rule of law.

This evidence comes from what some would consider an unlikely source. It comes from the dispute settlement system of the World Trade Organization.

---

[16] Preamble, Universal Declaration of Human Rights.
[17] Mary Ann Glendon, A World Made New: Eleanor Roosevelt and the Universal Declaration of Human Rights (New York: Random House, 2001), 176.
[18] Justice Benjamin Cardozo, New Jersey v. Delaware, 292 U.S. 361, 383 (1934).
[19] Id.

Few who have ever served in public office have ever had any illusions about the primacy of economics in the life of the world. Few who have ever faced the judgment of voters have ever doubted the significance of commerce and trade. It is true that the British statesman, William Gladstone, complained when, during his political apprenticeship, he was assigned to the Board of Trade. He complained that, wanting to govern men, he had been sent to "govern packages."[20] However, Gladstone, like many others, quickly learned that, in governing men, it helps to know how to govern packages. In my own case, great opportunities for governance came my way early in my tenure in the Congress of the United States because, as the Chairman of the House Ways and Means Committee told me at the time, "I understand that you have actually read the GATT."

Many others, however, have *not* read the GATT — the General Agreement on Tariffs and Trade. And — ironically — many of those who have *not* done so, are among the most ardent and articulate advocates of the international rule of law. For more than half a century now, the GATT-based trading system has been establishing the international rule of law in international trade — rule by rule, and case by case. For many years now, there has been an ever-expanding treasure of international jurisprudence arising, first, from the experience of the GATT, and, now, from the experience of the dispute settlement system of the new WTO. But, for some reason, all of this has been largely ignored by many of the most dedicated followers of Grotius.

Through the years, most of the leading luminaries on public international law have had little to say about international trade law.[21] There are exceptions.[22] But, generally, international trade law has been an afterthought in the academic and other realms of international law, even as the very notion of "international law" has often been an afterthought in much of the ongoing work of the world. Few have read it. Few have taught it. Few have seemed to think much of it or much about it.

---

[20] Richard Shannon, Gladstone, Volume One, 1809 – 1865 (London: Methuen, 1984), 110 [1982]; Roy Jenkins, Gladstone (London: Papermac, 1995), 66 – 67.

[21] Brownlie does not mention the GATT or the GATT-based trading system. Ian Brownlie, 4th ed., Principles of Public International Law (Oxford: Clarendon Press, 1996). Neither does Shaw. M.N. Shaw, 3rd ed., International Law (Cambridge: Cambridge University Press, 1995). Nor do a number of other standard treatises on public international law.

[22] The late Robert Hudec and John Jackson, of course, come most readily to mind. They have each devoted their lives and their long and illustrious careers to demonstrating the potential of international trade law as an example of the potential of the international rule of law.

Until now. Now this is changing.

Why is this so? Why is international trade law, all of a sudden, in the forefront of all the "cutting edge" thinking on international law worldwide — like the poor relation in some Jane Austen novel who is finally invited to sit at the main table in the manor house? Why, suddenly, is the WTO "trendy"?

One reason is that what has long been clear to the politicians and to their constituents worldwide has gradually also become clear to others. Trade is vital to the world. And, further, the work of trade and the law of trade increasingly intersect with much else that is also vital to the world. Health, environment, labor rights, human rights, and much, much more are *all* related to trade. They all affect trade, and are all affected by trade. And, thus, increasingly, we have *all* come to understand the sweeping implications of "governing packages."

Another reason is that it is increasingly clear to all that international trade law is, in fact, a part of the broader overall realm of "international law." Through the years, some have seen the law of the GATT, and now the law of the WTO, as somehow self-contained in the world of "widgets" that was for so long the seemingly separate province of those who dealt with GATT law and GATT lore. Yet our brief experience with the WTO has clearly shown that the work of the WTO cannot be seen as separate and apart from all that is not directly related to trade in "widgets." And it follows, likewise, that WTO law cannot be considered as separate and apart from other international law. As we said in the very first ruling of the WTO Appellate Body, WTO rules cannot be viewed in "clinical isolation" from the broader corpus and the broader concerns of the rest of international law.[23]

Still another reason why the WTO is "trendy" is because the WTO is busy. In only the few years since the creation of the WTO in 1995, the WTO dispute settlement system has rapidly become the busiest international system for resolving international disputes in the history of the world. Hundreds of international trade disputes have been settled because of the very existence of the WTO dispute settlement system, hundreds of other disputes have been resolved through formal cases in

---

[23]United States — Standards for Reformulated Gasoline, WTO Doc. WT/DS2/AB/R, at 17 (March 20, 1996).

the WTO dispute settlement system, and thousands of pages of new
international jurisprudence — by one recent count, *more than twenty
thousand pages* — have emerged from the ongoing work of the WTO
dispute settlement system.[24] The Appellate Body alone has issued about
sixty appellate reports. Still more are forthcoming. And all of this, of
course, is in addition to the *thirty thousand pages* of international
agreements, concessions, and other rules that comprise the "covered
agreements" of the WTO treaty. All in all, the ever-increasing workload
of the WTO dispute settlement system affects the lives of five billion people
in the 95 percent of all world commerce that is conducted by the 146
countries and other customs territories that are — currently — Members
of the WTO.

All of this is difficult to ignore. But none of this fully explains
why international trade law is no longer an afterthought. By far the most
important reason why the WTO has drawn the increasing attention of the
world is because the WTO is offering persuasive evidence to the world
for the very first time that there truly can be something deserving of being
called "international law," and, thus, also, that there truly can be the
international rule of law.

The British barrister and law professor Dennis Lloyd observed
some time ago that, "A distinctive feature of a developed, as compared
with a more primitive, form of law is the existence of tribunals charged
with the task of deciding matters in dispute, whose jurisdiction is
compulsory, and which have at their disposal sufficient organized force
to ensure that their decisions are, at least generally speaking, obeyed."[25]
He concluded that "international law ... has not yet attained, if it ever
will, the stage of regular adjudication and enforcement of disputes," and
he noted that "[e]ven the International Court of Justice has no compulsory
jurisdiction and if it had, has no means of enforcing its decisions."[26]

The seven of us who are privileged to serve by appointment of
the Members of the WTO as Members of the Appellate Body of the WTO
do not call our international trade tribunal a court. We do not wear robes.
We do not wear wigs. We do not wear bibs. We do not have all the
institutional accoutrements that have accrued to other tribunals with the
passage of time and with the accretion of tradition. Nor do we seek them.

---

[24] John H. Jackson, "Perceptions about the WTO trade institutions." <u>World Trade Review</u>,
Volume 1, Number 1 (March, 2002) 101, 109.
[25] Dennis Lloyd, <u>The Idea of Law</u>, at 335.
[26] Id. at 189.

We see ours as an important — but also as a mundane and straightforward — task. In the words of the treaty that guides and governs our work, we seek, through our work, to assist the Members of the WTO in their efforts "to secure a positive solution" to every international trade dispute that comes before us, and we seek, through our work, to help the Members of the WTO provide "security and predictability to the multilateral trading system," and also "to preserve the rights and obligations of Members" of the WTO "under the covered agreements, and to clarify the existing provisions of those agreements in accordance with customary rules of interpretation of public international law."[27] In this way, we hope to help the Members of the WTO establish a useful, workable, practical, enduring institution that will contribute to the continuing success of the WTO and the WTO dispute settlement system, and that will, in time, serve all the people of the world.

Yet we are ever mindful in our work that the WTO dispute settlement system is as busy as it is because the WTO dispute settlement system is *unique*. We have much to do around our table in Geneva because, among all the international tribunals in the world, and, indeed, among all the international tribunals in the *history* of the world, ours is unique in two important ways. The WTO has compulsory jurisdiction, and the WTO makes judgments that are enforced.

The WTO has compulsory jurisdiction because all WTO Members have agreed in the WTO treaty to resolve all their treaty-related disputes with other WTO Members in the WTO dispute settlement system. The WTO cannot be ignored by WTO Members when a claim is made under the WTO treaty.

The WTO makes judgments that are enforced because the WTO treaty empowers the WTO Members to enforce the decisions made in WTO dispute settlement through the "last resort"[28] of a "suspension of concessions"[29] that has the effect of economic sanctions. The WTO dispute settlement system inspires WTO Members to comply with WTO judgments through the considerable incentive of economic suasion.

Thus, the WTO offers an example to the world for the first time of what even the skeptics are bound to acknowledge by their own terms

---

[27] Article 3.7 and Article 3.2, WTO Understanding on Rules and Procedures Governing the Settlement of Disputes (the "Dispute Settlement Understanding").

[28] Article 3.7, Dispute Settlement Understanding.

[29] Article 22.1, Dispute Settlement Understanding.

is real "international law." The WTO has moved beyond the anarchy, beyond the primitivism, and beyond the skepticism to construct a system in which international rules and international rulings are both made *and enforced*. This is the essence of our uniqueness. This is also the source of what makes the WTO so controversial to so many in the world. It is easy to ignore a tribunal whose judgments are ignored. It is impossible to ignore a tribunal whose judgments are enforced.

Because of our uniqueness, and because of the commitment of the Members of the WTO to the success of the WTO dispute settlement system, we are helping the world get just a little closer toward Grotius. Through the WTO, we are approaching the international rule of law, as we often say on the Appellate Body, on a "case-by-case basis." And our progress in Geneva on matters relating to trade and commerce can and must be seen as evidence to all the world that, at long last, after long centuries of futile hoping and wishful thinking, the international rule of law can become real.

For WTO rules are not the only rules the world needs. There are many other international agreements, in addition to the WTO treaty, that have legitimacy, and that are also deserving of enforcement through the international rule of law. There are hundreds of multilateral international agreements dealing with human rights, women's rights, children's rights, workers' rights, the environment, health, intellectual property, investment, crime, corruption, genocide, and numerous other areas of compelling international concern that deserve due credence and due consideration by both national and international tribunals. And there is need for more.

There is need for more international law, not less. Certainly we could begin — as Judge Abi-Saab has recently suggested — with the negotiation of a comprehensive international convention against terrorism.[30] Surely we should also negotiate additional international agreements to help achieve the essential global goals of the recently completed World Summit on Sustainable Development in Johannesburg, South Africa. In these and other ways, we should find more and better means of making and enforcing international law in order to meet all the

---

[30] Georges Abi-Saab, "The Proper Role of International Law in Combatting Terrorism," Chinese J. Int'l L. 305,311 (2002). As he points out, "All international efforts for decades, starting with the League of Nations and continuing with the United Nations, to draw a comprehensive convention against terrorism (but not specific acts of terrorism) have hitherto failed, absent a generally accepted and shared definition of what is terrorism, a terrorist act or a terrorist group."

many challenges of "globalization," and in order to confront and overcome all the many threats to the peace and prosperity of our world.

The success, thus far, of the WTO dispute settlement system is an example of the success that can result from pursuing the insight of Grotius that making and enforcing international law can be an act of international cooperation. There is still "no common power" in the world. Thus, it falls to all the nations of the world to cooperate to shape and share a "common power" through an international rule of law that will be sufficient to address the needs of global trade in a global economy, and will be sufficient also to address the many other compelling needs of our common humanity. Although still new, and although still very much in the making, the WTO is proof that such a "common power" can be created, and can serve the common cause of human freedom through the international rule of law. What we have done for the "widgets" of the WTO we can do also for all the many other shared purposes of humanity. We can move ever closer to Grotius. As explained, for example, by Michael Mandelbaum, a leading theorist on international security, "The world that we want to see evolve today is not a world of one, two, or three contending powers, but rather a world governed by rules. That is already increasingly true in economics, and ... security affairs will eventually mirror that."[31]

We do not, in other words, want a world in which might makes right. Rather, we want a world in which *right* makes *might*. And we can have such a world only when the world has agreed on rules for international cooperation, and only when those rules are enforced through the international rule of law. As with the WTO, the aim in other areas of common human concern must be to resolve international disputes by relying on international rules on which the nations of the world have agreed, and by enforcing those rules uniformly and consistently. The aim must be to beat our "swords into ploughshares" through the international rule of law.[32]

Our success — thus far — in WTO dispute settlement is encouraging evidence that we can accomplish much more — in trade and in many other areas of our shared concern — for the international rule of law. It is the best evidence the world has ever seen that

---

[31]Michael Mandelbaum, Interview with Thomas Friedman, *International Herald Tribune* (April 11, 2000).
[32] Isaiah 2:4.

"international law" can be real law in the real world. Ours, though, is a fragile achievement. Our success, thus far, in the WTO is no guarantee of our continued success. We have emerged from the twilight of our imprisonment. But we have not yet escaped into the bright sunlight of freedom.

One of the many insights of Grotius was that "international law" is the product of historical experience. For Grotius, "natural law" can be reflected in experience. It can be revealed in the experience of applying human reason to rule-making.[33] Or, as Professor Oscar Schacter has written, in a contemporary echo of Grotius, law "is in essence a system based on a set of rules and obligations."[34]

This is certainly how many of us who serve and support the WTO see what Professor Schacter has called "the reality of international law" as it is reflected and revealed in the WTO dispute settlement system.[35] The WTO is the product of more than half a century of multilateral experience in rule-making for an ever-growing and ever-evolving multilateral trading system. The WTO treaty is a set of rules on which all those who have signed the treaty have agreed. By its terms, the treaty is binding — and enforceable — on all the Members of the WTO. By its terms, WTO rules *are* international law.

Long before there was a WTO, Professor Robert Hudec famously characterized the system of dispute settlement in the WTO's predecessor, the GATT, as a form of "diplomatic jurisprudence" — as a mix of law and politics, a mix of law and diplomacy.[36] Since its beginning, for more than half a century, the dispute settlement system has been evolving from politics and diplomacy to law and jurisprudence. What began as informal "working parties" of diplomats, has gradually evolved through the decades into formal deliberations by legally-minded jurists.

Today, in WTO dispute settlement, in the work of the *ad hoc* panels, and in the work of the standing Appellate Body, we have a system in which politics and diplomacy have yielded to the rule of law. In particular, this is so of the Appellate Body. We seven Members of the Appellate

---

[33] Bobbitt, The Shield of Achilles, at 529.
[34] Oscar Schacter, International Law in Theory and Practice (Norwell, Mass.: Martinus Nijhoff, 1991), 4.
[35] Id. at 5.
[36] Robert E. Hudec, Essays on the Nature of International Trade Law (London: 1999), 17.

Body are limited by the WTO treaty to addressing *legal* issues that are raised on appeal from panel decisions.[37] We have always fulfilled our responsibilities to the Members of the WTO in a way that one observer for the *New York Times* has described as "impartial and unflinching."[38] We have upheld the international rule of law. We always will.

But some would have it otherwise. Some would turn back the clock. Some would return to the "good old days" when politics and diplomacy prevailed over law in dispute settlement — to the days when the GATT was often derided as the "General Agreement to Talk and Talk." Some even maintain — despite all the accumulating evidence to the contrary — that the WTO dispute settlement system still is, not law, but diplomacy. Thus, the debate over whether there can or should be such a thing as the international rule of law continues — even within the WTO. And, thus, our achievements in recent years in establishing the rule of law in world trade through the WTO dispute settlement system cannot — and must not — be taken for granted.

What must we do? What must we do to secure and sustain our recent achievements for the international rule of law in the WTO? What must we do so that we will be able to build on those achievements for the future of the world trading system, and also for the future of the international rule of law as a liberating force for freedom in the world? What must we do to make our escape to freedom?

Much of what we must do is evident. We must continue to be "impartial and unflinching" in enforcing the rule of law in WTO dispute settlement. We must continue also to improve the WTO dispute settlement system so that it will better serve the rule of law. And we must continue — and succeed — in the mutual efforts of the Members of the WTO to agree on additional trade liberalization and other needed trade reforms in the new "Development Round" of multilateral trade negotiations. Burdened by a weak world economy, the world surely and sorely needs the additional growth that can result from the successful conclusion of the new round. And a *successful* conclusion of the new round will be one that clearly benefits *all* WTO Members. The more that *all* the Members of the WTO see that they *all share* in the benefits of growth, and the more that *all* see that they *all* share in the benefits of the WTO trading system,

---

[37] Article 17.6, Dispute Settlement Understanding.
[38] Michael M. Weinstein, "Economic Scene: Should Clinton embrace the China trade deal? Some say yes," *New York Times* (September 9, 1999).

the more willing *all* the Members of the WTO will be to continue to insist on the rule of law in WTO dispute settlement.

But to succeed in all this, we must do something more. Beyond all this, we must understand something more. We must understand what the "rule of law" really is, and we must understand also why we really need the "rule of law" internationally. We must understand what the stakes really are for all of us in realizing "the dictate of right reason" through the international rule of law.

The "rule of law" is, above all, *not* politics. The "rule of law" is definitely *not* politics. As Professor Schacter has warned us, we cannot reduce law to politics "without eliminating it as law."[39] Politics is arbitrary. Law is not. With the "rule of law," the law is certain, not arbitrary. With the "rule of law," the law is written beforehand, and the rules are defined and known in advance. With the "rule of law," the law is written to apply to all equally, and all — in practice — in reality — are equal before the law. With the "rule of law," no one — no one — is beneath the concern of the law, and no one — no one — is above the law. Only this can rightly be called the "rule of law."

Further, what all too many in the centuries since Grotius — what all too many in the bloody history of all the efforts to set men free — have all too often forgotten about the "rule of law", and what we must understand — above all — about why we really need "the rule of law", is this. It is the law that sets us free. We can be free only *under the law*. We can be free only *with the "rule of law."*

Grotius was not alone in teaching this. Voltaire taught us that we are free only when we are bound to obey nothing but the law.[40] Hayek explained that, when we obey laws under the rule of law, "we are not subject to another man's will and are therefore free."[41] Locke wrote, "The end of the law is ... to preserve and enlarge freedom. ... Where there is no law there is no freedom."[42] It is the law alone, he wrote, that prevents us from being "subject to the inconstant, uncertain, unknown, arbitrary will

---

[39] Schacter, <u>International Law in Theory and Practice</u>, at 4.

[40] Voltaire, <u>Philosophical Dictionary</u> (New York: Penguin Books, 1972), 194 [1764].

[41] Friedrich von Hayek, <u>The Constitution of Liberty</u> (Chicago: University of Chicago Press, 1978), 153 [1960].

[42] John Locke, Section 57, "The Second Treatise of Government," <u>Two Treatises of Government</u> (London: Everyman's Library, 1993), 142 [1689].

of another man."[43] All of these historic defenders of the "rule of law" were elaborating on Grotius, whether consciously or not. And all of them were right.

Freedom and law are linked. They are inextricably connected. What we may call freedom truly *is* freedom only where there *is* the rule of law. Grotius understood this, and all of us who are still groping toward Grotius all these hundreds of years later must understand this as well if we hope to escape to freedom. In particular, this must continue to be understood by all those who serve the "nation-states" that are Members of the WTO as — together — they strive to serve the cause of human freedom through the exercise of their "common power" as the WTO.

The demise of the "nation-state" has been much exaggerated.[44] The Peace of Westphalia, which first gave precedence to the "nation-state," still has meaning for the modern world. For the most part, the "Westphalia System" still prevails. The WTO is not by any means alone among international institutions in being "Member-driven" by "nation-states." Rightly, and unquestionably, the future of the WTO will be shaped by the shared will of the countries and other customs territories that are the Members of the WTO. Their shared will — their cooperative will — their combined will as manifested in the continuing idealistic aim of the WTO of achieving a multilateral consensus — is the key to the future of the WTO as both an engine for the trading system and an exemplar for the international rule of law. Their will is the key to opening the lock to freedom.

Like *all* law, all *international* law ultimately depends on a willingness on the part of those who are supposedly bound by the law to comply with the law. This is true *regardless* of whether there are sanctions for *not* complying with the law. This is true of a traffic ticket. This is true of WTO law. In this respect, the "law" of WTO rules and rulings differs from other "international law" only in degree, and not in kind. Ultimately, there must be a willingness to obey it.

Given this, the WTO will, ultimately, be able to achieve all that it is capable of achieving for the international rule of law only if all the many "nation-states" that are Members of the WTO remain willing to

---

[43] Id., Section 22, at 126.
[44] *See* Robert Gilpin, Global Political Economy: Understanding the International Economic Order (Princeton: Princeton University Press, 2001), 362 – 363.

uphold the international rule of law in all they do — individually — as Members of the WTO, and in all they do — together — as the WTO. And this willingness will exist and persist only if each and every Member of the WTO fully understands — and fully communicates at all times to all their citizens and to all their many and varied domestic constituencies — the full extent of all that is at stake for the future of the world in the future of the World Trade Organization.

Without the rule of law, the *developed* countries that are Members of the WTO can never obtain the security and the predictability they seek as a needed framework for world trade and as a firm foundation for the continued growth of the world economy. Without such a framework, without such a foundation, there can be no assurance of continued growth. Without it, the ability of developed countries to continue their historic trade expansion would be impaired, and their future would, thus, be greatly at risk. A world without the rule of law is *not* a world in which there can truly be a *world* economy.

Likewise, without the rule of law, the *developing* countries that are Members of the WTO cannot remain the equals of the developed countries within the WTO. One of the greatest achievements of the WTO is that developed countries and developing countries are equals in WTO dispute settlement. However, without the rule of law, developing countries would be at the mercy of a WTO dispute settlement system in which might *would* make right. Those who do not agree may wish to re-read Plato or Thucydides, or, better yet, recall the sad history of much of the twentieth century. If might ever made right in the WTO dispute settlement system, the developing countries would be destined forever to remain *developing* countries. They would never attain their full measure of freedom through sustainable economic development.

Moreover, without the rule of law, we cannot do everything else that we all hope to do for the cause of freedom throughout the world through the WTO. We would not be able to preserve the rights and obligations of the WTO Members under the existing rules of trade, and we would not be able to implement the new rules for trade that the world needs. And, further, we would not be able to remain an example to the world of all else that might be done for freedom in the world through the international rule of law.

Trade is a means to an end. The end is freedom. Much that can be done for the end of freedom through the means of trade simply will not be done unless politics yields to law, and unless diplomacy yields to jurisprudence, in the important work of WTO dispute settlement. The arts of politics and diplomacy are altogether appropriate when making law, but not when enforcing law. They are entirely appropriate when negotiating WTO rules, but not when clarifying WTO rules in dispute settlement for the purpose of preserving the rights and obligations of WTO Members under the WTO treaty. Only if WTO rules are viewed impartially and objectively in the light of a critical judgment that is totally independent of competing political considerations can compliance with those rules by all WTO Members — for the mutual benefit of all WTO Members — be justified. And only if all WTO Members remain willing to exercise their sovereign rights as "nation-states" by choosing to comply with WTO rules and WTO rulings can the continued success of the WTO be assured.

Nowhere is there a greater need for such willingness than in the leading trading nation in the world — the United States of America. Nowhere is there a greater need for an understanding of what the stakes really are for the world in seeking the international rule of law. Nowhere is there a greater need for an enlightened exercise of the sovereign will in the service of a broad and visionary understanding of the true national self-interest. From time to time, in the WTO, we speak of a "systemic" interest. And no Member of the WTO at any time has a greater "systemic" interest in the continued success of the WTO dispute settlement system in serving and furthering the international rule of law than my own, my beloved country.

Contrary to what some have suggested lately — in the context of the WTO and also in other international contexts — the idea of an international rule of law is not alien to America or to Americans. Americans have always been among the followers of Grotius. Early in our history, Charles Sumner suggested the need for both a world court and a league of nations.[45] From the conclusion of the Jay treaty, to the settlement of the Alabama Claims, to the establishment of the Hague court, to the conference at Bretton Woods, to the convening of the United Nations, to the agreement on the GATT, and to the creation at long last of the WTO, Americans have always been in the forefront of cooperative international efforts to achieve peace and prosperity in a better world through the international rule of law.

---

[45] Van Wyck Brooks, The Flowering of New England, 1815 – 1865, at 395.

Together with others of like mind around the world, we Americans must always be in the forefront of those who seek and serve the international rule of law. This must *remain so* in all that we do as it relates to the WTO. This must *be so* in everything that America does in the world.

In the mundane world of trade, there will always be the temptation to want to pick and choose the rules we will obey, and to pick and choose the occasions when we will obey them. But we must remain mindful that we cannot have one set of rules for the United States, and another for the rest of the world. And we must remain mindful also that we cannot comply with only the rulings we like while not complying with those we may not like. That is *not* the rule of law, and that is definitely *not* in our broader and more visionary self-interest as seekers and servants of the international rule of law.

In the murderous world of terror, this is also true. The "war" we are waging *against* terror in the world must be a war *for* the international rule of law. The "war against terror" is a war *for freedom*. And this "war" can only be won if, in waging it, we seek and serve the international rule of law. Freedom under law is the only freedom worthy of the name. Freedom under law is the only lasting antidote to terror. Freedom under law is the only hope we have ever had, or ever will have, for an "Age of Reason."

In furthering trade, in fighting terror, in all that we do in the world, we Americans must always stand for the international rule of law. We must continue to summon the will and the wisdom to see that our true national interest is the international rule of what the Constitution of the United States of America — like Grotius —calls "the law of nations."[46]

In remembering all it means to be Americans, we must remember also all we have always believed America can mean for *all* the world. In recalling all we share as Americans, we must recall also all we share with the rest of a common humanity. We will always be our best as citizens of America if we always see ourselves also as citizens of the world.

Nearly four hundred years after Grotius made his daring escape from his prison fortress, we have not yet secured the birthright of our common humanity. We have not yet made our own escape from the fortress

---

[46] Article I, Section 8, Constitution of the United States of America.

of our own imprisonment. We are still groping toward Grotius. We are still seeking the full measure of human freedom that he foresaw. We remain in the twilight.

The revolutionary thought of Grotius remains but a thought. Yet, as someone who values international law, I believe that one day it will be much more than a thought. It has been the work of centuries. It will be the work of many centuries to come. But, I believe that, if we resolve to seek and serve the international rule of law, our tale will have a happy ending. One day we will find our way out of the twilight, and all the world will live in the bright sunlight of freedom.

Chapter Twelve

Lecky's Circle:
Thoughts from the Frontier of International Law

As every Londoner knows, Samuel Johnson once said that, "When a man is tired of London, he is tired of life."[1] I never tire of London, because London is so full of life. No doubt my wife, Rebecca, would add that it is true also that I never tire of London because London is also full of books. When in London, I spend much of my time looking at old books on the dusty shelves of London's bookshops. Sometimes, Rebecca even lets me buy one.

In truth, I must confess that I spend much of my life looking at old books on dusty shelves in bookshops all over the world. One of my favorites is "The Bookworm," a small bookshop on the *Rue Sismondi* in Geneva that specializes in used English books. I can often be found in "The Bookworm" on those weekends in Geneva when I am not too busy reading the fine print of voluminous WTO panel reports.

It was there where I first met a Londoner named William Edward Hartpole Lecky.

It happened some time ago on a rainy Sunday afternoon in "The Bookworm." On several previous visits, my eye had been caught by the intriguing title of an old book on the top shelf in the musty section of the bookshop devoted to old tomes on "philosophy." The title on the faded cover of the book was <u>History of European Morals from Augustus to Charlemagne</u>.[2] The author was someone named W.E.H. Lecky. Typical benighted American that I am, I had, at the time, never heard, or read a word, of W.E.H. Lecky.

On my previous visits, my interest in the history of European morals had not proven to be sufficient to overcome the fact that the top shelf in "The Bookworm" is too high for someone of my short stature to reach. But, at last, on this particular rainy Sunday afternoon, my curiosity

---

This chapter appears in two parts in <u>Amicus Curiae</u>, the journal of the Institute of Advanced Legal Studies of the University of London, Issue 50 (November-December, 2003) and Issue 51 (January-February, 2004).

[1] James Boswell, <u>Life of Johnson</u> (Oxford: Oxford University Press, 1980), 859 [1791].

[2] W.E.H. Lecky, <u>History of European Morals from Augustus to Charlemagne</u> (New York: George Braziller, 1955) Volumes I and II [1869], hereinafter <u>Morals</u>.

got the best of me, and I reached up as high as I could, pulled down the old book, and purchased it for the sum of twenty-five Swiss francs.

It was money well spent. I began reading the book that Sunday evening, read it through most of that night, and finished reading it the next day. Lecky's book on the history of European morals during European antiquity was one I needed to read. In my view, it is one we all need to read. For, in my view, William Edward Hartpole Lecky was a man who knew the way forward to a morality that can embrace and serve all humanity.

There was a time when W.E.H. Lecky was renowned throughout much of the world. He was once widely seen as a man who had much to say that was worth saying, and worth remembering, about morality and about humanity. When he died, a statue of him was placed outside the University of Dublin in Ireland. Today, that statue still stands there, but, today, the man himself is not much remembered. The lofty reputation that Lecky enjoyed a century ago has for some reason diminished with the passing of the years. Most of his many books are long out of print. They sit unread on dusty shelves in the quiet libraries and in the antiquarian bookshops of the world.

This is unfortunate, for Lecky was a writer and a thinker who was in many ways far ahead of his time. Indeed, he was a writer and a thinker who was in many ways far ahead of *our* time.

Born in Dublin in 1838, W.E.H. Lecky was a man of many parts. He was an historian. He was an essayist. He was, for a time, a Member of Parliament. He was a wealthy, landed Anglo-Irish aristocrat whose life spanned the Victorian era, and reflected much about that era. He was — in the great tradition of Gibbon, Macaulay, Carlyle, Grote, Burke, and others — one of the last of the classic eighteenth and nineteenth century "men of letters" who wrote about history in an elegant and philosophical style that enriched the English language. He has been described by his biographer, Donal McCartney, as "one of the last of the great line of amateur literary historians writing in English," and as "one of the last of the historiographical school of the Enlightenment."[3]

---

[3] Many of the personal and anecdotal details about Lecky in this essay are drawn from the excellent biography by Donal McCartney, W.E.H. Lecky: Historian and Politician, 1838-1903 (Dublin, Ireland: The Lilliput Press, 1994), hereinafter Lecky. This quotation is on page 189.

After completing his studies at Trinity College in Dublin, Lecky spent several years in additional self-schooling while touring Europe in search of Enlightenment. He traveled widely, reading extensively and intensively in all the great continental libraries, and living what he described as a "half vagabond, half bookworm existence, diving into half the libraries of Europe and breaking unhappy porters' backs with the boxes of books."[4] More than once, his studious travels took him through Geneva. Had "The Bookworm" been there at the time, no doubt Lecky would have found it.

Eventually, Lecky and his boxes of books settled in London. Like many others before and since, he wanted to be near the Reading Room of the British Museum. (His books are on display there today, behind protective panes of glass.) He filled the library in his townhouse in South Kensington with an ever-growing collection of books. He then devoted the rest of his life and his leisure to writing lengthy and thoughtful books in which he tried to solve the persistent puzzle of human progress.

One of those books is the one that I pulled from the top shelf in "The Bookworm." Written while Lecky was still in his twenties, and first published in 1869 when he was only thirty-one, it is an account in more than eight hundred pages of the progressive unfolding in antiquity of the notion that there is such a thing as "humanity." Lecky's message in the book resonated in a mid-Victorian world that believed in the progress of humanity. The book went through fifteen editions in Great Britain. It was even more popular at the time in the United States. Dusty though the book may be, its message resonates even today. For, even today, we are far from understanding, and even farther from implementing, Lecky's moral message for all humanity.

Lecky's message was about a *circle*.

Here is some of what he had to say:

"In the first dawning of the human intelligence ... the notion of *duty*, as distinguished from that of *interest*, appears, and the mind, in reviewing the various emotions by which it is influenced, recognises the unselfish and benevolent motives as essentially and generically superior to the selfish and the cruel. But it is the general condition of society alone that determines the standard of benevolence — the classes toward which

---

[4] McCartney, <u>Lecky</u>, at 29.

every good man will exercise it. At first, *the range of duty* is the family, the tribe, the state, the confederation. Within these limits every man feels himself under moral obligations to those about him; but he regards the outer world as we regard wild animals, as beings upon whom he may *justifiably prey*."[5]

Elsewhere in the same book, Lecky elaborated on this provocative thought:

"Men come into the world with their benevolent affections very inferior in power to their selfish ones, and the function of morals is to invert this order. The extinction of all selfish feeling is impossible for an individual, and if it were general, it would result in the dissolution of society. The question of morals must always be a question of proportion or of degree. At one time the benevolent affections embrace merely the family, soon *the circle expanding* includes first a class, then a nation, then a coalition of nations, then *all humanity*, and finally, its influence is felt in the dealings of man with the animal world....."[6]

Lecky described this expanding circle of human morality as *"the enlarging circle of sympathy."*[7] This circle of sympathy that he saw unfolding progressively in human history, and that he foresaw as eventually including all of humanity, might be described as *Lecky's circle.*

W.E.H. Lecky was an old-fashioned moral philosopher. His idea was that ever-higher, ever-broader moral standards of the duties we owe to one another as human beings evolve as signs of an ever-unfolding, ever-advancing progress in human history. His idea was that history records and reflects an ever-evolving, ever-progressing, ever-expanding human morality. His was a simple idea, and the way he chose to express his idea was with the simplicity of the circle. We live our lives in circles, and the size of our circles shapes the dimensions of our lives. The larger our circle, the larger our lives, for the larger our circle, the larger our scope of concern for others, and the larger our claim to the morality of a *true humanity.*

I have a front row seat on the frontier of international law. For this reason, I was asked to speak in London about my view of the many

---

[5] Lecky, Morals, Volume II, at 256.
[6] Lecky, Morals, Volume I, at 100-101.
[7] Lecky, Morals, Volume I, at 285.

far-flung frontiers of international law. The contemplation of those frontiers causes me to linger with Lecky's thoughts about circles. I do so because, as I see it, the true frontiers of international law are not the frontiers of law at all. They are the frontiers of the human morality that precedes law. They are the frontiers of our range of duty to the rest of humanity. In my judgment, in my experience, in my view from the circle where I live on the frontier of international law, the boundaries of the circle of our human sympathy are the true frontiers. For they are the frontiers that ultimately define also the boundaries of what we truly recognize and respect as law, and, therefore, of what we truly are willing to uphold and enforce as law.

Lecky has long since left us. He died one hundred years ago, in 1903, while, fittingly enough, reading one of the books in his London library. Lecky is gone. But, a century later, the frontiers of international law are expanding in ways that he foresaw. They are expanding because the circle of human sympathy is expanding. The significance of international law is increasing in the world because of the ongoing enlargement in the world of what we see as our range of duty. Today, a century after Lecky's death, the boundaries of international law are at last approaching the visionary boundaries of Lecky's circle.

This can be seen in many of the frontiers of international law. However, perhaps most clearly, perhaps most visibly, and perhaps most significantly, this can be seen in the frontier of international law where I live and where I have spent the past eight years. It can be seen where I spend much of my time when I am not browsing in old bookshops. It can be seen in the frontier of international law called the "WTO."

The "WTO" is, of course, the World Trade Organization. There may be no more important, no more innovative, and no more controversial international institution in all the world than the World Trade Organization. The WTO is less than a decade old, but the WTO has been busy from its very beginning expanding the range of human duty, extending the frontiers of international law, and thereby contributing to the enlargement of the human circle.

There are many examples of how busy we are at the WTO. One is the rising pile of WTO dispute settlement reports on my desk that prevents me from spending more of my time reading the thoughts of W.E.H. Lecky. But just how busy we are at the WTO is perhaps best illustrated by the ever-increasing numbers of people going online all around the world to learn more about the WTO. The number of people who visit "wto.org" monthly now numbers in the millions, and is rising rapidly. There are no dusty shelves on the WTO website.

If he is among the growing millions who are surfing the WTO website, if he is somewhere today in some wired celestial library sifting through the thousands of pages of reports of WTO proceedings that have been placed on the World Wide Web, then surely Lecky is smiling at the success thus far of the WTO. The WTO is a conscious and considered international effort to use trade as a means of approaching Lecky's circle. By expanding trade, the WTO is also expanding the opportunities for enlarging the range of human sympathy to include the full extent of Lecky's circle.

There are several circles within the WTO that serve an enlarged circle of human sympathy. I would like to think that Lecky is smiling most of all at the accomplishments of the small but busy circle where I live and work within the WTO called the "Appellate Body." The Appellate Body is the circle of seven international jurists who help the nations that are the Members of the WTO make binding judgments in final appeals in their international trade disputes.

Our small circle helps the Members of the WTO resolve international disputes involving the whole vast and varied array of goods and services that are traded in the world every day — including everything from apples to bananas, from airplanes to poultry, and from shrimp to semiconductors to supercomputers to steel. These international disputes affect billions of people by affecting billions of dollars in world trade. These international disputes result in rulings in international law that affect almost all of world trade.

Ours is a circle of seven that sits at a round table in a small room in the far corner of the far wing of the Italianate villa on the lake of Geneva that serves as the international headquarters of the WTO. As we sit together in our small room, as we work together day by day, our circle seems small to us. But our circle in our small room is large enough to affect almost all the world. Our "range of duty" to the Members of the WTO, and, through them, to humanity, includes much of what happens every day in the world economy.

Ours is a circle that is new to the world. Like the WTO itself, the Appellate Body is less than a decade old. The Appellate Body was created along with the WTO as a "quasi-judicial" institution within the WTO in 1995. The WTO is the successor to an earlier international institution, the General Agreement on Tariffs and Trade — the "GATT." In a sense that Lecky would surely understand, we are heirs on the Appellate Body to the nearly fifty years of ever-evolving, ever-progressing experience of the GATT in resolving international trade disputes following the end of the Second World War. Like human morality, human political economy, from the GATT to the WTO, is ever-unfolding.

Ours is also a circle that has been drawn by the world. The seven of us who sit around our table were each nominated by our individual countries, but we were each appointed by all of the 146 countries and other customs territories that are Members of the WTO. Thus, we each serve all 146 Members of the WTO. The Members of the WTO account for more than 95 percent of all world trade by more than five billion people. Every country of the world is either a Member of the WTO or seems to want to be. The ever-enlarging circle of WTO membership is expanding rapidly. In time, it will include all the world.

Ours, furthermore, is a circle that has been drawn in the *mutual interest* of the world. The Members of the WTO have invented the WTO-based world trading system as a way of coming together and working together to lower the barriers to trade and, thus, to raise the levels of their mutual prosperity. They have invented the WTO dispute settlement system as a way of upholding the trading rules on which they have all agreed. They have invented the small circle of the Appellate Body as a way of helping them clarify their obligations under those rules so they can uphold them within the ever-enlarging circle of the world trading system.

Moreover, ours is a circle of mutual interest that also has been, from the very beginning, a circle of *mutual trust*. The table of the Appellate Body is round because we seven sit at our table as equals. No one sits at the "head" of our table. Thus, our table is like Thomas Jefferson's table in Monticello long ago. Jefferson believed that those who sit together around a round table sit together as equals, and so do we. We are equal at our table, and we are equal in our trust of one another.

Our mutual trust is the result of our years of hard work while sitting together around our table. The seven of us on the Appellate Body are very different people. We come from seven different backgrounds, seven different cultures, seven different ways of seeing the world.

Importantly for our work together around our table, we also come from seven different systems of jurisprudence. But we share one guiding philosophical approach that shapes our perspective and, therefore, shapes as well the results of our work. If Lecky sat with us at our table, undoubtedly he would also share this one guiding approach.

Our work is legal work. Our task is to help the Members of the WTO resolve the legal issues that are raised on appeal in WTO dispute settlement. These legal issues are legal questions about the nature of the obligations of the WTO Members in the many "covered agreements" of the WTO treaty. Our challenge is thus a legal challenge of working together to reach a consensus on the right legal answers to those legal questions. In this way, we help the Members of the WTO clarify those obligations and thus help them resolve difficult international trade disputes.

We have been able to find the right answers through the years at our table in large part because our shared approach to finding the right answers is founded on our firm mutual belief in both the necessity and the value of the *conversations* that comprise our deliberations. Our deliberations are conversations in the best and truest sense of the word. They are open. They are lively. They are engaging. They are, above all, demanding exercises in *mutual criticism*. They are extended exercises in advocating, in debating, in communicating, and — most of all — in listening. They are shared efforts in mutual thinking that lead to mutual agreement. They are enlightening conversations that have led the seven of us to our enduring *mutual trust*.

The seven of us on the Appellate Body may be very different in very many ways. We are very much alike, though, in our mutual confidence in real and reasoned conversation as the right approach to reaching the right answers and to creating mutual trust. This shared confidence has made all the difference to us through the years in building a new institution for the benefit of a world that is much in need of mutual trust.

On the Appellate Body, we believe that a willingness to engage in reasoned and reasonable deliberation through the principled practice of mutual criticism is one of the keys to creating and sustaining human freedom. We also believe that one of the best ways to enlarge the circle of human sympathy is by enlarging the circle of our thinking through the considerable power of mutual, rational thought. We believe that, by listening to one another, we can learn from one another, and we can learn also to trust one another. We believe, too, that trust sought and secured in this way can serve the cause of human freedom.

This is our shared view. This was, of course, also the view of that other Londoner, Lecky's fellow traveler on the long road to human morality, John Stuart Mill. Perhaps the best statement of Mill's view is in his classic essay On Liberty.[8] No doubt his essay On Liberty had a place of honor in Lecky's library, as it does in the personal libraries of everyone who has ever served on the Appellate Body. Everyone who has sat at the round table of the Appellate Body would agree that Mill's famous essay expresses abiding truths about how best to serve the cause of human freedom. Indeed, my dear friend and former colleague on the Appellate Body, the late Chris Beeby, of New Zealand, was able to quote long passages of On Liberty from memory.

We may have seven different perspectives on the Appellate Body. We may have seven different points of view on any given legal issue. However, we share with Mill a fundamental belief in reason and in reasonableness. We share with Mill the view that the best way to reach a consensus is the "salutary effect" of a "collision of opinions."[9] We agree with him that "truth has no chance but in proportion as every side of it, every opinion which embodies any fraction of the truth, not only finds advocates, but is listened to."[10] This, as we see it, is the key to securing and serving freedom. And this, as I see it, is the key also to our continuing mutual trust, and to our continuing consensus on the Appellate Body.

The small circle of the Appellate Body serves the large circle of humanity that is represented by the Members of the WTO. Our "range of duty" is to the entire population of all of the 146 Members of the WTO. Five billion people are with us whenever we sit together at our table. They are all part of our circle of human sympathy. Their needs, their longing, their passions, their aspirations for a fuller and truer humanity — their fondest hopes for freedom — are all ever with us as we reason together in our efforts to help the Members of the WTO clarify and uphold their international treaty obligations. We believe that, by reasoning together, we can best serve all their hopes for freedom.

---

[8] John Stuart Mill, On Liberty (London: Penguin Books, 1985) [1859].
[9] Id. at 115.
[10] Id.

Through our reliance on reasonableness, the mutual criticism around our table creates mutual trust, and the conversation around our table creates consensus. The strength of our consensus is reflected in the results of our work thus far. Since the Appellate Body was established in 1995, there have been about sixty appeals in WTO dispute settlement. In not one of those numerous appeals has any Member of the Appellate Body ever dissented from the findings or the conclusions of any Appellate Body Report. Every single one of our decisions has been by consensus. We do not claim infallibility for the Appellate Body, but, to the extent that we seven have been fallible in our work for the Members of the WTO, even our most vocal critics must acknowledge that we have been fallible *together.*

To my mind, the consensus we have shared on the Appellate Body has contributed much to the success of our new institution in the short time we have sat together at our table. Claus-Dieter Ehlermann, who sat beside me at our table during my first six years on the Appellate Body, has said that our shared goal from the very start was the establishment of an independent, quasi-judicial institution that would serve all the Members of the WTO equally and effectively.[11] As usual, I agree with Claus. This has been our mutual goal from the very first time we sat down together, and I would submit that, thus far, we have succeeded in our mutual efforts to achieve it.

There are other reasons as well for our initial success. Contributing also to the success of the Appellate Body in achieving our shared goal of serving the Members of the WTO equally and effectively has been our *uniqueness* as an international tribunal. The Appellate Body is unique in two ways: we have what we lawyers call "compulsory jurisdiction," and we make decisions that are upheld. This is true of no other international tribunal in the world. Indeed, this has never been true of any other international tribunal in the *history* of the world.

We have compulsory jurisdiction because all of the Members of the WTO have agreed in the WTO treaty to use the WTO dispute settlement system to resolve all their treaty-related disputes with other WTO Members. We make decisions that are upheld because all of the Members of the WTO have agreed in the treaty that any Member that chooses — in an exercise of its sovereignty — *not* to comply with a decision

---

[11] Claus-Dieter Ehlermann, "Reflections on the Appellate Body of the WTO," Address to the American Society of International Law, Washington, D.C. (April 3, 2003).

in dispute settlement can be subject to economic sanctions by other Members. These potential sanctions can include the loss of some of the valuable trade concessions that have been made by other Members in the treaty.

Our uniqueness helps explain why there is no dust on the shelves of the WTO website. Because WTO Members must take their treaty-related trade disputes with other WTO Members to the WTO, and because the decisions made about those disputes in dispute settlement are upheld, WTO rules and rulings have real force as real international law for the international economy. This means that what happens in the WTO is vitally important to all those five billion people who are served by the WTO and who, as we see it, are always with us whenever we sit down together at our table.

Although our uniqueness is the source of much of our success, it is the source also of much of the controversy that surrounds our rulings. The protests. The press conferences. The speeches in the Congress. The college students in their colorful turtle costumes. None of it would have happened if the Appellate Body were just like every other international tribunal. It is easy to ignore an international tribunal when the authority behind its rulings exists only on paper. It is hard to ignore an international tribunal with compulsory jurisdiction whose decisions are upheld.

Institutionally, our small circle of seven serves a *larger circle* of the WTO. The reports and recommendations of the Appellate Body are adopted by consensus of another, larger circle within the WTO called the *Dispute Settlement Body*. The Dispute Settlement Body — the "DSB" — consists of all 146 WTO Members acting together in WTO dispute settlement. The WTO is truly a "Member-driven" institution, and the Members of the DSB are truly the ultimate decision-makers in WTO dispute settlement.

The DSB is merely the name the Members of the WTO use when they are dealing with dispute settlement. The very same countries and other customs territories that comprise the DSB also comprise the *largest circle* of the WTO, which is the deliberative circle consisting of all of the Members of the WTO when they engage in negotiations on new rules for the world trading system. Even now, the Members of the WTO are engaged in a new global "round" of multilateral trade negotiations under the auspices of the WTO.

This new round of global trade negotiations is called the "Doha Development Round." Begun in Doha, Qatar, in 2001, it is the ninth such round of multilateral trade negotiations since the Second World War, and the first since the creation of the WTO. The stakes have never been higher for the world. Goods. Services. Agriculture. Manufacturing. Additional market access of all kinds. The continued lowering of tariff and other trade barriers of all kinds. The negotiation of new rules for competition, investment, intellectual property, and many other areas of the international economy that affect, and are affected by, international trade. These are only a few of the issues on the agenda of the Doha Development Round. In particular, the overriding goal of the new round is to bring the *developing* countries of the world into the mainstream of the WTO-based world trading system so that they will be able to profit and prosper as they should through expanded opportunities for international trade.

In a truly "Lecky-like" way, the eight previous global rounds of multilateral trade negotiations have contributed to enlarging the global circle by expanding global economic growth significantly in the past half century. Since the creation of the GATT in the aftermath of the Bretton Woods conference at the conclusion of the Second World War, the GATT-based and, now, WTO-based, world trading system has gradually lowered barriers to trade throughout the world while it has also gradually grown to include almost all of the world. Due in large part to these multilateral efforts, global trade has increased *fourteen-fold* in the half century or so since the creation of the GATT. This increase in world trade has supported a *six-fold* increase in global GDP.[12] WTO figures show that worldwide exports that, in 1950, accounted for only eight percent of worldwide production, today account for more than 26 percent of worldwide production.[13] As world trade continues to grow, this percentage continues to grow as well.

Overall, more economic progress has been made in the past half century than in the previous half millennium. Our progress in trade is the most significant economic progress the world has made in the past half century. And much of this progress has been made because of the world trading system that was established under the GATT and is served now by the WTO. Thanks in no small part to trade liberalization, millions upon millions of people in every part of the world have been lifted out of poverty. The dynamic growth of world trade has been the engine of the

---

[12] World Trade Organization, The Multilateral Trading System: 50 Years of Achievement (Geneva, 1998).
[13] Id.

longest and strongest period of sustained economic growth in human history. Humanity has enjoyed unprecedented prosperity in the wake of what one of Lecky's many intellectual heirs, President John F. Kennedy, an early and ardent champion of the multilateral trading system, described rightly — and memorably — as "the rising tide of trade."[14]

The benefits for the United States and for other *developed* countries from the successful conclusion of the current round of multilateral trade negotiations could be equally significant to this rising tide. The developed countries that are Members of the WTO stand to benefit enormously from continued multilateral trade liberalization. One recent study, at the University of Michigan, has concluded that if *all* the global barriers to trade in goods and services were eliminated, then the gain for the United States alone would be $537 billion — almost 6 percent of the annual U.S. gross domestic product.[15]

The benefits for the *developing* countries that are Members of the WTO would, however, be even greater. The scheduled implementation of the remaining trade concessions made in the Uruguay Round is expected to facilitate economic growth that will lift an additional *600 million people* worldwide out of poverty. We could add impressively to these numbers with the successful conclusion of the current round.

The World Bank has estimated that the abolition of *all* trade barriers in the new round, coupled with needed market reforms, would add *$2.8 billion dollars* to global income by 2015. Most of this additional global income — *1.5 trillion dollars* — would be in developing countries. This would lift an additional *320 million people* in developing countries out of poverty.[16] The elimination of all tariff and non-tariff trade barriers could result in gains for developing countries of $182 billion in services, $162 billion in manufactures, and $32 billion in agriculture.[17]

Not even Lecky would be optimistic enough to suggest that the Members of the WTO will abolish *all* the remaining barriers to world trade in this latest round of negotiations. Trade liberalization has always

---

[14] President John F. Kennedy, Presidential Address in Frankfurt, Germany (June 24, 1963).
[15] The details of the University of Michigan study are discussed in Douglas A. Irwin, Free Trade Under Fire (Princeton: Princeton University Press, 2002), 29-35.
[16] Mike Moore, Director-General of the WTO, WTO Doha and Beyond: A Roadmap for successfully concluding the Doha Development Round," Address to the Evian VII Plenary Meeting, Montreux, Switzerland (April 12, 2002).
[17] Id.

been an incremental process. Surely it will remain so. Still, these numbers show that abolishing even *some* of these remaining trade barriers could result in significant benefits for the developing countries that comprise an increasing majority of the membership of the WTO.

President George W. Bush has said, "We have the opportunity to include all the world's poor in an expanding circle of development."[18] On this, I agree with the President of the United States. Perhaps he, too, has read what W.E.H. Lecky wrote all those years ago about circles. And, in my view, there is no better way to expand the circle of development, there is no better way to further the continued development of developing countries, than through further, mutual, and substantial trade liberalization by the Members of the WTO in the Doha Development Round.

Developing and developed countries alike can benefit enormously from the increased economic growth that will result from additional trade liberalization. Everyone everywhere can benefit from more market access in every part of the world. As it is, the global economy is stalled by all the uncertainties occasioned by a unique combination of disease, terror, and economic downturn. I know of no better or surer way to help jump-start the weakened battery of our sluggish global economy than by the negotiation of new rules to lower the remaining barriers to trade in an early, successful, and balanced conclusion to the Doha Development Round.

The benefits of a successful conclusion of the current round would come none too soon for all of us. This would be especially so, though, for developing countries. The World Bank reports that there are 1.2 billion people in the world who live on less than $1 per day, and that there are 2.8 billion people in the world who live on less than $2 per day.[19] "Of the 4.6 billion people in developing countries, more than 850 million are illiterate, nearly a billion lack access to improved water resources, and 2.4 billion lack access to basic sanitation. Nearly 325 million boys and girls are out of school. And 11 million children under age five die each year from preventable causes — equivalent to more than 30,000 a day."[20] So says the World Bank. These, to say the least, are numbing statistics.[21]

---

[18] President George W. Bush, Address to the World Bank in Washington, D.C. (May, 2001).
[19] World Bank, <u>Human Development Report 2001</u> (Washington, D.C.), 9.
[20] Id.
[21] These are also only a few of the statistics that I might have cited. The annual reports of the World Bank on "human development" are always well worth reading in their entirety.

We must not, however, be numbed by these statistics. Those of us who see the circle of human sympathy as including all of humanity must not turn our eyes away from these many global human concerns. Lecky was able to live a life of financial ease and lettered leisure because he was an absentee Irish landlord. By all accounts, he was an enlightened landlord. All the same, he was able to spend his time reading in his library and writing his books because he profited from the sweat of others. He never forgot this. Neither must we. To be sure, most of us profit from our own efforts. Yet, most of us also, like Lecky, profit from the sweat of others. And, like Lecky, we must not forget this. One of the best ways we can remember others, one of the best ways we can help others, is through further trade liberalization in a successful conclusion of the Doha Development Round. Significantly, this is also one of the best ways we can help ourselves — because this also happens to be very much in our own self-interest.

Moreover, serious negotiations on a successful conclusion of the current round of multilateral trade negotiations are all the more imperative as a way of reassuring the world at this critical time that the nations of the world do remain capable of cooperating to address their many mutual concerns. At a time when so many of our important international institutions seem at a standstill, at a time when so many of them seem to be in a stalemate, at a time when continued support for so much of what the nations of the world have tried to accomplish together through multilateral efforts and through multilateral institutions seems so very doubtful, the WTO simply must remain a source of stability for the world.

The World Trade Organization is an example of all that can be achieved through "multilateralism" to approach Lecky's circle. The WTO is an example of the mutual international trust that can be achieved through consent, through consensus, and, above all, though cooperation. Whatever may happen outside the WTO, the Members of the WTO must continue to cooperate *within* the WTO. They must do so for the sake of all they hope to accomplish together both *within* the WTO and also *outside* the WTO.

This is especially so for the two leading traders in the world — the United States of America and the European Union. Because they are the two leading traders in the world, America and Europe share a special responsibility to cooperate in moving the world forward on trade. If America and Europe can work together for trade, then perhaps they will also be able to work together against terror and for much else that is needed by the world. America and Europe can do much more *together* to help enlarge the circle of human sympathy than either can do *on its own*.

The Secretary-General of the International Chamber of Commerce, Maria Livanos Cattaui, advises us, in the International Herald Tribune, that, "There can be no fortress America, no fortress Europe, in a world in which the fortunes of nations are more tightly intermeshed than ever before. ... The WTO is a shining example of multilateralism at work. Member governments accept its authority as the maker and enforcer of the rules of international trade. The WTO has always managed to overcome conflicts among its members and its authority remains intact. Helping to steer the Doha round to success would be the most dramatic proof the European Union and the United States could offer that the spirit of multilateral cooperation is still alive and well."[22]

With this, too, I agree. In particular, as an American, I think it appropriate that America fulfill its responsibility as the world's leading trading nation by leading in the effort to forge more multilateral cooperation. The United States of America accounts for about twenty percent of all the world's trade. Since 1995, the United States has accounted for about two-thirds of all the world's economic growth.[23] America, the world's leading trading nation, remains, as The Economist of London aptly puts it, "the engine of the world economy."[24]

The United States has unprecedented economic might, and might of all kinds must always be used for right. One responsibility of the United States of America as the world's leading economic power during this difficult time in the history of the world is the responsibility of continuing to support the world trading system that is served by the WTO. The pressures of protectionism and the politics of parochialism must not prevent Americans from seeing our true and enduring interest in the continued success of the WTO, and in the continued strengthening of the WTO-based multilateral trading system.

In particular, the WTO is an example to the world that a multilateral system for the peaceful settlement of international disputes can work. The world is much in need nowadays of such examples. Trade

---

[22] Maria Livanos Cattaui, "It's multilateralism that makes the world go round," *International Herald Tribune* (April 10, 2003), 8.
[23] The Economist (April 12, 2003), 63.
[24] Id.

is not terrorism. Widgets are not warfare. Even so, we Americans are much in need nowadays of opportunities for reassuring the rest of the world that we seek the success of multilateral systems for international cooperation and for international dispute settlement. The WTO is one such opportunity we must seize in our continued efforts to provide that reassurance.

The American philosopher John Rawls, in the tradition of Mill, and in the spirit of Lecky, suggested "reasonableness" as a way of bringing people from different backgrounds and cultures together to address common concerns.[25] He saw value in simply trying to work together. He saw potential in talking and listening and reasoning together. To be sure, not everyone will be persuaded by reason, and, thus, not every international dispute can be resolved by resort only to reason. Others are not always reasonable. Trust is not always attainable. But trust is always desirable. Trust is better than troops. Reason must always be our *first* resort. The abandonment of reason through the use of force must always be our *last*.

In urging "reasonableness," Rawls had great faith in particular in what he called "public reason."[26] By this, he meant active participation by active citizens in a free and ongoing public debate. He meant a public deliberation leading to an act of decision-making in which all who participated would feel that they had an active part. From such a deliberative process would come, he believed, what we would call in the WTO a "consensus."

A "consensus" in the WTO is not unanimity. Article IX, paragraph 1, of the Marrakesh Agreement establishing the World Trade Organization provides that, with respect to decision-making, "The WTO shall continue the practice of decision-making by consensus followed under GATT 1947."[27] Footnote 1 to this provision of the WTO treaty explains, "The body concerned shall be deemed to have decided by consensus on a matter submitted for its consideration, if no Member, present at the meeting when the decision is taken, formally objects to the proposed decision."[28]

---

[25] *See* John Rawls, Political Liberalism (New York: Columbia University Press, 1993) 212-254; and John Rawls, The Law of Peoples (Cambridge, Massachusetts: Harvard University Press, 1999) 129-180.

[26] Id.

[27] Article IX, paragraph 1, Marrakesh Agreement Establishing the World Trade Organization, done at Marrakesh, Morocco. (April 15, 1994), hereinafter the Marrakesh Agreement.

[28] Footnote 1 to Article IX paragraph 1, of the Marrakesh Agreement.

Thus, a "consensus" in the WTO is an agreement to go along and to go forward and to go together as one — even in the absence of absolute unanimity. It is a decision that none question because it is a decision that none, in the end, feel compelled to oppose actively. It is a decision in which all are willing to join, because it is one in which all have played a part in making. A decision resulting from a WTO consensus is a decision resulting from an active exercise in the WTO equivalent of "public reason." By no means is a consensus ever easily achieved within the WTO on a contentious or controversial issue. But a consensus that is finally achieved within the WTO on such an issue is a consensus well worth the effort and well worth the having. In my view, the world desperately needs more such active international exercises in "public reason."

One nation may, at a certain moment in history, have the power to work its will on many other nations. In our fractious and fragmented world of nations, one nation may, at a certain moment, have the power to do as it wishes without listening to other nations, and without reasoning with them in a sincere effort to reach anything even resembling a consensus. But my reading of history reminds me that such moments in history can be fleeting, even for the most powerful of nations.

Far better to reason together. Far better for every nation, no matter how powerful it may happen to be at some passing historical moment, to have the patience to engage in "public reason" by reasoning with others and, especially, by listening to others. For the seven of us at the round table of the Appellate Body, for the 146 Members of the WTO, for all the nations of the world in all that they must try to do together, this is the only way to reach a real consensus, and this is the only way to make continued and lasting progress in expanding the circle of humanity.

In these first years of the twenty-first century, we are understandably less sanguine and more skeptical than W.E.H. Lecky about the possibilities of progress for humanity. A decade after he died in the reassuring inner sanctum of his book-lined library, the calm certitudes of his Victorian era were shattered by the sudden violence of the First World War. All these years later, in the aftermath of two world wars, in the wake of the Holocaust, and in the shadow of the mushroom cloud, Lecky would perhaps understand the doubts of those today who are less hopeful than he was about the prospects for human progress.

Lecky observed once that, with societies and with eras, there is a "hidden bias of the imagination" that affects the course of events.[29] He believed that there are certain unstated predispositions of civilizations and of times that have a far greater impact on the climate of opinion, and thus on the flow of events, than any display of logic.[30] He believed, too, that this same observation applies equally to individuals. I think he was right. And I am persuaded that, as Lecky no doubt would have acknowledged, this observation applies equally to Lecky himself.

Lecky was imbued with the belief in progress that was characteristic of the Victorian era. He believed in progress because — although he was a rationalist who wrote about the virtues of rationalism — he retained nevertheless the prevailing Victorian belief in God's will. He had faith that Providence was guiding the evolution of humanity toward an ever-larger circle. He was confident that tomorrow would be better than today, because he thought that tomorrow would take us ever closer to the true morality of a true humanity.

Lecky described himself as "half vagabond, half bookworm."[31] He lived *with* books, and, to a great extent, he lived *in* books. He traveled primarily to go to libraries, and, when at home in London, he spent much of his time in his library. When he finally entered Parliament late in life, he complained that politics was an interruption of his lifelong devotion to books and literature. Lecky was the kind of man who corrected the page proofs of his latest book while on his honeymoon. (Lecky's obliging wife — a "lady-in-waiting" to Queen Sophia of the Netherlands — evidently tolerated that; Rebecca, who is not fond of waiting, would not.)

In all his Victorian bookishness, Lecky could not imagine a world in which humanity would not progress. As Donal McCartney has put it, Lecky's books, including the history of European morals in which he gave voice to his view of the ever-enlarging circle of humanity, were "written by one who held a firm belief in the idea of progress. The general theme of the books might be said to have been the story of the gradual triumph of rationalism, liberty and tolerance in European history. There could be no going back on these advances. It had never once crossed Lecky's mind that there could be any retrogression to persecution and intolerance in Western civilization."[32]

---

[29] Lecky, at 42.
[30] Id.
[31] Lecky, at 29.
[32] Lecky, at 66.

Lecky wrote confidently, "Liberty, industry and peace are in modern societies indissolubly connected, and their ultimate ascendancy depends upon a movement which may be retarded, but cannot be arrested."[33] We know better. For all our occasional inclinations toward triumphalism, for all our considerable confidence in the manifest potential of both democracy and capitalism, for all our wishful thinking about the "ultimate ascendancy" of all our many hopes for humanity, we definitely know better. The years since Lecky left us have taught us only too well that progress toward a wider circle of humanity is by no means assured. It definitely can be arrested.

Yet this is all the more reason for us to try to expand the size of our circle. This is all the more reason for us to broaden our "range of duty" in order to broaden the sweep of human concern and, thereby, the scope of human morality. This is all the more reason for us to use human morality to help us achieve human progress. Here in the twenty-first century, I, for one, do not have the absolute certainty that Lecky had in the nineteenth century about the "ultimate ascendancy" of humanity through continued human progress. The American mind of my time is not the Victorian mind of his time. I have other hidden biases of the imagination. Even so, I choose to imagine the possibility of human progress. More important, I have chosen to spend my life working to make what I can imagine *for* the world a living reality *in* the world. That is what brought me — and what brought others who share my stubbornly optimistic view — to the round table of the Appellate Body of the WTO.

The cosmologists, like the poet, say that, eons from now, the world will end with a whimper, and not with a bang.[34] I do not presume to know if they are right. It is not for me to foresee the completion of the human effort in this world. Like Lecky, I trust Providence to tend to our ultimate fate. For my part, I am far more interested in what will happen between now and then to those who live in the world that Providence has entrusted to us. And I am far more interested in fulfilling my own range of duty in the ongoing human effort.

Progress can sometimes be hard to see. While researching once in a library in Paris, Lecky found the minute scrawl of the fabled French diplomat Talleyrand so microscopic that he had to use a magnifying glass

---

[33] Id.
[34] T.S. Eliot, "The Hollow Men," in Oscar Williams, ed., <u>Immortal Poems of the English Language</u> (New York: Washington Square Press, 1952) 539, 542.

to read it. Similarly, sometimes it may seem that we need a magnifying glass to see the crawl of human progress toward Lecky's enlarged circle. The failures of international dispute settlement are featured in dying color on the bleeding broadcasts of CNN. The successes of international dispute settlement are written in boring black and white in the tedious pages of WTO reports.

Hard as it may sometimes be to discern, human progress is nevertheless possible. We need not be Victorian "men of letters" to believe that tomorrow can be better than today. But, to make progress, we must first be able to see the possibility of progress, and, to see it, we must first be able to imagine it. We must change the hidden biases of our imagination.

In trade, we have imagined progress. This helps explain why there is a WTO. In other areas, we have not yet done so. This helps explain much else. This helps explain, for example, why so many of the nations of the world are only now beginning to see the need for strengthening the authority and the capability of the World Health Organization in dealing with SARS, AIDS, and other global epidemic diseases that do not respect artificial political borders. This helps explain also why we have failed thus far to make concerted multilateral efforts to protect and preserve the world's environment comparable to those that we have made to expand the world's trade. There are, of course, numerous other equally compelling examples that I might use to illustrate all the other ways in which our imagination falls short of our genuine global need. Alas, there are far too many examples of where we are not yet meeting an urgent global need *because we do not yet see it.*

The right answer for the world is the approach we have taken to finding the right answers at the round table of the Appellate Body of the WTO. Conversation. Deliberation. Mutual criticism. And, as a result, mutual trust. The right approach, in other words, is what Mill and Lecky and Rawls would all call "reasonableness." The only way to human progress is through human freedom, and the only way to human freedom is through the reasonableness that is the key to freedom.

Admittedly, this may be easier for the seven of us on the Appellate Body than for all the assembled nations of the world in all the various multilateral venues in which they meet and deliberate and pontificate. For all our differences, the seven of us on the Appellate Body are in many ways all alike. To borrow trade terminology, the "process and production methods" around the world that eventually brought the seven of us together at our table in Geneva may have differed considerably; yet the seven of us are very much "like products." Accordingly, the picture we each have of the world is very much alike. If it were not, we would not have been asked by the Members of the WTO to sit together and work together around our table.

And yet, as I picture the world, this is true as well of different individuals and of different peoples throughout the world. We are all very much "like products." No matter our nationality, no matter our ethnicity, no matter our race, no matter our religion, no matter our sex or our age or our circumstance, no matter the vast cultural and other differences that may often divide us, we humans are, nevertheless, all "like." We are all alike in that we all share a common kinship that transcends our many differences. We are all part of the one circle of humanity.

In believing that there is one circle of humanity, in believing that the true circle of humanity is a single circle that includes *all* of humanity, in believing that, therefore, our circle of humanity must be enlarged through continued human progress to include all of humanity, Lecky did not underestimate the persistence of culture as a challenge that must be faced in the making of such progress. On the long, solitary mountain walks he often took when he was not reading and writing in his library, Lecky carried along in his pocket a copy of Edmund Burke's <u>Reflections on the Revolution in France</u>.[35] Like Burke, he was very much aware of the importance of the "little platoons" of local cultures, and of the challenges that the habits, the traditions, the attitudes, and the very diversities of local cultures present to the continued enlargement of the human circle.[36]

Lecky shared Burke's view that, "To be attached to the subdivision, to love the little platoon we belong to in society, is the first principle (the germ as it were) of public affections."[37] It was perhaps for this reason that Lecky spent so many years writing a history of Ireland that was notable in particular for its defense of Irish culture. At the same time, Lecky, like Burke, was of the view as well that, as Burke went on to

---

[35] Edmund Burke, <u>Reflections on the Revolution in France</u> (London: Penguin Books, 1968) [1790].
[36] Id. at 135.
[37] Id.

say in the very next sentence of his famous reflections, the "little platoon" of our local affections is *"the first link* in the series by which we proceed towards a love to our country *and to mankind."*[38] There must be other links beyond this first link that will lead us to a broader range of duty and to a similar allegiance to the larger circle of all of humanity.

This is seen clearly in Lecky's attitude toward the political relationship between Ireland and Britain. Like Burke before him, Lecky was an Irish "Unionist." He favored the continued union of Ireland and Britain, and he did so at a time when many Irish patriots who shared many of Lecky's other views were moving ever closer toward separation, and toward Irish independence. He was, however, no less of an Irishman because of it. After all, it was the Irish, not the British, who raised a statue of him in Dublin.

Lecky hoped that Ireland and Britain would be able to reason together in ways that would sustain their union. He believed, as I do, that a crucial part of our likeness is the capability we share as humans of reasoning together. This is true for seven people. This is true for hundreds, thousands, millions, or billions of people. This is true in trade. This is true also in much else of mutual international concern. Above all, and despite all, we must somehow reason together.

Reasonableness must be our approach in all our continuing multilateral efforts to further trade. Multilateral trade negotiation is one of the best opportunities we have for employing reasonableness by reasoning together, and multilateral trade liberalization through such negotiation is one of the best ways we have to help enlarge the circle to include all of humanity. Through the combined power of cooperative reason in the WTO, the nations of the world can continue to help free humanity through trade. Trade is an essential means to the essential end of liberating humanity so that we can all live together in freedom.

The connection between trade and freedom is one that is both critical and often overlooked. Our dignity as individual human beings depends on our ability to choose our own destiny. Thus, freedom is about choosing. Freedom is about having real choices about how to live. The liberty that is freedom is about choosing for ourselves. The French thinker Simone Weil once suggested that, "Liberty, taking the word in its concrete

---

[38] Id. (emphasis added)

sense, consists in the ability to choose."[39] Likewise, I would suggest that humanity, taken in its truest and highest sense, consists in believing that other people have the capacity to choose for themselves — if they are given the choice. Accordingly, by multiplying choices, by increasing the ability to choose, trade serves the end of freedom, and thereby serves as well the goal of establishing the single circle of all of humanity.

Reasonableness must likewise be our approach in all our other multilateral efforts beyond trade. In addition to the means of trade, other multilateral means are also needed to serve the end of freedom. Other means are also needed to help enlarge the circle of human sympathy to include all of humanity. Expanding trade is only one way to expand Lecky's circle. There are others. There are numerous other global concerns that demand global solutions if we are to have any hope of changing all the numbing statistics of world deprivation, and of having the full measure of both freedom and humanity throughout the world.

Some of these concerns relate to trade. Others do not. The numbing statistics reveal many global needs. The world is a circle of many truly global concerns. These include — but, as we lawyers say, are not limited to — human rights, women's rights, workers' rights, the environment, health, intellectual property, investment, crime, corruption, and, of course, terrorism, genocide, and all the other dire dilemmas that so urgently demand cooperative acts of collective international security.

Our need for international law to address these and other international concerns is great, and is greatly increasing. But our *awareness* of our need for international law, and of our need to establish and to abide by the international rule of law, is not increasing. The geographical distance between us seems to be diminishing, but the other distances between us are not. Even as the forces of "globalization" seem to be making our world smaller, other forces are pulling us farther and farther apart.

When lecturing at Harvard Law School some time back, I spoke at length about what I consider to be the significant and positive contribution the WTO is making in demonstrating to a skeptical world that there can be such a thing as the international rule of law. Afterwards, one of the bright students at Harvard asked me a question that I confessed at the time I could not answer.

---

[39] Simone Weil, The Need for Roots (London and New York: Routledge Classics, 2002), 12 [1949].

The question was this.

In trade, independent nation-states have a clear and compelling economic incentive to cooperate in finding global, multilateral solutions. In the WTO, mutual cooperation leads to greater mutual prosperity. In WTO dispute settlement, a refusal to comply with rules and rulings can lead to costly economic sanctions. But where is the incentive for compliance with international law in other areas of global concern — in areas where there is *not* an obvious economic incentive, and where there is *not* the *economic leverage* that there is to help secure and ensure compliance in the WTO? It is difficult enough to achieve consensus and compliance in the WTO — where there *is* such leverage. How can we do it *elsewhere*?

This is a very good question, to say the least. There are more than thirty thousand pages of rules in the WTO treaty. There are more than twenty thousand pages of rulings in WTO dispute settlement. The Members of the WTO comply with these rules and with these rulings because they see it as in their self-interest to do so. They want the trade concessions that are secured by compliance. They do not want the trade sanctions that can be the price of non-compliance. But what about the other treaties besides the WTO treaty that have been concluded by the nations of the world? And what about all the additional treaties that the world still needs to negotiate and conclude? What about, say, the international agreement to combat terrorism that the world has long discussed, but has not even come close to concluding? Where is the incentive to comply with other international laws that are not part of the WTO treaty, and where is the leverage to enforce them?

I promised that bright young Harvard law student that I would think about the answer to this question. I have thought long and hard about it ever since. I have concluded that my answer is the same as the answer that was given long ago by William Edward Hartpole Lecky.

Lecky said, "He who seeks to improve the moral condition of mankind has two, and only two, ways of accomplishing his end. The *first* is, to make it more and more the interest of each to conform to that of the others; the *second* is, to dispel the ignorance which prevents men from seeing their *true interest*."[40] Therefore, as Lecky saw it, there are only two

---

[40] Lecky, <u>Morals</u>, Volume I, at 13.

ways to further human progress. One is to find new ways to help us cooperate with one another in our mutual self-interest — such as through the WTO. The other is to find new ways to help us educate and otherwise enlighten one another so that we will be able to *see* our *true self-interest*.

The Oxford and Cambridge Club in London has a large library filled with shelves and shelves of old books. On one of the lofty shelves there, I found the two volumes of another old book by Lecky, entitled History of the Rise and Influence of the Spirit of Rationalism in Europe, which was published in 1865.[41] Fortunately, unlike "The Bookworm" in Geneva, the library of the Oxford and Cambridge Club has a tall ladder. So I climbed the ladder, pulled down the dusty volumes, and spent the better part of a pleasant afternoon sitting alone in the silence of the library and reading more of what Lecky had to say about the importance of seeing and serving our true self-interest. (Although I was all alone in the library, in keeping with the rules of the club, I wore a coat and a well-knotted tie while I did so.)

Lecky acknowledged that there is a "bond of intellectual sympathy" among some of us that inclines some of us to *desire* to cooperate in our mutual self-interest.[42] Intellectually, rationally, logically, there are some among us who want to work together in our mutual interest. The difficulty is in doing so. Lecky's solution to this difficulty was to urge *more* of us to learn *how* to do so by *trying* to do so. He maintained that "human nature is so constituted that it is impossible for bodies of men to work together under the sense of a common interest without a warm feeling of amity arising between them. Common aims and hopes knit them together by a bond of sympathy. Each man becomes accustomed to act with a view to the welfare of others, and a union of affections usually replaces or consecrates the union of interests."[43]

One example illustrating the essential truth of Lecky's insight is my own experience on the Appellate Body. In my eight years on the Appellate Body, I have seen firsthand how "common aims and hopes" can knit individuals together in a "bond of sympathy." I have seen firsthand how a "union of affections" can create and facilitate a "union of

---

[41] W.E.H. Lecky, History of the Rise and Influence of the Spirit of Rationalism in Europe, in Two Volumes (New York and London: D. Appleton and Company, 1899) [1865], hereinafter Rationalism.

[42] Lecky, Rationalism, Volume II, at 338.

[43] Lecky, Rationalism, Volume II, at 345.

interests." In our work together for the Members of the WTO, we seven see ourselves, not as seven, but as one. We have seen the Appellate Body as one from the very beginning.

My hope is that, long after I have left the Appellate Body, those who serve on the Appellate Body will continue to see themselves *as one* in their continued mutual efforts to serve the Members of the WTO. The Members of the Appellate Body can continue to achieve much by continuing to work together *as one* toward the common goal of strengthening and sustaining the WTO dispute settlement system as an international institution that will serve all of the Members of the WTO equally and effectively. Much can be achieved by a mutual commitment to the kind of real conversation that has always made the Appellate Body think and act and serve *as one*.

Still another example of the validity of Lecky's insight is the broader experience, first, of the Contracting Parties of the GATT, and now, of the Members of the WTO. Cooperation is based on trust. Trust builds on trust. Trust is generated by interaction. Trust is based on habit, and not merely on rational calculation. The trust that emerges from the habit of working together is an example of what some economists call "social capital."[44] The "social capital" within the WTO is evidenced in the humdrum, day-to-day working of the WTO-based world trading system that rarely is referenced in the pages of the world's press or in the rhetoric of the world's protests. The disputes that are addressed by the Appellate Body are the rare exceptions in a global trading system in which a mutual trust among the Members of the WTO largely prevails, and in which their mutual trust contributes significantly to a considerable mutual compliance with the agreed rules for trade.

By working together, the Members of the WTO have established the *habit* of working together. By establishing the *habit* of compliance with WTO rules, they have encouraged *more* compliance with WTO rules. Modern mathematical game theorists call this "Tit for Tat." Lecky would simply have called this human nature. For the 146 Members of the WTO, just as for the seven Members of the Appellate Body, the shared and sustained experience of working together has created, and sustains, a "bond of sympathy" and a "union of interests." It does so now for all the current 146 Members of the WTO. Ultimately, it can do so for all the world.

---

[44] "A question of trust," The Economist (February 22, 2003), 92.

All the same, Lecky stressed that none of us, whether individuals or nations, will want to engage in the real conversation that can lead to real mutual trust unless we believe that it is *in our interest* to do so. Altruism is admirable. Altruism is not a fit or a firm foundation for effective international law. There must be the perception of a real interest to inspire the real conversation and the real trust that, alone, can be the basis for real international law. As Lecky explained, "The bond of intellectual sympathy alone is far too weak to restrain the action of colliding passions, and it was reserved for political economy to supply a stronger and permanent principle of unity. This principle is an enlightened self-interest."[45]

By "political economy," Lecky, a nineteenth-century man, meant a policy aimed at attaining and maintaining the nineteenth-century goal of freer trade. In his mid-Victorian musings, he was echoing the views of Adam Smith, David Ricardo, Richard Cobden, and their many free-trade followers of his time. But this is also our goal in our time. Lecky was also anticipating some of the assumptions that are between the lines of the WTO treaty, and that are taking the Members of the WTO into the twenty-first century.

One of those assumptions is that of a fixed and unchanging human nature that focuses on self-interest, and thus on the need to perceive, and to appeal to, an enlightened self-interest. "Taking human nature with all its defects," observed Lecky, "the influence of an enlightened self-interest first of all upon the actions and afterwards upon the character of mankind, is shown to be sufficient to construct the whole edifice of civilisation; and if that principle were withdrawn, all would crumble in the dust."[46]

His emphasis on the need for an enlightened self-interest was not in any way an original thought with Lecky. Nor was it in any way an original thought with Smith, Ricardo, Cobden, or others of his time who influenced his Victorian thinking. There were many others who preceded them in perceiving the importance and, indeed, the indispensability, of an enlightened view of self-interest to expanding the circle of human morality and, thus, human sympathy. There have been many others who have concluded, as Lecky did, that, without an enlightened view of self-interest, civilization will "crumble in the dust."

---

[45] Lecky, <u>Rationalism</u>, Volume II, at 338.
[46] Lecky, <u>Rationalism</u>, Volume II, at 350.

An enlightened view of self-interest can, for example, be seen as a key to Aristotle's <u>Politics</u>. Like all classical Greeks, Aristotle could not even conceive of a happy or a virtuous life outside of the context of the mutually cooperative framework of the Greek *polis* — the Greek city-state.[47] Likewise, and contrary to the common misconception of many today, Adam Smith's "moral sentiments" were much more about cooperation than about competition. He saw trade primarily as a way of cooperating, not of competing. That is why he placed so much emphasis on the necessity of a division of labor in his most famous book, <u>The Wealth of Nations</u>.[48] Moreover, the first paragraph of the first page of the other, and often neglected, first book by that great champion of the pursuit of self-interest, <u>The Theory of Moral Sentiments</u>, is a ringing assertion of the centrality of the bonds of human sympathy.[49] Similarly, at the very center of the thoughts of Alexis de Tocqueville on the possibilities for human progress through the development of democratic self-government is his belief that, in perceiving and pursuing our self-interest, we must look both far ahead and far afield; we must adhere to what he described as "the principle of interest rightly understood."[50]

And so on. In Christian ethics, in Muslim ethics, in Jewish ethics, in Hindu ethics, in Buddhist ethics, in both religious and secular thinking of all kinds in all parts of the world and all through the centuries, there has been a pervasive emphasis on perceiving and pursuing an enlightened self-interest. In advocating adherence to an enlightened view of self-interest, Lecky was merely following in many other similar footsteps. Indeed, if there is one common thread that runs through much of theology and philosophy from antiquity to today — and that, I would contend, has universal application for all of humanity today and tomorrow — it is the common thread of the indispensability of an enlightened self-interest to the furthering of human progress and to the progressive unfolding of an ever-expanding human morality and human sympathy.

Thus, the answer to the question I was asked by the student at Harvard about the future of international law is found, not in the nuances

---

[47] Aristotle, <u>The Politics</u> (London: Penguin Books, 1981), I ii, "The State Exists by Nature," 55-61.

[48] Adam Smith, <u>An Inquiry into the Nature and Causes of the Wealth of Nations</u> (New York: The Modern Library, 1994), 3-23 [1776].

[49] Adam Smith, <u>The Theory of Moral Sentiments</u> (Amherst, New York: Prometheus Books, 2000), 3.

[50] Alexis de Tocqueville, <u>Democracy in America</u>, translated by Henry Reeve (New York: The Colonial Press, 1899), Volume II, at 129 [1835].

of law itself, not in the particulars of law *per se*, but in how we see our *true self-interest*. And how we see our true self-interest depends on how large we see the *size* of our circle. Do we really see *other* people as part of our circle? Do we really see other people *in other parts of the world* as part of our circle? Do we really see *their* welfare and *their* well-being as part of *our* self-interest? Do we wish for others what we wish for ourselves? Are other people, whoever they may be, wherever they may be, our neighbors? Are they our sisters and our brothers? Or are they *only our prey?*

As Lecky suggested, the range of duty we see ourselves as having to others is likewise the range of what we see as our self-interest. It is also, as a consequence, the range of what we see as our need for law. The long historical progression from preying on others to trusting in others is a progression away from might, and toward right. It is a progressive expansion of our range of duty, and a progressive enlargement of our circle of human sympathy. It is the progression away from barbarism, and toward law. It is the progression away from the rule of power, and toward the rule of law.

We still have a long road to travel from power to law. In particular, we still have a long way to go, we still have a long way to progress, to reach and realize the *international* rule of law. We have reached the point where nations feel compelled to *claim* they are adhering to the international rule of law. We have not yet reached the point where nations necessarily always do so. *Rhetorically*, our range of duty sometimes seems to include the whole world. But *realistically*, it does not. And thus, *legally*, it does not, because all too often what are described as "laws" that are meant to fulfill the full extent of our duty to others elsewhere in the world do not, *realistically*, have any real meaning.

Why not? Why does power still so often prevail over law? Why does the reality of the international rule of law fall considerably short of our rhetorical commitment to the international rule of law? The answer is in what we are able to *see*. Like everything else of man's devising, the law can be considered an *invention*. The British philosopher Mary Midgley has observed that the notion of an invention is not an abstract notion; it has meaning only "with reference to a given purpose. You can invent the spinning jenny, or a more humane form of divorce, or the notion of representative government, once you know that you want them."[51]

---

[51] Mary Midgley, Heart and Mind (London and New York: Routledge Classics, 2003), 62 [1981].

This is equally so with the invention of law. Just as other inventions occur only "once you know that you want them," so too does law occur only once you know that you want law. For this reason, international law, like any other law, will occur only once we know that we want it. But we will not *want* law until we know that we *need* it. And we will not *need* it until we *see* that we need it. And we will not *see* that we need it while the *size* of our circle of human sympathy remains smaller than the scope of the international law that we need.

An example of a society that did *not* see the need for invention was ancient Greece. The classical Greeks lived in a world in which everything seemed to be new. They had no precedents. They had no models. In the words of a great British historian of ancient Greece, the late Moses Finley, theirs was a situation of "compulsory originality."[52] The Greeks responded to the challenge of this situation with an originality that perhaps remains unequaled. In virtually every emerging form of human inquiry — including the scientific and mathematic pursuits of astronomy, biology, physics, geometry, meteorology, and more — the classical Greeks were pioneers of surpassing originality.

Long before Einstein, Democritus advanced an atomic theory of the universe. Long before Darwin, Anaximander anticipated the theory of evolution. Long before Copernicus and Galileo, Aristarchus argued that the earth circles the sun. In these and numerous other ways, the ancient Greeks demonstrated the reach of their originality. And yet, as Finley noted, "[T]he list of Greek inventions is a very short one indeed."[53]

There were several reasons for this. Because the Greeks had slaves, they had less need for inventions. Because the Greeks had an aristocratic tradition that valued leisure, they had less interest in what we would consider as useful work. Generally, they were content to engage in the originality of their remarkable deductive reasoning; they gave little thought to how the conclusions from their reasoning might be used to improve materially the quality of their daily lives.

The Greeks wanted to *know*, but for the most part they did not see the need to use their knowledge for invention. Theirs was what economists call a "bounded rationality."[54] For all their considerable

---

[52] M.I. Finley, The Greeks (London: Penguin Books, 1963), 41.

[53] Id. at 127-128.

[54] The phrase is that of the economist Timur Kuran. *See* Joel Mokyr, The Lever of Riches: Technological Creativity and Economic Progress (Oxford: Oxford University Press, 1990), 154.

capabilities for reasoning, they could not see beyond the bounds of the structure of their own ancient world. In Finley's judgment, "Apparently the society as a whole lacked the mentality and the motivation to strive systematically for greater efficiency and greater productivity.... What was missing was an intangible factor, a Baconian spirit which regularly and persistently turns speculation into empirical research, empirical research into practical application."[55]

Thus, as Lecky would remind us, the Greeks, too, had their "hidden bias of imagination." They did not share his view — or our view — of human progress as involving economic growth through the practical application of innovative ideas in technological inventions. They did not *know* that they wanted inventions. They did not know that they *needed* them, because they did not *see* a need for them. They could not imagine them.

We face the same challenge today. Today, with respect to international law, our own capabilities for reasoning — and especially for reasoning together — are bounded by the limits of our imagination. We cannot have the international rule of law if we cannot imagine a world in which there *is* the international rule of law. We cannot know that we need it if we do not see the need for it. And we cannot see the need for it if we cannot see as far as all of humanity. We cannot see the need for the international rule of law if we cannot see clearly enough to change the hidden bias of our imagination.

Generally, with trade, we see our shared interest in working together. Trade serves and strengthens our shared interest. By its very nature as an act of exchange, trade is an *acknowledgment* of a shared interest. In the multilateral trading system that is served by the WTO, this shared interest is reflected most clearly in the "most-favoured-nation" principle that is at the very heart of the system. A principle that provides that one trade concession made by one WTO Member to one other WTO Member must also be made to all other WTO Members is a principle that, above all else, acknowledges the shared interest of all WTO Members in securing the mutual benefits of trade.

Yet, even in trade, often we do not see the interest we share. Thus, even in trade, we do not always serve our shared interest as we should. In particular, even in trade, we do not always see clearly enough our

---

[55] Finley, The Greeks, at 125.

shared interest in establishing and upholding the international rule of law. More so, in areas of international concern other than trade, often we are even less likely than we are in trade to see our shared interest in the international rule of law. Because we cannot see it, we cannot serve it. We cannot advance the international rule of law in those other areas of shared human concern because we cannot see beyond the current limits of our imagination.

The circle of the ancient Greeks was enclosed by the limits of their own thinking. They could not see beyond it. All those who were not Greeks were barbarians. They spoke the "bar-bar" of something other than Greek, and so they were the outsiders. They were the "others." They were the foreigners who were beyond the limits of the Greek circle. At the dawn of rational thought, the ultimate implications of the profoundly original Greek thinking were universal. Yet the limited size of the Greek circle kept the Greeks from seeing the true extent of those implications.

So too with the way that many who profess to believe in law see the supposed limits of law today. The way they see the potential of law is limited by the way they see the limits of their self-interest. Thomas Hobbes, a Londoner who was a dedicated student of both the Greeks and self-interest, told us long ago, "Covenants, without the sword, are but Words...."[56] Short of the sword, the only other way to enforce the covenants we choose to call "international law" is by seeing more than we see now. It is by expanding the circle of our sight. It is by inspiring an ever-expanding circle of enlightened self-interest. The larger the circle, the larger the need we will see for international law that is really "law," and not merely "words."

Where international law is concerned, we live, like the ancient Greeks, in a time of "compulsory originality." And, to be sure, we have no lack of originality among our legal thinkers. We have no lack of legal theories that can have practical application in a world much in need of international law, and in need even more of the international rule of law. What we lack is a sufficient awareness in the world that real and inventive and practical applications of international law are needed.

Those of us who believe we need "law" — and who believe especially, and increasingly, that we need "international law" — must understand above all what it is that *precedes* "law." Law is preceded by a

---

[56] Thomas Hobbes, Leviathan (London: Penguin Books, 1968), 223 [1660].

perception of a duty. Thus, an awareness of a duty precedes a willingness to abide by a law. Law will exist only to the extent that we see a need for law in fulfilling our "range of duty." Law will exist only to the extent that we see the need to be *bound* by law.

In his book, Ways of Seeing, the British art critic John Berger told us, "Seeing comes before words. The child looks and recognizes before it can speak. But there is also another sense in which seeing comes before words. It is seeing which establishes our place in the surrounding world...."[57] As with art, so with law. Seeing comes before words, and, thus, seeing comes before the words that comprise the laws that place us all in the surrounding world. For this reason, the foremost frontier in international law is the frontier of what we *see*. It is the frontier of what we see as our true self-interest. It is the frontier that faces all of us who seek a surrounding world in which there *truly is* international law.

Can we look beyond the grim reiteration of all the numbing statistics of human degradation to see at last the sheer human reality they represent? Can we look beyond the mere numerical fact that there are 826 million people in the developing countries of the world who suffer from malnourishment to see the hunger of a single human being somewhere in Asia?[58] Can we look beyond the mere numerical fact that there are 968 million people in the developing countries of the world with no access to safe drinking water from improved water resources to see the thirst of a single human being somewhere in Africa?[59] Can we feel the sheer urgency of their hunger, their thirst, their poverty, their deprivation, their desperation, *if we do not see it?* And can we see it if we do not see and, thus, do not acknowledge the basic humanity that each and every one of them shares with each and every one of us? Can we really treat them as anything other than mere numbers, as anything other than mere statistics, *if we do not see each and every one of them as part of our circle?*

Article 102 of the Charter of the United Nations provides that every treaty and every other international agreement that is entered into by a Member State of the United Nations shall be registered and published by the United Nations Secretariat.[60] The United Nations Treaty Collection

---

[57] John Berger, Ways of Seeing (London: Penguin Books, 1972), 7.
[58] World Bank, Human Development Report 2001 (Washington, D.C.), 22.
[59] Id. at 9.
[60] Article 102, United Nations Charter.

contains more than forty thousand treaties.[61] Many of these treaties are followed and upheld. But many are not. Many are simply ignored in the day-to-day dealings and doings of the nations of the world.

For all of the "international law" we have made as a world, ours remains a world that is largely *without* international law. We know a lot about how to negotiate and conclude and sign and ratify and even register treaties. We know a lot less about how to give them real meaning as real law in the daily life of the world. We know a lot about how to *make* international law. We know a lot less about how to make international law work for all of us in the large circle that includes all of those who are much in need of international law all over the wide world.

Why is international law so often invoked but so seldom obeyed? Why do sovereign nation-states so often simply ignore international law and international tribunals? They do so because they can, and they do so because they do not *see* why they should not. Like the ancient Greeks, their circle is too small. It is enclosed by the limits of their own thinking. To expand their thinking, to expand the domain of international law, the nations of the world must expand the size of their circle. In a world where there truly is international law, the circle of human sympathy will truly be a circle that includes the whole world.

Lecky was much taller than I am. He could reach the top shelf. He was so "very tall" that, on the long walks they often took together, he had to stoop over to hear the soft voice of the aged Thomas Carlyle.[62] Lecky was tall enough to foresee the future. Like many men, he grew more pessimistic as he grew older. The glass that seemed half full in his youth seemed in his later years to be half empty. Like some others of his time — and like some also of our time[63] — Lecky worried about extending the limits of liberal democracy out of fear that doing so would lead to illiberal results. He feared that too much democracy would result in too little freedom. Yet, even in his old age, Lecky retained the optimistic belief in human progress about which he wrote so eloquently in his youth.

Later in life, Lecky wrote a multi-volume history of eighteenth-century England, and also a multi-volume history of eighteenth-century

---

[61] *See* the United Nations Treaty Collection online at un.org.

[62] Fred Kaplan, Thomas Carlyle: A Biography (Ithaca, New York: Cornell University Press, 1983), 542.

[63] *See*, for example, most recently, Fareed Zakaria, The Future of Freedom: Illiberal Democracy at Home and Abroad (New York: W.W. Norton & Company, 2003).

Ireland. These lengthy narrative histories were widely read and widely praised at the time. Even today, they are, on occasion, still read. But it was his youthful book on the history of European morals that was, of all his books, Lecky's favorite. Perhaps this was because it was in that early book that Lecky voiced the most optimism about the future. It was in that youthful distillation of all the hopes he held as he delved so deeply into all the dusty shelves of all the musty libraries of Europe that he saw most clearly the expanding circle of humanity.

It was also in his youth when Lecky first began to admire and model himself after another nineteenth-century "man of letters" who wrote about circles, Ralph Waldo Emerson. Like me, Emerson was an American who never tired of London. You can see this in every line of his collection of essays about his visit to London and to England, "English Traits."[64] Lecky was about thirty years younger than Emerson. To my knowledge, they never met. But, in his youth, Lecky, like me, read Emerson, and the Victorian historian from Ireland was, like me, clearly much influenced by the musings of the American sage from Concord.

Lecky's histories were really extended philosophical essays in a style reminiscent of Emerson's own timeless essays. Like the writings of Emerson, Lecky's writings were really lay sermons that sought to inspire a thoughtful emulation. In his writing, and in his thinking, Lecky admittedly emulated Emerson. Like Emerson, "he tried to crystallize political wisdom in a single shining sentence."[65] And, like Emerson, he saw the world as a world of circles in which the range of what we see shapes the range of what we do.

At some point in his youth, before writing his history of European morals, Lecky must surely have read Emerson's essay entitled "Circles." If so, it must have influenced his own thinking, even as it has influenced mine. In that essay, Emerson wrote, "The life of man is a *self-evolving circle* which, from a ring imperceptibly small, *rushes* on all sides *outwards* to new and larger circles, and that without end.... The eye is the first circle; the horizon which it forms is the second; and throughout nature this primary figure is repeated without end.... Our life is an *apprenticeship to the truth*, that *around every circle another can be drawn*. ... The one thing which we seek with insatiable desire is... to *draw a new circle*...."[66]

---

[64] "English Traits," Ralph Waldo Emerson, in <u>Essays and Lectures</u> (New York: Library of America, 1983, 763 [1856].

[65] <u>Lecky</u>, at 186.

[66] Emerson, "Circles," in <u>Essays and Lectures</u>, supra, 403, at 403, 404, and 414.

As Emerson taught us, our "invisible thought" makes our visible world.[67] As Lecky taught us, the "hidden bias" of our imagination determines what is visible to us in the world around us. For Emerson, for Lecky, and for me, the question is one of what we can *see*. The size of our circle depends on our eyes. It depends on our sight. It depends on who and what and how far we can see across the horizon.

Can we see anything beyond our own narrow-minded and short-sighted selfishness? Can we see as far as next door? Can we see as far as the farthest forgotten and forsaken corner of our imperiled planet? Will we turn inward? Will we turn our eyes away from the world? Or will we turn outward toward the world, and to new and larger circles, to circles without end?

From my seat in our small circle called the WTO Appellate Body, from my front row seat on the frontier of international law, I see an urgent need for a new and larger circle. I see our apprenticeship to truth as ending only when we finally discover the truth about our real interest as individuals and as nations. I see our apprenticeship as ending only when we clearly and finally *see* that our true self-interest includes *all of humanity*.

Together, we must draw a new circle that embraces all the world.

Together, we must draw Lecky's circle.

---

[67] Id. at 404.

About the Author

In December, 2003, James Bacchus completed eight years and two terms as one of the seven Members of the Appellate Body of the World Trade Organization in Geneva, Switzerland. He was a founding Member, and remains the longest-serving Member, of the highest global trade tribunal. He was twice appointed to the Appellate Body by consensus of the Members of the WTO, and was twice elected chairman of the Appellate Body by his six colleagues. Previously, he served as a Member of the Congress of the United States, from Florida, and served also as special assistant to the United States Trade Representative in the Executive Office of the President of the United States. Currently, he is the chairman of the global trade practice group of the international law firm Greenberg Traurig, P. A., and also a professor of law at Vanderbilt University Law School. He lives with his family in Winter Park, Florida, and has offices with his law firm in Orlando, Florida, and in Washington, D. C.